CRITICAL SURVEY
OF
LONG FICTION

CRITICAL SURVEY
OF
LONG FICTION

English Language Series

REVISED EDITION

But-Doy

2

Edited by
FRANK N. MAGILL

SALEM PRESS
Pasadena, California   Englewood Cliffs, New Jersey

SECOND PRINTING

∞ The paper used in these volumes conforms to the
American National Standard for Permanence of Paper
for Printed Library Materials, Z39.48-1984.

Library of Congress Cataloging-in-Publication Data
Critical survey of long fiction. English language series/
  edited by Frank N. Magill. — Rev. ed.
      p.   cm.
    Includes bibliographical references and index.
    1. English fiction—Dictionaries. 2. American
  fiction—Dictionaries. 3. English fiction—
  Bio-bibliography. 4. American fiction—
  Bio-bibliography. 5. Novelists, English—
  Biography—Dictionaries. 6. Novelists, American—
  Biography—Dictionaries.
  I. Magill, Frank Northen, 1907-   .
  PR821.C7   1991
  823.009′03—dc20   91-19694
  ISBN 0-89356-825-2 (set)   CIP
  ISBN 0-89356-827-9 (volume 2)

PRINTED IN THE UNITED STATES OF AMERICA

LIST OF AUTHORS IN VOLUME 2

CRITICAL SURVEY
OF
LONG FICTION

OCTAVIA E. BUTLER

Born: Pasadena, California; June 22, 1947

Principal long fiction
Patternmaster, 1976; *Mind of My Mind,* 1977; *Survivor,* 1978; *Kindred,* 1979; *Wild Seed,* 1980; *Clay's Ark,* 1984; *Dawn,* 1987; *Adulthood Rites,* 1988; *Imago,* 1989.

Other literary forms
Octavia E. Butler has contributed short stories to various science-fiction collections and periodicals, including *Isaac Asimov's Science Fiction Magazine, Future Life,* and *Clarion.* Her story "Speech Sounds" won the Hugo Award in 1984; a short work of fiction, "Bloodchild," was honored with the Hugo and various other prizes in 1985.

Achievements
Broad and growing popularity among readers of science fiction greeted first Butler's Patternist series of novels and then her Xenogenesis series. She has won multiple prizes for her short fiction as well as critical acceptance for her longer work. Her portrayal of the "loner" of science and adventure fiction is given depth and complexity by the implied treatment of sexual and racial prejudices and the direct treatment of social power structures. Entertaining stories with alien settings, sometimes narrated by truly alien characters, provide a platform for her contemplative approach to human dynamics. Love and miscegenation, male-female roles, the responsibilities of power, and the urge to survive are among the recurring themes that insistently invite the reader to reexamine long-standing attitudes.

Biography
Octavia E. Butler grew up in a family that reflected some of the hard realities for African Americans. Her father, who died when she was very young, shined shoes; her mother, who had been taken from school at the age of ten, supported herself by working as a maid.

Reared by her mother, grandmother, and other relatives, Butler felt most comfortable in the company of her adult relatives, even while she was uncomfortable with a social system that routinely denied their humanity. She was tall for her age, shy, bookish, and further set off from her peer group by strict Baptist prohibitions against dancing and use of makeup. Her escape from a less-than-satisfactory everyday life was provided by her ability to write. She began writing when she was about ten years old and began to experiment with science fiction one day at age twelve, when she decided that she could write a better story than the poor science-fiction film she was watching on television.

Her family did not support her decision to write, and her teachers did not support her choice of science fiction as a medium. She attended Pasadena City College and then California State College at Los Angeles, where she was unable to major in creative writing but took a potpourri of other subjects. After attending evening writing classes at the University of California at Los Angeles, she found a long-sought entrée to science fiction writing when she met writer Harlan Ellison through the Writers Guild of America and Ellison brought her to the six-week Clarion Science Fiction Writers Workshop in 1970. She continued her study of science-fiction writing in classes taught by Ellison at UCLA. Although she had sold some of her science fiction as early as 1970, her breakthrough publication came in 1976 with *Patternmaster*, with which she began the Patternist series.

Analysis

Octavia E. Butler's work has been described as "dystopian"—that is, it does not follow the lead of Isaac Asimov's *The Foundation Trilogy* (1961), Arthur C. Clarke's *2001: A Space Odyssey* (1968), and similar science fiction in offering an optimistic, rational, and agreeable view of humanity. As Butler herself says, she does not believe that imperfect human beings can create a perfect world.

Butler's diverse societies are controlled by Darwinian realities: competition to survive, struggle for power, domination of the weak by the strong, parasitism, and the like. Within this framework, there is room for both pain and hope, for idealism, love, bravery and compassion, for an outsider to challenge the system, defeat the tyrant, and win power. There is, however, no happy ending but a conclusion in which the lead characters have done their best and the world (wherever it is) remains ethically and morally unchanged.

In contemplative but vividly descriptive prose, Butler tells her story from the first- or third-person perspective of someone who is passive or disfranchised and is forced by events or other characters to take significant action. In order to fulfill her destiny, often the protagonist—most often a black woman—must do or experience something not only unprecedented but also alien and even grotesque. What begins as an act of courage usually ends as an act of love, or at least understanding. Through an alien, alienated, or excluded person, a crucial compromise is struck, civilization is preserved in some form, and life goes on.

Butler's fiction reflects and refracts the attempts—and failures—of the twentieth century to deal with radical, ethnic, and sexual prejudice. She frequently uses standard images of horror such as snakelike or insectlike beings, to provoke an aversion that the reader is unable to sustain as the "humanity" of the alien becomes clear. Being "human" does not mean being faultless—merely familiar. Therefore, each of her human, nonhuman, and quasi-human societies displays its own form of selfishness and, usually, a very clear power structure. The maturity and independence achieved by the protagonists imply not the advent of universal equality and harmony but merely a pragmatic personal obligation to wield power responsibly. Characters unable to alter or escape the order of things are expected to show a sort of *noblesse oblige*.

Butler's most atypical work in terms of genre is *Kindred*, published in 1979. While the protagonist is shuttled helplessly back and forth between 1824 and 1976 in a kind of time travel, this device is of no intrinsic importance to the message of the story. At one point, the heroine, Edana, asks herself how it can be that she—the as yet unborn (black) descendant of a nineteenth century slaveholder—can be the instrument of keeping that slaveholder alive until he fulfills his destiny and fathers her ancestor. By asking, she preempts the reader's own curiosity, and when there is no answer, the story simply moves forward.

Kindred uses a black woman of the 1970's and her white husband to probe beneath the surface stereotypes of "happy slave" on the one hand and "Uncle Tom" on the other. When Edana and Kevin are separated by the South of 1824 into slave and master, they each begin unwillingly to imbibe the feelings and attitudes of the time from that perspective. The impact of the novel results from Butler's ability to evoke the antebellum South from two points of view: the stubborn, desperate attempts of blacks to lead meaningful lives in a society that disregards family ties and disposes of individuals as marketable animals; and the uncomprehending, sometimes oppressively benevolent ruthlessness of a ruling class that defines slaves in terms of what trouble or pleasure they can give.

Butler began her science-fiction novels with the Patternist series, and in this series the reader can observe the beginning of her development from a writer of well-crafted science/adventure fiction to a writer who recalls in her own way the reflectiveness of Ray Bradbury. The internal chronology of the series is reflected in the following ordering: *Wild Seed* (published in 1980), *Clay's Ark* (1984), *Patternmaster* (1976), *Mind of My Mind* (1977), and *Survivor* (1978).

First written but third published was *Survivor*, the tale of an orphaned Afro-Asian girl who becomes a "wild human" in order to survive in a harsh environment. She is found and adopted, in an atypical act of reaching out, by two members of the Missionaries—a nouveau-Fundamentalist Christian sect. The Missionaries' escape from a hostile Earth takes them to a planet inhabited by furred bipeds, whom they regard as less than human. These beings are, in fact, a science-fiction version of the noble savage, but the protagonist is alone in recognizing their nobility. Internally untouched by Missionary dogma, she is truly socialized as a captive of the Tehkohn and, in the end, chooses them as her own people. Her survival and success require an understanding of the color classes of fur among the Tehkohn, where blue is the highest color. (One suggests a tongue-in-cheek reference to "blue blood.") She makes her own way by dint of qualities often found in protagonists of adventure novels: physical agility, courage, and adaptability.

The appealing heroine of *Survivor* is followed by an appealing duo in *Patternmaster*, where the younger son of the Patternmaster—the psychic control-central of a society of psionically advanced human beings—must confront and defeat his brutal older brother in an unwanted competition to succeed their father. His helper, mentor, and lover is a bisexual Healer; he trusts her enough to "link" with her in order to pool their psionic power. She teaches him that Healing is, paradoxically, also a deadly knowledge of the body with which he can defeat his brother. Thus, trust and cooperation overcome ambition and brutality. The "mutes" of this novel are nontelepathic human beings whose vulnerability to cruelty or kindness and inability to control their own destinies reflect the earlier status of slaves in America.

Mary, in *Mind of My Mind*, is a "latent" who must undergo a painful transition in order to become a full-fledged telepath. The pain and danger of this passage from adolescence to adulthood are emblematic of the turmoil of coming of age everywhere and of the physical or psychological pain that is required as the price of initiation in many, if not all, societies. The deadened, sometimes crazed, helplessness of latents who cannot become telepaths but must continue to live with the intrusive offal of other people's thoughts is a powerful metaphor for people trapped in poverty, and some of the horrors Butler paints are familiar.

Mary has no choice at first. The founder of her "people," a nontelepathic immortal named Doro, prescribes her actions until she acquires her power. He senses danger only when she reaches out reflexively to control other, powerful telepaths, thus forming the first Pattern. Mary's destruction of the pitiless Doro, like the death of the older brother in *Patternmaster* and of the rival alien chief in *Survivor*, is foreordained and accomplished with a ruthlessness appropriate to the society and to the character of the victim. The incipient change in Butler's style is evident here in the comparative lack of adventure-action sequences and in the greater concentration on psychological adaptation to and responsible use of social power.

Kindred came at this point in Butler's writing, and the technique of historical reconstruction is seen again in the next Patternist novel, whose evocation of Ibo West Africa owes something to the work of writers such as Chinua Achebe. *Wild Seed* traces Doro and Anyanwu from their seventeenth century meeting in West Africa to the establishment of Doro's settlements in America. Doro is a centuries-old being who lives by "taking" another man's or woman's body and leaving his previous body behind. Anyanwu, the Emma of *Mind of My Mind*, is a descendant of Doro. She is a "wild seed" because she has unexpectedly developed the power to shape-shift, becoming young or old, an animal, fish, or bird, at will. Their relationship is completely one-sided, since Doro could "take" her any time he chose, although he would not acquire her special abilities. His long life and unremitting efforts to create a special people of his own have left him completely insensitive to the needs and desires of others. Anyanwu finally achieves some balance of power simply by being willing to die and leave him without the only companion who could last beyond a mortal lifetime.

The last Patternist novel, *Clay's Ark*, introduces the reader to those brutish enemies of both Patternist and "mute" humanity: the Clayarks, so named because the disease that created them was brought back to Earth on a spaceship called "Clay's Ark." The disease culls its victims, killing some and imbuing others with a will to live that overcomes the horror of their new existence. They become faster and stronger, and their children evolve even further, taking on animal shapes and attributes of speed, power, and heightened senses, but retaining human thought and use of their hands. In the guise of a horror story, *Clay's Ark* follows the first Clayarks' attempt to come to terms with their condition and live responsibly, shut off from civilization. Their failed attempt demonstrates that it is not possible to contain cataclysmic natural change, but the story enlists the reader's sympathy for human beings who suffer even as they afflict others.

With the exception of *Clay's Ark*, where there is much action, the pace of Butler's novels slows progressively; action is increasingly internalized and psychological. Moral judgmentalism and the contest of Right versus Wrong dwindle to insignificance. The next, and quite logical, development is the Xenogenesis series—*Dawn* (1987), *Adulthood Rites* (1988), *Imago* (1989)—which has confirmed Butler as a science-fiction writer of sufficient depth to be of significance beyond the genre.

The change from her originally projected title for the series is informative. "Exogenesis" would have implied merely genesis effected from outside humanity. "Xenogenesis" has both text and subtext. Its meaning is the production of an organism altogether and permanently unlike the parent. The subtext is a function of the best-known English word built on the same root: xenophobia, fear and dislike of that which is foreign or alien. Butler makes the series title a statement of the thesis she will address.

Many of the techniques and themes of her earlier, developing style come to fruition here: the alternating use of first- and third-person narrative, the slow pace of a plot laden with psychological development and sensory perceptions, the meticulous foreclosure of value judgments, the concern with hierarchy and responsibility, the objective observation of feelings of revulsion for that which is alien, and those feelings' gradual dissipation as the alien becomes familiar and therefore less threatening.

Words used to describe two of Butler's shorter works in the 1984 and 1987 issues of *Year's Best Science Fiction* may serve here as a characterization of the Xenogenesis series: "strange, grotesque, disturbing . . . and ultimately moving," a "tale of despair, resignation, and, most painfully, hope." It is apparently to examine the capacity of human beings to adapt, to survive, and perhaps stubbornly to pursue a self-destructive course of action that Butler has created the nightmarish situation that the reader encounters in *Dawn*.

In a world devastated by nuclear exchange between East and West, the dying remnants of humanity survive largely in the Southern Hemisphere. The heroine of *Dawn* is an African, Lilith, whose name suggests the demonic goddess of Hebrew tradition, the famous medieval witch who appears in Johann Wolfgang von Goethe's *Faust* (1808-1831) and the medieval, alternate "first mother" who was put aside in favor of Eve.

Enter the Oankali, a nonviolent race of benevolent parasites and genetic engineers, who exist for the opportunity of combining with other species to acquire new cellular "knowledge" and capabilities. They live for miscegenation. They are trisexual: male, female, and ooloi. The ooloi is the indispensable link between male and female, channeling, altering, or amplifying all genetic material and sexual contact, including transfer of sperm and pleasurable sensations. The ooloi is capable of internal healing; for example, one cures Lilith of a cancer and finds the cancer to be an exciting new biological material with which to work.

The Oankali blend with another species by linking a male and female of that species and a male and female Oankali through an ooloi. Thereafter, independent conception is not possible for those members of that species. The progeny are "constructs," who, at least at first, resemble their direct parents but carry genetic change within them. Lilith's first husband is killed in *Dawn*, but she bears his child posthumously because Nikanj, the ooloi that has chosen her, has preserved his seed. The resultant humanoid male child is the protagonist of *Adulthood Rites*, while a much later child of Lilith with another husband and the same Oankali parents is the protagonist of *Imago*.

Action in the series is sparse, normally kept to the minimum necessary to maintain the pace of psychological and social observation. In some ways, it is a chilling series of seductions of human beings by an alien, benevolent oppressor not entirely unlike Rufus of *Kindred* in his better moments. In some ways, it is a demonstration of the infinite capacity of humanity to seek satisfaction in the destruction of itself and others.

Lilith is at first appalled by even the more humanoid Oankali, with their Medusan tentacles and sensory arms. She is gradually acclimated to them, cooperates with them to save humanity, bears children with them, is overwhelmed by the sensory pleasure they can give, and becomes sympathetic to their need to unite with other species, but she is never fully resigned. In *Imago*, Lilith compares the Oankali's description of the "flavors" of human beings to physical cannibalism and implies that the spiritual equivalent is no less predatory.

Lilith's conversion from complete repugnance in *Dawn*, a stylistic tour de force, shapes the following novels, as human beings are ultimately allowed a choice of living with the Oankali, staying behind on a doomed and barren Earth, or living in an experimental, all-human world on Mars. The Oankali, who seem to make decisions as a kind of committee-of-the-whole, foresee that the same old combination of intelligence and hierarchical tendencies (in a rather Darwinian sense) will lead this last outpost of humanity to destroy itself. No one convincingly denies it.

Butler's stylistic virtuosity also extends to narrative person. *Dawn* is a third-person account of Lilith's absorption into the Oankali social structure; *Adulthood Rites* is the third-person narrative of Akin, a male-human construct, who convinces the more rational human beings left on Earth to trust the Oankali, and convinces the Oankali to offer the humans the choice of planetary residences; *Imago* is a first-person account of Jodahs, a child whose transformation to adulthood reveals it to be an ooloi. Use of the first-person narrative to tell the story of an apparent human who becomes wholly alien in both psychology and physiology is risky but rewarding. Through the eyes of a being routinely referred to as "it," in its own society, the reader observes its benevolent stalking and drug-induced brainwashing of human mates and the final planting of a seed that will grow into an organic town and then an organic spaceship, which will carry Jodahs and his people to new worlds for new genetic blendings.

Imago's conclusion serves as a reminder that Butler's imaginary worlds are primarily arenas for hard, necessary decisions in the business of survival. There is compassion as well as bitterness, and love as well as prejudice, but there is no triumph or glory. There is only doing what must be done as responsibly as possible.

James L. Hodge

Bibliography

Butler, Octavia E. "Black Woman and the Science Fiction Genre." Interview by Frances M. Beal. *Black Scholar* 17 (March/April, 1986): 2, 14-18. This interview with Butler by a member of *Black Scholar*'s editorial staff discusses, among other things, Butler's reasons for entering science fiction, her analysis of what will bring more nonwhite and female writers into the genre, her own perception of racial bias as a child, and her treatment of it in *Kindred*.

Crossley, Robert. Introduction to *Kindred*, by Octavia Butler. Boston: Beacon Press, 1988. One of the more scholarly critical appreciations of *Kindred*, this essay includes a short biography and suggests connections with Butler's other work. Crossley deals with the political and social content of Butler's writing, noting how few science-fiction writers have been able to treat questions of race and sex without a patronizing attitude.

Foster, Frances Smith. "Octavia Butler's Black Female Future Fiction." *Extrapolation* 23 (Spring, 1982): 37-49. Foster shows how Butler's distinctive message is expressed through a rather traditional story line in the Patternist series, and she analyzes the balance and tension of feminine/masculine and black/white in Butler's works.

Govan, Sandra Y. "Connections, Links, and Extended Networks: Patterns in Octavia Butler's Science Fiction." *Black American Literature Forum* 18 (1984): 82-87.

Salvaggio, Ruth. "Octavia Butler and the Black Science-Fiction Heroine." *Black American Literature Forum* 18 (1984): 78-81.

Weiximann, Joe. "An Octavia E. Butler Bibliography." *Black American Literature Forum* 18 (1984): 88-89. These three articles make this issue of *Black American Literature Forum* one of the most comprehensive resources on Butler. Govan deals with the black heroine as a survivor—sometimes a dangerous one. Salvaggio compares the caring and strength of Butler's heroines to the rigidity and brutality of their antagonists. Weiximann gives a bibliography of Butler's work and critiques of her novels up to *Clay's Ark*.

Zaki, Hoda M. "Fantasies of Differences." *The Women's Review of Books* 5 (January, 1988): 4, 13-14. A compact and lively discussion that encapsulates positive critical opinion up to 1988 and considers Butler's dystopian perspective.

SAMUEL BUTLER

Born: Langar Rectory, England; December 4, 1835
Died: London, England; June 18, 1902

Principal long fiction
Erewhon, 1872; *The Fair Haven*, 1873; *Erewhon Revisited*, 1901; *The Way of All Flesh*, 1903.

Other literary forms

The Shrewsbury editions of Samuel Butler's works, published between 1923 and 1926, reveals the breadth of his interests. Butler's fiction was perhaps less important to him than his work in other fields, notably his theorizing on religion and evolution. He was also an art critic (*Ex Voto*, 1888; *Alps and Sanctuaries of Piedmont and the Ticino*, 1881); a literary critic (*The Authoress of the "Odyssey,"* 1897; *Shakespeare's Sonnets Reconsidered*, 1899); the biographer of his famous grandfather, Dr. Samuel Butler; a letter-writer; and a poet. An age which produces "specialists" may find Butler to be a talented dabbler or dilettante, but his unifying philosophy gives a center to all his work.

Achievements

Butler was a figure of controversy during his lifetime, and perhaps his greatest achievement resides in his ability to challenge: he contended with Charles Darwin and Darwinism; he took on the established scholars of William Shakespeare, classical literature, and art; and he was part of the nineteenth century revolt against traditional religion. He approached all of these areas in such a way that his opponents could not ignore him; whether he was right or wrong, any subject benefited by his treatment, which opened it up to new and candid thought.

Of his four works which may be labeled as fiction, by far the greatest is *The Way of All Flesh*. Virginia Woolf, in *Contemporary Writers* (1965), described this novel as a seed from which many others developed—a biological image which would have pleased Butler. In earlier novels, indifferent or cruel families had been portrayed as agents of the hero's youthful unhappiness—witness Charles Dickens' *David Copperfield* (1849-1850)—but only in *The Way of All Flesh* did the oppressiveness and cruelty of family life become a theme in itself, worthy of generation-by-generation treatment.

Biography

Samuel Butler was born in 1835, the son of a clergyman who wished him to go into the Church. After a successful career at Cambridge, Butler prepared for a career in the Church but found himself unable to face the prospect of that life. Letters between Butler and his father show the young man to be considering a half-dozen plans at once: art, the army, cotton-growing, and bookselling among them. Finally, father and son agreed that the young man should emigrate to New Zealand and try his fortune there, with Butler's father providing capital. Both father and son hoped that the experience would "settle" Butler and build his character.

Butler arrived in New Zealand in January of 1860, remaining there for four years. It was a useful time: he made money which freed him of his family, at least financially, and he saw an unusual country which gave him a subject and setting for his later writings. New Zealand, however, was too rough a land to be his permanent home. His "hut" there was an island of comfort and civilization, where Butler devoted himself to music and study. His optimistic letters home became the basis of *A First Year in Canterbury Settlement* (1863), a book assembled and published by Butler's father.

Returning to England in 1864, Butler settled at Clifford's Inn in London, which would be his home for the rest of his life. He began to study art; his paintings had some success. He wished to do something greater, however, something which would express his developing ideas. Out of this desire grew *Erewhon*, a satire which was published anonymously in 1872 at the author's own expense. By that time, Butler was already at work on *The Fair Haven*. This book may or may not be considered fiction; it is a dispute over the validity of Christianity, but the dispute is conducted in a fictional frame.

The following year, 1873, was an important one for Butler. *The Fair Haven* was published, his mother died, he made a risky financial investment, and he began *The Way of All Flesh*. All of these events shaped his later years. *The Fair Haven*, following on the heels of *Erewhon*, marked him as a belligerent enemy of traditional religion. His mother's death caused him some grief, but it spurred him to begin *The Way of All Flesh*, the work for which he is most remembered. That work was slowed, though, by financial troubles. Butler invested his New Zealand fortune in a Canadian venture which soon failed. He salvaged less than a quarter of his investment and had to seek help from his father. Not until 1886, when his father died, was Butler wholly free of financial pressures.

The next several years were occupied by work on evolution and religion. In 1882, Butler returned to *The Way of All Flesh*, completing it the following year. He felt, however, that the book should not be published while anyone who could be hurt by it was still alive; therefore it did not appear until a year after his own death.

In 1883, Butler began to write music. Music and music criticism were to occupy him intermittently for several years, interspersed with art criticism. The last decade of his life was filled with the study of literature, culminating in his publications on Shakespeare's sonnets and his translations of the *Iliad* (1898) and the *Odyssey* (1900). These works were characterized by the combativeness that to some degree sums up Butler's life. He was always the rebellious, contradictory son.

Butler's life was shaped by a number of intense relationships. His relationship with his family was unresolved; the work (*The Way of All Flesh*) which might have laid the ghosts to rest was haunted by another ghost, Butler's lifelong friend Eliza Mary Ann Savage. A fellow art student, she gave the writer friendship, friendly criticism, advice, and approval. Her own understanding of the relationship can never be known, but Butler feared she wished to marry him. His implicit rejection disturbed him deeply after her death. Other friendships were equally ambiguous. Charles Paine Pauli consumed much of Butler's attentions and resources from their first meeting in New Zealand until Pauli's death in 1897, when Butler discovered that Pauli had been supported by two other men. The perhaps sexual ambiguities of this relationship were repeated in Butler's affection for a young Swiss, Hans Faesch, and to a lesser degree in his long-lasting bonds with Henry Festing Jones and Alfred Emery Cathie. Butler's emotional make-up seems similar to that of Henry James. Both men formed passionate attachments to other men; both appreciated women more as memories than as living beings.

Analysis

On his deathbed, Samuel Butler spoke of the "pretty roundness" of his career, his beginning with *Erewhon* and ending, thirty years later, with *Erewhon Revisited*.

Erewhon must be understood first of all as a satire rather than as a novel. It is in the tradition of Jonathan Swift's *Gulliver's Travels* (1726-1727) and Samuel Johnson's *The History of Rasselas, Prince of Abyssinia* (1759), works which sacrifice unity and development to a vision of the writer's society, in the guise of an imaginary foreign land. Like Rasselas and Gulliver, Higgs of *Erewhon* is a young man, ready for adventure, out to learn about the world. He quickly reveals his image of himself as sharp, cunning, and bold. Before he tells his story, he lets the reader know the things he will hold back so that no reader will be able to find Erewhon and thus profit financially from Higgs's exploration.

His story begins as he is working on a sheep farm in a colony, the name of which he will not reveal. Intending to find precious metals or at least good sheep-grazing land, he journeys alone inland, over a mountain range. On the other side, he finds a kingdom called Erewhon (Nowhere), which looks very much like England. Higgs's point of reference is England; all aspects of Erewhonian life he measures by that standard.

Many such satires work through the narrator's quick judgment that his new land is either much better or much worse than his native country: the narrator's rather simple view plays against the author's more complex perspective. In *Erewhon*, however, the narrator is not quite so naïve. His own failings, rather than his naïveté, become part of the satire, which thus has a dual focus, much like Book IV of *Gulliver's Travels*. Higgs, like many good Victorian heroes, is out to make money. It is this prospect which motivates him most strongly. Coexisting with his desire for fortune is his religiosity. Here, Butler's satire upon his character is most pronounced and simplistic. Higgs observes the Sabbath, but he seduces Yram (Mary) with no regret. He plans to make his fortune by selling the Erewhonians into slavery, arguing that they would be converted to Christianity in the process; the slaveholders would be lining their pockets and doing good simultaneously. Thus, Butler exposes, to no one's great surprise, the mingled piety and avarice of British colonialists.

Butler satirizes European culture through the Erewhonians more often than through his hero, Higgs, gradually unfolding their lives for the reader to observe. Their lives are, on the surface, peaceful and pleasant; they are a strikingly attractive race. Only through personal experience does Higgs learn the underpinnings of the society: when he is ill, he learns that illness is a crime in Erewhon, while moral lapses are regarded in the same way as illnesses are in England. When his pocket watch is discovered, he learns that all "machines" have been banned from Erewhon. Erewhonian morality is based on reversals: the morally corrupt receive sympathy, while the ill are imprisoned; a child duped by his guardian is punished for having been ignorant, while the guardian is rewarded; children are responsible for their own birth, while their parents are consoled for having been "wronged" by the unborn. This pattern of reversals is of necessity incomplete, a problem noted by reviewers of *Erewhon* in 1872.

"The Book of the Machines" is the section of the satire which has drawn the most attention, because of its relationship to Darwinian thought. It may well be, as it has often been considered, a *reductio ad absurdum* of Darwinism, but the chapter also takes on reasoning by analogy as a less complex target of satire. "The Book of the Machines" is Higgs's translation of the Erewhonian book which led to the banning of all mechanical devices. Its author claimed that machines had developed—evolved—more rapidly than humankind and thus would soon dominate, leaving humans mere slaves or parasites. He argued that machines were capable of reproduction, using humans in the process as flowers use bees. The arguments proved so convincing that all machines in Erewhon were soon destroyed, leaving the country in the rather primitive state in which Higgs found it.

The purpose of "The Book of the Machines" becomes clearer in the following two chapters, which detail Erewhonian debates on the rights of animals and the rights of vegetables. At one point in the past, insistence on the rights of animals had turned Erewhon into a land of vegetarians, but the philosophers went a step further and decreed that vegetables, too, had rights, based upon their evolving consciousness. Again, Butler plays with argument by analogy, as the philosophers compare the vegetables' intelligence to that of a human embryo.

The Erewhonians who believed in the rights of vegetables were led nearly to starvation by their extremism, and it is this same extremism which causes Higgs to leave Erewhon. Fearful that disfavor is growing against his foreign presence, he plans to escape by balloon, taking with him his beloved Arowhena. The perilous escape takes place, and the hero, married to Arowhena and restored to England, becomes a fairly successful hack writer. His account of Erewhon, he says at the end, constitutes an appeal for subscriptions to finance his scheme to return to Erewhon.

The broad, traditional satire of *Erewhon* is abandoned in its sequel. Written years later, *Erewhon Revisited* reflects the maturity of its author, then in his sixties. In the later work, Butler treats Erewhon as a habitation of human beings, not satiric simplifications. *Erewhon Revisited* is thus a novel, not a satire; its focus is on human relationships. Butler had already written (though not published) *The Way of All Flesh*, and the preoccupations of that work are also evident in *Erewhon Revisited*. Both works grew out of Butler's fascination with family relationships, especially those between father and son.

The narrator of *Erewhon Revisited* is John Higgs, the son of George Higgs and Arowhena. He tells of his mother's early death and of his father's desire to return to Erewhon. This time, though, Higgs's desire is sentimental; he has grown past his earlier wish to profit from the Erewhonians. He goes to Erewhon, returns in ill-health, tells the story of his adventure to John, and dies. The book in this way becomes John's tribute to his father.

Although *Erewhon Revisited* may be identified as a novel rather than as a satire, it does have a satiric subject as part of its plot. Upon reentering Erewhon, Higgs discovers that his ascent by balloon has become the source of a new religion. The Erewhonians revere his memory and worship him as the "Sun Child." Higgs is horrified to find that there are theologians of Sunchildism fighting heretics. Unfortunately, Sunchildism has not made the Erewhonians a better or kinder people. Here is the heart of Butler's satire: that a religion based upon a supernatural event will divide people, place power in the wrong hands, and humiliate reason.

In *Erewhon*, Higgs was a pious and hypocritical prig, a target of satire himself. In the sequel, he is a genial, loving humanist, appalled by the "evolution" of his frantic escape into the ascent of a god. Much of *Erewhon Revisited* develops his plans to deflate Sunchildism, to reveal himself as the "Sun Child" and tell the truth about his "ascent."

Higgs has a special motive which transcends his disgust with Sunchildism. Upon arriving in Erewhon, he meets a young man whom he soon recognizes as his own son, a son he did not know he had. The young man is the product of Higgs's brief romance with Yram, the jailer's daughter. Higgs keeps his identity from his son (also named George) for a while, but eventually the two are revealed to each other in a touching and intense scene. To earn his newfound son's respect, Higgs determines to deflate Sunchildism. Thus, the process of satire in *Erewhon Revisited* is rooted in its human relationships.

Higgs's son John, the narrator of the novel, feels no jealousy toward his half brother. Instead, he shares the elder Higgs's enthusiasm for young George. Following his father's death, John goes to Erewhon himself to meet George and to deliver a large gift of gold to him. This legacy exemplified one of Butler's tenets about parent-child relations: that the best parents are kind, mostly absent, and very free with money. This theme is repeated throughout *The Way of All Flesh*. In *Erewhon Revisited*, however, it has a simpler expression. The relationship of Higgs and his two sons forms the emotional center of the novel and creates the impetus for some of its plot, but it is distinct from the satire on religion which makes up much of the book.

It is fitting that Butler's last work, *Erewhon Revisited*, should have presented a genial hero determined to strip away what he saw as ridiculous supernatural beliefs. Much of "Sunchildism" is a response to the religious foment of the nineteenth century with which Butler had begun contending early in his career. *The Fair Haven* was his first satire concerned with Christian belief. This work is "fiction" only in a very limited sense: Butler creates a persona, John Pickard Owen, whose arguments in favor of Christianity are in fact the vehicle for Butler's satire against it. *The Fair Haven* begins with a fictional memoir of John Pickard Owen by his brother. The memoir reveals that Owen moved from faith to disbelief to faith, and that his efforts to prove the validity of his religion pushed him to mental exhaustion and, eventually, death.

The characters of *The Fair Haven* are forerunners of the Pontifex family in *The Way of All Flesh*, Butler's fullest and most characteristic work. *The Way of All Flesh* encompasses all of Butler's concerns: family life, money, sexual attitudes, class structure, religion, and art. This novel too is a satire, but in it, Butler does not portray an Erewhon; much more disturbingly, he keeps the reader at home.

The Way of All Flesh is Ernest Pontifex's story, but it does not begin with Ernest. Butler the evolutionist shows Ernest as the product of several generations of social changes and personal tensions. The genealogical background, as well as the title and biblical epigraph, "We know that all things work together for good to them that love God," helps to create the ironic treatment of religion which will permeate the novel. What is the way of all flesh? The biblical echo suggests sin and decay; Butler's fiction, however, reminds the reader that the way of all flesh is change, for better or worse.

Ernest is the product of three generations of upward mobility. His great-grandfather is a simple, kind craftsman who sends his only son into the city. The son, George Pontifex, becomes successful as a publisher and even more successful as a bully. He chooses the Church as a career for his second son, Theobald, who revolts briefly, then acquiesces and evolves into the image of his father. Butler is careful to show personalities as products of environment.

George's bullying is only that of an egotistical, self-made man; Theobald's is more harsh, the product of his own fear and suppressed anger. The unfortunate object of this anger is Theobald's first born son, Ernest Pontifex.

Ernest's childhood is dominated by fear of his father. His mother, Christina, is of little help; Butler portrays her as the product of her own family life and the larger social system, both of which make marriage a necessity for her. Like Theobald, Christina becomes a hypocrite pressed into the service of "what is done." Much later in life, Ernest reflects that the family is a painful anachronism, confined in nature to the lower species. His opinion is shared by Overton, the narrator of the novel, an old family friend who takes an interest in young Ernest and becomes his lifelong friend and adviser. The two of them, in fact, eventually come to constitute a kind of family, an evolved, freely chosen family, not one formed by mere biological ties.

This outcome occurs only after long agony on Ernest's part. As a child, he believes all that is told: that he is, for example, a wicked, ungrateful boy who deserves Theobald's frequent beatings. His young life is lightened, however, by the interest taken in him by his aunt Alethea and by Overton, who has known all of the Pontifexes well and who tells their story with compassion.

Ernest is still an innocent and unformed young man when he goes to Cambridge to prepare for a career in the Church. Near the end of his peaceful, happy years there, he comes under the influence of an Evangelical group which alters his perceptions of what his life as a clergyman ought to be. Instead of stepping into a pleasant rural parish, Ernest becomes a missionary in the slums of London. He falls under the spell of the oily clergyman Nicholas Pryor, who "invests" Ernest's money and eventually absconds with it. Pryor, the Cambridge enthusiasts, and Theobald Pontifex all represent the clerical life; they are radically different kinds of people, and they are all portrayed negatively. Butler took no prisoners in his war on the clergy; his use of the genial Overton as a narrator partially masks this characteristic.

Sexual ignorance, imposed (and shared) by Theobald and his kind, provides Butler with his next target for satire. In despair over his religious life, Ernest seeks a prostitute and approaches the wrong woman, the eponymous Miss Snow. Ernest's ignorance lands him in prison and cuts him off forever from mere gentility. It redeems him, however, from a life circumscribed by his father: ironically, Theobald's strict control over Ernest liberates Ernest at last. In prison, stripped of all his former identity, Ernest begins to come to terms with what his life has been and may be. A long illness serves to clarify his mind; he rejects traditional religion, society, and his family's condescending offers of help. Overton alone stands by Ernest, and it is at this point in Ernest's development that they become fast friends. Overton takes on the role of the ideal father—fond, genteel, and moneyed.

It is in this last area that Overton's role is most important to the events of the book: he keeps Alethea's substantial bequest in trust for Ernest, allowing him knowledge of it and access to it, according to Alethea's wish, only when he judges that Ernest is prepared to use it wisely. Ernest's ill-advised marriage and his decision to work as a tailor cause Overton to hold the money back. Eventually, Ernest's maturity evolves to a level acceptable to Overton, and the two of them lead a pleasant life of wealth and, on Ernest's side at least, accomplishment: he has become a writer who, like Butler, writes thoughtful, theoretical books.

In his role as a father, Ernest also has evolved. The children of his marriage to Ellen are reared by simple country people and grow up free of the pressures of Ernest's childhood. After four generations, the Pontifexes have returned to the peaceful and happy life of Ernest's great-grandfather.

Liberal amounts of money, however, keep Ernest's son and daughter from any want that ordinary country folk might experience. Ernest's son wants to be a riverboat captain: Ernest buys him riverboats. This scenario is nearly as idealized a version of country life as was Maric Antoincttc's. What makes this vision disconcerting is that Ernest's attitudes are clearly shared by Butler. Early in the novel, Ernest the bullied child is the object of the reader's pity. As a student and young cleric, his life creates a sense of pity but also humor. The more fully Ernest evolves, however, the less appealing the reader is likely to find him. The Ernest who finally comes into his aunt's fortune is a rather dull prig, who, upon learning of his wealth, considers how his emotion might be rendered in music. He tells Overton that he regrets nothing—not his parents' brutality, not prison—because everything has contributed to his evolution away from the "swindle" of middle-class expectations. Unfortunately, this self-satisfied view makes his character seem shallow, consisting only of words and affectations.

In spite of this problem, Butler's achievement is considerable. *The Way of All Flesh* is an immensely ambitious book, and much of it succeeds. Butler articulated fully and convincingly the varied stresses of family life, and that aspect alone would make the novel worthwhile. *Erewhon* and *Erewhon Revisited* share some of that evocative power. They also express Butler's optimism. For all his satirical vision and contentiousness, Butler does offer happy endings: Higgs's successful escape from Erewhon with his beloved, the reunion of the brothers in *Erewhon Revisited*, and the pleasant life of Ernest and Overton in *The Way of All Flesh*. Though societies may often be in the wrong, Butler seems to tell the reader, there is hope in freely chosen human relationships.

Deborah Core

Other major works

NONFICTION: *A First Year in Canterbury Settlement*, 1863; *Life and Habit*, 1877; *Evolution, Old and New*, 1879; *God the Known and God the Unknown*,

1879; *Unconscious Memory*, 1880; *Alps and Sanctuaries of Piedmont and the Ticino*, 1881; *A Psalm of Montreal*, 1884; *Luck or Cunning*, 1887; *Ex Voto*, 1888; *The Life and Letters of Dr. Samuel Butler*, 1896; *The Authoress of the "Odyssey,"* 1897; *Shakespeare's Sonnets Reconsidered*, 1899; *The Note-books*, 1912 (H. Festing Jones, editor).

TRANSLATIONS: *Iliad*, 1898; *Odyssey*, 1900.

Bibliography

Bekker, W. G. *An Historical and Critical Review of Samuel Butler's Literary Works*. 1925. Reprint. New York: Russell & Russell, 1964. A full-length study of Butler written by a native of Holland, where *Erewhon* found popularity and immediate acceptance. Bekker argues for the unity in Butler's works.

Cole, G. D. H. *Samuel Butler and "The Way of All Flesh."* London: Home & Van Thal, 1947. An appreciative study of Butler's novel *The Way of All Flesh*. Contains some discussion of his other works, including *Erewhon*. Also includes valuable background material on Butler, such as his upbringing and his relationship to Darwinism.

Jeffers, Thomas L. *Samuel Butler Revalued*. University Park: Pennsylvania State University Press, 1981. A philosophical discourse on Butler's ideas. Jeffers argues that Butler was influenced by eighteenth century English thinkers such as David Hume, John Locke, and Philip Dormer Stanhope, the Fourth Earl of Chesterfield. A penetrating analysis of Butler's work.

Jones, Joseph. *The Cradle of "Erewhon": Samuel Butler in New Zealand*. Austin: University of Texas Press, 1959. A valuable account of Butler's five years in New Zealand and the origins of his later *Erewhon* books.

Norrman, Ralf. *Samuel Butler and the Meaning of Chiasmus*. London: Macmillan, 1986. A technical study which examines symmetry and ambilateralism—inverting the order AB into BA—and how it affected Butler's works. In exploring these concepts, Norrman concentrates on *Erewhon*, *The Way of All Flesh*, and *Erewhon Revisited* and adopts a negative tone, describing Butler as compulsive and obsessive in his use of symmetry.

JAMES BRANCH CABELL

Born: Richmond, Virginia; April 14, 1879
Died: Richmond, Virginia; May 5, 1958

Principal long fiction
The Eagle's Shadow, 1904; *The Cords of Vanity*, 1909; *The Soul of Melicent*, 1913 (republished as *Domnei*, 1920); *The Rivet in Grandfather's Neck*, 1915; *The Cream of the Jest*, 1917; *Jurgen*, 1919; *Figures of Earth: A Comedy of Appearances*, 1921; *The High Place*, 1923; *The Silver Stallion*, 1926; *Something About Eve*, 1927; *The White Robe*, 1928; *The Way of Ecben*, 1929; *Smirt*, 1934; *Smith*, 1935; *Smire*, 1937; *The King Was in His Counting House*, 1938; *Hamlet Had an Uncle*, 1940; *The First Gentleman of America*, 1942; *There Were Two Pirates*, 1946; *The Devil's Own Dear Son*, 1949.

Other literary forms
James Branch Cabell was both prolific and versatile. In addition to his many novels, he produced a volume of poetry entitled *From the Hidden Way* (1916) and a play, *The Jewel Merchants* (1921). His short stories are collected in *The Line of Love* (1905), *Gallantry* (1907), *Chivalry* (1909), and *The Certain Hour* (1916). Included among his writings are critical volumes on his contemporaries Joseph Hergesheimer and Ellen Glasgow; *Taboo* (1921), a satire dedicated to Cabell's nemesis, John S. Sumner, who initiated obscenity charges against his novel *Jurgen*; *Some of Us* (1930), a defense of the individualism of such writers as Elinor Wylie, Sinclair Lewis, and H. L. Mencken; and *The St. Johns* (1943), a history of a Florida river, written with A. J. Hanna, for Stephen Vicent Benét's series entitled "The Rivers of America."

Perhaps Cabell's most interesting volumes are those that illuminate his life and literary development. He wrote two epistolary volumes: *Special Delivery* (1933), which presents both his conventional responses to letters he received and the nonconventional replies he would have preferred to send, and *Ladies and Gentlemen* (1934), a collection of addresses to dead historical figures— from Solomon to George Washington, from Pocahontas to Madame de Pompadour—who have inspired myths and legends. He explores the past of his native region and its impact upon his writings in his trilogy "Virginians Are Various," consisting of *Let Me Lie* (1947), *Quiet, Please* (1952), and *As I Remember It* (1955). Providing readers with insight into Cabell's art are *Beyond Life* (1919), which clarifies his values, literary precedents, and thematic concerns: *These Restless Heads* (1932), a discussion of creativity based upon the four seasons of the year; and *Straws and Prayer-Books* (1924), an explanation of his reasons for writing *The Biography of the Life of Manuel* (1927-1930). Two volumes of Cabell's letters have been published: *Between Friends: Letters of James Branch Cabell and Others* (1962), edited by his second wife, Margaret Freeman Cabell, and Padraic Colum; the other, *The Letters of James Branch Cabell* (1975), edited by Edward Wagenknecht. His manuscripts and memorabilia are in the James Branch Cabell Collections at the University of Virginia in Charlottesville.

Achievements

Cabell's aesthetic individualism—as expressed in his highly artificial style, his loose, episodic structure, and his peculiar synthesis of romance and comedy, idealism and cynicism, mythology and personal experience—has limited both his popular and critical appeal. As Arvin R. Wells observes in *Jesting Moses: A Study in Cabellian Comedy* (1962), "It seems fair to say that rarely has a serious literary artist had so little luck in finding a responsive, judicious, and articulate audience." The essays, short stories, and books that Cabell published from 1901 to 1919 received only a small readership along with generally negative reviews, although both Mark Twain and Theodore Roosevelt praised his collection of chivalric tales, *The Line of Love*. Most readers, advocates of realism, found his works too romantic, whereas those with a taste for romance complained that Cabell was too abstruse.

In 1920, when obscenity charges were brought against *Jurgen*, Cabell found himself in the public eye, perceived as a valiant iconoclast battling the forces of puritanical repression. Sales of *Jurgen* skyrocketed, and Cabell enjoyed praise from such respected literary figures as Vernon Louis Parrington, Carl Van Doren, H. L. Mencken, and Sinclair Lewis, who in his Nobel Prize address of 1930, acknowledged Cabell's achievement. Suddenly, in critical studies, literary histories, and anthologies, Cabell was elevated to, as the critic Joe Lee Davis explains, "the rank of a 'classic' and an 'exotic' in the movement of spiritual liberation led by H. L. Mencken, Theodore Dreiser, Eugene O'Neill, and Sinclair Lewis." The public fanfare of the 1920's, however, inspired primarily by the eroticism in Cabell's works, proved to be short-lived—not to the surprise of Cabell, who, in *These Restless Heads*, predicted the decline of his literary generation. In the 1930's and 1940's, Cabell was viewed as a trifling talent, rooted to the 1920's and to his native Virginia. His aestheticism displeased the ethical neohumanists; his escapism annoyed the Marxists. The New Critics and mythic critics paid him scant attention. In the 1950's, three major literary historians—Edward Wagenknecht, Edd Winfield Parks, and Edmund Wilson—called for a reevaluation of Cabell's career, but they did little to change public opinion. Virtually all of Cabell's books are out of print, although the recent surge of interest in fantasy literature has brought some attention to his work, and he is appreciated primarily by a coterie of scholars and graduate students.

Biography

Born on April 14, 1879, in Richmond, Virginia, James Branch Cabell grew up there as a Southern gentleman. His parents—Robert Gamble Cabell II, a physician, and Anne Branch—were both from distinguished Southern families. Cabell's paternal great-grandfather was a governor of Virginia; his parternal grandfather held two claims to fame, having been a schoolmate of Edgar Allan Poe at the English and Classical School in Richmond and later a neighbor and the personal physician of General Robert E. Lee. On his mother's side of the family, Cabell was related through marriage to a number of prominent Virginia families and was cousin to a governor of Maryland. Fostering Cabell's aristocratic pride still further was his "mammy," Mrs. Louisa Nelson, who, in her several decades of service in the Cabell household, doted upon James and encouraged him to consider himself a privileged member of society.

Cabell's outstanding intellect asserted itself early. He performed brilliantly at the College of William and Mary in Williamsburg, which he attended from 1894 to 1898. His professors suggested that he revise a sophomore paper entitled "The Comedies of William Congreve" for publication, and later asked him to teach courses in French and Greek at the college. The only blemish upon Cabell's academic career was a scandal during his senior year. One of his professors was accused of having homosexual relations with his students; Cabell, because he had been friends with the man, was briefly implicated. The unpleasant episode had positive repercussions, however, for in wandering about Williamsburg alone and troubled, Cabell met Ellen Glasgow, who had come to town to research the background for a novel. She offered him sympathy, and thus began a lifelong friendship. Soon, the charges against Cabell were dropped for lack of evidence, and he was graduated with highest honors.

After his graduation, Cabell pursued writing both as a vocation and an avocation. He served as a copyholder on the *Richmond Times* in 1898, then spent two years working for the *New York Herald*, and in 1901, he worked for the *Richmond News*. For the next decade, he worked as a genealogist, traveling about America, England, Ireland, and France to examine archives. Not only did this occupation result in two volumes of the Branch family history—*Branchiana* (1907), a record of the Branch family in Virginia, and *Branch of Abingdon* (1911), a record of the Branch family in England, but it also prepared Cabell for his future literary endeavors in tracing the lineage of a character through twenty-two subsequent generations. During that same time, Cabell wrote several novels and steadily produced short stories, which he contributed to such periodicals as *The Smart Set*, *Collier's Weekly*, *Red Book*, *Lippincott's*, and *Harper's Monthly*. In 1911, Cabell, disappointed by his lack of acclaim as a writer, took a position in coal-mining operations in West Virginia; in 1913, he abandoned the experiment and returned to Richmond to resume work as a genealogist.

On November 8, 1913, at the age of thirty-four, Cabell gave up what had been a carefree bachelorhood, filled with romantic intrigues, to marry

Rebecca Priscilla Bradley Shepard, a widow with five children. Marriage proved mutually satisfying to Cabell and Priscilla. He enjoyed the domesticity of his new life-style, including the rearing of their son Ballard Hartwell; she delighted in performing the literary and social duties that came with being his wife. Their thirty-five-year union was marked by undying affection and loyalty.

Literary prominence, or perhaps one should say notoriety, came to Cabell in 1920 when John S. Sumner, the executive secretary of the New York Society for the Suppression of Vice, seized the plates and copies of his novel *Jurgen* and accused the publishing company, McBride, of violating the anti-obscenity statutes of the New York State penal code. Sumner's action proved ill-advised, for it only increased the public's interest in Cabell's writings during the two and a half years before the obscenity trial was finally held. On October 19, 1922, after a three-day trial, the jury acquitted McBride, and Cabell emerged as a celebrity.

During the 1920's, Cabell took a more active role as a literary leader and was instrumental, along with Ellen Glasgow, in making the nation aware of Richmond as a literary center. While writing books with great regularity (during the 1920's, he published seven novels, one play, and several works of short fiction and nonfiction), Cabell also entertained and corresponded with a number of important literary figures, including Sinclair Lewis, Hugh Walpole, and Carl Van Vechten. In addition, he served as a writer and guest editor for *The Reviewer*, Richmond's impressive contribution to the vogue of little magazines. As active as Cabell was on the literary scene, he was still able to continue his career as a genealogist, working for the Virginia Chapter of the Sons of the Revolution and other historical societies, as well as serving as editor of the Virginia War History Commission.

The last decades of Cabell's life were anticlimactic, fraught with physical ailments and an increasing disillusionment with the American reading public. With the advent of the Great Depression, his literary fame seemed to weaken and then die. From 1932 to 1935, Cabell—like Sherwood Anderson, George Jean Nathan, Eugene O'Neill, and Theodore Dreiser—attempted to rekindle the vital skepticism of the 1920's, serving as editor of the *American Spectator*; he soon realized, however, that his efforts to enlighten the public were useless. In the mid-1930's, Cabell suffered from repeated attacks of pneumonia, and Priscilla developed severe arthritis; thus, they frequently sought relief in the warm climate of St. Augustine, Florida. There, Priscilla died of heart failure on March 29, 1949. Her death left Cabell feeling bitter, lost, and angry, but he continued to write steadily. In 1950, he regained some of his former zest for life when he decided to wed Margaret Waller Freeman, a member of the Richmond literati whose acquaintance he had made years earlier while writing for *The Reviewer*. Cabell died of a cerebral hemorrhage on May 5, 1958, in Richmond.

Analysis

James Branch Cabell's art rests upon a paradox. On the one hand, he contends that man is idealistic and must therefore create dreams to sustain himself. On the other, he mocks man's tendency "to play the ape to his dreams"—that is, to seek the unattainable foolishly. Manipulating the polarities of romance and comedy, Cabell responded to the predominant intellectual trend of the early twentieth century—naturalism. From a cosmic perspective, he had no difficulty accepting the premise that man is like a bit of flotsam in a deterministic universe, subject to environmental forces, but unable to control or understand them. From a humanistic point of view, however, he could not tolerate the limitations that naturalism imposed upon man's mind. For Cabell, man does not survive because he adapts to biological, social, or economic forces, but rather because he persists in believing in the products of his own imagination—what he terms "dynamic illusions." These illusions, according to Cabell, emanate from the demiurge, or psyche, yet they are rooted in man's primitive, animal instincts. Their source of energy is the libido. Thus, Cabell's protagonists move between two realms of experience. They are romantic questers after ideal beauty, perfection, and salvation; they are also comic bumblers whose lusts, vanities, and misconceptions entangle them in a web of complexities. Cabell's narratives follow a Hegelian pattern. His thesis is that man desires to escape from the dull, routine world of actuality. His antithesis is that such a desire can never be attained; disillusionment is inevitable. Yet in the synthesis, man achieves a degree of satisfaction. He learns that his ideals are illusions, but also that they should be cherished, for in the realm of the imagination, dreams themselves have a reality.

Cabell's background explains his propensity for blending the romantic and the comic. Quite early, he developed a love for myth and legend. As a child, he delighted in such books as *Old Greek Stories Simply Told*, *Stories of Old Rome*, *Book of Bible Stories*, and *Stories of the Days of King Arthur*. Cabell gained a strong sense of aristocratic pride—an appreciation of the southern characteristics of chivalry and gallantry—yet he was no dreamy-eyed romantic. He saw the ironic underside of life. In growing up, he heard frank gossip, as well as heroic tales, from his elders. In college, Cabell became interested in the Restoration comedy of manners, which heightened his awareness of the hypocrisies and absurdities of human behavior. Such weaknesses became more immediately apparent when, as a bachelor in his twenties and early thirties, he vacationed at the Virginia resort of Rockbridge Alum. There, he witnessed and participated in affairs that assumed the facade of chaste, genteel encounters, but were actually indulgences in lust. From his various experiences, Cabell developed a dichotomous concept of the artist, appropriate to his blending of romance and comedy. The artist assumes an exalted status, painting beautiful visions of life as it ought to be. Ironically, however, because of this detached, godlike perspective, skepticism intrudes. The world that the artist portrays becomes a caricature; it mocks and contradicts his idealistic presentation. For Cabell, the ideal and the real coexist.

Cabell's major literary achievement is his eighteen-volume *The Biography of the Life of Manuel*, which he wished readers to regard as a single book. In 1915, Cabell conceived the idea of bringing together his writings into one vast architectural construct, and for the next fifteen years, he strove to achieve his plan: revising published works, deciding upon a logical arrangement, and writing new tales and romances to clarify his design. The result was the Storisende Edition of *The Works of James Branch Cabell*, bound in green and gold. Cabell's magnum opus represents an ingenious application of his genealogical talents to the realm of fiction. Spanning seven centuries and moving from the imaginary medieval realm of Poictesme to modern Virginia, it celebrates the life force passed on by Manuel to his descendants.

The design of *The Biography of the Life of Manuel* is best viewed in musical terms. Whether one considers it to be a fugue, as does Louis Untermyer in *James Branch Cabell: The Man and the Masks* (1970), or a sonata, which is the thesis of Warren McNeil in *Cabellian Harmonics* (1928), it revolves upon three themes and their variations. These themes are three philosophies of life: the chivalrous, the gallant, and the poetic. The chivalrous attitude views life as a testing; dominated by the will, it represents an ideal tradition in which men revere first God and then noble women. Quite the opposite, the gallant attitude views life as a toy; its social principle is hedonism. This attitude emphasizes the intelligence and is thus skeptical. Celebrating both chivalry and gallantry, the final attitude, the poetic, views life as raw material out of which it creates something that transcends life. It is controlled by the imagination.

These attitudes of the chivalrous, the gallant, and the poetic determine the structure of Cabell's work. In *Beyond Life*, the Prologue to *The Biography of the Life of Manuel*, he defines them. Then, in *Figures of Earth*, Cabell presents the life of Manuel of Poictesme, who at various times is affected by all three codes; and follows it with *The Silver Stallion*, which traces the development of the legend of Manuel the Redeemer. The fourth volume—composed of *Domnei* and *The Music from Behind the Moon*—treats one aspect of the chivalric code: woman-worship. Cabell then elaborates upon the subject in his short-story collection entitled *Chivalry*. He next examines the gallant attitude in *Jurgen*; inserts *The Line of Love*, which treats all three attitudes; then returns to gallantry in *The High Place* and the short-story collection *The Certain Hour*. The next four volumes move to the modern world: *The Cords of Vanity* presents Robert Townsend, a gallant; *From the Hidden Way* offers Townsend's verses; *The Rivet in Grandfather's Neck* portrays a chivalrous character; and *The Eagle's Shadow* examines the poet. Finally, *The Biography of the Life of Manuel* circles back upon itself, as the soul of Felix Kennaston, the protagonist of *The Cream of the Jest*, journeys back to Poictesme through his dreams. Cabell's vast design concludes with an epilogue, *Straws and Prayer-Books*, and *Townsend of Lichfield*, containing notes and addenda.

Figures of Earth, one of Cabell's finest novels, follows its author's typical tripartite pattern of quest, ensuing disillusionment, and final transcendence, as it traces the career of the swineherd Manuel. Subtitled *A Comedy of Appearances*, it is a complex allegorical work peopled with supernatural and preternatural beings who reside in the imaginary medieval land of Poictesme. The tale begins when Miramon Lluagor, the master of dreams, appears to Manuel at the pool of Haranton. There, he convinces Manuel to abandon his job as a swineherd—that is, to rebel against the elemental forces of life— and to pursue knight-errantry in seeking the beautiful yet unattainable Lady Gisele. Eager to make a fine figure in the world, Manuel repudiates his lover Suskind, a mysterious creature who represents the unconscious desires of the libido, and sets forth, unaware that he is being victimized by Horvendile, the diabolical spirit of romance. On his journey, he has a series of encounters with allegorical women. He first meets Niafer, a rather plain kitchen servant, who symbolizes worldly wisdom and domesticity. Dressed as a boy, she accompanies Manuel on his quest until, when faced with his own death unless he gives up Niafer, Manuel decides to sacrifice her to Grandfather Death. His next encounter is with the Princess Alianora, who represents political power, worldly position, and the undercurrent of sexual excitement that accompanies them. Manuel surrenders to lust, but eventually rejects Alianora, discovering the limitations of self-seeking gallantry. His third important encounter is with the supernal Queen Freydis, who symbolizes creative inspiration. Using magic, Manuel persuades her to leave her realm of Audela and enter the ordinary world. She does so out of love for him and animates a set of clay figures that he sculpted as a swineherd. These eventually enter history as major writers.

Manuel soon discovers that Freydis cannot give him fulfillment; only Niafer can, so he submits to thirty years of slavery to The Head of Misery to bring Niafer back from the dead. Then he settles down to a comfortable existence as a husband, father, and the Count of Poictesme. One day, however, while watching his wife and daughter through the window of Ageus (Usage) in his palace study, he discovers to his horror that their figures are only scratched upon the glass—that beyond the window is a chaos containing the images of preexistence, including the disturbing Suskind. Manuel must then choose whether to die himself or to allow his child Melicent to die in his place, while he resumes his relationship with Suskind. Acting decisively, he murders Suskind, bricks up the study window, and departs with Grandfather Death. In the last chapter, Grandfather Death accompanies him to the River Lethe, where he watches the images of his life as they sweep by him. Then the scene blurs, as Cabell moves his readers back to the pool of Haranton where Manuel began his quest. He repeats the dialogue of the first chapter, in which Miramon refers to Count Manuel, who has just died. Thus, Cabell ends with an appropriate reminder of his view of life as a cycle in which one life passes into other lives through heredity.

Manuel is Cabell's man of action, driven by dreams of a better life than that of a swineherd, yet the pursuit of dreams proves frustrating. Even in the mythical realm of Poictesme, Cabell constantly emphasizes through allegory the realities of death, misery, and madness. Life, Manuel learns, is full of obligations: to Alianora, Melicent, and especially to Niafer. Indeed, Cabell underscores this lesson by structuring his episodes into five books entitled "Credit," "Spending," "Cash Accounts," "Surcharge," and "Settlement." Yet it is in confronting his obligations that Manuel finds fulfillment. The romantic quest results in a comic exposure of man's limitations, but the final picture is of human dignity in accepting those limitations. Manuel can never completely obliterate discontent, but he decides that the human possessions of a kingdom, a wife, and a family, even if they are illusions, are better than a return to the primitive unconsciousness. Thus, although he never achieves the object of his initial quest, he does transcend experience through belief in his destined role as the Redeemer of Poictesme and his ultimate rejection of lust for love.

Figures of Earth, because of its confusing cast of characters—some of whom are figures of earth; some, unearthly—and the artificialities of Cabell's prose, makes difficult reading. The effort is rewarding, however, for Cabell offers some intriguing insights into man's values: that the demands of the family and the aspirations of the individual often conflict; that the world is duplicitous; and that the search for perfection involves paradoxically the self realization of imperfection. The work is thought-provoking and timely.

Jurgen follows the same movement as *Figures of Earth*: the pursuit of perfection, the discovery that it does not exist, and then the satisfaction achieved through accepting actuality; it merely views these ideas from a different perspective. The controlling concept is justice, which to Cabell's title character, a poetry-producing pawnbroker, means that in the universe, every idealistic desire should have a means of being fulfilled. Jurgen's problem, however, is that existence is unjust; since man's intellect increases as his physical prowess diminishes, he can never completely realize his potential. Granting Jurgen a temporary respite from his dilemma, Cabell allows his middle-aged poet to retain his youthful body and then lets his reader see the subsequent effects upon his protagonist's values.

Jurgen began as a tale entitled "Some Ladies and Jurgen," which Cabell published in *The Smart Set* in 1918. His novel simply expands upon the narrative of that story. The hero meets a monk, who curses the devil for causing him to trip over a stone. Jurgen, playing the devil's advocate, defends evil. Shortly thereafter, he meets a black gentleman who thanks him for the defense and expresses the hope that his life will be carefree. When Jurgen replies that such a life is impossible, since he is married, the stranger promises to reward him. The reward turns out to be the disappearance of Jurgen's wife, Dame Lisa. When he returns home, she is gone; he later learns that she has been seen near a cave outside town. Feeling an obligation, he goes there, only to encounter the black gentleman—who, he learns, is Koshchei the Deathless, the controller of the universe. Koshchei tempts Jurgen by evoking three women that he feels would be more suitable for a poet: Queen Guenevere, Queen Anaïtis, and Queen Helen—standing respectively for faith, desire, and vision. Jurgen rejects each, however, and asks for Dame Lisa back. She appears, lectures him, and then leaves for home. In response, Jurgen praises her as a source of poetic inspiration more valuable than faith, desire, and vision, and then follows her home.

Expanding his narrative for the novel, Cabell added two fantasy sequences that would explain Jurgen's ultimate attraction to Lisa. In the first, Jurgen visits the Garden between Dawn and Sunrise, where he relives falling in love with Dorothy la Désirée, one of the daughters of Manuel. She destroys his romantic bliss when she marries the wealthy Heitman Michael and then engages in adulterous affairs. Because of Dorothy's behavior, Jurgen marries Lisa. In the second episode, Jurgen, having been granted by Mother Sereda the recovery of a bygone Wednesday, fantasizes about how his relationship with Dorothy might have developed. He imagines himself killing Heitman Michael and claiming her, but as the Wednesday ends, he finds himself embracing the Dorothy of reality, an aged femme fatale.

Cabell also expanded his original tale by depicting Jurgen's adventures in five realms: Glathion, Cocaigne, Leukê, Hell, and Heaven. Throughout these episodes, Jurgen assumes the roles of charlatan and womanizer, as he tests historical systems of values. In Glathion, he examines the medieval tradition of Christian chivalry, but rejects it as being irrational. In Cocaigne, he becomes equally dissatisfied with hedonistic paganism. Leukê, a stronghold of the Helenic tradition, teaches him the danger of the realm of utilitarian Philistia. In Hell, Jurgen learns of the sin of pride, and in Heaven encounters selfless love. Feeling the shadow of worldly wisdom trailing him, Jurgen finally decides to give up his youthful body and return to the domestic comforts that Dame Lisa can provide. He trades the ideal for the actual, yet in so doing bestows romantic value upon his ordinary existence and his ordinary wife.

Although entertaining, *Jurgen* lacks clarity of design. The reader who is steeped in mythology may enjoy Cabell's manipulation of the legends of Faust, Don Juan, King Arthur, Troilus and Cressida, and Ulysses and Penelope, but somehow, the integration of the hero's adventures with the narrative line exploring the feelings between husband and wife is incomplete. The episodic looseness of the novel is distracting. Thus, modern readers, like those titillated readers of the 1920's, may be absorbed by Jurgen's amorous exploits without fully considering Cabell's analysis of the values that make life worth living.

Cabell's great achievement is that he celebrated the illusion-making capacity of the mind while simultaneously exposing man's follies in pursuing dreams. He merged the traditions of humanism and skepticism. Reacting against naturalism, Cabell had the courage to present a transcendent view of life—one that acknowledged not man's impotency, but his potential. A meticulous craftsman, a daring iconoclast, an imaginative thinker, Cabell deserves recognition as a major writer of the twentieth century.

Lynne P. Shackelford

Other major works

SHORT FICTION: *The Line of Love*, 1905; *Gallantry*, 1907; *Chivalry*, 1909; *The Certain Hour*, 1916; *The Music from Behind the Moon*, 1926; *The White Robe*, 1928

PLAY: *The Jewel Merchants*, 1921.

POETRY: *From the Hidden Way*, 1916.

NONFICTION: *Branchiana*, 1907; *Branch of Abingdon*, 1911; *Beyond Life*, 1919; *The Judging of Jurgen*, 1920; *Taboo*, 1921; *Joseph Hergesheimer*, 1921; *Straws and Prayer-Books*, 1924; *Some of Us*, 1930; *These Restless Heads*, 1932 (contains two short stories and personal reminiscences); *Special Delivery*, 1933; *Ladies and Gentlemen*, 1934; *Of Ellen Glasgow*, 1938; *The St. Johns*, 1943 (with A. J. Hanna); *Let Me Lie*, 1947; *Quiet, Please*, 1952; *As I Remember It*, 1955; *Between Friends: Letters of James Branch Cabell and Others*, 1962 (Margaret Freeman Cabell and Padraic Colum, editors); *The Letters of James Branch Cabell*, 1975 (Edward Wagenknecht, editor).

MISCELLANEOUS: *The Biography of the Life of Manuel: The Works of James Branch Cabell*, 1927-1930 (18 volumes).

Bibliography

Duke, Maurice. *James Branch Cabell: A Reference Guide*. Boston: G. K. Hall, 1979. A most useful guide, in a chronological format, to the writings about Cabell; spans reviews to full-length studies.

Himelick, Raymond. *James Branch Cabell and the Modern Temper: Three Essays*. New York: Revisionist Press, 1974. Himelick explores realism and romance, the fact and the dream in Cabell's novels. Sees Cabell as an antiromantic whose novels convey his understanding of life as a "grotesque comedy."

Inge, Thomas M., and Edgar E. MacDonald, eds. *James Branch Cabell: Centennial Essays*. Baton Rouge: Louisiana State University Press, 1983. A compilation of essays that were presented at Virginia Commonwealth University, 1979, in commemoration of the centennial of Cabell's birth. A most useful volume with valuable biographical information and criticism.

Also includes a bibliographical essay.

Tarrant, Desmond. *James Branch Cabell: The Dream and the Reality.* Norman: University of Oklahoma Press, 1967. A full-length critical study of Cabell that examines the author as mythmaker. Discusses both Cabell's early and later works, but Tarrant's eulogistic approach weakens his criticism.

Van Doren, Carl, H. L. Mencken, and Hugh Walpole. *James Branch Cabell: Three Essays.* Port Washington, N.Y.: Kennikat Press, 1967. Criticism of a very high standard—both erudite and entertaining—by three eminent authors. Included in the appendix is a sampling of book reviews. A valuable contribution to critical studies on Cabell.

GEORGE WASHINGTON CABLE

Born: New Orleans, Louisiana; October 12, 1844
Died: St. Petersburg, Florida; January 31, 1925

Principal long fiction

The Grandissimes, 1880; *Dr. Sevier*, 1884; *Bonaventure*, 1888; *John March, Southerner*, 1894; *The Cavalier*, 1901; *Bylow Hill*, 1902; *Kincaid's Battery*, 1908; *Gideon's Band*, 1914; *Lovers of Louisiana*, 1918.

Other literary forms

In addition to nine novels, George Washington Cable published a novella, *Madame Delphine* (1881), and four collections of short stories: *Old Creole Days* (1879); *Strong Hearts* (1899); *Posson Jone' and Père Raphaël* (1909); and *The Flower of the Chapdelaines* (1918). He also wrote a dramatized version of one of his novels, *The Cavalier*. His eight books of nonfiction cover miscellaneous subjects. *The Creoles of Louisiana* (1884) is a collection of history articles, and *Strange True Stories of Louisiana* (1889) is a collection of factual stories; both collections are set in Cable's native state. *The Silent South* (1885) and *The Negro Question* (1890) are collections of essays on Southern problems. *The Busy Man's Bible* (1891) and *The Amateur Garden* (1914) grew out of Cable's hobbies of Bible-teaching and gardening. *A Memory of Roswell Smith* (1892) is a memorial tribute to a friend. *The Cable Story Book: Selections for School Reading* (1899) is a book of factual and fictional material for children. Cable also wrote magazine articles and a newspaper column.

Achievements

In his study *George W. Cable* (1962), Philip Butcher shows the high position that Cable held in American literature in the last years of the nineteenth century. In 1884, the *Critic* ranked him ahead of fourteenth-place Mark Twain in its list of "Forty Immortals." A cartoon in *Life* (May 27, 1897) depicted Cable among the ten most popular authors of the day. In the American edition of *Literature* in 1899, he was tenth on the list of greatest living American writers.

Popular both with critics and with the reading public in his own time, Cable is little known today. His reputation as a writer of fiction rests on three works: the novel *The Grandissimes*, the novella *Madame Delphine*, and the collection of short stories *Old Creole Days*, later editions of which include *Madame Delphine* as the lead story. Although *Dr. Sevier* and *John March, Southerner* contain serious commentary, the three novels which followed in the first decade of the new century are trivial romances. His last two novels, *Gideon's Band* and *Lovers of Louisiana*, signal only an incomplete return to the artistic level and social worth of his first three books. Because much of his energy went into provocative social essays on Southern racial problems, into humanitarian reforms in such areas as prisons and insane asylums, into cultural projects, and, as a major source of income, into platform tours, Cable found insufficient time for the fiction he might otherwise have created. Nevertheless, as late as 1918 he published a collection of short stories and a novel, and up to his death in 1925 he was working on still another novel.

Cable was much admired by his contemporaries. William Dean Howells praised him privately and in print. Twain took him as a partner on a reading tour, and for four months (1884-1885) the two shared the stage as they read from their respective works. Cable also read on programs that included Hamlin Garland, James Whitcomb Riley, Eugene Field, and other popular writers of the day.

Popular in Britain as well, he was invited to England by James S. Barrie for the first of two trips abroad (1898, 1905). For nearly three months in 1898, he traveled and visited in the homes of Barrie, Sir Arthur Conan Doyle, Rudyard Kipling, Henry James, and other well-known figures. He was an interesting conversationalist, an effective speaker, and an entertaining performer. His British friends arranged for him to read his fiction, play a guitar, and sing Creole-Negro songs in their homes and in public halls. Andrew Carnegie, his host at Skibo Castle, was so impressed with Cable's personality and writing that he later bestowed a lifetime pension on him. Among his honorary degrees was the Doctorate of Letters given by Yale University in 1901 to Cable, Twain, Howells, Theodore Roosevelt, Woodrow Wilson, and other contemporary notables.

Cable's reputation began to decline before his death and has never recovered. In the 1980's he is considered too important a writer to be omitted from Southern literature anthologies and American literature textbooks, but he has not yet been deemed worthy of widespread revival.

Biography

George Washington Cable was born in New Orleans, Louisiana, on October 12, 1844. Ancestors of his mother, Rebecca Boardman Cable, had lived in New England since the seventeenth century and had moved to Indiana in 1807. The background of his father, the elder George Washington Cable, dates back to pre-Revolutionary times in Virginia. The elder Cable lived in Virginia and Pennsylvania with his parents before moving to Indiana, where he married Rebecca in 1834. The Cable family migrated to New Orleans in 1837, where young George became their fifth child.

In the 1840's, the Cables lived a comfortable existence, owning several household slaves until the father's business failed. Through the 1850's, the elder Cable worked at a series of jobs until, weakened in health, he died on February 28, 1859. Because young George's older brother, along with an older sister, had died of scarlet fever, his father's death required him, not yet fourteen, to leave school to support the family. Until the third year of the Civil War, he held his father's former position as a clerk at the customhouse.

Slight in size—with a height of five feet five inches and a weight of one hundred pounds—and deceptively youthful in features, Cable enlisted in the Confederate Army on October 9, 1863, three days before his nineteenth birthday. Incurring two slight wounds during his service, he was discharged in 1865.

After the war, Cable worked as errand boy, store clerk, and, until malaria stopped him, as a rodsman with a surveying party on the Red River. In 1868, he became a bookkeeper for two cotton firms in New Orleans. He married Louise Stewart Bartlett on December 7, 1869, and soon fathered the first of a large family of children. At one time, he worked simultaneously for the cotton house of William C. Black and Company, the New Orleans Cotton Exchange, and the National Cotton Exchange.

Newspaper work provided Cable's first opportunity to see his writing in print. While continuing as an accountant, he worked for newspapers as a free-lance contributor and then as a full-time reporter. For eighteen months, beginning February 27, 1870, he wrote "Drop Shot," a column, weekly and then daily, for the New Orleans *Picayune*. While working for the *Picayune*, his research into Louisiana history at city hall, the cathedral, and the Cabildo, former seat of colonial government, led him to factual stories later to be shaped into fiction. In addition, his newspaper reports on contemporary local affairs interested him in reform on civic, regional, and national levels.

Appearing in *Scribner's Monthly*, Cable's stories were based on his knowledge of the people and activities of New Orleans and of events in Louisiana history. Six of the stories appearing in *Scribner's Monthly* and a seventh story, "Posson Jone'," which was published in *Appleton's Journal*, were later collected as *Old Creole Days*, published by Scribner's. His first novel, *The Grandissimes*, also based on the people and history of Louisiana, was serialized in *Scribner's Monthly* over a twelve-month period and then published in book form in 1880. Next came the novella *Madame Delphine*, first printed in *Scribner's Monthly* as a three-part serial, and then published in book form in 1881.

In 1881, Cable gave up his position as an accountant, depending for the rest of his life on lectures and public readings of his fiction to supplement his income as a writer. One of his successes was a series of six lectures at Johns Hopkins University in 1883, and he continued to find himself in demand on platforms in many cities. In 1884, his regional history *The Creoles of Louisiana* appeared, and in the same year his second novel, *Dr. Sevier*, was published. In 1884-1885 he went on a successful reading tour with Mark Twain.

Cable, son of a slaveholding family, was a loyal Confederate soldier during the Civil War and apparently remained unchanged in political stance for some time thereafter. Later, however, he began to express feeling against racial injustice. Although criticism of discrimination is present in his fiction, it was only through the direct statements of his magazine articles and public lectures that fellow Southerners became fully aware of his radical stance. The publication of a volume of his essays, *The Silent South* (1885), made his stand clear. Newspaper editorialists who had acclaimed his fiction now began to attack his social and political views.

Cable had two households to support—one including his wife and children, the other his mother, his sisters, and the children of his widowed sister. His wife, who traced her ancestry back to the Mayflower, was born and reared in New England. Cable believed that a return to the climate of New England would be beneficial for his wife's frail health. In addition, the attraction that a location near his publishers in New York held for him, and a sensitivity to the criticism aimed at him in the South, influenced his decision to leave New Orleans after forty years of residence there. Having previously visited Northampton, Massachusetts, he moved his wife and children to a home there in 1885, and his mother, sisters, and cousins followed soon thereafter.

Despite his desire to write fiction, Cable allowed other interests to take much of his time. In 1885, he championed black rights in an essay read nationwide, "The Freedman's Case in Equity." In 1886, he founded the first of the Home Culture Clubs, in which he would be involved for the next thirty-five years. Through his Open Letter Club (1888-1890), in whose name he lectured, wrote, and published, Cable completed the period identified as his greatest effort for reform in the South. From 1887 to 1889, he undertook an extensive program of religious writing and teaching; he conducted a large Bible class in Northampton each Sunday, traveling to Boston on Saturdays to hold a similar class.

For five years, Cable published a book annually; *Bonaventure*, *Strange True Stories of Louisiana*, *The Negro Question*, *The Busy Man's Bible*, and *A Memory of Roswell Smith* were all published during this period. At the same time, he was giving readings and lectures from coast to coast. A popular speaker, he was frequently invited to deliver commencement addresses and to give talks on literary subjects, Southern problems, and Creole history. Despite his endeavors, however, he remained constantly in debt—receiving advances on royalties from his publishers, obtaining loans, repaying old debts, and incurring new ones.

By this time, Cable had ceased actively campaigning for civil rights, and his writing developed a noncontroversial tone. His third novel, *John March, Southerner*, although concerned with Reconstruction problems, avoided racial issues, as did his collection of short stories *Strong Hearts*. *The Cable Story Book*, needless to say, offended no one. The following novels, *The Cavalier* and *Bylow Hill*, veered even more sharply from controversy to entertainment, their artistic value diminishing proportionately.

Meanwhile, in 1898, Cable had made a triumphal reading tour in Britain.

Philanthropist Andrew Carnegie, with whom Cable became friends while in Scotland, donated money to one of Cable's long-enduring projects. In 1903, Carnegie agreed to give fifty thousand dollars for a building for the Home Culture Clubs on the condition that five thousand dollars a year be guaranteed locally for five years.

Dimming Cable's good fortune, his beloved wife died on February 27, 1904, ending a devoted marriage of nearly thirty-five years. Cable continued to write, although without immediately readying a book for publication. Two years and nine months after Louise's death, he married Eva C. Stevenson. In 1908, he published the novel *Kincaid's Battery*, and in 1909 he put two of his short stories (one of them selected from the *Old Creole Days* collection) into book form, *Posson Jone' and Père Raphaël*. In 1911, Carnegie began sending Cable one thousand dollars a year to support his writing. Three years later, *Gideon's Band* and *The Amateur Garden* were published.

Despite his debts, Cable managed to travel outside the United States even before Carnegie began to subsidize him. When traveling, he often carried with him an unfinished manuscript, working on it when he had time. In later years, no longer dependent on the platform circuit, he began staying in Northampton in the summer, spending the winter in New Orleans, Florida, and Bermuda. In 1918, at the age of seventy-four, he published two books—*The Flower of the Chapdelaines*, a collection of short stories, and *Lovers of Louisiana*.

When Carnegie died in 1919, his will provided Cable with five thousand dollars a year for life, the annuity to be transferred to Eva if she survived her husband. Eva, however, died on June 7, 1923. Six months after her death, Cable married his third wife, Hanna Cowing. A little more than a year later, on January 31, 1925, he died. Among his literary papers was an unfinished novel on which he had been working.

Analysis

Although George Washington Cable's reputation rests primarily on one collection of short stories and two pieces of longer fiction, his total output includes twenty-two books. For an understanding of Cable as a writer of fiction, one should first consider his nonfiction and his reasons for writing it. Cable's interest in history is shown in two books centered on Creole culture, *The Creoles of Louisiana*, a collection of history articles, and *Strange True Stories of Louisiana*, a collection of factual stories about the Creoles. On a juvenile level, *The Cable Story Book* is a combination of factual and fictional material that emphasizes the same Creole subjects as his fiction. *The Silent South* and *The Negro Question*, his best-known works of nonfiction, are collections of essays on controversial Southern problems, notably the problem of racial discrimination. Characteristic of Cable's prose is a moral posture and a humanitarian zeal, openly stated in his nonfiction and imaginatively expressed in the most important of his fiction. He worked for the reform of men and institutions and for a reversal in racial attitudes.

Cable's first novel, *The Grandissimes*, is his unqualified masterpiece. Louis D. Rubin, Jr. has called it the first "modern" Southern novel, dealing realistically as it does with the role of the black in American society. Added to the rich portrayal of aristocratic Creole settings and family problems, a panoramic array of characters of Indian, black, and mixed bloods vivify problems of social castes and racial discrimination in Louisiana in 1803, the year of the Louisiana Purchase. Using the historical actuality of racially tangled bloodlines as the theme for dramatic episodes, Cable emphasizes the ramifications of black-white relationships. The free quadroon caste, for example, had its special role in Southern society, as shown historically in the New Orleans "quadroon balls." Beautiful young women of one-quarter black blood (quadroons) or, perhaps, one-eighth (octoroons) danced at these balls with white men, were chosen by them as mistresses, and were set up in separate households in the city.

Two principal quadroons interact in *The Grandissimes*. A male quadroon is the identically named half-brother of the aristocratic Creole, Honoré Grandissime. The darker Honoré Grandissime flouts the law by refusing to inscribe the letters "f.m.c." (free man of color) after his name. Educated in Paris along with his half-brother and heir to most of their deceased father's wealth, the quadroon nevertheless remains unrecognized as a legitimate member of the Grandissime family. The Creoles' acceptance of an Indian chieftain as ancestor is introduced to point up their unwonted prejudice against the taint of black blood. The main female quadroon is Palmyre Philosophe, a freed slave who bears a hopeless love for the all-white Honoré Grandissime and, in turn, is loved by his quadroon half-brother. To illustrate the injustices perpetrated against blacks, Cable inserts the episode of the black Bras-Coupé, a historical figure used earlier in Cable's unpublished short story "Bibi." Palmyre hates Agricola Fuselier, her former owner and uncle to Honoré Grandissime, who forced her unconsummated marriage to Bras-Coupé.

The character who serves throughout the novel as spokesman for Cable is Joseph Frowenfeld, a German-American newcomer to New Orleans, who observes, participates in, and comments critically on the action. Honoré Grandissime, the leading male character, is a Creole who recognizes the faults of his society and works with moderation to correct them. He provides a liberal Creole viewpoint, supplementary to the rigid moral judgment of Frowenfeld. Agricola Fuselier, in direct contrast to Frowenfeld, represents the proud old Creoles who insist on purity of race.

Action antecedent to the year-long events of the novel goes back to 1673, the year of the birth of the Indian girl whose choice of a De Grapion suitor began a feud between two Creole families, the De Grapions and the Grandissimes. Preceding the main plot by eight years comes the tale of Bras-

Coupé. Otherwise, the action takes place between September, 1803, and September, 1804.

The leading female character, Aurora Nancanou, daughter of a De Grapion, is the young widow of a man killed by Agricola Fuselier in a duel over a card game. Agricola took Nancanou's estate in payment for the gambling debt, passing the estate on to his nephew, the white Honoré, and leaving Aurora and her daughter Clotilde without land or money. The novel opens at a masked ball in New Orleans where Aurora and Honoré meet, unaware of each other's identity, thus beginning a romantic complication. Paralleling the love triangle of Palmyre and the Grandissime half-brothers, Joseph Frowenfeld falls in love with Clotilde, who, at the same time, is desired by Frowenfeld's friend Dr. Charlie Keene.

Honoré Grandissime, as leader of the Grandissime family and as Cable's symbol of right-thinking Creoles, upsets his relatives on several occasions: endangering the Grandissime finances, he returns Aurora Nancanou's property to her; in an act socially degrading to the family, he becomes a partner with the quadroon Honoré, under the business title "The Grandissime Brothers"; on an uneasy political level, he cooperates with Claiborne, the newly appointed territorial governor.

Romance, realism, and melodrama are mingled in *The Grandissimes*. In a romantic resolution, the De Grapion-Grandissime feud is ended, and marriage is imminent for two sets of lovers—Aurora and the white Honoré Grandissime, Clotilde and Frowenfeld. On the realistic side—with an admixture of melodramatic incidents—the two leading quadroons of the story are defeated. After Palmyre's several attempts to get revenge on the object of her hate, Agricola Fuselier, and after he is stabbed by the quadroon Honoré, she is forced to flee for safety to Paris. She is accompanied by her fellow refugee, Honoré Grandissime (f m c), who commits suicide by drowning because of her final rejection of him.

Intentional obscurity is a characteristic of Cable's style in *The Grandissimes*. Lack of direct statement and slow revelation of relationships mark the progress of the plot. Facts are given through hints and implication; full information is withheld in a dense accumulation of incidents. This technique, typical of his early and best works, has been praised for its artistry and criticized for its lack of clarity.

Cable's portrayal of slaveholders, slaves, and the stubbornly held traditions of French Louisiana added a new dimension to Southern literature. Succeeding in his aim as a novelist, Cable found that fame brought a painful backlash. His radical views caused this native son to be identified as a traitor to New Orleans and the South.

In 1881, Cable published the novella *Madame Delphine*, the third in the three-year sequence of Cable's finest literary works (after the short-story collection *Old Creole Days* and the novel *The Grandissimes*). First published as a three-part novelette in *Scribner's Monthly* from May to July, 1881, *Madame Delphine* was published by Scribner's in book form later that year. In editions of *Old Creole Days* succeeding its initial publication, *Madame Delphine* is included and given lead position in the book.

The story begins with beautiful Olive Delphine returning from France on a ship that is boarded by the Creole pirate Ursin Lemaitre. Confronted by Olive's piety and charm, Lemaitre is struck with repentance for his sinful life and with love for the unidentified stranger. Settling in New Orleans, the reformed Lemaitre changes his name to Vignevielle and turns from piracy to banking. When not in his banker's office, he wanders through the streets, searching for the mysterious young woman.

Eventually, the lovelorn banker and Olive develop a friendship and marriage becomes their intention. Olive, however, is not legally able to become Lemaitre's wife, for she has black ancestry. Her mother, Madame Delphine, is a quadroon, the mistress to a white man, Olive's father. Madame Delphine, despite the laws against miscegenation, approves of the marriage. Indeed, she has made it clear that she is seeking a white husband for her daughter.

Vignevielle's relatives and friends, knowing that Madame Delphine is a quadroon, attempt to stop the illegal marriage, going so far as to threaten to turn him over to government agents who are searching for him. Madame Delphine meanwhile puts forth the ultimate effort to make the union possible. Producing fabricated evidence, she perjures herself by swearing that she is not the girl's blood mother. After Vignevielle and Olive are married, Madame Delphine goes for confession to the priest Père Jerome, admits her lie, and dies. Père Jerome speaks the closing line: "Lord, lay not this sin to her charge!"

The style of *Madame Delphine* is leisurely. Little mysteries cling to characters and actions, with revelation coming in glimpses, suggestions, and half-expressed statements. Early reviewers compared Cable to Nathaniel Hawthorne in achievement of mood, atmosphere, and ambiguity. Adverse criticism of *Madame Delphine*, however, finds the work excessively obscure; most troubling to critics is the needlessly complicated unfolding of the plot.

Furthermore, the characterization of the lovers is weak. Vignevielle's switch from dashing pirate to banker is inadequately motivated. Olive is a shadowy figure without distinguishable traits. Madame Delphine, despite her maneuvers, approaches the stereotype of the helpless mother. The only strong character, is Père Jerome, a compassionate observer and spokesman for Cable. Père Jerome sees that society deserves blame, both for its actions and for its failure to act. Society acquiesces in evil—from its unprotesting profit in Lemaitre's smuggled goods to its deliberate manipulation of the lives of mulattoes.

More significant than the style of *Madame Delphine* is its portrayal of the Southern attitude toward miscegenation. Although romanticism embellishes the outwardly happy ending of the story, Cable's recognition of the female mulatto's untenable position is clear. Looking beyond the temporary bliss of the wedding day, the reader realizes that prospects for Olive in New Orleans are not favorable. Madame Delphine's perjury has made the marriage legally permissible, but in the eyes of Lemaitre's friends, Olive is not and will never be an acceptable member of their aristocratic society.

The developing social consciousness revealed by Cable in *Madame Delphine* gives the work a lasting value. After this novella, though, he confined the most telling of his indictments to essays, disappointing readers who waited for his familiar critical tone in future novels. He was never able to duplicate the blend of artistic craftsmanship, authentic local color, and social commentary which distinguishes *Madame Delphine*, *The Grandissimes*, and *Old Creole Days*.

Bernice Larson Webb

Other major works

SHORT FICTION: *Old Creole Days*, 1879; *Madame Delphine*, 1881; *Strong Hearts*, 1899; *Posson Jone' and Père Raphaël*, 1909; *The Flower of the Chapdelaines*, 1918.

NONFICTION: *The Creoles of Louisiana*, 1884; *The Silent South*, 1885; *Strange True Stories of Louisiana*, 1889; *The Negro Question*, 1890; *The Busy Man's Bible*, 1891; *A Memory of Roswell Smith*, 1892; *The Amateur Garden*, 1914.

MISCELLANEOUS: *The Cable Story Book: Selections for School Reading*, 1899.

Bibliography

Bikle, Lucy Leffingwell. *George W. Cable: His Life and Letters* New York: Charles Scribner's Sons, 1928. A valuable intimate portrait by Cable's daughter, Bikle's biography stresses family interests more than literary ones, and tends to drop names. The student may be interested in the illustrations of Cable's residence, family, and the people he knew.

Butcher, Philip. *George W. Cable*. New York: Twayne. 1962. In addition to a biography, contains a history of New Orleans to place Cable's life in context. A study of Cable's literary reputation concludes that its decline was the result of distaste for his essays on slavery. Includes a chronology and an annotated bibliography.

Petry, Alice Hall. *A Genius in His Way*. Cranbury, N.J.: Associated University Presses, 1988. A literary study focusing on the short stories from *Old Creole Days*, but opening with a chapter on *Madame Delphine*, this book is rather scholarly, but accessible to an advanced high school student. The bibliography includes only items cited in the text.

Rubin, Louis D., Jr. *George W. Cable: The Life and Times of A Southern*

Heretic. New York: Pegasus, 1979. By Rubin's own admission, the biography in this book is dependent on the work of Arlin Turner, but Rubin's comments on the individual stories are insightful and helpful. Has complete chapters on *Old Creole Days, The Grandissimes, Dr. Sevier*, and *John March, Southerner*.

Turner, Arlin. *George W. Cable: A Biography*. Durham, N.C.: Duke University Press, 1957. This award-winning biography by an important critic emphasizes Cable's life but offers helpful insight into his writing as well, with three novels receiving their own chapters. Still the most detailed biography of Cable available.

_____. *Mark Twain and George W. Cable: The Record of a Literary Friendship*. East Lansing: Michigan State University Press, 1960. Drawing almost exclusively on letters between the two writers, this short volume is useful for its personal insights.

ERSKINE CALDWELL

Born: White Oak, Georgia; December 17, 1903
Died: Paradise Valley, Arizona; April 11, 1987.

Principal long fiction

The Bastard, 1929; *Poor Fool*, 1930; *Tobacco Road*, 1932; *God's Little Acre*, 1933; *Journeyman*, 1935; *Trouble in July*, 1940; *All Night Long: A Novel of Guerrilla Warfare in Russia*, 1942; *Tragic Ground*, 1944; *A House in the Uplands*, 1946; *The Sure Hand of God*, 1947; *This Very Earth*, 1948; *Place Called Estherville*, 1949; *Episode in Palmetto*, 1950; *A Lamp for Nightfall*, 1952; *Love and Money*, 1954; *Gretta*, 1955; *Claudelle Inglish*, 1958; *Jenny by Nature*; 1961; *Close to Home*, 1962; *The Last Night of Summer*, 1963; *Miss Mamma Aimee*, 1967; *Summertime Island*, 1968; *The Weather Shelter*, 1969; *The Earnshaw Neighborhood*, 1972; *Annette*, 1974.

Other literary forms

Erskine Caldwell's first published work was "The Georgia Cracker," a 1926 article. Other pieces were printed in "little" magazines, and then in *Scribner's Magazine*. For several decades, he regularly wrote articles for magazines and newspapers. He produced several nonfiction books, some in collaboration with photojournalist Margaret Bourke-White (at one time his wife): *You Have Seen Their Faces* (1937), *North of the Danube* (1939), *All-Out on the Road to Smolensk* (1942), and *Russia at War* (1942). His collections of short stories include *American Earth* (1931), *We Are the Living: Brief Stories* (1933), *Kneel to the Rising Sun and Other Stories* (1935), *Southways: Stories* (1938), and *Jackpot: The Short Stories of Erskine Caldwell* (1940), which contains all the stories of the first four books in addition to nine new ones.

Achievements

More than sixty-four million copies of Caldwell's books have been published in thirty-four countries, with 320 editions released in such languages as Croatian, Chinese, Slovene, Turkmenian, Arabic, Danish, Hebrew, Icelandic, Russian, and Turkish. He has been called the best-selling writer in America.

In 1933, Caldwell received the *Yale Review* award for fiction for his short story "Country Full of Swedes." Between 1940 and 1955, he was editor of twenty-five volumes of a regional series, *American Folkways*. His novel *Tobacco Road* was adapted for the stage in 1934 by Jack Kirkland and ran seven and a half years on Broadway, a record run. It was made into a motion picture in 1941. *Claudelle Inglish* became a film in 1961. *God's Little Acre*, possibly his best-known novel, sold more than eight million copies in paperback in the United States alone and became a film in 1959.

Biography

Erskine Caldwell was the son of a preacher, Ira Sylvester Caldwell. His mother was Caroline "Carrie" Preston (Bell) Caldwell of Staunton, Virginia. At the time Erskine was born, on December 17, 1903, the Reverend Caldwell was minister in Newman, Georgia, in Coweta County, forty miles from Atlanta. His wife, active in helping her husband in his ministry, also ran a small school. She taught Caldwell through much of his elementary and secondary education, both in her school and at home. He actually spent only one year in public school and one in high school.

Between 1906 and 1919, the Caldwells moved several times as the ministry dictated. This not-quite-nomadic existence and the straitened circumstances under which the family lived were probably influential in molding Caldwell into early self-reliance and in fostering a wanderlust that persisted throughout his youth and adult life. Caldwell left home at fourteen, roaming about the Deep South, Mexico, and Central America. He did return home, however, to complete his high school education.

In 1920, Caldwell enrolled in Erskine College in Due West, South Carolina. From 1923 to 1924, he attended the University of Virginia on a scholarship; in 1924, he studied for two terms at the University of Pennsylvania. In 1925, he returned to the University of Virginia for an additional term, but he was never graduated.

While attending the University of Virginia, he married Helen Lannegan, and it was at this time that he decided to write for a living. With his wife and growing family of three children (Erskine Preston, Dabney Withers, and Janet), he lived in Maine between 1925 and 1932 while he wrote and earned a living at odd jobs; seven years of writing elapsed before any of his work was published. In his lifetime, Caldwell had experience as a mill laborer, cook, cabdriver, farmhand, stonemason's helper, soda jerk, professional football player, bodyguard, stagehand at a burlesque theater, and once even a hand on a boat running guns to a Central American country in revolt.

He published his first article in 1926. Soon Maxwell Perkins, the legendary editor at Charles Scribner's Sons, discovered some of his works and was enthusiastic and encouraging about his talent. Subsequently, Perkins published *American Earth* and *Tobacco Road*, which brought Caldwell his first real recognition. When Caldwell and Perkins had a serious disagreement, Caldwell switched his publishing allegiance to The Viking Press.

Divorced from his first wife in 1938, Caldwell married the photojournalist Margaret Bourke-White. They collaborated on several successful books, but the marriage ended in divorce in 1942. The same year, he married June Johnson, with whom he had one son, Jay Erskine. In 1957, after divorcing his third wife, he married Virginia Moffett Fletcher.

During the 1940's, Caldwell traveled to China, Mongolia, Turkestan, and Russia. Because of the powerful, enthusiastic way in which he wrote about

Russia and in turn indicted certain aspects of American capitalism, some accused him of being a Communist, a charge he emphatically denied.

Caldwell was a member of the National Institute of Arts and Letters, the Authors League of America, the Phoenix Press Club, and the San Francisco Press Club. Active as a writer and lecturer, Caldwell toured Europe in the 1960's under the auspices of the United States State Department. In the 1970's, he made a series of speeches in Georgia, promoting the paperback reprint of his 1937 book *You Have Seen Their Faces*. He used this opportunity to decry the remaining poverty in the South despite its industrialization.

In 1974, Caldwell underwent surgery for the removal of a growth on his lung; he submitted to similar surgery the following year. He regained enough health to publish two collections of short stories and two nonfiction volumes in the 1980's. Caldwell died in Arizona in 1987.

Analysis

Erskine Caldwell is the chronicler of the poor white. He has told the story of the diversions and disasters of the poor Southerner with more detail and sympathetic attention than any other American writer of his time. In doing so, he has created memorable characters and unforgettable episodes and has provoked scandalized eyebrow-raising at his language, his imagery, and his view of life.

Obscenity charges have been filed against an inordinate number of Caldwell's books, only to be fought down in court: one man's obscenity is another man's earthy realism. The attendant publicity generated more curiosity about his books, and sales soared. The self appointed censors who attacked his books in court were only slightly more antagonistic than the reviewers who labeled his works "orgiastic litanies" and "particularly ugly stories" to be read with disgust and "a slight retching."

Charges of obscenity barraged the publication of *God's Little Acre* from New York to Denver. *Tobacco Road* had an arduous struggle to stay on the booksellers' shelves. *Tragic Ground* ran into trouble with Canadian censors. But how obscene are these books? By today's standards even *God's Little Acre* seems only mildly lewd. Under the layer of animalistic sexual behavior and uncouth, uncultured dialogue, qualities of literary merit are readily discernible.

The most prominent and lasting quality of Caldwell's fiction—the one which has made *Tobacco Road* a minor classic and several other of his earlier novels important literary pieces—is comic grotesquerie. Caldwell conveys a kind of ludicrous horror that becomes more horrible when the reader realizes that hyperbole does not negate the truth behind the most ridiculous episodes: the poor people of the South were deprived to the point of depravity. Writing in a naturalistic style, Caldwell allows the reader to observe the day-to-day activities of poor white families whose impoverished condition has created tragicomic eccentricities.

Those impoverished conditions are the key to understanding Caldwell's main thrust in nearly all of his earlier novels. Living in hopeless hunger, illiterate, and essentially cut off from the world of progress, ambition, and culture, Caldwell's characters seem not quite human. The veneer of civilized attitudes and activities has been ground away by the endless struggle to satisfy the daily hunger and to find some hope, in a vast vista of barren prospects, of a better day tomorrow.

Caldwell was deeply concerned that this segment of society he chose to depict in his work had been repressed by ignorance and poverty as an almost direct result of society's indifference. In later works such as *The Weather Shelter* or even *Claudelle Inglish*, he shifted his attention from the thoroughly downtrodden to the merely browbeaten, but he continued to make a statement about society's indifference to the poor and about the survival instinct of the poor that makes them persevere.

Caldwell's earlier books are generally considered his better efforts; his themes and characters were fresh, and he had not yet begun to rework them with regularity. Still, there is a kind of plot formula in his first important novels: the main characters are introduced with a recounting of their day-to-day activities wherein their basic problem is presented; a new character is introduced, bringing what seems to be an opportunity for some degree of betterment; then tragedy strikes, usually resulting in the death of a sympathetic character. There are seldom any "bad guys" in Caldwell's novels, no dastardly villains. The villain is society, which allows abject poverty, ignorance, hunger, and hopelessness to exist without trying to correct the circumstances that caused them. His characters, victims of society, flounder into tragic situations without knowing how to save themselves.

In the case of *Tobacco Road*, tragedy strikes as unpredictably as lightning and the characters accept their lot as though it were a natural, unalterable phenomenon. This book, perhaps his best-known work, is the story of a family of ignorant poor white Georgians who at the outset are at the depths of degradation. They have no food, no prospects, and no apparent opportunity to get either. They have settled into a bleak routine, planning to plant a crop in the vague future and hoping for something to happen to change their lot. Jeeter Lester, the patriarch, has the last trace of a noble love of the land and a strong inherent need to farm his land and produce a crop, yet he cannot or will not do any of the practical things that must be done for serious, life-saving farming. He has no money and no credit, and he will not leave his farm to find work in the town to get the money for seed and fertilizer. Thus, he drifts from day to day with good intentions but takes no positive action. Survival for him and his family has reached an "every man for himself" level. His mother is treated with less consideration than a dog: When any food is acquired, as when Jeeter steals a bag of turnips from his son-in-law, the old mother is not given any. The others in the family—Jeeter's wife Ada and the two remaining children, Ellie Mae and Dude—are equally unfeeling.

These people seem to be as far down the scale of humanity as anyone can get, yet the story relates a series of episodes that carries them progressively further to degeneracy and death. The casual attitude toward sex, as shown in the scenes with Dude and his "new" wife Bessie, brings to mind the blasé attitude that farmers show toward the breeding of their farm animals. There is no particularly lewd interest in the family's attempts to spy on the "honeymooning" couple. Rather, their curiosity seems born of boredom or the simple need for distraction. Because Caldwell has narrated these episodes in blunt, realistic language, a puritanical mind might see a moral looseness in them which could be (and was) attributed to an immoral intent on the part of the author. Viewed from the perspective of fifty years, however, the actions of the characters appear not obscene but merely uncivilized.

Another scene involves the accidental killing of a black in a wagon. Rammed and overturned by the new car acquired by Bessie (as a not-very-subtle enticement to persuade Dude to marry her), the black is crushed by the wagon. The Lesters, having caused the accident, go blithely on their way. Their only concern is the wrecked fender of the car. They philosophize that "niggers will get killed." The killing of another human being is as casually natural to them as the killing of a dog on a highway.

The most inhuman and inhumane episode involves the death of Mother Lester, who is hit by the car in the Lester yard. She is knocked down and run over, "her face mashed on the hard white sand." She lies there, unaided by any of the family, hardly even referred to beyond Ada's comment that "I don't reckon she could stay alive with her face all mashed like that." The old woman struggles a bit, every part of her body in agonizing pain, and manages to turn over. Then she is still. When Jeeter at last decides something must be done with his old mother, he looks down and moves one of her arms with his foot, and says, "She aint stiff yet, but I don't reckon she'll live. You help me tote her out in the field and I'll dig a ditch to put her in."

When Caldwell depicts the indifference of the family members to Mother Lester's slow, painful death, he is really depicting the degeneracy of people whom society has deprived of all "human" feeling. Thus, when in the last chapter the old Lester house catches fire and burns up the sleeping occupants without their ever waking, the reader may well feel that poetic justice has been served: The Lesters have lived a subhuman existence, and their end is fittingly subhuman. Yet, one does not entirely blame the Lesters for their lack of humanity; Caldwell moves his readers to wonder that a rich, progressive country such as the United States could still harbor such primitive conditions.

The comic quality that is so much a part of Caldwell's work saves *Tobacco Road* from utter grimness. Some of the episodes with the car, Jeeter's maneuverings to get money from his new daughter-in-law, the turnip filching—all create a climate that lightens the pervading ugliness. The sexual adventures are irreverent and bawdy; the dialogue is the ridiculous, repetitive gibberish of single-minded illiterates engrossed in their own narrow concerns. There is a particularly comic quality in Jeeter's serious pronouncements, which bespeak a completely unrealistic creature out of touch with himself and his true condition. The enduring ridiculousness of Jeeter and his family is under-coated with a pathos that is obvious to the thoughtful reader. The condition and ultimate end of Jeeter and Ada are perhaps atypical but are still symp-tomatic of the condition and ultimate end of the many others like them living in the destitute areas of the South.

Caldwell's *God's Little Acre* was considered by some critics his best work up to that time. A *Forum* review said it was "the first thing [Caldwell] has done which seems . . . to justify in any way the praise the critics have heaped upon him." There are flaws, as some reviewers were quick to point out, including repetitiousness and a too sudden and unexpected transition from a comic atmosphere to violent tragedy, yet it is second in quality only to *Tobacco Road* among Caldwell's novels.

God's Little Acre tells the story of Ty Ty Walden, a Georgia dirt farmer who for fifteen years has been digging enormous holes in his land looking for gold. Ty Ty, who is in most other respects a man with considerable mother wit, has a curious tunnel vision where this quest for gold is concerned. Because of it, he neglects his farming to the point of endangering his livelihood and that of his family. Worse yet, he fails to see the peril in the growing tension among the members of his family living on the farm with him. The inevitable tragedy results from the fact that he has two beautiful daughters and an even more beautiful daughter-in-law, Griselda. Ty Ty himself praises Griselda so much to anyone who will listen that he is largely instrumental in encouraging the fatal allurement she has for the other men in the family. When these men—a son, Jim Leslie, and a son-in-law, Will Thompson—make advances toward Griselda, her husband Buck understandably becomes enraged. He is thwarted in his revenge against Will Thompson by another calamity—Will, a mill worker, is killed during a strike action—but Jim Leslie does not escape his brother Buck's wrath, nor does the tragedy stop there, for Buck's action is harshly punished.

The opening episodes of the novel are comic: Pluto Swint, the fat, lazy suitor of the younger daughter, Darling Jill, is clearly a comic character in the mold of the sad clown. The enthusiastic search for the albino Dave, who according to black lore can divine gold lodes, is humorous: The process of finding him, roping him, dragging him away from his home and wife, and keeping him under guard like a prized animal is handled with a matter-of-fact detachment that makes these actions acceptable, predictable, and ridic-ulous, all at once. Darling Jill's sexual promiscuity and amoral attitude are refreshingly animalistic, even though some readers might disapprove of her untouched conscience.

When Darling Jill steals Pluto's car to go joyriding, when Ty Ty along with the rest goes to town to ask the well-off son Jim Leslie for money to help him through the winter because of inadequate crops, when Rosamond finds Will Thompson, her husband, in bed with her sister Darling Jill and chases him, buck-naked, out of the house—these richly comic scenes create a humorously cockeyed view of the Georgia poor white.

The deaths which occur later in the novel, however, are not funny, nor are their reasons; the comic existence Caldwell has depicted turns somber. This shift in tone has been described as a flaw, but such a judgment assumes that *God's Little Acre* is a comic novel gone astray. In fact, it is a serious story about people who in their daily lives do things that seem comic to those who observe them from a distance. Caldwell begins with a feckless existence that gradually becomes tragic; the comical infighting and escapades of Ty Ty's clan assume a grim inevitability.

Ty Ty has set aside one acre of his land for God. His intent is to farm the land, raise a crop, and give the proceeds to God through the church. Ty Ty has been digging for gold all over his farm, however, and there is very little land left that can still be farmed. Because he needs to raise a crop to feed his family and the two black families who tenant-farm for him, Ty Ty must constantly shift the acre for God from place to place. He readily admits that he will not dig for gold on God's little acre because then he would be honor-bound to give the gold to the church. He has no compunctions about doing God out of what he has declared is God's due. Later in the story, however, when he learns of Will Thompson's death, he has a sudden need to bring the acre closer to the homestead:

> He felt guilty of something—maybe it was sacrilege or desecration—whatever it was, he knew he had not played fair with God. Now he wished to bring God's little acre back to its rightful place beside the house where he could see it all the time. . . . He promised himself to keep it there until he died.

After this decision, however, blood is shed on God's little acre: Buck kills his own brother, Jim Leslie. The bloodletting on God's ground is almost a ceremonial sacrifice wherein Ty Ty, albeit involuntarily, atones for a life spent giving only lip-service to God. This ironic justice has the tragicomic grotesquerie characteristic of Caldwell's best work. The fall of his protagonists is both inevitable and absurd, utterly lacking in dignity.

Beginning in 1936, Caldwell produced different work. Perhaps he was aware that he had gone to the well often enough and needed to find new or different subjects. At any rate, traveling about the United States and Europe, with the drama of Adolf Hitler's Germany taking form, he wrote other books on uncustomary subjects: *North of the Danube, You Have Seen Their Faces, Some American People* (1935), *Southways, Jackpot, Say! Is This the U.S.A.?* (1941, with Margaret Bourke-White), *All-Out on the Road to Smolensk, Russia at War*, and more.

The novels that poured from Caldwell's pen on into the 1940's, 1950's, 1960's, and 1970's more or less followed the pattern of his early work. Reviewers observed that Caldwell seemed to have grown lackadaisical, content with repeating himself. He no longer seemed to instruct the reader subtly about the social and economic problems of the South; his work had begun to take on the dullness that results from the same joke and the same protestations repeated too often in the same way. He continued to use the same old formula without the zest and the imagination that made *Tobacco Road* and *God's Little Acre* so memorable.

Of the more than thirty novels Caldwell wrote over more than forty years, it is disappointing to find that two written in the 1930's—*Tobacco Road* and *God's Little Acre*—are the only ones likely to endure. Still, Caldwell is considered to be among the significant twentieth century writers produced by the South. His major contribution was his naturalistic comedic approach to his subjects. His best work depicts, with admirable craftsmanship, the harsh life of the sharecropper and tenant farmer through painful explicitness and comic vigor, juxtaposing social issues to the grotesque.

Jane L. Ball

Other major works

SHORT FICTION: *American Earth*, 1931; *Mama's Little Girl*, 1932; *Message for Genevieve*, 1933; *We Are the Living: Brief Stories*, 1933; *Kneel to the Rising Sun and Other Stories*, 1935; *Southways: Stories*, 1938; *Jackpot: The Short Stories of Erskine Caldwell*, 1940; *Georgia Boy*, 1943; *Stories by Erskine Caldwell: 24 Representative Stories*, 1944; *Jackpot: Collected Short Stories*, 1950; *The Courting of Susie Brown*, 1952; *Complete Stories*, 1953; *Gulf Coast Stories* 1956; *Certain Women*, 1957; *When You Think of Me*, 1959; *Men and Women: 22 Stories*, 1961; *Stories of Life: North and South*, 1983; *The Black and White Stories of Erskine Caldwell*, 1984.

NONFICTION: *Tenant Farmer*, 1935; *Some American People*, 1935; *You Have Seen Their Faces*, 1937 (with Margaret Bourke-White); *North of the Danube*, 1939 (with Margaret Bourke-White); *Say! Is This the U.S.A.?*, 1941 (with Margaret Bourke-White); *All-Out on the Road to Smolensk*, 1942 (with Margaret Bourke-White, also known as *Moscow Under Fire: A Wartime Diary, 1941*); *Russia at War*, 1942 (with Margaret Bourke-White); *The Humorous Side of Erskine Caldwell*, 1951; *Call It Experience: The Years of Learning How to Write*, 1951; *Around About America*, 1964; *In Search of Bisco*, 1965; *In the Shadow of the Steeple*, 1967; *Deep South: Memory and Observation*,

1968; *Writing in America*, 1968; *Afternoons in Mid-America*, 1976; *With All My Might*, 1987; *Conversations with Erskine Caldwell*, 1988.

CHILDREN'S LITERATURE: *Molly Cottontail*, 1958; *The Deer at Our House*, 1966.

MISCELLANEOUS: *The Caldwell Caravan: Novels and Stories*, 1946.

Bibliography

Devlin, James. *Erskine Caldwell*. Boston: Twayne, 1984. The first book-length study of Caldwell, this volume is the fullest available introduction to his major work. Its biographical treatment of Caldwell is limited, but five of Caldwell's best novels are considered in detail, as well as many short stories. Contains a chronology and a detailed bibliography.

Gray, R. J. "Southwestern Humor, Erskine Caldwell, and the Comedy of Frustration." *Southern Literary Journal* 8, no. 1 (1975): 3-26. Detachment and distancing form an inherent part of Southwestern humor. As in the epic theater of German playwright Bertolt Brecht, Caldwell makes sure his readers do not involve themselves in the actions of the characters—Gray calls them "grotesques"—but are compelled "to adopt an attitude of clinical detachment."

Korges, James. *Erskine Caldwell*. Minneapolis: University of Minnesota Press, 1969. This forty-eight-page monograph is scholarly and rich in literary allusion. Has a tendency to exaggerate Caldwell's achievement on occasion, but also condemns his *Summertime Island*. Treats not only early books but also neglected later novels, as well as a number of short stories and nonfiction pieces.

MacDonald, Scott. *Critical Essays on Erskine Caldwell*. Boston: G. K. Hall, 1981. Divided into three sections: The first reprints contemporary "reviews" or reactions to Caldwell's work, the second does the same for the man, and the final section reprints a number of helpful essays by Malcolm Cowley, Sylvia Cook, William Frobock, and others and some of Caldwell's own "Introductions" to his novels. Gathers much hard-to-find material under one roof. Also contains a good introductory essay and a fine bibliography.

Pembroke Magazine 11 (1979). This special issue, devoted to Caldwell on the occasion of his seventy-sixth year, contains a large number of articles, many of them characterized by a note of nostalgia. Old friends, scholars, and foreign admirers acknowledge the septuagenarian's realism, politics, and permanent contribution to American fiction.

MORLEY CALLAGHAN

Born: Toronto, Canada; February or September 22, 1903
Died: Toronto, Canada; August 25, 1990

Principal long fiction

Strange Fugitive, 1928; *It's Never Over*, 1930; *No Man's Meat*, 1931; *A Broken Journey*, 1932; *Such Is My Beloved*, 1934; *They Shall Inherit the Earth*, 1935; *More Joy in Heaven*, 1937; *The Varsity Story*, 1948; *The Loved and the Lost*, 1951; *The Many Coloured Coat*, 1960; *A Passion in Rome*, 1961; *A Fine and Private Place*, 1975; *Season of the Witch*, 1976; *Close to the Sun Again*, 1977; *A Time for Judas*, 1983; *Our Lady of the Snows*, 1985; *A Wild Old Man on the Road*, 1988.

Other literary forms

Morley Callaghan's early reputation was based primarily on his short stories, many of which appeared in European and American magazines such as *The Transatlantic Review*, *The Exile*, *Transition*, *The New Yorker*, *Esquire*, *The Atlantic*, and *Scribner's Magazine*. Several significant collections of these stories have been published, including *A Native Argosy* (1929), *Now That April's Here and Other Stories* (1936), *Morley Callaghan's Stories* (1959), and *The Lost and Found Stories of Morley Callaghan* (1985). In addition to the novels and stories, Callaghan wrote a few plays and published many articles in *The Toronto Star*, *New World*, *Maclean's*, and *Saturday Night*. In 1963, he published *That Summer in Paris: Memories of Tangled Friendships with Hemingway, Fitzgerald, and Some Others*, a memoir of his early years as a writer in the company of Ernest Hemingway, F. Scott Fitzgerald, Robert McAlmon, James Joyce, and Ford Madox Ford.

Achievements

It seems almost typical of the Canadian literary scene that Callaghan has been more widely praised outside his home country than within it. Many American and European critics have compared Callaghan's work, especially the short stories, to that of the great Russians: Leo Tolstoy, Anton Chekhov, and Ivan Turgenev. Edmund Wilson claimed that Callaghan was probably the most neglected novelist in the English-speaking world. From the beginning of his career in the 1920's, Callaghan attracted the attention of some of the foremost figures in the literary world: F. Scott Fitzgerald, Ernest Hemingway, Sinclair Lewis, James T. Farrell, Ezra Pound, Erskine Caldwell, and Ford Madox Ford, to name but a few. These writers praised his direct, laconic style, which was unencumbered by many of the excesses in language and description prevalent in the fiction of the 1920's and 1930's. American and European editors also found a special quality in Callaghan's work and promoted it in the leading magazines of the day: *The Exile*, *Transition*, and *The New Yorker*.

In Canada, on the other hand, Callaghan's early critical reception was often less than positive, as if there were some acute embarrassment in having a local author achieve international success. Callaghan himself was particularly sensitive to the vicissitudes of his reputation, and in *A Fine and Private Place*, using the persona of neglected author Eugene Shore, placed himself at the forefront of Canadian letters. Certainly, much of the international praise of Callaghan has been extravagant and much Canadian criticism has been parochial, but recently a more incisive and serious approach to this work is creating a well-deserved and long overdue balance. Callaghan was awarded the Lorne Pierce Medal for Literature by the Royal Society of Canada and Canada's most prestigious literary prize, the Governor General's Award (1951), for his novel *The Loved and the Lost.*

Biography

Edward Morley Callaghan was born in Toronto, Ontario, on February or September 22, 1903. His parents, both of whom encouraged his literary bent, were Roman Catholics of Irish descent. Callaghan was educated at Riverdale Collegiate and St. Michael's College, University of Toronto, where he excelled in academics and in sports. His college interests are often illustrated in his writing, most prominently in *The Varsity Story*, a novel of university life written on the occasion of a fund-raising campaign, and *That Summer in Paris*, which includes his account of his famous boxing match with Ernest Hemingway. During his university days, Callaghan worked as a reporter on the *Toronto Daily Star*; in 1923, he met Ernest Hemingway, who was the European correspondent for the paper. The two became good friends, and Hemingway not only provided stimulating conversation concerning Callaghan's favorite authors, Sherwood Anderson (Callaghan's "literary father"), James Joyce, Pound, and Fitzgerald, but also encouraged him to continue writing fiction.

Callaghan was graduated with a B.A. from St. Michael's in 1925 and enrolled in Osgoode Law School, from which he was graduated in 1928. From 1926 to 1928, he made numerous trips to New York, where he met many friends of Hemingway who were to help him in his career. Among them were Katherine Anne Porter, William Carlos Williams, Nathan Asch, and Maxwell Perkins of Charles Scribner's Sons. Perkins, after reading Callaghan's material, decided to publish his first novel, *Strange Fugitive*, and a collection of stories, *A Native Argosy*. Following his marriage to Loretto Dee in 1929, Callaghan traveled to Paris, where in a few months he completed a novel, *It's Never Over*, a novella, *No Man's Meat*, and a number of stories.

In 1930, Callaghan returned to Toronto permanently and began to produce his mature work, including *Such Is My Beloved*, *The Loved and the Lost*, and *Close to the Sun Again*. Although his work has a universal appeal which distinguishes it from much Canadian fiction, it is rooted in his observations of ordinary Canadian life and the particular attitudes of people as they respond to social and institutional forces. Past eighty years of age, Callaghan continued to write effectively, challenging the moral and social complacency which threatens the individual consciousness. He died in Toronto on August 25, 1990.

Analysis

Much has been made of Morley Callaghan's streamlined style—in his own words, the art of getting the writing down "so directly that it wouldn't feel or look like literature." Callaghan wished to get an effect that was "transparent as glass"; life should be delineated without embellishment and to a large extent without metaphor. The language should be stripped of all artistic and symbolic associations, and objects should be seen as they are, like Paul Cezanne's apples, which are merely apples and yet capture the essence of apples. The central idea of Callaghan's style is that reality must be accepted for what it is, and that it can be conveyed directly and simply. Leon Edel suggests that this method has its origins in Callaghan's journalism, that Callaghan, like Hemingway, transfers the clipped, almost perfunctory prose of the newsroom into the realm of the novel, evading the images and symbols so often used in fiction. In its formative stages, Callaghan's style was perhaps also affected by the naturalism which was popular in the 1920's and 1930's, especially with American writers who wanted a mode of expression to capture the grim realities of the Depression.

Whatever its antecedents, Callaghan's style, especially in the early novels such as *Strange Fugitive* and *It's Never Over*, is handicapped by its programmatic simplicity; the prose is ill-equipped to handle complexities of character. Callaghan's novels, even the later ones, are also marked by a structural simplicity, with a limited number of characters, few subplots, and, usually, a single controlling consciousness. They seem to plod on to an inevitably tragic but morally ambiguous conclusion, giving an illusion of time that is almost static, reduced to its elemental character.

Callaghan did not, however, adhere slavishly to the avowed principles of his early fiction. Beginning with *Such Is My Beloved*, the sentences are more complex; the dialogue is richer, less stylized in the Hemingway manner; the prose is more rhythmic; and the structure of the novels is more intricate. Still, all of Callaghan's work is characterized by an unremarkable surface which at first glance has little aesthetic appeal. A more discriminating appraisal must therefore be made which accounts for the enduring quality of his work. Some critics have noted the parabolic nature of Callaghan's fiction, which limits the need for rounded characterization and necessitates simplicity of structure. Others argue that Christian humanism, especially in *Such Is My Beloved*,

More Joy in Heaven, and *A Passion in Rome*, with their obvious biblical titles, informs Callaghan's work, giving it veracity and insight; finally, some conclude that Callaghan's power derives from the influence of Charles Darwin, Karl Marx, and Sigmund Freud and a particular setting in history.

To a certain extent, all these theories are true, but all are equally unsatisfying as comprehensive theories. Underlying each of the novels is an ironic point of view which defeats easy answers and leaves the reader with both an unsatisfying vision of life with few moral or aesthetic certainties, and a sense of mystery, an awareness of the infinite complexities of human action and thought which make life worthwhile. This deliberate ambiguity is a narrative strategy designed to force the reader into reevaluating his own observations of life and his own moral stance. Callaghan's novels, then, demand an involved sensibility and a questioning attitude; perhaps what is needed is the passionate intensity which Callaghan so frequently hints is the key to self-realization and independence.

Many of Callaghan's novels are animated by the tension between an individual and the institutions which circumscribe his behavior. The Church, the government, and the business community insist on a patterned, prudent existence which gives society stability and order. As such, they serve a useful function in most people's lives, but they are no substitute for a personal, compassionate, and intuitive vision which, in everyday relationships, often subverts the legalistic intentions of the institutions. An individual can be caught betraying society because he refuses to betray his own conscience. Thus, Father Dowling in *Such Is My Beloved* befriends two prostitutes to rescue them, and himself, with the power of love. His seemingly inordinate concern for them strikes a local parishioner and Dowling's bishop as unorthodox, and Dowling is relieved of his position and finally is admitted to a sanatorium. In *The Loved and the Lost*, Jim McAlpine is torn between his ambition to be a respectable columnist on a Montreal newspaper and the love of a mysterious woman who inhabits the seamier region of the city. By losing faith in Peggy at a crucial moment, Jim allows the circumstances which bring about her death and a loss of faith in himself.

In *Close to the Sun Again*, a more complex relationship between private and public values is explored. Ira Groome, former "lord" of the Brazilian Power Company and now chairman of Toronto's police commission, reflects to no avail on why he has become impersonal and detached from the stream of life. After suffering severe injuries in a car accident, he relives his career as a naval commander and realizes that he had tried to escape the pain of human involvement by representing an institutional view of life. In a final epiphany, he accepts the voices in his own heart and dies with the profound self-knowledge that had been lacking in the earlier part of his life. In all of these works, the ultimate irony is that the individual can rarely reconcile the public demands of the world with a passionate, often barbaric private vision.

The dedication to Callaghan's finest early novel, *Such Is My Beloved*, reads, "To Those Times With M. In The Winter Of 1933"; "M." was Jacques Maritain, the world-renowned philosopher, who came to St. Michael's College Institute for Medieval Studies as a visiting lecturer. Perhaps from his discussions with Maritain, especially concerning the nature of Christian humanism and the role of the saint in the world, Callaghan chose to concentrate on an explicitly religious theme, probing the relationship between the Roman Catholic Church, an agency of worldly prudence, and its priests, who must minister to individuals' needs through the love of Christ. The title suggests the focus of the novel; as Brandon Conron has noted, it is an echo of God's expression of love for His Son on the occasion of Christ's baptism. The epigraph confirms the theme of the nature of love and the consequences of the spiritual attitude of the novel. Taken from the Song of Songs, it reads: "Many waters cannot quench love, neither can the floods drown it: if a man give all the substance of his house for love, it would utterly be contemned."

The story is simple. Father Dowling, the central figure of the novel, befriends two prostitutes, Veronica (Ronnie) Olsen and Catherine (Midge) Bourassa, in order to save them from their degrading way of life. He soon realizes that they need not only love but also material necessities to sustain them through the Depression. Aware that the money he earns from his parish will not be enough, Dowling enlists the help of a wealthy parishioner, James Robison, to provide jobs for them. Robison, however, is not willing to risk the possibility of scandal and reports Dowling to his bishop. The two women are forced to leave the city (ostensibly Toronto), and Dowling, driven by these betrayals to madness, has only momentary periods of lucidity in the sanatorium.

Brandon Conron and Malcolm Ross both have argued that the novel presents at least a superficial allegory, with Dowling as Christ, Robison as Judas, and the bishop as Pontius Pilate, with certain minor characters also serving symbolic roles. The success of the novel, however, resides in Callaghan's ability to draw these characters as vulnerable human beings and not merely as types. Dowling conveys a disturbing naïveté which, despite his powerful love, causes his downfall. He brings Ronnie and Midge presents and money in an effort to keep them off the streets, but the gifts are ineffective. Dowling exhibits many other traits which seduce the reader into a kind of Conradian belief in him as "one of us." In the confessional, he is so consumed by his thoughts for the girls that he is harsh with others. He is jealous of Father Jolly's room, which Dowling himself covets; he admits to the natural sexual feelings of a young man his age; he hates the owner of the bawdy house, Henry Baer; and he lies about his involvement with the two prostitutes. Ironically, these human weaknesses make his love seem more potent.

The other characters, although not as well portrayed as Dowling, are effective in that the reader's responses to them are never wholly one-sided.

Robison, much of the time, is a kind, helpful Christian who is confused by Dowling's love. The bishop, representing the position of the worldly Church, doubts himself and does not seem secure in his opinion of Dowling. Ronnie's pimp, Joe Wilenski, is a brutish man who often takes advantage of her yet respects her as a person. Ronnie, coming from a broken home in Detroit, and Midge, abandoned by her lover, react with affecting girlishness, especially when Dowling gives them pretty clothes. The ambivalent, realistic natures of these people condition the reader's response to the novel as a whole. One sees human beings with limited control over their circumstances; the Church and society seem to conspire to destroy the idealistic impulse in the individual consciousness.

Professor David Dooley identifies the central moral problem of the novel as the conflict between quixotic idealism and worldy prudence, with no satisfactory conclusion being evinced. Father Dowling tries to love the prostitutes as Christ loved sinners; all people are worthy of love without distinction, despite their failures. Love, he thinks, will overcome worldly considerations, but his faith cannot change the economic conditions which have driven the girls into sin. Dowling also tries to console the Canzanos, a family with twelve children living in abject poverty. Mr. Canzano says that they need money, not faith, and there is nothing left for him but despair. Even Dowling's great love is unconvincing here; he spends so much time with the girls that he can give little to his other parishioners. Although the bishop is satirized by Callaghan for his concern that the scandal will hurt his charity campaign, he is perhaps correct in thinking that the church should play a more material part in helping people such as the Canzanos.

Dowling's best friend, Charlie Stewart, a medical student who is an avowed Marxist, also views the world in terms of economics. Because he is a secular idealist, he believes that the ideal state could transform society and put an end to poverty. For him, there is no religious problem, only an economic one. The church, the business community—represented by Robison and his uncharitable wife—Stewart, and Dowling are all caught up in the same dilemma. The personal qualities of spiritual love and secular compassion are defeated by institutions which must force their representatives to make rational, pragmatic choices. Even though these choices are often hypocritical, they are necessary to sustain order in society.

Such Is My Beloved ends with the two prostitutes forced out of the city by the police, and Dowling, in the sanatorium, is left to think of them as two of the many restless souls who cannot find peace. Dowling has occasional moments of clarity in which he offers his sanity as a sacrifice to God so that He might spare their souls. The priest is content in this offering and, at peace with himself, plans to write a commentary on the Song of Songs. The only positive note in the book is that this powerful love of Dowling's is somehow good, and although it cannot change society, it can transcend it, making even the tragic elements of life worthwhile.

In his next two novels, *They Shall Inherit the Earth* and *More Joy in Heaven*, Callaghan continued to examine the theme of love and its relation to society in explicitly religious terms. Neither novel is as well wrought as *Such Is My Beloved*, but they are nevertheless effective renderings of complex human motives. In the period between 1937 and 1948, his "dark period," Callaghan published no major novels. In 1948, however, his period of "spiritual dryness" over, Callaghan published *Luke Baldwin's Vow* and *The Varsity Story*, and began work on *The Loved and the Lost*, which appeared in 1951.

Although the religious dimension is understated in *The Loved and the Lost*, the inner opposition between the individual and the dictates of society is again explored. For the most part, the narrative consciousness is that of Jim McAlpine, through whose eyes the reader receives impressions of Montreal's clearly divided social strata. Formerly an associate professor of history at the University of Toronto, Jim is brought to the city by a publisher, Joseph Carver, to write a political column for the Montreal *Sun*. Carver, a professed "liberal," admired Jim's article, "The Independent Man," in *The Atlantic*. Living on "the mountain," an affluent district in Montreal, Carver and his divorced daughter, Catherine, represent the social status to which Jim has aspired all his life. Through a friend, Jim meets Peggy Sanderson, a seemingly generous and warm-hearted woman. Jim falls in love with her innocence and her compassion, knowing that their relationship, as elusive as it may be, could destroy his ambitions. After a brawl involving Peggy at Café St. Antoine, a black jazz club on the river, Jim feels compelled to protect her and to profess his love for her. When Peggy's need for him is greatest, however, Jim loses faith in her, inadvertently leaving her to be raped and murdered. Unable to choose between the stable values of "the mountain" and the uncertain values of the river, Jim betrays not only Peggy, but also himself.

The novel works in parallels of discrete oppositions between the mountain and the river, with Jim at the center, torn by the attractiveness of each and unable to reconcile the contradictions inherent in both. Carver has wealth and power which he uses to operate a newspaper dedicated, like *The New York Times* or *Manchester Guardian*, to the principles of independent thinking. His editorial stance, however, is compromised by his personal objection to giving his own writers freedom of thought; he wants supreme loyalty from his staff, and he is disturbed by the possibility that Jim may be an embarrassment to him. His daughter, Catherine, embodies the beauty and social grace of her class, but she is unsure of herself and hides her ardent character. She sees a hockey game with Jim, remarking on the artistic patterns of play. For her, life is a pattern, like her orderly room, which should not be disturbed. When Jim seems to side with the hockey player breaking the pattern by receiving a penalty, she asks why he is not "with us." In the end, however, discovering Jim's complicity in the murder, she empathizes with Peggy, violently slapping Jim for what she thinks is his betrayal.

Evoking similarly complex responses in all those who know her, Peggy Sanderson is an extremely ambiguous character. She has an air of innocence which enchants Jim and makes him want to protect her, but there is also a suggestion of carnality; as a young girl she admired the body of a naked black boy, and there are many comments made on her promiscuity with the blacks at the Café St. Antoine, although they are not verified. In her indiscriminate, but platonic, love for all souls "without distinction" (here she echoes Father Dowling), she is seen as St. Joan and Christ. This spiritual gift, however, invites fear and resentment, not peace and understanding. Symbolically, she is associated with a carved leopard and a small antique church, both of which she takes Jim to see. The fierce, uncertain jungle violence of the leopard contrasts with the stable religious feeling of the church, but Callaghan never lets the reader know if these are indeed *Peggy*'s responses to these objects. Jim thinks that her innocence is attracted to violence, that in fact her actions are self-destructive. By refusing to compromise her personal vision to social prudence, she is destroyed; the reader is never really sure of the extent to which she is culpable for her own fate.

Much of the novel is controlled by Jim's subjective, ambivalent feelings. He is estranged from the world of status as a child, a boy outside the hedge of the wealthy Havelocks, so his ambition is understandable even if excessively rationalized. Although he is drawn to Catherine and her tidy universe, he feels more comfortable in the "middle world" of the Chalet restaurant. Peggy shatters his balance by showing him a different side of life, where society's rules are broken and ambition becomes mere illusion. At the hockey game, he dismisses the patterns and sees the ice surface as a pit with writhing sacrificial figures. His vision, however, is only refracted, not significantly altered, and rather than accept Peggy for what she is, he tries to mold her into his possession. Like Peter denying Christ, Jim denies knowing Peggy at Angela Murdoch's party on the mountain, hoping at some later date to bring the two worlds into harmony.

Wolfgast, the owner of the Chalet restaurant, tells Jim the story of a white horse he believed belonged to him although it was owned by his father's landlord. The circumstances of losing the horse impressed upon him the need for some definitive personal possession, In buying the Chalet, he achieved his dream. Peggy becomes Jim's "white horse," and he tries to own her by using her apartment to write his articles. Every day he tidies it up and makes a change which reflects his own personality. Only after her death does he recognize that his sin resided in not accepting Peggy for herself. Ironically, by not abandoning himself completely, by losing faith in Peggy as Orpheus lost faith in Euridice, he loses his own sense of identity as well. Confused about the values of high and low society and the mysterious values embodied by Peggy, Jim is left only with a dream of Peggy being trampled by white horses from the mountain as he draws back. In desperation, he attempts to find Peggy's antique church, hoping that in this symbol of belief Peggy will be with him always. The gesture is futile: Jim does not find the church.

The reader, too, is left without a clear moral resolution. Is Peggy really a virgin, a pure innocent? Is she a saint like St. Joan, destroyed by an insensitive society? Is there really something primitive in her character which attracts violence? Could Jim cope with Peggy as a human being and not as the ideal he made her out to be? How do the symbols clarify and support meaning? After all, Wolfgast's "white horse," the possession of his restaurant, is something quite different from the possession of a human being. Does the church symbolize religious values or innocence, or is there a more ephemeral quality to it? Does the leopard represent the passionate nature of man or perhaps only independence? Beneath the surface of a straightforward, well-told story, then, there are ambiguities admitting no easy resolutions.

Through the 1950's, 1960's, and early 1970's, Callaghan continued to write many interesting stories; his novels, however, met with mixed reviews. His style became more ambitious and his ideas remained adventurous, but his plots were clumsy, his dialogue often unrealistic, and his characterizations more stereotyped than ever before. In *A Fine and Private Place*, an entertaining *roman à clef* for Callaghan followers, there is even a strident attack on critics unwilling to accept him as a major novelist. With *Close to the Sun Again*, however, Callaghan returned to some earlier themes with great success. The values of the novel are less ambiguous, and the story is simply but powerfully told in his characteristic clipped style, which suits the material admirably.

The story relates the psychic journey of former naval commander Ira Groome, who quits his job as head of the Brazilian Power Corporation to become chairman of the police commission in a large, metropolitan city, probably Toronto. After the death of his alcoholic wife, Julia, he feels a sense of astonishment which shocks him into the realization that imperceptibly he has lost the passion that makes life real. He has, in fact, become so detached that his wife only felt comfortable calling him "Commander," and his son has rejected him as a father. Voices from within challenge him to break the pattern of impersonality which has characterized his life, but they do not completely penetrate his conscious mind.

As introspective as he was in Brazil, Groome still projects the image of stable authority in Toronto, demanding and getting loyalty from the members of the police commission and starting a casual, uninvolved affair with Mrs. Oscar Finley (Carol) of the prestigious Hunt Club set. Still seeking some "enchantment," however, he begins to drink gin, which softens his disciplined view of life but forces him into the Maplewood rest home every few weeks for a temporary "cure." One night, shocked by some harsh but vaguely familiar words from Carol, he leaves Maplewood in an excited state for home, only to be involved in a serious car accident. In the hospital, holding the hand of his former ship's boatswain, Horler, Groome experiences the enchantment he so badly desires and drifts into a dream world of memory and heightened perception.

Groome relives an important part of his life in which he is again Lieutenant Groome on a ship in the North Atlantic during the war. Upon realizing that he is alive after being severely wounded in action, he sees people as unique individuals, each inhabiting a wonderful private world, and is then able to respond to his men with a sensitivity rarely shown by officers. Groome's life is changed radically, however, when two survivors of a torpedo raid board his ship. Gina Bixby, trying to reach England to see her father, a boxing promoter, is accompanied by huge, silent Jethroe Chone, her father's bodyguard. They are escaping Marty Rosso, a mobster involved in fixing fights, who wants to use Gina to prevent her father from testifying to the boxing commission. Rosso has already caused the death of Robert Riopelle, a naïve boxer duped into believing in himself: with his hands smashed by Rosso Riopelle perceived that his whole being was corrupted and committed suicide. During their escape from Rosso, the mysterious Chone raped Gina but feels no remorse for an act which "kills" part of her. Although there still seems to be a perverse bond between them, Gina confesses to Groome that, when they reach London, she will kill Chone for this brutal betrayal.

Groome is disturbed by this world so unlike the well-ordered naval existence; it is a world of violent passions beyond his experience. In her questioning of Groome, however, Gina brings to the surface his fascination for the Mayan religious rituals he had encountered as a young archaeology student on the Yucatán peninsula. This society with its sacrificial violence seems to parallel Gina's world in a strange way. Groome recalls a native girl, Marina, an image of light suffusing his memory, who gave him the ancient piece of wisdom that in a cruel, senseless world, all one can do is create something beautiful from the nightmare.

Before they can reach the safety of London, the ship is torpedoed, leaving Groome, Horler, Gina, a wounded Chone, and a few sailors on a life raft. Defiantly, Chone tells Groome that no one knew or loved Gina more than he did; soon after, Chone rolls himself into the water to die at sea. Yelling for him to come back in the same words that Carol later spoke to Groome, Gina swims after Chone, her passion overcoming any sense of safety. She is also lost in the water. Groome is horrified at the emotions he feels—the jungle terrors of involvements with people living in intense personal worlds. He rationalizes that getting too close to people, being intoxicated by violent passions, only causes pain and suffering. Groome closes his heart to these sufferings and resists the voices in his own heart. He changes into secure Ira Groome, the Commander, dedicated to a high purpose in life, a world of order unencumbered by the depth of personal relationships.

Remembering all this from his hospital bed, Groome realizes that he has committed treason to his own nature. He finally understands the significance of Chone's life. He sees the brightness from a sunlit jungle clearing into which a white leopard emerges, and finally, Groome understands himself. Recognizing the necessity of leading a life of passion in all respects, bearing the suffering and sacrifice which enrich the individual sensibility, Groome dies, "close to the sun again."

In this novel, Callaghan reiterates the themes of his other works, but makes it clear that passion should not be compromised to suit the values of society. In earlier novels, the conflict between private passions and the imposed, prudent views of society is unresolved, but *Close to the Sun Again* concludes with an epiphany which clearly emphasizes that the individual's responsibility is above all to himself. Throughout his career, Callaghan offered his readers a vision which is thought-provoking, humane, and replete with the passions which touch everyone's life. There is little doubt that in the future his reputation as a significant twentieth century novelist will remain secure.

James C. MacDonald

Other major works

SHORT FICTION: *A Native Argosy*, 1929; *Now That April's Here and Other Stories*, 1936; *Morley Callaghan's Stories*, 1959; *The Lost and Found Stories of Morley Callaghan*, 1985.

PLAYS: *Turn Home Again*, 1940 (also known as *Going Home*); *To Tell the Truth*, 1949; *Season of the Witch*, 1976.

NONFICTION: *That Summer in Paris: Memories of Tangled Friendships with Hemingway, Fitzgerald, and Some Others*, 1963.

CHILDREN'S LITERATURE: *Luke Baldwin's Vow*, 1948.

Bibliography

Conron, Brandon. *Morley Callaghan*. New York: Twayne, 1966. A comprehensive, carefully organized analysis of Callaghan's short fiction and novels up to *A Passion in Rome*. Its straightforward style and format make this book accessible to students. Also includes a useful biographical chronology and a selected bibliography.

Cude, Wilfred. "Morley Callaghan's Practical Monsters: Downhill from Where and When?" In *Modern Times*. Vol. 3 in *The Canadian Novel*, edited by John Moss. Toronto: NC Press, 1982. This florid essay examines the darker side of Callaghan's vision through a discussion of characterization in several of his short stories and in some of his novels, such as *Luke Baldwin's Vow* and *A Passion in Rome*.

Hoar, Victor. *Morley Callaghan*. Toronto: Copp Clark, 1969. Discusses the style and thematic concerns in Callaghan's fiction up to 1963 in two sections, "The Technique" and "The Themes." Hoar supports his commentary with numerous quotations from Callaghan's work. A useful bibliography is included.

Kendle, Judith. "Morley Callaghan: An Annotated Bibliography." In *The Annotated Bibliography of Canada's Major Authors*, edited by Robert Lecker and Jack David. Vol. 5. Toronto: ECW Press, 1984. Contains the most exhaustive listing of primary sources and secondary sources for Callaghan's work up to 1984 that a student is likely to need. The categories cover the spectrum from books and articles to interviews to audiovisual material. A helpful "Index to Critics Listed in the Bibliography" is also included.

Stuewe, Paul. "The Case of Morley Callaghan." In *Clearing the Ground: English-Canadian Fiction After "Survival."* Toronto: Proper Tales Press, 1984. In this chapter, Stuewe takes Callaghan to task for sloppy writing and his critics to task for concentrating on Callaghan's thematic concerns to the exclusion of his technical flaws. Stuewe's own writing and tone are lively and incisive.

Woodcock, George. "Possessing the Land: Notes on Canadian Fiction." In *The Canadian Imagination: Dimensions of a Literary Culture*, edited by David Staines. Cambridge, Mass.: Harvard University Press, 1977. Callaghan's fiction is discussed in the context of Woodcock's overview of Canadian fiction and its development and direction since the nineteenth century.

TRUMAN CAPOTE
Truman Streckfus Persons

Born: New Orleans, Louisiana; September 30, 1924
Died: Bel-Air, California; August 25, 1984

Principal long fiction
Other Voices, Other Rooms, 1948; *The Grass Harp*, 1951; *A Christmas Memory*, 1956 (serial); *In Cold Blood*, 1966; *The Thanksgiving Visitor*, 1967 (serial); *Answered Prayers: The Unfinished Novel*, 1986.

Other literary forms
In addition to writing fiction, Truman Capote worked principally in two other forms: the drama (stage, film, and television) and reportage. Capote's first work for the stage was his adaptation of his novel *The Grass Harp*, which was produced in New York in the spring of 1952. In 1954, he collaborated with Harold Arlen on the Broadway musical *House of Flowers*, based on his short story. He also wrote the film scenario for *Beat the Devil* (1954) and dialogue for *Indiscretion of an American Wife* (1954). He adapted Henry James's 1898 short story *The Turn of the Screw* for film as *The Innocents* (1961). Two Hollywood films, *Breakfast at Tiffany's* (1961) and *In Cold Blood* (1967), were based on his work, but Capote himself did not contribute to the screenplays. He did, however, with Eleanor Perry, adapt three of his stories— "Miriam," "Among the Paths to Eden," and *A Christmas Memory*—for television. *A Christmas Memory* was honored with the Peabody Award in 1967, and the three-story dramatizations were later released as a film, *Trilogy: An Experiment in Multimedia* (1969).

Capote's first venture in reportage was *Local Color* (1950), a series of impressionistic sketches of New Orleans, New York, and other places where he had lived or visited in America and Europe. *Local Color* was followed by *The Muses Are Heard* (1956), an urbane account of his trip to Leningrad and the opening night performance of the American cast of *Porgy and Bess*. Other sketches of the 1950's appeared in *Observations* (1959), with photographs by Richard Avedon. His masterpiece in this form is *In Cold Blood*, although Capote prefers to regard this work as a "nonfiction novel." *The Dogs Bark: Public People and Private Places* (1973) collects his earlier nonfiction writing and includes some additional sketches, while *Music for Chameleons* (1980) includes new reportage and a short "nonfiction novel" *Handcarved Coffins*, an account of multiple murders in the American Southwest.

Achievements
With the publication of his first novel, *Other Voices, Other Rooms*, Capote achieved fame at the precocious age of twenty-four. His precocity, the bizarre

nature and brilliant quality of the novel, and the astonishing photograph of the author on the book's dust jacket (a figure, childlike in stature, who reclines on a period sofa and looks out with an expression of unsettling maturity and aloofness) made him widely discussed in both America and Europe. This debut set the tone of Capote's later career, in which he consistently attained remarkable popularity while yet appealing to an elite audience of serious readers. The publication a year later of *A Tree of Night and Other Stories* consolidated his reputation as an author of baroque fiction, fiction concerned with the strange, often dreamlike inner states of estranged characters. A peculiarity of this volume, however, is that several of the stories it contains are lightly whimsical. *The Grass Harp*, which shares this more "sunlit" vision, shows Capote emerging, tentatively, from his "private," subjective fiction; in this work, whimsy predominates as the individual gropes for his relationship to others. *Breakfast at Tiffany's: A Short Novel and Three Stories* (1958) moves further out into the world, and this tendency becomes more pronounced still in his nonfiction novel *In Cold Blood*. His unfinished novel, *Answered Prayers*, with its large gallery of precisely observed characters, was Capote's fullest effort to engage the many-sided world of actual social experience. In whatever form he wrote, however, whether sequestered fantasy or fiction with a social orientation, Capote's preoccupations remained constant—loneliness and isolation, the dichotomy between the world and the self, the deprivations of the innocent or unconventional and their moments of grace.

Capote's strength was mainly in the briefer modes—in the vignette, short story, and short novel. Of his longer works, the best is *In Cold Blood*, the most accomplished "nonfiction novel" of its time. Called by Norman Mailer "the most perfect writer of my generation . . . word for word, rhythm upon rhythm," Capote is above all a great stylist. There is no question that he belongs in the first rank of modern American writers.

Biography

Truman Capote, whose name at birth was Truman Streckfus Persons, was born in New Orleans on September 30, 1924. His mother, Nina (Faulk) Persons, only sixteen when he was born, had married a traveling salesman, Joseph Persons, to escape the drabness of her hometown, Monroeville, Alabama. The marriage soon proved unhappy, and by the time Capote was four years old his parents had become divorced. When his mother moved to New York, she sent her son (an only child) to live with a variety of relatives in the South. From the time Capote was four until he was ten, he lived outside Monroeville, where one of his neighbors was Nelle Harper Lee, who later put him into her novel *To Kill a Mockingbird* (1960) as Dill, the strange, brilliant little boy who is "passed from relative to relative." The relatives with whom he stayed were four elderly, unmarried cousins—three women and their brother. One of the women was Sook Faulk, a childlike, simple woman, wise in ways that mattered to a small boy who otherwise lived much to himself and within his own imagination. Sook Faulk inspired the character of Dolly Talbo in *The Grass Harp*, and Capote later commemorated his childhood friendship with her in his autobiographical stories *A Christmas Memory* and *The Thanksgiving Visitor*. In his secluded life in rural Alabama, he read Charles Dickens and other novelists at an early age and made his first attempts at fiction at the age of ten. Feeling himself different from others, without the love of a mother or father, uncertain even of a home, Capote developed the sense of isolation which informs all of his fiction.

Capote's childhood wanderings continued after he left Monroeville in 1934. At different times, he stayed with cousins in New Orleans, and at one point lived with a family in Pass Christian, Mississippi, which provided the setting for *Other Voices, Other Rooms*. In 1939, when he was sixteen, he went to New York to join his mother and her second husband, Joseph Garcia Capote, a Cuban textile manufacturer who legally adopted him and whose surname he took. At this time, he was sent to a series of boarding schools in New York and then to Greenwich High School in Millbrook, Connecticut, where his parents had moved. At seventeen, he dropped out of school and found work with *The New Yorker* magazine. After two years, he left his job to live with relatives in Alabama and begin a first novel, "Summer Crossing," later discarded when he began work on *Other Voices, Other Rooms*. Capote had been sending out stories for publication since he was fifteen; by the time he was seventeen he had his first acceptances, and in Alabama he wrote his first important stories—"Miriam" and "A Tree of Night." With a $1,500 advance from Random House for his novel-in-progress, he traveled to New Orleans, then to New York and Nantucket, where the novel, the result of two years' work, was completed. The novel drew upon his own childhood experiences—his exposure to rural localities in the South, his crisis of identity as a nomadic child, and his early preoccupation with homosexuality.

Reviews of *Other Voices, Other Rooms* were mixed, yet many praised Capote enthusiastically for his evocation of the dream states of the subconscious, his "uncanny ability to make a weird world come alive" with a kind of magical radiance. One reviewer called Capote's talent "the most startling American fiction has known since the debut of Faulkner." For a time, Capote was regarded as a writer of Southern Gothic fiction; in the 1950's, however, he moved away from this school. *The Grass Harp*, although set in the rural South, was more lyrical than Gothic; *Breakfast at Tiffany's*, which followed it, was set in New York and was urban in its idiom, its manner, and its implication. *The Muses Are Heard*, with its detached, worldly intelligence, shows how fully Capote had adopted a cosmopolitan stance.

During much of the 1950's, Capote lived abroad, but by autumn of 1959 he was living in New York, and while exploring the possibilities of "nonfiction fiction" read in the newspapers of the macabre and seemingly inexplicable murder of the Herbert Clutter family in the Midwest. Acting on the intuition that he had found his "subject," he went immediately to Holcomb, Kansas, and began to familiarize himself with the town and the circumstances of the Clutters. This project soon developed into a major undertaking, to which he devoted himself almost exclusively from November, 1959 to April, 1965. After their apprehension, the murderers, Richard Hickok and Perry Smith, were tried and sentenced to be executed in 1960, but the executions were stayed for five years, during which Capote held more than two hundred interviews with them. He also personally retraced the route they had taken in the course of their wandering after the murders, and compiled extensive notes from his conversations with all the parties concerned with the case. The psychological strain Capote experienced at this time was particularly great because of his empathetic involvement with one of the murderers, Perry Smith. Like Capote, Perry had come from a shattered home and had been a nomadic dreamer; the two were physically similar, both being five feet four inches tall. The intensity of Capote's imaginative involvement can be felt on every page of *In Cold Blood*, a work that, almost paradoxically, combines objective reporting with deep feeling.

On its publication, *In Cold Blood* became a phenomenal best-seller while winning great critical acclaim. The literary year of 1966 belonged to Capote. It was at this time that he gave his black and white masked ball for five hundred friends at the Plaza Hotel in New York, sometimes called "the Party of the Decade." After the publication of *In Cold Blood*, Capote became a media celebrity and a member of wealthy and fashionable society. After that, however, he produced relatively no new work—chiefly, two volumes of reportage: *The Dogs Bark* and *Music for Chameleons*. In the late 1960's, he announced that he was at work on a new book, *Answered Prayers*, a lengthy, Proustian novel that would be a "major work."

By the mid-1970's, four chapters of the work-in-progress had been published in *Esquire* magazine, which perhaps was done to prove that Capote was actually working on the novel. By this time, Capote had developed drug and alcohol problems, and his lack of professional output reflected his personal disintegration.

Answered Prayers has a stronger sexual frankness than any of Capote's other works; its complicated, darkly intriguing narrative is sometimes scabrous in its revelation of envied lives. In its suggestive handling of reality and illusion, *Answered Prayers* also reveals Capote's familiar sense of loneliness—loneliness among the members of the haut monde. Capote died in California at the home of his close friend Joanne Carson on August 25, 1984, of heart and liver failure caused by multiple drug ingestion. As one biographer, Gerald Clarke, observed, it is unknown whether Capote committed suicide or his health had failed under the assault that his addictions had launched on his body.

Analysis

The pattern of Truman Capote's career suggests a divided allegiance to two different, even opposing literary forms—objective realism and romance. Capote's earliest fiction belongs primarily to the imagination of romance. It is intense, wondrously evocative, subjective; in place of a closely detailed outlining of a real social world, it concentrates on the inner states of its characters, usually with the full resources of romance, including archetypal journeys or a descent into the subconscious. His characters' inner life is fixed through the use of telling imagery and controlling symbols. In "The Headless Hawk," for example, the real world exists hardly at all; what little there is of it seems subaqueous, has the liquid flow of things seen underwater. In "A Tree of Night," the heroine is subjected to real terror, complete with Gothic phantoms in the form of two strangers on a train. The journey of the train itself is complementary to Kay's journey into the dark places of her soul, where the "wizard man" and irrational fear prevail. In "Miriam," an elderly woman's sense of reality and personal identity give way before the presence of an implike child. It is not surprising that these early stories have been compared to those of Edgar Allan Poe, for like Poe, Capote was fascinated by the psyche at the point of disintegration. Similarly, in *Other Voices, Other Rooms*, the boy Joel Knox inhabits a vaguely outlined social world; what is ultimately most real is the terror that surrounds and threatens him. The scenes that pinpoint his experience are all charged with moral, symbolic implication; rather than unfolding through a study of social relationships, the narrative moves episodically through assaults on Joel's mind, imagistic storm points keeping him in agitation and crisis; the identities of the characters surrounding Joel are fixed from the beginning and have only to be revealed through psychic drama. The shape of the work is, finally, that of a romantic moral parable.

How strange it is, then, that as Capote's career progressed he revealed a pronounced interest in the literature of realism, even a kind of superrealism, implied by "nonfiction fiction." He began working in this genre with *Local Color*, a poetic literature of pure "surface." The texture of surface is the real subject of *The Muses Are Heard*. With a sleepless vigilance, Capote observes his fellow travelers and in the finest, most precise detail captures their idiosyncrasies, the gestures and unguarded remarks that reveal them, as it were, to the quick. Tart, witty, detached, *The Muses Are Heard* assumes no depths of meaning in the Cold War world it portrays; eye, ear, and social intelligence are what are important. Capote's career also shows a desire to bring together the opposing parts of his nature and his equipment as a writer, however, and in *In Cold Blood* he actually achieved such a fusion. Capote himself never intrudes on the narration, makes no commentary, stands back reporting "impartially" on what occurs. This effacement of self is so complete that the reader believes he is witnessing the events as they occur. Yet at the same time the work contains many, not always obvious, romantic urgings, forcing the reader to put himself in the place of Perry Smith on death row. Strict categories of good and evil break down before the sense of the inextricable mixture of both in life, and the helplessness of man before an obscure and ominously felt cosmic drama. The lyric note of baffled yearning at the end is romantic, in spite of the work's judicious, almost judicial, realism.

The plot of *Other Voices, Other Rooms*, Capote's first novel, is not extremely complicated. Joel Knox, a thirteen-year old, motherless boy, is sent from the home of his Aunt Ellen in New Orleans to Skully's Landing to be united with his father, Mr. Edward Sansom. Arriving eventually at the Landing, a plantation house partly in ruins, Joel is cared for by a woman named Amy, her languid, artistic cousin Randolph, and two family retainers, Jesus Fever, an ancient black man, and his granddaughter Missouri Fever, known as Zoo. The boy's inquiries about his father are mysteriously unanswered by the adults, and it is only later in the novel that the boy confronts his father—a paralytic invalid who neither speaks nor understands, his eyes fixed in a wide, crazed stare. The crisis experienced by the boy in the decaying house is largely inward; he attempts to free himself of his situation, but in a series of strange episodes his failure to do so becomes evident, and at the end he embraces his fate, which is complementary to that of Randolph, the dream-bound homosexual. He accepts whatever love and solace Randolph (evoked as mother-father, male-female, and "ideal lover" in one) can give him.

In its atmosphere of sinister enchantment, of the bizarre and weird, *Other Voices, Other Rooms* exploits many of the resources of the Gothic mode. William Faulkner stands distantly in the background; Carson McCullers is more immediately evident. Capote's theme of a quest for love and understanding in a world apparently incapable of providing either, and his use of freakish characters, suggest the generic influence of *The Heart Is a Lonely Hunter* (1940). Even the "normal" world of Noon City is filled with oddity— a one-armed barber, a female restaurant proprietor who has an apelike appearance. Such oddity is minor, however, compared to the characters who inhabit the Landing—Jesus Fever, a brokeback dwarf; Zoo, whose long, giraffelike neck reveals the scars from Keg Brown's razor assault upon her; Randolph, who, in an upper-floor room, dressed in a gown and wig, becomes a "beautiful lady." At the same time, and often with the most powerful effect, the novel draws on the imagery of surrealism. The late scene at the carnival, for example, is spectacular in its evocation of an irrational world struck by lightning, a sequence followed by the nocturnal pursuit of Joel through an abandoned house by the midget Miss Wisteria, and the coma Joel experiences in which his life is relived while a pianola composes its own jazz and the plantation lurches into the earth.

Essentially, *Other Voices, Other Rooms* is a romance. It has been compared to Nathaniel Hawthorne's "My Kinsman, Major Molineux," which also deals with a youth who, in a dark and dreamlike world, searches for his identity and is initiated into life. Joel's journey, in its various stages, has a symbolic shading. At the opening, he leaves the morning world of Paradise to travel to Noon City, where he continues his journey through the backcountry in a mule-drawn wagon, with Jesus Fever asleep at the reins; arriving at the Landing in darkness, Joel is himself asleep, and cannot remember entering the house when he awakens the next morning in an upstairs bedroom. With the effect of a wizard's spell, the house comes to claim him. Complicated patterns of imagery—of fire and fever, knifing and mutilation, death and drowning—evoke the extremity of the boy's fear and loneliness as avenues of escape from the Landing are closed to him, one by one. Mythic patterns also emerge—the search for the "father," the Grail Quest, Christian crucifixion, Jungian descent into the unconscious—to reinforce the romantic contour of his experience. Although in some ways Joel's guide ("I daresay I know some things I daresay you don't"), Randolph is himself held under an enchantment, dating back to the inception of his homosexual life. At the end, Joel and Randolph become one. As the ancient "slave bell" in the ruined garden seems to ring in Joel's head, he goes forward to join Randolph, leaving his childhood behind him.

Other Voices, Other Rooms is less perfectly achieved than *The Heart Is a Lonely Hunter*. Randolph, for example, a major character, is more a pastiche of English decadence than a real person. Moreover, the ending becomes snarled in obscurity. In accepting Randolph, Joel accepts his own nature, an act that brings liberation and even some limited hope of love. Yet Randolph is so sterile, so negative, and so enclosed within his own narcissism, that the reader cannot share the upsurge of joy that Joel is supposed to feel. Capote's strength in the novel lies elsewhere—in his ability to create a sustained poetry of mood, to capture psychic states of rare intensity and beauty. His experimentalism in this respect is far more adventurous than that of McCullers. The image-making power of Capote's language is so impressive in this precocious novel as to leave one fearful that he may have exhausted the resources of the Southern Gothic mode in a single flight.

Capote's next novel, *The Grass Harp*, derives from the rural Southern fable of "Children on Their Birthdays." Like that tale, *The Grass Harp* has a narrative frame that begins and ends in the present, with the story placed in between. Collin Fenwick looks back upon his rearing as an orphan in the home of two maiden women, Dolly Talbo, a gentle, childlike woman, and her sister Verena, who has property and investments in town. He is spared the intense ordeal of Joel Knox, but is like him in his sense of personal isolation and in his search for love and identity. When Verena takes it upon herself to exploit a home remedy that Dolly makes from herbs (her little scrap of identity), Dolly rebels, and with Collin and Catherine Creek, an eccentric halfbreed factotum, she withdraws to a treehouse set amid a field of tall Indian grass. Eventually, they are joined by Riley Henderson, a rebellious youth, and Charlie Cool, a retired circuit court judge whose refinement makes him an anachronism to his married sons, at whose houses he stays in rotation. The adventure in the tree house does not have a long duration, but by the time it is over the characters all come to have an enlarged sense of who they are. The narrative is flawed in various respects. It involves a number of plot contrivances (Morris Ritz's absconding with the money in Verena's safe); the "battle" scenes between the tree house occupants and the law-and-order characters from town rely too much on slapstick; and Riley Henderson's reformation and marriage to Maude Riordan is a trite conception. Yet there are many fine touches in this fragile, not wholly successful tale—the portrait of Judge Cool and his late-in-life courtship of Dolly; Verena's recognition that it is she who is more alone than Dolly, whose "heart" has been the pillar of the house; the controlling symbols of freedom and imagination versus rigidity and dry rationality (the Indian grass "harp" and the cemetery) that enclose the work and give it life beyond its conclusion. A meditation on freedom and restriction, *The Grass Harp* reveals Capote moving away from his earlier studies in isolation toward a concern with a discovery of identity through relation to others.

Breakfast at Tiffany's marks a new stage of Capote's career, since it brings him fully into the world outside his native South. In this short novel, Capote captures New York and its denizens—Joe Bell, the sentimental bartender with a sour stomach; Madame Sapphia Spanella, a husky coloratura who rollerskates in Central Park; O. J. Berman, the Hollywood agent; and Sally Tomato, the surprisingly unsinister mobster with a Sing Sing address. José Ybarra-Jaegar, the Argentine diplomat, is perceived acutely and never more so than when he writes a mendacious letter to the novel's protagonist, Holly Golightly, breaking off a relationship with her when her dreamlife becomes "unsafe." The novel employs a retrospective narrative frame like the one in F. Scott Fitzgerald's *The Great Gatsby* (1925), in which the pale, conventional Nick Carraway observes the strange career of his larger-than-life neighbor. In both cases, the narration is dominated by nostalgia and the sense of loss, accentuated by the use of reiterated autumnal motif. Holly's origins go far back in Capote's writing. In *Other Voices, Other Rooms*, Randolph's dream initiator Dolores dries her washed hair in the sun and strums a guitar, as does Holly. Miss Bobbit models her too, her "precious papa" having told her to "live in the sky." Holly is a Miss Bobbit in her late teens, a child-adult whose ideal of happiness lies "beyond." An "innocent" immoralist, Holly is, however, a somewhat sentimental conception (a "good" sensitive character misprized by a nasty and unfeeling world), and a rather underdeveloped character. As Alfred Kazin has observed, she is partly New York chic and partly Tulip, Texas, naïve, but in neither case does she become a real person.

The fusion of realism and romantic fable attempted in *Breakfast at Tiffany's* is not achieved fully until Capote's next work, *In Cold Blood*.

In Cold Blood, which remained on the best-seller lists for more than a year and has since being translated into twenty-five languages, is Capote's most popular and widely read book. It is also one of his most notable works artistically. F. W. Dupee has called it "the best documentary account of an American crime ever written," and Capote himself claimed that it creates a new literary genre, the "nonfiction novel." Although nothing exactly like *In Cold Blood* had appeared previously, there are clearly precedents for it— Theodore Dreiser's *An American Tragedy* (1925), for example, a documentary novel of crime and punishment, and Ernest Hemingway's *Green Hills of Africa* (1935), as well as the reportage of Rebecca West and Lillian Ross. Moreover, *In Cold Blood*'s objectivity is more apparent than real, since the material Capote draws from has been heightened, muted, and selected in many ways, subjected to his aesthetic intelligence. *The New Yorker* style of objective reportage clearly was an influence on the book; another may have been Capote's experience as a scenarist. His use of "intense close-ups, flash-backs, traveling shots, [and] background detail," as Stanley Kauffmann has observed, all belong to the "structural" method of the cinema.

A cinematic method is particularly noticeable in the earlier part of the work, where Capote cuts back and forth between the murderers and the victims as the knot tightens and their paths converge. It is the convergence of a mythic as well a literal kind of two Americas—one firmly placed in the wheat belt of the Midwest, decent in its habits, secure in its bounty, if a little stiff in its consciousness of being near to God; the other aimless and adrift, powered by garish and fantastic dreams, dangerous in its potential for vio-lence. The horrible irony of Capote's description of "Bonnie" Clutter suggests the ominousness of this section. "Trust in God sustained her," he writes, "and from time to time secular sources supplemented her faith in His forthcoming mercy." The account of the actual murders, suspensefully postponed until later in the work, is chilling in its gratuitous nature while at the same time, through a steady building in of telling details, it has the force of a vast inevitability. The slaughter of the Clutters is "gratuitous" insofar as it might well not have occurred, has nothing to do with them personally, and gains for the young men responsible nothing except a few dollars, a fugitive life, arrest, and execution. As "haves" and "have-nots" come together, as Smith's long pent-up rage against his father becomes projected onto Mr. Clutter, a lighted match explodes a powder keg. Contributing to this act of unreason, is the stand-off between Hickok and Smith, each having told lies about himself to the other; rather than surrender this "fiction" of himself, which would involve confronting the truth of his maimed and powerless life, Smith is driven to a senseless murder. The irrationality of the crime is complemented later by the irrationality implicit in the trial and execution, so that ultimately *In*

Cold Blood deals with the pervasive power of irrationality.

The psychological interest of the book is heightened by Capote's drifting narrative and use of multiple "perceptors"—the Clutters themselves, Alvin Dewey, the Kansas Bureau of Investigation agent, and many of Holcomb's townspeople. Of overshadowing interest, however, is Perry Smith, who could, as Capote said, "step right out of one of my stories." A young dreamer and "incessant conceiver of voyages," he is at the same time a dwarfish child-man with short, crippled legs. A series of Capote's earlier characters stand behind him. Holly Golightly, dreamer-misfit and child-woman, is a not-so-distant cousin. Yet in this work, Capote's sentimental temptation has been chastened by a rigorous actuality, and what results is an extraordinary portrait. Sensitive and sympathetic, Smith is yet guilty of heinous murders. His romantic escapism (he dreams of diving for treasure but cannot swim, imagines himself a famous tapdancer but has hopelessly maimed legs) becomes comprehensible in the light of his homeless, brutalized background, more bizarre than any fiction; his undoing is elaborately plausible. In the final scene, reminiscent of the ending of *The Grass Harp*, Capote brings the memory of Nancy Clutter together with the memory of Smith—entangled in an innocence blighted by life; in this way, *In Cold Blood* becomes a somber meditation on the mysterious nature of the world and the ways of Providence. This questioning quality and lyric resonance were undoubtedly what Rebecca West had in mind in referring to *In Cold Blood* as "a grave and reverend book." It is a work in which realism and romance become one.

After the publication of *In Cold Blood*, Capote produced no new major work. During this period, which included bouts of suicidal depression as well as serious physical illnesses, he continued to write for films and to write shorter pieces, while also supposedly at work on *Answered Prayers*. Of the four chapters originally published, Capote later decided that "Mojave" did not belong in the novel, being a self-contained short story written by the character P. B. Jones. With its drifting narrative, including flashbacks and a story-within-the-story, it is extremely suggestive. Its theme is never directly stated, but its cumulative effect makes it clear that its concern is with illusion, particularly of those who love others and find their love betrayed. "La Côte Basque: 1965" is set at a fashionable restaurant on New York's East Side, where all the diners indulge in or are the subject of gossip. P. B. Jones lunches with Lady Ina Coolbirth, who, herself on the eve of divorce, tells stories of broken marriages, while at the next table Gloria Vanderbilt Cooper and Mrs. Walter Matthau tell similar tales. This mood piece closes at the end of the afternoon in an "atmosphere of luxurious exhaustion." Jones himself is the focal figure in "Unspoiled Monsters," which details his career as an opportunistic writer and exploiter of others, exploitation and disillusion being the observed norm among the members of the international set. Unfortunately, even these few chapters reveal the depth to which Capote's writing had sunk. His "gossip column" approach simply reveals that Capote had lost the capability of producing anything original—he was merely telling thinly disguised tales out of school. Indeed, the publication of "La Côte Basque" alienated many of Capote's society friends. Its topicality also ensured that *Answered Prayers* would not have stood the test of time—or of the critics, for that matter—and probably that, more than any other reason, is why Capote never finished it.

Capote excelled in a number of literary forms—as a memoirist, journalist, travel writer, dramatist, short-story writer, and novelist. The body of his work is comparatively small, and it has neither the social range nor the concern with ideas of the work of certain of his contemporaries, but it is inimitable writing of great distinction. He is a brilliant and iridescent stylist, and his concern with craft belongs to that line of American writers that includes Henry James, Edith Wharton, Willa Cather, and F. Scott Fitzgerald. Like Fitzgerald particularly, whose romantic themes and classical form he shares, Capote has the abiding interest of sensibility.

Robert Emmet Long

Other major works

SHORT FICTION: *A Tree of Night and Other Stories*, 1949; *Breakfast at Tiffany's: A Short Novel and Three Stories*, 1958; *One Christmas*, 1983.

PLAYS: *The Grass Harp: A Play*, 1952; *House of Flowers*, 1954 (with Harold Arlen).

SCREENPLAYS: *Beat the Devil*, 1954 (with John Huston); *The Innocents*, 1961.

NONFICTION: *Local Color*, 1950; *The Muses Are Heard*, 1956; *Observations*, 1959 (with Richard Avedon); *The Dogs Bark: Public People and Private Places*, 1973.

MISCELLANEOUS: *Selected Writings*, 1963; *Trilogy: An Experiment in Multimedia*, 1969 (with Eleanor Perry and Frank Perry); *Music for Chameleons*, 1980; *A Capote Reader*, 1987.

Bibliography

Brinnin, John Malcolm. *Truman Capote: Dear Heart, Old Buddy*. 1981. Rev. ed. New York: Delacorte Press/Seymour Lawrence, 1986. Concerned mainly with biographical detail about Capote. Brinnin has expanded his original work to include events up to Capote's death. Also contains an index.

Clarke, Gerald. *Capote: A Biography*. New York: Simon & Schuster, 1988. A comprehensive biography of Capote which includes information about his childhood and about his death. The bibliography of books by Capote is complete, and the general bibliography is exhaustive. Also includes a detailed index.

Dunphy, Jack. *"Dear Genius": A Memoir of My Life with Truman Capote*. New York: McGraw-Hill, 1989. Written by Capote's friend and close companion of more than thirty years and a novelist in his own right. Details the disintegration of Capote's life as a result of drugs and alcohol. Includes an index.

Grobel, Lawrence. *Conversations with Capote*. New York: New American Library, 1985. This book of interviews with Capote also includes an epilogue recounting Capote's funeral. Although the book is not literary criticism per se, Capote did talk in detail about his works, including *Answered Prayers*. An index is provided.

Moates, Marianne M. *A Bridge of Childhood: Truman Capote's Southern Years*. New York: Henry Holt, 1989. This biography was written with the help of Jennings Faulk Carter, who grew up with Capote. The work concentrates mainly on Capote's childhood and how it affected—and was incorporated into—his writing. A genealogy and an index are provided.

ANGELA CARTER

Born: Eastbourne, England; May 7, 1940

Principal long fiction

Shadowdance, 1966 (U.S. edition, *Honeybuzzard*, 1967); *The Magic Toyshop*, 1967; *Several Perceptions*, 1968; *Heroes and Villains*, 1969; *Love*, 1971, revised 1987; *The Infernal Desire Machines of Doctor Hoffman*, 1972 (U.S. edition, *The War of Dreams*, 1974); *The Passion of New Eve*, 1977; *Nights at the Circus*, 1984.

Other literary forms

Angela Carter is nearly as well-known for her short fiction as she is for her novels. Her short-story collections include *Fireworks: Nine Profane Pieces* (1974), *Black Venus* (1985; U.S. edition, *Saints and Strangers*, 1986), and the highly praised *The Bloody Chamber and Other Stories* (1979), which contains her transformations of well-known fairy tales into adult tales with erotic overtones. She has also written a number of fantastic stories for children, including *Miss Z, the Dark Young Lady* (1970), *The Donkey Prince* (1970), and a translated adaptation of the works of Charles Perrault, *Sleeping Beauty and Other Favourite Fairy Tales* (1982). In 1978, she published her first book of nonfiction, *The Sadeian Woman: And the Ideology of Pornography*, a feminist study of the Marquis de Sade that remains controversial among both literary and feminist critics. Other nonfiction essays have been published by British journals; *Nothing Sacred: Selected Writings* (1982) is a collection of her journalistic pieces. She also cowrote the screenplay for the British film *The Company of Wolves* (1985), based on her short story of the same title. *Come unto These Yellow Sands* (1985) is a collection of various other scripts adapted from her fiction.

Achievements

With the publication of her first novels in the late 1960's, Carter received wide recognition and acclaim in Great Britain for blending gothic and surreal elements with vivid portrayals of urban sufferers and survivors. She was awarded the John Llewellyn Rhys Memorial Prize for *The Magic Toyshop* and the Somerset Maugham Award for *Several Perceptions*. Critics have praised her wit, inventiveness, eccentric characters, descriptive wealth, and strongly sustained narrative while sometimes questioning her depth of purpose and suggesting a degree of pretentiousness. Such adverse criticism is mostly directed at such novels as *Heroes and Villains* and *The Infernal Desire Machines of Doctor Hoffman*, which are set in postapocalyptic or metaphysical landscapes. Her imaginative transformation of folkloric elements and examination of their mythic impact on sexual relationships began to be fully appreciated on the appearance of *The Bloody Chamber and Other Stories*, which received the Cheltenham Festival of Literature Award. *Nights at the Circus*, recipient of the James Tait Black Memorial Prize, helped to establish firmly for Carter a growing transatlantic reputation as an extravagant stylist of the Magical Realist school. She is noted for her provocative observations and commentary on contemporary social conditions.

Biography

Angela Carter (neé Stalker) was born in Eastbourne, Sussex, England, on May 7, 1940. After working as a journalist from 1958 to 1961 in Croyden, Surrey, she attended Bristol University, from which she received a B.A. in English literature in 1965. She has traveled widely and lived for several years in Japan. From 1976 to 1978, she served as Arts Council of Great Britain Fellow in Creative Writing at Sheffield University. She has been a visiting professor at Brown University, the University of Texas, Austin, and the University of Iowa, and lives in London, England.

Analysis

The search for self and for autonomy is the underlying theme of most of Angela Carter's fiction. Her protagonists, usually described as bored or in some other way detached from their lives, are thrust into an unknown landscape or enter on a picaresque journey in which they encounter representatives of a vast variety of human experience and suffering. These encountered characters are often grotesques or exaggerated parodies reminiscent of those found in the novels of Charles Dickens or such Southern gothic writers as Flannery O'Connor. They also sometimes exhibit the animalistic or supernatural qualities of fairy-tale characters. The protagonists undergo a voluntary or, more often, forced submission to their own suppressed desires. By internalizing the insights gained through such submission and vicariously from the experiences of their antagonists and comrades or lovers, the protagonists are then able to garner some control over their own destinies. This narrative structure is borrowed from the classic folk- and fairy tales with which Carter has been closely associated. Carter does not merely retell such tales in modern dress; rather, she probes and twists the ancient stories to illuminate the underlying hierarchical structures of power and dominance, weakness and submission.

In addition to the folkloric influence, Carter has drawn from a variety of other writers, most notably Lewis Carroll, Jonathan Swift, the Marquis de Sade, and William Blake. The rather literal-minded innocent abroad in a nightmarish wonderland recalls both Alice and Gulliver, and Carter acknowledges, both directly and obliquely, her borrowings from *Alice's Adventures in Wonderland* (1865) and *Gulliver's Travels* (1726). She has also been influenced by the Swiftian tool of grotesque parody used in the service of satire. It is through Swiftian glasses that she has read Sade. While deploring the depradations on the human condition committed by both the victims and victimizers in Sade's writings, she interprets these as hyperbolic visions of the actual social situation, and she employs in her novels derivatively descriptive situations for their satiric shock value. Finally, the thematic concerns of Blake's visionary poetry—the tension between the contrarieties of innocence and experience, rationality and desire—are integral to Carter's outlook. The energy created by such tension creates the plane on which Carter's protagonists can live most fully. In Blake's words and in Carter's novels, "Energy is Eternal Delight."

Although Carter's landscapes range from London in the 1960's (*The Magic Toyshop*, *Several Perceptions*, *Love*) to a postapocalyptic rural England (*Heroes and Villains*) or a sometime-in-the-future South America (*The Infernal Desire Machines of Doctor Hoffman*), a United States whose social fabric is rapidly disintegrating (*The Passion of New Eve*), or London and Russia at the turn of the century (*Nights at the Circus*), certain symbolic motifs appear regularly in her novels. Carter is particularly intrigued by the possibilities of roses, wedding dresses, swans, wolves, tigers, bears, vampires, mirrors, tears, and vanilla ice cream. Menacing father figures, prostitute mothers, and a kaleidoscope of circus, fair, and Gypsy folk people most of her landscapes. It is unfair, however, to reduce Carter's novels to a formulaic mode. She juggles traditional and innovative elements with a sometimes dazzling dexterity and is inevitably a strong storyteller.

At the opening of *The Magic Toyshop*, fifteen-year-old Melanie is entranced with her budding sexuality. She dresses up in her absent mother's wedding gown to dance on the lawn in the moonlight. Overwhelmed by her awakening knowledge and the immensities of possibilities the night offers, she is terrified and climbs back into her room by the childhood route of the apple tree—shredding her mother's gown in the process. Her return to childhood becomes catastrophic when a telegram arrives announcing the death of Melanie's parents in a plane crash. Melanie, with her younger brother and sister, is thrust from a safe and comfortable existence into the constricted and terrifying London household of her Uncle Philip Flower, a toy maker of exquisite skill and sadistically warped sensibility. He is a domestic tyrant whose Irish wife, Margaret, was inexplicably struck dumb on her wedding day. The household is also inhabited by Margaret's two younger brothers, Finn and Francie Jowle; the three siblings form a magic "circle of red people" which is alternately seductive and repulsive to Melanie. Uncle Philip is a creator of the mechanical. He is obsessed by his private puppet theater, his created world to which he enslaves the entire household. In aligning herself with the Jowle siblings, Melanie asserts her affirmation of life but becomes aware of the thwarted and devious avenues of survival open to the oppressed. The growing, but ambivalent, attraction between her and Finn is premature and manipulated by Uncle Philip. Even the love that holds the siblings together is underlined by a current of incest. Finn is driven to inciting his uncle to murder him in order to effect Philip's damnation. The crisis arises when Uncle Philip casts Melanie as Leda in a puppet extravaganza. Her symbolic rape by the immense mechanical swan and Finn's subsequent destruction of the puppet release an orgiastic, yet purifying, energy within the "circle of red people." The ensuing wrath of Uncle Philip results in the conflagration and destruction of the house. Finn and Melanie are driven out, Adam-and-Eve-like, to face a new world "in a wild surmise."

In fairy-tale fashion, Melanie is threatened by an evil father figure, protected by the good mother, and rescued by the young hero. Even in this early novel, however, Carter skews and claws at the traditional fabric. The Jowle brothers, grimy, embittered, and twisted by their victimization at the hands of Philip Flower, are as dangerous as they are endangered. They are unable to effect their own freedom. Melanie's submission to Uncle Philip's swan catalyzes not only her own rescue but also, indeed, the release of the Jowle siblings. Melanie's sacrifice breaks the magic spell that held the Jowles imprisoned.

Several Perceptions, Carter's third novel, depends less on such folkloric structure. In this novel, her evocation of the late 1960's counterculture is so finely detailed that she manages to illuminate the thin line between the idealism and solipsism of that era, without denigrating the former or disguising the latter. The clarity of observation is achieved by viewing the culture through the eyes of Joseph Harker, a classic dropout. He has failed at the university, been dumped by his Jane Austen–reading lover, is disheartened by his job caring for dying old men, despises the contentment of his hippie peers, and, early in the novel, bungles a suicide attempt. Joseph, like his biblical namesake, is a dreamer of dreams: He dreams in the violent images of Vietnam atrocities, the self-immolation of Buddhist monks, and assassinations. His schizophrenic perceptions are colored by shattered images from the books in his room, *Alice's Adventures in Wonderland* and Anne Gilchrist's *Life of William Blake* (1863), by memories of his grandfather, visions of his psychiatrist, the purring of his pregnant cat, Anne Blossom's custard, and the vanilla ice-cream breasts of Mrs. Boulder. The novel narrates Joseph's slow crawl back into the world of the living. Despite a tough-minded acknowledgment of the grubby and quite desolate lives of the characters, the novel is written with a gentle touch and ends on an affirmative note. The Christmas party that takes place at the end of the novel, in which Joseph symbolically reenters society, stands as a classic description of a hippie-generation party, just as F. Scott Fitzgerald's description of Gatsby's party stands as the image for the flapper generation. The connected-disconnected flow, the costumes, the easy sexuality, the simple goodwill, the silliness, and the sometimes inspired personal insights are vividly re-created. Carter wrote the novel as this life-style was being played out, and it is much to her credit that she succumbed neither to sentimentality nor to parody.

Parody and satire are, however, major elements in her three novels that are often classified as science fiction or science fantasy. In *Heroes and Villains*, *The Infernal Desire Machines of Doctor Hoffman*, and *The Passion of New Eve*, Carter's protagonists dwell in societies which are described in metaphysical iconography. Carter seems to be questioning the nature and values of received reality. Marianne's world in *Heroes and Villains* is divided into high-technology enclaves containing Professors, the Soldiers who protect them, and the Workers who serve them. Outside the enclaves, in the semijungle/semicesspool wildernesses, dwell the tribes of nomadic Barbarians and the Out-people, freaks created by nature gone awry. Marianne, the daughter of a Professor, motivated mainly by boredom, escapes from her enclave with Jewel, a young Barbarian chieftain, during a raid. In *The Infernal Desire Machines of Doctor Hoffman*, the aging Desiderio narrates his heroic exploits as a young man when he saved his City during the Reality War. Doctor Hoffman besieges the City with mirages generated from his Desire Machines. Sent by the Minister of Determination to kill Doctor Hoffman, Desiderio is initiated into the wonders of desires made manifest, Nebulous Time, and the juggled samples of cracked and broken reality. His guide is Hoffman's daughter, Albertina, who appears to Desiderio as an androgynous ambassador, a black swan, the young valet of a vampiric count, and finally as his one true love, the emanation of his whole desire. The United States in *The Passion of New Eve* is torn apart by racial, class, and sexual conflicts. Evelyn, a young British teacher, travels through this landscape and is re-created. The unconsciously exploitive and disinterestedly sadistic narrator suffers a wild revenge when captured by an Amazonlike community of women. He is castrated, resexed, raped, forcibly wed and mated, and ultimately torn from his wife's love by a gang of murderous Puritanical boys. Each of these protagonists experiences love but only seems to be able to achieve wholeness through the destruction of the loved one. Symbolically, the protagonists seem to consume the otherness of the loved ones, reincorporating these manifest desires back into their whole beings. Each, however, is left alone at the end of the novel.

Symbolic imagery of a harshly violent though rollicking nature threatens to overwhelm these three novels. The parody is at times wildly exaggerated and at times cuts very close to reality (for example, in *The Passion of New Eve*, the new Eve is incorporated into a polygamous family which closely resembles the Manson cult). Although some critics have decried Carter's heavy reliance on fantasies, visions, and zany exuberance, it is probably these qualities that have appealed to a widening audience. It must also be given to Carter that, within her magical realms, she continues to probe and mock the repressive nature of institutionalized relationships and sexual politics.

With *Nights at the Circus*, Carter wove the diverse threads of her earlier novels into brilliantly realized tapestry. This novel has two protagonists— Fevvers, the Cockney Venus, a winged, six-foot, peroxide blonde aerialist, who was found "hatched out of a bloody great egg" on the steps of a benevolent whorehouse (her real name is Sophia) and Jack Walser, an American journalist compiling a series of interviews entitled "Great Humbugs of the World," who joins Colonel Kearney's circus, the Ludic Game, in order to follow Fevvers, and who is "Not hatched out, yet . . . his own shell don't break, yet." It is 1899, and a New World is about to break forth. The ambivalent, tenuous attraction between Fevvers and Walser is reminiscent of that between Melanie and Finn in *The Magic Toyshop* or Marianne and Jewel in *Heroes and Villains*, but it is now mature and more subtly complex. The picaresque journeyings from London to St. Petersburg and across the steppes of Russia recall the travels in *The Infernal Desire Machines of Doctor Hoffman* and *The Passion of New Eve* but are more firmly grounded in historical landscapes. The magic in this novel comes in the blurring between fact and fiction, the intense unbelievability of actual reality and the seductive possibilities of imaginative and dreamlike visions. Are Fevvers' wings real or contrived? Do the clowns hide behind their makeup and wigs or only become actualized when they don their disguises? As in most Magical Realist fiction, Carter is probing the lines between art and artifice, creation and generation, in a raucous and lush style.

Here, after a long hiatus from the rather bleak apocalyptic visions of her 1970's novels, in which autonomous selfhood is only achieved through a kind of self-cannibalization of destroyed love, Angela Carter envisions a route to self-affirmation that allows sexual love to exist. With shifting narrative focuses, Carter unfolds the rebirths of Walser and Fevvers through their own and each other's eyes. Walser's shells of consciousness are cracked as he becomes a "first-of-May" clown, the waltzing partner to a tigress, the Human Chicken, and, in losing consciousness, an apprentice shaman to a primitive Finno-Urgic tribe. As star of Kearney's circus, Fevvers is the toast of European capitals: an impregnable, seductive freak, secure in and exploitive of her own singularity. On the interminable train trek through Siberia, she seems to mislay her magnificence and invulnerability. She becomes less a freak and more a woman, but she remains determined to hatch Walser into her New Man. As he had to forgo his socially conditioned consciousness in order to recognize Sophia, however, so she has to allow him to hatch himself. It is as confident seers that Sophia/Fevvers and Jack Walser love at the close of the novel. With *Nights at the Circus*, Angela Carter, too, seems to have entered a confident, strong period in her remarkable literary career.

Jane Anderson Jones

Other major works

SHORT FICTION: *Fireworks: Nine Profane Pieces*, 1974; *The Bloody Chamber and Other Stories*, 1979; *Black Venus*, 1985 (U.S. edition, *Saints and Strangers*, 1986).

SCREENPLAYS: *Come unto These Yellow Sands*, 1985 (based on her short fiction); *The Company of Wolves*, 1985 (based on her short story).

NONFICTION: *The Sadeian Woman: And the Ideology of Pornography*, 1979; *Nothing Sacred: Selected Writings*, 1982.

CHILDREN'S LITERATURE: *Miss Z, the Dark Young Lady*, 1970; *The Donkey Prince*, 1970; *The Fairy Tales of Charles Perrault*, 1979 (translation); *Sleeping Beauty and Other Favourite Fairy Tales*, 1982 (translation and adaptation of Perrault's tales).

Bibliography

Haffenden, John. "Angela Carter." In *Novelists in Interview*. New York: Methuen, 1985. A brief overview of Carter's work, with a checklist mentioning her critically acclaimed novel *Nights at the Circus*. Also contains an interview by Haffenden of Carter that took place in September, 1984.

Palumbo, Donald, ed. *Erotic Universe: Sexuality and Fantastic in Literature*. London: Greenwood Press, 1986. A compilation of essays on feminist literature. The chapter by Brooks Landon looks at sexuality and the reversal of expectations in Carter's novels, in particular *Heroes and Villains*. Discusses the feminist mythology of this novel and Carter's confrontation of sexual stereotypes.

Punter, David. "Angela Carter: Supersessions of the Masculine." *Critique: Studies in Modern Fiction* 25 (Summer, 1984): 209-222. Describes Carter as charting the unconscious processes of Western society and addresses the sexual themes in her novels, such as the struggle between Eros and Thanatos in *The Infernal Desire Machines of Doctor Hoffman*. Also includes some commentary on *The Passion of New Eve* and *The Sadeian Woman*. A thoughtful essay on Carter.

Sheets, Robin. "Angela Carter." In *An Encyclopedia of British Women Writers*, edited by Paul Schlueter and June Schlueter. New York: Garland, 1988. A synopsis of Carter's writing up to and including *Saints and Strangers*. Focuses on the way in which she merges history and fantasy, the erotic content of her works, and her rootless bohemian characters.

Vannatta, Dennis P., ed. *The English Short Story, 1945-1980: A Critical History*. Boston: Twayne, 1985. Discusses Carter in the context of the avant-garde English writers of the 1970's, although Vannatta considers her the "least experimental among the innovators." In examining *Fireworks: Nine Profane Pieces*, Vannatta selects "The Loves of Lady Purple" as the best. Provides some useful comments on Carter's writing and on the dilemmas that contemporary novelists face in expressing their work.

JOYCE CARY

Born: Londonderry, Ireland; December 7, 1888
Died: Oxford, England; March 29, 1957

Principal long fiction

Aissa Saved, 1932; *An American Visitor*, 1933; *The African Witch*, 1936; *Castle Corner*, 1938; *Mister Johnson*, 1939; *Charley Is My Darling*, 1940; *A House of Children*, 1941; *Herself Surprised*, 1941; *To Be a Pilgrim*, 1942; *The Horse's Mouth*, 1944, 1957; *The Moonlight*, 1946; *A Fearful Joy*, 1949; *Prisoner of Grace*, 1952; *Except the Lord*, 1953; *Not Honour More*, 1955; *The Captive and the Free*, 1959 (Winnifred Davin, editor); *Cock Jarvis*, 1974 (A. J. Bishop, editor).

The last two novels were published posthumously. *The Captive and the Free*, edited by Winnifred Davin, Cary did not live to finish. *Cock Jarvis*, edited by A. J. Bishop, Cary worked on from 1924 to 1937.

Other literary forms

All of Joyce Cary's short stories published under his own name are contained in *Spring Song and Other Stories* (1960, Winnifred Davin, editor). Ten early stories published under the pseudonym Thomas Joyce are not included. More than half a dozen of these stories, which deal with bohemian life in Paris, Cary sold to the *Saturday Evening Post* (1920) in order to support his serious writing. Cary's self-admitted formula for these "potboilers" was a little sentiment, a little incident, and surprise.

Cary also published three booklets of verse and many essays, the latter appearing in such places as *Harper's Magazine*, *The New Yorker*, and the *Sunday Times*. The most significant pieces of Cary's occasional writing have been gathered by A. G. Bishop into a volume of *Selected Essays* (1976). This volume is of interest to the literary student because it includes some samples of Cary's practical criticism and of his views on the theory and practice of writing, as well as interesting material about his background and political views. *Art and Reality* (1958) is a sequence of meditations on aesthetics that Cary composed for the 1956 Clark Lectures at Cambridge University but was too ill to deliver.

Cary's other nonfiction mainly articulates his views on the philosophy and practice of politics, concerning itself with such issues as history, imperialism, and war. These works include *Power in Men* (1939), *The Case for African Freedom* (1941; reprinted with other essays about Africa in 1962), *Process of Real Freedom* (1943), and *Memoir of the Bobotes* (1960). These works shed light upon Cary's treatment of ethical and political issues in his fiction.

A collection of Cary's unpublished manuscripts, papers, letters, and diaries is in the possession of the Bodleian Library at Oxford University.

Achievements

Cary's major artistic achievements—*Mister Johnson* and the novels *Herself Surprised*, *To Be a Pilgrim*, and *The Horse's Mouth* comprising a trilogy—are realistic books that reflect social, moral, and historical change as well as technical performances that embody the formal and linguistic innovations of literary modernism. This distinctive mixture of traditional realism and modernist style is Cary's principal legacy as a novelist. Although he experiments with techniques such as stream of consciousness, interior monologue, disrupted chronology, shifting point of view, and present-tense narration, he consistently rivets the action—past or present—to a particular historical and social context. The continuity of exterior events never completely disintegrates, though it is sometimes difficult to reconstruct. To be sure, the various novels offer the reader different perspectives and interpretations of social reality. The intention, however, is not to obscure that reality or to render it relative to the subjectivity of the narrator, but rather to layer it, to augment its texture. Cary's perspectivism, therefore, is not nihilistic. His experiments in the trilogy form enhance the reader's sense of dwelling in a shared or intersubjective reality, even though each novel in the series adroitly captures the idiosyncratic perspective of its first-person narrator. Cary refuses to endorse any sort of feckless relativism (he was repelled by the moral defeatism and philosophical pessimism of such post-World War I writers as Aldous Huxley) and yet manages to incorporate into his writing the innovations of modernism. His self-proclaimed comedy of freedom extends the range of traditional realism and offers new possibilities for the form of fiction.

Recognition of Cary's literary merit came only late in his life. Under the pseudonym Thomas Joyce, he published in the *Saturday Evening Post* several stories based on his youthful experiences of bohemian life in Paris, but he considered these efforts to be potboilers rather than serious pieces of fiction. The journal, in fact, rejected his subsequent stories for being too "literary." Not unitl 1932, when Cary was forty-three, was his first novel, *Aissa Saved*, published. It was not a commercial success. He continued to produce novels, and finally, in 1941, after the publication of *A House of Children*, his seventh novel, he won his first literary award: the James Tait Black Memorial Prize for the best British novel of the year.

After this award, Cary's reputation increased steadily. In 1950, *The Adam International Review* devoted a special issue to his work, and in 1953, Walter Allen's seminal study of his work, *Joyce Cary*, appeared. Cary enjoyed a successful lecture tour in the United States (1951), and he was asked to deliver the 1956 Clark Lectures at Cambridge University. During his lifetime, he was praised by such prestigious critics as Allen, John Dover Wilson, and Barbara Hardy. Since his death in 1957, Cary scholarship has grown steadily. In 1963, *Modern Fiction Studies* devoted a special issue to his work, and there are numerous books, articles, and theses dealing with Cary's achievements.

Biography

Arthur Joyce Lunel Cary was born in Londonderry on December 7, 1888. His ancestors had been Irish landlords since the early seventeenth century. The Arrears Act of 1882, however, plunged his grandfather into ruinous debt, and his father, Arthur Cary, a prospective civil engineer, moved the family to London shortly after Cary's birth. There the nexus of traditional family life was Cromwell House, owned by Cary's Uncle Tristam. Cary never lost contact with his Irish roots and the legacy of his family history, spending childhood vacations at his grandparents' cottages in Ireland and gaining familiarity with Devon, England, the point of his family's origin. These settings, along with the familial stability and continuity they represented, were important to Cary's fiction. *Castle Corner* deals with a half century of life in Ireland, England, and Africa, moving from the 1870's to the brink of World War I; *Charley Is My Darling* deals with the World War II evacuation of thousands of London children to Devon; *A House of Children* is a poetical evocation of childhood based on Cary's recollections of his Irish vacations; and *The Moonlight* and his two trilogies are set mainly in Devon.

A tragic note entered Cary's life when his mother died in 1898, and his sense of life's miseries was compounded when his stepmother died five years later. His performance as a student at Hurstleigh and Clifton was average at best, though he did show interest in telling stories and writing poetry. In 1904, at the age of fifteen, he went on a sketching trip with his aunt to France, which was his first exposure to Impressionist painting. Two years later, he went to Paris as an art student and experienced bohemian life. He then went to Edinburgh for formal artistic training; at the age of twenty, he decided that he was not good enough to be a first-rate painter: writing would be his vocation and painting his hobby. *Verses by Arthur Cary*, a decidedly mediocre effort, was published in 1908.

These early experiences were later exploited in his fiction. The first fictional pieces he published were short stories which dealt with bohemian life in Paris, and *The Horse's Mouth*, his portrait of the artist, not only draws some of its material from his life in Paris and Edinburgh but also bases its style on a literary approximation of Impressionism. Cary's highly developed visual imagination is evident throughout his writings.

In accordance with his choice of vocation, Cary went to Oxford University in 1909 to take a degree in law, intending to provide himself with an alternate career should his literary attempts fail. His fourth-class degree, however, the lowest one possible, debarred him from pursuing a gainful career in either the civil service or the field of education. In 1912, the Balkan War erupted, and Cary decided to go to the aid of Montenegro, feeling that the firsthand experience of war would offer a writer valuable material. *Memoir of the Bobotes* is a nonfictional account of his Montenegrin sojourn. He returned to England in 1913, entered the Nigerian service in 1914, and fought against the Germans in West Africa. In 1916, in England on leave from Nigeria, he married Gertrude Ogilvie, whom he had met in Oxford. He returned to Nigeria before the end of the year.

Cary's African years (1914-1919) had a formative influence on the shape of his fiction. *Aissa Saved* deals with the collision between Western religion and African paganism; *An American Visitor* explores the difference between the Western idealization of the noble savage and the African reality of tribal life; *The African Witch* reveals the prejudices of some Britons in Africa; *Mister Johnson* depicts the vibrantly imaginative existence of a young black clerk with "civilized" aspirations and his tragicomic relationship with District Officer Rudbeck; and *Cock Jarvis* dramatizes the experience of a "Joseph Conrad character in a Rudyard Kipling role," a morally sensitive liberal whose paternalistic and imperialistic attitudes do not coincide with the historical situation in twentieth century Africa. Without his experience as an assistant district officer in Nigeria—a position which required him to work as a police-man, tax collector, judge, administrator, census taker, map-maker, and road-builder, not to mention someone capable of dealing tactfully with the mys-teries of witchcraft and juju—Cary would not have developed the sympathetic imagination that allowed him to understand and record the African point of view with sensitivity and knowledge.

Not surprisingly, his long residence in Africa put some strain on his mar-riage; his first two children, born in England during his absence, were virtual strangers to him. Despite occasional outbreaks of tempestuous disagreement, Cary and his wife shared a love that carried them through several adversities and the birth of three more children. Gertrude died in 1949. Cary's ability to render vividly the perspectives of women is particularly evident in *Herself Surprised*, *The Moonlight*, *A Fearful Joy*, and *Prisoner of Grace*; in part, this ability derives from the depth and intensity of his relationship with his wife.

In 1920, Cary returned to England, and he, his wife, and their two sons moved to a house in Oxford, where Cary lived until his death. After the publication of his first novel, *Aissa Saved*, in 1932, he produced novels at the impressive rate of almost one a year. His literary reputation increased steadily after he won the James Tait Memorial Prize in 1941.

Analysis

The entirety of Joyce Cary's fiction is, as the author himself suggests, about one world—the world of freedom, "the active creative freedom which main-tains the world in being . . . the source of moral responsibility and of good and evil . . . of injustice and love, of a special comedy and a special tragic dilemma which can never be solved." It is "a world in everlasting conflict between the new idea and the old allegiances, new arts and new inventions against the old establishment." Cary sees human beings as condemned to be free and society as perpetually poised between the extremes of anarchy and totalitarianism. Because creative imagination is of the highest value, the individual must rebel against the forces that threaten to trammel or stultify the free expression of his imagination, whether the forces be those of the established church, the state, tribalism, nationalism, conventional morality, or whatever. Throughout his novels, Cary dramatizes the tension between the intuitive and the analytical, the imaginative and the conceptual, the concrete and the abstract, and the vital and the mechanical.

Cary's romanticism, however, is not naïve. He is acutely aware that the tension between freedom and authority is necessary, that the will to create is continually in conflict with the will to preserve. His first trilogy, for example, sympathetically portrays a survivalist, a conservative, and a rebel. Yet even radically different characters must enact their lives and secure their salvation or damnation in the moral world of freedom, imagination, and love.

In *Joyce Cary* (1973), R. W. Noble conveniently divides Cary's novels into five categories, according to their subject matter: Africa and empire; youth and childhood; women and social change; the artist and society; and politics and the individual. The novels of Africa and empire are substantial achievements but not major novels of this century, save for *Mister Johnson*. *Cock Jarvis*, Cary's first effort, was abandoned in 1937; it was published posthumously. The problem with the novel was that Cary could not construct a plot adequate enough to encompass the character of Cock Jarvis, for at this point Cary had not assimilated the modernist style. Without recourse to first-person narration or stream of consciousness, his eminently interesting character was locked into a melodramatic and conventional plot structure. Whether Jarvis was to murder his wife and her lover, forgive them, or commit suicide, Cary never decided; none of the resolutions would solve the essential problem, which is technical.

Aissa Saved, with its seventy or more characters, has so many cultural conflicts, disconnected episodes, and thematic concerns that the aesthetic experience for the reader is congested and finally diffuse. Its analysis of the transforming powers of religious conversion, however, is penetrating and ironic. The juxtaposition of Aissa, an African convert who understands the sacrifice of Christ in a dangerously literal way and ingests Him as she would a lover, and Hilda, an English convert, is effective. Though the backgrounds of the two converts are divergent, they both end by participating in gruesome blood-sacrifices. The novel as a whole, however, suffers from two problems. First, its central action, which revolves around attempts to end a devastating drought, cannot unify the manifold details of the plot: the cultural, religious, and military conflicts between Christians, pagans, and Muslims. Second, its tone is somewhat ambiguous. It is not clear whether the novel is meant to be an outright attack on missionaries and thus an ironic and cynical treatment of Aissa's so-called salvation or a more moderate assessment of the transforming powers of religious conversion.

An American Visitor has more manageable intentions. The book effectively dramatizes the difference between practical and theoretical knowledge and concrete and abstract knowledge. The preconceptions of the American visitor, Marie Hasluck, are not experientially based and are contrasted with the practices of the local district officer, Monkey Bewsher, who strives to strike a balance between freedom and authority. Even though reality forces Marie to abandon some of her pseudoanthropological beliefs, utopianism is so much a part of her psychological complex that she turns to religious pacifism for compensation, a turning that has tragic consequences for the pragmatic, imaginative, and somewhat self-deluded officer.

The African Witch is more panoramic in scope. It deals with the social, political, and religious life of both Europeans and Africans. The plot revolves around the election of a new emir: the Oxford educated Aladai is pitted against Salé, a Muslim. Aladai's Western demeanor offends many of the Europeans; they prefer Africans to be noble savages rather than liberal rationalists. In the end, the forces of juju and political corruption prevail. Aladai is rejected and chooses a self-sacrificial death, presumably abandoning his rationalism and lapsing into stereotype. The conclusion of the novel is not convincingly wrought.

Castle Corner is part of a projected trilogy or quartet of novels which Cary decided not to continue. Covering a half century of life in Ireland, England, and Africa, the novel moves from the 1870's to the brink of World War I. Because of its congeries of characters and variety of themes, the book resists summary. In general, however, it puts the world of individual freedom and responsibility in collision with the world of historical change, but has too much explicit debate and attitudinizing to be dramatically effective.

Generally, Cary's novels of Africa and empire are competent but not exceptional fiction. More materially than formally satisfying, they suffer finally from a lack of cohesion and unity; the form is not adequate to the content, which is rich and detailed. Nevertheless, these novels well delineate the everlasting conflict between new ideas and the old allegiances, the necessary tension between freedom and authority, reflecting Cary's characteristic preoccupation with the struggle for imaginative freedom on a personal, moral, social, religious, and political level.

Mister Johnson is an exceptional piece of fiction. The character from whom the novel takes its title, as Cary points out in the Preface, is a young clerk who turns his life into a romance, a poet who creates for himself a glorious destiny. Johnson is a supreme embodiment of imaginative vitality and, as such, a prototype for the picaresque heroes in Cary's later novels. Even though Johnson's fate is ultimately tragic, his mind is full of active invention until the end.

The novel occupies a pivotal moment in the dialectic of Cary's art, for not only is the content exceptional—Mr. Johnson is an unforgettable character;

his adventures indelibly impress themselves upon the reader—but also the innovative form is adequate to that content. In *Mister Johnson*, Cary deploys third-person, present-tense narration. He notes in the Preface that he chose this style because it carries the reader unreflectingly on the stream of events, creating an agitated rather than a contemplative mood. Because Johnson lives in the present and is completely immersed in the vibrant immediacy of his experience, he does not judge. Nor does the reader judge, since the present-tense narration makes him swim gaily with Johnson on the surface of life.

Cary's choice of third-person narration, which he does not discuss in the Preface, is equally strategic. The first-person style that he uses so effectively in some of his later novels would have been appropriate. By using the third-person style, he is able not only to give the African scene a solidity of local detail but also to enter into the mind of Rudbeck, so that the reader can empathize with his conscientious decision to shoot Johnson, a personal act, rather than hanging him, an official act. The impact of the tragic outcome is thereby intensified.

The novel traces the rise and fall of Mr. Johnson, chief clerk of Fada in Nigeria. A southerner in northern Nigeria and an African in European clothes, he has aspirations to be civilized and claims to be a friend of District Officer Rudbeck, the Wazirin Fada, the King of England, and anyone who vaguely likes him. Johnson's aspirations, however, are not in consonance with his finances, and his marriage, machinations, schemes, stories, parties, petty thefts, capital crime, and irrepressible good spirits become part of the exuberant but relentless rhythm of events that lead to his death. For Johnson, as Cary suggests, life is simply perpetual experience, which he soaks into himself through all five senses at once, and produces again in the form of reflections, comments, songs, and jokes. His vitality is beyond good and evil, equally capable of expressing itself anarchistically or creatively.

Rudbeck, too, is a man of imagination, though not as liberated from constraint as Johnson. His passion for road-building becomes obsessive once Johnson's imagination further fuels his own. He goes so far as to misappropriate funds in order to realize his dream. Without the infectious influence of Johnson's creativity, Rudbeck would never have rebelled against the forces of conservatism. The completed road demonstrates the power of creative imagination.

The road, however, brings crime as well as trade, and in his disillusionment, Rudbeck fires Johnson for embezzlement. In the end, Johnson murders a man and is sentenced to death by Rudbeck. Johnson wants his friend Rudbeck to kill him personally, and Rudbeck eventually complies with his clerk's wish, putting his career as district officer in jeopardy by committing this compassionate but illegal act.

After *Mister Johnson*, Cary chose domestic settings for his novels. His novels of youth and childhood, *Charley Is My Darling* and *A House of Chil-*

dren, are set in Devon and Ireland. The former deals with the evacuation of thousands of London children to Devon during World War II; the latter is a poetical evocation of childhood vacations in Ireland.

In *Charley Is My Darling*, the main character, Charley, like Mr. Johnson, is thrust into an alien world, and the urban values he represents are contrasted with the rural values represented by Lina Allchin, the well-intentioned supervisor of the evacuees. Charley, whose head is shaved as part of a delousing process, is isolated from his peers and consequently channels his imaginative energies into crime and ultimately into anarchistic destruction in order to gain acceptability. Because neither school nor society offers him any outlet for his creative individuality, it expresses itself in violence, an expression which is perhaps a microcosmic commentary on the causes of war.

A House of Children is autobiographical. Technically innovative, it has no omniscient point of view and relies instead on one central consciousness, which narrates the story in the first person. This was to become Cary's characteristic narrative style. The novel has a poetic rather than a linear coherence, depending on a series of revelations or epiphanies rather than on plot. Cary obviously learned a great deal from James Joyce's *A Portrait of the Artist as a Young Man* (1916), which he had read in Africa.

The Moonlight and *A Fearful Joy* are two novels about women and social change. The former, a response to Leo Tolstoy's interpretation of women in *The Kreutzer Sonata* (1889), deals with the familiar theme of law and order versus personal freedom; Ludwig van Beethoven's "Moonlight Sonata" represents romantic love and womanhood. The latter chronicles Tabitha Baskett's life from 1890 to 1948 and is set in Southeast England and the Midlands. The roguish Bonser, one of her paramours, is a memorable character.

These novels were followed by Cary's masterpiece, a trilogy that focuses on the artist and society. Cary designed the trilogy, he said, to show three characters, not only in themselves but also as seen by one another, the object being to get a three-dimensional depth and force of character. Each novel adapts its style to the perceptual, emotive, and cognitive idiosyncrasies of its first-person narrator. *Herself Surprised*, the narrative of Sara Monday, is reminiscent of Daniel Defoe's *Moll Flanders* (1722), and its autobiographical style is ideally suited to dramatize the ironic disparity between Sara's conventional moral attitudes and her "surprising," unconventional behavior. *To Be a Pilgrim*, the narrative of Tom Wilcher, is akin to a Victorian memoir, and the formal politeness of its language reflects the repressed and conservative nature of its narrator. *The Horse's Mouth*, the narrative of Gulley Jimson, uses stream of consciousness and verbally imitates the Impressionist style of painting, an imitation which strikingly reveals the dazzling power of Gulley's visual imagination. The entire trilogy is a virtuoso performance, underscoring Cary's talent for rendering characters from the inside.

Sara Monday is the eternal female—wife, mother, homemaker, mistress, and friend. In accordance with her working class position as a cook, she consistently describes her world in domestic images and metaphors—the sky for her is warm as new milk and as still as water in a goldfish bowl. Her desire to improve her socioeconomic lot is a major motivating factor in her life, and this desire often encourages her to operate outside the bounds of morality and law. Sara, however, is not a moral revolutionary; her values mirror her Victorian education. In her terms, she is constantly "sinning" and constantly "surprised" by sin, but in terms of the reader's understanding of her, she is a lively and sensuous being with an unconscious genius for survival who succumbs, sometimes profitably, sometimes disastrously, to immediate temptation. Her language of sin, which is vital and concrete, belies her language of repentance, which is mechanical and abstract. Nevertheless, Sara, unlike Moll Flanders, does not seem to be a conscious opportunist and manipulator.

Sara betters her socioeconomic status by securing a middle-class marriage to Matthew Monday. The marriage, however, does not prevent her from having affairs with Hickson, a millionaire, and Jimson, an artist. (The narrative description of these "surprises" is exquisitely managed.) Though she sincerely believes in conventional morality, that morality is no match for her joy of life. Cary also shows the negative aspects of Sara's mode of being. Like other characters in his fiction, she is a creative being whose imaginative vitality borders on the anarchistic and irresponsible. She virtually ruins her first husband and makes little effort to keep contact with her four daughters.

After her violent relationship with Gulley Jimson, Sara becomes a cook for the lawyer Wilcher and is about to marry him when his niece has Sara jailed for theft. She had been stealing in order to purchase art supplies for Gulley and to pay for his son's education. Her will to live is thus an implicit critique of the conventional morality that her conscious mind mechanically endorses. She is a survivalist *par excellence*.

Unlike the events in *Herself Surprised*, those in *To Be a Pilgrim* are not presented chronologically. The narrative is layered, juxtaposing Wilcher's present situation of imminent death with the social, political, and religious history of his times. The disrupted chronology poignantly accentuates Wilcher's realization, which comes too late, that he ought to have been a pilgrim, that possessions have been his curse. Now his repressed energies can only counterproductively express themselves in exhibitionism and arson. Marriage to Sara Monday, which might have been a redemptive force in his life, is now impossible, for she has already been incarcerated for her crimes.

In the present time of the novel, Wilcher is a virtual prisoner at Tolbrook Manor, the family home. His niece Ann, a doctor and the daughter of his dead brother Edward, a liberal politician whose life Wilcher tried to manage, is his warden. She marries her cousin Robert, a progressive farmer devoted to the utilitarian goal of making the historic manor a viable commercial enterprise, much to Wilcher's chagrin. Ultimately, Wilcher is forced to recognize that change is the essence of life and that his conservative fixation with tradition, the family, and moral propriety has sapped him of his existential energy, of his ability to be a pilgrim.

The Horse's Mouth, a portrait of the artist as an old man, is justly celebrated as Cary's most remarkable achievement. (Although the Carfax edition of Cary's novels is complete and authoritative, the revised Rainbird edition of *The Horse's Mouth*, 1957, illustrated by the author, includes a chapter—"The Old Strife at Plant's"—that Cary had previously deleted.) Its reputation has been enhanced by the excellent film version in which Alec Guiness plays the role of Gulley Jimson.

Gulley Jimson is a pilgrim; he accepts the necessity of the fall into freedom with joy and energy, conceiving of it as a challenge to his imagination and thereby seeking to impose aesthetic order on experiential chaos. For Gulley, anything that is part of the grimy reality of the contingent world—fried fish shops, straw, chicken boxes, dirt, oil, mud—can inspire a painting. The Impressionist style of his narrative reflects his vocation, for he mainly construes his world in terms of physical imagery, texture, solidity, perspective, color, shape, and line, merging Blakean vision with Joycean stream of consciousness. Gulley's sensibility is perpetually open to novelty, and his life affirms the existential value of becoming, for he identifies with the creative process rather than with the finished product. His energies focus on the future, on starting new works, not on dwelling on past accomplishments. Even though he is destitute, he refuses to paint in the lucrative style of his Sara Monday period.

Gulley is also a born con artist, a streetwise survivor. He is not adverse to stealing, cheating, swindling, blackmailing, or even murdering if his imaginative self-expression is at stake. He is completely comfortable in a brutal, violent, and unjust world. His vision, therefore, has limitations. His pushing Sara down the stairs to her death shows the anarchistic irresponsibility implicit in regarding life as merely spiritual fodder for the imagination. Moreover, Gulley lacks historical consciousness. Even though the novel chronicles his life before and after the beginning of World War II, Gulley seems to have no conception of who Adolf Hitler is and what he represents.

For the most part, this novel clearly champions the creative individual and criticizes the repressive society that inhibits him, although Cary is always fair-minded enough to imply the limitations of his characters. Gulley Jimson remains a paradigm of energetic vitality, an imaginative visionary who blasts through generation to regeneration, redeeming the poverty of the contingent world and liberating consciousness from the malady of the quotidian. The entire trilogy is a masterpiece; the created worlds of the three narrators mutually supplement and criticize one another, stressing the difficulty of achieving a workable balance between the will to survive, to preserve, and to create.

Cary's second trilogy—*Prisoner of Grace*, *Except the Lord*, and *Not Honour More*—deals with politics and the individual. It is a commentary on radical liberalism, evangelicalism, and crypto-Fascism, moving from the 1860's to the 1930's and involving the lives of three characters (Nina Nimmo/Latter, Chester Nimmo, and Jim Latter) whose lives are inextricably enmeshed, unlike those of the characters of the first trilogy.

In *Prisoner of Grace*, Nina Nimmo (Nina Latter by the end of her narrative) tries to protect and defend both her lovers—the radical liberal politician Nimmo, maligned for his alleged opportunism and demagoguery, and the crypto-Fascist Latter, a military man obsessed by a perverted notion of honor. The time-span of the novel covers the Boer War, the Edwardian reform government, the World War I victory, the prosperous aftermath, and the 1926 General Strike. The action takes place mainly in Devon, where Nimmo makes his mark as a politician and becomes a member of Parliament, and in London, where Nimmo eventually becomes a cabinet minister.

Nina, carrying the child of her cousin Jim Latter, marries the lower-class Chester Nimmo, who is handsomely remunerated for rescuing the fallen woman in order to secure a respectable future for the child. Nina never loves Nimmo but is converted to his cause by his political and religious rhetoric. She writes her account in order to anticipate and rebut criticism of his conduct.

Thrust into the duplicitous and morally ambiguous world of politics, she succumbs both to Chester's ideals, values, morals, and beliefs and to his lusts, lies, schemes, and maneuverings, seemingly incapable of distinguishing the one from the other, as is the reader, since he can only rely on Nina's unreliable account. Unlike the disingenuousness of Sara Monday in *Herself Surprised*, which the reader can easily disentangle—Sara's sensuous vitality gives the lie to the maxims of conventional piety she mechanically utters—Nina's disingenuousness is a fundamental part of her character. Nina, like Chester, is both sincere and hypocritical, genuinely moral and meretriciously rhetorical, an embodiment of the political personality. Even the politics of their marriage parallel in miniature the politics of the outside world.

Nina is a prisoner of grace once she has converted to the belief that Chester's being is infused with grace and that his religious and political beliefs enjoy moral rectitude by definition. Her love for Jim is also a grace that imprisons her and ultimately impels her to divorce Chester and marry Jim. The reader, too, is a prisoner of grace, since he cannot get outside of Nina's "political" point of view and thus cannot separate truth and falsity, the authorial implication being that the two are necessarily confused and interdependent in the political personality. Like Sara, Nina is a survivalist, and after she becomes adulterously involved with Nimmo, she, like Sara, is murdered by a man whom she had helped. Survivalism has limits.

Except the Lord, the story of Nimmo's childhood and youth, takes place in the 1860's and 1870's. It is the history of a boy's mind and soul rather than one of political events. Like *To Be a Pilgrim*, it takes the form of a Victorian memoir in which the mature narrator explores the events and forces that caused him to become what he is. Nurtured in an environment of poverty, fundamentalist faith, and familial love, Nimmo becomes in turn a radical preacher, labor agitator, and liberal politician.

According to the first verse of Psalm 127, "Except the Lord build the house, they labour in vain that would build it; except the Lord keep the city, the watchman waketh but in vain." Since this novel stops before the events of *Prisoner of Grace* and *Not Honour More* begin, and since it principally induces a sympathetic response to Nimmo, the reader has a difficult time interpreting the significance of the title. He tends to see Nimmo differently after having read the account of the latter's youth, but he is still uncertain whether Nimmo is a knight of faith or an opportunistic antinomian. The trilogy as a whole seems to suggest that Chester is both.

Not Honour More is the story of a soldier, Jim Latter, who sees the world in dichotomous terms and cannot accept the necessarily ambiguous transaction between the realms of freedom and authority. The novel is a policewoman's transcript of Jim's confession; it is dictated as he awaits execution for the murder of Nina, provoked by his discovery of her adulterous relationship with Nimmo, her ex-husband. His language is a combination of clipped military prose, hysterical defensiveness, and invective against both the decadence of British society around the time of the 1926 General Strike and the corruption of politicians such as Nimmo.

Latter believes in authority, in imposing law and order on the masses. He has no sense of the moral ambiguity of human behavior, no sense of the complexity of human motivation. A self-proclaimed spiritual descendent of the Cavalier poet Richard Lovelace, Jim believes that his murder of Nina proves that he loves honor more. He conceives of the murder as an execution, a moral act, whereas it is in reality a perversion of honor, a parody of the code that Lovelace represents. District Officer Rudbeck, of *Mister Johnson*, is by comparison a truly honorable man: he personalizes rather than ritualizes Mr. Johnson's death. Because Jim believes in the rectitude of authoritarians with superior gifts, he is a crypto-Fascist. The best that can be said of him is that he has the courage of his misplaced convictions.

Throughout his novels, Cary focused his creative energies on human beings who are condemned to be free, to enact their lives somewhere between the extremes of anarchism and conformity. His achievement demonstrates that it is possible for a novelist to be at once stylistically sophisticated, realistically oriented, and ethically involved.

Greig E. Henderson

Other major works

SHORT FICTION: *Spring Song and Other Stories*, 1960 (Winnifred Davin, editor).

POETRY: *Verses by Arthur Cary*, 1908; *Marching Soldier*, 1945; *The Drunken Sailor*, 1947.

NONFICTION: *Power in Men*, 1939; *The Case for African Freedom*, 1941, 1962; *Process of Real Freedom*, 1943; *Britain and West Africa*, 1946; *Art and Reality*, 1958; *Memoir of the Bobotes*, 1960; *Selected Essays*, 1976 (A. G. Bishop, editor).

Bibliography

Bloom, Robert. *The Indeterminate World: A Study of the Novels of Joyce Cary*. Philadelphia: University of Pennsylvania Press, 1962. Focuses on the "indeterminateness" of Cary's novels, which Bloom considers both Cary's strength and his weakness as a writer. Half of this study is devoted to detailed analyses of the last three novels published in Cary's lifetime.

Cook, Cornelia. *Joyce Cary: Liberal Principles*. Totowa, N.J.: Barnes & Noble Books, 1981. This full-length study, which draws on the Cary collection at the Bodleian library at Oxford, England, places Cary in the context of Edwardian social change. Cook argues that Cary's novels "explore the themes of creativeness, power, freedom and their manifestations in the world."

Echeruo, Michael J. *Joyce Cary and the Novel of Africa*. London: Longman, 1973. Echeruo places Cary's African novels in the tradition of the foreign novel and argues that they have a special place in this genre. Provides new insights into the growth of Cary's art as well as valuable criticism of Cary's African novels.

Foster, Malcolm. *Joyce Cary: A Biography*. London: Michael Joseph, 1969. Written in four parts, this is an exhaustive and informative study of Cary; Foster had access to the Cary collection at the Bodleian library in Oxford, England. Critical discussion of each novel is brief and incomplete; however, Foster offers some new insights into Cary's novels.

Hall, Dennis. *Joyce Cary: A Reappraisal*. London: Macmillan, 1983. Makes the point that there are two Carys: one the thinker and the other the artist. This full-length study discusses all of Cary's novels with conscientious thoroughness. Hall is sympathetic to Cary, but notes the unevenness of his work and concludes that Cary is "his own worst enemy." Contains a helpful bibliography for the Cary scholar.

Majumdar, Bimalendu. *Joyce Cary: An Existentialist Approach*. Atlantic Highlands, N.J.: Humanities Press, 1982. A scholarly study of Cary devoted to critical appraisal of his work. Majumdar focuses on the central existential theme in Cary's novels: the uniqueness of the individual who "refuses to fit into some system constructed by rational thought."

Noble, R. W. *Joyce Cary.* Edinburgh, Scotland: Oliver & Boyd, 1973. Classifies Cary's work into categories that are useful in providing fresh insights into his writing. The introduction traces Cary's life and its relationship to his writing. Noble is particularly sensitive to Cary's narrative skill.

Wolkenfeld, Jack. *Joyce Cary: The Developing Style.* New York: New York University Press, 1968. Examines Cary from the perspective of his being a lone figure among contemporaries and an outsider in experimental writing. The opening chapter, "Juxtapositions and Confrontations," provides some excellent criticism on Cary's African novels.

WILLA CATHER

Born: Back Creek Valley, near Gore, Virginia; December 7, 1873
Died: New York, New York; April 24, 1947

Principal long fiction

Alexander's Bridge, 1912; *O Pioneers!*, 1913; *The Song of the Lark*, 1915; *My Ántonia*, 1918; *One of Ours*, 1922; *A Lost Lady*, 1923; *The Professor's House*, 1925; *My Mortal Enemy*, 1926; *Death Comes for the Archbishop*, 1927; *Shadows on the Rock*, 1931; *Lucy Gayheart*, 1935; *Sapphira and the Slave Girl*, 1940.

Other literary forms

Willa Cather was a prolific writer, especially as a young woman. By the time her first novel was published when she was thirty-eight, she had written more than forty short stories, at least five hundred columns and reviews, numerous magazine articles and essays, and a volume of poetry. She collected three volumes of her short stores: *The Troll Garden* (1905), *Youth and the Bright Medusa* (1920), and *Obscure Destinies* (1932). Those volumes contain the few short stories she allowed to be anthologized, most frequently "Paul's Case," "The Sculptor's Funeral" (*The Troll Garden*), and "Neighbour Rosicky" (*Obscure Destinies*). Since her death, three additional volumes have been published which contain the rest of her known stories: *The Old Beauty and Others* (1948), *Willa Cather's Collected Short Fiction: 1892-1912* (1965), and *Uncle Valentine and Other Stories: Willa Cather's Collected Short Fiction, 1915-1929* (1973). A great many of her early newspaper columns and reviews have been collected in *The Kingdom of Art: Willa Cather's First Principles and Critical Statements, 1893-1896* (1966) and in *The World and the Parish: Willa Cather's Articles and Reviews, 1893-1902* (1970, 2 volumes). Three volumes of essays, which include prefaces to the works of writers she admired, have been published. Cather herself prepared the earliest volume, *Not Under Forty* (1936), for publication. The other two, *Willa Cather on Writing* (1949), and *Willa Cather in Europe* (1956), have appeared since her death. Her single volume of poetry, *April Twilights*, appeared in 1903, but Cather later spoke apologetically of that effort, even jokingly telling a friend that she had tried to buy up and destroy all extant copies so that no one would see them. Only one of Cather's novels, *A Lost Lady*, has been adapted for the screen. A second screen version of that novel was so distasteful to her that in her will she prohibited any such attempts in the future. One story, "Paul's Case," has been presented on PBS television. Cather's will also forbids the publication of her letters. Cather continued to write short stories after she began writing novels, but she wrote them less frequently.

Achievements

Cather actually had at least two careers in her lifetime. Prior to becoming a novelist, she was a highly successful journalist and writer of short fiction, as well as a high school English teacher. She began her career as a writer while still in college, where she published several short stories and wrote a regular newspaper column for the *Nebraska State Journal*. Later she also wrote for the Lincoln *Courier*. Her columns were on a variety of subjects, but many of them were related to the arts. She discussed books and authors, and reviewed the many plays, operas, and concerts that came through Lincoln on tour. She gained an early reputation as an astute (and opinionated) critic. Even after she moved to Pittsburgh, the Lincoln papers continued to print her columns.

Over the years, Cather published stories in such national magazines as *Century*, *Collier's*, *Harper's*, *Ladies' Home Journal*, *Woman's Home Companion*, *Saturday Evening Post*, and *McClure's*, the popular journal for which she served as an editor for several years.

During her affiliation with *McClure's*, Cather traveled widely gathering materials for stories and making contacts with contributors to the magazine. She helped many a struggling young writer to find a market, and she worked regularly with already prominent writers. Cather had been a student of the classics since childhood, and she was unusually well-read. She was also a devoted and knowledgeable student of art and music, a truly educated woman with highly developed, intelligent tastes. She was friendly with several celebrated musicians, including Metropolitan Opera Soprano Olive Fremstad, after whom she patterned Thea Kronborg in *The Song of the Lark*; songwriter Ethelbert Nevin; and the famous child prodigies, the Menuhins. She also knew Sarah Orne Jewett briefly.

Typically, Cather did not move in writers' circles, but preferred to work by her own light and without the regular association of other writers of her time. She never sought the public eye, and as the years went on she chose to work in relative solitude, preferring the company of only close friends and family. Known primarily as a novelist, she has in recent years enjoyed a growing reputation as a writer of short fiction. She was awarded the Pulitzer Prize for *One of Ours*, and an ardent admirer, Sinclair Lewis, was heard to remark that she was more deserving than he of the Nobel Prize he won. Cather is particularly appealing to readers who like wholesome, value-centered art. She is held in increasingly high regard among critics and scholars of twentieth century literature and is recognized as one of the finest stylists in American letters. Time will surely accord her a lasting position in the first rank of American novelists.

Biography

Willa Cather was born in Back Creek Valley, Virginia, on December 7,

1873, the first of seven children. Her father's side of the family came to Virginia during colonial times. Her grandfather, William Cather, did not believe in slavery and favored the Union cause during the Civil War, creating a rift in a family of Confederate sympathizers. Her grandfather on her mother's side, William Boak, served three terms in the Virginia House of Delegates. He died before Cather was born, while serving in Washington in the Department of the Interior. Cather's grandmother, Rachel Boak, returned with her children to Back Creek Valley and eventually moved to Nebraska with her son-in-law Charles, Willa Cather's father, and his wife, Mary Virginia. Rachel Boak is an important figure in Cather's life and fiction. A courageous and enduring woman, she appears as Sapphira's daughter Rachel in Cather's last completed novel and as the grandmother in a late story, "Old Mrs. Harris." Rachel's maiden name was Seibert, a name which Cather adopted (spelling it "Sibert" after her uncle William Sibert Boak) as a young woman and then later dropped.

In 1883, when Cather—named Wilella, nicknamed Willie, and later renamed Willa by her own decree—was nine years old, her family sold their holdings at Back Creek and moved to Webster County, Nebraska. In that move from a lush Virginia countryside to a virtually untamed prairie, Cather experienced what Eudora Welty has called a "wrench to the spirit" from which she never recovered. It proved to be the most significant single event in her young life, bringing her as it did face to face with a new landscape and an immigrant people who were to make a lasting impression on her imagination. The move was a shock, but a shock that was the beginning of love both for the land and the people, and for the rest of her life, Cather was to draw from this experience in creating her fiction.

Cather always had a special affection for her father; he was a gentle, quiet-mannered man who, after eighteen months on his parents' prairie homestead, moved his family into Red Cloud, sixteen miles away. There, he engaged in various business enterprises with no great success and reared his family. Unlike her husband, Mary Cather was energetic and driving, a hard disciplinarian, but generous and life-loving. A good many scenes and people from Cather's years on the farm and in Red Cloud appear in her fiction. Her third novel, *The Song of the Lark*, though its central character is a musician, recounts some of Cather's own struggles to develop her talent amid the strictures and jealousies of small-town life.

Cather's years at the university in Lincoln were extremely busy ones. Not a metropolis by any means, Lincoln was still many times larger than Red Cloud, and Cather gratefully discovered the joys of the theater and of meeting people with broad interests and capabilities. Her experience is much like that of Jim Burden as she describes it in *My Ántonia*. At first she planned to study science but switched to the humanities, she later confessed, when she saw an essay of hers printed in the newspaper. As she tells it, she was hooked for life. While at the university, she was active in literary circles, serving as an editor for the *Lasso* and the *Hesperian*, two student literary magazines. Several of her stories appeared in those magazines and in others. She spent the year after her graduation, in 1895, in and around Red Cloud, where she began writing for the weekly Lincoln *Courier* as well as for the *Nebraska State Journal* and published her first story in a magazine of national circulation, the *Overland Monthly*. Then in June, 1896, she left Nebraska to take a position with the *Home Monthly*, a small rather weak family magazine in Pittsburgh.

Cather knew she had to leave Red Cloud to forward her career, and even the drudgery of the *Home Monthly* was an important opportunity. Later, she secured a position with the Pittsburgh *Daily Leader*, and then taught high school English and Latin for five years. While in Pittsburgh, Cather continued to write short fiction while pursuing an active social life. It was there that she met Isabelle McClung, who was to become her dearest friend. For a time, Cather lived with Isabelle and her parents, and in their home she enjoyed the quiet seclusion she needed for her writing. Cather's big break in her journalistic career came in 1903 when S. S. McClure, the dynamic publisher of *McClure's* magazine, became aware of her work and summoned her to his office. That interview began an association that led to an important position with *McClure's* and eventually made it possible for Cather to leave the world of journalism and devote her full energies to the writing of fiction. The publication of *The Troll Garden* in 1905 announced that a major new talent had arrived on the literary scene. McClure knew ability when he saw it.

Cather's first novel, *Alexander's Bridge*, was written while she was still with *McClure's*, and it was first conceived as a serial for the magazine. It appeared as a novel in 1912, the year she left *McClure's* to try writing on her own. Still, it was not until *O Pioneers!* came to fruition the next year that Cather felt she had hit what she called "the home pasture" and discovered herself as a novelist. In this book, she turned to her memories of the Nebraska prairie and wrote powerfully of immigrant efforts to come to terms with the land. From then on, Cather was on her way. In 1920, she began a long and satisfying professional relationship with Alfred A. Knopf, who became her publisher and remained so for the rest of her life.

Cather lived most of her professional life in New York City with a friend and literary associate, Edith Lewis. Her many trips to Europe confirmed her great admiration for France and the French people, an appreciation that receives repeated expression in her novels. She also visited the American West a number of times and drew upon her experiences there for some of her work. She developed a special affection for the area around Jaffrey, New Hampshire, where she liked to go for uninterrupted work. She even chose to be buried there.

Cather's classmates in Lincoln remembered her as strong-willed, bright, gifted, and somewhat eccentric. Certainly, she knew her own mind, and she had strong ideas about the difference between the cheap and the valuable. She was fiercely attached to her family and friends, but once her parents were dead, she never returned to Red Cloud. Prior to her death on April 24, 1947, Cather was working on a novel that was set in medieval France. After her death, the unfinished manuscript, as she had requested, was destroyed.

Analysis

Willa Cather once said in an interview that the Nebraska landscape was "the happiness and the curse" of her life. That statement points up the ambivalence in Cather that produced in her a lifelong tug-of-war between the East and the Western prairie. That ambivalence is the central tension in her novels. As long as her parents were alive, she made repeated trips back home to see them and each time she crossed the Missouri River, she said, "the very smell of the soil tore [her] to pieces." As a young woman in Red Cloud and Lincoln, however, she was chafed by narrow attitudes and limited opportunities. She knew that she had to leave the prairie in order to fulfill her compelling desire for broader experiences and for art. Like Thea Kronborg in *The Song of the Lark*, Cather knew she would never find fulfillment unless she left her home. At the same time, however, she also discovered that her very being was rooted in the landscape of her childhood. Thus, going back to it, even if only in memory, was essential and inescapable.

Cather once remarked that the most important impressions one receives come before the age of fifteen, and it seems clear that she was referring particularly to her own experiences on the Nebraska prairie. She did use some Virginia memories in her work, but only sporadically, in a few early short stories, before turning to them in her last published novel, *Sapphira and the Slave Girl*. In her "Nebraska works," it is not only Nebraska that Cather evokes; but it is, also, what Nebraska symbolizes and means, for she is not simply a regional writer. The range of her work is as broad as the range of her experience, and Nebraska represents the westward necessity of her life. Wherever in her work the pull of the landscape is felt, there is Nebraska— whether the setting is Colorado, Kansas, New Mexico, or even rural Pennsylvania or frontier Quebec.

As has been suggested, her life had an eastward necessity too. The raw hardships of prairie life could sometimes mutilate the body and drain the spirit, and a human being often needed something else. A man of genuine sensitivity and culture, such as Ántonia Shimerda's father, for example, could not survive in a hard land. Cather's awareness of this fact made a great impression on her. One of the first stories she heard after arriving in Nebraska was the account of Francis Sadilek's suicide, an event which she reconstructed in *My Ántonia*. Not only could the beloved land be killingly cruel, but it also failed to provide the environment of training, discipline, and appreciation so necessary for the growth and development of an artist. Although the land provided the materials for memory to work with and the germinating soil for the seed of talent, it could not produce the final fruit.

Then, too, part of the Nebraska Cather experienced was small-town life and the limited opportunities it offered the artistically ambitious. Throughout her life, she felt misunderstood by some of the townspeople who had known her as a youngster. Letters to her lifelong friend in Red Cloud, Carrie Miner Sherwood (from whom she drew Frances Harling in *My Ántonia*), indicate how sharply Cather felt their disapproval of her. She rebelled against their codes and refused to remain among them but was stung by their criticism.

Thea Kronborg is not the only Cather character to be torn, like her creator, between East and West, civilization and the land. In *My Ántonia*, the young Jim Burden expresses Cather's own feelings of awe and fear upon his arrival in Nebraska. Later, when he goes to school in Lincoln and eventually leaves for a career in the East, the Nebraska landscape of his past stays with him, just as it stayed with Cather, even after long absences. Claude Wheeler, in *One of Ours*, also has a good deal of his maker in him. Much as he loves the beauty of the Nebraska landscape, he cannot find himself until he leaves it. Like Cather, the ultimate in civilization for him is France.

The opposing aspects of Cather's desire, the land and civilization—or, more specifically, art—were of equal value to her. She could never entirely give up one for the other or value one above the other. Thus, the land was "the happiness and the curse" of her life. She might well have said the same thing about her art. Ironically, however, at least according to her friend, Elizabeth Sergeant, it was not until Cather made her feelings for the land a part of her art that she truly realized her potential as an artist. Though East and West, civilization (art) and the land—the very foundations of Cather's work—are sometimes at opposite poles in terms of the choices one must make, they are both positive values to her. The greatest threat to each is not the other; the greatest threat to each is an exploitative materialism that has no appreciation for the innate value of the land or of art.

In Cather's work, the same impulse that exploits the land is also destructive to art and the best qualities of civilization. The author's most despicable characters are those such as Ivy Peters in *A Lost Lady* and Bayliss Wheeler in *One of Ours*, who have no feeling for the land or for the past which it harbors. All that interests them is making money, as much as possible as fast as possible. Cather had great admiration for the early railroad pioneers, wealthy men of immense courage, vision, and taste as she pictures them in *A Lost Lady*. In too many people, however, the lust for wealth and the acquisition of it are destructive to character. They subvert what are for Cather some of life's most positive values, a relationship with the earth and an aesthetic sensibility.

Of Cather's twelve novels, only three, *Alexander's Bridge*, *My Mortal Enemy*, and *Sapphira and the Slave Girl*, do not deal centrally with the tension between East and West, with civilization and the land as values threatened by the spirit of acquisitiveness; and even those touch the latter point. For example, Myra Henshawe's harshness of character comes partly as a result of her need to live in a style only money can provide; the desire to possess that style leads to the buying and selling of human beings, a central issue in *Sapphira and the Slave Girl*.

Cather's second novel, *O Pioneers!*, her first to use Nebraska materials, presents the conflict between the land and civilization and the threat of destructive materialism as its major concerns. The novel's principal character, Alexandra Bergson, is something of an earth mother, a being so closely linked with the soil and growing things that her very oneness with the earth seems to convert the harsh wild land into rich acreage that willingly yields its treasures. From the first, she believes in the land and loves it, even when her brothers and neighbors grow to despise and curse it. Two of Alexandra's brothers have such a fear of financial failure that they cannot see the land's potential.

Cather, however, does not simply present Alexandra's struggle and eventual triumph. There is another value, opposed to the land but equally important, with which Alexandra must contend. Her youngest brother, Emil, is sensitive in a way that does not lend itself to life on the continental divide, and she wants him to have opportunities that are available only in centers of civilization. His finely tuned spirit, though, leads him to disaster in a prairie environment where passions can run high, untempered by civilizing influences. Emil falls in love with Marie Shabata, a free, wild creature, and both of them are killed by her enraged husband. The book's final vision, however, returns to an affirmation of the enduring qualities of the land and the value of human union with it.

The conflict between the landscape of home and art is played out dramatically in the central character of *The Song of the Lark*. Thea Kronborg is in many ways the young Willa Cather, fighting the narrowness of small-town life on the prairie, needing to leave Moonstone to develop her talent, but needing also to integrate the landscape of home with her artistic desire. Thea has to leave home, but she also has to have it with her in order to reach her potential as an opera singer. Much that she has set aside in her quest for art she must pick up again and use in new ways. In fact, Cather makes it clear that without the integration of home Thea might never have become an artist. Moonstone, however, also has its materialists who obviously stand in opposition to the enduring, if sometimes conflicting, values of earth and art. The only villain of the piece is the wife of Thea's best friend and supporter, Doctor Archie. She is a mean, pinched woman, shriveled with stinginess.

Once Thea has left Moonstone and gone to Chicago to study music, the killing pace and the battle against mediocrity wear her to the breaking point. In an effort at self-renewal, she accepts an invitation to recuperate on a ranch near the Canyon de Chelly in Arizona. There, she spends many hours lying in the sun on the red rock, following the paths of ancient potters, examining the broken pieces of their pottery that still lie in the streambeds. It is there that Thea has the revelation that gives birth to her artist self. These ancient potters made art pieces of their pottery by decorating them. The clay jars would not hold water any better for the artistic energy expended upon them, but their makers expended that energy nevertheless. This revelation comes to Thea out of the landscape itself, and it gives her the knowledge she needs in order to continue her studies: artistic desire is universal, ageless, and she is a part of it.

The eponymous protagonist of *Lucy Gayheart* is not so hard and indomitable a character as Thea, nor is she destined to become a performing artist in her own right. Nevertheless, Lucy is much like Thea (and the young Willa Cather) in her need to leave the prairie landscape and pursue art in the only place where such pursuits are possible, the city. Lucy is, however, in many ways a child of the earth—she loves skating on the frozen river, and she begs for the preservation of an orchard that her sister Pauline, a plodding materialist, wants to cut down because it is no longer productive. Given her nature, it is no surprise that Lucy falls in love with the singer for whom she plays accompaniments at practice. He is the embodiment of the art for which her soul yearns. After his accidental drowning, Lucy returns home and she herself dies in a skating accident, her death a final union with the earth. There is also a "Doctor Archie's wife" in *Lucy Gayheart*. Ironically, she marries the one man in Haverford that Lucy might have married happily, the one man with the capacity to appreciate what a rare and lovely phenomenon Lucy was.

Something of an earth mother like Alexandra Bergson, yet more malleable and human, Ántonia Shimerda of *My Ántonia* is for many readers Cather's most appealing character. She becomes a total embodiment of the strength and generosity associated with those who are at one with the land and the forces of nature. Unlike Alexandra, her capacity for life finds expression not only in the trees and plants she tends but also in her many children, who seem to have sprung almost miraculously from the earth. It is in Jim Burden, who tells the story, and to some extent, in Ántonia's husband, Anton Cuzak, that the conflict between East and West occurs. Jim, like Cather, comes to Nebraska from Virginia as a youngster, and though he has to seek his professional life in eastern cities, he never gets Nebraska out of his soul. Even as a student at the University of Nebraska in Lincoln, he gazes out his window and imagines there the landscape and figures of his childhood. Ántonia represents for Jim, even after twenty years of city life, all the positive values of the earth for which no amount of civilization can compensate. At the end of the book, he determines to revitalize his past association with the land and yet still tramp a few lighted streets with Cuzak, a city man at heart.

The conflict between the harshness of life on the prairie and the cultural advantages of civilization is also presented in Ántonia's father, who had been a gifted musician in Europe, but who now, poverty-stricken and overworked, no longer played the violin. Ántonia's deep appreciation for Cuzak's quality and for his gentle city ways and her pride in Jim's "city" accomplishments, bridges the gap between prairie and civilization.

The materialists are also evident in *My Ántonia*. In fact, one of Cather's most memorable villains is the lecherous and greedy Wick Cutter, Black Hawk's nefarious moneylender. His last act is to devise a scheme whereby he can kill himself and his equally greedy wife and at the same time guarantee that her relatives will not get a cent of his money.

Claude Wheeler, the main character of *One of Ours*, is torn, like so many of Cather's young people, by the need to go and the need to stay. Claude is filled with yearnings he does not completely understand. All he knows is that he is burning to fulfill some inner desire, and everything he does seems to go wrong. Much as he loves the rivers and groves of his own landscape, he feels like a misfit there. His father's hearty, nonchalant materialism is only slightly less distressing to him than the hard, grasping greed of his older brother Bayliss, the bloodless, pious parsimony of his wife Enid, and the cheerful selfishness of his younger brother Ralph. The world begins opening to him during the short period when he is allowed to attend the university at Lincoln, but Claude completely finds himself only when he enlists in the army and begins fighting in France. There, he meets Lieutenant David Gerhardt, a musician, and encounters a gracious cultural climate to which he responds with all his heart.

There is, however, a troubling aspect to this novel. Claude's real fulfillment comes in the midst of battle, surrounded by death and destruction. Only then does he feel at one with himself and his surroundings; only then is the old anguish gone, the tension released. In the end, he is killed, and his mother feels some sense of gratitude that at least he does not have to face the disillusionment of returning to a country that has given itself over to material pursuits. With the exception of *Alexander's Bridge*, this is probably Cather's least successful novel, perhaps partly because she was emotionally very close to her central character. Cather stated publicly that she modeled Claude after a young cousin of hers who died in World War I, but in a letter she indicated that Claude was, in fact, an embodiment of Cather herself. The novel is a poignant portrayal of the central tensions in her work between the land and civilization, and it also describes the ever-present threat of spiritually damaging materialism.

In *A Lost Lady*, Cather again shows a character's need for civilization's amenities, in spite of the appeal of the Western landscape. Here too, though the reader may fault Cather's main character for her sometimes expedient morality, Cather has publicly expressed her affection for the woman upon whom she based the character of Marian Forrester. Further, the ruthless, materialistic mind-set that nearly always characterizes "the enemy" in Cather's work is graphically portrayed in the coarse figure of Ivy Peters. As a boy, Ivy cruelly blinded a bird and then set it free, and as a man he drained what was once the Forresters' lovely marshlands in order to make them yield a profit. Unscrupulous and shrewd, he manages to compromise the beautiful Marian Forrester with as little conscience as he showed toward the helpless bird.

Until her husband's decline, Mrs. Forrester managed to have the best of both worlds, East and West, spending her summers in the beautiful countryside outside Sweet Water, on the Burlington line, and her winters in the lively social atmosphere of Denver and Colorado Springs. Captain Forrester, much her elder, had made his fortune pioneering Western railroad development. When the novel opens, the Captain's failing health has already begun to limit Mrs. Forrester's social and cultural opportunities, though she still enjoys visits to the city and entertains important guests at Sweet Water. It becomes apparent, however, much to the dismay of Marian Forrester's young admirer, Niel Herbert, that Marian's passion for life and high living has led her into an affair with the opportunistic, if handsome, Frank Ellinger even before the death of the Captain. This affair foreshadows her later desperate sellout to Ivy Peters. It is significant, however, that Cather never judges Marian, though the prudish Niel does. It is not the life-loving Marian Forrester that Cather condemns, but the grasping Ivy Peters and the unprincipled Frank Ellinger— and perhaps even the unforgiving Niel Herbert. The novel's hero is Captain Forrester, who willingly relinquishes his fortune to preserve his honor.

There are two plotlines in *The Professor's House*, one of which centers around the growing life weariness of Professor Godfrey St. Peter, and the other around the experiences of his student, Tom Outland, on a faraway desert mesa. Both sets of experiences, however, illuminate the tension between civilization and the open landscape and focus upon the destructive nature of materialistic desire. St. Peter, a highly civilized man with refined tastes and a keen appreciation for true art, loses heart at his daughters' greed and selfishness and his wife's increasing interest in what he regards as ostentatious display. Near the end of the book, he focuses his imagination on the Kansas prairie, on his solitary, primitive boyhood self. He wants to recapture the self he was before he married and before his family and his colleagues began conjugating the verb "to buy" with every breath.

Tom Outland, the one remarkable student of St. Peter's teaching career, becomes equally disillusioned with society and its greed. Cather spares him from living out his life in such a society, however, by mercifully allowing him to die in the war in France as she had allowed Claude Wheeler to die. Ironically, it is Tom's invention of a new engine, bequeathed in a romantic impulse to one of St. Peter's daughters, that makes her and her husband rich. While herding cattle on the great Western desert, Tom Outland and his partner Roddy Blake explore the great Blue Mesa across the river from their summer grazing range. On it, they find the remnants of ancient cliff dwellers, including many beautifully decorated jars. These jars provide for Tom, as they had for Thea Kronborg, a priceless link with the art and people and landscape of the past. In these jars, the tension between land and art is erased. While Tom is away on a fruitless trip to Washington, where he had hoped to interest someone in his find, Roddy Blake misguidedly sells the relics to a European art dealer. Recovering from two heartbreaking disappointments, the loss of the relics and the loss of Roddy, Tom makes his spiritual recovery through union with the mesa itself. He becomes one with the rock, the trees, the very desert air.

Even though *Death Comes for the Archbishop* is not Cather's final novel, it is in a very real sense a culmination of her efforts at reconciling the central urges toward land and toward art, or civilization, that are the hallmark of her life and her work. Selfishness and greed are a threat in this book too, but their influence is muted by Cather's concentration on Father Jean Latour as the shaping force of her narrative. He is Cather's ideal human being, by the end of the book a perfect blend of the virtues of the untamed landscape and the finest aspects of civilization.

As a young priest, Latour is sent from a highly cultivated environment in his beloved France to revitalize Catholicism in the rugged New Mexico Territory of the New World. Learned in the arts, genteel in manner, dedicated to his calling, this man of fine-textured intelligence is forced to work out his fate in a desolate, godforsaken land among, for the most part, simple people who have never known or have largely forgotten the sacraments of the civilized Church. His dearest friend, Father Joseph Vaillant, works with him—a wiry, lively man, Latour's complement in every way. Latour must bring a few greedy, unruly local priests into line, but his greatest struggle is internal as he works to convert himself, a product of European civilization, into the person needed to serve the Church in this vast desert land. In the end, his remarkable nature is imprinted indelibly on the barren landscape, and the landscape is imprinted indelibly on his nature. Instead of returning to France in his official retirement, he elects to remain in the New World. His total reconciliation with the land is symbolized in the fulfillment of his dream to build a European-style cathedral out of the golden rock of New Mexico. In that building, the art of civilization merges gracefully with the very soil of the Western landscape, just as Jean Latour's spirit had done.

Shadows on the Rock, a lesser book, takes for its landscape the rock of Quebec, but the tension is still between the old ways of civilized France and the new ways of the Canadians of the future, children of the uncharted, untamed land. It, too, focuses on the efforts of the Catholic Church to bring spiritual civilization to the New World, but its central character is not a churchman. Rather, it is young Cécile Auclair who values the old ways, the civilities taught her by her mother and still priceless to her father, but who also responds to the wave of the future and marries a Canadian backwoodsman whose deepest ties are to the uncharted landscape.

Cather's work stands as something of an emotional autobiography, tracing the course of her deepest feelings about what is most valuable in human experience. For Cather, what endured best, and what helped one endure, were the values contained in the land, and in humanity's civilizing impulses, particularly the impulse to art. What is best in humanity responds to these things, and these things have the capacity to ennoble in return. Sometimes they seem mutually exclusive, the open landscape and civilization, and some characters never reconcile the apparent polarity. Cather says, however, that ultimately one can have both East and West. For her, the reconciliation seems to have occurred mainly in her art, where she was able to love and write about the land if not live on it. A conflict such as this can be resolved, for it involves a tension between two things of potential value. Thus, in her life and her art it was not this conflict that caused Cather to despair; rather, it was the willingness of humanity in general to allow the greedy and unscrupulous to destroy both the land and civilization. At the same time, it was the bright promise of youth, in whom desire for the land and for art could be reborn with each new generation, that caused her to rejoice.

Marilyn Arnold

Other major works

SHORT FICTION: *The Troll Garden*, 1905; *Youth and the Bright Medusa*, 1920; *Obscure Destinies*, 1932; *The Old Beauty and Others*, 1948; *Willa Cather's Collected Short Fiction: 1892-1912*, 1965; *Uncle Valentine and Other Stories: Willa Cather's Collected Short Fiction, 1915-1929*, 1973.

POETRY: *April Twilights*, 1903.

NONFICTION: *Not Under Forty*, 1936; *Willa Cather on Writing*, 1949; *Willa Cather in Europe*, 1956; *The Kingdom of Art: Willa Cather's First Principles and Critical Statements, 1893-1896*, 1966; *The World and the Parish: Willa Cather's Articles and Reviews, 1893-1902*, 1970 (2 volumes).

MISCELLANEOUS: *Writings from Willa Cather's Campus Years*, 1950.

Bibliography

Bloom, Edward A., and Lillian D. Bloom. *Willa Cather's Gift of Sympathy.* Carbondale: Southern Illinois University Press, 1962. Considered a classic on criticism of Cather's works. The Blooms look at this author's gift of sympathy and skillfully relate it to her thematic interests and technical proficiency. Deals with not only Cather's fiction but also her poetry and essays, which in themselves form an important commentary on her ideas.

Bloom, Harold, ed. *Modern Critical Views: Willa Cather.* New York: Chelsea House, 1985. Bloom says of this volume that it gathers "the best literary criticism on Cather over the last half-century." The criticism selected emphasizes Cather's novels *Sapphira and the Slave Girl, My Ántonia, Death Comes for the Archbishop*, and *A Lost Lady*. The volume concludes with a study by Marilyn Arnold on what are considered Cather's two finest short stories, "A Wagner Matinee" and "Paul's Case." Contains a chronology and a bibliography. A must for serious Cather scholars.

Fryer, Judith. *Felicitous Space: The Imaginative Structures of Edith Wharton and Willa Cather*. Chapel Hill: University of North Carolina Press, 1986. Although there are many full-length studies on Cather's writing, this volume is particularly noteworthy for its examination of Cather using current feminist thinking. Fryer explores Cather's fiction in terms of the "interconnectedness between space and the female imagination" and cites her as a transformer of social and cultural structures. A thorough and interesting study, recommended for its contribution to women's studies in literature. Includes extensive notes.

Gerber, Philip. *Willa Cather*. Boston: Twayne, 1975. Rather than calling Cather a "disconnected" writer, as have some critics, Gerber takes the view in this study that there is unity in her writing. Gerber demonstrates the development of her artistry from one novel to the next. Includes a chronology and a selected bibliography.

Middleton, Jo Ann. *Willa Cather's Modernism: A Study of Style and Technique*. Rutherford, N.J.: Fairleigh Dickenson University Press, 1990. Middleton investigates the techniques of Cather's style, which she calls "apparently effortless, beautifully simple," and explores the ability of Cather to draw the reader into her imagination. Contains extensive notes and a bibliography. A useful volume analyzing Cather's writing techniques.

Murphy, John. *Critical Essays on Willa Cather*. Boston: G. K. Hall, 1984. A compilation of criticism on Cather's work, including general essays from a variety of contributors as well as reviews and literary criticism of specific titles. The introduction emphasizes her creativity, and the volume concludes with reviews of her last four books. Most useful for its breadth of criticism on Cather. Contains a selected bibliography.

Stouck, David. *Willa Cather's Imagination*. Lincoln: University of Nebraska Press, 1975. Each chapter in this volume addresses a theme in Cather's work and analyzes specific novels. The themes discussed in part 1 are the epic, the pastoral, and satire. Part 2 explores what Stouck refers to as Cather's "mortal comedy," and the final chapter examines her last four books.

RAYMOND CHANDLER

Born: Chicago, Illinois; July 23, 1888
Died: La Jolla, California; March 26, 1959

Principal long fiction
The Big Sleep, 1939; *Farewell, My Lovely*, 1940; *The High Window*, 1942; *The Lady in the Lake*, 1943; *The Little Sister*, 1949; *The Long Goodbye*, 1953; *Playback*, 1958.

Other literary forms
Raymond Chandler began his literary career with a false start in England in his early twenties, publishing an assortment of journalistic sketches, essays, poems, and a single story, most of which have been collected in *Chandler Before Marlowe* (1973). His real career as a writer began more than twenty years later, when he began to publish short stories in crime magazines. Chandler published twenty-three stories during his lifetime, most of which appeared in pulp magazines such as *Black Mask* or *Dime Detective Magazine*. Although the stories rarely approach the literary merit of his novels, they are representative of a popular type of American writing. They also show a versatility within the mystery formula that would later be developed by Chandler in his novels.

Chandler forbade the reissue during his lifetime of eight of his stories, but three of these were published, apparently without the author's consent. Chandler insisted that these stories be withheld because of a curious professional scruple. The materials had been incorporated in subsequent novels—in Chandler's word, "cannibalized"—and he felt that their republication would be unfair to readers of the novels. Some of the best of Chandler's stories are in this group and have, since his death, been published in the collection *Killer in the Rain* (1964).

Like William Faulkner and F. Scott Fitzgerald, Chandler was invited to Hollywood to write film scripts. He collaborated on several important screenplays and with Billy Wilder was nominated for an Academy Award for their adaptation of James M. Cain's novel *Double Indemnity* (1936). His original screenplay *The Blue Dahlia* also received a nomination, despite the fact that Chandler remained dissatisfied with the film. In 1948 he wrote, under contract with Universal, an original screenplay, *Playback*, which was not filmed but was rewritten, with new characters, as a novel during Chandler's final years.

Achievements
More than any of his contemporaries, Chandler attempted to use the devices of mystery fiction for serious literary purposes. The peculiarly American school of detective fiction came of age during the years of the 1930's Depres-

sion. The most influential outlet for this fiction was *Black Mask*, a pulp magazine founded by H. L. Mencken and George Jean Nathan and later edited by Captain Joseph T. Shaw. Because the American detective had his origins in *Black Mask* and similar pulp magazines, he is often called the "hard-boiled detective." The character of the hard-boiled detective differs sharply from that of the traditional British sleuth. Chandler's heroes are not charming eccentrics in the tradition of Dorothy Sayers' Lord Peter Wimsey, nor are they masters of unbelievable powers of deduction, such as Arthur Conan Doyle's Sherlock Holmes. When Chandler's Philip Marlowe tells his client (in *The Big Sleep*) that he is not Holmes or Philo Vance and humorously introduces himself as Philo Vance in *The Lady in the Lake*, Chandler is calling attention to the distance he intends to create between his character and the traditional heroes of detective literature. The American detective as created by Chandler, Dashiell Hammett, and a host of lesser contemporaries, is a loner, a man of ordinary intellect but of unusual perseverance and willingness to confront whatever adversary he encounters, whether that adversary be the criminal or the legal establishment. Kenneth Millar, who under the pen name Ross Macdonald would become the most worthy of Chandler's successors, has said that from the *Black Mask* revolution came "a new kind of detective hero, the classless, restless men of American democracy, who spoke the language of the street."

Chandler found the formulaic plots of traditional detective fiction limiting and confining. He was less interested in challenging the deductive skills of the reader than in examining the milieu and sociocultural effects of criminal behavior. Chandler once told his publisher that he disliked those popular mystery titles that emphasized sheer deduction because such titles "put too much emphasis on the mystery itself, and I have not the ingenuity to devise the sort of intricate and recondite puzzles the purest aficionados go for." His mention of a lack of ingenuity is characteristic of the diffidence with which Chandler sometimes spoke of his own work; what is certain, both from his letters and from his essay "The Simple Art of Murder," is that such plots did not interest Chandler.

Although he should be credited, along with Hammett and other *Black Mask* writers, with the development of a peculiarly American form for detective fiction, Chandler himself always consciously sought to transcend the limitations of the genre. He regarded himself as a serious novelist who wrote detective fiction. His intent was to study the modern landscape of evil, and his work bears striking affinities with T. S. Eliot's *The Waste Land* (1922) and with Ernest Hemingway's novels. His evocation of a world dominated by malicious, sadistic, self-centered, ruthless, and psychopathic types led W. H. Auden, in his essay "The Guilty Vicarage," to conclude that Chandler's interest was not in detective fiction at all, but in "serious studies of the criminal milieu, the Great Wrong Place"; Auden argued that Chandler's "powerful but extremely depressing books should be read and judged, not as escape literature, but as works of art."

Auden states, admirably, only half the case. Chandler's books should be judged as works of art, but not merely as studies of the world of crime, or of the world gone bad. In his novels there is a constant quest, a search for heroic possibility in the ruined moral landscape of modern California. Chandler's fiction continually considers whether authentic heroism is possible in the modern world, and Marlowe's attempt to take heroic action places him at odds with the world he inhabits. By the time he was ready to write *The Long Goodbye*, Chandler had indeed transformed the detective story: in that book the elements of detection and mystery are clearly subordinate to psychological and cultural realism.

The achievement of Chandler thus discloses a paradox. Although he was instrumental in the discovery of an American style for detective fiction and has been widely and rightly respected for that accomplishment, his real achievement was to merge detective fiction with serious literature.

Biography

Although his early ambition was to be a writer, Raymond Thornton Chandler did not begin the literary career that would win him fame until he was forty-five years old. This is only one of several incongruities in the life of one of America's original literary talents.

Chandler was born in Chicago, in 1888, the only child of a railroad employee and an Irishwoman. The marriage was marred by his father's alcoholism and ended in divorce when the boy was seven. Chandler and his mother moved to London and became dependent on his maternal uncle, a successful solicitor. Chandler went to Dulwich College, where he received the solid classical education characteristic of English public schools. He was at the head of his classes in most of his subjects. After his graduation from Dulwich, Chandler claimed dual citizenship so that he could take the English civil service examinations, but he was unable to adapt to the bureaucratic environment and resigned his civil service appointment. He supported himself briefly by writing for magazines and newspapers and by publishing some undistinguished poems and a single story. He left England for America in 1912.

Upon his return to America, Chandler made his way to Southern California where he began a relationship that was to dominate his literary life. Chandler despised the superficiality and pretentiousness of the California culture, as well as its lack of tradition or continuity, but he intuited that this would be the culture of the future. One aim of his writing would be to record and comment on that culture. His immediate concern upon his return was to find work, and he was involved in a variety of minor jobs until he completed a three-year bookkeeping course in six weeks. Thereafter, he was involved in various business enterprises until 1917, when he joined the Canadian Army.

He saw action in France; Chandler was the sole survivor of a raid on his outfit and was decorated for valor. When he returned to California, he briefly tried banking and eventually established himself as an extremely successful executive of the Dabney Oil Syndicate. He became vice-president of the concern and was at one time director of eight subsidiary firms and president of three.

Shortly after he joined the Dabney firm, Chandler married Cissy Pascal, who filed for divorce in order to marry him. An accomplished pianist and a beauty, she was also eighteen years older than Chandler, a fact she deliberately concealed from him: he was thirty-five; she was fifty-three. Their marriage was a lasting but troublesome one.

Perhaps discoveries about his marriage, as well as problems and pressures in his business, led to the first appearance of Chandler's lifelong struggle with alcoholism. In fact, several of Chandler's early stories, such as "Pearls Are a Nuisance," feature a hero who must contend with a drinking problem. In 1932, Dabney fired Chandler because of chronically poor job performance traced directly to excessive drinking.

Chandler was forty-four, an alcoholic, unemployed, and married to a woman sixty-two years old. He took the shock of his firing as an indication that he had to take control of his life, and he turned again to the literary aspirations of his youth. Chandler was then reading and being influenced by Hemingway rather than by Henry James, whom he had read avidly in England, and he soon found the outlet his creative talent needed in the emerging American detective story. His first story appeared in *Black Mask* in 1933; he would be a successful novelist within the decade.

Fame and success came to Chandler in the 1940's. His sales were solid, studios sought the film rights to his novels, his books were being translated into several languages, and he was lured to Hollywood to write screenplays. There he enjoyed material success and stimulating camaraderie with other writers. Soon the pressures of studio deadlines, artistic compromise, and the pretentiousness around him—much of the satire of *The Little Sister* is directed at the phoniness of Hollywood—combined with personal ill-health sent Chandler back to the bottle. His career in Hollywood ended in frustration, petty squabbles, and bitterness.

With material success and public acclaim, Chandler spent the final decade of his life alternating between despair and the hope for new beginnings. Always a lonely man, he became depressive after his wife died in 1954. He attempted suicide, but after his recovery divided his time between life in London and La Jolla, between bouts with the bottle and the admiration of an appreciative public. He fell in love with his agent, Helga Greene, but the two were unable to marry. Chandler's death in 1959 ended the career of a shy, quiet man who was quite unlike his fictional hero Marlowe except for the essential loneliness and decency Chandler could not avoid projecting onto his most important creation.

Analysis

Many people who have never read a single word of Raymond Chandler's recognize the name of his fictional hero Philip Marlowe. This recognition results in part from the wide exposure and frequent dilution Chandler's work has received in media other than print. Several of his novels, and especially *Farewell, My Lovely* and *The Big Sleep*, have been filmed repeatedly; both were filmed again in the 1970's. Marlowe has been interpreted on film by such diverse actors as Humphrey Bogart, Dick Powell, Robert Montgomery, George Montgomery, Robert Mitchum, James Garner, and Elliot Gould. A series for radio and one for television were based somewhat loosely on Chandler's character.

This recognition amounts to more than exposure in multiple media; it is an indication of the legendary or even mythic proportions of Chandler's creation. Marlowe has become a central figure in the myth of the detective; the only comparable characters would be Arthur Conan Doyle's Sherlock Holmes and Agatha Christie's Hercule Poirot, even though they are quite different from Marlowe. Dashiell Hammett's Sam Spade, although well-known, is developed in only one book and lacks the psychological depth of Marlowe. Marlowe has taken his place among characters of American myth, with Natty Bumppo, Captain Ahab, Huckleberry Finn, and Thomas Sutpen. There is something uniquely American about the self-reliance of this character, something that goes beyond Chandler's brilliant descriptions of the burned-out landscape of modern California.

Marlowe is in fact Chandler's great achievement, but that accomplishment in itself imposed a limitation of a sort. Because Marlowe had the dual role of central character and observer in all seven of Chandler's novels, the author was not consistently pressed to explore other characters except as they interacted with his hero. In his final novel, *Playback*, Chandler leads Marlowe through an ill-conceived plot at the expense of two neglected characters who had shown real literary promise. In this final project, the author had fallen victim to the temptation to rely on his primary character, and Marlowe's character suffers as a result.

Nevertheless, Marlowe remains an impressive artistic creation because of his remarkable combination of the detective with more traditional American heroic types, a combination discussed in Chandler's famous essay "The Simple Art of Murder" (1944). This essay attempts to define Chandler's intentions as a writer of detective fiction and has since become one of the classic texts concerning the scope and intention of mystery writing. Although a major point of "The Simple Art of Murder" is Chandler's rejection of the stylized mystery and his often-quoted tribute to Hammett—his claim that Hammett took murder "out of the Venetian vase and dropped it in the alley"—the essay makes its most important point in an argument for detective fiction as a heroic form in which modern readers can still believe. Claiming that all art must contain the quality of redemption, Chandler insists, perhaps too stridently, that the detective is "the hero; he is everything." In the character of Marlowe, Chandler tests the possibility of heroism in the modern cultural and spiritual wasteland of Southern California, to see whether traditional heroic values can survive the test of a realistic portrait of modern society.

In precisely this way, Chandler had to face a limitation that did not affect his American predecessors: the disappearance of the frontier. American heroes acted out the myth of Emersonian self-reliance against the background of a vast, unspoiled frontier. In the present century, William Faulkner, attempting to study the ambivalent role of the hero, moved his fiery character Thomas Sutpen to the frontier in *Absalom, Absalom!* (1966). Most American novelists in the present century have despaired of the possibility of reviving the heroic tradition, and have concentrated instead on victims, common men, and even criminals.

Ernest Hemingway stood alone among the serious novelists looking for an affirmation by means of the code hero, and Chandler's intellectual debt to Hemingway is profound. He acknowledged that debt in two ways. In "The Simple Art of Murder," he points out that what is excellent in Hammett's (and by inference his own) work is implicit in Hemingway's fiction. In a more celebrated reference, a policeman in *Farewell, My Lovely* is called Hemingway by Marlowe. When Galbraith, the officer, asks who this Hemingway is, Marlowe explains, "A guy that keeps saying the same thing over and over until you begin to believe it must be good." This is of course a joke about the terse Hemingway style, and the character whom Marlowe calls Hemingway is indeed terse. The jest is not, however, a slap at Hemingway. Galbraith is one of the few men with integrity whom Marlowe encounters in *Farewell, My Lovely*. He is a policeman who wants to be honest but who has to work in a corrupt system. By contrast, in the story from which this portion of *Farewell, My Lovely* was "cannibalized," "The Man Who Liked Dogs," Galbraith was as corrupt as any of the criminals Carmady (the detective) encountered. He was merely a sadistic cop who participated in cover-ups and even murder. The verbal association of this character with Hemingway corresponds nicely with Chandler's changing the personality of the officer so that he would represent the quality Chandler most admired in Hemingway's heroes, resignation to defeat while maintaining some measure of integrity.

The world Marlowe inhabits is, like that of Hemingway's characters, not conducive to heroism. Chandler coined a memorable phrase, "the mean streets," to describe the environment in which his hero would have to function. Marlowe was created to indicate that it is possible to maintain integrity in these surroundings, even if one cannot be uninfluenced by them. As Chandler put it, "down these mean streets a man must go who is not himself mean, who is neither tarnished nor afraid." Chandler emphasized that Marlowe is part of that environment—by necessity—but is not contaminated by it—by choice. He is not without fear. Marlowe often expresses the fear of a normal man in a dangerous situation, and in this way he differs from the heroes of the tough-guy school and from those of Chandler's apprentice stories. Like Hemingway's heroes, he must learn to control and to disguise his fear. Most important, he is not intimidated by his environment. As Chandler puts it in his essay, the detective "must be, to use a rather weathered phrase, a man of honor."

Although commonly used, the phrase "the mean streets" is somewhat misleading. Chandler's target is not merely, or even primarily, the cruelty and brutality of life at the bottom of the social and economic ladder. For him, the mean streets extend into the posh apartments and mansions of Hollywood and suburban Los Angeles, and he is more interested in exploring cruelty and viciousness among the very rich than among the people of the streets. Each of the novels treats the theme of the quest for and ownership of money and power as the source of evil; Chandler constantly emphasizes Marlowe's relative poverty as a symbol for his incorruptibility. *The High Window*, for example, is more a study in the corrupting influence of wealth than in the process of detection. Marlowe is shocked to discover that his client Mrs. Murdock not only murdered her husband to collect his life insurance, but also systematically conditioned her timid and neurotic secretary to believe that she was the murderess, dependent on Mrs. Murdock for forgiveness as well as for protection from the law. This instance is typical of Chandler's novels. The mean streets originate in the drawing rooms of those who may profit by exploiting others.

Marlowe's code of behavior differs from those of other fictional detectives, though his descendants, particularly Ross Macdonald's Lew Archer and Robert B. Parker's Spenser, resemble Chandler's hero. Marlowe is not, in the final analysis, a tough guy. He is a compassionate man who, as he half-ironically tells a policeman in *The Long Goodbye*, hears "voices crying in the night" and goes to "see what's the matter." Marlowe is instinctively the champion of the victims of the rich and powerful; in *The High Window* he insists that the secretary, Merle Davis, be set free of the psychological exploitation by the Murdock family and be allowed to return to her home in Kansas. To those who aspire to wealth and power, Marlowe is not so kind. In *The Little Sister*, he knowingly allows the amoral, ruthless murderess Dolores Gonzales to be killed by her husband.

This instinctive compassion for the weak accounts for much of Marlowe's fundamental decency, but it often gets him into trouble, for he is human enough to be occasionally deceived by appearances. The apparently innocent client in *The Little Sister*, Orfamay Quest from Kansas, deceives Marlowe with her piety and sincerity, and he is eventually depressed to learn that his compassion for her is wasted, that despite her apparent innocence she is compulsively materialistic and is willing to exploit even her brother's murder if she can profit by his scheme to blackmail a gangster.

Marlowe's compassion is what makes him interesting as a character, but it is also what makes him vulnerable in the mean streets. His defense against that vulnerability is to play the role of the tough guy. His wisecracks, which have since become obligatory in stories about private detectives, are nothing more than a shield. Chandler says in "The Simple Art of Murder" that the detective is a proud man who will take "no man's insolence without a due and dispassionate revenge." The mean streets have taught Marlowe that corrupt politicians, tired policemen, ambitious actresses, rich people, and street toughs will insult and abuse him readily; his defense is the wisecrack. It is the attempt of an honorable man to stand up to a world that has gone sour.

The Big Sleep, Chandler's first full-length novel, makes explicit use of the associations with myth that had been implicit in the stories he had published over six years. It was in this book that the author settled on the name Marlowe for his detective, after he had experimented with such names as Carmady and Dalmas. In his first detective story, "Blackmailers Don't Shoot," he had called the detective Mallory, an obvious allusion to the chronicler of the Arthurian legends, Sir Thomas Malory. The association with the quest romance is worked out in several important ways in *The Big Sleep*. When the detective first arrives at the home of his client, he notices a stained-glass panel "showing a knight in dark armor rescuing a lady" and concludes that, "if I lived in the house, I would sooner or later have to climb up and help him." Much later, upon returning to the house, the detective notes that the knight "wasn't getting anywhere" with the task of rescuing the lady.

These two references remind the reader of a heroic tradition into which Marlowe, a citizen of the twentieth century, is trying to fit his own experiences. Malory's knights lived in an age of faith, and the quest for the Holy Grail was a duty imposed by that faith as well as a test of the worthiness of the knight himself. Marlowe's adventures entangle him with a pornographer who is murdered, a small-time blackmailer whose effort to cut himself into the action leads to his death, a trigger-happy homosexual, a powerful criminal the law cannot touch, a district attorney eager to avoid scandal that might touch a wealthy family, and a psychopathic murderess. The environment is impossible to reconcile with the values suggested by the knight in the panel. At midpoint in the novel, Marlowe has a chess problem laid out (his playing chess against the problems defined in classical matches gives him an intellectual depth uncharacteristic of the tough-guy detective), and, trying to move a knight effectively on the board, he concludes that "knights had no meaning in this game. It wasn't a game for knights."

The implication of this set of images is that Marlowe aspires to the role of the traditional knight, but that such an aspiration is doomed to failure in the mean streets. His aspiration to the role of the knight is a hopeless attempt to restore order to the modern wasteland. At the same time, it is proof of his integrity that he tries to maintain that role in the face of certain and predictable frustration. In a subsequent novel, *The High Window*, a minor character invents a phrase that eloquently describes Marlowe's association with the romance tradition; he calls the detective a "shop-soiled Galahad," a reminder both of the knight who, in the romance, could not be corrupted, and of the pressures that wear down the modern hero.

Another important reference to the romance tradition in *The Big Sleep* is the client himself. General Sternwood is a dying man; he has to meet Marlowe in a greenhouse because the general needs the artificial warmth. He is lame, impotent, and distressed at the moral decay of his daughters. Chandler implicitly associates this character with the Fisher King of the archetypal romance, and *The Big Sleep* takes on revealing connections with T. S. Eliot's *The Waste Land* (1922), another modern version of this quest. Like Eliot's poem, Chandler's version of the quest is a record of failure. Marlowe's success in the work of detection points paradoxically to the failure of his quest. He is able to complete, even to go beyond, his assignment. His instinctive sympathy for the helpless general leads him to try to find out what happened to the general's son-in-law, Rusty Regan, whose charm and vigor had restored some vitality to the old man, much as the traditional knight might restore the Fisher King. Marlowe discovers that Regan has been murdered, hence, there is no hope that the general might be restored. He can only prepare to join Regan in "the big sleep."

"It was not a game for knights." This knight is able to sort through the many mysteries of *The Big Sleep*, to discover the killers of the various victims. He outsmarts a professional killer in a shoot-out, and feels that in doing so he achieves some revenge for Harry Jones, a tough little victim that Marlowe had respected. His actions do not, however, restore order to his surroundings. He is unable to reach, through law or intimidation, Eddie Mars, the operator of a gambling casino and several protection rackets, a parasite of society. His discovery that Regan was murdered leads him to the conclusion that all he can do is try to protect the general from "the nastiness," the inescapable and brutal facts of life. Even his discovery that Regan's killer was the general's daughter, Carmen, does not resolve anything: she is a psychopath, and her actions are gratuitous, not subject to reform. All Marlowe can do, ironically, is the same thing Eddie Mars and Regan's widow, Vivian, tried to do—protect the general from knowing that his own daughter was responsible for the death of the one person who brought happiness to his life. Marlowe's method differs from that of Mars. Rather than cover up the fact, he uses the leverage of his knowledge of the cover-up to force Vivian Regan, Carmen's sister as well as Rusty's widow, to have Carmen committed to a mental hospital. He makes this deal only after Vivian has tried to buy his silence.

What makes *The Big Sleep* such a rich novel, in addition to its mythic associations, is the question of what keeps Marlowe going. He knows that justice is not possible in a world controlled by Eddie Mars, and he learns that his efforts lead only to compound frustrations and personal danger. He continues to work, against the warnings of the criminal element, the official police, and the family of his client. Both Vivian and Carmen offer sexual bribes if Marlowe will get off the case. He is so personally affected by "the nastiness" around him that he has a nightmare after having encountered the perverse scene in which the pornographer Geiger was killed—a dream in which Marlowe implicates himself as an ineffective pornographer. He dreams about a "man in a bloody Chinese coat" (Geiger) who was chasing "a naked girl with long jade earrings" (Carmen) "while I ran after them and tried to take a photograph with an empty camera." This exposure to the corruption around him makes Marlowe doubt, in his nightmare, even his own ability to resist corruption.

He is able to continue in the face of these pressures because, like Joseph Conrad's Marlow in *Heart of Darkness* (1902), he believes in something greater than his personal interests. His idealism is of course shattered by the corruption around him, but like Conrad's character or Hemingway's heroes, he believes in a code: loyalty to his client. In the absence of a belief in an absolute good, Marlowe guides his behavior by weighing his options in the context of the principle of loyalty to the client. When the police and the district attorney threaten him, he explains that all he has to sell is, "What little guts and intelligence the Lord gave me and a willingness to get pushed around in order to protect a client." He refuses an invitation to have sex with each of the attractive Sternwood daughters because of this principle. He tells Carmen, "It's a question of professional pride" after he has told Vivian that as a man he is tempted but as a detective, "I work at it, lady. I don't play at it." Many bribes, monetary and sexual, are offered Marlowe in *The Big Sleep*. Even more threats, from criminals, police, and his client's family, are hurled at him. What gives him his sense of purpose in a world that seems to resonate to no moral standard is one self-imposed principle. This is the main theme of Chandler's fiction: if standards of behavior do not exist outside the individual, as they were believed to in the age of chivalry, then one must create them, however imperfect they may be, for oneself.

By the end of the 1940's, Chandler was well established as a master of detective fiction, but he was becoming increasingly impatient with the limitations of the form. Classically educated and somewhat aristocratic in his personal tastes, he found the conventions of the hard-boiled genre increasingly confining. Yet he was not willing to dispose of Marlowe, partly because the detective had brought his creator success. More important, as biographer Frank MacShane has pointed out, Chandler's real interest was the variety of the life and the essential formlessness of Los Angeles, so his detective's ability to cut across class lines, to meet with criminals, police, the seedier citizens as well as the wealthy, gave the author a chance to explore in fiction the life of the entire community, much as two of his favorite novelists, Charles Dickens and Honoré de Balzac, had done for the cities in which they had lived.

Chandler had already pushed the mystery novel somewhat beyond its inherent limits, but he remained unsatisfied with what must be regarded as an impressive achievement. He had altered the formula to apply the quest myth in *The Big Sleep*; to study phony psychics and corrupt police in *Farewell, My Lovely*; to examine psychological and legal exploitation by the very wealthy in *The High Window*; to work with the devices of disguise and the anxieties of those who merely aspire to wealth and power in *The Lady in the Lake*; and to satirize the pretentiousness of Hollywood as well as to comment on the corrosive influence of materialism in *The Little Sister*.

Having done all this in a decade, Chandler set out on his most daring experiment. *The Long Goodbye* abandons so many of the conventions of the detective formula that it simply uses what is left of the formula as a skeleton around which to build serious psychological and cultural themes. The actual detective work Marlowe is hired to perform is merely to search for the novelist Roger Wade, who has disappeared on a drunken spree, and eventually Marlowe discovers that the search itself was unnecessary. Wade's wife knew where Roger was but hired Marlowe to get him involved in Roger's life, so that he might possibly be persuaded to take a job as Wade's bodyguard. The search for Wade allows for some discussion of physicians who dispense drugs freely to the wealthy, but it depends more on persistent following of leads than on brilliant deduction. The real detective work in which he engages is entirely independent, work from which he is discouraged by the police, a gangster named Menendez, a wealthy businessman, and the Wades. It is a work of sentiment, not professionalism, and the book discloses that this task is worth neither the effort nor integrity that Marlowe puts into it.

The Long Goodbye is finally a study in personal loyalties. The sustaining ethic of the earlier novels, loyalty to a client, does not really apply in this book, for most of the time Marlowe has no client or refuses to take up the assignments offered him. He is no longer satisfied with his work as a detective, and one of the book's best chapters details the monotony and triviality of a day in the life of a private investigator. His own ambivalence about his role is summed up after a series of absurd requests for his services: "What makes a man stay with it nobody knows. You don't get rich, and you don't often have much fun. Sometimes you get beaten up or shot at or tossed in the jailhouse." Each of these unpleasant things happens to Marlowe. He stays in business, but he has ceased to understand why.

At the heart of the book is Marlowe's relationship with Terry Lennox, who drifts into Marlowe's personal life. Lennox, a man with a mysterious past but at present married for the second time to the nymphomaniac daughter of a tycoon, impresses Marlowe with a jaded version of the Hemingway code. Lennox knows he is little more than a gigolo, but has accepted himself with a kind of refined drunkenness. He and Marlowe become friends, but after his wife is brutally murdered, Lennox asks Marlowe to help him escape to Mexico. Marlowe, who agrees out of friendship rather than loyalty to Lennox as a client, is thus legally implicated as a possible accessory after the fact.

His action brings him into inevitable conflict with the police, and he is roughly treated by a detective and his precinct captain. Marlowe's being at odds with the official police is far from a new occurrence in Chandler's work. His fiction always contains an innate distrust of the legal establishment, from the *exposé* of police corruption in *Farewell, My Lovely* through the abuse of police power by one of the killers in *The Lady in the Lake*. A lawyer in *The Long Goodbye* tells Marlowe, "The law isn't justice, it's a very imperfect mechanism. If you press exactly the right buttons and are also lucky, justice may show up in the answer." This distrust of the mechanism of law usually led Chandler to condemn separate kinds of justice for the wealthy and the powerless. Marlowe's reaction to his disillusionment includes verbal and physical conflict with the police as well as the routine concealment of evidence that might implicate a client.

What differentiates this conflict from previous ones in Chandler's work is that Marlowe is not really protecting the interests of a client. He acts out of a personal loyalty, based partly on his belief that Lennox could not have committed the sadistic murder of which he is accused. He keeps his silence during a week in jail, during which he is pressed to give evidence that would implicate both himself and Lennox.

Lennox's confession and suicide render Marlowe's actions futile. The arrival of a letter and a large sum of money rekindles a sentimental interest in the Lennox matter, and as it becomes clear that some connection exists between Lennox and the Wades, who have tried to hire him to help Roger stay sober long enough to finish his book, Marlowe continues to fit together evidence that points to Lennox's innocence. Proving Lennox innocent is another source of disillusionment: Marlowe learns that both the confession and the suicide were faked. In their final interview, Marlowe tells Lennox, "You had standards and you lived by them, but they were personal. They had no relation to any kind of ethics or scruples." Marlowe has himself come close to this moral relativism in his uncritical loyalty to Lennox, and has perhaps seen in his friend an example of the vague standard of ethical conduct to which such moral relativism can lead. The difference between Lennox and Marlowe is that the detective still recognizes the importance of having a code. He tells Lennox, "You're a moral defeatist." His work on behalf of Lennox has been a disappointment of the highest order, for he has seen the paralysis of will toward which the cynicism both men share leads. By returning Lennox's money, Marlowe implies that Lennox was not worth the risk and labor of proving his innocence.

The Long Goodbye is populated by "moral defeatists." Another character,

Roger Wade, has given up on himself as a man and as a writer. Chandler creates in this character a representation of the writer who knowingly sells out his artistic talent for personal gain. Knowing that he is "a literary prostitute," Wade is driven to alcoholic sprees and personal despair. When he seeks Marlowe's sympathy for his predicament, Marlowe reminds him of Gustave Flaubert, an example of the genuine artist who is willing to sacrifice success for his art.

Marlowe's association with Wade develops the central theme of *The Long Goodbye*: personal responsibility. Wade's publisher and his wife want Marlowe to protect Wade from his depressive and suicidal tendencies. Realizing that Wade is trying to escape something inside himself, Marlowe knows that only Wade can stop his rush toward self-destruction. He refuses to take the lucrative job as Wade's bodyguard because he realizes he cannot prevent the author from being self-destructive. In fact, Marlowe is in the Wade house the day Roger Wade apparently commits suicide. Although he does try to remove Wade's gun from its customary desk drawer, he makes no effort to stop Wade from drinking. He knows that restraining Wade, whether by physical force or coercion, would be an artifical substitute for a real solution. If Wade's self-loathing makes him suicidal, Marlowe recognizes that nothing he can do will prevent the self-destructive act from taking place.

The theme of personal responsibility is even more directly apparent in Marlowe's relation with Eileen Wade. Initially, she impresses him as an ideal beauty, and the erotic implications of their relationship are always near the surface. In a scene after he has put the drunken Roger to bed, the detective comes close to his first sexual consummation in the novels. In this episode, it becomes clear that Eileen is mentally disturbed, and Marlowe's subsequent investigation reveals that she was once married to Lennox, who served in the war under another name. Her attempt to seduce Marlowe is in fact a clumsy attempt to establish a relationship with the Terry Lennox she knew before his cynicism turned to moral defeatism. From these premises, Marlowe deduces that Eileen murdered both Sylvia Lennox and Roger, who had been having an affair with Sylvia, a perverse revenge for her being twice defeated by a woman whose vulgarity she despised.

Marlowe has sufficient evidence to prove Lennox's innocence and to show that Wade's death was not suicide, but he does not go to the police. He confronts Eileen with the evidence and gives her time to commit suicide. He refers to himself as a "one-man death watch" and takes no action to prevent the self-destruction of this woman to whom he is so powerfully attracted. When he has to explain his conduct to the one policeman he trusts, Bernie Ohls, he says, "I wanted her to take a long look at herself. What she did about it was her business." This is a ruthless dismissal of a disturbed, though homicidal, person. What Chandler intends to emphasize is the idea that all humans must ultimately take full responsibility for their actions.

Even Marlowe's relationship with Bernie Ohls deteriorates. Ohls, the only policeman Marlowe likes or trusts, consents to leak a document so that Marlowe will use it unwittingly to flush out the racketeer Menendez, knowing that Marlowe will be abused psychologically and physically in the process. The ruse works, and Ohls ruthlessly sends Mcnendez off to possible execution by his fellow criminals. In the image used by another character, Marlowe has been the goat tied out by the police to catch the tiger Menendez. Marlowe understands why the police have used him this way, but the novel ends with a new note of mistrust between Marlowe and Ohls. Yet another human relationship has failed.

In *The Long Goodbye*, the business of detection is subordinate to the themes of personal responsibility, betrayal, and the mutability of all human relationships. The book is a powerful indictment of the shallowness of public values in mid-century America, and the emphasis is on characterization, theme, and atmosphere rather than on the matters typical of the mystery novel. It represents a remarkable transition from the detective novel to the realm of serious fiction, a transition that has subsequently been imitated but not equaled.

David C. Dougherty

Other major works
SHORT FICTION: *Five Murderers*, 1944; *Five Sinister Characters*, 1945; *Finger Man and Other Stories*, 1946; *Red Wind*, 1946; *Spanish Blood*, 1946; *Trouble Is My Business*, 1950; *The Simple Art of Murder*, 1950; *Pick-up on Noon Street*, 1952; *Smart-Aleck Kill*, 1953; *Pearls Are a Nuisance*, 1958; *Killer in the Rain*, 1964 (Philip Durham, editor); *The Smell of Fear*, 1965; *The Midnight Raymond Chandler*, 1971.

NONFICTION: *The Blue Dahlia*, 1946 (Matthew J. Bruccoli, editor); *Raymond Chandler Speaking*, 1962 (Dorothy Gardiner and Katherine Sorely Walker, editors); *Chandler Before Marlowe: Raymond Chandler's Early Prose and Poetry*, 1973 (Matthew J. Bruccoli, editor); *The Notebooks of Raymond Chandler and English Summer*, 1976 (Frank MacShane, editor); *Selected Letters of Raymond Chandler*, 1981 (Frank MacShane, editor).

Bibliography
Babener, Liahna K. "Raymond Chandler's City of Lies." In *Los Angeles in Fiction*, edited by David Fine. Albuquerque: University of New Mexico Press, 1984. The chapter on Chandler is a study of the image patterns in his novels. The volume as a whole is an interesting discussion of the importance of a sense of place, especially one as mythologically rich as Los Angeles. Includes notes.
Hamilton, Cynthia S. "Raymond Chandler." In *Western and Hard-Boiled Detective Fiction: From High Noon to Midnight*. Iowa City: University of

Iowa Press, 1987. This study provides unusual insight into Chandler's detective fiction from the historical and generic perspective of the American Western novel. Includes three chapters on the study of formula literature, a bibliography, and an index.

Jameson, F. R. "On Raymond Chandler." In *The Poetics of Murder: Detective Fiction and Literary Theory*, edited by Glenn W. Most and William W. Stowe. San Diego: Harcourt Brace Jovanovich, 1983. Starts with the observation that Chandler's English upbringing in essence gave him an outsider's view of American life and language. A useful discussion of the portrait of American society that emerges from Chandler's works.

Knight, Stephen. "'A Hard Cheerfulness': An Introduction to Raymond Chandler." In *American Crime Fiction: Studies in the Genre*, edited by Brian Docherty. New York: St. Martin's Press, 1988. A discussion of the values and attitudes which define Chandler's Philip Marlowe and which make him unusual in the genre of hard-boiled American crime fiction.

Lehman, David. "Hammett and Chandler." In *The Perfect Murder: A Study in Detection*. New York: Free Press, 1989. Chandler is represented in this comprehensive study of detective fiction as one of the authors who brought out the parable at the heart of mystery fiction. A useful volume in its breadth and its unusual appendices: One a list of further reading, the other, an annotated list of the critic's favorite mysteries. Includes two indexes, one of concepts and one of names and titles.

Skinner, Robert E. *The Hard-Boiled Explicator: A Guide to the Study of Dashiell Hammett, Raymond Chandler, and Ross Macdonald*. Metuchen, N.J.: Scarecrow Press, 1985. An indispensable volume for the scholar interested in tracking down unpublished dissertations as well as mainstream criticism. Brief introductions of each author are followed by annotated bibliographies of books, articles, and reviews.

JOHN CHEEVER

Born: Quincy, Massachusetts; May 27, 1912
Died: Ossining, New York; June 18, 1982

Principal long fiction

The Wapshot Chronicle, 1957; *The Wapshot Scandal*, 1964; *Bullet Park*, 1969; *Falconer*, 1977; *Oh What a Paradise It Seems*, 1982.

Other literary forms

Since the publication of his first fictional piece, "Expelled," in the October 10, 1930, issue of *The New Republic*, more than two hundred John Cheever stories have appeared in American magazines, chiefly *The New Yorker*. Less than half that number have been reprinted in the seven collections Cheever has published over the past four decades: *The Way Some People Live* (1943), *The Enormous Radio and Other Stories* (1953), *The Housebreaker of Shady Hill and Other Stories* (1958), *Some People, Places, and Things That Will Not Appear in My Next Novel* (1961), *The Brigadier and the Golf Widow* (1964), *The World of Apples* (1973), and *The Collected Stories of John Cheever* (1978), which includes all but the earliest collected stories and adds four previously uncollected pieces. His one television play, *The Kidnapper of Shady Hill*, aired on January 12, 1982, to inaugurate the Public Broadcasting System's "American Playhouse" series. Cheever, however, made a clear distinction between fiction, which he considered man's most exalted and intimate means of communication, and literary works written for television, film, and theater. Consequently, he remained aloof from all attempts to adapt his literary work—the 1968 film version of "The Swimmer," for example, directed by Frank and Eleanor Perry and starring Burt Lancaster (which he found disappointing), or the adaptations of the three stories televised on the Public Broadcasting System in 1979. In addition, he rarely turned his considerable energies to the writing of articles and reviews. One large and undoubtedly fascinating body of Cheever's writing is his journal, the keeping of which is part of a long family tradition.

Achievements

Until the publication of *Falconer* in 1977 and *The Collected Stories of John Cheever* the following year, Cheever's position as a major American writer was not firmly established, even though as early as 1953, William Peden had complained that he was one of the country's most "undervalued" literary figures. Despite the fact that critics, especially academic ones, frequently invoked Cheever only to pillory his supposedly lightweight vision and preoccupation with upper middle-class life, his reputation continued to grow steadily: four O. Henry awards between 1941 and 1964; a Guggenheim fellowship in 1951; the University of Illinois Benjamin Franklin Award in 1955; a grant from the National Institute of Arts and Letters in 1956 and election to that organization the following year; the National Book Award for his first novel, *The Wapshot Chronicle*, in 1958; the Howell's Medal for its sequel, *The Wapshot Scandal*, seven years later; election to the American Academy of Arts and Letters in 1973; and cover stories in the nation's two most widely circulated weekly news magazines, *Time* (1964) and *Newsweek* (1977). The overwhelmingly favorable reception of *Falconer* made possible the publication of *The Collected Stories of John Cheever*, which in turn brought to its author additional honors: a second National Book Award; the National Book Critics Circle Award for best fiction; a Pulitzer Prize; the Edward MacDowell Medal; an honorary doctorate from Harvard University; and in April, 1982, the National Medal for Literature for his "distinguished and continuing contribution to American letters." The popular and critical success of those books and the televising of his work before a national audience brought Cheever the recognition he had long deserved and established his well-earned place in literature.

Biography

   John Cheever was born in Quincy, Massachusetts, on May 27, 1912, and grew up during what he has called the "Athenian twilight" of New England culture. His father Frederick, who was forty-nine when Cheever was born, lost his position in the shoe business in the 1929 Depression and much of his self-respect a short time later when his wife opened a gift shop in order to support the family. The parents' emotionally strained relationship eventually led to their separation and caused Cheever to become very close to his brother Fred, seven years his senior. At age seventeen, Cheever was dismissed from Thayer Academy in South Braintree, Massachusetts, for smoking and poor grades; he promptly turned his experience into a story, "Expelled," which Malcolm Cowley published in *The New Republic* on October 10, 1930, and with Fred embarked on a walking tour of Europe. Upon their return, the brothers lived together briefly in Boston, where "Jon" (as he then identified himself) wrote while Fred worked in the textile business. The closeness of their relationship troubled Cheever, who then moved to a squalid rooming house on New York's Hudson Street. There, with the help of his Boston mentor, Hazel Hawthorne, he wrote synopses for Metro-Goldwyn-Mayer, subsisted on buttermilk and stale bread, associated with Cowley, E. E. Cummings, Sherwood Anderson, Edmund Wilson, Hart Crane, John Dos Passos, and Gaston Lachaise, and somehow managed to keep his art free of the political issues that dominated much of the literature of the period. It was also during that time that Cheever began three of his most enduring relationships: with Yaddo, the writers' colony in Saratoga Springs, New York; with *The New*

Yorker, which published his "Brooklyn Rooming House" in the May 25, 1935, issue; and with Mary Winternitz, the daughter of the Dean of Yale Medical School, whom he married on March 22, 1941. There are three children: Susan, a writer; Benjamin, an editor at *Reader's Digest*, and Federico.

Midway through a tour of duty with the army, Cheever published his first book to generally favorable reviews, and following his discharge, he was able to support himself and his family almost exclusively, if at times precariously, by his writing. Although he liked to give interviewers and others the impression that he was something of a country squire—the heavy Boston accent, the eighteenth century house with its extensive grounds in Ossining, New York—Cheever was in fact plagued throughout much of his life by financial as well as psychological insecurity.

The 1950's was an unsettling time for Cheever. As he explained to fellow writer Herbert Gold, the decade had begun full of promise, but halfway through it "something went terribly wrong"; confused by "the forceful absurdities of life" and, like another Quincy man, Henry Adams, unprepared to deal with them, he imagined himself as "a man in a quagmire, looking into a tear in the sky." The absurdities of modern life are presented, often with a comic twist, in the three novels and six collections of short stories that Cheever published between 1953 and the early 1970's—at which time the author's life took an even darker turn: a massive heart attack in 1972, acute alcoholism that eventually forced Cheever to commit himself to the Smithers Rehabilitation Center in New York, financial difficulties, and the death of his brother in 1976. In the light of this background, it is clear that the writing of his triumphant novel *Falconer* freed Cheever from the same sense of confinement that plagues his characters.

Cheever was both deeply, though not narrowly, religious (a practicing Episcopalian) and physically active (biking, walking, skiing, and sawing were among his favorite pastimes). He was also active sexually and, often feeling rebuffed by his wife, pursued numerous love affairs both with men (including the composer Ned Rorem and a number of young writers) and with women (including the actress Hope Lange). As a writer, he incorporated into his fiction the same blend of the spiritual and the worldly that marked his own character. This blend shines most strongly in *Oh What a Paradise It Seems*, the novella Cheever published just three months before he died of cancer on June 18, 1982. In the novella, protagonist Lemuel Sears is introduced in a sentence that begins in the writing style of William Butler Yeats and ends in pure Cheever: "An aged man is but a paltry thing, a tattered coat upon a stick, unless he sees the bright plumage of the bird called courage—*Cardinalis virginius* in this case—and oh how his heart leapt." More than a literary work, *Oh What a Paradise It Seems* is the gift of an enormously generous writer whose loss is, to use one of John Cheever's favorite words, "inestimable."

Analysis

In a literary period that has witnessed the exhaustion of literature, wholesale formal experimentation, a general distrust of language, the death of the novel, and the blurring of the lines separating fiction and play, mainstream art and the avant-garde, John Cheever consistently and eloquently held to the position that the writing of fiction is an intimate, useful, and indeed necessary way of making sense of human life and affirming its worth. Cheever's ambitious and overtly religious view of fiction is not only unfashionable today; but it also stands in marked opposition to those critics who pigeonhole, and in this way dismiss, his fiction as social criticism in the conventional realistic mode. Certainly, there is that element of realism in his work which one finds in the fiction of John O'Hara and Anton Chekhov, writers with whom he is often compared. Such a view, however, fails to account for the various nonrealistic components of his work: the mythic resonance of William Faulkner, the comic grotesquerie of Franz Kafka, and, most important, the lyric style that, while reminiscent of F. Scott Fitzgerald's finest prose, is nevertheless entirely Cheever's own, a cachet underscoring his essentially religious sensibility.

Man's inclination toward spiritual light, Cheever has said, "is very nearly botanical." His characters are modern pilgrims—not the Kierkegaardian "sovereign wayfarers" one finds in the novels of Walker Percy, another contemporary Christian writer, but instead the lonely residents of Cheever's various cities and suburbs whose search for love, security, and a measure of fulfillment is the secret undercurrent of their otherwise prosaic daily lives. Because the idea of original sin is a given in Cheever's fiction, his characters are men and women who have fallen from grace. At their worst, they are narcissists and chronic complainers. The best of them, however, persevere and, as a result, attain that redemptive vision which enables them "to celebrate a world that lies around them like a bewildering and stupendous dream."

This affirmation does not come easily to Cheever's characters, nor is it rendered sentimentally. Cheever well understands how social fragmentation and separation from the natural world have eroded the individual's sense of self-worth and debased contemporary life, making man's "perilous moral journey" still more arduous. The outwardly comfortable world in which these characters exist can suddenly, and often for no clearly understandable reason, turn dangerously dark, bringing into sharper focus the emotional and spiritual impoverishment of their lives. What concerns Cheever is not so much the change in their fortunes as the way they respond to that change. Many respond in an extreme, sometimes bizarre manner—Melissa Wapshot, for one. Others attempt to escape into the past; in doing so, they deny the present by imprisoning themselves in what amounts to a regressive fantasy that Cheever carefully distinguishes from nostalgia, which, as he uses it, denotes a pleasurable remembrance of the past, one that is free of regret. Cheever's heroes are those who embrace "the thrust of life," taking from the past what is valuable and using it in their present situations. How a character responds to his world determines Cheever's tone, which ranges from open derision to compassionate irony. Although in his more recent work Cheever may have been, as Richard Schickel has claimed, less ironic and more forgiving, his finest stories and novels, including *Falconer*, derive their power from the balance or tension he creates between irony and compassion, comedy and tragedy, light and dark.

The social and moral vision that forms the subject of Cheever's fiction also affects the structure of his novels. The novel, Cheever said in 1953, is a form better suited to the parochial life of the nineteenth century than to the modern age with its highly mobile population and mass communications; but because critics and readers have continued to look upon the short story as inferior to the novel, the conscientious writer of short fiction has often been denied the recognition routinely awarded lesser writers who have worked in the longer form. One way out of this dilemma for Cheever was to publish a collection of stories having the unity of a novel: *The Housebreaker of Shady Hill*. Another was to write novels that had some of the fragmentary quality Cheever found at the heart of the modern age. His four novels are not, therefore, made up of short stories badly spliced together, as some reviewers have maintained; rather, they reflect—in various degrees according to the author's state of mind at the time of composition—Cheever's firm belief that wholeness of being is no longer readily apparent; instead, it is something that character, author, and reader must strive to attain. Moreover, Cheever develops his novels on the basis of "intuition, apprehensions, dreams, concepts," rather than plot, as is entirely consistent with the revelatory nature of his religious vision. Thus, although the story form is appropriate to the depiction of the discontinuity of modern life, only in the novel can that discontinuity be not only identified but also brought under some control, or, as happens in *Falconer*, transcended.

In *The Wapshot Chronicle*, Cheever's first novel, the discontinuity of modern life is apparent not only in the structure and the characterization but also in the complex relationship the author sets up between his fictional New England town and the modern world lying beyond its nineteenth century borders. The impulse to create St. Botolphs (loosely based on Quincy) came to Cheever while he stood at the window of a Hollywood hotel, gazing down on "the dangerously barbaric and nomadic world" beneath him. The strength of his novel, however, derives not from a rejection of the present or, as in the work of nineteenth century local colorists such as Sarah Orne Jewett, in a reverent re-creation of a vanished way of life, but in the way Cheever uses each to evaluate the other.

The novel traces the decline of once-prosperous St. Botolphs and the Wapshot clan and the picaresque adventures of the two Wapshot boys—the "ministerial" Coverly and his older and more worldly brother Moses—who go to seek their fortunes in New York, Washington, D.C., and elsewhere. By having the novel begin and end with an annual Fourth of July celebration, Cheever does not so much impose an arbitrary orderliness on his discursive narrative as affirm that ceremoniousness which, in his view, is necessary to man's spiritual and emotional well-being. The temporal frame is important for another reason: it implies that man's desire for independence equals his desire for tradition. Each must be accommodated if the individual is to prosper. If the modern world seems chaotic, even inhospitable to Leander Wapshot's sons, it nevertheless possesses a vitality and expansiveness that, for the most part, St. Botolphs lacks. While the town is to be treasured for its rich tradition and continuity, it is also to be considered as a place of confinement. The burden of the novel, then, is to show that with "strength and perseverance" it is possible to "create or build some kind of bridge" between past and present.

Cheever intends this bridge to serve a larger, emblematic purpose in *The Wapshot Chronicle*, where, as in his other works, it is the distance between self and other, or, more specifically, between man and woman, that must be bridged. Although Cheever has repeatedly warned that fiction is not "crypto-autobiography," he obviously, if loosely, modeled the Wapshots on his own family and has even admitted that he wrote the novel to make peace with his father's ghost. Leander Wapshot is the book's moral center; he has the imaginative power to redeem his fallen world, to affirm what others can only whiningly negate. Lusty and romantic, a lover of nature as well as of women, he transmits to Coverly and Moses, by his example rather than by precept, his vision of wholeness. Fittingly, the novel concludes with his "Advice to my sons," which Coverly finds tucked into a copy of William Shakespeare: "Stand up straight. Admire the world. Relish the love of a gentle woman. Trust in the Lord." Despite his affirmative stance, Leander is a diminished hero. Unlike earlier generations of Wapshot men who proved themselves by sailing around the world, Leander's sailing is limited to ferrying tourists across the bay in his barely seaworthy boat, the *Topaze*, which his wife Sarah later converts into a floating gift shop, thus further reducing Leander's self-esteem. At one point, a storm drives the boat upon some rocks, an image that captures perfectly what Leander and many other Cheever characters feel so acutely: "man's inestimable loneliness." One of Leander's friends, for example, is haunted by the knowledge that he will be buried naked and unceremoniously in a potter's field; another man sings of his "guest room blues," and a young girl who briefly stays with the Wapshots mistakenly believes that sexual intercourse will end her loneliness. Others, equally desperate, collect antiques or live in castles in a vain attempt to make themselves secure in a bewilderingly changeable world. Leander's vision and vitality keep him from the despair that afflicts these others; as a result, even his death by drowning seems less an end than an affirmation.

Leander, with his "taste for romance and nonsense," is quixotic and exuberant; his wife Sarah, with her "air of wronged nobility," her "habitual reliance on sad conclusions," and his sister Honora, who substitutes philanthropy for love, are strong-willed and sexless. He affirms life; they deny it. Sarah, the town's civic leader, and Honora, the keeper of the Wapshot fortune, uncaringly strip Leander of his usefulness and self-worth (just as Cousin Justina, the reincarnation of Charles Dickens' Miss Havisham, aggressively plots to unman Moses). To some extent they are predatory, but even more they are incomplete because they are in need of someone to love. Similarly, Leander is portrayed as a man not without flaws. He is, like many of Cheever's male characters, impractical and, at times, inattentive to his family; he can also appear childishly petulant, even ridiculous, as in the scene in which he fakes suicide in order to attract attention. More important, he loves and is loved, as the large crowd of mourners at his funeral service attests—much to Honora's surprise.

Whether his sons will fare any better in their relationships with women is left uncertain in this novel. Both marry—Coverly his "sandwich shop Venus" and Moses the beautiful Melissa Scaddon, who plays Estella to Cousin Justina's Miss Havisham. Both, after briefly losing their wives, eventually father sons, thus fulfilling the terms of their inheritance as set by Honora. Melissa and Betsey are, however, tainted, or haunted, by their pasts (in Betsey's case this is only vaguely mentioned). Moreover, most marriages in Cheever's fiction, as in life, are difficult affairs. In sum, the Wapshot boys may yet be greatly disappointed in their expectations. What is more important is the fact that Moses and, more particularly, Coverly build the necessary bridge between past and present, holding firm to what is best in St. Botolphs (as evidenced in Leander's journal) while freeing themselves from that confinement which the town, in part, represents. This optimistic view is confirmed by the novel's lively style. Straight narrative sections alternate with large portions of two Wapshot journals, humorous parodies of biblical language, and frequent direct addresses to the reader. Tragic elements are present but always in muted tones and often undercut with humor. In *The Wapshot Chronicle*, the comic spirit prevails, as well it should in a novel that twice invokes Shakespeare's Prospero, the liberator of Ariel and tamer of Caliban.

Outwardly, Cheever's first two novels are quite similar in theme, character, and structure. Like *The Wapshot Chronicle*, *The Wapshot Scandal* employs a framing device and interweaves three related stories: Honora's escape to Italy to avoid prosecution for income tax evasion and her return to St. Botolphs, where she promptly starves and drinks herself to death; Coverly and Betsey's life in yet another bland, middle-class housing development, Talifer; and Moses and Melissa's difficult existence in the affluent suburb of Proxmire Manor. Although reviewers generally responded less favorably to the second Wapshot book, finding it too discursive, Cheever has pointed out that both novels were carefully thought out in advance and has described the sequel as "an extraordinarily complex book built upon non sequiturs." Whether it is, as Samuel Coale has argued, Cheever's finest work, because it carefully balances comic and tragic elements, is open to question. More certain is that a considerably darker mood pervades *The Wapshot Scandal*. At the time he began writing it, Cheever told an audience that American life had become abrasive and debased, a kind of hell, and during its four-year composition he became severely depressed. In *The Wapshot Chronicle* the easy-to-answer refrain is "Why did the young want to go away?" but in *The Wapshot Scandal* the repeated question is Coverly's Hamlet-like "Oh, Father, Father, Father, why have you come back?"—a query that accurately gauges the extent of Coverly's and Cheever's disenchantment with a world that no longer seems either inviting or livable for men or ghosts. In the earlier book, Moses and Coverly had to escape the confinement of St. Botolphs; in the sequel, characters have too completely cut themselves off from the usable traditions, comforting stability, and vital, natural light that the town also represents. As a result, the communal center to which earlier Wapshot men had come back and, analogously, the narrative center to which *The Wapshot Chronicle* continually returned, are conspicuously absent from *The Wapshot Scandal*.

In the sequel, St. Botolphs, though by no means idealized, is rendered in less qualified terms, thus more firmly establishing Cheever's preference for its values and his impatience with the rootlessness and shallowness of the modern age. Honora, for example, is now a far more sympathetic figure endowed with two of Leander's most attractive qualities: a belief in ceremony and a love of nature. In the guise of an elderly senator, Cheever carefully distinguishes between the sentimentalizing of the past and the modern tendency to dispense with the past altogether. The modern Prometheus, the senator notes, is technologically powerful, but he lacks "the awe, the humility, that primitive man brought to the sacred fire."

Whereas earlier Wapshot men faced the terrors of the sea, Moses and Coverly face the greater terrors of daily life in the twentieth century: insecurity, boredom, loneliness, loss of usefulness and self-esteem, and the pervasiveness of death. As Cheever shows, the American dream totters on the brink of nightmare. When one resident of Proxmire Manor suddenly finds her carefree days turn into a series of frozen water pipes, backed up toilets, exploding furnaces, blown fuses, broken appliances, unopenable packages of bacon, and vacationing repairmen, she turns first to alcohol and promiscuity, then to suicide. The few mourners her husband can convince to attend the funeral are people they had briefly known on various sea cruises who, intuiting her disappointment and recognizing it as their own, burst into tears. Similarly, Melissa Wapshot becomes the Emma Bovary of Proxmire Manor, taking as her lover a delivery boy and eventually fleeing to Italy, where, perversely, she finds some "solace" for her disappointments in the Supra-Marketto

Americano in Rome. Moses responds to his wife's infidelity by becoming a wandering alcoholic, and Betsey finds compensation for the wrongs she claims to have suffered by whittling away her husband's small store of self-esteem.

Coverly, now twelve years older than at the beginning of *The Wapshot Chronicle*, serves (as Leander did in the earlier work) as the novel's moral center. He survives, perhaps even prevails, partly because he chooses to follow the best of the past (Leander's advice to his sons) and partly because he adapts to his world without being overwhelmed by it. Trained as a computer programmer, he accepts the computer error that transforms him into a public relations man but resists the apocalyptic mood that infects nearly everyone else in the novel. Unlike Melissa, whose brief illness leads her to cultivate "a ruthless greed for pleasure," Coverly's narrow escape from a hunter's arrow prompts him to "make something illustrious of his life." His computer analysis of John Keats's poetry leads to the creation of new poetry and the realization of a universal harmony underlying not only the poems but also life itself. His brother Moses, whom he has saved for the moment from debauchery, claims to see through the pasteboard mask of Christmas morning to "the nothingness of things." Coverly, on the other hand, celebrates the "dazzling" day by romancing his wife and sharing Christmas dinner with his late aunt's blind guests, "the raw material of human kindness." Coverly's vision, as well as St. Botolphs' brand of decorum as "a guise or mode of hope," is certainly Cheever's own. Even so, that vision is tempered insofar as the author also shares Moses' pessimistic knowledge of decorum's other side: hypocrisy and despair.

The contrasting visions of Coverly and Moses reappear as Eliot Nailles and Paul Hammer, the main characters of Cheever's third novel, *Bullet Park*. Nailles is the book's comic and decidedly qualified hero. Like Cheever, he has belonged to a volunteer fire department, loves to saw wood with a chain-saw, feels a kinship with the natural world, and has a realistically balanced view of suburban living as being neither morally perfect nor inherently depraved. Yet while both character and author are optimistic, the quality of their optimism differentiates them, for Nailles's is naïve and ludicrously shallow: "Nailles thought of pain and suffering as a principality lying somewhere beyond the legitimate borders of western Europe." Just as Cheever's story "The Death of Justina" satirizes a community determined to defeat death by means of zoning regulations, so *Bullet Park* satirizes Nailles's myopic optimism, which, like St. Paul's faith (Cheever quotes II Corinthians 11-12), is sorely tried during the course of the novel.

Beneath the appearance of respectability and comfort in *Bullet Park*, one finds the same unease that afflicts Talifer and Proxmire Manor. There is Mr. Heathcup, who interrupts his annual house painting to kill himself, claiming he could not stand "it" anymore. When Harry Shinglehouse is sucked under a passing express train and killed, only his shoe is found, an ironic memorial to a hollow life. Shaken by this and other reminders of mortality, Nailles turns to drugs. Drug addiciton is one of Nailles's escapes; another is the devising of soothing explanations. When asked about his work—he sells Spang mouthwash—Nailles claims to be a chemist. When his son Tony suddenly becomes melancholy and withdraws, Bartleby-fashion, from the outside world, his father, like the lawyer in Herman Melville's tale, rationalizes his son's illness as mononucleosis rather than confront the actual cause: he tried to murder his son when Tony echoed his misgivings about the quality of his life. Neither the father's drugged optimism nor the expensive services of a doctor, a psychiatrist, and a specialist in somnambulatory phenomena effect Tony's cure. That is accomplished by the Swami Rutuola, "a spiritual cheerleader" whose vision is not altogether different from Nailles's.

The climax of Nailles's dark night of the soul occurs when he defeats his secret antagonist, Hammer, who, as John Leonard suggests, may represent a part of Nailles's own personality. Hammer is the illegitimate son of a wealthy socialist (such ironies abound in Cheever's fiction) and his name-changing secretary. Unloved and rootless, Hammer is haunted by a vaguely defined canard. To escape it he turns to various pursuits: aimless travel, alcohol, fantasizing, psychoanalysis, translating the pessimistic poetry of Eugenio Montale, and locating a room with yellow walls where, he believes, he will finally be able to lead "a useful and illustrious life." He finds the room, as well as a beautiful wife, but both prove disappointing, and his search for "a useful and illustrious life" continues to elude him. At this point, Hammer adopts the messianic plan formulated by his dissatisfied, expatriate mother: to live quietly in a place like Bullet Park, to single out one of its representative men, and to "crucify him on the door of Christ's Church. . . . Nothing less than a crucifixion will wake that world!" Hammer fails in this, as in his other attempts, mainly for the same reasons he turned to it. One reason is his loneliness; feeling the need for a confidant, he explains his plan to the swami, who, of course, tells Nailles. The other is his having underestimated the depth of love, even in Bullet Park, where homes are associated not with the people who live in them but with real estate: number of bedrooms, number of baths, and market value.

This "simple" book about a father's love for his son greatly pleased its author. A number of reviewers, however, were troubled by the ending, which Guy Davenport called "shockingly inept." In a review that Cheever blames for turning the critical tide against the book, Benjamin DeMott charged that *Bullet Park* was broken-backed, its "parts tacked together." In retrospect, none of the charges appear merited. Cheever's narrative method and "arch"-like form (as he called it) are entirely consistent with his thematic purpose. In Part I, the third-person narration effectively establishes both the author's sympathy for and distance from his protagonist Nailles, whose confused state of mind is reflected in the confused chronology of this section. Part II, Hammer's journal (the third-person narrator disappears after parenthetically remarking "Hammer wrote"), is the first-person monologue of a quietly desperate madman such as one finds in works by Edgar Allan Poe and Nikolai Gogol. The return to third-person narration in Part III enables Cheever to use as centers of consciousness each of his two main characters. At the end of the novel, Tony is saved and returns to school, Hammer is sent to a hospital for the criminally insane, "and Nailles—drugged—went off to work and everything was as wonderful, wonderful, wonderful, wonderful as it had been." By undercutting Nailles's triumph without actually dismissing it, Cheever's ending resists those simplistic affirmations and negations that the rest of *Bullet Park* has explored.

The prison setting is the most obvious difference between *Falconer* and Cheever's previous fiction. The more significant difference, however, is the absence of any qualifying irony in its concluding pages. Never has the author's and his protagonist's affirmation been so completely self-assured as in this, Cheever's finest achievement.

Falconer is a story of metaphoric confinement and escape. The realism here serves a larger purpose than verisimilitude; Cheever sketches the essentials of the religious experience and shows how that experience is reflected in a man's retreat from the natural world or in his acceptance of a responsible place in it. The relationship between two brothers (as in the Wapshot books) or two brotherlike figures (*Bullet Park*) is given a violent twist in *Falconer*, where the main character, a forty-eight-year-old college professor named Ezekiel Farragut, has been convicted of fratricide. Farragut's murderous act, as well as his addictions to heroin and methadone, imply his retreat into self, a retreat that is not without some justification—a narcissistic wife, a father who wanted his unborn child aborted, a mother who was hardly maternal, a jealous brother, and the violence of war—but self-pity is the sin Cheever has most frequently assailed. Farragut's task, then, is "to leach self-pity out of his emotional spectrum," and to do this he must learn inside Falconer prison what he failed to learn outside it: how to love.

Farragut's first, humble step away from self-love is the affection he has for his cat, Bandit, whose cunning he must adopt if he is to survive his time in prison and those blows that defeat Moses and Melissa Wapshot. More important is Farragut's relationship with a fellow prisoner, Jody. Neither narcissistic nor regressive, this homosexual affair is plainly shown to further Farragut's movement away from self and, in that from Jody's hideout Farragut is given an expansive view of the world he has lost, it also furthers his movement toward that world and "the invisible potency of nature." Jody teaches the professorial Farragut an important lesson concerning the usefulness of one's environment and the active role that must be assumed in order to effect one's own salvation, one's escape from the metaphoric prison. When Jody escapes from Falconer, the loss of his lover at first leads Farragut back to lonely self-love; directed by another prisoner, the Cuckold, to whose depths of self-pity Farragut could easily descend, Farragut goes to the Valley, a dimly lit lavatory where the prisoners masturbate. Here Farragut has a revelation; he suddenly understands that the target of human sexuality ought not to be an iron trough but "the mysteriousness of the bonded spirit and the flesh."

His continuing escape from useless fantasizing, from nostalgic re-creation of the past, and from passivity causes him to become more self-assured and more interested in the present moment and how to make use of it in realizing his future. The riot at nearby Amana prison (based on the September, 1971, Attica uprising, during which Cheever was teaching at Sing Sing) shows that Farragut is actually freer than his jailers, but it is at this point that Farragut overreaches himself. In his view, the Amana riot signals the salvation of all the dispossessed, and to aid himself in hearing the "word," that is, the news reports, Farragut begins to build a contraband radio. He hopes to get a crystal from Bumpo, who had earlier said he would gladly give up his diamond to save someone. Bumpo refuses to give up the crystal, his reasoning obviously being his own selfishness, yet there is something ridiculous in Farragut's vague plan for sweeping social reform when his own salvation is still in doubt. In the aftermath of his and the rioters' failures, Farragut briefly slips back into self-regarding passivity, from which he is saved by a dying prisoner. In place of the ineffectual and wholly impersonal charity of his plan to save mankind, Farragut takes upon himself the humbler and more truly charitable task of caring for his fellow man. For the first time, Farragut, prompted by the dying man's question, faces up to the enormity of his crime, making clear to the reader, and perhaps to himself, that in murdering his brother he was unconsciously trying to destroy the worst part of his own personality. The demon exorcised, Farragut becomes spiritually free, a creature of the light.

The visible sign of this freedom is his escape from Falconer in Chicken Number Two's burial box. Borrowing freely from Alexandre Dumas' *The Count of Monte-Cristo* (1844), Cheever treats the escape symbolically as a rebirth and a resurrection. The religious theme is effectively underscored by the novel's parablelike ending. Farragut meets a man who, although he has been evicted from his apartment because he is "alive and healthy," remains both cheerful and charitable, offering Farragut a coat, bus fare, and a place to stay. Miracles, it seems, do occur. The step from psychological retreat and spiritual darkness to freedom and light is not difficult to take, Cheever implies; it simply requires commitment and determination. As for the effect of this choice, which is as much Cheever's as Farragut's, that is summed up in the novel's final word, "rejoice."

Falconer recapitulates all of the major themes of Cheever's earlier fiction and, at the same time, evidences a number of significant changes in his art. One is the tendency toward greater narrative compression. Another, related to the first, is the inclusion of ancillary narratives, less as somewhat obtrusive sketches and more as integral parts of the main storyline. The third—a more overt treatment of the religious theme—appears to have influenced the characterization, style, and structure of *Falconer*. Although Cheever always considered the novelist as one who devotes himself to "enlarging" his fellow men rather than "diminishing" them, his two middle novels emphasize many of his characters' worst features. *Falconer* represents Cheever's return to the more certain affirmation of *The Wapshot Chronicle*; moreover, *Falconer* is Cheever's most lyrical and least bitingly humorous novel. The religious theme and the harmony it implies may also account for its being the most "novelistic" in structure of the four; this is not to say that Cheever had finally "out-grown" his earlier short-story style and mastered the more demanding form of the novel, for the structure of *The Wapshot Chronicle*, *The Wapshot Scandal*, and *Bullet Park* mirrors Cheever's vision of the 1950's and the 1960's. By the time he wrote *Falconer*, however, that sense of personal and cultural fragmentation no longer dominated his thinking, a change reflected in the relatively tight, more harmonious structure of his most affirmative work.

Oh What a Paradise It Seems is a slighter but in its own way no less triumphant work. The "bulky novel" which illness forced Cheever to cut short is, though brief, nevertheless remarkably generous in tone and spirit. It is also Cheever's most topical fiction yet strangely his least realistic—a self-regarding, even self-mocking fabulation, a *Walden* for the postmodern age, in which the irony falls as gently as the (acid) rain. Set in a future at once familiar (jogging, for example, has become popular) yet remote (highways with lanes in four digits)—a timeless present, as it were—the novel ends as it begins, by pretending to disclaim its own seriousness: "[T]his is just a story to be read at night in an old house on a rainy night."

Oh What a Paradise It Seems focuses on the "old but not yet infirm" Lemuel Sears. Twice a widower, Sears is financially well-off (he works for Computer Container Intrusion Systems, maker of "cerbical chips") and is as spiritually as he is sexually inclined. Sears's heart "leaps" in two not altogether different directions. One is toward Beasley's Pond, located near his daughter's home, where he ice-skates and in this way briefly satisfies his desire for fleetness, grace, pastoral innocence, and connectedness with the transcendental world of Emersonian Nature. When family connections (Mafia) and political corruption despoil the scene, however—transmogrifying pastoral pond into town dump—Beasley's Pond comes to symbolize for Sears not only imminent ecological disaster but, more important, the "spiritual vagrancy" of a "nomadic society" whose chief characteristics are "netherness" and "portability."

Sears's attraction to the pond parallels and in a way is offset by his physical attraction to the beautiful Renee Herndon, whose appetite for food and whose work as a real estate broker suggest that, despite the exoticism of her given name and the mysteriousness of her personal life, she represents everything which the prosaically named Beasley's, in its pristine state, does not. In his sexual pursuit of Renee, Sears is persistent to the point of clownishness. After numerous initial triumphs, Sears will eventually be rebuffed and come to see the waywardness of this attempt of his to attain what the pond, Sears's first wife, "the sainted Amelia," and even Renee in her own strange way symbolize, but not before a comical but nevertheless loving interlude with Eduardo, the elevator operator in Renee's apartment building, and a perfectly useless session with a psychiatrist named Palmer, "a homosexual spinster." The small but increasingly prominent part homosexuality plays in each of the novels reflects Cheever's ambivalence concerning his own bisexuality. Comically dismissed in the early works, it becomes in *Falconer* and *Oh What a Paradise It Seems* viable but, as Cheever would say in a letter to one of his many male lovers, not ultimate.

As in Cheever's other fictions, the narrative here progresses along parallel fronts. Sears's dual lives, the sexual and the transcendental, become entwined in and simultaneously exist alongside those of Horace Chisholm, whose commitment to the environment evidences his longing for purity and human as well as spiritual attachment but also causes him to become estranged from his wife and family. Like Sears, he is also quixotic, which is to say both idealistic and absurd. Thanks to a number of those improbable plot complications which abound in Cheever's fiction, Chisholm, working for Sears to save Beasley's Pond, finds and returns a baby inadvertently left by the roadside after a family outing to the beach. The parents, the Logans, live next door to the Salazzos; Sammy Salazzo presides over the pond-turned-dump. Chisholm will be welcomed into the Logan family but eventually will be killed by the mob; an angry Betsey Logan will, however, complete his work, stopping the dumping, by threatening to poison the teriyaki sauce in the local Buy Brite supermarkets. (A by-product of her action is that her hated neighbors, the Salazzos, will move away.) Sears, in turn, will utilize the latest technology to restore the pond to its original state, thus redeeming himself as well.

Cheever's ending is self-consciously "happy"—aware of its own improbability. It is, like the architecture of Hitching Post Lane where the Logan and the Salazzos live, "all happy ending—all greeting card." Yet Cheever's satire is more than offset by his compassion, his recognition of and sympathy for the waywardness of man's continuing search for both home and wholeness.

Robert A. Morace

Other major works

SHORT FICTION: *The Way Some People Live*, 1943; *The Enormous Radio and Other Stories*, 1953; *Stories*, 1956 (with Jean Stafford, Daniel Fuchs, and William Maxwell); *The Housebreaker of Shady Hill and Other Stories*, 1958; *Some People, Places, and Things That Will Not Appear in My Next Novel*,

1961; *Dry Martini*, 1962 (Milan); *Selected Stories*, 1962 (Moscow); *The Brigadier and the Golf Widow*, 1964; *Homage to Shakespeare*, 1968 (published in a limited-edition, hardbound volume); *The World of Apples*, 1973; *The Collected Stories of John Cheever*, 1978.

PLAY: *The Shady Hill Kidnapping*, 1982 (written for television).

NONFICTION: *The Letters of John Cheever*, 1988 (edited by Benjamin Cheever).

Bibliography

Bosha, Francis J. *John Cheever: A Reference Guide*. Boston: G. K. Hall, 1981. The annotated listing of 593 reviews, articles, books, and dissertations, as well as Bosha's discussion of the "inconsistent critical response" to Cheever's work make this an especially useful volume. The listing of Cheever books is thorough, but for a checklist of Cheever's shorter writings the student will need to consult Dennis Coates's "John Cheever: A Checklist, 1930-1978." *Bulletin of Bibliography* 36 (January-March, 1979): 1-13, 49, and his supplement in Collins (below).

Cheever, Susan. *Home Before Dark*. Boston: Houghton Mifflin, 1984. This memoir by the author's daughter is especially important for fleshing out Cheever's troubled early years and providing an insider's look at Cheever's marital and assorted other personal difficulties (alcoholism, illnesses, sexual desires). The book suffers from lack of documentation (and indexing); strange to say, this memoir turns out to be most valuable as a synthesis of previously published material (interviews) than as a daughter's intimate revelations.

Coale, Samuel. *John Cheever*. New York: Frederick Ungar, 1977. This volume in Ungar's Literature and Life series includes a brief biography, two chapters on selected short stories, individual chapters on Cheever's first four novels, and a brief conclusion. Coale focuses on the development of Cheever's style (from realism to fantasy) and concern for moral issues.

Collins, Robert G., ed. *Critical Essays on John Cheever*. Boston: G. K. Hall, 1982. A very useful volume for the editor's discerning introduction, for the reviews, interviews, and critical articles it reprints, for Dennis Coates's updating of his 1979 checklist, and for Samuel Coale's excellent discussion entitled "Cheever and Hawthorne: The American Romancer's Art."

Donaldson, Scott, ed. *Conversations with John Cheever*. Jackson: University Press of Mississippi, 1987. Because he was largely a private man, Cheever granted few interviews prior to the publication of *Falconer*. Donaldson can therefore afford to offer an exhaustive compilation of Cheever's interviews. Many of Cheever's comments, especially those about fiction, are repetitive, and others, about himself, more fictive than truthful.

_____. *John Cheever: A Biography*. New York: Random House, 1988. Donaldson's exhaustive but readable biography cuts through the biographical fictions Cheever himself fostered to create one of the most accurate portraits of the actual man. Donaldson's approach is always evenhanded; his research, impeccable; his portrait, compelling.

Hunt, George. *John Cheever: The Hobgoblin Company of Love*. Grand Rapids: Wm. B. Eerdmans, 1983. Hunt's is the first book-length analysis of Cheever's fiction that is not introductory in nature. Hunt, a Jesuit, reads Cheever in Christian terms as a Kierkegaardian humorist (rather than an ironist) whose "dialectical intelligence" manifests itself in the oppositional structure and thematics of the stories and novels.

Waldeland, Lynne. *John Cheever.* Boston: Twayne, 1979. This volume in Twayne's United States Authors series is introductory in nature. Although it lacks the thematic coherence of Coale's, it has greater breadth and evidences a greater awareness of, or at least interest in, previous critical commentary.

CHARLES WADDELL CHESNUTT

Born: Cleveland, Ohio; June 20, 1858
Died: Cleveland, Ohio; November 15, 1932

Principal long fiction

The House Behind the Cedars, 1900; *The Marrow of Tradition*, 1901; *The Colonel's Dream*, 1905.

Several of Charles Waddell Chesnutt's novels were never published, but are in the Chesnutt Collection at Fisk University: *Mandy Oxendine*, c. 1897; *A Business Career*, c. 1898; *Evelyn's Husband*, c. 1900; *The Rainbow Chasers*, c. 1900; *Paul Marchand, F. M. C.* (Free Man of Color), c. 1928; *Rena*, various versions.

Other literary forms

Charles Waddell Chesnutt's two major collections of short stories are *The Conjure Woman* (1899) and *The Wife of His Youth* (1899). Some critics consider both collections as novels. Although he does not view the works as novels, William Andrews in *The Literary Career of Charles W. Chesnutt* (1980) explains why some think the collections should be called "novels."

At the heart of *The Conjure Woman* is ex-slave Uncle Julius McAdoo, whose reminiscences in black dialect present a picture of plantation life in the Old South. His tales in turn center around old Aunt Peggy, the plantation conjure woman, and each has a moral, although their primary purpose is supposed to be entertainment. Another major character is a Midwestern businessman who has come to North Carolina for his wife's health and who describes rural life in the South after the Civil War. The businessman's loosely connected descriptions serve as a frame for the tales of Uncle Julius, who is his coachman and unofficial family entertainer. In the stories in *The Conjure Woman*, Chesnutt is following the dialect/local-color tradition.

The stories in *The Wife of His Youth and Other Stories of the Color Line* are issue-oriented. In them, Chesnutt is concerned with the special difficulties that those of mixed blood had in the pervasively racist environment in America after the Civil War. He asserted in a letter to his publisher, Houghton Mifflin, that while the stories are not unified by a character such as Uncle Julius in *The Conjure Woman*, they are unified by a theme—what Chesnutt called "the color line." Chesnutt gives various fictional case studies of social problems caused by the color consciousness of Americans. Some stories are addressed to blacks, some to those of mixed blood, and others to whites. Besides having all the stories deal with a common subject, "the color line," Chesnutt attempted to unify the stories in another way. In all of them, he sought to revise and the public's conception of blacks—to counter the stereotypes found in American fiction at that time.

Chesnutt also wrote a biography (*The Life of Frederick Douglass*, 1899), a play ("Mrs. Darcy's Daughter"), and a few poems. He wrote essays and speeches that were published in national magazines. Representing a dominant concern of his, these writings were primarily political and didactic: "What Is a White Man?," "A Plea for the American Negro," and "The White and the Black." His essay on "The Disfranchisement of the Negro" appeared as a part of a book entitled *The Negro Problem* (1903), whose subtitle announced that it was *A Series of Articles by Representative American Negroes of Today* and whose list of contributors included such men as Booker T. Washington, W. E. B. Dubois, T. Thomas Fortune, and Paul Laurence Dunbar.

Chesnutt's correspondence and many of his writings have not been published. Most of these unpublished works, as well as many of the published ones, are in the Charles Waddell Chesnutt Collection of the Erastus Milo Cravath Memorial Library, Fisk University, Nashville, Tennessee.

Achievements

In 1872, when he was fourteen years old, Chesnutt's first story was published serially in a local black weekly. The publication of "The Goophered Grapevine" (August, 1887) in *The Atlantic* marked Chesnutt's first appearance in a major American literary magazine. Three more short stories followed: "Po' Sandy," "The Conjurer's Revenge," and "Dave's Neckliss." The publication of these four Uncle Julius stories were his entering wedge into the literary world—a world which Chesnutt had long dreamed of being a part of as a novelist. The two collections of his short stories, *The Conjure Woman* and *The Wife of His Youth*, were moderately successful. Containing virtually all his best writing during the period between 1887 and 1899, these collections are ultimately the basis for Chesnutt's reputation as a short-story writer. The stories must be viewed in the context of his total contribution to the traditional dialect/local-color story and the issue-oriented, problem story. With these stories, he moved up from literary apprenticeship to a respected position among America's short-story writers.

In 1900, Chesnutt published his first novel, *The House Behind the Cedars*, which sold about two thousand copies in its first two months. His next two published novels (*The Marrow of Tradition* and *The Colonel's Dream*) were not as well received. Although he was honored as a writer by being asked to be a guest at Mark Twain's seventieth birthday party, he retired from writing as a profession in 1905. After that time, none of his creative work was published.

Chesnutt achieved a great deal for his people in nonliterary areas. He was active politically and socially to help advance the cause of blacks. He wrote many controversial essays and speeches on the race issue. In 1913, he received an honorary LL.D. degree from Wilberforce University. In 1928, he was awarded the NAACP's Spingarn Medal, an award given to Afro-Americans who distinguish themselves in their fields. The gold medal commemorated

Chesnutt for his "pioneer work as a literary artist depicting the life and struggles of Americans of Negro descent and for his long and useful career as a scholar, worker, and freeman of one of America's greatest cities [Cleveland]."

Biography

Charles Waddell Chesnutt was born on June 20, 1858, in Cleveland, Ohio. When he was nine years old, his family moved to Fayetteville, North Carolina, where he spent his youth. Although he was of Afro-American descent, his features barely distinguished him from whites. He learned, however, that family blood was very important in determining a person's social and economic prospects.

Chesnutt's mother died in 1871 when he was thirteen years old. Two years later, he left school to teach in order to supplement the family income. In 1878, he married Susan Perry, a fellow teacher and daughter of a well-to-do black barber in Fayetteville. He had begun teaching in 1877 at the new State Colored Normal School in Fayetteville, and in 1880 he became principal of the school.

On a job-hunting trip to Washington, D.C., in 1879, Chesnutt was unable to find work. He had been studying stenography and hoped to obtain a job on a newspaper. In 1883, he was able to begin a new career as a stenographer and reporter in New York City, and shortly afterward moved to Cleveland, where he was first a clerk and then a legal stenographer. Two years later, he began studying law, and in 1887, he passed the Ohio bar examination with the highest grade in his group. He opened his own office as a court reporter in 1888.

Between 1887 and 1899, beginning with the publication of "The Goophered Grapevine" by *The Atlantic*, he achieved some success as a short-story writer. In 1899, when Houghton Mifflin published two collections of his short stories, he gave up his profitable business and began writing novels full time—something he had dreamed of doing for many years.

His first published novel, *The House Behind the Cedars*, had some commercial success, but the next one, *The Marrow of Tradition*, did not. In 1901, two years after he had closed his stenographic firm, he reopened it. Deciding to write short stories once more in 1903 and 1904, he sent them to *The Atlantic*, where he had had success earlier, but only one, "Baxter's Procrustes," was accepted. His novel *The Colonel's Dream*, published in 1905, failed to attract the attention of the public. The public of the early 1900's was not ready for the controversial subject matter of his novels and later short stories or for the sympathetic treatment of the black characters in them. It did not want to read literature that had colored persons as the main characters, that presented their problems in a predominately white world, and that were written with a sympathy for blacks rather than whites. Chesnutt retired from creative writing as a profession in 1905, and thereafter he published only nonfiction.

During the rest of his life, Chesnutt concentrated on managing his business affairs, on participating in civic affairs, and on working on the behalf of black people. He was an active member of the Rowland Club, an exclusive male literary group in Cleveland, although at first he was denied membership in this Club because of his race. During the last twenty-seven years of his life, he managed to find time to travel in Europe and to help educate his three children. He was a member of the Cleveland Chamber of Commerce and the National Arts Club; he also helped establish Playhouse Settlement (now Karamu House).

Before 1905, he had been politically and socially active in helping to advance the cause of the black race, and he continued to be active throughout his life. In 1901, he contributed greatly to having W. H. Thomas' *The American Negro* withdrawn from circulation. That same year, he chaired the Committee on Colored Troops for the 35th National Encampment of the Grand Army of the Republic in Cleveland. In 1904, he became a member of the Committee of Twelve, organized by Booker T. Washington, and in 1905, he was a consultant on the black problem and a member of the Cleveland Council of Sociology. He addressed the National Negro Committee, which later became the NAACP, and served as a member of its General Committee. He protested the showing of *The Birth of a Nation* and, more important, he protested the treatment of black soldiers. He participated in the First Amenia Conference, called by Joel Spingarn in 1916. He was awarded the Spingarn Medal by the NAACP in 1928.

Analysis

Charles Waddell Chesnutt wrote three novels that were published and seven that were not. He was a much more skillful short-story writer than a novelist, and although he developed most of his novels from short stories, one of the novels is exceptional as a literary work. Those reading his novels should remember, however, that some of the matters for which he is criticized today—thin, idealized characters and the use of plot manipulations such as foreshowing and coincidence—were standard in the fiction of the late 1800's and were accepted by the readers of the day.

Chesnutt dreamed of being a novelist, and he believed that racial issues such as the problems of passing, miscegenation, and racial assimilation had to be the subject of serious fiction. He found, though, that if he tried to write novels that would be commercially successful, publishers would not accept them, and if he tried to write works that examined racial issues honestly and with sympathy for blacks, the public would not accept these topical but controversial novels.

Chesnutt is notable for being the first Afro-American fiction-writer to gain a reputation for examining honestly and in detail the racial problems of the black in America after the Civil War. Many Americans in the last part of the nineteenth century preferred to ignore the problems of the Afro-American and especially did not want a presentation as sympathetic toward blacks as that given by Chesnutt.

His most successful years as a novelist, if they can be called successful, were from 1900 to 1905. During that time, his three published novels appeared: *The House Behind the Cedars*, *The Marrow of Tradition*, and *The Colonel's Dream*. Chesnutt believed that the only way to change the attitudes of whites was to do so slowly and through fiction that expressed ideas indirectly. He believed too that preaching was not art, yet with each novel he became more of a crusader. In 1901, he gave up writing as a full-time profession and returned to his stenographic business; after 1905, he did little creative writing and published only nonfiction. He decided that he could help his people best by achieving in a field other than writing.

Chesnutt may have been a victim, just as his characters sometimes are. The themes that he could present most effectively and that he felt compelled to present were ones that the public would not accept; thus, he did not continue to write novels and may have been prevented from developing as a literary artist. In addition, he may have had to compromise to get his views before readers in America.

Before studying his three published novels, one should understand his views concerning racial issues of the late 1800's and early 1900's. One of the racial situations with which he was most concerned was that of the mulatto. The mulatto shared many of the problems of the full black, but he was also confronted with the issues of passing for white and of miscegenation. (Chesnutt himself was a mulatto who appeared white and who considered trying to pass for white.) Those passing might achieve social, economic, and professional opportunities, but they also had to make emotional sacrifices by giving up their family and friends. Furthermore, they faced certain limitations; they could not try to be famous or distinguished because their past might be revealed.

Chesnutt believed that Americans had an unnatural fear of miscegenation. Because of this fear, the person of mixed blood was an outcast in society and was almost forced by society to pass for white to try to obtain the American Dream. Ironically, those forced into passing and marrying whites began again the miscegenation cycle that was so feared by whites. Anglo-Saxon racial purity was something that should not be preserved, Chesnutt believed. Intermingling and integration would improve man biologically, but more important, blacks would then be able to have the rights they should have as human beings. Only by eliminating laws against intermarriage and social interaction between the races would blacks gain true social, economic, and political equality.

Chesnutt's three published novels are all problem novels that treat his characteristic theme of the effects of color consciousness in American life. The first one, a novel of miscegenation and passing, is written from the viewpoint of "the socially alienated, ambitious young mulatto," according to William Andrews in *The Literary Career of Charles W. Chesnutt*. The second novel is from the viewpoint of "a conscientious Southern social critic," and in it, Chesnutt analyzes the political aspects and the caste structure of the small town in the South after the Civil War. The last one, in the vogue of the muckraking novel, is an economic problem novel told from the viewpoint of "the progressive northern reformer."

Between 1890 and 1899, Chesnutt greatly expanded and revised "Rena Walden," a short story, until it became *The House Behind the Cedars*. At first, he focused on how color consciousness can destroy an intraracial marriage and then on the predominant issue of whether a mulatto should cross the color line. In March, 1899, he wrote Walter Hines Page that the Rena Walden story was the strong expression of a writer whose themes dealt primarily with the American color line. When he wrote to his daughters in the fall of 1900, he indicated that he hoped for "a howling success" from *The House Behind the Cedars*, "a strong race problem novel." The story of Rena Walden and her brother was the first in which the problems of Americans concealing their African heritage were studied with a detached and compassionate presentation of individuals on the various sides of the issue.

The novel can be divided into two parts: Rena in white society, in which her brother is the major focus, and Rena in black society, in which she becomes the focus. The novel is set in Patesville, North Carolina, a few years after the Civil War. John Warwick, who has changed his name from Walden, has left Patesville and gone to South Carolina, where he has become a lawyer and plantation owner, acquiring wealth and position. He and his sister Rena are the children of a quadroon mother Molly and a white man who has died. John has returned to Patesville to help his beautiful sister escape the restrictions of color by teaching her how to pass for white. She is a success at the boarding school in South Carolina to which he takes her. As proof of her success in passing, George Tryon, a good friend of John and a white, wants to marry Rena, but she is not sure she should marry him without telling him of her mixed blood. John and Rena indirectly discuss the pros and cons of passing and intermarriage. A series of coincidences leads to an unexpected meeting between George and Rena; he learns of her heritage, and the engagement is broken. Rena returns home to her mother and the house behind the cedars.

A chapter interlude which gives the Walden family history separates the first part of the novel from the second. John tries to persuade his sister to return to South Carolina with him or to take money and go North or West, where she can pass for white and marry someone even better than George, but she refuses to leave Patesville. She has decided to accept her destiny and be of service to her people, whom she has rediscovered. After this point, the reader is told little more about John.

Rena meets Jeff Wain, an influential and prosperous mulatto from a rural county, who is seeking a schoolteacher. Rena accepts the position, not realizing Jeff has a personal as well as a professional interest in her. Jeff is not as admirable a character as he first appears. As he pays her more and more attention, she is upset and repulsed. Once again, coincidence plays a part in the plot. George Tryon happens to learn of her presence near a place he is visiting. When he sees her, he realizes that he loves her and that his love is stronger than his racial prejudice. The same day that George decides to declare his love, Jeff decides to do so too. Rena fears both of the men and leaves hastily for her mother's house behind the cedars. After exposure and fatigue have overcome her, Frank Fowler, a childhood friend and a conscientious black workman, finds her and carries her to her home, where she dies. Rena realizes before she dies that Frank loved her the best.

In his fiction before *The House Behind the Cedars*, Chesnutt did not directly condemn passing and miscegenation, but also he did not directly call for it. Primarily, he wanted the public to be aware of the causes and to feel sympathy for those of mixed blood. In this novel, he makes passing and miscegenation acts deliberately chosen by mature Afro-Americans. Such choices were justified because they were the only means by which blacks could gain and enjoy the social, economic, and political rights due them as citizens of the United States.

Chesnutt seeks to lead his readers to share his perspective rather than lecturing them. He delays revealing that John and Rena are mulattoes. To create sympathy for them first, he presents them simply as persons of humble origins who are attempting to achieve prosperity and happiness. Chesnutt passes John and Rena for white with the reader before he lets the reader know that they are mulattoes who have chosen or will deliberately choose to pass for white.

John Walden is the first black character in American fiction to decide to pass for white and, at the same time, to feel that his decision is legally and morally justified. Believing that the color of his skin tells him that he is white, he has no psychological problems concerning his choice to pass. He is not a stereotype. Intelligent and industrious, he patiently trains himself so that he can achieve the American Dream. At the beginning of the novel, the reader learns that he has become a prosperous lawyer and plantation owner after leaving Patesville; in the second part of the novel, after he has not been successful in helping Rena pass for white, he returns to South Carolina to regain his position.

The characters are not fully developed and remain stick figures, although Chesnutt is partially successful in creating human interest for them. While Chesnutt attempts to create pity for her, Rena is simply a victim who accepts her fate, like other antiassimilationist mulattoes of the time. Another character, Dr. Green, is no more than a vehicle to present the traditional Southern viewpoint. Two figures, Molly Walden and George Tyron, retain some individuality. Molly, as an unprotected free black woman in the slave South, is a product of her environment. With the circumstances that she faces, she can do little other than be the kept mistress for the white plantation owner, who has died but left her the house behind the cedars. Chesnutt does not want the reader to feel contempt for her or to be repulsed by her actions; her position is rendered dispassionately. George Tyron, on the other hand, undergoes great emotional upheaval and has a change of view that is probably meant to be instructive. He is tied to the traditional code of the Southern gentleman, but is not deluded about his prerogatives as a Southern aristocrat. Rather, he is meant to be the best of the new South. His realization that he loves Rena and that her racial heritage is not important comes too late; she dies before he is able to do anything about it. He does not blame her for passing, and Chesnutt expects the reader not to blame her.

In *The House Behind the Cedars*, Chesnutt tries to present a mulatto that is not a prop or stereotype, one who deserves interest and sympathy apart from his position on the miscegenation issue. Furthermore, he treats a theme, color consciousness in post-Civil War American life, honestly when most writers were sentimentalizing. This novel, the one for which he will be best remembered, should be read for its historical place in American literature.

Immediately after finishing *The House Behind the Cedars*, Chesnutt began working on his next novel. Events in Wilmington, North Carolina, gave him a race problem for the novel. On November, 1898, during the elections, there had been a bloody race riot in which more than twenty-five blacks were killed, after which white supremacists took over the town government. Chesnutt followed the events of the city after this incident. He learned graphic details when a local Wilmington physician visited him in Cleveland and described what he had seen when the violence was at its peak. Chesnutt also sought information from other friends in the area, and in 1901, he went on a fact-finding trip to Wilmington and Fayetteville.

The Marrow of Tradition is the story of two families: the Carterets stand for the New South aristocracy with its pride and prejudice, and the Millers, who are of mixed blood, represent the qualities of the new black. The lives of the families are intertwined because the wives are half-sisters. Janet Miller, however, has been cheated of her inheritance by Olivia Carteret, and Olivia constantly struggles with the problem of accepting Janet as her rightful sister.

The novel's message—a study of white supremacist politics in a small southern town after the Civil War—is more relevant to the problems encountered by the husbands than those the wives face. Dr. Adam Miller is a brilliant young surgeon denied opportunity in his hometown of Wellington (Wilmington, North Carolina). Major Philip Carteret, editor of the town's newspaper, seeks to seat a white supremacist regime in the local government. If he is successful, Adam Miller's position will be even more intolerable than it has been.

At the end of the novel, Major Carteret stirs up a riot during which Dr. Miller's son is killed. Immediately after the death of the Millers' child, the son of the Carterets becomes ill, and Adam Miller is the only person who can perform the surgery necessary to save the child's life. At first, Miller refuses, but after Olivia Carteret humbles herself before her half-sister and pleads with her to help save the Carterets' son, Janet Miller convinces her husband to change his mind and operate. The child is saved.

The Marrow of Tradition was too controversial a novel for the public. Americans were not ready for the subject of white supremacist politics and the political injustice existing in the South. Chesnutt himself was concerned that the novel approached fanaticism. He believed that he should not speak so plainly concerning these matters if he hoped to succeed as a fiction-writer in the future.

Like the previous two novels, *The Colonel's Dream* seems to have come from a long story that became a novel, even though the manuscript is not in existence. This novel deals with the economic status quo in the South, where caste and class prejudice prevented the rise of nonwhites. Muckraking novels were popular at this time, but there had not been one about the New South. Chesnutt tends to become didactic in this novel, and he relies on overused novelistic machinery such as melodramatic subplots that involve interracial love and a lost inheritance. The novel is almost an economic parable.

The main character in the novel is Colonel Henry French, who, though born and reared in the South, has become a successful businessman in the North. His wife has died, and he has returned to Clarendon, North Carolina, where he hopes his son's health will improve. During the first part of the book, Colonel French, who is respected and admired by the townspeople, successfully reenters Southern life. Although he is a white moderate, he comes to believe that he can unite the races into one society. He is especially concerned with improving the economic situation of Afro-Americans. As he and the people of Clarendon become further and further apart in their understanding of the situation, he finds all of his efforts nullified by racial bigotry, and he must leave in failure. The novel was not successful commercially and is not very satisfying as a work of literature. Chesnutt decided to stop writing novels at this point, and devoted himself to helping his people in other ways.

None of Chesnutt's three published novels was popular with the reading public of the early twentieth century, although *The House Behind the Cedars* enjoyed a modest commercial success. Furthermore, none of the novels can be considered successful artistic endeavors. Chesnutt sought to reveal his views slowly and indirectly so as to lead his readers to the feelings he wanted them to have. Too often, however, his "message" dominates, and he is didactic despite his intentions. His characters are not fully developed, even though Chesnutt attempts to present characters, especially mulattoes and blacks, who are not stereotypes. It may be his strong concern with conveying his views and instructing his readers that prevents his characters from achieving depth. All of these novels are important, however, because Chesnutt was one of the first American novelists to create blacks who were not stereotypes and to deal honestly with racial issues that most Americans of the time preferred to ignore.

Sherry G. Southard

Other major works
SHORT FICTION: *The Conjure Woman*, 1899; *The Wife of His Youth and Other Stories of the Color Line*, 1899.
NONFICTION: *The Life of Frederick Douglass*, 1899.

Bibliography
Andrews, William L. "Charles Waddell Chesnutt: An Essay in Bibliography." *Resources for American Literary Studies* 6 (Spring, 1976): 3-22. A valuable guide to materials concerning Chesnutt.
_____. *The Literary Career of Charles W. Chesnutt*. Baton Rouge: Louisiana State University Press, 1980. A good, full-length study of the full range of Chesnutt's writings.
Gayle, Addison. *The Way of the New World: The Black Novel in America*. Garden City, N.Y.: Anchor Press, 1975. Examines Chesnutt's literary and historical significance as one of the first black American novelists.
Keller, Frances Richardson. *An American Crusade: The Life of Charles Waddell Chesnutt*. Provo, Utah: Brigham Young University Press, 1978. The most helpful and important biographical resource on Chesnutt available.
Render, Sylvia Lyons. *Charles W. Chesnutt*. Boston: Twayne, 1980. A part of the Twayne series on American writers, this volume offers an excellent introduction and critical overview of Chesnutt's life and work.

KATE CHOPIN

Born: St. Louis, Missouri; February 8, 1851
Died: St. Louis, Missouri; August 22, 1904

Principal long fiction
At Fault, 1890; *The Awakening*, 1899.

Other literary forms
In addition to her novels, Kate Chopin wrote nearly fifty poems, approx-imately one hundred stories and vignettes, and a small amount of literary criticism. Her poems are slight, and no serious claims can be made for them. Her criticism also tends to be modest, but it is often revealing. In one piece written in 1896, for example, she discloses that she discovered Guy de Mau-passant eight years earlier; that is, when she first began to write. There is every indication that Maupassant remained one of her most important models in the short-story form. In another essay, she pays tribute to Mary Wilkins Freeman, the New England local colorist whose depiction of repressed passion in women was probably an influence on Chopin's own work. Elsewhere, she seems to distinguish between her own writing and that of the "local-color" school. She is critical of Hamlin Garland for his concern with social problems, "which alone does not insure the survival of a work of art"; and she finds the horizons of the Indiana local-color writers too narrow. The subject of genuine fiction is not regional quaintness, she remarks, but "human existence in its subtle, complex . . . meaning, stripped of the veil with which ethical and conventional standards have draped it." Like Thomas Huxley, much read in her circle, she finds no moral purpose in nature, and in her fiction she fre-quently implies the relativity of morals and received standards.

Chopin's most important work, apart from her novels, lies in the short story. It was for her short stories that she was chiefly known in her time. Her earliest stories are unexceptional, but within only a few years she was pro-ducing impressive work, including a fine series of stories set in Nachitoches Parish, her fictional region. Many of these mature stories are included in the two volumes published during her lifetime—*Bayou Folk* (1894) and *A Night in Acadie* (1897). All of the stories and sketches have now been made available in *The Complete Works of Kate Chopin* (1969). Had she never written *The Awakening*, these stories alone, the best of which are inimitable and gemlike, would ensure Chopin a place among the notable writers of the 1890's.

Achievements
Chopin's reputation today rests on three books—her two short-story col-lections, *Bayou Folk* and *A Night in Acadie*, and her mature novel, *The Awakening*. *Bayou Folk* collects most of her fiction of the early 1890's set in

Nachitoches (pronounced Nack-i-tosh) Parish. The characters it generally portrays, although belonging to different social levels, are Creole, Acadian (Cajun), or black. In many cases they are poor. Not all of the stories in *Bayou Folk* are perfectly achieved, for when Chopin departs from realism into more fanciful writing she loses her power, but three of the stories in this volume— "Beyond the Bayou," "Désirée's Baby," and "Madame Célestin's Divorce"— are among her most famous and most frequently anthologized.

A Night in Acadie collects Chopin's stories from the middle and late 1890's. In many of the stories, the protagonists come to sudden recognitions that alter their sense of the world; Chopin's recurring theme is the awakening of a spirit that, through a certain set of circumstances, is liberated into conscious life. Passion is often the agent of liberation; while in the fiction of William Dean Howells, for example, characters frequently meet and fall putatively in love; in Chopin's fiction, they do so from the inmost springs of their being. There is nothing putative or factitious about Chopin's characters who are brought to the point of love or desire. *A Night in Acadie* differs from *Bayou Folk* somewhat in the greater emphasis it gives to the erotic drives of its characters.

Chopin's authority in this aspect of experience, and her concern with the interaction of the deeply inward upon the outward life, set her work apart from other local-color writing of the time. In her early novel *At Fault*, she had not as yet begun to probe deeply into the psychology of her characters. David Hosmer and Thérèse Lafirme are drawn too much at the surface level to sustain the kind of writing that Chopin does best. After she had developed her art in her stories, however, she was able to bring her psychological concerns to perfection in *The Awakening*, her greatest work. Chopin's achievement was somewhat narrowly bounded, without the scope of the fiction of manners which occupied Howells and Henry James, but in *Bayou Folk*, *A Night in Acadie*, and *The Awakening*, Chopin gave to American letters works of enduring interest—the interest not so much of local color as of a strikingly sensuous psychological realism.

Biography

Kate Chopin was born Katherine O'Flaherty on February 8, 1851, in St. Louis, Missouri, into a socially prominent family with roots in the French past of both St. Louis and New Orleans. Her father, Thomas O'Flaherty, an emigrant to America from Ireland, had lived in New York and Illinois before settling in St. Louis, where he prospered as the owner of a commission house. In 1839, he married into a well-known Creole family, members of the city's social elite, but his wife died in childbirth only a year later. In 1844, he married Eliza Faris, merely fifteen years old but according to French custom eligible for marriage. Faris was the daughter of a Huguenot man who had migrated from Virginia and a woman who descended from the Charlevilles, among the earliest French settlers in America. Kate was one of three children and the only one to live to mature years. In 1855, tragedy struck the O'Flaherty family when the father, a director of the Pacific Railroad, was killed in a train wreck; thereafter, Kate lived in a house of many widows—her mother, grandmother, and great grandmother Charleville. In 1860, she entered the St. Louis Academy of the Sacred Heart, a Catholic institution where French history, language, and culture were stressed—as they were, also, in her own household. Such an early absorption in French culture would eventually influence Chopin's own writing, an adaptation in some ways of French forms to American themes.

Chopin was graduated from the Academy of the Sacred Heart in 1868, and two years later was introduced to St. Louis society, becoming one of its ornaments, a vivacious and attractive girl known for her cleverness and talents as a storyteller. The following year, she made a trip to New Orleans, and it was there that she met Oscar Chopin, whom she married in 1871. After a three-month honeymoon in Germany, Switzerland, and France, the couple moved to New Orleans, where Chopin's husband was a cotton factor (a businessman who financed the raising of cotton and transacted its sale). Oscar Chopin prospered at first, but in 1878 and 1879, the period of the great "Yellow Jack" epidemic and of disastrously poor harvests, he suffered reverses. The Chopin family then went to live in rural Louisiana, where, at Cloutierville, Oscar Chopin managed some small plantations he owned. By all accounts, the Chopin marriage was an unusually happy one, and in time Kate became the mother of six children. This period in Kate's life ended, however, in 1883 with the sudden death, from swamp fever, of her husband. A widow at thirty, Chopin remained at Cloutierville for a year, overseeing her husband's property, and then moved to St. Louis, where she remained for the rest of her life. She began to write in 1888, while still rearing her children, and in the following year she made her first appearance in print. As her writing shows, her marriage to Oscar Chopin proved to be much more than an "episode" in her life, for it is from this period in New Orleans and Natchitoches Parish that she drew her best literary material and her strongest inspiration. She knew this area personally, and yet as an "outsider" was also able to observe it with the freshness of detachment.

Considering the fact that she had only begun to have her stories published in 1889, it is remarkable that Chopin should already have written and published her first novel, *At Fault*, by 1890. The novel is apprenticeship work and was published by a St. Louis company at her own expense, but it does show a sense of form. She then wrote a second novel, *Young Dr. Gosse*, which in 1891 she sent out to a number of publishers, all of whom refused it, and which she later destroyed. After finishing this second novel, she concentrated on the shorter forms of fiction, writing forty stories, sketches, and vignettes during the next three years. By 1894, her stories began to find a reception in Eastern magazines, notably in *Vogue*, *The Atlantic Monthly*, and *Century*. In the same year, her first short-story collection, *Bayou Folk*, was published by Houghton Mifflin to favorable reviews. Even so, because short-story collections were not commercially profitable, she had difficulty placing her second collection, *A Night in Acadie*, which was brought out by a relatively little-known publisher in Chicago in 1897. Although having achieved some reputation as an author of what were generally perceived to be local-color stories set in northern Louisiana, Chopin was still far from having established herself as a writer whose work was commercially profitable. Under the advice of editors that a longer work would have a broader appeal, she turned again to the novel form, publishing *The Awakening* in 1899. *The Awakening*, however, received uniformly unfavorable reviews, and in some cities was banned from library shelves. In St. Louis, Chopin was cut by friends and refused membership in a local fine arts club. Chopin had never expected such a storm of condemnation and, although she withstood it calmly, she was, according to those who knew her best, deeply hurt by the experience. She wrote little thereafter and never published another book. In 1904, after attending the St. Louis World's Fair, she was stricken with a cerebral hemorrhage and died two days later.

With her death, Chopin's reputation went into almost total eclipse. In literary histories written early in the century, her work was mentioned only in passing, with brief mention of her local-color stories but none at all of *The Awakening*. Even in the first biography of Chopin, Daniel S. Rankin's *Kate Chopin and Her Creole Stories* (1932), *The Awakening* was passed over quickly as a "morbid" book. The modern discovery of Chopin did not begin until the early 1950's, when the French critic Cyrille Arnavon translated *The Awakening* into French, with an introduction in which he discussed Chopin's writing as early realism comparable in some respects to that of Frank Norris and Theodore Dreiser. In essays written in the mid-1950's, Robert Cantwell and Kenneth Eble called attention to *The Awakening* as a neglected work of classic stature. The belated recognition of *The Awakening* gained momentum in the 1960's when Edmund Wilson included a discussion of Chopin in *Patriotic Gore: Studies in the Literature of the American Civil War* (1963), in which he described *The Awakening* as a "quite uninhibited and beautifully written [novel] which anticipates D. H. Lawrence in its treatment of infidelity." By the mid-1960's, *The Awakening* was reprinted for the first time in half a century, and critics such as Werner Berthoff, Larzer Ziff, and George Arms all praised it warmly; Ziff called the novel "the most important piece of fiction about the sexual life of a woman written to date in America." With the publication of Per Seyersted's *Kate Chopin: A Critical Biography* (1969) and his edition of her writing, *The Complete Works of Kate Chopin* (1969), Chopin's work at long last became fully available. She has been of particular interest to feminist scholars, but interest in her has not been limited to a single group. It is now generally conceded that Chopin was one of the significant writers of the 1890's, and *The Awakening* is commonly viewed as a small masterpiece.

Analysis

When Kate Chopin began to publish, local-color writing, which came into being after the Civil War and crested in the 1880's, had already been established. Bret Harte and Mark Twain had created a special ambience for their fiction in the American West; Sarah Orne Jewett and Mary Wilkins Freeman had drawn their characters in the context of a New England world in decline; and the Creole culture of New Orleans and the plantation region beyond it had been depicted by George Washington Cable, Grace King, and Ruth McEnery Stuart. A late arriver to the scene, Chopin was at first, as her stories show, uncertain even of her locale. *At Fault*, her first novel, was a breakthrough for her in the sense that she found her rural Louisiana "region." The novel is set in the present, a setting that is important to its sphere of action. Place-du-Bois, the plantation, represents conservative, traditional values which are challenged by new, emergent ones. David Hosmer, from St. Louis, obtains lumber rights on Place-du-Bois, and with him comes conflict. *At Fault* deals with divorce, but beyond that with the contradictions of nature and convention. Place-du-Bois seems at times idyllic, but it is shadowed by the cruelties of its slaveholding past, abuses created by too rigidly held assumptions. St. Louis is almost the opposite, a world as much without form as Hosmer's pretty young wife, who goes to pieces there and again at Place-du-Bois.

A "problem novel," *At Fault* looks skeptically at nature but also at received convention. Intelligent and "thought out," it raises a question that will appear again in *The Awakening*: Is the individual responsible to others or to himself? The characters in *At Fault* tend to be merely vehicles for ideas, while in the short stories that follow it, Chopin's ability to create characters with an emotional richness becomes apparent. If *At Fault* suggests the symmetrical social novels of William Dean Howells, *Bayou Folk* gives the impression of Southern folk-writing brought to a high degree of perfection. The dominant theme in this collection is the universality of illusion, while the stories in *A Night in Acadie* prepare for *The Awakening*, in which a married woman, her self-assertion stifled in a conventional marriage, is awakened to the sensuous and erotic life.

Comparable in kind to Gustave Flaubert's *Madame Bovary* (1857), *The Awakening* is Chopin's most elaborate orchestration of the theme of bondage and illusion. Dramatic in form, intensely focused, it makes use of imagery and symbolism to an extent never before evident in Chopin's work. The boldness of her possession of theme in *The Awakening* is wholly remarkable. Her earliest effort in the novel, *At Fault*, asked if the individual was responsible to others or to himself, a question that is raised again in *The Awakening*.

At Fault, however, deals with its characters conventionally, on the surface only, while in *The Awakening* Chopin captures the deep, inner life of Edna Pontellier and projects it powerfully upon a world of convention.

In *At Fault*, Chopin drew upon her familiarity with two regions, St. Louis and the plantation country north of New Orleans. The hero, David Hosmer, comes to Louisiana from St. Louis, like Chopin herself, and at least one segment of the novel is set in St. Louis. The heroine, Thérèse Lafirme, proprietress of Place-du-Bois, is similar to Chopin, too—a widow at thirty who carries on the management of her late husband's property. Moreover, her plantation of four thousand acres is of the same size as and seems suggested by that of Chopin's father-in-law, who had purchased it from the notorious Robert McAlpine, the model for Harriet Beecher Stowe's Simon Legree in *Uncle Tom's Cabin* (1852). In Chopin's novel, attention is called specifically to McAlpine, the former owner of the property, whose ghost is said to walk abroad at night in expiation of his cruel deeds.

Apart from its two settings, *At Fault* does not seem autobiographical. It has the form of a "problem novel," reminiscent of the novels of Howells, to whom Chopin sent a copy of the work when it was published. As in certain of Howells's novels, a discussion takes place at one point which frames the conflict that the characters' lives illustrate. In this case it is the conflict between nature and convention, religious and social precept versus the data of actual experience. Thérèse Lafirme, although a warm and attractive woman, is accustomed to thinking about human affairs abstractly. When she learns that David Hosmer, who owns a sawmill on her property, is divorced from his young wife, a weak and susceptible woman who drinks, she admonishes him to return to her and fulfill his marriage pledge to stand by and redeem her. Hosmer admires Thérèse to such an extent that, against his own judgment, and most reluctantly, he returns to St. Louis and remarries Fanny Larimore. They then return to the plantation to live, and in due course history repeats itself. Despite Hosmer's dutiful attentions and her acceptance into the small social world of Place-du-Bois, Fanny begins to drink and to behave unreasonably. Near the end of the novel, having become jealous of Thérèse, Fanny ventures out in a storm and, despite Hosmer's attempt to rescue her, dies in a river flood.

Running parallel to this main plot is a subplot in which Hosmer's sister Melicent feels a romantic attraction to Thérèse's impetuous young nephew Grégoire, but decides on the most theoretical grounds that he would not be suitable for a husband. When he becomes involved in a marginal homicide, she condemns him utterly, literally abandoning him. He then returns to Texas, where he goes from bad to worse and is eventually killed in a lawless town. At the end, a year after these events, Hosmer and Thérèse marry and find the happiness they had very nearly lost through Thérèse's preconceptions. It is clear to her that Fanny never *could* have been redeemed, and that her plan to "save" her had brought suffering to all parties concerned—to Hosmer, herself, and to Fanny as well. Left open, however, is the question of Melicent's responsiblity to Grégoire, whom she had been too quick to "judge." *At Fault* appears to end happily, but in some ways it is pessimistic in its view of nature and convention.

At Fault shows a questioning intelligence and has an architectural competence, but it is still apprenticeship work. The St. Louis setting, especially in comparison to her Southern one, is pallid, and the characters encountered there are lifeless. Fanny's associates in St. Louis include Mrs. Lorenzo (Belle) Worthington, who has dyed blonde hair, and Mrs. Jack (Lou) Dawson, who has an expressionless face and "meaningless blue eyes set to a good humored readiness for laughter." These lady idlers, Belle and Lou, are stick figures. Although given a stronger individuality, the more important characters also tend to be typed. Grégoire is typed by his vulnerability and impetuousness, just as Melicent is drawn to type as an immature girl who does not know her mind. The plot of *At Fault* is perhaps too symmetrical, too predictable in its outcome, with the irredeemability of Fanny Larimore a foregone conclusion. Moreover, in attempting to add emotional richness to the work, Chopin has sometimes resorted to melodramatic occurrences, such as Joçint's setting fire to the mill, his death at the hands of Grégoire, the death of Joçint's father Morico, the death of Grégoire, and the scene in which Fanny perishes in the storm. *At Fault* is essentially a realistic novel but resorts at times to romantic or melodramatic conventions. If Chopin fails to bring her novel to life, she does at times create suggestive characters such as Aunt Belindy, Thérèse's cook, who asks pointedly "Whar you gwine live if you don' live in de worl'?" One also notes a tonal richness in the drawing of Thérèse Lafirme. Thérèse is not allowed in this work to be fully "herself," but she points the way to Chopin's later successes in fiction, the women Chopin creates from the soul.

In *The Awakening*, Chopin achieved her largest exploration of feminine consciousness. Edna Pontellier, its heroine, is always at the center of the novel, and nothing occurs that does not in some way bear upon her thoughts or developing sense of her situation. As a character who rejects her socially prescribed role as a wife and mother, Edna has a certain affinity with the "New Woman," much discussed in the 1890's, but her special modeling and the type of her experience suggests a French influence. Before beginning the novel, Chopin translated eight of Guy de Maupassant's stories. Two of these tales, "Solitude" and "Suicide," share with *The Awakening* the theme of illusion in erotic desire and the inescapability of the solitary self. Another, "Reveil," anticipates Chopin's novel in some incidents of its plot. At the same time, *The Awakening* seems to have been influenced by *Madame Bovary*. Certain parallels can be noticed in the experience of the two heroines—their repudiation of their husbands, estrangement, and eventual suicides. More important, Flaubert's craftsmanship informs the whole manner of Chopin's novel—its directness, lucidity, and economy of means; its steady use of incident and detail as *leitmotiv*. The novel also draws upon a large fin-de-siècle background concerned with a hunger for the exotic and the voluptuous, a yearning for the absolute. From these diverse influences, Chopin has shaped a work that is strikingly, even startlingly, her own.

The opening third section of *The Awakening*, the chapter set at Grand Isle, is particularly impressive. Here one meets Edna Pontellier, the young wife of a well-to-do Creole *negociant* and mother of two small boys. Mrs. Pontellier, an "American" woman originally from Kentucky, is still not quite accustomed to the sensuous openness of this Creole summer colony. She walks on the beach under a white parasol with handsome young Robert Lebrun, who befriends married Creole women in a way that is harmless, since his attentions are regarded as a social pleasantry, nothing more. In the background are two young lovers, and not far behind them, keeping pace, a mysterious woman dressed in black who tells her beads. Edna Pontellier and Robert Lebrun have just returned from a midday swim in the ocean, an act undertaken on impulse and perhaps not entirely prudent, in view of the extreme heat of that hour and the scorching glare of the sun. When Edna rejoins her husband, he finds her "burnt beyond recognition." Léonce Pontellier is a responsible husband who gives his wife no cause for complaint, but his mind runs frequently on business and he is dull. He is inclined to regard his wife as "property," but by this summer on Grand Isle she has begun to come to self-awareness, suppressed by her role as a "mother-woman." Emboldened by her unconventional midday swim, she goes out swimming alone that night, and with reckless exhilaration longs to go "further out than any woman had ever swum before." She quickly tires, however, and is fortunate to have the strength to return to the safety of the shore. When she returns to their house, she does not go inside to join her husband but drowses alone in a porch hammock, lost in a long moonlit reverie that has the voluptuous effulgence of the sea.

As the novel proceeds, it becomes clear that Edna has begun to fall in love with Lebrun, who decides suddenly to go to Mexico, following which the Pontelliers themselves return to their well-appointed home in New Orleans. There Edna begins to behave erratically, defying her husband and leading as much as possible an independent existence. After moving to a small house nearby by herself, she has an affair with a young roué, Alcée Arobin; Lebrun returns from Mexico about the same time, and, although in love with her, does not dare to overstep convention with a married woman and the mother of children. Trapped once again within her socially prescribed role, Edna returns to the seashore and goes swimming alone, surrendering her life to the sea.

In its own time, *The Awakening* was criticized both for its subject matter and for its point of view. Reviewers repeatedly remarked that the erotic content of the novel was disturbing and distasteful, and that Chopin had not only failed to censure Edna's "morbid" awakening but also had treated it sympathetically. What the reviewers failed to take into account was the subtlety and ambiguity of the novel's vision. For if Chopin enters deeply into Edna's consciousness, she also stands outside it with a severe objectivity. A close examination of *The Awakening* reveals that the heroine has been involved in illusion from the beginning. Edna sometimes meditates, for example, on the self-realization that has been blunted by her role as wife and mother; but in her rejection of her responsibilities she constantly tends toward vagueness rather than clarity.

The imagery of the sea expresses Edna's longing to reach a state in which she feels her own identity and where she feels passionately alive. The "voice" of the sea, beckoning Edna, is constantly in the background of the work. "The voice of the sea," Chopin writes, "speaks to the soul. The touch of the sea is sensuous, enfolding the body in its soft, close embrace." In this "enfolding," however, Edna discovers her own solitude, and loses herself in "mazes of inward contemplation." In *Moby Dick* (1851), Herman Melville contrasts the land and the sea, the one convention-bound, the other "open" and boldly, defiantly speculative, but Edna is no thinker; she is a dreamer who, in standing apart from conditioned circumstance, can only embrace the rhapsodic death lullaby of the sea. At the end of her life, she returns to her childhood, when, in protest against the aridness of her Presbyterian father's Sunday devotions, she had wandered aimlessly in a field of tall meadow grass that made her think of the sea. She had married her Catholic husband despite her father's objection, or rather, one thinks, *because* of his objection. Later, discovering the limitations that her life with her husband imposes upon her, she rebels once again, grasping at the illusion of an idealized Robert Lebrun. Edna's habit of idealization goes far back in her past. As a girl, she had fallen in love with a Confederate officer whom she had glimpsed, a noble figure belonging to a doomed cause, and also with a picture of a "tragedian." The last lines of the novel, as Edna's consciousness ends, are: "The spurs of the cavalry officer clanged as he walked across the porch. There were the hum of bees, and the musky odor of pinks filled the air." Her consciousness at the end thus reverts back to its beginning, forming a circle from which she cannot escape. The final irony of *The Awakening*, however, is that even though Edna is drawn as an illusionist, her protest is not quite meaningless. Never before in a novel published in America was the issue of a woman's suppressed erotic nature and need for self-definition, apart from the single received role of wife and mother, raised so forcefully. *The Awakening* is a work in which the feminist protest of the present had already been memorably imagined.

In the mid-1950's, Van Wyck Brooks described *The Awakening* as a "small perfect book that mattered more than the whole life work of many a prolific writer." In truth, *The Awakening* is not quite "perfect." Chopin loses some of her power when she moves from Grand Isle to New Orleans. The guests at her dinner party, characters with names such as Mrs. Highcamp and Miss Mayblunt, are two-dimensional and wooden, and at times the symbolic connotation of incidents seems too unvaried. *The Awakening*, certainly, would be embarrassed by comparison with a large, panoramic novel of marital infidelity such as Leo Tolstoy's *Anna Karenina* (1875-1877). Yet, within its limits, it reveals work of the finest craftsmanship, and is a novel that, well after having been read, continues to linger in the reader's consciousness. Chopin was not prolific; all but a few of her best stories are contained in *Bayou Folk* and *A Night in Acadie*, and she produced only one mature novel, but these volumes have the mark of genuine quality. Lyric and objective at once, deeply humane and yet constantly attentive to illusion in her characters' perception of reality, these volumes reveal Chopin as a psychological realist of magical empathy, a writer having the greatness of delicacy.

Robert Emmet Long

Other major works
SHORT FICTION: *Bayou Folk*, 1894; *A Night in Acadie*, 1897.
MISCELLANEOUS: *The Complete Works of Kate Chopin*, 1969 (Per Seyersted, editor, 2 volumes).

Bibliography
Bloom, Harold, ed. *Modern Critical Views: Kate Chopin*. New York: Chelsea House, 1987. Bloom has gathered what he considers "the best criticism devoted to the fiction of Kate Chopin," with contributions by Dyer, Eble, Wolff, Gardiner, to name a few. The introduction relates *The Awakening* to the poetry of Walt Whitman, and the book concludes with an analysis of the mythic pattern of *The Awakening* by Sandra M. Gilbert, a foremost feminist critic. Clearly a valuable study of Chopin and her work. Includes a chronology and a bibliography.
Bonner, Thomas, Jr. *The Kate Chopin Companion*. New York: Greenwood Press, 1988. A guide, arranged alphabetically, to the more than nine hundred characters and over two hundred places that affected the course of Chopin's stories. Also includes a selection of her translations of pieces by Guy de Maupassant and one by Adrien Vely. Contains interesting period maps and a useful bibliographic essay.
Ewell, Barbara, *Kate Chopin*. New York: Frederick Ungar, 1986. This full-length study of Chopin covers her life as a woman and a writer, her short stories, and her two novels, *At Fault* and *The Awakening*. The final chapter examines her poems and final stories. In her notes, Ewell acknowledges Per Seyersted's biography of Kate Chopin as a significant source. Considered the best and most comprehensive study available on Chopin's work in its entirety. Includes a notes section and a bibliography.

Koloski, Bernard, ed. *Approaches to Teaching Chopin's "The Awakening."* New York: Modern Language Association of America, 1988. Part 1 gives background material, bibliographies, and critical studies; part 2 is a compilation of critical essays on *The Awakening* from a variety of perspectives. An excellent resource on Chopin's most distinguished work.

Martin, Wendy, ed. *New Essays on "The Awakening."* New York: Cambridge University Press, 1988. A valuable contribution to the criticism on Chopin's second and last novel, *The Awakening*. Four contributors present their views on this important novel and Edna Pontellier's conflict between individual autonomy and social conformity. The introduction is a wonderfully readable overview of Chopin's life and work. Includes a selected bibliography.

Seyersted, Per. *Kate Chopin: A Critical Biography*. Baton Rouge: Louisiana State University Press, 1969. Seyersted's well-researched biography is still considered an important study on Chopin. Seyersted cites *The Awakening* as a "highly accomplished work of art" in its exploration of the awakening of Edna's erotic passions, but concedes some minor flaws. Should be read in conjunction with more current criticism of Chopin. Also suggested is the two-volume *Complete Works of Kate Chopin* edited by Per Seyersted, Louisiana State University Press, 1969.

Skaggs, Peggy. *Kate Chopin*. Boston: Twayne, 1985. A comprehensive, readable study of Chopin which discusses her life in relation to her literature, analyzes the short stories in *Bayou Folk* and *A Night in Acadie*, and examines both her early novel, *At Fault*, and her "masterpiece," *The Awakening*. The final chapter presents some conclusions based upon the analyses of the works. Includes a selected bibliography.

AGATHA CHRISTIE

Born: Torquay, England; September 15, 1890
Died: Wallingford, England; January 12, 1976

Principal long fiction

The Mysterious Affair at Styles: A Detective Story, 1920; *The Secret Adversary*, 1922; *The Murder on the Links*, 1923; *The Man in the Brown Suit*, 1924; *The Secret of Chimneys*, 1925; *The Murder of Roger Ackroyd*, 1926; *The Big Four*, 1927; *The Mystery of the Blue Train*, 1928; *The Seven Dials Mystery*, 1929; *The Murder at the Vicarage*, 1930; *Giants' Bread*, 1930 (as Mary Westmacott); *The Sittaford Mystery*, 1931 (published in the United States as *The Murder at Hazelmoor*); *The Floating Admiral*, 1932 (with others); *Peril at End House*, 1932; *Lord Edgware Dies*, 1933 (published in the United States as *Thirteen at Dinner*); *Murder on the Orient Express*, 1934 (published in the United States as *Murder on the Calais Coach*); *Murder in Three Acts*, 1934; *Why Didn't They Ask Evans?*, 1934 (published in the United States as *Boomerang Clue*, 1935); *Unfinished Portrait*, 1934 (as Mary Westmacott); *Death in the Clouds*, 1935 (published in the United States as *Death in the Air*); *The A. B. C. Murders: A New Poirot Mystery*, 1936; *Cards on the Table*, 1936; *Murder in Mesopotamia*, 1936; *Death on the Nile*, 1937; *Dumb Witness*, 1937 (published in the United States as *Poirot Loses a Client*); *Appointment with Death: A Poirot Mystery*, 1938; *Hercule Poirot's Christmas*, 1939 (published in the United States as *Murder for Christmas: A Poirot Story*); *Murder Is Easy*, 1939 (published in the United States as *Easy to Kill*); *Ten Little Niggers*, 1939 (published in the United States as *And Then There Were None*, 1940); *One, Two, Buckle My Shoe*, 1940 (published in the United States as *The Patriotic Murders*, 1941); *Sad Cypress*, 1940; *Evil Under the Sun*, 1941; *N or M? The New Mystery*, 1941; *The Body in the Library*, 1942; *Five Little Pigs*, 1942 (published in the United States as *Murder in Retrospect*); *The Moving Finger*, 1942; *Death Comes in the End*, 1944; *Towards Zero*, 1944; *Absent in the Spring*, 1944 (as Mary Westmacott); *Sparkling Cyanide*, 1945 (published in the United States as *Remembered Death*); *The Hollow: A Hercule Poirot Mystery*, 1946; *Murder Medley*, 1948; *Taken at the Flood*, 1948 (published in the United States as *There Is a Tide . . .*); *The Rose and the Yew Tree*, 1948 (as Mary Westmacott); *Crooked House*, 1949; *A Murder Is Announced*, 1950; *Blood Will Tell*, 1951; *They Came to Baghdad*, 1951; *They Do It with Mirrors*, 1952 (published in the United States as *Murder with Mirrors*); *Mrs. McGinty's Dead*, 1952; *A Daughter's a Daughter*, 1952 (as Mary Westmacott); *After the Funeral*, 1953 (published in the United States as *Funerals Are Fatal*); *A Pocket Full of Rye*, 1953; *Destination Unknown*, 1954 (published in the United States as *So Many Steps to Death*, 1955); *Hickory, Dickory, Dock*, 1955 (published in the United States as *Hickory, Dickory,*

Death); *Dead Man's Folly*, 1956; *The Burden*, 1956 (as Mary Westmacott); *4:50 from Paddington*, 1957 (published in the United States as *What Mrs. Mc-Gillicuddy Saw!*); *Ordeal by Innocence*, 1958; *Cat Among the Pigeons*, 1959; *The Pale Horse*, 1961; *The Mirror Crack'd from Side to Side*, 1962 (published in the United States as *The Mirror Crack'd*, 1963); *The Clocks*, 1963; *A Caribbean Mystery*, 1964; *At Bertram's Hotel*, 1965; *Third Girl*, 1966; *Endless Night*, 1967; *By the Pricking of My Thumb*, 1968; *Hallowe'en Party*, 1969; *Passenger to Frankfurt*, 1970; *Nemesis*, 1971; *Elephants Can Remember*, 1972; *Postern of Fate*, 1973; *Curtain: Hercule Poirot's Last Case*, 1975; *Sleeping Murder*, 1976 (posthumous).

Other literary forms

Agatha Christie published approximately thirty collections of short stories, fifteen plays, a nonfiction book (*Come Tell Me How You Live*, 1946), and many omnibus editions of her novels. Under the pen name "Mary Westmacott," Christie published six romantic novels. At least ten of her detective works were made into motion pictures, and *An Autobiography* (1977) was published because, as Christie told *Publishers' Weekly* (1966), "If anybody writes about my life in the future, I'd rather they got the facts right." Sources disagree on the total number of Christie's publications because of the unusual quantity of titles, the reissue of so many novels under different titles, and especially the tendency to publish the same book in England and America under differing titles.

Achievements

Among her many achievements, Christie bears one unusual distinction: she is the only writer whose main character's death precipitated a front-page obituary in *The New York Times*. Christie was a Fellow in the Royal Society of Literature; received the New York Drama Critics' Circle Award for Best Foreign Play of the year in 1955 (*Witness for the Prosecution*); was knighted Dame Commander, Order of the British Empire, 1971; received the Film Daily Poll Ten Best Pictures Award, 1958 (*Witness for the Prosecution*); and was made a Doctor of Literature at the University of Exeter.

Biography

Born at Torquay, Devon, England, on September 15, 1890, the impact of this location on Mary Clarissa Agatha Miller was enormous. Near the end of *Agatha Christie: An Autobiography*, Christie indicates that all other memories and homes pale beside Ashfield, her parents' home in Torquay. "And there you are again—remembering. 'I remember, I remember, the house where I was born. . . .' I go back to that always in my mind. Ashfield." The roots of Christie's self-contained, quiet sense of place are found in her accounts of life at Ashfield. The love of peace, routine, and order was born in her mother's well-ordered household, a household cared for by servants whose nature seemed never to change, and sparked by the sudden whims of an energetic and dramatic mother. Christie's father was Fred Miller, an American, many years older than her English mother, Clara. They were distant cousins and had an exceptionally harmonious marriage because, Christie says, her father was an exceptionally agreeable man. Nigel Dennis, writing for *Life* (May, 1956), says that Christie is at her best in "orderly, settled surroundings" in which she can suddenly introduce disruption and ultimately violence. Her autobiographical accounts of days upon days of peace and routine followed by sudden impulsive adventures initiated by her mother support the idea that, as she says, all comes back to Ashfield, including her mystery stories at their best.

In writing her autobiography, Christie left a detailed and insightful commentary on her works. To one familiar with her autobiography, the details of her life can be found in the incidents and plots of her novels. Frequently, she barely disguises them. She writes, for example, of a recurring childhood dream about "the Gunman," whose outstanding characteristics were his frightening eyes appearing suddenly and staring at her from absolutely any person around her, including her beloved mother. This dream forms almost the entire basis for the plot of *Unfinished Portrait*, a romantic novel written under the pen name "Mary Westmacott." That dream may have been the source of her willingness to allow absolutely any character the role of murderer. No one, including her great Hercule Poirot, is exempt from suddenly becoming the Gunman.

Christie was educated at home chiefly by her parents and her nurse. She taught herself to read before she was five and from then on was allowed to read any available book at Ashfield. Her father taught her arithmetic for which she had a propensity and which she enjoyed. She hated spelling, on the other hand, because she read by word sight and not by the sound of letters. She learned history from historical novels and a book of history that her mother expected her to study in preparation for a weekly quiz.

She did have tutors. A stay in France at about age seven and an ensuing return with a French woman as her companion resulted in her speaking and reading French easily. She also had piano and voice tutors and a weekly dancing class. As she grew older, she attended the theater weekly, and, in her teens, she was sent to a boarding school in France.

She was always allowed to use her imagination freely. Her sensible and beloved nurse went along with her early construction of plots and tales enlisting the nurse as well as dolls and animals to be the characters. She carried on a constant dialogue with these characters as she went through her days. The absence of playmates and the storytelling done within the family also contributed to the development of her imagination. Her mother invented ongoing bedtime tales of a dramatic and mysterious nature. Her elder sister,

Madge, liked to write, and she repeatedly told Agatha one particular story: it was the "Elder Sister" tale. Like the Gunman, the Elder Sister became a frequent personage in her later novels. As a child, Agatha would ask her sister, feeling a mixture of terror and delight, when the elder sister was coming; Madge would indicate that it would be soon. Then a few days later, there would be a knock on Agatha's door and her sister would enter and begin talking in an eerie voice as if she were an elder, disturbed sister who was normally locked up somewhere but at large for the day. The pattern seems similar to that of the Gunman: the familiar figure who is suddenly dangerous. One book in particular, *Elephants Can Remember*, concerns a crazy identical twin sister who escapes from a mental institution, kills her twin, and takes her place in marriage to a man they had both known and loved as young girls.

Besides her sister, Madge, Agatha had an elder brother, Monty, whom she adored. He allowed her to join him frequently in his escapades and was generally agreeable, but, like her father, did not amount to much otherwise and was managed and even supported by his sisters later in his life. "Auntie Grannie" was another strong figure in Agatha's early life. She was the aunt who had reared Clara Miller and was also Fred's stepmother, hence her title. Many critics see in her the basis for the character of Miss Marple.

The picture emerging of Christie is of a woman coming from an intensely female-dominated household where men were agreeable and delightful but not very effective. Female servants and family members provided Agatha with her rigorous, stable values and independent behavior. She grew up expecting little of men except affection and loyalty; in return, she expected to be sensible and self-supporting when possible. Another possible explanation for Christie's self-sufficiency is the emotional support that these surrounding females provided for her. Even after her mother's death in the late 1920's, Agatha always sought the companionship of loyal female servants and secretaries who, in the British Victorian fashion, then became invaluable to her in her work and personal life. Especially in her marriage to Archibald Christie, she relied on her female relatives and servants to encourage, assist, and even love her. The Miss Marples of her world, the Constance Sheppards (*The Murder of Roger Ackroyd*), and the servants were her life's bedrock.

In 1914, Agatha Miller married Colonel Archibald Christie in a hasty wartime ceremony. They had one daughter, Rosamund, whom Agatha adored but considered an "efficient" child. She characterized Rosamund in "Mary Westmacott's" novel *A Daughter's a Daughter*.

Agatha started writing on a dare from her sister but only began writing novels seriously when her husband was away in World War I and she was employed as a chemist's assistant in a dispensary. Finding herself with extra time, she wrote *The Mysterious Affair at Styles*. Since she was familiar with both poisons and death because of her hospital and dispensary work, she was able to distinguish herself by the accuracy of her descriptions. Several other books followed, which were increasingly successful, until *The Murder of Roger Ackroyd* became a best-seller in 1926.

The death of her mother and a divorce from Archie Christie took place about the same time as her success. These sent her into a tailspin which ended in her famous eleven-day disappearance. She reappeared at a health spa unharmed but, to her embarrassment, the object of a great deal of attention; and the public was outraged at the large expense of the search.

In 1930, she married Sir Max Mallowan, an archaeologist, perhaps a more "agreeable" man. Certainly her domestic life after the marriage was peaceful; in addition, she was able to travel with Mallowan to his archaeological dig sites in the Middle East. This gave her new settings and material for her books and enabled her to indulge in one of her greatest pleasures: travel.

In 1930, *The Murder at the Vicarage* was published; it introduced her own favorite sleuth, Miss Jane Marple, who was village spinster and observer of the village scene. By this time, Christie was an established author, and in the 1940's, her books began to be made into plays and motion pictures. In 1952, *The Mousetrap* was launched in London theater and eventually became one of the longest running plays in that city's history. The film version of *Witness for the Prosecution* received awards and acclaim in the early 1950's. *Murder in the Calais Coach* became *Murder on the Orient Express*, a popular American film.

Producing approximately a book a year, Christie has been likened to an assembly line, but, as her autobiography indicates, each book was a little puzzle for her own "grey cells," the conceiving of which gave her great enjoyment and the writing of which took about six to twelve weeks and was often tedious. In 1971, she was knighted Dame Agatha Christie by Queen Elizabeth II and had what she considered one of her most thrilling experiences, tea with the Queen. In 1975, she allowed the book *Curtain: Hercule Poirot's Last Case* to be published and the death of her chief sleuth, Hercule Poirot, to occur. This was of sufficient interest to warrant a front-page obituary in *The New York Times*.

By the time of her own death in 1976, Ellsworth Grant in *Horizon* (1976) claimed that Christie's writings had "reached a wider audience than those of any author who ever lived." More than four hundred million copies of her novels and short stories had been sold, and her works had been translated into 103 languages.

Analysis

Agatha Christie's trademarks in detective fiction brought to maturity the classical tradition of the genre, which was in its adolescence when she began to write. The tradition had some stable characteristics, but she added many more and perfected existing ones. The classical detective hero, for example, from Edgar Allan Poe on, according to Ellsworth Grant, is of "superior intellect," is "fiercely independent," and has "amusing idiosyncracies." Christie's Hercule Poirot was crafted by these ground rules and reflects them in *The Mysterious Affair at Styles* but quickly begins to deplore this Sherlock Holmes type of detecting. Poirot would rather think from his armchair than rush about, magnifying glass in hand, searching for clues. He may, by his words, satirize classical detection, but he is also satirizing himself, as Christie well knew.

Christie's own contributions to the genre can be classified mainly as the following: a peaceful, usually upper-class setting into which violence intrudes; satire of her own heroes, craft, and genre; a grand finale in which all characters involved gather for the dramatic revelation of truth; the careful access to all clues; increased emphasis on the "who" and the "why" with less interest in the "how"; heavy use of dialogue and lightning-quick description, which create a fast-paced, easy read; a consistent moral framework for the action; and the willingness to allow absolutely any character to be guilty, a precedent-setting break with the tradition. Her weakness, contemporary critics claim, is in her barely two-dimensional characters and in their lack of psychological depth.

Christie created, as Grant puts it, a great many interesting "caricatures of people we have met." Grant excuses her on the grounds that allowing every character to be a possible suspect limits the degree to which they can be psychologically explored. One might also attribute her caricatures to her great admiration for Charles Dickens, who also indulged in caricatures, especially with his minor characters. Christie herself gives a simple explanation. She judged it best not to write about people she actually knew, preferring to observe strangers in railroad stations and restaurants, perhaps catching a fragment of their conversation. From this glimpse, she would make up a character and a plot. Character fascinated her endlessly, but, like Miss Marple, she believed the depths of human iniquity were in everyone, and it was only in the outward manifestation that people became evil or good. "I could've done it," a juvenile character cries in *Evil Under the Sun.* "Ah, but you didn't and between those two things there is a world of difference," Poirot replies.

In spite of Christie's simplistic judgment of human character, she manages on occasion (especially in her novels of the 1940's and later) to make accurate and discerning forays into the thought processes of some characters. In *Death Comes in the End*, considerable time is spent on Renisenb's internal musings. Caught in the illiterate role which her time (Egypt, 2000 B.C.) and sex status decree for her, Renisenb struggles to achieve language so she can articulate her anxieties about evil and good. Her male friend, Hori, speaks at great length of the way that evil affects people. "People create a false door—to deceive," he says, but "when reality comes and touches them with the feather of truth—their truth self reasserts itself." When Norfret, a beautiful concubine, enters a closed, self-contained household and threatens its stability, all the characters begin to behave differently. The murderer is discovered precisely because he is the only person who does *not* behave differently on the outside. Any innocent person would act guilty because the presence of evil touches self-doubts and faults; therefore, the one who acts against this Christie truth and remains normal in the face of murder must, in fact, be guilty.

Although *The Mysterious Affair at Styles* is marred by overwriting and explanations that Christie sheds in later books, it shows signs of those qualities that will make her great. The village of Styles St. Mary is quiet, and Styles House is a typical country manor. The book is written in the first-person by Hastings, who comes to visit his old friend John Cavendish and finds him dealing with a difficult family situation. His mother married a man who everyone agrees is a fortune hunter. Shortly afterward, she dies of poison in full view of several family members, calling her husband's name. Hastings runs into Hercule Poirot at the post office; an old acquaintance temporarily residing at Styles, he is a former police inspector from Belgium. Christie's idea in this first novel seems to be that Hastings will play Watson to Poirot's Holmes, although she quickly tires of this arrangement and in a later book ships Hastings off to Argentina.

Every obvious clue points to the husband as the murderer. Indeed, he *is* the murderer and has made arrangements with an accomplice so that he will be brought to a speedy trial. At the trial, it would then be revealed that the husband had an absolute alibi for the time when the poison must have been administered; hence, he and his accomplice try to encourage everyone to think him guilty. Poirot delays the trial and figures out that the real poison was in the woman's own medicine, which contained a substance that would only become fatal if released from other elements. It then would settle to the bottom of the bottle and the last dose would be lethal. Bromide is an ingredient that separates the elements. Bromide was added at the murderer's leisure, and he had only to wait until the day when she would take the last dose, making sure that both he and his accomplice are seen by many people far distant from the household at the time she is declared to have been poisoned. The plot is brilliant, and Christie received congratulations from a chemists' association for her correct use of the poisons in the book.

By the publication of *The Murder of Roger Ackroyd*, her sixth book, Christie had hit her stride. Although Poirot's explanations are still somewhat lengthy, the book is considered one of her best. It is chiefly noted for the precedent it set in detective fiction. The first-person narrator, Dr. Sheppard, turns out to be the murderer. The skill with which this is revealed and concealed is perhaps Christie at her most subtle. The reader is made to like Dr. Sheppard, to feel he or she is being taken into his confidence as he attempts to write the history of Roger Ackroyd's murder as it unwinds. Poirot cultivates Dr. Sheppard's acquaintanceship, and the reader believes, because he hears it from Dr. Sheppard, that Poirot trusts him. In the end, Dr. Sheppard is guilty. Christie allows herself to gloat at her own fiendish cleverness through the very words that Sheppard uses to gloat over his crime when he refers back to a part of his narrative (the story itself is supposedly being written to help Poirot solve the crime) where a discerning reader or sleuth ought to have found him out.

The Body in the Library, executed with Christie's usual skill, is distinctive for two elements: the extended discussions of Miss Marple's sleuthing style and the humorous dialogue surrounding the discovery of the body of an unknown young woman in the library of a good family. Grant says of Jane Marple that she insists as she knits that human nature never changes. O. L. Bailey expands upon this in *Saturday Review* (1973): "Victorian to the core," he writes, "she loves to gossip, and her piercing blue eyes twinkle as she solves the most heinous crimes by analogy to life in her archetypal English village of St. Mary Mead."

Marple, as well as the other characters, comments on her methods. Marple feels her success is in her skeptical nature, calling her mind "a sink." She goes on to explain that "the truth is . . . that most people . . . are far too trusting for this wicked world." Another character, Sir Henry, describes her as "an old lady with a sweet, placid, spinsterish face and a mind that has plumbed the depths of human iniquity and taken it as all in the day's work."

Through a delightfully comic conversation between Mr. and Mrs. Bantry, the possibility of a dead body in the library is introduced, and, once it is discovered, the story continues in standard sleuth style; the opening dialogue, however, is almost too funny for the subject matter. Ralph Tyler in *Saturday Review* (1975) calls this mixture of evil and the ordinary a distancing of death "by bringing it about in an upper-middle-class milieu of consummate orderliness." In that milieu, the Bantrys' dialogue is not too funny; it is quite believable, especially since they do not yet know the body is downstairs.

Perhaps a real Christie aficionado can be identified by his reaction to Tommy and Tuppence Beresford of *The Secret Adversary*, an engaging pair of sleuths who take up adventuring because they cannot find work in postwar England. Critics dismiss or ignore the pair, but Christie fans often express a secret fondness for the two. In Tommy and Tuppence, readers find heroes close to home. The two blunder about and solve mysteries by luck as much as by anything else. Readers can easily identify with these two and even feel a bit protective of them.

Tommy and Tuppence develop a romance as they establish an "adventurers for hire" agency and wait for clients. Adventure begins innocently when Tommy tells Tuppence he has overheard someone talking about a woman named Jane Finn and comments disgustedly, "Did you ever hear such a name?" Later they discover that the name is a password into an international spy ring.

The use of luck and coincidence in the story is made much of by Christie herself. Christie seems to tire of the frequent convenient circumstances and lets Tommy and Tuppence's romance and "high adventure" lead the novel's progress. When Tommy asks Mr. Carter, the British spy expert, for some tips, Carter replies, "I think not. My experts, working in stereotyped ways, have failed. You will bring imagination and an open mind to the task." Mr. Carter also admits that he is superstitious and that he believes in luck "and all that sort of thing." In this novel, readers are presented with a clever story, the resolution of which relies on elements quite different from deductive reasoning or intuition. It relies on those qualities which the young seem to exude and attract: audacity and luck.

In *N or M? The New Mystery*, Tommy and Tuppence (now married and some twenty years older) are again unemployed. Their two children are both serving their country in World War II. The parents are bemoaning their fate when a messenger from their old friend Mr. Carter starts them on a spy adventure at the seacoast hotel of Sans Souci. They arrive with the assumed names Mr. Meadowes and Mrs. Blenkensop. Mrs. Blenkensop, they agree, will pursue Mr. Meadowes and every now and then corner him so they can exchange information. The dialogue is amusing and there is a good deal of suspense, but too many characters and a thin plot keep this from being one of Christie's best.

At times, it seems that Christie withholds clues; that all evidence is presented to the reader is the supreme test of good detective fiction. Mrs. Sprot, adopted mother of Betty, coolly shoots Betty's real mother in the head while the woman is holding Betty over the edge of a cliff. The reader cannot be expected to know that the woman on the cliff is Betty's real mother. Nor can the reader be expected to decipher Tuppence's mutterings about the story of Solomon. In the story of Solomon, two women claim the same baby, and Solomon decrees that the woman who is willing to give up her child rather than have it killed is the real mother. Since both women in this scene *appear* willing to jeopardize the baby's life, the reader is likely, justifiably, to form some wrong conclusions. This seems less fair than Christie usually is in delivering her clues.

In *Sleeping Murder*, written several years before its 1977 publication date, Christie achieves more depth in her portrayal of characters than before: Gwenda, her dead stepmother, Dr. Kennedy, and some of the minor characters such as Mr. Erskine are excellent examples. The motivation in the book is, at least, psychological as opposed to murder for money or personal gain, which are the usual motives in Christie's novels. There seems, in short, to be much more probing into the origin and motivation of her characters' actions.

Her last novel, *Sleeping Murder* ends with the romantic young couple and the wise old Miss Marple conversing on the front porch of a hotel in, of all places, Torquay, Christie's beloved birthplace. Christie came full circle, celebrating her romantic and impulsive youth and her pleasant old age in one final reunion at home in Torquay, England.

Anne Kelsch Breznau

Other major works

SHORT FICTION: *Poirot Investigates*, 1924; *Partners in Crime*, 1929; *The Mysterious Mr. Quin*, 1930; *The Thirteen Problems*, 1932 (published in the United States as *The Tuesday Club Murders*, 1933); *The Hound of Death and Other Stories*, 1933; *The Listerdale Mystery and Other Stories*, 1934; *Parker Pyne Investigates*, 1934 (published in the United States as *Mr. Parker Pyne, Detective*); *Murder in the Mews and Other Stories*, 1937 (published in the United States as *Dead Man's Mirror and Other Stories*); *The Regatta Mystery and Other Stories*, 1939; *The Labours of Hercules: Short Stories*, 1947 (published in the United States as *Labors of Hercules: New Adventures in Crime by Hercule Poirot*); *The Witness for the Prosecution and Other Stories*, 1948; *Three Blind Mice and Other Stories*, 1950; *Under Dog and Other Stories*, 1951; *The Adventures of the Christmas Pudding, and Selection of Entrées*, 1960; *Double Sin and Other Stories*, 1961; *13 for Luck: A Selection of Mystery Stories for Young Readers*, 1961; *Star over Bethlehem and Other Stories*, 1965 (as A. C. Mallowan); *Surprize! Surprize! A Collection of Mystery Stories with Unexpected Endings*, 1965; *13 Clues for Miss Marple: A Collection of Mystery Stories*, 1965; *The Golden Ball and Other Stories*, 1971; *Hercule Poirot's Early Cases*, 1974.

PLAYS: *Black Coffee*, 1930; *Ten Little Niggers*, 1943 (published in the United States as *Ten Little Indians*, 1946); *Appointment with Death*, 1945; *Murder on the Nile*, 1946; *The Hollow*, 1951; *The Mousetrap*, 1952; *Witness for the Prosecution*, 1953; *The Spider's Web*, 1954; *Towards Zero*, 1956 (with Gerald Verner); *The Unexpected Guest*, 1958; *Verdict*, 1958; *Go Back for Murder*, 1960; *Afternoon at the Seaside*, 1962; *The Patient*, 1962; *The Rats*, 1962; *Akhnaton*, 1973.

POETRY: *The Road of Dreams*, 1925; *Poems*, 1973.

NONFICTION: *Come Tell Me How You Live*, 1946; *An Autobiography*, 1977.

Bibliography

Bargainnier, Earl F. *The Gentle Art of Murder: The Detective Fiction of Agatha Christie*. Bowling Green, Ohio: Bowling Green University Popular Press, 1980. A scholarly study which provides a literary analysis of Christie's writings. Individual chapters focus on settings, characters, plots, and so on. Contains a very useful bibliography.

Christie, Agatha. *An Autobiography*. New York: Dodd, Mead, 1977. Published posthumously, this illustrated autobiography covers the first seventy-five years of Christie's life. Christie chose to "remember" those parts of her life which she considered amusing and joyful, while avoiding mention of episodes such as her mysterious disappearance in December, 1926.

Hart, Anne. *The Life and Times of Miss Marple*. New York: Dodd, Mead, 1985. Hart has constructed a brief, 161-page "biography" of Christie's most popular creation, Miss Marple, based upon the twelve novels and twenty short stories in which she appears. A chronology of Miss Marple's fictional life is provided, along with insights into her personality and powers of detection.

Riley, Dick, and Pam McAllister, eds. *The Bedside, Bathtub, and Armchair Companion to Agatha Christie*. New York: Frederick Ungar, 1979. Containing more than two hundred illustrations, this handbook also provides plot summaries of all Christie's novels, plays, and many of her short stories arranged chronologically by first date of publication.

Robyns, Gwen. *The Mystery of Agatha Christie*. Garden City, N.Y.: Doubleday, 1978. Provides a well-written and well-rounded popular biography of Christie. Richly illustrated and contains an appendix with a chronological listing of all Christie's writings. Perhaps the best place to begin a further study of Christie.

Toye, Randall. *The Agatha Christie's Who's Who*. New York: Holt, Rinehart and Winston, 1980. Toye has compiled a dictionary of more than two thousand, out of a total of more than seven thousand, important characters appearing in Christie's sixty-six mystery novels and 147 short stories. For each entry, he attempts to give the character's importance to the story, as well as some memorable characteristics.

Wagoner, Mary S. *Agatha Christie*. Boston: Twayne, 1986. A scholarly, but readable, study of Christie and her writings. A brief biography of Christie in the first chapter is followed by analytical chapters focusing on the different genres of her works, such as short stories. Also contains a good bibliography, an index, and a chronological table of Christie's life.

WALTER VAN TILBURG CLARK

Born: East Orland, Maine; August 3, 1909
Died: Reno, Nevada; November 10, 1971

Principal long fiction
The Ox-Bow Incident, 1940; *The City of Trembling Leaves*, 1945; *The Track of the Cat*, 1949; *Tim Hazard*, 1951.

Other literary forms
Besides his three major novels, Walter Van Tilburg Clark has published one short-story collection, *The Watchful Gods and Other Stories* (1950), and an early poetry volume, *Ten Women in Gale's House and Shorter Poems* (1932).

Achievements
By the time of his death in 1971, Clark's reputation had been largely eclipsed by almost twenty years of inactivity since the publication of his last book. The author of but a slender corpus of work—three novels, one short-story collection, and one volume of poetry—he had suffered the particular misfortune of a talented writer who felt unable to fulfill the promise of a successful first novel. The critical and commercial popularity of *The Ox-Bow Incident* invariably led critics and reviewers to compare his next two novels with his first achievement. The disappointing reception of his second novel, *The City of Trembling Leaves*, and the failure of his third novel, *The Track of the Cat*, to match the response to his first book may have led Clark to become overly sensitive about his work. After 1951, he published no further books during his lifetime, although he left at least two novels uncompleted at his death. His first and third novels, however, were adapted to the screen and became successful motion pictures.

One critic, L. L. Lee, speaks of the personal and human "tragedy" of Clark's abortive writing career. There is no denying that his reluctance to continue publishing was a loss to American letters, but it may well have been that Clark's greatest obstacle was his own rigorous critical standards, which would not allow him to publish anything he suspected was second-rate. He was particularly aware of the need for good writers in the literature of the American West, a field dominated by pulp romances and dime-store paperbacks. In Clark's case, however, literature's loss was teaching's gain, since he enjoyed a distinguished career as a professor of creative writing during the last twenty years of his life, teaching at a half-dozen different colleges and universities in the West and serving as visiting lecturer at many others. Clark is by no means the only writer who has abandoned his craft for the academy, but his particular hesitancy to publish is still unusual, since he was a writer of genuine talent and ability.

Clark was a sensitive and demanding writer with a keen sense of crafts-manship and exacting critical standards. He had little patience with poor writing and no desire to write for a popular market, although he clearly could have done so after the success of his first novel. Nor had he any desire to be pegged as merely another "Western writer." He wanted above all to be a good writer who happened to write about the American West because that was what he knew and understood best. As he observed in a September 1, 1959, letter, "In part, I set about writing *The Ox-Bow Incident* as a kind of deliberate technical exercise." He was determined to take the ingredients of the conventional Western plot and "bring both the people and the situations alive again." He succeeded brilliantly in his tense melodrama of a Nevada rustling incident in 1885, a suspected murder, a posse, a chase, and the lynch-ing of three innocent men by a cowardly and unthinking mob.

Clark's initial success with *The Ox-Bow Incident* was not an accident. The same lean, spare, carefully modulated prose marks his subsequent novels and stories. Clark has mastered several techniques particularly well. First, as an intensely masculine writer, he has an uncanny knack for capturing the lan-guage and behavior of real men. He is careful, however, not to allow artificial or melodramatic elements to intrude upon his characterizations. His char-acters, especially in *The Ox-Bow Incident*, are direct and laconic in speech; there is nothing contrived or romanticized about their conversation or action. In this sense, especially, Clark has rejected the romantic formula used by Owen Wister and others in favor of a realistic, historically accurate treatment of the late nineteenth century West. In the Introduction to his master's thesis on Tristran and Isolde, Clark had argued that the past must be made alive again through literature, and he proceeded to accomplish this reanimation through his own work. The period about which he wrote in both *The Ox-Bow Incident* and *The Track of the Cat* was that transitional period after the Civil War when the West was neither frontier nor fully settled. His town of Bridger's Wells in *The Ox-Bow Incident* is scarcely more than a stagecoach stop with a saloon, a general store, a boardwalk, and a few ramshackle storefronts. The Bridges, the ranching family in *The Track of the Cat*, live in an even more remote mountain valley in the Sierra. Their nearest neighbors live in the next valley. In short, Clark's characters are cattlemen, or else employees of ranchers and cattlemen.

Clark had little material to work with in the Nevada of the 1880's. His society was a raw world of men—violent, transient, and rootless. It was not yet tamed by the more permanent forms of settlement—the family, the school, and the church. As Walter Prescott Webb has pointed out, however, Clark concentrated on three aspects of his world: The spectacular mountain land-scape, the harsh and dramatic weather, and the men themselves. Out of these elements, Clark shaped his Western fiction.

Perhaps Clark demonstrated his finest abilities as a writer in his depictions of the Western landscape and climate—those harsh natural forces and vast stretches of land that distinguish the high plains and mountainous regions. Each of Clark's novels is set in the Nevada region, but the natural environment figures most prominently in *The Ox-Bow Incident* and *The Track of the Cat*; the harsh winter climate of the Sierra Nevada and the imposing presence of the mountains dominate both books. The natural environment functions as more than simply a backdrop or setting—it is a brooding, implacable presence, always to be reckoned with in its sudden storms and heavy, isolating snows. Moreover, it is symbolic of all the latent powers of nature that the white American has tried to subdue.

Clark's characters ignore or defy nature at their peril, since it will eventually have its revenge on them. Clark's white characters lack the wise passivity of the native Americans, the Indians whom he so admired, with their responses to nature shaped by long adjustment to the Western environment. He believed that eventually white Americans in the West would come to resemble the Indian, if their culture survived, but their impulse to dominate and exploit the natural environment would first have to give way to a wise ethic of land-use. As Arthur Bridges comments in *The Track of the Cat*, the American dream-turned-nightmare is a "belly dream" of property greed and material abundance, regardless of the cost to the land itself or to the Indians who had formerly inhabited the land. Clark believed that, unless the white man's attitude to the land could change, natural forces would return to haunt him. In Clark's works, this stance is represented perhaps by the mythic black panther in *The Track of the Cat* or by the darkness and sudden snowstorm that panic the posse into hasty mob revenge and lynch law in *The Ox-Bow Incident*.

Any assessment of Clark's career must return finally to the question of why this talented and gifted novelist failed to fulfill his early promise as a writer. What may finally have thwarted his literary development was not his lack of ability but perhaps the limitations of his genre. He may simply have failed to find a suitable direction for his work after his third novel was published. Although he had exploited the possibilities of the conventional Western myth in his historical Nevada regionalism and local color, he could not break from the restrictions of the formula Western enough to write a really good novel of the modern American West. In fact, his attempt to accomplish this in his second novel, *The City of Trembling Leaves*, resulted in his weakest book. Rather than submit to the endless reiteration of the romantic Western myths and their trappings, Clark quit writing. The tenacity of the Western myth proved more potent, finally, than the resources of his imagination. Clark's dilemma was that of the serious Western writer today: to find ways to reinterpret the history and materials of the West from new perspectives—either through revisionist views of Western history, which would acknowledge the costs as well as the achievements in the winning of the West, or by incorporating other perspectives such as the Spanish-American, native American, or feminist views of the American West.

Biography

The first of four children in an academically talented family, Walter Van Tilburg Clark was born in East Orland, Maine, on August 3, 1909. His parents, Walter Ernest and Euphemia Abrams Clark, were cultured, refined people who introduced their children to music and the arts. Dr. Clark often read to his children in the evenings, and his wife Euphemia, who had studied piano and composition at Columbia University before she turned to social work, encouraged her son to paint and learn to play the piano. Thus, early in life he "developed a love of reading and writing, music and art."

Dr. Walter Ernest Clark enjoyed a distinguished career as economics professor at City College of New York, where he served as chairman of the Economics Department and was awarded the French Legion of Honor during World War I. The Clarks lived in West Nyack, New York, until 1917, when Dr. Clark resigned his position at City College in order to become president of the University of Nevada at Reno, where he served until 1933. Thus, at the age of nine, young Van Tilburg Clark moved to the West, the region that was to become the focus of his later writing. The Clarks did not live a sheltered academic life in Reno. Many of their friends were, in fact, miners and ranchers, and Clark came to know these people well. He also spent much of his time "camping and hiking in the desert hills and the Sierras." Not being native-born, he saw the Western landscape and character afresh, with a sensitivity and receptiveness that is registered in his fiction.

In the city of Reno, Walter Van Tilburg Clark enjoyed an active and conventional adolescence. He attended public schools in the city—Orvis Ring Grammar School and Reno High School—and became an accomplished tennis player. A fictionalized portrait of these years appears in the autobiographical novel, *City of Trembling Leaves*, a *Bildungsroman* that traces the development of the young musician Tim Hazard and his friends as they grow up in Reno during the 1920's. At that time, the city had not yet become a garish gambling and divorce center, and it retained much of its original Western flavor. After high school graduation, Clark entered the University of Nevada in Reno in 1926, majoring in English and earning his B.A. (1930) and his M.A. (1931) there.

While at the university, Clark was active in theater, contributed to the campus literary magazine, and played varsity tennis and basketball. After completing his college work, he decided to remain at Reno and begin his graduate study in English. For his master's thesis he wrote "The Sword-Swinger: The Tale of Tristran Retold," a creative reinterpretation in verse of the Tristran and Isolde legend, to which he added a critical introduction.

Continuing his graduate study in English, he came east in 1931 to the University of Vermont, where he served as a teaching assistant and earned a second M.A. in English in 1934. This time, he concentrated on American literature and the Greek classics, writing his master's thesis on Robinson Jeffers. As Max Westbrook points out, Clark had met Jeffers at the California poet's home, Thor House, and was "immediately impressed." Echoes of Jeffers and E. A. Robinson appeared in Clark's first volume of poetry, *Ten Women in Gale's House*, published in Boston in 1932.

While in graduate school, Clark married Barbara F. Morse in Elmira, New York, on October 14, 1933. They had two children, Barbara Ann and Robert Morse. After he finished his master's study at Vermont in 1934, Clark and his family spent most of the next ten years in the small upstate New York town of Cazenovia, where he taught high school English and dramatics and coached basketball and tennis. There he wrote *The Ox-Bow Incident*, which became a best-seller in 1940. In 1940, Clark went to Indian Springs, Nevada, for a year before returning to Cazenovia. He then taught for a year in Rye, New York, in 1945, before permanently moving to the West with his family a year later. By that time, he had published two novels and had won the O. Henry Prize in 1945 for one of his short stories, "The Wind and the Snow of Winter," an event that influenced him to quit teaching and devote himself to his writing. In 1946, the Clarks lived in Taos, New Mexico, before moving to a ranch in the Washoe Valley and then finally settling in Virginia City. Clark's last published novel, *The Track of the Cat*, appeared in 1949, followed by *Tim Hazard*, the enlarged version of *The City of Trembling Leaves*. Clark then published *The Watchful Gods and Other Stories* in 1950.

After 1950, finding it difficult to sustain his writing career, Clark returned to teaching. He taught creative writing at the University of Nevada until 1953, when he resigned to protest the "autocratic" administration of the university. Following that position, he taught intermittently at a number of schools, including Reed College, the University of Montana, and San Francisco State College. He earned a reputation as a dedicated and demanding creative-writing professor at the University of Montana from 1953 to 1956, before moving to San Francisco State, where he subsequently became director of creative writing from 1956 to 1962. He was awarded an honorary Litt.D. from Colgate University in 1957. In 1962, Clark returned to the University of Nevada in Reno as writer-in-residence, but by that time his career as a writer had virtually ended. He edited the papers of the Western writer Alfred Doten and even began a biography of him, which he did not live to finish. He died from cancer on November 10, 1971, in Reno, leaving two novels incomplete, his early promise as a writer never entirely fulfilled.

Analysis

In the Afterword to *The Ox-Bow Incident*, Walter Prescott Webb quotes

Walter Van Tilburg Clark as saying, "'Though I was born in Maine . . . I am essentially a westerner, and mostly of the desert breed.'" Though not a Westerner by birth and in fact the product of a distinctly eastern academic family, Clark absorbed enough of the history and flavor of his adopted region to consider himself a genuine Western writer. Besides his sense of character and place, he developed what amounted to a native American sensibility—an almost mystical reverence for the natural environment that places his novels in an authentic Western natural setting, one in which mountains, desert, and weather assume the proportions of protagonists in the human drama. This Western sensibility is evident in his first novel, *The Ox-Bow Incident*, and becomes even more pronounced in his third book, *The Track of the Cat*.

The Ox-Bow Incident is by any standards a brilliant first novel, and it won recognition for Clark as a major new talent among Western writers. His novel was praised by critics as the prototype of a new kind of Western that would lend dignity and stature to the genre. Indeed, Clark had accomplished something new in reinvigorating the tired and hackneyed conventions of the Western. As Webb argues, *The Ox-Bow Incident* is a taut, relentless tragedy in five acts. It portrays all of the familiar archetypes of the Western experience— good men and bad, thieves and outlaws, cattlemen and rustlers, sheriffs and posses—yet it manages to retell the story in a new way.

Dealing with the attempt to establish law and order in a lawless land, the novel does not, however, allow justice to be served in the conventional fashion of the Western romance. Instead, in Clark's novel, a posse's attempt to take the law into its own hands results in a miscarriage of justice. After an all-night pursuit and capture, three innocent men are tried, convicted, and hanged on the basis of compelling but misleading circumstantial evidence. The posse is browbeaten into taking revenge by a sadistic and psychopathic leader, Gerald Tetley, a former Confederate officer turned cattleman who hungers for swift justice and has little use for the formalities of the law. There are no other potential leaders to speak for restraint and due process or to stand up to Tetley's domineering egotism, although the old storekeeper, Arthur Davies, tries, later blaming himself for lacking the courage to defy Tetley. These events, the report of a supposed murder, the formation of the posse, and the pursuit and capture of the supposed rustlers all occur within twenty-four hours. The novel is narrated in the first person by Art Croft, a cowhand who has wandered down from the mountains to Bridger's Wells after spending the winter with his buddy, Gil Carter, holed up in a cabin on the winter range. He is deputized into the posse against his better judgment and serves as an unwilling participant in and observer of the subsequent action.

While the ostensible theme of the novel is the weakness and culpability of the mob deputized to pursue the alleged rustlers, the abiding issue is the establishment of justice in the West. One might argue that as regions of the West passed from territory into statehood, the status of the law also changed from the near anarchy of "natural law," to the rough and ready status of common law or territorial law, to the more fixed and certain statutory law that was finally imposed. Men in a lawless region are always ready to take the law into their own hands, and Clark dramatizes the tragic consequences of lynch law, particularly for the young cattleman Donald Martin, who leaves a widow and two young children. Martin, who has the misfortune to be caught driving another man's cattle without a bill of sale, has committed no greater crime than rashness and lack of foresight.

There are obviously no heroes in this novel—only villains and victims—and everyone is tainted in some way by mob violence or moral cowardice. The mob in fact takes on a kind of collective identity that reminds one of Reinhold Niebuhr's observation about groups and nations behaving less responsibly than individuals. The common enemy is rumor and impulsiveness, and in the absence of responsible leaders, the mob is easily swayed by demagogues. In a town inflamed by rumors of rustling and murder, the forces of law and order are ironically absent, or are unable to dissuade the mob from setting forth hastily (and, as it turns out, illegally) in pursuit of the rustlers. Clark once wrote in a letter that the novel contained a veiled warning against the threat of Fascism, and one might even call it a parable about the fate of justice in a democracy that degenerates into mob rule.

Clark's second novel, *The City of Trembling Leaves*, was a very different kind of book, one which some critics suspected he had written previous to *The Ox-Bow Incident*. A rather unconvincing "portrait of the artist as a young man" in Reno, the novel tells the story of Tim Hazard, a sensitive, young artist *manqué* who hopes to become a musician. Unfortunately, too much of the novel is preoccupied with Hazard's adolescence and high school experiences and too little with his later accomplishments. Too much of the book is about wanting to be an artist—or rather about the burden of growing up with an artistic temperament in a philistine society—rather than with the specifics of musical training and the development of a career. Tim Hazard does not mature into a convincing American composer; he remains too much the sensitive and troubled adolescent. Nor does he evidence a strong will to succeed or triumph over adverse circumstances. In short, the protagonist is not a convincing or interesting enough character to fill a 690-page novel. The book does not compare well with Willa Cather's *The Song of the Lark* (1915), for example, which brings the heroine, Thea Kronborg, out of the provincial West and back to Chicago, and eventually to a distinguished opera career in New York. *The City of Trembling Leaves* is, in short, the kind of novel a young writer will often try once, and then put aside without publishing. It merely demonstrates that Clark's true métier was the frontier West.

In his third novel, *The Track of the Cat*, Clark returned to Nevada frontier material in his powerful account of the Bridges family, isolated on their mountain ranch deep in the Sierra, and their attempts to stalk a panther that has been ravaging their cattle. The action takes place during a winter blizzard as the three brothers—Arthur, Curt, and Harold—set out successively to hunt down the killer mountain lion. The quest itself becomes something of a parable of the American dream, about the discovery, settlement, and exploitation of the West. Through the Bridges family, Clark explores the question of the American's proper relationship with the land—as dreamer, exploiter, or preserver—with the black panther representing the violent and unpredictable forces of nature that oppose man's attempts to subdue the land. The novel's action shifts between the Bridges' ranch and the surrounding valley and rugged mountain ranges as the brothers attempt to track the cat and thus meet their fate. The thematic focus alternates between dream and reality as each of the brothers dreams his fate before he meets it.

In Part One, Arthur, the impractical dreamer, trusting too much in the goodness of the natural world, is ambushed and killed by the cat. The second part of the book shifts back to the Bridges family, whose unnatural tensions and conflicts are heightened by the suspense of waiting for Arthur's return and the confinement enforced by the storm. The father, a maudlin alcoholic, escapes from the present by heavy drinking; the mother, a cold, bitter, religious woman, tried to interfere with her youngest son Harold's engagement to Gwen Williams, who is visiting from a nearby ranch; and the sister, Grace, is a hysterical spinster. The entire family represents, as L. L. Lee suggests, the decline in the American pioneer stock and its ideals, which were never very noble. The land seems to harden and distort the character of these people, making them ruthless and exploitative; there is none of the Indian's reverence or understanding of the land. Instead, these people live isolated and apart from nature without roots, connections, or a sense of place. The old Piute, Joe Sam, who works with the Bridges as a farmhand, suggests the gap between the native American and white cultures and the inability of the white to learn or benefit from the Indian.

In Part Three, the longest section of the novel, Curt's dream turns to nightmare as he sets out to find his brother Arthur and becomes lost and disoriented in the storm. His arrogant self-sufficiency proves inadequate in the face of the prolonged storm, until he cannot tell whether he is tracking or being tracked by the great cat, who comes to assume in Curt's confused imagination the proportions of Joe Sam's mythological panther. After two days of hunger and exposure, Curt loses his bearings in the storm and panics, believing he is being pursued; he runs away wildly, finally plunging over a snow-covered cliff.

In Part Four, Curt's frozen body is finally found the following day by Harold, the youngest brother, and Joe Sam. Harold, who combines reverence for the cat with common sense and decency to the old Indian, finally kills the cat and puts an end to its slaughter of their herd. Presumably, he will also marry Gwen Williams and carry on the family's ranch, eventually earning his birthright to the land and becoming a true Westerner. He will find a way to combine the white American's energy and enterprise with the Indian's reverence for the land and sense of the sacredness of the natural world. This introduction of serious themes to an otherwise romanticized genre perhaps marks Clark's most lasting contribution to the literature of the American West.

Andrew J. Angyal

Other major works
SHORT FICTION: *The Watchful Gods and Other Stories*, 1950.
POETRY: *Ten Women in Gale's House and Shorter Poems*, 1932.
NONFICTION: *The Journals of Alfred Doten, 1849-1903*, 1973 (3 volumes).

Bibliography

Alt, John. "*The City of Trembling Leaves*: Humanity and Eternity." *South Dakota Review* 17 (Winter, 1979-1980): 8-18. Although Clark's novel begins with a tribute to the spiritual healing of nature, its story complicates that theme. Human beings gain much from nature, but it is also aloof and threatening. The focus of this theme is on the growth of the character of Hazard, who realizes that his drive for rationality must be frustrated by nature itself. The novel concludes with an affirmative stance: that what is good is in the commonality of living.

Carpenter, Fredric I. "The West of Walter Van Tilburg Clark." *College English* 13 (February, 1952): 243-248. The special features of Clark's writing derive from his geographical perspective of an adopted Westerner reared in the environment of an American college. Analyzes *The City of Trembling Leaves* as an autobiographical novel of adolescence, and then examines *The Ox-Bow Incident* and *The Track of the Cat* as Clark's best novels. The first is clearer but not more important than the second, which is very psychological and symbolic, with its theme of man against nature. Also uses some of his stories, including "The Indian Well" and "The Anonymous," to illustrate themes of alienation and loneliness symbolized by the western wasteland of Nevada. Clark's strengths are in the originality and richness of his stories, while his weakness is his artistic self-consciousness, which affects his style.

Haslam, Gerald. "Predators in Literature." *Western American Literature* 12 (1977): 123-131. Citing the work of Joseph Campbell, Max Westbrook, and B. Malinowski, Haslam studies the mythic/symbolic level of the sacred in the art of Robinson Jeffers' poetry and Clark's stories, a natural comparison to make, since Clark wrote a thesis on Jeffers. These writers illustrate the symbolic meaning of predators, who communicate love-hate relationships and reflect the basic duality in human beings. Rattlesnakes in "The Watchful Gods," the black panther in *The Track of the Cat*, and the hawk in "Hook" are used for illustrating this theme in Clark's work.

Laird, Charlton, ed. *Walter Van Tilburg Clark: Critiques*. Reno: University of
Nevada Press, 1983. A collection of testaments and essays commemorating
the life and writing of Clark. Much is by Clark's son, Robert, and some
comes from lectures and a seminar given at the University of Nevada,
Reno, in 1973-1974. After a letter to his son by Clark, serving as a
"credo," the book is arranged in four main parts: a group of four essays
on Clark, "As Others Knew Him," including an appreciation by Wallace
Stegner; nine essays on various aspects of Clark's major published works,
including essays of commentary on three by Clark himself; three essays
which analyze the art of Clark's writings; and an autobiographical sketch
by Walter Clark and a chronology by Robert M. Clark. Includes an index.

Lee, L. L. "Walter Van Tilburg Clark's Ambiguous American Dream." *College English* 26 (February, 1965): 382-387. Clark's fiction is a criticism of
the American Dream, but because he accepts some of the dream, his work
is indirect and not entire. Under the surface of his stories, he works as
an effective ironist who is both a moralist and a realist. "The Watchful
Gods," *The Track of the Cat*, *The City of Trembling Leaves*, and *The Ox-
Bow Incident* are analyzed to illustrate the ambiguity of the dream, caused
by Clark's ironic treatment of it, as in the focus on Davies, the storekeeper,
in the last novel. Justice is shown to be possible only in the hands of
individuals, never in groups or mobs of people.

Westbrook, Max. *Walter Van Tilburg Clark*. New York: Twayne, 1969. Argues
that, since the success of *The Ox-Bow Incident*, Clark's novels have been
misread. A correct reading recognizes a paradox in his writing: that individuals have a duty to be free in American democracy. After a short
biography, examines the place of Clark's writing in the tradition of the
Western and analyzes Clark's four novels in detail: the archetypal ethic in
The Ox-Bow Incident, the ironic qualities of *The City of Trembling Leaves*,
the sense of doom in *The Track of the Cat*, and the self-reflectiveness of
The Watchful Gods. Also reviews some of Clark's poetry and short stories,
and assesses his accomplishments as relevant to the troubling problems of
modern America. Includes a chronology, notes and references, a selected,
annotated bibliography, and an index.

_____. "Walter Van Tilburg Clark and the American Dream." In *A
Literary History of the American West*. Fort Worth: Texas Christian University Press, 1987. An authoritative chapter which scrutinizes the place of
Clark in American literary history. *The Ox-Bow Incident* is credited with
beginning a phase of realism in Western novels and films, but *The City of
Trembling Leaves* raises doubts about realism. In addition, Clark's writing
does not show signs of the author's living through the extraordinary experiences of the Great Depression, World War II, and international tensions
with Communist countries. The answer is that his central concern was the

American Dream and its consequences. This aligns Clark with America's major writers, such as Herman Melville, Henry Adams, Henry James, and perhaps William Faulkner and Ernest Hemingway as well, who all examined how the American Dream can turn into nightmare. Contains a selected bibliography of primary and secondary sources.

J. M. COETZEE

Born: Cape Town, South Africa; February 9, 1940

Principal long fiction

Dusklands, 1974; *In the Heart of the Country*, 1977; *Waiting for the Barbarians*, 1980; *Life & Times of Michael K*, 1983; *Foe*, 1986; *Age of Iron*, 1990.

Other literary forms

J. M. Coetzee has published a number of book reviews and essays, primarily dealing with South African authors and Thomas Hardy. In *White Writing: On the Culture of Letters in South Africa* (1988), he surveys South African literature from its beginnings up to, but not including, World War II.

Achievements

Coetzee is recognized as one of South Africa's finest writers, one whose allegorical fiction suggests that apartheid is but a particularly virulent expression of man's will to dominate. At the same time, like many contemporary writers, he is acutely aware of problems of language and representation, and his fiction reflects an increasing preoccupation with the complex interplay of language, imagination, and experience. It is Coetzee's distinctive achievement to fuse such philosophical concerns with probing social and psychological insights.

Although Coetzee's career is very much in progress, he has already received many prestigious literary awards. His second book, *In the Heart of the Country*, won South Africa's premier literary award, the Central News Agency (CNA) prize, in 1977. *Waiting for the Barbarians*, chosen as one of the Best Books of 1982 by *The New York Times*, won the CNA prize, the Geoffrey Faber Memorial Prize, and the James Tait Black Memorial Prize; *Life & Times of Michael K* won Great Britain's Booker Prize in 1983. In 1987, Coetzee received the Jerusalem Prize for writing "that contributes to the freedom of the individual in society."

Biography

John Michael Coetzee was born in Cape Town, South Africa, in 1940; he was educated in computer science and in linguistics in South Africa and the United States, and he received his Ph.D. in linguistics from the University of Texas in 1969. He served as an assistant professor of English at the State University of New York at Buffalo, and later as a lecturer in English at the University of Cape Town.

Analysis

Although contemporary South Africa is seldom mentioned or referred to explicitly in J. M. Coetzee's novels, the land and the concerns of that country permeate his works; one may see this indirect approach as an evasion of the censorship which must be a factor for any writer in that state, but this necessary blurring of temporal and geographic actualities also endows each work with universal overtones. On one level, Coetzee's novels deal with the suffering that human beings inflict on one another, whether as agents of the state or as the victims of their own obsessions. On another level, concurrent with this one, the obsessions and those in their grip form the major thematic centers of the greater part of his fiction.

Coetzee's first major work, *Dusklands*, is composed of two novellas, *The Vietnam Project* and *The Narrative of Jacobus Coetzee*; the common thread that runs through the two seemingly unrelated pieces is the obsession of each protagonist with the personal dimension of colonization. Eugene Dawn, the narrator of *The Vietnam Project*, is a mythographer inquiring into the efficacy of America's propaganda in Vietnam. His discoveries are disturbing and soul-shattering to the point that Dawn is driven to kidnap his child from his estranged wife and use him as a hostage. In the course of his confrontation with the police, Dawn stabs his son, marveling at the ease with which the knife slips into the flesh. He is last seen in an insane asylum, his consciousness peopled with images of power and powerlessness.

The second novella purports to be a narrative of an eighteenth century Boer settler, translated from the Dutch by J. M. Coetzee, with an afterword by Coetzee's father. The account relates a trek undertaken ostensibly to hunt elephants but really to see what lies beyond the narrator's immediate environment. The decorous, antiquarian headings which break up the narrative—"Journey Beyond the Great River," "Sojourn Among the Great Namaqua"—contrast strangely to the horrors endured both by the narrator and by the tribespeople he meets. Stricken with illness, Jacobus remains with the not-yet-colonized Namaqua, whose relations with him are at times contemptuous, at times nurturing, but never the expected ones of respectful native to European explorer. Jacobus' Hottentot servants desert him to stay with the Namaqua, and naked, unarmed, and alone, he returns to civilization after an arduous journey. He goes back to the land of the Namaqua with troops and takes his revenge on the tribespeople, who have shown him less respect than he wanted.

Throughout, the narrator hints, almost unconsciously, at what he is seeking: a sense of limits, and therefore a definition of his self. This motif is introduced in the first novella by Dawn's analysis of the hate felt by Americans toward the Vietnamese: "Our nightmare was that since whatever we reached for slipped like smoke through our fingers, we did not exist. . . . We landed on the shores of Vietnam clutching our arms and pleading for someone to stand up without flinching to these probes of reality. . . but like everything else they withered before us."

This concern with boundaries seems to stem from the physical environment of the vast African plain, into which Jacobus expands endlessly but joylessly. There are no rules, and Jacobus is worried by the possibility of "exploding to the four corners of the universe." There is an unmistakable grandeur in such a concept, one that reflects the position of the powerful in relation to the powerless, but it is a qualified grandeur. It is one that Coetzee's protagonists reject, drawing back from the spurious apotheosis of limitless being, understanding that it is not worth the dreary awareness of the void. Transcendence cannot occur when there is nothing to transcend.

Indeed, transcendence is the object of the quest for all of Coetzee's main characters, and what they seek is the obstinate, obdurate object that will resist them to the point that they know that they exist, and against which they may define themselves. This quest is an important factor in Coetzee's second book, *In the Heart of the Country*, a novel written in the form of a diary kept by a young woman on a sheep farm. The farm is isolated in the featureless landscape, and Magda has recourse to fantasies, terrible and bloody, of revenge on her father, who to her has always remained an "absence." Little by little, Magda peoples her life, writes variations on reasons that she wants to kill her father, imagines situations in which she becomes the servant of her father and his brown mistress, and ultimately kills him, more or less by accident, while he is making love to Anna, the wife of the servant Hendrik. The uncertainty of the act's reality lingers after the occurrence; the father really has been shot, however, and takes several days to die.

At this point, the diary takes on a more straightforward tone, as if the difficulty of disposing of the body has finally focused Magda's life. Hendrik and Anna are moved into the house, and Magda begins sleeping with Hendrik, who now seems to despise her and who treats her as if she were the servant. Eventually, worried that they will be blamed for the murder of Magda's father, Hendrik and Anna disappear in the middle of the night, and Magda is left alone in the great house.

Without money, without any visible means of support, she manages to live into an old age in which she hears voices from airplanes passing overhead. The voices say things which she takes to be comments on her condition: "Lacking all external enemies and resistances, confined within an oppressive narrowness and regularity, man at last has no choice but to turn himself into an adventure." The solipsism which is evidenced in the earlier part of the diary (and which is a function of the diary form) is thus recalled to cast doubt on the truth of what Magda has been writing. Has all the foregoing been the product of a spinster's fevered imagination? Every event surrounding the father's murder and burial may have been so, and Magda herself wonders whether her father will come striding back into her life. Yet the one point in which Magda truly lives is the point where her father has ceased being an absence, when the weight and increasing rigidity of his corpse have lent reality to his dutiful daughter's heretofore thwarted love.

This relationship between the violent act and the affirmation of one's identity, along with the connection between hate and love, between master and slave, between the tortured and the torturer, forms the central theme of *Waiting for the Barbarians* (the title of which alludes to a poem by C. P. Cavafy). An unnamed, aging magistrate of a town on the far borders of "the Empire" narrates the story of an attempt by the Empire to consolidate its northern border against the depredations of "the barbarians," nomads who have heretofore existed peacefully—with the exception of some dubious raids—in the face of increasing expansion by the agrarian settlers. The magistrate is far more interested in comfort, his books, and his antiquarian researches into the ancient sand-buried buildings near the town than he is in the expansion of empire. He is disturbed by the arrival of the sinister Colonel Joll of the "Third Bureau," a police force given special powers for the duration of the "emergency."

At first, the magistrate merely resents the intrusion of such affairs into the somnolent world that keeps him comfortable. He is severely shaken, however, by the torture of two obviously innocuous prisoners (and the killing of one of them) by Joll. As a result, the magistrate is compelled to place himself, quiet servant of the Empire, in opposition to the civilization to which he has been dedicated.

Joll has taken out an expedition to capture barbarians, some of whom he interrogates upon his return. The magistrate cannot simply ignore what is happening, but neither can he act. When Joll leaves, the barbarians are released and they depart; they have left behind a girl who has been tortured: Her eyes have been burned and her ankles broken in order to wring information from her father. The magistrate takes her into his house and enters into a bizarre relationship with her, one which consists of washing her swollen feet and badly healed ankles; the washing progresses to the other parts of her body, but there is no straightforward sexual act. During these ministrations, both the magistrate and the girl fall asleep, a normal sleep for the girl but a heavy drugged torpor for the man.

He cannot fathom his fascination with this girl who has been so cruelly marked, but he begins to understand that perhaps it is her damaged quality which so attracts him. She is unresponsive to him, accepting his tenderness as he imagines she accepted her torture, passive, impenetrable. He decides to take her back to her people after he realizes that to her, he and Colonel Joll are interchangeable, two sides of the same empire.

After an arduous journey, he and his small party come face-to-face with the barbarians in the mountains; he gives the girl back to them, since she expresses her desire to leave him and civilization. Upon his return, he is arrested by the occupying force of the Empire on charges of collaborating with the barbarians. A new policeman has installed himself in his office, and the magistrate goes to his cell almost gladly: "I had no duty to her save what it occurred to me to feel from moment to moment: from the oppression of such freedom who would not welcome the liberation of confinement?"

He manages to escape, but returns, knowing that he cannot survive in the open spaces. Eventually he is released: The expedition against the barbarians has been a dismal failure, the town is emptying of soldiers and civilians, and the Empire is crumbling at the edges. He assumes his former responsibilities and tries to prepare the town for approaching winter. The novel ends with the same image that has haunted his dreams: children playing in the snow in the town square. Yet the children are making a snowman, not a model of the empty town, and the faceless girl is not among them.

The Empire could be anywhere: Its geography encompasses Africa as well as Mongolia or Siberia. The townspeople are not described physically, and the barbarians' description is that of Mongols. Colonel Joll and the warrant officer—and their methods—evoke the Gestapo, the KGB, or, for that matter, the South African police. The time appears to be set in a future so distant that sand dunes have engulfed buildings of staggering antiquity. What does endure, Coetzee seems to be saying, are the sad constants of human history: the subjugation of the weak by the strong, the effects of slavery on masters as well as slaves, and the impotence of good intentions. If the magistrate has survived, it is because the Empire has considered his rebellion of no consequence.

It is difficult to present limited expectations as an affirmation of the value of life. This subject, touched on in *Waiting for the Barbarians*, is realized in *Life & Times of Michael K*, a novel set in a South Africa of the future. Coetzee had, until this novel, furnished his readers with introspective, articulate narrators who reveal their complicated thoughts in precise language. With *Life & Times of Michael K*, he departed from this pattern.

Michael K's survival is precarious from the beginning of his life; born with a deformed lip, he must be painstakingly fed with a spoon by a mother repelled by his appearance. Anna K, a domestic worker, takes him with her when she works. When he reaches school age, he is put in an institution for the handicapped, where he learns a bit of reading and writing and the skills of the unskilled: "scrubbing, bedmaking, dishwashing, basket weaving, woodwork, and digging." Eventually, at the age of fifteen, he joins the Parks and Gardens service and becomes a gardener, a job to which he returns after an attempt at night work.

At the age of thirty-one, K receives a message to fetch his mother from the hospital. For a time, they live together in Anna's old "servant's room"—a windowless cubicle under a staircase, originally meant for air-conditioning equipment that was never installed—but a riot in the vicinity of the apartment buildings convinces them to leave. Anna, as her dropsy gets worse, harbors a confused dream of returning to the farm where she spent her child-hood. She has saved some money, and K attempts to buy a railroad ticket, but a bureaucratic nightmare of reservations and permits forces them to walk, the son pushing his mother on a two-wheeled cart which he has built with persistence and ingenuity.

They travel through a disquieting landscape: At times thronged with people leaving the city, at times ominously empty, the roads are the domain of enormous army convoys, whose purpose and destination remain un-known, but which, along with the riots in the cities, indicate an ongoing civil war in the unnamed country.

Towns still exist, however, and it is in one of these that Anna and K stop; exhaustion and exposure to the cold rain have aggravated the mother's ill-ness, and K takes her to a hospital where, after a few days, she dies. A nurse hands K a box of ashes, tells him that these are his mother's remains, and sends him on his way. He is robbed of his money by a soldier, but he keeps his mother's ashes, until he reaches an abandoned farm which might be the one mentioned by his mother. He decides to live there. There is a windmill pump on the farm, and its leaking has formed an oasis in the barren land. K plants a garden there and sprinkles his mother's ashes over the soil.

A grandson of the departed owners appears, seeking safety from what is happening in the cities. Dimly, K realizes that if he stays, it will be as a ser-vant to this boy; he therefore shuts off the pump so that everything will die and he leaves.

He is interned in a work camp from which he escapes, returns to the farm, and again plants his garden, the boy is gone, and K builds himself a shelter with stones and a piece of corrugated iron. One day, he sees men approach-ing. From concealment, he is somehow aware that these men must be "the other side," the antagonists to the dispirited government soldiers he has known. Although their donkeys destroy half his crop, K feels sympathy with these men. He makes plans to tend his garden so that there will be many crops and they will have more to eat when they come back. Ironically, the next soldiers are government soldiers, who appear months later, and they arrest K under suspicion of being connected to the rebels. They destroy the garden, explode the pump, and burn the farmhouse. K is again interned.

Up to this point, the third-person account has been from K's point of view: a registering of random impressions by someone who has no language to impose a pattern on events, who seldom wonders how he must appear, and who periodically achieves states approaching the meditative or vegetative. The second section is a first-person narrative by the medical officer—a phar-macist in civilian life, but it seems that many old men have been called back to military service, indicating that the civil war has spread everywhere—of K's new camp. An articulate, compassionate man, reminiscent of the mag-istrate in *Waiting for the Barbarians*, he is by turns annoyed and inspired by

K's refusal to eat "the food of the camp." When K escapes, the medical officer convinces the aged commandant of the camp to report him dead.

K has returned to the city whence he set out, and there he falls in with others who live by scavenging; he undergoes a sexual initiation among these people, who mean him no harm but by whom he is repelled. At the end of the third section, K has gained self-consciousness. His thoughts are now phrased in the first person and told to the reader: "I am a gardener." This burst of self-awareness does not cut his ties to what he has been before; the final image is an emulation of the slow, patient rhythms of the earth: " . . . he would bend the handle of the teaspoon in a loop and tie the string to it, he would lower it down the shaft deep into the earth, and when he brought it up there would be water in the bowl of the spoon; and in that way, he would say, one can live."

Coetzee has been accused of being too political in his concerns and also of not being political enough; to accuse him of either is to miss the point of his novels. He is concerned with humanity, and what it means to be human. In *Waiting for the Barbarians*, the magistrate says of his torturers, "They came to my cell to show me the meaning of humanity, and in the space of an hour they showed me a great deal." To be human is to suffer, but the one who causes the suffering also suffers, and also is human. His hatred is twisted love, a rage against the victim for not pushing back, not allowing him humanity. This is the root of all evil in the world, and this is what Coetzee shows. Humanity's history is one of suffering, and the only way to escape suffering is to live outside history.

Jean-Pierre Metereau

Other major work

NONFICTION: *White Writing: On the Culture of Letters in South Africa,* 1988.

Bibliography

Castillo, Debra A. "The Composition of the Self in Coetzee's *Waiting for the Barbarians*." *Critique: Studies in Modern Fiction* 27 (Winter, 1986): 78-90. An in-depth examination of this novel, noting that Coetzee carefully charts "the physical and mental topography" of a fictitious place and, in so doing, invites readers to confront "the essential nature of both history and the self in history." A valuable criticism of this novel with comments on Coetzee's theme of the seductress and the magistrate's relation to her, which leads to his downfall and "degradation to animality."

Flower, Dean. "Fiction Chronicle: A Review of the *Life & Times of Michael K* by J. M. Coetzee." *Hudson Review* 37 (Summer, 1984): 312-314. Discusses Coetzee's theme of racial tensions in his homeland, noting that he is "at once oblique and scathingly direct." Flower acknowledges this compelling story, a "grim poetry of survival" but claims that being a political parable undermines its poetic technique. He does praise Coetzee for the "severely controlled precision" in this work, citing the Visagie farm with its juxtaposition of blacks and whites as the most telling political statement of the novel.

Heywood, Christopher, ed. *Aspects of South African Literature*. New York: Africana, 1976. An interesting commentary on the variety of writing coming out of South Africa since the 1920's. The chapter on "English-Language Literature and Politics in South Africa" by author Nadine Gordimer singles out Coetzee as an "interesting newcomer." In her appraisal of his two-part novel, *Dusklands*, Gordimer argues that Coetzee "links the behaviouristic conditioning of peoples by other peoples as a congenital flaw in human nature."

Penner, Dick. *Countries of the Mind: The Fiction of J. M. Coetzee*. New York: Greenwood Press, 1989. A full-length, valuable study on Coetzee that explores how his novels "replicate and subvert traditional forms," as well as address the concept of individual freedom. Explores the diversity of his works and gives useful background information on South Africa, the Afrikaners, and Coetzee's academic achievements. Argues for the greatness of Coetzee's writing in his novels *In the Heart of the Country*, *Waiting for the Barbarians*, and *Life & Times of Michael K*. A useful bibliography includes sources on South African literature within their political contexts.

Post, Robert M. "Oppression in the Fiction of J. M. Coetzee." *Critique: Studies in Modern Fiction* 27 (Winter, 1986): 67-77. Post examines Coetzee's works as statements of opposition but considers Coetzee more ambiguous and less straightforward than his South African counterparts. Emphasizes *In the Heart of the Country* and *Waiting for the Barbarians*.

WILKIE COLLINS

Born: London, England; January 8, 1824
Died: London, England; September 23, 1889

Principal long fiction

Antonina: Or, The Fall of Rome, 1850; *Basil: A Story of Modern Life*, 1852; *Hide and Seek*, 1854; *The Dead Secret*, 1857; *The Woman in White*, 1860; *No Name*, 1862; *Armadale*, 1866; *The Moonstone*, 1868; *Man and Wife*, 1870; *Poor Miss Finch: A Novel*, 1872; *The New Magdalen*, 1873; *The Law and the Lady*, 1875; *The Two Destinies: A Romance*, 1876; *A Rogue's Life*, 1879; *The Fallen Leaves*, 1879; *Jezebel's Daughter*, 1880; *The Black Robe*, 1881; *Heart and Science*, 1883; *I Say No*, 1884; *The Evil Genius: A Dramatic Story*, 1886; *The Legacy of Cain*, 1889; *Blind Love*, 1890 (completed by Walter Besant).

Other literary forms

Wilkie Collins produced a biography of his father in 1848 as well as travel books, essays and reviews, and a number of short stories. He also wrote and adapted plays, often in collaboration with Charles Dickens.

Achievements

Collins' reputation nearly a century after his death rests almost entirely on two works—*The Woman in White*, published serially in *All the Year Round* between November 26, 1859, and August 25, 1860; and *The Moonstone*, published in 1868. About this latter work, Dorothy Sayers said it is "probably the finest detective story ever written." No chronicler of crime and detective fiction can fail to include Collins' important contributions to the genre; simply for the ingenuity of his plots, Collins earned the admiration of T. S. Eliot. *The Woman in White* and *The Moonstone* have also been made into numerous adaptations for stage, film, radio, and television. Yet, for an author so conscientious and industrious—averaging one "big" novel every two years in his maturity—to be known as the author of two books would hardly be satisfactory. The relative obscurity into which most of Collins' work has fallen cannot be completely attributed to the shadow cast by his friend and sometime collaborator, Charles Dickens, nor to his physical infirmities and his addiction to laudanum, nor to the social vision which led him to write a succession of thesis novels. Indeed, the greatest mystery Collins left behind concerns the course of his literary career and subsequent reputation.

Biography

A pencil drawing survives, entitled "Wilkie Collins by his father William Collins, R. A." It shows a pretty, if serious, round face. The features beneath the end of the boy's nose are shaded, giving especial prominence to the upper face and forehead. The viewer at once is drawn to the boy's eyes. They are large, probing, mysterious, hardly the eyes of a child. Perhaps the artist-father sought to impart to his elder son some of his own austere, pious nature. William Collins (1788-1847), whose life began on the verge of one great European revolution and ended on the verge of another, was no revolutionary himself, nor the Bohemian others of his calling imagined themselves. Instead, William Collins was a strict Sabbatarian, an individual who overcame by talent and perseverance the disadvantages of poverty. The novelist's paternal grandfather was an art dealer, a restorer, a storyteller who lovingly trained and cajoled his son in painting and drawing. William Collins did not begin to taste success until several years after the death of his father in 1812, but gradually commissions and patrons did come, including Sir Robert Peel. Befriended by noted artists such as Sir David Wilkie and Washington Allston, William Collins was at last elected to the Royal Academy in 1820. Two years later, he married Harriet Geddes. The names of both of their sons, born in 1824 and 1828, respectively, honored fellow artists: William Wilkie Collins and Charles Allston Collins.

Little is known of Wilkie Collins' early years, save that they appear to have been relatively tranquil. By 1833, Collins was already enrolled at Maida Hill Academy. In 1836, William Collins elected to take his family to Italy, where they remained until the late summer of 1838. The return to London required taking new lodgings at Regent's Park, and the fourteen-year-old Wilkie Collins was sent to boarding school at Highbury. By the close of 1840, he was presumably finished with school. His father's health began to fail, and the senior Collins made known his wish that Wilkie take holy orders, though the son apparently had no such inclinations. The choice became university or commerce. Wilkie Collins chose business, and he became an apprentice to the tea merchants Antrobus and Company in 1841. Collins performed well, and was able to take a leave in order to accompany his father to Scotland the following summer. While still an apprentice, Collins began to write occasional pieces, and in August, 1843, *The Illuminated Magazine* published his first signed story, "The Last Stage Coachman." A novel about Polynesia was also written but discarded. In 1844, Collins traveled to Paris with his friend Charles Ward, and made a second visit in 1845. While William Collins' health began to deteriorate more rapidly, his son was released from his apprenticeship and decided upon the study of law. In February, 1847, William Collins died.

Wilkie Collins emulated his father's self-discipline, industry, and especially his love of art and beauty, yet if one judges by the series of self-serving religious zealots who populate Collins' fiction, one must assume that, while he respected his father's artistic sensibilities, he did not admire his pious ardor. Instead, Wilkie Collins seems in most things to have taken the example of his mother, a woman of loving good nature and humor with whom both he and his brother Charles remained close until her death. Nevertheless, William Collins near the end of life, had asked Wilkie to write his biography, providing the opportunity for the young man's first published book, *Memoirs of the Life of William Collins, R. A.*, published in 1848 in two volumes. While the narrator tends toward self-effacement and burdens his readers with minute detail, the work is nevertheless a formidable accomplishment. Researches on the book led Collins into correspondence with the American writer Richard Henry Dana and with a circle of established and rising artists, including E. M. Ward (brother of his friend Charles), Augustus Egg, John Everett Millais, Holman Hunt, and the Rossettis. At this time, Collins completed his historical novel *Antonina*, filled with Gothic violence and adventure, a work that attracted the serious attention of John Ruskin. It was published in 1850, the same year in which Collins made his first public stage appearance in *A Court Duel*, which he had adapted from the French. With the success of his first dramatic work and the surprisingly positive reception of *Antonina*, Collins began to enjoy a rising reputation.

Richard Bentley published Collins' account of a Cornwall hiking trip taken during the summer of 1850 in January, 1851, as *Rambles Beyond Railways*. Two months later, Egg introduced the twenty-seven-year-old Collins to Dickens, and the initial contact resulted in Collins taking part in Dickens' theatrical, *Not So Bad as We Seem*, written by Edward Bulwer-Lytton. (Until Dickens' death in 1870, he and Collins remained staunch friends, though there remains some indication of friction following Collins' success with *The Moonstone* and Dickens' supposed attempt to outdo his junior in his incomplete novel, *The Mystery of Edwin Drood*, 1870.) In 1852, after having tried to sell the version of a story that would become "Mad Monkton" to Dickens, Collins published "A Terribly Strange Bed," anthologized often since, in *Household Words* (1850-1859). The following years saw considerable collaboration between the two authors, not the least of which were Collins' stories for the Christmas annuals such as *Mr. Wray's Cash-Box: Or, The Mask and the Mystery* (1852); the collaboration *The Seven Poor Travellers* (1854); *The Wreck of the Golden Mary* (1856), a work often attributed to Dickens until recently; the novel *The Dead Secret* (1857); and numerous other stories and articles. In 1853, Collins, Dickens, and Egg traveled together in Italy and Switzerland. Four years later, Dickens produced Collins' play *The Frozen Deep*, later noting that the self-sacrifice of the central character, Richard Wardour (played by Dickens), provided the germ for *A Tale of Two Cities* (1859). Although never published as a play, *The Frozen Deep* was published in 1874 as a collection of short stories.

The impact each had on the writing of the other has long been a topic of controversy and speculation for critics and biographers; generally unchallenged is the influence of Collins' meticulous plotting on his senior. In turn, Dickens often corrected and refined by suggestion Collins' fiction, although he never agreed with Collins' practice of including prefaces which upbraided critics and the public alike. When Collins published *Basil* (having included for Bentley's publication in book form the first of those vexing prefaces), he forwarded the volumes to Dickens. After a two-week silence, there came a thoughtful, admiring reply: "I have made Basil's acquaintance," wrote Dickens at the end of 1852, "with great gratification, and entertain high respect for him. I hope that I shall become intimate with many worthy descendants of his, who are yet in the limbo of creatures waiting to be born." Collins did not disappoint Dickens on that count over their years of friendship and collaboration; indeed, they became "family" when Charles Allston Collins married Dickens' daughter Kate.

Household Words faded in 1859 along with Dickens' association with the publishers Bradbury and Evans. Dickens' new periodical, *All the Year Round* (1859-1870), began auspiciously with the publication of *A Tale of Two Cities*. After its run, he needed something to keep public interest in the new magazine from abating, and Collins provided it with *The Woman in White*. Its monumental success put Collins into that rarest literary circle: that of well-to-do authors. Its success also coincided with other important events—personal ones—in Collins' life.

Collins had lived the life of a bachelor, residing with his brother and mother at least into his early thirties. Their house was often open to guests. On one such evening, the author and his brother escorted home the artist Millais through then rural North London. Suddenly, a woman appeared to them in the moonlight, attired in flowing robes, all in white. Though distraught, she gained her composure and vanished as quickly as she had appeared. The author was most astounded, and insisted he would discover the identity of the lovely creature. J. G. Millais, the painter's son, who narrates this anecdote in a life of his father, does not reveal the lady's ultimate identity: "Her subsequent history, interesting as it is, is not for these pages." The woman was Caroline Elizabeth Graves, born 1834, mother of a little girl, Harriet. Her husband, G. R. Graves, may or may not have been dead. Of him, only his name is known.

Clearly, however, the liaison between Caroline Graves and Wilkie Collins was fully under way when he began to write *The Woman in White*. From at least 1859, the couple lived together in a secret relationship known only to their closest friends, until the autumn of 1868, when for obscure reasons Caroline married the son of a distiller, John C. Clow. Collins, not one to waste time, started a new liaison with Martha Rudd. This union produced three children: Marian (1869), Harriet Constance (1871), and William Charles (1874). The children took the surname Dawson, but Collins freely admitted his paternity. By this time, too, Caroline and her daughter returned, and Harriet Graves for a time served as her mother's lover's amanuensis; Collins adopted her as his daughter. A lover of hearty food, fine champagne, and good cigars, Collins appears to have lived in private a life that would have shocked many of his readers. Still, Collins treated his "morganatic family" quite well: he provided handsomely for his natural and adopted children and for their mothers. When she died in 1895 at sixty-one, Caroline Elizabeth Graves was interred beside the author of *The Woman in White*.

As Collins' private life began taking on its unconventional proportions in the 1860's, his public career grew more distinguished. His output for *All the Year Round* in shorter forms declined; he simply did not need the money. In March, 1861, a didactic novel about inheritance, *No Name*, began its run; it was published in volume form in December, 1862. A year later, Collins resigned his editorial assignment for Dickens' periodical, and also published, with Sampson Low, Son, and Company, *My Miscellanies*, bringing together in two volumes work that had first appeared in the two Dickens periodicals. After about seven years of almost obsessive productivity, Collins relented, but only for a time; he began *Armadale* in the spring of 1864, for serial publication in *The Cornhill Magazine* in Britain and *Harper's Monthly* in the United States. This exploration of inherited and personal guilt remains one of Collins' most adept and popular novels; it is also his longest. He wrote a dramatic version of the novel in 1866, but not until it appeared as *Miss Gwilt* (1876) was it produced.

In 1867, Collins and Dickens began their last collaboration, *No Thoroughfare*, an adventure set in the Alps and perhaps not unaffected by their shared Swiss journey many years before. By this time, too, Collins began to suffer tremendously from the good living he had long enjoyed—gout of the areas around the eyes drove him into excruciating pain, requiring the application of bandages for weeks at a time. To allay the ache, Collins developed a habit for laudanum, that tincture of opium that fills the darker recesses of middle Victorian culture. It was in this period of alternating pain and bliss that Collins penned *The Moonstone*, for *All the Year Round*, beginning in January, 1868. It was an uncontestable triumph; Collins himself thought it wonderfully wrought.

Yet *The Moonstone* had hardly begun its run when Collins' mother died, and later that same year, Caroline married Clow. When the novel was finished, Collins again turned to the stage, writing *Black and White* with his actor-friend Charles Fechter, which successfully opened in March, 1869. At the end of the year, the serialization of *Man and Wife* began in *Harper's Weekly* and in January, 1870, in *Cassell's Magazine*. Posterity has judged *Man and Wife* more harshly than did its first readers. It was a different kind of novel from *The Moonstone*: it attacked society's growing obsession with athleticism and castigated marital laws which Collins believed to be cruel, unfair, and unrealistic. Collins' "standard" modern biographer, Kenneth Robinson, sees *Man and Wife* as the turning point in Collins' career, the start of the "Downhill" (his chapter title) phase of the writer's life. It sold well after its serialization;

Collins also wrote a four-act dramatic version, although it did not appear onstage until 1873.

At the same time, Collins adapted *No Name* for the theater, and in 1871, *The Woman in White*. This play opened at the Olympic Theatre in October and ran for five months before going on tour. The same year saw the beginning of a new novel in serial, *Poor Miss Finch*, about a blind woman who falls in love with an epileptic whose cure turns him blue. When she is temporarily cured of her affliction, she finds herself in a dilemma about her blue lover, whose healthy twin also desires her love. A year later the indefatigible Collins published *The New Magdalen* in a magazine called *Temple Bar*, whose heroine, a virtuous prostitute, outraged contemporary critics. Its dramatization (1873) was greeted with enthusiasm.

As his work increasingly turned to exposing social hypocrisies, Collins sought to regulate as a writer of established repute the body of his published work. Since *Basil*, wholesale piracy had angered him and hurt his finances. By the early 1870's, he had reached agreement with the German publisher Tauchnitz, with Harper and Brothers in America, and, by 1875, with Chatto & Windus in Britain. Chatto & Windus not only bought all extant copyrights to Collins' work but also became his publisher for the rest of his life. This arrangement was finalized in the year after Collins, like his friend Dickens before him, had undertaken a reading tour of the United States and Canada. Apparently, while in New York, his gout had relented sufficiently for him to demand only brut champagne.

The years 1875 and 1876 saw the publication of two popular but lesser novels, *The Two Destinies* and *The Law and the Lady*. The next year was marked, however, by the successful dramatization of *The Moonstone* and the beginning of Collins' friendship with Charles Reade. In 1879, Collins wrote *The Haunted Hotel* for *The Belgravia Magazine*, a ghost story fresh in invention that extends one's notions about the genre. Meanwhile, however, Collins' health became less certain and his laudanum draughts became more frequent and potent. The decade took away many close friends, beginning with Dickens, and later, his brother Charles, then Augustus Egg.

In the last decade of his life, Collins became more reclusive, though not much less productive. He adapted his 1858 play, *The Red Vial*, into a novel *Jezebel's Daughter*. He also began, for serialization in *The Canadian Monthly*, the novel *The Black Robe*, whose central figure is a priest plotting to encumber the wealth of a large estate. The work has been regarded as the most successful of his longer, late novels. It was followed by a more controversial novel, *Heart and Science*, a polemic against vivisection that appeared in 1883. The same year saw Collins' last theatrical, *Rank and Riches*, an unqualified disaster that brought the leading lady to tears before the first-act curtain and which led her leading man, G. W. Anson, to berate the audience. Collins thereafter gave up writing for the stage, save a one-performance version of *The Evil*

Genius (1885), quickly recast as a novel that proved his single most lucrative publication.

Although 1884 saw the passing of Reade, Collins' closest friend of the time, he continued to write steadily. *The Guilty River* made its appearance in the *Arrowsmith Christmas Annual* for 1886; in 1887, Chatto & Windus published *Little Novels*, collecting earlier stories. Two works also appeared that ended the battle Collins had long waged with critics. A young man, Harry Quilter, published an encomiastic article for *The Contemporary Review*, "A Living Story-Teller." Collins himself wrote "How I Write My Books" for *The Globe*, an account of composing *The Woman in White*. As his health at last began to fail precipitously in 1888, Collins completed his final serial novel, *The Legacy of Cain*. It appeared in three volumes the following year, at a time when he was finished writing *Blind Love* for *The Illustrated London News*. On the evening of June 30, 1889, Collins suffered a stroke. He requested Walter Besant, then traveling in the north, to return and complete the tale. Collins had long ago befriended Dickens' physician and neighbor, Frank Beard. Beard did what little could be done to comfort Collins in his final days. Just past mid-morning, on September 23, 1889, Wilkie Collins died, Beard at his bedside.

Four days following his death, Collins was buried at Kensal Green; his procession was headed by Caroline Graves, Harriet Graves, and his surviving literary, theatrical, and household friends. Despite infirmities, Collins had lived a life long and full, remaining productive, industrious, and successful throughout his career.

Analysis

At its best, Wilkie Collins' fiction is characterized by a transparent style that occasionally pleases and surprises the reader with an apt turn of word or phrase; by a genius for intricate plots; by a talent for characterization that in at least one instance must earn the epithet "Miltonic"; and by an eye for detail that seems to make the story worth telling. These are the talents of an individual who learned early to look at things like a painter, to see the meaning, the emotion behind the gesture or pose—a habit of observation which constituted William Collins' finest bequest to his elder son.

The transparency of Collins' style rests on his adherence to the conventions of the popular fiction of his day. More so than contemporaries, he talks to readers, cajoles them, often protesting that the author will recede into the shadows in order that the reader may judge the action for himself. The "games"—as one current critic observes—that Collins plays with readers revolve about his mazelike plots, his "ingenuous" interruptions of the narrative, and his iterative language, symbolic names, and metaphors. Thus, at the beginning of "Mrs. Zant and the Ghost," published in *Little Novels*, the narrator begins by insisting that this tale of "supernatural influence" occurs in the daylight hours, adding "the writer declines to follow modern examples by thrusting himself and his opinions on the public view. He returns to the shadow from which he has emerged, and leaves the opposing forces of incredulity and belief to fight the old battle over again, on the old ground." The apt word is "shadow," for certainly, this story depicts a shadow world. At its close, when the preternatural events have occurred, the reader is left to assume a happy resolution between the near victim Mrs. Zant, and her earthly rescuer, Mr. Rayburn, through the mood of the man's daughter:

> Arrived at the end of the journey, Lucy held fast by Mrs. Zant's hand. Tears were rising in the child's eyes. "Are we to bid her good-bye?" she said sadly to her father.
> He seemed to be unwilling to trust himself to speak; he only said, "My dear, ask her yourself."
> But the result justified him. Lucy was happy again.

Here, Collins' narrator has receded like Mrs. Zant's supernatural protector, leaving the reader to hope and to expect that Mrs. Zant can again find love in this world. This kind of exchange—direct and inferred—between author and reader can go in other directions. Surely, when near the center of *The Woman in White*, one realizes that Count Fosco has read—as it were—over one's shoulder the diary of Miss Halcolmbe, the author intends that one should feel violated, while at the same time forced into collusion with the already attractive, formidable villain.

Because Collins' style as narrator is so frequently self-effacing, it sustains the ingenuity of his plots. These are surely most elaborate in *The Woman in White* and *The Moonstone*. In both cases, Collins elects to have one figure, party to the main actions, assemble the materials of different narratives into cohesive form. It is a method far less tedious than that of epistolary novels, and provides for both mystery and suspense. Although not the ostensible theme in either work, matters of self-identity and control over one's behavior operate in the contest between virtue and vice, good and evil. Thus, Laura Fairlie's identity is obliterated in an attempt to wrest from her her large fortune; thus, Franklin Blake, heavily drugged, unconsciously removes a gem that makes him the center of elaborate investigation. In each novel, the discovery of the actual circumstances restores identity to these characters. The capacity to plot allows Collins to surprise his readers profoundly: In *The Woman in White*, one is astounded to be confronted by Laura Fairlie standing in the churchyard, above her own grave. In *The Moonstone*, one is baffled when the detective, Sergeant Cuff, provides a plausible solution to the theft of the diamond which turns out to be completely incorrect.

The novels of the 1860's find Collins having firmly established his transparent detachment from the subjects at hand, in turn giving full scope to his meticulous sense of plot. *No Name* and *Armadale* are no less complex in their respective actions than their more widely read counterparts. Interestingly, though, all of these novels explore matters of identity and motive for action; they attest Collins' ability to relate popular tales that encompass more serious issues.

Because he had a painter's eye for detail, Collins was a master of characterization, even when it appears that a character is flat. Consider, for example, this passage from "Miss Dulane and My Lord" published in *Little Novels*:

> Mrs. Newsham, tall and elegant, painted and dyed, acted on the opposite principle in dressing, which confesses nothing. On exhibition before the world, this lady's disguise asserted she had reached her thirtieth year on her last birthday. Her husband was discreetly silent, and Father Time was discreetly silent; they both knew that her last birthday had happened thirty years since.

Here an incidental figure in a minor tale remains fixed, the picture of one comically out of synchronization with her own manner; before she has uttered a syllable, one dislikes her. Consider, on the other hand, the initial appearance of a woman one will grow to like and admire, Marian Halcolmbe, as she makes her way to meet Walter Hartright in *The Woman in White*:

> She turned towards me immediately. The easy elegance of every movement of her limbs and body as soon as she began to advance from the far end of the room, set me in a flutter of expectation to see her face clearly. She left the window—and I said to myself, The lady is dark. She moved forward a few steps—and I said to myself, The lady is young. She approached nearer—and I said to myself (with a sense of surprise which words fail me to express), The lady is ugly!

Not only does this passage reveal Collins' superb sense of pace, his ability to set a trap of astonished laughter, but also it reveals some of Hartright's incorrect assumptions about the position he has taken at Limmeridge House; for example, that the two young women he will instruct are pampered, spoiled, and not worth his serious consideration. Preeminently, it shows the grace of Marian Halcombe, a grace that overcomes her lack of physical beauty in conventional senses and points to her indefatigable intelligence and loyalty so crucial to future events in the novel. Marian is, too, a foil for her half sister, Laura Fairlie, the victim of the main crimes in the book. While one might easily dismiss Laura Fairlie with her name—she is fair and petite and very vulnerable—she also displays a quiet resilience and determination in the face of overwhelming adversaries.

The most memorable of Collins' characters is Count Fosco in the same novel, whose name immediately suggests a bludgeon. To Marian Halcombe, Collins gives the job of describing the Count. "He looks like a man who could tame anything." In his characterization of Fosco, Collins spawned an entire race of fat villains and, occasionally, fat detectives, such as Nero Wolfe and Gideon Fell. One is not surprised that Sydney Greenstreet played both Fosco and his descendant, Caspar Gutman, in film versions of *The Woman in White* and Dashiell Hammett's *The Maltese Falcon* (1930). In one of his best speeches, Fosco reveals the nature of his hubris, his evil genius:

> Crimes cause their own detection, do they? . . . there are foolish criminals who are discovered, and wise criminals who escape. The hiding of a crime, or the detection of a crime, what is it? A trial of skill between the police on one side, and the individual on the other. When the criminal is a brutal, ignorant fool, the police in nine cases out of ten win. When the criminal is a resolute, educated, highly-intelligent man, the police in nine cases out of ten lose.

In pitting decent people against others who manipulate the law and social conventions to impose their wills, Collins frequently creates characters more interesting for their deficiencies than for their virtues. His novels pit, sensationally at times, the unsuspecting, the infirm, or the unprepossessing, against darker figures, usually operating under the scope of social acceptance. Beneath the veneer of his fiction, one finds in Collins a continuing struggle to legitimize the illegitimate, to neutralize hypocrisy, and to subvert the public certainties of his era.

Kenneth Friedenreich

Other major works

SHORT FICTION: *Rambles Beyond Railways*, 1851; *Mr. Wray's Cash-Box: Or, The Mask and the Mystery*, 1852; *The Seven Poor Travellers*, 1854; *After Dark*, 1856; *The Wreck of the Golden Mary*, 1856; *The Queen of Hearts*, 1859; *Miss or Mrs.? and Other Stories*, 1873; *The Frozen Deep*, 1874; *The Haunted Hotel: A Mystery of Modern Venice*, 1879; *The Guilty River*, 1886; *Little Novels*, 1887; *The Lazy Tour of Two Apprentices*, 1890 (with Charles Dickens).

PLAYS: *No Thoroughfare*, 1867 (with Charles Dickens); *The New Magdalen*, 1873; *Man and Wife*, 1873; *The Moonstone*, 1877.

NONFICTION: *Memoirs of the Life of William Collins, R.A.*, 1848 (2 volumes).

MISCELLANEOUS: *My Miscellanies*, 1863; *The Works of Wilkie Collins*, 1900, 1970 (30 volumes).

Bibliography

Kendrick, Walter. "The Sensationalism of *The Woman in White*." *Nineteenth Century Fiction* 32 (June, 1977): 18-35. Places the novel at a midpoint within the sensation/detective novel genre. Sees the novel's true significance in its very ambiguity in relation to mainstream Victorian realism.

O'Neill, Philip. *Wilkie Collins: Women, Property, and Propriety*. New York: Macmillan, 1988. Seeks to move the discussion of Collins away from popularist categories by using modern feminist criticism deconstructively to open up a more considered version of his thematic material. Contains a full bibliography.

Page, Norman. *Wilkie Collins*. Boston: Routledge & Kegan Paul, 1974. One of the Critical Heritage series, this is a full anthology of Collins' critical reception from 1850 through 1891. Contains a short bibliography.

Robinson, Kenneth. *Wilkie Collins: A Biography*. 1951. Reprint. London: Bodley Head, 1972. Still the most readable and accessible account of Collins' career. A short bibliography is provided.

Taylor, Jenny. *In the Secret Theatre of Home: Wilkie Collins, Sensation Narrative, and Nineteenth Century Psychology*. New York: Routledge, 1988. The subtitle of this study suggests its perspective. However, it deals as fully with social structures and how these shape the structures of Collins' major fiction. Contains full notes and an excellent select bibliography of both primary and secondary material.

IVY COMPTON-BURNETT

Born: Pinner, England; June 5, 1884
Died: London, England; August 27, 1969

Principal long fiction

Dolores, 1911; *Pastors and Masters*, 1925; *Brothers and Sisters*, 1929; *Men and Wives*, 1931; *More Women Than Men*, 1933; *A House and Its Head*, 1935; *Daughters and Sons*, 1937; *A Family and a Fortune*, 1939; *Parents and Children*, 1941; *Elders and Betters*, 1944; *Manservant and Maidservant*, 1947 (published in the United States as *Bullivant and His Lambs*, 1948); *Two Worlds and Their Ways*, 1949; *Darkness and Day*, 1951; *The Present and the Past*, 1953; *Mother and Son*, 1955; *A Father and His Fate*, 1957; *A Heritage and Its History*, 1959; *The Mighty and Their Fall*, 1961; *A God and His Gifts*, 1963; *The Last and the First*, 1971.

Other literary forms

Ivy Compton-Burnett is known only for her novels.

Achievements

Compton-Burnett is a novelist's novelist, much appreciated by her peers. She has been compared by her partisans to figures as various as Jane Austen, Jean Racine, Henry James, Leo Tolstoy, George Eliot, Anton Chekhov, the Elizabethan tragedians, William Congreve, Oscar Wilde, George Meredith, Elizabeth Gaskell, Harold Pinter, and the cubists. Her appeal is to a growing circle of admirers, though her work has enjoyed neither popular adulation nor widespread critical attention. Her novels require slow and attentive reading and make heavy demands upon the reader, yet they do not offer the inviting depths of works such as James Joyce's *Ulysses* (1922) and William Faulkner's *The Sound and the Fury* (1929). Compton-Burnett's modernism is of a different kind: her works present hard and brittle surfaces, and her style reaches its purest expression in pages of unbroken dialogue, highly stylized and crackling with suppressed emotion. Her uncompromising artistry won for her a small but permanent place in twentieth century world literature.

Biography

Ivy Compton-Burnett always thought she would write, even when she was quite young. She came from a well-to-do family: her father, James Compton Burnett (no hyphen), was a doctor and direct descendant of the ecclesiastical writer Bishop Gilbert Burnett. Ivy adored her father and from him inherited a love of words and of nature. Her mother, Katharine Rees Compton-Burnett, was the second wife of her father: Katharine became stepmother to five children at marriage and mother of seven more, of whom Ivy was the oldest.

Katharine seems to have been the prototype for several of the tyrants in Compton-Burnett's works: she was beautiful, autocratic, indifferent to her stepchildren and distant to her own. The real mother to the children was their nurse Minnie. Olive, the eldest of all the children, was bitterly jealous of her stepmother and of Ivy for her close relationship with their father.

Compton-Burnett's closest companions were her two younger brothers. Guy and Noel (Jim). The three were educated together, first by a governess, then by a tutor, and Compton-Burnett always remained proud that she had had a boy's education. She loved Latin and Greek. In 1902, she entered Royal Holloway College, London University; in 1904, she was awarded the Founder's Scholarship; in 1906, she passed the Bachelor of Arts honors examination in the classics. Her love of the classics appears clearly in her works: her plots, with their recurring motifs of incest and family murder, seem straight from Greek tragedy; her characters often allude to Greek tragedy; her view of life as cruel and ironic is the tragic view of the Greek dramatists, skewed by modern experience and by her own temperament.

Compton-Burnett claims to have written very little before her first novel, *Dolores*, was published. She discounted *Dolores* entirely in later life, uncertain which parts were hers and which were the work of her overly enthusiastic brother Noel. Between the publication of *Dolores* and *Pastors and Masters*, her second novel, is a gap of fourteen years which was filled with family turbulence. After the death of both her parents, Ivy became head of the household and a bit of a tyrant herself. Her four younger sisters and Minnie moved out and set up their own household which they refused to let Ivy visit. Compton-Burnett's only remaining brother Noel (Guy had died earlier) was killed in World War I, and the author cared for his widow after she took an overdose of sleeping pills. Around the same time, Ivy's two youngest sisters committed suicide. She herself had a bout with Spanish influenza which drained her energy for some years.

In the early 1920's, Compton-Burnett settled in a flat in London with her friend, Margaret Jourdain, an authority on Regency furniture, with whom she lived for thirty years. Jourdain was the more famous and remained the dominant of the pair. The two women traveled abroad together every year, where Compton-Burnett pursued her passion of collecting wildflowers. Every odd-numbered year, with only a few exceptions, she produced a novel. World War II disturbed her greatly: she and Jourdain fled to the country to escape the bombing. When Jourdain died in 1951, Compton-Burnett felt betrayed by her "desertion."

In her later years, many honors were bestowed upon Compton-Burnett. She was made a Commander of the Order of the British Empire in 1951; she was awarded the James Tait Black Memorial Prize in 1956; in 1960, she received an honorary Doctor of Letters degree from the University of Leeds; in 1967, she was made a Dame Commander of the British Empire.

Compton-Burnett dedicated her life to her art, reading and working continually. She had little wish to reveal the details of her private life—"I haven't been at all deedy"—and believed that all she had to offer the world could be found in her books.

Analysis

Ivy Compton-Burnett has no wide range of style or subject in her twenty novels. Like Jane Austen, she limits her characters to a few well-to-do families in the country. The action takes place in the late Victorian era, though there are few indications of any time period. Scenery is almost nonexistent, and no heavy Victorian furnishings clutter the scene.

Instead, Compton-Burnett concentrates entirely on her characters, not in describing them but in having them reveal (and sometimes betray) themselves in what they do and do not say. Her novels demand more of the ear than of the eye. They have been likened to plays in their spareness of description, narration, exposition, and their concentration on talk. Dialogue indeed is the reason why her novels draw readers and is her chief contribution to the art of the novel. Each chapter contains one event, which is discussed in detail by one family, and then perhaps another, or by the masters in the house and then the servants. Although Compton-Burnett as an omniscient author does not comment on or analyze her characters or their motives, her chorus of servants, children, neighbors, and schoolmistresses do so incessantly. In this way, she achieves many points of view instead of only one.

Compton-Burnett's novels do have plots—melodramatic and sometimes implausible ones with murders, incest, infidelity, and perversions of justice. At times, she drops enough clues for the reader to know what will happen; at other times, events occur arbitrarily. Shipwrecked characters often reappear; documents are stolen or concealed only to turn up later. Eavesdroppers populate her novels. Several people, for example, coincidentally walk into a room when they are being slandered. Although the events themselves are often too coincidental, the highly crafted conversations about them prove Compton-Burnett's talent as a writer. These witty and ironic conversations insist on the revelation of truth, on the precise use of language, making Compton-Burnett's novels memorable. Language insulates people against the primitive forces, the unmentionable deeds of which they are capable. Her witty dialogue tends to anesthetize the reader's response (and the characters' as well) to horrendous crimes of passion.

Compton-Burnett's novels explore all the tensions of family life—between strong and weak, between generations, between classes. Power is her chief subject, with love, money, and death as constant attendants. Her main foes are complacency, tyranny, and hypocrisy. Compton-Burnett deplores sloppy thinking and dishonesty, whether with oneself or with others. Her novels clearly indicate her view of human nature. She believes that wickedness is often not punished and that is why it is prevalent. When wickedness is likely to be punished, most people, she thinks, are intelligent enough to avoid it. She also sees very few people as darkly evil: many people, when subjected to strong and sudden temptation without the risk of being found out, yield to such an urge. Even her bad characters have some good in them. Although the good points of the tyrants can be recognized, their cruelty can never be forgiven. Yet, ironically, their cruelty often produces good results. The victims build up bravery, loyalty, and affection as defenses against the wicked and cruel. Compton-Burnett's novels, above all, elicit concern for human suffering.

Though she does believe in economic and hereditary forces, Compton-Burnett also believes in free will. She is one of the rare novelists whose good-hearted characters are credible as well as likable. The good and innocent characters in her novels, particularly the children, are not corrupted and usually remain unharmed. They conquer by truth, affection, and, most important, by intelligence. Compton-Burnett shows the great resilience of the human spirit; her characters survive atrocities and then settle down to resume their everyday lives. In her novels, the greatest crimes are not crimes of violence, but crimes against the human spirit: one person beating down, wounding, or enslaving another's spirit. Yet her novels do not end with a feeling of despair. They end, rather, with a feeling of understanding. The good characters see the faults of the tyrants yet continue to love them and gallantly pick them up when they have fallen. The good characters realize that evil and good are inextricable.

Compton-Burnett's strengths and weaknesses as a novelist are both suggested by the fact that she has no masterpiece, no best or greatest novel. Her oeuvre has a remarkable consistency, the product of an unswerving artistic intelligence yet also evidence of a certain narrowness and rigidity. By general consensus, her strongest works are those of her middle period, including *Brothers and Sisters*, *More Women Than Men*, *A Family and a Fortune*, and *Manservant and Maidservant*.

Brothers and Sisters, Compton-Burnett's third novel, is distinguished by the appearance of the first of many tyrannical women in her oeuvre. Sophia Stace (who, like the later tyrants, is a tragic figure as well) wants attention and affection, but she is never willing to give in return. She never sees beyond herself or acts for anyone but herself. Her daughter Dinah succinctly comments: "Power has never been any advantage to Sophia. . . . It has her worn out, and everyone who would have served her."

Sophia's self-absorption leads to disaster. Thinking her father's instructions, which are locked in a desk, will cut her and her adopted brother out of his will, Sophia leaves them there unread, marries her adopted brother (who is really her half-brother), and bears three children. Her husband dies of a heart attack after finding out the truth about his and Sophia's parentage, and

Sophia reacts to his death by imprisoning herself in her home. Intending to draw attention to herself, Sophia dramatizes her grief. When her children attempt to resume life as usual, she moans that they feel no affection for her: "I don't know whether you like sitting there, having your dinner, with your mother eating nothing?" Like other Compton Burnett tyrants, she turns mealtime into domestic inquisition.

The only one who can control Sophia, modeled on Compton-Burnett's mother Katharine, is Miss Patmore, modeled on Compton-Burnett's own nurse Minnie. The children love and respect "Patty" as a mother since their own is incapable of giving love. When Sophia herself finds out the truth, she has no feeling for what the revelation will do to her children. They meet the tragedy with characteristic wittiness to cover the pain: "Well if we are equal to this occasion, no other in our lives can find us at a loss. We may look forward to all emergencies without misgiving." The children, though they have been Sophia's victims, are able to realize after her death that she, more than anyone else, has been her own victim: "The survey of Sophia's life flashed on them, the years of ruthlessness and tragedy, power and grief. Happiness, of which she held to have had so much, had never been real to Sophia. They saw it now." Power thus eats away at the powerful while their victims rise to a higher moral plane of understanding.

Brothers and Sisters has many of the standard Compton-Burnett plot ingredients: incest, illegitimacy, domestic torture, and the family secret that becomes public knowledge. What gives the novel added strength is the subplot of Peter Bateman and his children, another example of a parent who blithely torments his children. Socially gauche, Peter's vicious stupidity inflicts painful embarrassment on his skulking son Latimer and his self-effacing daughter Tilly. He determinedly pigeonholes his children into demeaning positions.

While the bond between parents and children in the novel is a brutal one, the bond between brothers and sisters becomes a saving one. Sophia's children, Andrew, Robin, and Dinah, support one another, and they are not the only brothers and sisters in the novel to do so. There are three other sets of brothers and sisters: Edward and Judith, Julian and Sarah, and Gilbert and Caroline, all friends of the Stace children. At various points in the novel, Andrew and Dinah are engaged to Caroline and Gilbert, then to Judith and Edward, and finally Julian proposes to Dinah but is rejected. The Stace children and their friends change romantic partners as if they were merely changing partners at a dance, partly in reaction to the tragic secrets that are revealed, and partly because Compton-Burnett has little faith in marriage or in romantic love. Her marriages are matters of convenience, timing, and location: none of her husbands and wives grow together in a fulfilling relationship. The strongest love bond is always the fraternal bond.

Like Compton-Burnett's first two novels, *More Women Than Men* is a school novel. The schoolmistresses of Josephine Napier's girls' school function as the villagers do in Compton-Burnett's manor novels: they serve as a chorus for the main action and provide comic relief from the main tragic action (Miss Munday, the senior teacher, is particularly good at this). The schoolmistresses, however, have less freedom than the villagers: in a society where unmarried or widowed women have few options in supporting themselves, they are bound to the tyrant Josephine.

More Women Than Men, like *Men and Wives* and *A House and Its Head*, the novels that immediately preceded and followed it, is a very somber work. Josephine is morally, though not legally, guilty of murder; she exposes her nephew Gabriel's wife, who is deathly ill with pneumonia, to cold blasts of air. She is also a hypocrite par excellence. When her husband Simon dies, she affects ostentatious mourning and claims "I am not a person to take a pride in not being able to eat and sleep," yet she does exactly that. In reality, she feels little at his death. Gabriel, her morose victim, is also one of the few people who stands up to her. When she makes such claims as "I am not an ogress," Gabriel flatly replies, "Well, you are rather." His standing up to her, though, cannot prevent his wife's murder.

There is another important element in Josephine's complex personality: sexual repression and dominance. Indeed, *More Women Than Men* is preoccupied with the psychology of sex and with gender differences. Men and women are attracted both to women and to men. Josephine, for example, many years before the book begins, has stolen Simon from Elizabeth Giffard; she disposes of Ruth Giffard so she can reclaim her nephew Gabriel's affections; she thrusts herself on Felix Bacon and, when rejected, accepts the love of Miss Rossetti, Gabriel's natural mother. For Josephine, sex is purely an expression of power.

Josephine's cruel oppression is counterbalanced by another sexually amorphous character, the comic Felix Bacon. Felix begins the novel as the homosexual companion of Josephine's brother, inherits a manor and a fortune in the course of the novel, and marries the intelligent young heroine Helen Keats at the end. He triumphs in that he escapes Josephine's smothering affection and is able to be master of his own world, yet he still feels a longing for the old situation. One can never break completely free from the stranglehold of the tyrant.

Gender differences are explored in many of Compton-Burnett's novels. In *Pastors and Masters*, she had already dealt with the relative merits of men and women. Emily Herrick, the novel's main character, had maintained that men are egotistical and "devious." In *More Women Than Men*, Compton-Burnett raises the problem of the shoddy attention women receive. Felix, for example, wryly remarks that parents express surprise that their daughters' education should be taken seriously. "It is a good thing that they entrust it to other people . . . they don't seem to give any real thought to their being the mothers of the race." Although never an ardent supporter of feminist causes,

Compton-Burnett did object to the unequal treatment women received, especially in terms of education.

A Family and a Fortune is one of Compton-Burnett's kindliest novels. Matty Seaton, the tyrant, is not like the tyrants of earlier novels: she has neither the highly dramatic and tragic sense of Sophia Stace nor the magnetizing and suffocating attraction of Josephine Napier. She wants to be needed by others and craves power, but her tyranny is limited because she is a maiden aunt (not a mother), because she is financially dependent on her sister's family, because she cannot actively move about (she was crippled in a riding accident), and because she lives in a lodge separated from the main family in the manor. With these limitations, she becomes a study of frustrated tyranny. Compton-Burnett introduces her thus: "Her energy seemed to accumulate and to work itself out at the cost of some havoc within her." All that is left of her youthful attractiveness is her overpowering self-regard. She tries to make herself needed by cutting down others with recrimination and guilt, but all her maneuvers are transparent. She releases her frustration by browbeating her paid companion Miss Griffin, whom she even drives out into the cold one night.

While Matty's energies are loosed into negative and destructive channels, her niece Justine releases her own similar energies in positive and constructive routes. Justine is one of the best of the strong-minded, clear-seeing, female characters whom Compton-Burnett uses to balance her tyrants (Patty in *Brothers and Sisters* and Rachel in *Men and Wives* are other examples). Justine is the one who patches the leaky boat of family life with her optimistic matter-of-factness. Self-effacing and comic, she is "utterly honest" with herself, particularly about her own potential weaknesses. She busies herself about everyone's business but never lapses into tyranny and willingly yields her power when her father remarries. Though a bit officious, she brings a positive force to the family and the novel, insisting that life has meaning· "All human effort must achieve something essential, if not apparent," she explains. She is one of the few Compton-Burnett characters who is morally good and truthful, but not cynical (nor very witty). It is she who makes the ending of the novel happy—with the two brothers Edgar and Dudley once again arm in arm—happy because she insists it is.

Another remarkable character in the novel is Aubrey, Justine's fifteen-year-old retarded brother. Compton-Burnett first introduced children into her novels in *Daughters and Sons*, and they never left her novels thereafter. Children prove useful to Compton-Burnett in the contrast they make with their parents; in the choric comments they can make on the action; in the helpless victims they provide for the tyrants; and in themselves, because Compton-Burnett knows the difficult and sometimes fearful world of children. Aubrey senses his inadequacies and is always trying to reassure himself by saying how much he is like someone else in the family. His dialogue brings out real family resemblances: at times he is peevish like his grandfather, at other times he consciously (and sometimes unconsciously) imitates his uncle Dudley's clear-headed, mannered speech. Aubrey's attempts to be normal constitute some of the most moving scenes in Compton-Burnett's fiction.

One important theme of *A Family and a Fortune* is that to be "normal" is to be flawed. Matty Seaton treats her devoted companion brutally; her nephew Clement Gaveston hoards gold coins in his bedroom; and Dudley Gaveston, the generous bachelor uncle who inherits the fortune, leaves the manor in a jealous rage when his brother Edgar steals his fiancée. Dudley sums up their behavior by saying that all have their ridiculous moments.

Dudley and Edgar have the very close fraternal relationship so common in Compton-Burnett novels. They almost exclude Blanche, Edgar's first wife, from close communion, and the greatest threat in the novel is not murder or incest as in the early novels, but that the brotherly bond will be broken. At the end of the novel, though, it is clear that Edgar's honeymoon is over and that he will return to Dudley.

Manservant and Maidservant has been the most popular of all Compton-Burnett's novels; some critics have named it as their favorite, and Compton-Burnett even said it was one that she particularly liked. It is less spare than the other novels, with more exposition, more sense of place (a smoking fireplace begins and ends the novel, for example), and fully drawn characters. A story of reformation, it shows strong bonds of affection among Horace Lamb, his cousin Mortimer, and his counterpart in the servants' world, Bullivant, the butler.

Horace, a penny pincher who makes his children do calisthenics to keep warm in winter, is one of Compton-Burnett's crotchety male tyrants. He often looks aside in apparent abstraction as "punishment to people for the nervous exasperation that they produced in him, and must expiate." His wife Charlotte and his cousin Mortimer plan to run away and take the children with them to save them from suffering. Horace finds a letter detailing their plans and becomes Compton-Burnett's first and only tyrant who attempts to reform. His reformation does not erase the past (his children, in particular, point this out); in fact, it makes the children suffer more because he inevitably has lapses. The ups and downs of being nourished, then starved, torture the children far more excruciatingly than would consistent oppression. Yet Horace draws forth deep love from Mortimer and devoted service from Bullivant. Mortimer explains the tyrant's appeal: "Is there something in Horace that twines itself about the heart? Perhaps it is being his own worst enemy." The wise characters may be victims of the tyrants, but they also understand and pity them.

Mortimer, like Dudley Gaveston, is an example of Compton-Burnett's un-married, rather impotent characters who attach themselves to their richer relatives in the manor. Like Dudley, Mortimer cares more about the children than their own father does. It is these dependent characters who have the strength to challenge the tyrant's ruthlessness, who speak with caustic honesty to expose the tyrant's pretentiousness. They act courageously, even though they must mortify themselves (thus Mortimer's name) and expose their own weakness in the cause of truth. The exploiter needs the exploited, and vice versa.

Manservant and Maidservant introduces an important new element in Compton-Burnett's novels: the servants. Like the children, they can mirror their masters or can serve as a chorus discussing the action. The characters of Compton-Burnett's servants are never better than in this novel: the timid maid; the motherly, nonconformist cook; George, the workhouse boy with grandiose pretensions; and Bullivant, the wonderfully comic butler. Bullivant holds both upstairs and downstairs together with his wry wit and firm hand. He knows everything that has transpired and anticipates what will come. He is also a character of great tenderness and protectiveness, though he hides it under a mask of strict propriety. His devotion to Horace is almost that of an elder brother, though he is always careful to keep his place.

Two important themes of *Manservant and Maidservant* are the conflict between instinct and social conventions and the pernicious effects of do-gooders' meddling. Compton-Burnett had no belief in God, but she was a great supporter of social conventions as necessary restraints on man's primitive instincts. The decent majority of men create social and moral rules; the unscrupulous minority violate them. Horace claims that civilized life consists in suppressing one's instincts, but his wife Charlotte corrects him by saying that all life consists in fulfilling them. Charlotte expresses the complexity of Compton-Burnett's vision: "There is so much truth on all the different sides of things."

Compton-Burnett first sounded the theme of meddling do-gooders in *Pastors and Masters*, in which one character remarks, "I think it's rather terrible to see it [good] being done." In *Manservant and Maidservant*, Mortimer breaks his engagement to Magdalen because of her interference: "At any time you might act for my good. When people do that, it kills something precious between them." Like Charles Dickens in *Bleak House* (1852-1853), Compton-Burnett believes that do-gooders are usually thinly veiled tyrants. Yet the novel ends happily with an act of goodness: the maid will teach Miss Buchanan, the illiterate shopkeeper, to read.

After *Manservant and Maidservant*, Compton-Burnett's novels weaken, showing signs of strain, repetition, melodrama, and lack of inventiveness. One exception to this is *A God and His Gifts*, in which the tyrant Hereward Egerton overflows with sexual and artistic energy. Through his character, Compton-Burnett reflects on the nature of the artist: his essential and consuming egoism and his godlike creativity.

The most telling criticism leveled against Compton-Burnett's novels is their sameness. The plots of her novels tend to become indistinguishable after many are read; the speech of all her characters, no matter what their social class or background, is witty and stylized, and her characters themselves become habitual types. Such charges have a degree of validity, yet Compton-Burnett's novels must be accepted on their own terms. She was not interested in realistic dialogue; she was concerned with speech as a means of revealing human character. Her tyrants tend to be careless in their speech, relying on clichés or using words inexactly, just as they are careless in the way they trample moral laws and people. They pretend to be open, but their speech incriminates them for lack of self-knowledge and candor. Their victims, who seek truth, always correct the tyrants' misuse of language by questioning the real meaning of the words they use.

Whatever her flaws as a novelist, Compton-Burnett was an artist of uncommon intelligence, originality, and control. Her work might best be described in a phrase from one of her own novels, *More Women Than Men*: "Like agate, beautiful and bright and hard."

Ann Willardson Engar

Bibliography
Baldana, Frank. *Ivy Compton-Burnett*. New York: Twayne, 1964. Packs much information into a short space. Offers brief characterizations of all the novels, organized around common themes such as home and family. Also "criticizes the critics," giving an analysis of the major evaluations of Compton-Burnett available at that time. Baldana regards Compton-Burnett as the foremost contemporary novelist.
Burkhart, Charles. *I. Compton-Burnett*. London: Victor Gollancz, 1965. Classes Compton-Burnett as an eccentric novelist and offers a psychological account of this type of writer. Presents themes found in Compton-Burnett's works, such as conventions, secrets, people and power, and ethos, devoting a chapter to each. Concludes with a summary of each of the novels, ranking *Manservant and Maidservant* as the most brilliant.
Hutchinson, Joanne. "Appearances Are All We Have." *Twentieth Century Literature* 25 (Summer, 1979): 183-193. Contends that Compton-Burnett's novels describe the appearance of things with great precision. Unlike Jane Austen, Compton-Burnett does not find a deeper reality within appearances; once one learns to adjust to them, they are all there is to life. This thesis is illustrated by discussion of *Manservant and Maidservant* and other novels.
Nevius, Blake. *Ivy Compton-Burnett*. New York: Columbia University Press, 1970. This short study presents a general account of the novelist. Her works stress the conflict of passion and duty and are situated in an enclosed space. Their peculiar form, consisting almost entirely of dialogue,

has led many to dismiss Compton-Burnett as an eccentric. Although her characters are static, her theme of the abuse of power has contemporary relevance.

Sprigge, Elizabeth. *The Life of Ivy Compton-Burnett*. New York: George Braziller, 1973. Devoted to Compton-Burnett's life much more than her works, but includes some literary analysis. Sprigge denies that the novels are all alike: each one is a separate creation. The main theme of Compton-Burnett's work is that the truth behind a family's relationships will eventually come to light. Sprigge is extremely favorable to her subject and accepts what Compton-Burnett claims at face value.

Spurling, Hilary. *Ivy: The Life of I. Compton-Burnett*. New York: Alfred A. Knopf, 1984. The most comprehensive account of Compton-Burnett's life, based on exhaustive research and conversations with Compton-Burnett's friends. The novelist's severely repressed life as a child in the late Victorian era dominates the first half of the book. After the death of her two sisters by suicide in 1917, her life was outwardly uneventful. Her childhood experiences influenced her stories and novels, all of which are discussed at length.

EVAN S. CONNELL, JR.

Born: Kansas City, Missouri; August 17, 1924

Principal long fiction
Mrs. Bridge, 1959; *The Patriot*, 1960; *The Diary of a Rapist*, 1966; *Mr. Bridge*, 1969; *The Connoisseur*, 1974; *Double Honeymoon*, 1976.

Other literary forms
Despite the critical and popular success of his two Bridge books, it might be argued that the novel is not Evan S. Connell, Jr.'s best form; certainly, it is only one of many forms in which he has worked. His *Notes from a Bottle Found on the Beach at Carmel* (1963) and *Points for a Compass Rose* (1973) are haunting, sometimes cryptic prose poems, the latter of which was nominated for the National Book Award for Poetry in 1974. Termed "vatic literature" by one critic, these books have been compared to T. S. Eliot's *The Waste Land* (1922), Ezra Pound's *Cantos* (1925-1973), and Albert Camus' *Notebooks* (1963, 1965)—even to "an exotic, unexpurgated *Encyclopaedia Britannica*."

Connell's fascination with the odd particulars of human existence has also produced two well-received collections of essays, *A Long Desire* (1979) and *The White Lantern* (1980). Both of these books blend history, legend, and whimsy in essay form as Connell contemplates the singular obsessions of some of the great travelers, explorers, plunderers, and thinkers of world history. His growing fascination with "the Little Bighorn Fiasco" narrowed Connell's plans for a third book of essays, this time about the Old West, to a nonfiction work about General Custer, entitled *Son of the Morning Star: Custer and the Little Bighorn* (1984). His highly praised short stories have appeared in numerous anthologies and magazines such as *Esquire* and *Saturday Evening Post*. Three volumes of his short fiction have been published: *The Anatomy Lesson and Other Stories* (1957), *At the Crossroads* (1965), and *Saint Augustine's Pigeon* (1980). From 1959 to 1965, Connell was editor of *Contact*, a well-respected San Francisco literary magazine.

Achievements
Connell's first novel, *Mrs. Bridge*, was a best-seller and was nominated for the National Book Award for Fiction in 1960; in 1973, Connell was one of the five judges for that award. Three of his six novels (*Mrs. Bridge*, *The Diary of a Rapist*, and *Mr. Bridge*) have been selected by the editors of *The New York Times Book Review* as being among the best novels of the year. Writers praise his mastery, but scholars have found no enigmas demanding explication.

His instinct for telling details and the crisp straightforwardness of his narrative style have been widely admired.

Apart from work by Gus Blaisdell, however, little systematic study of Connell's writing exists. One of the most private of contemporary writers, Connell has never intentionally courted the public, writing only about subjects that interest him and only in ways that interest him, paying no attention to current literary fashion. While not an "experimental" writer in the usual self-conscious sense of the term, Connell freely searches among forms and styles for each of his works, and the category-defying forms of *Mrs. Bridge* and *Notes from a Bottle Found on the Beach at Carmel* made publication of both books difficult: eight publishers rejected *Mrs. Bridge* before The Viking Press gambled on it, and even Viking might not have published *Notes from a Bottle Found on the Beach at Carmel* had it not first appeared in *Contact*, providing them printing plates which they could reuse.

Apart from the two nominations for National Book Awards, Connell's writing has earned him Saxton and Guggenheim fellowships and a Rockefeller Foundation grant. One mark of his distinction is that in 1981, North Point Press reissued his two Bridge books, in keeping with its commitment to reissue out-of-print contemporary classics. *Son of the Morning Star* was a best seller and garnered for Connell a National Book Critics Circle Award.

Biography

Evan Shelby Connell, Jr., was born on August 17, 1924, in Kansas City, Missouri, and was graduated from Southwest High School there in 1941. He attended Dartmouth College as a premedical student, but left in 1943 to enter the navy as an aviation cadet, later noting that without World War II he might have followed further in the footsteps of his father and grandfather, both doctors. Connell was graduated from flight school in Pensacola in May, 1945, attended instructors' training school in New Orleans, and spent the remainder of his service as a flight instructor at the Glenview Naval Air Station outside of Chicago. His flight experience provided him much of the background for his second novel, *The Patriot*, just as his childhood in Kansas City contributed to the Bridge books. After the war, Connell returned to school on the G.I. Bill, studying art and English at the University of Kansas, where he began writing fiction as a student of Ray B. West. Art has remained for him "an avocation, or second occupation," and he explains its place in his life in pragmatic terms, noting that he saw some chance of making a living as a writer, but none as a painter. Receiving his B.A. in English from the University of Kansas in 1947, Connell went on to study writing with Wallace Stegner at Stanford, with Helen Hull at Columbia from 1948 to 1949, and with Walter Van Tilburg Clark at San Francisco State College. He "floated" in Paris and Barcelona for two years, writing short stories that eventually began appearing in commercial magazines, a development which Connell partially credits to Elizabeth Mckee, who has remained his literary agent throughout his career.

From the 1950's onward, Connell lived in San Francisco, explaining that "it seems I've always needed a sense of landscape and topography." He has at times supported his writing with what he calls "stupid jobs," working as a postal clerk and a meter-reader, hauling ice, and interviewing unemployed workers for the California Department of Unemployment—the job he recalls as his worst and the one he gives to Earl Summerfield in *The Diary of a Rapist*. He has also written reviews for *The New York Times*, *New York* magazine, the *San Francisco Chronicle*, *The Washington Post*, and other publications.

Analysis

When he was asked by interviewer Dan Tooker whether he could generalize about what he wanted to "get across" in his work, Evan S. Connell, Jr.'s answer, characteristically laconic, was: "No." He says of his writing only: "I want to exemplify." For Connell, exemplification usually consists more of brief, understated vignettes than of heavily embroidered plots and fully textured characterization. He has stated his preference for doing "very, very short things" and admits that he has "always had trouble constructing a fifteen chapter novel." A reviewer in London's *The Times Literary Supplement* once compared Connell to "a coral insect, who piles one tiny, exactly shaped fragment on top of another until by the end something solid, impressive and durable has been created," a description which accurately reflects both Connell's predominant technique and its impact. Three of his six novels are literally composed of "tiny, exactly shaped fragments," as the Bridge books and *The Diary of a Rapist* consist of short chapters or diary entries, a form that has been called mosaic or pointillistic. Precision and economy characterize Connell's style, described by Gus Blaisdell as the prose equivalent of the sieve of Eratosthenes: "Everything nonessential is filtered out until only what is prime remains." The "solid, impressive, and durable" result of Connell's writing is a poetics of obsession structured in all of his novels by a dialectic of wonder and despair.

Each Connell novel presents a kind of case history of some form of obsession, ranging from Earl Summerfield's violent hatred of women to Mrs. Bridge's quiet hope for perfect conformity. His protagonists tend to define themselves in terms of single goals which they may or may not be able to perceive, much less articulate. These goals may be of tremendous import, as is true of Melvin Isaac's stubborn attempt to understand his place in a world apparently in love with war and death, or they may be of limited but intense significance, as is true of Karl Muhlbach's almost desperate love of pre-Columbian artifacts or of his infatuation with the young, beautiful, but destructive Lambeth Brett. Their particular obsessions seem to be all that separates Connell's characters from despair at the emptiness of their lives, and often their obsessions are themselves further causes of despair. Moments of exciting prospect light their lives, but those prospects usually dim, suggesting more often than not that "life is a condition of defeat."

Even after acquiring such a negative realization, Connell's characters rarely give up: like Macbeth, but for widely differing reasons and to widely differing effects, his characters echo the cry of "tomorrow and tomorrow and tomorrow." For Walter Bridge, this thought is actually reassuring, but it stamps the narrow sameness of his life. For Muhlbach, it is the dreary, disappointed, but safe cadence that will allow him to march away from the tragedy of Lambeth Brett. For Melvin Isaacs, tomorrow is the day when his life may start to make some sense to him. For Earl Summerfield, tomorrow is an oath of vengeance, and for Mrs. Bridge, it is the day when something important might happen, but never does.

Applauding the human spirit in all its vagaries, Connell paints a world that is anything but cheerful, but one that has values even if it has no meaning. In the very different lives of Melvin Isaacs and Karl Muhlbach, Connell suggests that endurance and integrity are themselves cause for minor celebrations, and while his characters all seem to face defeat after defeat, they keep struggling to make the sound and fury of their lives signify *something*. That, Connell seems to suggest, may be enough.

Mrs. Bridge consists of 117 short chapters, each a brief, ironic glimpse into the life of India Bridge, bona fide Kansas City Country Club Matron, a woman whose first name is the only chink in the armor of her militant orthodoxy. Her greatest fear is that she and her children will—even in small ways—be perceived as different from everyone else. "Everyone else" means a small circle of socially prominent Kansas Citians. Each of Connell's vignettes captures the instinctive, self-imposed narrowness of Mrs. Bridge's life in the years between the world wars.

Mrs. Bridge cannot imagine any departure from the narrow custom of her life: she flies into an inarticulate rage because her son actually uses one of the fancy towels put out for guests and is even vaguely distressed by his penchant for coming into the house through the "servants' entrance." She teaches her children that you can judge people by their shoes and their table manners. Mrs. Bridge reads only what her friends say they are reading and diligently tries to think only as they think, yearning for a world in which every vote is unanimous. So implacable is her innocent provinciality that she discusses the outbreak of World War II in almost surreal terms: "Piggly Wiggly still delivers, thank heavens, but the service is so much slower than it used to be."

Connell's satire would become sadistic were it not for his ability to reveal the emptiness beneath the crushing boredom of Mrs. Bridge's narrowly circumscribed life. Several times she almost recognizes her own plight, but the nature of her vague dissatisfaction eludes articulation. She is always about to ask an important question, about to do something interesting, about to embark on a worthwhile project, but she never does. Her life settles into a necessary sequence of delays and interruptions, insuring her a contentedness that is also a kind of despair; as her children grow up and she realizes that her successful lawyer husband will never cut back on his long hours at the office, she finds it harder and harder to pass the time. One morning she stays in bed, wondering if she is about to die, cheering only when she remembers that "her husband had told her to get the Lincoln waxed and polished." The measure of her tragedy is that even that task had been done the week before.

The longest of Connell's novels, *The Patriot* is also the least tightly wound, somewhat uneasily split between its protagonist's military and civilian experiences. This clumsiness, however, may be entirely necessary for telling the story of Melvin Isaacs, the impressively inane misfit who is Connell's patriot. The novel follows Melvin's often spectacular misadventures as he first washes out of naval flight school during World War II, then after the war he washes himself out of a fraternity and finally out of artistic success when he abandons abstractionism just when it is becoming most popular. Never really sure of his motivations, Melvin simply refuses to be incorporated, displaying for most of the novel an almost saintlike ingenuousness; more unconscious than conscientious, he is nevertheless an objector to the meticulous and mysterious processes that prepare young men for war. To the jingoistic exhortations of his Polonius of a father, Melvin says as he departs for flight training: "I'll do the best I can, as long as it makes some kind of sense." His problem, of course, is that most of military life and all of the war can never make sense at the basic intuitive level of Melvin's perceptions.

Melvin bumbles through his flight training, getting everything wrong, asking "why?" when given orders, going to sleep during relaxation class, getting his foot stuck underneath the rudder pedal on an early training flight, even accidentally managing to put a couple of rounds through his instructor's plane during gunnery practice, finally willfully tearing his plane apart on his *pro forma* last flight, crash-landing it in the face of certain dismissal from the flight program. So incredible is his performance that he becomes something of a legend in the ranks of naval aviators, the prototypal dumb "dilbert." If Melvin has a virtue it is his stubborn persistence in wanting to understand what he is doing, although he is not intellectually suited for much of a quest; faced with puzzles or problems, Melvin usually goes to sleep. He is the black chick to be pecked to death in any grouping, and yet for all of his weaknesses and for all of the embarrassments he suffers, Melvin instinctively protects his individuality—whatever the cost. In fact, his ingenuousness, so pure as to make him seem at times imbecilic, sheathes him in a kind of dopey, but unassailable existential integrity.

Put simply, Melvin values life and freedom. Spending the last few months of the war shagging golf balls at an officers' club in Texas, Melvin learns with horror of the effects of the bombing of Hiroshima. After the war, he begins to understand the significance of his own inscrutable rebellion, seeing that he had been caught up in an insanely murderous tide that had almost made of him "a derelict self, in a sea anemone, some nodulon ruptured polyp washing senselessly to and fro in the ebb and flow of the littoral foam." As *The Patriot* ends, Melvin has identified the tide he had struggled against: he decides that he will not report for his draft physical (this time the tide flows to Korea) and when his father, obviously excited by the prospect of a new war, tries to give Melvin and his wife the latest in civil defense equipment and advice, Melvin kicks him out of their house. To his father's cry of "What will you do?," Melvin simply says: "I know what I won't do," affirming once and for all his commitment to the dignity of life.

Earl Summerfield, the psychopathic protagonist of Connell's third novel, *The Diary of a Rapist*, thinks that the world's decency "went up in a column of smoke above Hiroshima," and the stark evidence of his diary supports his despair. "We set the past on fire," he writes in a diary that sears the present with Earl's rage. Indeed, this novel has a frightening intensity as Connell turns his examination of obsession on the pathology of rape, citing as one of his influences the story of a man who had raped a Miss California on two separate occasions, driving her home after the second time. "I remember wondering what could have caused him to behave in that way unless he had fallen in love with her and was thinking that maybe once she got to know him, she would love him too," Connell explains, adding that this kind of insane romanticism struck him as a peculiarly American notion.

Each day, twenty-six-year-old Earl Summerfield, a chillingly modern Bartleby the Scrivener, dazedly works at an employment bureau, waiting for a promotion that will never come, as anonymous as the countless unemployed he must interview. Each rattle of a bottle sliding down the trough of the office Coke machine times the disappearance of Earl's life. At night and on holidays he channels his hatred for his life, his job, his wife, and for women in general into entries in his diary, augmenting its private horrors with a scrapbook of newsclippings about beatings, murders, rapes, and executions. Earl is one of those whom Nathanael West termed "the cheated": he feels betrayed by a world that refuses to recognize his superiority, humiliated and dominated by a succession of women, adrift in a world so corrupt that only violence can purify it. He writes in his diary that he has looked for love, but has found only "strokes of revenge, back and forth, regular as a metronome."

Earl's diary begins on January 1 and continues for almost a year, during which time his alienation warps into madness, his moralism into monstrosity. His fantasies begin to displace reality, his memory fails, he suffers from vertigo and blackouts; more and more he loses control of his actions. "Have tried praying, it doesn't help," he writes, "My knees hurt and the words break between my teeth like eggshells." His general rage hardens into an obsession with one woman, a beauty-contest winner that he first sees on Washington's Birthday, rapes on the Fourth of July, and then suicidally surrenders himself to on Christmas Day.

Ironically, through the violence and hatred of the rape, Earl finds an even sadder prospect of love: falling in love with his victim, Mara St. John, he attempts a bizarre and terrifying courtship. Anonymously, he begins to send her presents, and he repeatedly calls her, wanting to explain how he had been so terrified with life that he fell in love with hate. He always loses control during these calls, however, and they end in his curses. Finally, he decides to give himself up to Mara on Christmas morning, and calls to tell her that he will then bow down and ask to be forgiven. His chilling diary entry for December 25 reads: "In the sight of our Lord I must be one of many." The last pages of his diary bear only the dates for the rest of the month.

Connell's depiction of Earl is horrifyingly compelling, justifying Gus Blais-dell's judgment that *The Diary of a Rapist* is "a voyage through one of the darkest nights of the soul ever encountered in literature." What is most powerful and frightening about Earl's madness is that it serves as an outlet for the sicknesses of his society. The little horrors of his scrapbook pale before the "column of smoke above Hiroshima," and Connell, too, seems to agree that "there isn't much decency left in the world."

Written ten years after *Mrs. Bridge*, *Mr. Bridge* displays little of the gentle-ness of the former work and much less humor, but is its necessary completion: to read one Bridge book without reading the other would be to miss the stunning depth of Connell's characterizations. Unlike the hapless, purposeless Mrs. Bridge, her husband, Walter, efficiently structures his life around a few severe and inflexible principles—beliefs that would cheer anyone worried that Herbert Hoover was a bit too liberal. Mr. Bridge prides himself in providing for his family's fiscal and philosophical welfare: good, safe stocks and bonds supply the former, quotations from Abraham Lincoln the latter. In *Mrs. Bridge*, Walter Bridge appears hard-working, honest, and dour—a good man even if an unlikable one. *Mr. Bridge* does nothing to change the essentials of this picture, but the world forced through the nozzle of Walter Bridge's stern perspective becomes a far darker place than it was in *Mrs. Bridge*.

Because Mr. Bridge's life is so much more complicated than his wife's, his story takes over a hundred pages longer to tell, continuing the pointillist format of the first book. Mr. Bridge's world is almost exclusively composed of relationships indicated by money, which means little to him in itself, but provides the markers that measure his achievement in the three areas essential to his self-image: "financial security, independence, and self-respect." Mr. Bridge can imagine no hardship that will not yield to the virtue of hard work, and he finds all the concern over the Depression a bit puzzling. While he is not totally unaware of his limitations, Mr. Bridge rationalizes most of them into virtues, and the book's humor rises from the few occasions when doubt momentarily undermines his priggishness. What he cannot dismiss or rationalize is his troubled relationship with his oldest daughter, Ruth, whose sullen rebelliousness and flaunted sexuality arouse both consternation and pangs of desire in his otherwise tightly controlled life. It may well be, as Guy Davenport has suggested, that "in Mr. Bridge's intuitive sense that Ruth is somehow right in her rebellion is the meaning of the two novels."

The reader knows Mrs. Bridge through her failures, Mr. Bridge through his successes, and realizes that both have imprisoned themselves in sadly limited views of the world. Mr. Bridge's opinions infuriate as much as Mrs. Bridge's naïveté amuses; the two books are different, yet perfectly matched. Not since Gertrude Stein's *Three Lives* (1909) have the rhythms of daily life been so marvelously represented, the repetitions of the mind made to seem so inexorable.

The Connoisseur is the strangest of Connell's novels; it seems least like a novel—being instead a compendium of information about pre-Columbian art—and its most important themes must be inferred and reconstructed by the reader, in much the same way that Connell's connoisseur must approach pre-Columbian culture. The connoisseur is Karl Muhlbach, a middle-aged widower with two children, a New York insurance executive whose life seems without focus until he buys a small pre-Columbian figurine while on a business trip to New Mexico. Muhlbach is the protagonist of several earlier Connell short stories, most notably "Arcturus," "Otto and the Magi," and "Saint Augustine's Pigeon," and *The Connoisseur* actually has the texture and development of a short story more than of a novel.

From his initial whimsical purchase of the figurine in a Taos gift shop, Muhlbach moves steadily, if somewhat dreamily, into two worlds, one of the ancient world of pre-Columbian artisanry, the other the modern world of fanciers, collectors, auctioneers, and dealers of art. As Muhlbach becomes more expert in the details of the ancient world, he also becomes more aware of the vagaries of the contemporary status of pre-Columbian objects. He learns from experience of the trade in fake artifacts and of the exquisite uncertainties in trying to determine whether a piece is fake or authentic, and, as he encounters others obsessed by this art, he sees and then shares in the peculiar intensity of its collectors and dealers. Connell's readers learn right along with Muhlbach; a significant portion of the novel seems to consist of direct excerpts from studies of pre-Columbian art and comments that serve as minilectures from the string of connoisseurs whom Muhlbach encounters. His immersion into this lore raises a number of questions about the psychology of collecting and of obsession, about the ethics of removing national treasures from their native countries, and about the aesthetic difference between originals and imitations. Underlying all of these issues is the contrast between past and present, between the fragile permanence of centuries-old artifacts and the impermanence of Muhlbach's own life, which threatens to leave a mark no more substantial than steps in the snow.

More difficult to isolate, but more important are the questions raised by Muhlbach's obsession itself. His relationships with his children, with his woman friend, and with the world around him become completely eclipsed by his desire for pre-Columbian art. Late in the novel, he realizes that he is so gripped by this obsession that he can no longer distinguish reality, and he has to remind himself that his children "mean more than all the world's Olmec masks." Sleepwalking through the other aspects of his life and finding meaning only in his collecting, the connoisseur muses to himself: "I suppose I should be alarmed, but as a matter of fact I'm not. This is really rather pleasant. I want more."

The title of Connell's fifth novel, *Double Honeymoon*, is itself doubly ironic as it is both the title of a pornographic film that counts in the book's plot and a caustic description of the contours of that plot. This is the story of a hopeless affair between Connell's most familiar protagonist, Karl Muhlbach, and a beautiful, tragically unstable twenty-year-old girl, Lambeth Brett. Bored with his life, which he compares to a "stale chopped liver sandwich," Muhlbach convinces himself that even a fleeting relationship with the exotic Lambeth is worth enduring "a reasonable amount of nonsense." Although he recognizes that Lambeth is as "unstable as a bead of mercury," and that his own rather staid life can never really change, Muhlbach grows more and more infatuated—if not exactly with Lambeth, with the idea of her youth and the mystery of her supreme indifference to the world around her. Constrained by traditions, "condemned to worry about consequences," Muhlbach realizes that Lambeth offers him—however remotely—a last chance to break the confining "threads of half a lifetime."

Of course, Muhlbach's obsession with Lambeth frees him from nothing, offering instead piece after piece of unavoidable evidence that any relationship with her can only underscore his dissatisfaction with his life. "You're more screwed up than I am," Lambeth tells him. Even after one of Lambeth's many former lovers shows Muhlbach a pornographic film in which she is one of the brides on a "double honeymoon," Muhlbach cannot free himself from his infatuation, although he recognizes all of its irony. Art, in the guise of his old stamp collection and of a show of Japanese woodcuts, offers him some distraction, but only Lambeth's suicide allows him to blend back into the sameness of his life.

Since *Double Honeymoon*, like *The Connoisseur*, dispenses with quotation marks, the reader is often uncertain whether Muhlbach is talking or thinking, the result being a dreamlike quality of the narration that perfectly suits the dreamlike, sometimes nightmarish, relationship between Muhlbach and Lambeth. What makes this story so complicated is that Lambeth is as much victim as she is victimizer: Muhlbach does offer her a stability she needs even more desperately than he needs her unpredictability, and she is drawn to him just as surely as she acts in ways that must repel him. Her "likes" and "wows" make Muhlbach think that he may need an interpreter for talking with her, and their language differences only hint at the ultimately unbridgeable chasm between their lives. Protected by the very staidness he wants to escape, Muhlbach survives while Lambeth does not, at least partially confirming an adage he shared with her: "Life being what it is, one dreams of revenge."

Running through Connell's novels is a persistent note of frustration that often shades into despair. While Connell's novels acknowledge and sometimes celebrate the intensity, enthusiasm, and scattered triumphs that attend the many levels and ranges of human obsession, they seem to protest that life itself should be the end or object of obsession and not merely its means: man should be obsessed *with* life, not only obsessed *in* it. What finally emerges most strongly from this note of frustration or despair is not a sense of fatalism or of defeat, but a sense of the author's own fierce respect for human life and his outrage at the follies—large and small—that threaten to stifle or still the human spirit. Gus Blaisdell calls this stance of Connell "a position of untempered humanism, primitively Christian at the core . . . his outrage and indignation ameliorated by love." Indeed, some combination of outrage, indignation, and love, both for his characters and for the human traits they represent, can account for most of Connell's writing.

At a time when many novelists argue that the only interesting and promising subject of fiction is fiction itself, Connell remains committed to the belief that the novel should have some substantial connection to the powerful feelings of human experience. This is not to say that Connell's novels are conventionally "realistic," but that they strive to be true to human emotion—in the tradition of Anton Chekhov, Leo Tolstoy, and Thomas Mann. While Connell's craftsmanship in each of his novels reveals a fascination with language, his novels always point beyond themselves to human experience and beyond human experience to the wonder of life.

Brooks Landon

Other major works

SHORT FICTION: *The Anatomy Lesson and Other Stories*, 1957; *At the Crossroads*, 1965; *Saint Augustine's Pigeon*, 1980.

POETRY: *Notes from a Bottle Found on the Beach at Carmel*, 1963; *Points for a Compass Rose*, 1973.

NONFICTION: *A Long Desire*, 1979; *The White Lantern*, 1980; *Son of the Morning Star: Custer and the Little Bighorn*, 1984.

Bibliography
Blaisdell, Gus. "After Ground Zero: The Writings of Evan S. Connell, Jr."

New Mexico Quarterly 36 (Summer, 1966): 181-207. A discussion of Connell's major works up to 1966. Blaisdell is very impressed by *Mrs. Bridge*
but thinks that *The Diary of a Rapist* is Connell's masterpiece, primarily
because of the sympathy he creates for the rapist.

Hicks, Granville. "Flyer Out of Formation." *Saturday Review* 43 (September 24, 1960): 16. Praises *Mrs. Bridge* but considers *The Patriot* a step
backward in Connell's career, finding the novel to be dull and poorly
structured.

Landon, Brooks. "On Evan Connell." *Iowa Review* 13 (Winter, 1982). Landon has high praise for Connell and thinks that the evocation of daily life in
Mrs. Bridge is especially well done. Connell's satire reveals the emptiness
of the Bridges' lives with tact and sympathy.

Shattuck, Roger. "Fiction à la Mode." *The New York Review of Books* 6
(June 23, 1966): 22-25. Shattuck likes the characterization and suspense of
The Diary of a Rapist but has some reservations about the diary form.

Tooker, Dan, and Roger Hofheins. "Evan S. Connell, Jr." In *Fiction: Interviews with Northern California Writers*. New York: Harcourt Brace Jovanovich, 1976. Connell is very candid about his influences and his own writing. He speaks of his early interest in painting and how that shaped his
view of craftsmanship in any art. Surprisingly, he finds American writers
to be tiresome next to Europeans.

JOSEPH CONRAD
Józef Teodor Konrad Nałęcz Korzeniowski

Born: Near Berdyczów, Poland; December 3, 1857
Died: Oswalds, Bishopsbourne, England; August 3, 1924

Principal long fiction

Almayer's Folly, 1895; *An Outcast of the Islands*, 1896; *The Nigger of the "Narcissus,"* 1897; *Heart of Darkness*, 1899 (serial), 1902; *Lord Jim*, 1900; *The Inheritors*, 1901 (with Ford Madox Ford); *Romance*, 1903 (with Ford Madox Ford); *Nostromo*, 1904; *The Secret Agent*, 1907; *Under Western Eyes*, 1911; *Chance*, 1913; *Victory*, 1915; *The Shadow-Line*, 1917; *The Arrow of Gold*, 1919; *The Rescue*, 1920; *The Rover*, 1923; *The Nature of a Crime*, 1909 (serial), 1924 (with Ford Madox Ford); *Suspense*, 1925 (incomplete).

Other literary forms

Joseph Conrad's many short stories were published in seven collected editions. The majority of the stories appeared earlier in magazine form, especially in *Blackwood's Magazine*, a magazine that Conrad referred to as "Maga." Of the short stories, three—"Youth," "The Secret Sharer," and "An Outpost of Progress"—have been widely anthologized and are generally recognized as classics of the genre. Two memoirs of Conrad's years at sea, *The Mirror of the Sea* (1906) and *A Personal Record* (1912) are prime sources of background information on Conrad's sea tales. Conrad wrote three plays: *The Secret Agent* (1921), a four-act adaptation of the novel which enjoyed a brief success on the London stage; and two short plays, *Laughing Anne* (1923) and *One Day More* (1905) which had no success. His oeuvre is rounded out by two books of essays on widely ranging topics, *Notes on Life and Letters* (1921) and *Last Essays* (1926); a travel book, *Joseph Conrad's Diary of His Journey Up the Valley of the Congo in 1890* (1926); and the aborted novel *The Sisters*, left incomplete at his death in 1924, but published in fragment form in 1928.

Achievements

In the last quarter-century, Conrad has enjoyed an extraordinary Renaissance in readership and in critical attention. Readers and critics alike have come to recognize that although one of Conrad's last novels, *The Rover*, was published in the early 1920's, he is the most modern of writers in both theme and technique.

Conrad is, in fact, the architect of the modern psychological novel with its emphasis on character and character analysis. For Conrad, people in plot situations are the primary concern, rather than plot situations, per se. Indeed, Conrad once professed that he was incapable of creating "an effective lie," meaning a plot "that would sell and be admirable." This is something of an exaggeration, but the fact remains that Conrad's novels center around the solitary hero who, either by chance or by choice, is somehow alienated and set apart from his fellowmen. This theme of isolation and alienation dominates Conrad's novels and spans his work from the early sea tales to the political novels to what Conrad called his "romances."

Conrad's "loners" are manifest everywhere in his work—Jim in *Lord Jim*, Kurtz in *Heart of Darkness*, Razumov in *Under Western Eyes*. This emphasis in Conrad on the alienated and isolated figure has had a considerable impact on the direction of the twentieth century novel, and Conrad's influence may be discerned in such disparate writers as Stephen Crane, F. Scott Fitzgerald, and T. S. Eliot.

Conrad made another contribution in shaping the modern novel: he was the forerunner (although hardly the originator) of two techniques which have found much favor and wide employment in the twentieth century novel. Conrad was among the first of the modern novelists to employ multiple narrators, or shifting points of view, as he does in *Heart of Darkness* and *Lord Jim*. This technique enabled Conrad to make the probing analyses of characters and their motivations which are the hallmarks both of his work and of the work of so many others to follow. The reader sees both Kurtz and Jim, for example, through several pairs of eyes, some sympathetic, some not, before both tales are turned over to Charlie Marlow, who does his best to sort out the conflicting testimonies and to give the reader an objective and a rounded view of both men.

The extensive use of the flashback in the contemporary novel and, indeed, the contemporary film, is another technique which Conrad pioneered. In Conrad's case, as is the case with all writers who employ the technique, the flashback creates suspense; but it also serves another and more important function in his work, enabling him to examine more thoroughly the minds and the motivations of his characters. Having presented the crisis or the moment of action or the point of decision, Conrad then goes back in time, in an almost leisurely fashion, and retraces step by step the psychological pattern which led to the crisis, to the action, to the decision.

Finally, Conrad finds a place and a role among the moderns in still another way. He is one of the great symbolists in English literature. Conrad's use of thoroughly unconventional symbols, related in some way to the metaphysical metaphors to be found in much modern poetry, has had an inestimable influence on the modern novel.

Biography

Joseph Conrad was born Jósef Teodor Konrad Nałęcz Korzeniowski on December 3, 1857, near the rural village of Berdyczów in the Polish Ukraine, then, as it is today, under Russian domination. Conrad's mother, Ewa Bobrowski, came from an affluent and influential family of landowners who had made their peace, as best they could, with their Russian overlords. Conrad's father, Apollo Korzeniowski, was a would-be poet, a dedicated patriot, and a translator of William Shakespeare into Polish and found no peace in Russian Poland. The marriage of Apollo and Ewa was frowned upon by the Bobrowskis, who felt that Ewa had married beneath herself, and Ewa's brother, Tadeusz, a prominent lawyer and member of the landed gentry, seldom missed an opportunity to remind his nephew, Jósef, that he bore the tainted Nalecz blood.

Apollo Korzeniowski devoted all his energies and, ultimately, his life to the Polish freedom movement. As a result of his political activities, he was labeled an enemy of the state and exiled to Vologda in northern Russia. The five-year-old Jósef Teodor and his mother followed Apollo into exile. Three years later, her health ruined by the fierce Russian winters, Ewa Korzeniowski died, and Apollo, equally weakened by the ordeal, succumbed four years after his wife. There is little doubt that Conrad's own lifelong precarious physical state had its genesis in these years in exile.

From these blighted early years, two convictions were impressed in Conrad's consciousness which surfaced in his work: a continuing hatred for all things Russian and for autocratic regimes; and a strong sense of man as victim, instilled by his father's fate, and of man's essential loneliness and isolation, instilled by his own orphanage at the age of twelve. The victimization of the innocent lies at the heart of Conrad's political novels, especially *Under Western Eyes* and *The Secret Agent*, and is a major theme in *Heart of Darkness*. The alienated figure, forced to cope as best he can alone, is the essential Conrad.

With the deaths of Apollo and Ewa Korzeniowski, Conrad came under the tutelage of his concerned but somewhat demanding maternal uncle, Tadeusz Bobrowski. Bobrowski, a man of many affairs and very positive ideas and ideals, sent his young ward to St. Anne's School in Krakow for a brief term and later provided Conrad with a tutor and companion in the hope of creating a proper Polish gentleman. These few years constituted the extent of Conrad's formal education. An avid reader from his early childhood, Conrad was largely self-educated, and the wide knowledge of English, French, and Russian literature apparent in his works (especially in his critical essays) was acquired through his own efforts.

Bobrowski's hopes and plans for Conrad's becoming an accepted member of the right circles in Polish society were not to be realized. Chafing under the regimen of his over-solicitous uncle and, perhaps, convinced that there was no place for Apollo Korzienowski's son in Russian Poland, Conrad finally persuaded his reluctant uncle that his future lay elsewhere: at sea, a dream with which Conrad had been obsessed since seeing the Adriatic during a walking tour of northern Italy in 1873.

In 1874, at the age of seventeen, Conrad left Poland for the port city of

Marseilles, France, and the seaman's life to which he would devote the next twenty years. He carried with him his uncle's begrudging blessing and, more important, considerable financial support. The break with his native land was to be more complete than Conrad may have realized at the time, since he returned to Poland on only three occasions during the remainder of his life.

Conrad's adventures and misadventures during his four years in and about Marseilles provided the material, many years later, for the almost lyrical memoir *The Mirror of the Sea* and the novel *The Arrow of Gold*, the latter of which works has been the subject of much critical dispute. With his uncle's backing, Conrad acquired, during that time, part ownership of the bark *Tremolino*, which was then employed in smuggling arms for the Spanish Pretender, Don Carlos. It was a period of much intrigue, and Conrad appears to have been at the center, enjoying it hugely.

What is not clear about the Marseilles years, unless one accepts Conrad's highly fictionalized version of the events in *The Arrow of Gold*, is how his ventures at that time all came to a disastrous end. Conrad apparently invested a considerable sum of money in a quixotic mining venture. Moreover, if the Doña Rita of *The Arrow of Gold* did, in fact, exist as Conrad describes her in the novel, then a particularly painful and hopeless love affair complicated Conrad's desperate financial straits. In any event, in February, 1878, Conrad attempted suicide and almost succeeded by placing a bullet in his chest, very near the heart.

Uncle Tadeusz made a hasty trip to Marseilles and restored some kind of order to Conrad's tangled affairs, and, on April 24, 1878, Conrad signed on the British ship *Mavis*, bound from Marseilles to England. Conrad's career as a seaman and, more particularly as a British seaman, had begun. In the next twenty years, sailing on a variety of ships on passages which encompassed half the globe, Conrad accomplished an incredible feat. An alien from a landlocked country, bearing an unpronounceable foreign name and speaking English with a pronounced Slavic-French accent, Conrad rose from able seaman to master mariner in the British Merchant Service. Conrad took great pride in being addressed as Captain Korzeniowski, just as he took great pride in his British citizenship, acquired in 1885.

Many of the ships on which Conrad sailed make an appearance in his works. For example, there actually was a *Narcissus* on which Conrad sailed from Bombay to Dunkirk and a *Palestine* which became the *Judea* of "Youth" and the *S. S. Roi des Belges*, the counterpart of Marlow's "tinpot" steamboat in *Heart of Darkness*. In similar fashion, many of Conrad's characters are based on real-life prototypes, men whom Conrad had encountered or of whom he had heard while at sea. There *was* a "Jim"; there *was* a "MacWhirr"; there *was* an "Almayer"; there *was* an "Axel Heyst"; there *was* a "Tom Lingard" and there *was* a "Charlie Marlow," born Jósef Korzeniowski.

In 1889, while between ships in London, Conrad began work on the strange tale of Kaspar Almayer. The work continued sporadically during Conrad's six-month tour in the Belgian Congo in 1890, a sojourn which later provided the material for his first major work, *Heart of Darkness*, and also succeeded in further undermining his already unstable health. In 1893, Conrad, then first mate of the ship *Torrens*, showed the nine completed chapters of *Almayer's Folly* to an English passenger and was encouraged to finish the book. *Almayer's Folly* was published in 1895, to be followed by *An Outcast of the Islands* in 1896, *The Nigger of the "Narcissus"* in 1897, *Heart of Darkness* in 1899, and *Lord Jim* in 1900.

Conrad enjoyed almost immediate critical acclaim, but despite the string of critical successes, he had only a modest public following. In fact, Conrad did not have a best-seller until 1913, with *Chance*. Ironically, the reading public did not find Conrad until after he had written his best work.

Given this limited popular success, Conrad did not feel secure enough to devote himself entirely to a writing career, and, for a five-year period, 1889 to 1895, he vacillated between the safety of a master's berth aboard ship and the uncertainty of his writing table. Even as late as 1898, when he was well-established with a publisher and several reputable magazines eager for his work, Conrad seriously considered returning to the sea.

With his marriage to Jessie George in 1894, Conrad had, in effect, returned from the sea and settled down to a life of hectic domesticity and long, agonizing hours of writing. Jessie, an unassuming, maternal woman, was the perfect mate for the often unpredictable, volatile, and ailing Conrad, and she cheerfully nursed him through his frequent attacks of malaria, gout, and deep depression. The marriage produced two sons, Borys and John, and lasted until Conrad's death.

Except for a brief trip to his native Poland in 1914, a few holidays on the Continent, and an even briefer trip to the United States in 1923, Conrad was resigned to the endless hours at his desk and content to live the life of an English gentleman in his adopted land. The Conrads were something of a nomadic family, however, moving frequently whenever Conrad tired of one of their rented dwellings. His last five years were spent at Oswalds, Bishopsbourne, near Canterbury.

After World War I, the acclaim and the recognition which he had so richly earned finally came to Conrad—an offer of knighthood (which he declined) and the friendship and the respect of many of the literary greats of the time. Essentially a very private man, Conrad, while never denying his Polish origins nor renouncing his Roman Catholic faith, tried to live the quiet life of the quintessential English country squire. There was always, however, something of the foreigner about him—the monocle, the Continental-style greatcoat, the slightly Oriental eyes, the click of the heels and the formal bow from the waist—which did not go unnoticed among his English friends and neighbors. Like so many of the characters in his novels; Conrad remained somehow apart and alienated from the mainstream of the life about him.

On August 3, 1924, Conrad succumbed to a massive heart attack at his home near Bishopsbourne. He is buried in the cemetery at Canterbury, in—according to the parish register of St. Thomas' Church—"that part reserved for Catholics." Even in death, Conrad, like so many of his fictional creations, found himself alone and apart.

Analysis

Three themes are dominant among Joseph Conrad's sea tales, considered by most critics as his best work. The first of these themes is an unremitting sense of loyalty and duty to the ship and this quality is exemplified by Conrad's seamen who are successful in practicing their craft. In *The Mirror of the Sea*, Conrad, in propria persona, and through Singleton, the exemplar of the faithful seaman in *The Nigger of the "Narcissus,"* summarized this necessity for keeping faith in observing, "Ships are all right. It's the men in them." The note of fidelity is struck again in *A Personal Record*, when Conrad says of his years at sea: "I do not know whether I have been a good seaman, but I know I have been a very faithful one." Conversely, it is the men who break faith—Jim is the prime example—who fail and who are doomed to be set apart.

A second major theme in Conrad's sea tales, noted by virtually all of his critics, is the therapeutic value of work. To Conrad, the ancient adage "Idle hands are the devil's workshop" was not a cliché but a valid principle. The two most damning words in Conrad's lexicon are "undisciplined" and "lazy," and, again, it is the men whose hands and minds are without meaningful employment who get into difficulties, who fail, and who suffer the Conradian penalty for failure, alienation and isolation. Kurtz, in *Heart of Darkness*, is Conrad's chief exemplar here, but Jim's failure, too, partially results from the fact that he has very little to do in the way of work during the crucial passage aboard the *Patna*.

Finally, a sense of tradition, of one's place in the long continuum of men who have gone to sea, is a recurring theme in Conrad's sea tales. Marlow expresses this sense of tradition best when he speaks of the faithful seamen who band together and are bonded together in what he calls "the fellowship of the craft." The Jims, on the other hand, the captains who display cowardice, the seamen who panic under stress, all those who bring disgrace on the men who have kept faith and do keep faith, are dismissed from the fellowship and are set apart, isolated and alienated. Conrad, then, played a central role in setting the stage for the alienated, solitary figures and, ultimately, the rebels-at-arms who people the pages of the modern novel.

In *Heart of Darkness*, the first of Conrad's recognized masterpieces and one of the greatest novellas in the language, a number of familiar Conradian themes and techniques coalesce: his detestation of autocratic regimes and their special manifestation, colonialism; the characteristic Conradian alien figure, isolated and apart; the therapeutic value of work; and the use of multiple points of view and of strikingly unconventional symbols.

Charlie Marlow, the ostensible narrator of the story, finds himself (as Conrad did on occasion during his sea career) without a ship and with few prospects. As a last resort, he signs on to command a river steamboat for a Belgian trading company, then seeking ivory in the Congo. In a curious way, Marlow's venture into the Congo represents a wish fulfillment, since, Marlow recalls, as a child he had placed his finger on a map of Africa and said, "Someday, I will go there," "there" being the Congo. (This is "autobiography as fiction" again in that Conrad himself had once expressed such a desire and in exactly the terms Marlow employs.)

The mature Marlow, however, has few illusions about what he is undertaking. He characterizes his "command" as "a two-penny-half-penny river-steamboat with a penny whistle attached," and he is quite aware that he will be working for a company whose chief concern is turning a profit, and a large one at that. Moreover, the Company's success will come only at the expense of the innocent and helpless natives who have the misfortune of living in an area that has immense possibilities as a colony.

Marlow, like Conrad, abhors the concept of one people dominating another unless, as he says, the colonizing power is faithful to the "idea" which provides the sole rationale for colonialism, that is, the "idea" of actually bringing the benefits of civilization to the colonized. He believes that only in the British Crown Colonies is the "idea" being adhered to, and he has grave reservations about what he will find in the Congo. Despite these reservations, Marlow is hardly prepared for what awaits him.

Marlow finds in the Congo disorder bordering on lunacy, waste, intrigue, inefficiency, and the cruelest kind of exploitation. The "pilgrims of progress," as Marlow calls them, go about their aimless and pointless tasks while the steamboat he is to command sits idle in the river with a hole in her bottom. Mountains are leveled to no purpose, while equipment and supplies rust or rot in the African sun or never reach their destination. As long as the ivory flows from the heart of darkness, however, no one is overly concerned. Marlow is appalled by the hypocrisy of the situation. An entire continent is being ruthlessly ravaged and pillaged in the name of progress, when, in fact, the real motivation is sheer greed. Nor is there the slightest concern for the plight of the natives in the Company's employ. Marlow sees once proud and strong tribesmen, divorced from their natural surroundings and from all that is familiar to them, sickened and weakened, sitting passively in the shade waiting to die.

Herein is Marlow/Conrad's chief objection to colonialism. By taking men from their normal mode of life and thrusting upon them a culture which they neither want nor understand, colonialism places men in isolation and makes them aliens in their own land. The cannibals who serve as woodcutters for Marlow's steamboat have lost their muscle tone and belong back in the jungle practicing the peculiar rites that, however revolting by other standards, are natural for them. The native fireman on the steamboat, "an improved specimen," Marlow calls him, watches the water gauge on the boiler, lest the god inside becomes angry. He sits, his teeth filed, his head shaved in strange patterns, a voodoo charm tied to his arm, a piece of polished bone inserted through his lower lip. He represents the perfect victim of the white men's progress, and "he ought to have been clapping his hands and stamping his feet on the bank."

The evil that colonialism has wrought is not, however, confined to the natives. The whites who seek adventure or fortune in the Congo are equally uprooted from all that is natural for them, equally isolated and alienated. The doctor who gives Marlow a perfunctory examination in the Company's headquarters in Brussels asks apologetically for permission to measure Marlow's head while, at the same time, noting that the significant changes will occur "inside." To some degree or other, such changes have come to the whites whom Marlow encounters in Africa. The ship on which Marlow sails to the Congo passes a French gunboat firing aimlessly into the jungle as an object lesson to the natives. The accountant at the Central Station makes perfectly correct entries in his impeccable ledgers while just outside his window, in the grove of death, the mass of displaced natives is dying of fever and malnutrition. The Company's brickmaker makes no bricks because there has been no straw for more than a year, but he remains placid and unconcerned.

Marlow's summation of what he has seen in the Congo is acerbic, withering in its emotional intensity, but it is also an accurate statement of Conrad's feelings toward this, the cruelest exercise of autocratic power. Marlow says, "It was just robbery with violence, aggravated murder on a great scale . . . and with no more moral purpose at the back of it than there is in burglars breaking into a safe." The voice is Charlie Marlow's, but the sentiments are Joseph Conrad's.

One man alone among the Company's disreputable, if not depraved, white traders appears to be an exception, a man who is faithful to the "idea" and is bringing progress and betterment to the natives in exchange for the ivory he gathers. Kurtz is by far the Company's most productive trader, and his future in Brussels seems assured. At the same time, Kurtz is both hated and feared by all the Europeans in the Company's employ. He is hated because of the unconventional (an ironic adjective) methods he has adopted, and he is feared because these methods are apparently working.

With the introduction of Kurtz into the tale, Conrad works by indirection. Neither Marlow nor the reader is allowed to see Kurtz immediately. Rather, one is exposed to Kurtz through many different viewpoints, and, in an effort to allow the reader to see Kurtz from all perspectives, other narrators are brought forth to take over the story briefly: the accountant; the brickmaker; the manager of the Central Station; the Russian; penultimately, Marlow himself; and ultimately, Kurtz's fiancée, the Intended. In addition to these many shifting points of view which Conrad employs, it should be noted that the story, from beginning to end, is told by a dual narrator. Charlie Marlow speaks, but Marlow's unnamed crony, the fifth member of the group gathered on the fantail of the *Nellie*, is the actual narrator of the story, retelling the tale as he has heard it from Marlow. In some sense, then, it is difficult to say whether *Heart of Darkness* is Kurtz's story or Marlow's story or the anonymous narrator's story, since Marlow's tale has obviously had a significant impact on the silent listener.

Marlow is fascinated by Kurtz and what his informants tell him of Kurtz, and throughout the long journey upriver to the Inner Station, he is obsessed with meeting this remarkable man, but he is destined for a shocking disappointment. Kurtz is, perhaps the extreme example among all the isolated and alienated figures to be found in Conrad's works. Philosophically and spiritually alienated from the "pilgrims of progress," he is also physically isolated. He is the only white man at the Inner Station, and, given the steamboat debacle, nothing has been heard from or of him for months. He has been alone too long, and the jungle has found him out. He is, in Marlow's words, "a hollow man" with great plans and hopes but totally lacking in the inner resources vital for survival in an alien environment. As a result, he has regressed completely to the primitive state; he has become a god to the natives, who worship him in the course of "unspeakable rites." He has taken a native woman as a consort, and the Russian trader who tried to befriend him has been relegated to fool and jester in Kurtz's jungle court. Kurtz exercises absolute power of life and death over the natives, and he punishes his enemies by placing their severed heads on poles about his hut as ornaments. The doctor in Brussels, Marlow recalls, was fearful of what physical and spiritual isolation might do to men's minds, and on Kurtz, the effect has been devastating. Kurtz is mentally unbalanced, but even worse, as Marlow says, "His soul was mad."

Marlow has confessed that he, too, has heard the appeal of "the fascination of the abomination," the strange sounds and voices emanating from the banks of the river as the steamboat makes its way to Kurtz. Meaningless and unintelligible as the sounds and voices are, they are also somehow familiar to Marlow and strike deep at some primordial instinct within him. Yet, while Kurtz is destroyed, Marlow survives, "luckily, luckily," as he observes. The difference between the two men is restraint, a recurrent term in the novel: with restraint, a man can survive in isolation. The cannibals on the steamboat have it, and Marlow is at a loss to explain the phenomenon. The manager at the Central Station also has it, largely the result of his unfailing good health which permits him to serve, virtually unscathed, term after term in the darkness. The accountant has restraint by virtue of concentrating on his correct entries in his meticulous ledgers and, at the same time, by forfeiting his humanity and closing his mind to the chaos around him.

Chiefly, however, restraint (in Conrad's *Weltanschauung*) is a function of work, and the major statement in all of Conrad of the redeeming nature of work comes in *Heart of Darkness*. Marlow confesses that, like most human beings, he does not like work per se. He does, however, respond to "what is in the work," and he recognizes its salutary effect, "the chance to find yourself." Indeed, the fact that Marlow has work to do in the Congo is his salvation. The steamboat must be salvaged; it must be raised from the bottom of the river. No supplies are available, and the boiler is in disrepair. Marlow needs rivets and sheeting to patch the gaping hole in the boat. The task seems hopeless, but Marlow attacks it enthusiastically, almost joyously, because his preoccupation with rescuing his "two-penny, half-penny" command effectively shields him from "the fascination of the abomination." Later, during the trip upriver to the Inner Station, it is again the work of piloting the vulnerable steamboat around and through the myriad rocks and snags of the convoluted river and the intense concentration required for the work that shut Marlow's eyes and, more important, his mind to the dangers to psyche and spirit surrounding him. Marlow does not leave the Congo completely untouched; he has paid a price, both physically and mentally, for venturing into the darkness, but he does escape with his life and his sanity. As he later recognizes, he owes his escape to the steamboat, his "influential friend," as he calls it, and to the work it provided.

Symbols abound in *Heart of Darkness*, many of them conventional: the interplay of light and darkness throughout the novel, for example, carrying essentially the traditional symbolic meanings of the two terms, or the rusting and decaying equipment Marlow comes across at the Central Station, symbolizing the callous inefficiency of the Company's management. More striking, however, is Conrad's use of thoroughly unconventional symbols; dissimilar images are yoked together in a startling fashion, unique in Conrad's time. Kurtz's totally bald head, for example, is compared to a ball of ivory, and the comparison moves beyond metaphor to the realm of symbol, adumbrating the manner in which the lust for and preoccupation with ivory have turned flesh-and-blood human beings into cold, lifeless ivory figures. There are also the shrunken heads fixed as ornaments on the fence posts surrounding Kurtz's hut. These are Kurtz's "rebels" and, notably, all but one are facing inward, so that, even in death, they are compelled to worship their god. The one facing outward, however, is irretrievably damned and without hope of salvation.

Similar in many ways to *Heart of Darkness*, *Lord Jim* is considered by many critics to be not only Conrad's greatest sea tale but also his greatest novel. *Lord Jim* is not a sea tale, however, in the purest sense, since most of the action of the novel takes place on land. *Lord Jim* is one of Conrad's psychological studies; Jim's mind and his motivations are searched and probed in meticulous detail in an effort to "see Jim clearly." In making this effort, Conrad employs two characteristic techniques: the shifting, multiple points of view and the extensive use of flashbacks.

The narrative begins conventionally with an unnamed third-person narrator who brings the reader to the point of Marlow's first encounter with Jim at the Board of Inquiry investigating the strange case of the pilgrim ship *Patna*. At this point, Marlow takes over the tale, recounting his meeting with Jim. Marlow's account, however, is filtered through the consciousness of the anonymous narrator, much as is the case in *Heart of Darkness*. The manipulation of the narrative voices in *Lord Jim* is much more complex, however, since Jim speaks through Marlow and Marlow through the ultimate narrator.

Again, as in *Heart of Darkness*, other narrators enter the scene briefly, and Marlow gives way to a series of speakers, each of whom is qualified to tell the reader something more about Jim. Montague Brierly, Captain of the crack ship *Ossa*, is troubled by Jim's failure to meet the demands of "the fellowship of the craft" and is also troubled by his doubts about his own ability to meet those demands. The French Lieutenant who boarded the abandoned *Patna* and brought it safely to port is a bit more sympathetic toward Jim's moment of cowardice, but is also more rigid in his condemnation of Jim's loss of honor. At the opposite end of the scale, Chester, the preposterous seaman-at-large, dismisses Jim's canceled mate's certificate as nothing more than "a bit of ass's skin" and solicits Marlow's aid in involving Jim in Chester's lunatic scheme of extracting guano from an island which is totally inaccessible. In Chester's view, Jim is the right man for the job, since he is now good for nothing else. Through Chester as interim narrator, Marlow recognizes how desperate Jim's plight is and how equally desperate Jim is for his help.

Marlow does help by putting Jim in touch with Mr. Denver, the owner of a rice mill, and Jim thrives for a time, becoming, in essence, a surrogate son to his employer. The specter of the *Patna* affair overtakes Jim, however, in the form of the fated ship's second engineer, who comes to work at the rice mill. Through Denver, through Egström, who employs Jim briefly as a water-clerk, and finally, through the seedy Schomberg, proprietor of an equally seedy hotel in Bangkok, Marlow learns of Jim's gradual decline and his erratic flight from the *Patna* or, as Marlow puts it, his flight "from himself."

In an attempt to help Jim, Marlow turns to Stein, an extraordinary trader and shrewd judge of both butterflies and men. Stein's eminently "practical" solution is to send Jim to Patusan, virtually the end of the Earth, where the *Patna* has never been heard of and from whence Jim need run no more.

Marlow's visit to Patusan and to Jim is relayed, as is the bulk of the novel, through the unnamed listener among Marlow's small circle of friends gathered over their evening cigars to whom Marlow has been addressing his tale. In the final chapters, Conrad's tour de force of narrative technique takes yet another twist. The disaster in Patusan is recounted through the medium of a lengthy letter which Marlow writes to the ultimate narrator, the narration thus coming full circle from third-person narrator, to Marlow, to a series of intermediate narrators, and finally returning to the speaking voice which began the tale.

Adding to the difficulties which Conrad's dizzying shift of narrators presents for the reader is his frequent use of time shifts in the narrative. Jim's long colloquy with Marlow in Marlow's room at the Malabar House, for example, takes the reader back in time to the events aboard the *Patna* which occurred several months earlier. While observing the seemingly bored Brierly in the courtroom at the Board of Inquiry, Marlow abruptly moves ahead in time to Brierly's suicide, which follows a week after the end of the trial, and then ahead again some two years for the mate's detailed account of Brierly's methodical leap over the side of the *Ossa*. Marlow's letter, which Conrad employs to bring the novel to its close, represents yet another flashback, examples of this movement back and forth in time in the novel could be multiplied.

Conrad's complex manipulation of his narrators and of the disjointed time sequence of the events of the novel have a single purpose: to give the reader a complete view of a psychologically complex figure. It is an effort, as Marlow insists several times, to "see Jim clearly." Yet, for all Conrad's (and Marlow's) efforts, Jim remains an enigma. Marlow, in fact, confesses at the end of his letter that Jim continues to be "inscrutable."

Chiefly, there are two problems which have plagued critics in coming to grips with Jim. Stein, on whom Marlow relies for enlightenment, pronounces Jim "a romantic," which Stein says is "very bad . . . and very good too." In attempting to resolve the problem of how a romantic may cope with reality, Stein uses the metaphor of a man falling into the sea (the overtones of Jim's leap from the *Patna* are obvious here). Stein continues, "The way is to the destructive element submit yourself, and with the exertions of your hands and feet in the water make the deep, deep sea keep you up." The trouble here is that Stein does not make clear whether it is Jim's dream of heroes and heroics which is the "destructive element" or whether it is the practical and mundane world in which he must endeavor to carry out this dream which is destructive. Does Jim immerse himself in the dream yet keep his head above "water" in the world of reality, or immerse himself in the world of reality and yet keep the dream alive directly above the surface? The critical controversy which Stein's cryptic advice has provoked continues.

Critics are also divided on the meaning of the end of the novel. When Jim presents himself to the old nakhoda, Doramin, and suffers the pistol shot which ends his life, is this the act of a man who has finally accepted that he is capable of failure and who "has mastered his destiny," or is it merely the desperate act of a man who has simply run out of options? The distinction may seem fine, since in any case, Jim's gesture is a positive act, but it governs the reader's final judgment on whether Marlow is correct in accepting Jim as "one of us."

If Jim is not "one of us," he is clearly one of "them," them being the familiar Conradian figures, the isolated and alienated solitaries, and he is so both spiritually and physically. In abandoning the *Patna*, Jim has violated a cardinal principle of the seaman's code, placing his own safety above that of the pilgrims who have entrusted themselves to him. As Brierly puts it, "we are trusted," and he is unforgiving of Jim's dereliction, as is Marlow, although Marlow is willing to admit mitigating circumstances. To the seamen whom Jim encounters, who raise the specter of the *Patna*, Jim is a pariah who has broken the bond of "the fellowship of the craft." Jim himself is quite conscious of his alienation. When he sails aboard Marlow's ship from Bangkok, he takes no interest in the passage as a seaman would, but instead, in Marlow's words, skulks below deck, "as though he had become a stowaway."

Jim is also isolated physically. In a moving passage, Marlow speaks with great feeling of the seaman's ties with and affection for his native land, for home. Jim, however, can never go home; he has, in effect, no home, and his destiny lies everywhere and anywhere but in the village in Essex where he came into being.

On Patusan, Jim's physical isolation is complete. Except for the unspeakable Cornelius, he is the only white man for hundreds of miles. With the *Patna* safely behind him, as he supposes, Jim thrives in isolation, bringing order and security to the troubled land, and is called by the natives "Tuan Jim," "which is to say, Lord Jim." The years of unparalleled success take their toll. Jim is convinced that "nothing can touch me," and his egotism proves fatal when Gentleman Brown finds him out. Jim's last hours are spent, isolated and alone, and he dies alone.

In addition to the alienated hero, another familiar Conradian motif may be observed in *Lord Jim*: Conrad's continuing insistence on the redeeming nature of work. Earlier in the novel, the unnamed narrator makes an attempt to sum up Jim, and it comes in the form of Jim's failure to accept or to appreciate the nature of the demands of life at sea. The narrator says that "the only reward [one may expect in the seafaring life] is in the perfect love of the work. This reward eluded him." Notably, throughout the novel, Jim is most vulnerable when he is without work. During his long stay in the hospital at Singapore, he is infected by the malaise of the seamen ashore who have been in the East too long and who have given up all thought of returning to the more demanding Home Service. Under this debilitating influence, Jim takes the fateful step of signing aboard the *Patna*. The ship's passage is deceptively uneventful and undemanding, and Jim has so little to do as mate that his "faculty of swift and forestalling vision," as Marlow calls it, is given free reign. Thus, in the emergency, Jim sees with his imagination rather than with his eyes. In like fashion, after the initial heroics on Patusan, the demands on Jim are minimal. In the absence of anything practical for Jim to do, except carry out his role as "Tuan Jim," he is again vulnerable. Gentleman Brown is enabled, as a result, to catch Jim off guard, to find the "weak spot," "the place of decay," and Jim's idyllic but precarious world comes crashing down.

Conrad the symbolist may also be observed in *Lord Jim*. Again, as in *Heart of Darkness*, some of the symbols are conventional. Jim's retreat from the *Patna*, for example, is always eastward toward the rising sun, or Jim has bright blue eyes—the eyes, one assumes, of the romantic which darken in moments of stress—or Jim wears immaculate white attire during his climactic confrontation with Gentleman Brown across the creek in Patusan.

As in *Heart of Darkness*, however, some of the symbols in *Lord Jim* are thoroughly original. In pronouncing Jim a "romantic," Stein is, in part, also pronouncing judgment on himself. Stein's romanticism, though, is mixed with a strong alloy of the practical, and he is prepared, as Jim is not, to act or to react immediately when action is called for, as is evident when he is ambushed and defends himself with skill and daring. Thus, Stein the romantic collects butterflies, while Stein the practical man collects beetles. The ring which Doramin gives his old "war-comrade" Stein as a talisman of the bond between white and native ultimately assumes symbolic import. Stein, in turn, gives the ring to Jim as his entrée to Patusan, and Jim wears it proudly during his brief days of glory. In the midst of the Gentleman Brown affair, Jim sends the ring to Doramin's son, Dain Waris, as a token of the white man's faith. In the closing scene of the novel, the ring, taken from the finger of the dead Dain Waris and placed in Doramin's lap, falls to the ground at Jim's feet. Jim glances down at it, and, as he raises his head, Doramin shoots Jim. The ring, then, paradoxically, is both a symbol of faith and of a breach of faith.

Victory, one of Conrad's later novels, was published in 1915. As such, it represents in one sense a Conrad who had mastered the techniques of the genre he had made his own, the novel, and in another sense a Conrad in decline as a creative artist. The early experimentation in narrative technique—the multiplicity of narrators and the complex, and sometimes confusing, manipulation of chronology—is behind Conrad. *Victory* is a linear narrative, told by a single, first-person speaking voice without interruption of the forward chronological thrust of the tale. For the noncritical reader, this straightforward handling of his material on Conrad's part was a boon and may very well account for the fact that not until *Chance*, in 1913, and *Victory*, two years later, did Conrad enjoy a genuine popular success.

At the same time, Conrad made a stride forward in narrative technique and in command of the language in the fifteen years between *Lord Jim* and *Victory*. This step took him past clarity to simplicity. *Victory* is, perhaps, too straightforward a tale, freed of occasional confusion and of the varied and variable speaking voices, but also lacking the richness and the range contributed by those same voices. Confined as Conrad is to one point of view, the extensive searching and probing of his characters, seen in Kurtz and Jim, are denied him. Axel Heyst is an interesting character, but he is only that. He is not, like Kurtz and Jim, a provocative, puzzling, and ultimately enigmatic figure.

The other characters in the novel are similarly unimpressive. Heyst finds the heroine, Alma, or Lena, a thoroughly intriguing young woman, but the reader is at a loss to understand the fascination, even the appeal, she seems to have for Heyst. Other than the commitment Heyst has made to Lena in rescuing her from the odious Schomberg, the tie between the two is tenuous. Many critics have noted that Conrad's women are generally lifeless, and it is true that, with the possible exception of Doña Rita in *The Arrow of Gold* (and here Conrad may have been writing from direct emotional involvement), women generally remained mysteries to him. As his greatest work attests, he was essentially a man's writer.

The three other principal characters in *Victory*, however, are male; yet they, too, are wooden and artificial. Much has been made of "plain Mr. Jones," Ricardo, and Pedro's representing Conrad's most searching study of evil. In this construct, Jones stands for intellectual evil, Ricardo for moral (or amoral) evil, and Pedro for the evil of force. On the whole, however, they emerge as a singularly unimpressive trio of thugs. The lanky, emaciated Jones, called the "spectre," is indeed a ghostlike figure whose presence is observed but scarcely felt. Ricardo, with his bluster and swagger, is almost a comic character, and some of his lines are worthy of a nineteenth century melodrama. Pedro's chief function in the novel appears to be his availability to be bashed on the head and suffer multiple contusions. Compared to Gentleman Brown, "the show ruffian of the Australian coast" in *Lord Jim*, they are theatrical, and while they may do harm, the evil they represent pales beside that ascribed by Conrad to Brown, "akin to madness, derived from intense egoism, inflamed by resistance, tearing the soul to pieces and giving factitious vigor to the body."

Victory is a talky novel with long passages devoted to inconclusive conversations between Heyst and Lena. It is relevant here to contrast the lengthy exchange between Jim and Marlow in the Malabar House and the "getting to know one another" colloquies in which Heyst and Lena engage. In the former, every line is relevant and every word tells; in the latter, the emotional fencing between the two ultimately becomes tedious.

Gone, indeed, in *Victory* are the overblown passages of the earlier works, which can make even the most devout Conradian wince. Gone too, however, are the great passages, the moments of magic in which by the sheer power of words, Conrad moves, stirs, and thrills the reader. On the whole, the style in *Victory*, like the format of the novel itself, is straightforward; the prose is clear, but the interludes of splendor are sadly missing, and missed.

Whatever differences are to be found in the later works in Conrad's technical handling of the narrative and in his style, one constant remains. Heyst—like Kurtz, Jim, and so many of the figures who fill Conrad's pages—is an alien, isolated and apart, both spiritually and physically. He does differ somewhat from his counterparts, however, in that he stands alone by choice. Heyst, following the dying precept of his gifted but idealistic father—"Look-on—make no sound"—proposes to spend his life aloof and divorced from humankind; in this way, he believes, nothing can ever touch him. In general, except for his brief involvement with the unfortunate Morrison, Heyst manages to maintain his role of the amused and detached skeptic, living, as Conrad puts it, an "unattached, floating existence." He accommodates himself to all men but makes no commitments to any man. Thus, chameleonlike, he is known under many guises; he is called, for example, "Enchanted Heyst" because of his expressed enchantment with the East and, on other occasions by would-be interpreters, "Hard Facts Heyst," "the Utopist," "the Baron," "the Spider," and "the Enemy." A final sobriquet, "the Hermit," is attached to Heyst when, with the collapse of the Tropical Belt Coal Company, he chooses to remain alone on the deserted island of Samburan. Heyst's physical isolation is now of a piece with his spiritual isolation.

The encounter with Lena changes this attitude. With his commitment to Lena, Heyst is no longer the detached observer of the world, and with the flight to Samburan, his wanderings come to an end. Paradoxically, this commitment brings about both his spiritual salvation and his physical destruction. It is a redeemed Heyst, freed at last from the other enchantment of his life (the living presence of his dead father), who, at Lena's death, is able to assert, "Woe to the man whose heart has not learned while young to hope, to love—and to put its trust in life!" Thus, Heyst differs from Conrad's other alien spirits in that he "masters his destiny," as Jim could not and Kurtz, perhaps, would not.

In still another way, Heyst "masters his destiny" as Jim and Kurtz do not. Kurtz dies the victim of his own excesses and of the debilitating effect of the jungle; Jim places his life in the hands of Doramin. Heyst, however, governs his own fate and chooses to die with Lena, immolating himself in the purgative fire which he sets to destroy all traces of their brief idyll on Samburan, a fire that, ironically, blazes over the ruins of a defunct coal company.

Other echoes of the earlier Conrad may be seen in *Victory*. For example, albeit to a lesser degree than in *Lord Jim*, *Heart of Darkness*, *The Arrow of Gold*, and *Almayer's Folly*, *Victory* is another instance of Conrad's writing "autobiography as fiction." In the Author's Note to the novel, Conrad speaks of a real-life Heyst whom he remembers with affection, but also with a sense of mystery. So too, Mr. Jones, Ricardo, and Pedro come from Conrad's store of memories, although he encountered each individually and not as the trio they comprise in the book. The character of Lena is drawn from a brief encounter in a café in the South of France with a group of entertainers and with one girl in the company who particularly caught Conrad's eye. The settings of *Victory*, exotic names such as Malacca, Timor, Sourabaya, were, of course, as familiar to the sea-going Conrad as the streets of London, and there is no reason to doubt that somewhere in the tropics, the fictional Samburan has its counterpart.

Finally, in *Victory*, Conrad the symbolist may again be seen. Noticeably, however, in this later novel, just as Conrad's narrative technique and his style have become simplified and his ability to create vivid characters has declined, the symbols he employs lack the freshness and the depth of those of the earlier novels. Conrad makes much of the portrait of the elder Heyst which dominates the sparse living room on Samburan, just as the subject of the portrait has dominated Heyst's existence. In fact, Conrad makes too much of the portrait as a symbol, calling attention to it again and again until the reader can virtually predict that each time Heyst enters the room, the portrait will be brought to his and to the reader's attention. As a symbol, then, the portrait is overdone, overt, and obvious. Similarly, the darkening storm which threatens Samburan as the events of the novel reach their climax is a bit heavy-handed and hardly worthy of Conrad at his best.

Even so, there is a brief moment of the *echt* Conrad shortly before the climactic violence that brings about both Heyst's redemption and destruction. Conrad writes· "the thunder growled distantly with angry modulations of its tremendous voice, while the world outside shuddered incessantly around the dead stillness of the room where the framed profile of Heyst's father looked severely into space." Here, the two symbols coalesce in a telling and effective manner. Regrettably, telling and effective instances such as this are rare in *Victory*. Conrad's work as a whole, however, with its stylistic and narrative innovations, testifies to the quality of his contribution to twentieth century literature.

C. F. Burgess

Other major works

SHORT FICTION: *Tales of Unrest*, 1898; *Youth: A Narrative, and Two Other Stories*, 1902; *Typhoon, and Other Stories*, 1903; *A Set of Six*, 1908; *'Twixt Land and Sea, Tales*, 1912; *Within the Tides*, 1915; *Tales of Hearsay*, 1925; *The Complete Short Stories of Joseph Conrad*, 1933.

PLAYS: *One Day More: A Play in One Act*, 1905; *The Secret Agent: A Drama in Four Acts*, 1921; *Laughing Anne: A Play*, 1923.

NONFICTION: *The Mirror of the Sea*, 1906; *Some Reminiscences*, 1912 (published in the United States as *A Personal Record*); *Notes on Life and Letters*, 1921; *Joseph Conrad's Diary of His Journey Up the Valley of the Congo in*

1890, 1926; *Last Essays*, 1926; *Joseph Conrad: Life and Letters*, 1927 (Gérard Jean-Aubry, editor); *Joseph Conrad's Letters to His Wife*, 1927; *Conrad to a Friend*, 1928 (Richard Curle, editor); *Letters from Joseph Conrad, 1895-1924*, 1928 (Edward Garnett, editor); *Lettres françaises de Joseph Conrad*, 1929 (Gérard Jean-Aubry, editor); *Letters of Joseph Conrad to Marguerite Doradowska*, 1940 (John A. Gee and Paul J. Sturm, editors); *The Collected Letters of Joseph Conrad: Volume I, 1861-1897*, 1983; *The Collected Letters of Joseph Conrad: Volume II, 1898-1902*, 1986; *The Collected Letters of Joseph Conrad: Volume III, 1903-1907*, 1988.

Bibliography

Berthoud, Jacques. *Joseph Conrad: The Major Phase*. Cambridge, England: Cambridge University Press, 1978. Sees Conrad's work as tragic, the inevitable outcome of a conflict between private vision and public action. For Berthoud, Conrad's sea life and his novelist's career began simultaneously. The focus is on *The Nigger of the "Narcissus," Heart of Darkness, Lord Jim, Nostromo, The Secret Agent*, and *Under Western Eyes*.

Geddes, Gary. *Conrad's Later Novels*. Montreal: McGill-Queen's University Press, 1980. This study of Conrad's last six novels attempts to correct the prevailing estimate of Conrad's "decline" after his early "achievements." Focuses on the beginnings and somber, ironic endings of the later novels, using Conrad's letters, essays, prefaces, and his *A Personal Record* to provide the "critical upgrading" these novels merit. Provides an excellent selected bibliography and an index.

Gekoski, R. A. *Conrad: The Moral World of the Novelist*. New York: Barnes & Noble Books, 1978. Explores the novels in terms of the apparent contradiction between personal autonomy, with its attendant alienation, and social responsibility. Devotes separate chapters to Conrad's major fiction. Gekoski's analyses are studded with quotations from the works and with plot summaries. Contains a selected bibliography and an index.

Guerard, Albert J. *Conrad the Novelist*. Cambridge, Mass.: Harvard University Press, 1958. A pioneering critical study of Conrad's major fiction, exploring the "night journey," the solitary journey involving a change in the voyager, in such Conrad classics as *The Nigger of the "Narcissus," Lord Jim, Nostromo*, "The Secret Sharer," and *Heart of Darkness*. The early novels, such as *Almayer's Folly*, are read as necessary steps toward the discovery of Conrad's fictional world.

Najder, Zdzislaw. *Joseph Conrad: A Chronicle*. Translated by Halina Carroll-Najder. New Brunswick, N.J.: Rutger's University Press, 1983. Unique among Conrad biographies, attempts to bridge the gap between Polish and English-speaking readers by deciphering implicit meanings related to Conrad's Polish origins and by offering Polish readers an explanation of his complex attitudes toward his background. Also provides full genealogies, a chronology, maps, an excellent index, and an extensive bibliography.

Page, Norman. *A Conrad Companion*. New York: St. Martin's Press, 1986. A relatively short volume, the Conrad "companion" is, indeed, a guide for the beginning Conrad scholar. Provides a wealth of information: maps, illustrations, a Conrad chronology, a "who's who" in Conrad, a discussion of Conrad's "world," brief synopses and analyses of Conrad's novels and short stories, and a comprehensive bibliography, including a filmography of cinematic treatments of Conrad's work.

Ressler, Steve. *Joseph Conrad: Consciousness and Integrity*. New York: New York University Press, 1988. Devotes separate chapters to Conrad's major fiction: *Heart of Darkness, Lord Jim, Nostromo*, "The Secret Sharer," and *Under Western Eyes*. Ressler's focus is the conflict between the characters' self-affirming possibilities of action and the necessary test of moral substance. Claims that *Under Western Eyes* is Conrad's greatest artistic and moral success; the later *Victory* is dismissed, along with Conrad's other late fiction.

JAMES FENIMORE COOPER

Born: Burlington, New Jersey; September 15, 1789
Died: Cooperstown, New York; September 14, 1851

Principal long fiction

Precaution: A Novel, 1820; *The Spy: A Tale of the Neutral Ground*, 1821; *The Pioneers: Or, The Sources of the Susquehanna*, 1823; *The Pilot: A Tale of the Sea*, 1824; *Lionel Lincoln: Or, The Leaguer of Boston*, 1825; *The Last of the Mohicans: A Narrative of 1757*, 1826; *The Prairie: A Tale*, 1827; *The Red Rover: A Tale*, 1827; *The Wept of Wish-Ton-Wish: A Tale*, 1829; *The Water-Witch: Or, The Skimmer of the Seas*, 1830; *The Bravo: A Tale*, 1831; *The Heidenmauer: Or, The Benedictines—A Tale of the Rhine*, 1832; *The Headsman: Or, The Abbaye des Vignerons*, 1833; *The Monikens*, 1835; *Homeward Bound: Or, The Chase*, 1838; *Home as Found*, 1838; *The Pathfinder: Or, The Inland Sea*, 1840; *Mercedes of Castile: Or, The Voyage to Cathay*, 1840; *The Deerslayer: Or, The First Warpath*, 1841; *The Two Admirals: A Tale*, 1842; *The Wing-and-Wing: Or, Le Feu-Follet*, 1842; *Wyandotté: Or, The Hutted Knoll*, 1843; *Le Mouchoir: An Autobiographical Romance*, 1843 (also known as *Autobiography of a Pocket Handkerchief*); *Afloat and Ashore: A Sea Tale*, 1844; *Miles Wallingford: Sequel to Afloat and Ashore*, 1844; *Satanstoe: Or, The Littlepage Manuscripts, a Tale of the Colony*, 1845; *The Chainbearer: Or, The Littlepage Manuscripts*, 1845; *The Redskins: Or, Indian and Injin, Being the Conclusion of the Littlepage Manuscripts*, 1846; *The Crater: Or, Vulcan's Peak, a Tale of the Pacific*, 1847; *Jack Tier: Or, The Florida Reef*, 1848; *The Oak Openings: Or, The Bee Hunter*, 1848; *The Sea Lions: Or, The Lost Sealers*, 1849; *The Ways of the Hour*, 1850.

Other literary forms

Although James Fenimore Cooper was primarily a novelist, he also tried his hand at short stories, biography, and a play. Among these works, only the biographies are considered significant. He also wrote accounts of his European travels, history, and essays on politics and society. Among his political writings, *The American Democrat* (1838) retains its appeal as an analysis of contemporary political and social issues and as an expression of Cooper's mature political and social thought. His *The History of the Navy of the United States of America* (1839, two volumes) is still considered a definitive work. While most scholars prefer to use the Darley edition of his fiction (1860), the State University of New York Press is preparing a definitive edition of his writings, of which four volumes have appeared: *The Pioneers*, *The Pathfinder*, and two volumes of his travels. Cooper was an active correspondent. Many of his letters and journals have been published, but large quantities of material remain in the hands of private collectors.

Achievements

Though he is best known as the author of the Leatherstocking Tales, Cooper has come to be recognized as America's first great social historian. The Leatherstocking Tales—*The Pioneers*, *The Last of the Mohicans*, *The Prairie*, *The Pathfinder*, and *The Deerslayer*—are those novels in which the frontier hunter and scout, Natty Bumppo, is a central character. Along with *The Spy* and *The Pilot*, two novels of the American Revolution, the Leatherstocking Tales are familiar to twentieth century readers, and critics agree that these are Cooper's best novels. Less well-known are the novels he began writing during his seven-year residence in Europe, his problem and society novels. In these books, he works out and expresses a complex social and political theory and a social history of America seen within the context of the major modern developments of European civilization. Because his problem and society novels often are marred by overstatement and repetition, they are rarely read for pleasure, but they remain, as Robert Spiller argues, among the most detailed and accurate pictures available of major aspects of American society and thought in the early nineteenth century.

Cooper achieved international reputation with *The Spy*, his second novel, which was translated into most European languages soon after its publication. With this work, he also invented a popular genre, the spy novel. He is credited with having invented the Western in the Leatherstocking Tales and the sea adventure with *The Pilot*, another popular success. His ability to tell tales of romance and adventure in convincingly and often beautifully described settings won for him a devoted readership and earned a title he came eventually to resent, "The American Scott." His reputation began to decline when he turned to concerned criticism of American society. Though his goal in criticism was always amelioration through the affirmation of basic principles, Cooper's aristocratic manner and his frequent opposition to popular ideas made him increasingly unpopular with the public. The political and social atmosphere was not favorable to his opinions, and his works routinely received scathing reviews as pretentious and aristocratic, also as politically motivated and self-serving. As Spiller argues, Cooper was too much a man of principle to use consciously his public position for personal ends. His suits against the press to establish a definition of libel, his exploration of the principles of democracy in his novels and essays, and his careful and objective research in his naval histories and biographies reveal a man who passionately sought truth and justice regardless of the effect on his popularity.

Though his popularity declined after 1833, Cooper continued writing with energy. In his thirty-year writing career, he wrote more than thirty novels, the naval history, several significant social works, and many other works as well. Howard Mumford Jones credits Cooper with early American developments of the international theme, the theme of the Puritan conscience, the family saga, the utopian and dystopian novel, and the series novel. By general agreement, Cooper stands at the headwaters of the American tradition of fiction; he contributed significantly to the themes and forms of the American novel.

Biography

James Cooper was born in Burlington, New Jersey, on September 15, 1789, the twelfth of thirteen children of William and Elizabeth Cooper. He added "Fenimore" in 1826 in memory of his mother's family. Elizabeth Fenimore was an heiress whose wealth contributed to William Cooper's success in buying and developing a large tract of land on which he founded Cooperstown, New York. Cooper's father, descended from English Quakers, expressed enlightened ideas about developing wilderness lands in his *A Guide in the Wilderness* (1810). William Cooper and Cooperstown became models for Judge Temple and Templeton in *The Pioneers*. The Coopers moved to Cooperstown in 1790, and Cooper grew up there as the son of the community's developer and benefactor, a gentleman who eventually became a judge and a Federalist congressman. Cooper's conservative Enlightenment views of the frontier, of American culture, and of democracy had their roots in his Cooperstown youth.

Like many sons of the wealthy gentry, Cooper had some difficulty deciding what to do with his life. In his third year at Yale, he was dismissed for misconduct. In 1806, he began a naval career which led to a commission in the U.S. Navy in 1808, where he served on Lake Ontario, scene of *The Pathfinder*. In 1809, his father died from a blow delivered from behind by a political opponent, and Cooper came into a large inheritance. In 1811, he married Susan Augusta DeLancey of an old and respectable Tory family, and he resigned from the Navy. For eight years he lived the life of a country gentleman, eventually fathering seven children. By 1819, however, because of the financial failures and deaths of all his brothers, which left him responsible for some of their families, Cooper found himself in financial difficulty. Cooper began writing at this time, not with the hope of making money— there was no precedent for achieving even a living as an author—but in response to a challenge from his wife to write a better novel than one he happened to be reading to her. Once he had begun, Cooper found in various ways the energy and motivation to make writing his career. Susan's support and the family's continued domestic tranquility inspired Cooper's writing and protected him from what he came to see as an increasingly hostile public.

The success of *The Spy* and of his next four novels made him secure enough in 1826 to take his family to Europe, where he hoped to educate his children and to improve the foreign income from his books. While living in Paris and London and traveling at a leisurely pace through most of Europe, Cooper involved himself in French and Polish politics and published several works. Before his return to the United States in 1833, he met Sir Walter Scott, became intimate with Marie de La Fayette, aided the sculptor Horatio Greenough in beginning his career, and maintained his lifelong friendship with Samuel Morse. This period of travel was another turning point in his life. In *Notions of the Americans* (1828), Cooper wrote an idealized defense of American democracy which offended both his intended audiences, the Americans and the English. When he went on to publish a series of novels set in Europe (1831-1833), Cooper provided American reviewers with more reasons to see him as an apostate. Upon his return to America, he tended to confirm this characterization by announcing his retirement as a novelist and publishing a group of travel books, satires, and finally a primer on republican democracy, *The American Democrat*. When he returned to writing novels with *Homeward Bound* and *Home as Found* in 1838, he indicated that he had found America much decayed on his return from Europe. The promises of a democratic republic he had expressed in *Notions of the Americans* were fading before the abuse of the Constitution by demagogues and the increasing tyranny of the majority. *The American Democrat* was, in part, a call to return to the original principles of the republic.

Having resettled in Cooperstown in 1833, Cooper soon found himself embroiled in controversies over land title and libel, controversies which the press used to foster the image of Cooper as a self-styled aristocrat. He is credited with establishing important legal precedents in the libel cases he won against editors such as Thurlow Weed and Horace Greeley. By 1843, Cooper's life had become more tranquil. He had settled down to the most productive period of his life, producing sixteen novels between 1840 and 1851; among them are many marred by obtrusive discussions of political and social issues, but also several which are considered American classics, such as *The Pathfinder* and *The Deerslayer*, the last two of the Leatherstocking Tales. His last five novels show evidence of increasing interest in religious ideas. Though Cooper had been active in religious institutions all his life and though all his novels express Christian beliefs, he was not confirmed as an Episcopalian until the last year of his life. He died at Cooperstown on September 14, 1851.

Analysis

James Fenimore Cooper was a historian of America. His novels span American history, dramatizing central events from Columbus' discovery (*Mercedes of Castile*) through the French and Indian Wars and the early settlement (the Leatherstocking Tales) to the Revolution (*The Spy* and *The Pilot*) and the contemporary events of the Littlepage and the Miles Wallingford novels. In some of his European novels, he examined major intellectual developments, such as the Reformation, which he thought important to American history, and in many of his novels, he reviewed the whole of American history, attempting to complete his particular vision of America by inventing a tradition for the new nation. Modern criticism is divided concerning the meaning and nature of Cooper's tradition. Following the lead of D. H. Lawrence, a group of myth critics concentrates on unconscious elements in Cooper's works, while Robert Spiller and a group of social and historical critics concentrate more on his conscious opinions.

In his *Studies in Classic American Literature* (1923), Lawrence argued that Cooper's myth of America is centered in the friendship between Natty Bumppo and his Indian friend, Chingachgook, and in the order of composition of the Leatherstocking Tales. Of the friendship, Lawrence says, Cooper "dreamed a new human relationship deeper than the deeps of sex. Deeper than property, deeper than fatherhood, deeper than marriage, deeper than love. . . . This is the nucleus of a new society, the clue to a new epoch." Of the order of writing, he says that the novels "go backwards, from old age to golden youth. That is the true myth of America. She starts old, old and wrinkled in an old skin. And there is a gradual sloughing of the old skin, towards a new youth." These insightful statements have been elaborated by critics who have looked deeply into Cooper's works, but who have concentrated most of their attention on the Leatherstocking Tales in order to find in Cooper affinities with Herman Melville, Mark Twain, and others who seem to find it necessary, like Natty Bumppo, to remain apart from social institutions to preserve their integrity. Because these critics tend to focus on Leatherstocking and mythic elements in the tales, they may be better guides to American myth than to Cooper. While Cooper contributes images and forms to what became myths in the hands of others, his own mind seems to have been occupied more with making American society than with escaping it.

Another more traditional mythic pattern pervades all of his works, including the Leatherstocking Tales. Several critics have called attention to a key passage in *The Last of the Mohicans* when Natty describes the waterfall where the scout and his party take refuge from hostile Indians. The pattern of a unified flow falling into disorder and rebellion only to be gathered back again by the hand of Providence into a new order is not only descriptive of the plot of this novel but also suggests other levels of meaning which are reflected throughout Cooper's work, for it defines Cooper's essentially Christian and Enlightenment world view, a view which he found expressed, though with too monarchical a flavor, in Alexander Pope's *Essay on Man* (1733-1734).

In *Home as Found*, Cooper sees the same pattern in the development of frontier settlements. They begin with a pastoral stage in which people of all kinds cooperate freely and easily to make a new land support them. The second stage is anarchic, for when freed of the demanding laws of necessity, society begins to divide as interests consolidate into factions and as families struggle for power and position. Though it appears painful and disorderly, this phase is the natural, providential reordering process toward a mature society. In the final phase, established, mutually respecting, and interdependent classes make possible a high civilization. In *The American Democrat*, Cooper often echoes Pope's *Essay on Man* as he explains that human life in this world is a fall into disorder where the trials exceed the pleasures; this apparent disorder, however, is a merciful preparation for a higher life to come. Many of Cooper's novels reflect this pattern; characters leave or are snatched out of their reasonably ordered world to be educated in a dangerous and seemingly disordered one, only to be returned after an educational probation into a more familiarly ordered world, there to contribute to its improvement. This pattern of order, separation, and reintegration pervades Cooper's thought and gives form to his conscious dream of America. He came to see America as moving through the anarchic and purifying phase of the Revolution toward a new society which would allow the best that is in fallen mankind to realize itself. This dream is expressed, in part, in *The Pioneers*.

The Pioneers is Cooper's first great novel, the first he composed primarily to satisfy himself. The popular success of *The Spy* increased both his freedom and his confidence, encouraging him to turn to what proved to be his richest source of material, the frontier life of New York State. This first novel in the Leatherstocking series has a complex double organization which is an experimental response to what Robert Spiller sees as Cooper's main artistic problem, the adaptation of forms developed in aristocratic civilized Europe to his democratic frontier material. On the one hand, *The Pioneers* describes daily life in the new village of Templeton on Otsego Lake and is ordered within a frame of seasonal change from Christmas, 1793, until the following autumn. Behind this organization, on the other hand, stands a hidden order which gradually reveals itself as the story unfolds; central to this plot is the transfer of title of the largest portion of land in the district from Judge Marmaduke Temple to Edward Oliver Effingham. These two structures interact to underline the providential inevitability and significance of this transfer.

The seasonal ordering of events brings out the nature of the community at Templeton at this particular point in its development. Templeton is shown to be suspended between two forms of order. Representing the old order are the seventy-year-old Natty Bumppo, the Leatherstocking, and his aged Indian friend, John Mohegan, whose actual name is Chingachgook. The forest is their home and their mediator with divine law. Natty, through his contact with Chingachgook and his life in the forest, has become the best man that such a life can produce. He combines true Christian principles with the skills and knowledge of the best Indian civilization. Natty and the Indian live an ideal kind of life, given the material circumstances of their environment, but that environment is changing. Otsego Lake is becoming settled and civilized. Chingachgook remains because he wishes to live where his ancestors once dwelt. Natty stays with his friend. Their presence becomes a source of conflict.

The new order is represented at first by Judge Temple, but the form of that order remains somewhat obscure until the revealing of motives and identities at the end of the novel. Temple's main function in the community is moral. He is important as the owner and developer of the land. He has brought settlers to the land, helped them through troubled times, and, largely at his own expense, has built the public buildings and established the institutions of Templeton. During the transition to civilization, Temple is a center of order, organization, and—most important—restraint. In part through his efforts, the legislature is enacting laws to restrain the settlers in the state. Restraint on two kinds of behavior is necessary. On the one hand, there are characters such as Billy Kirby, whose wasteful use of community resources stems primarily from the inability to understand the needs of a settled country. These individuals live in the old forest world but without the old forest values. On the other hand, there are the settlers themselves: some, such as Richard Jones and Hiram Doolittle, tend toward cupidity, while others such as the community's poor are so unaccustomed to having plenty, that they waste it when they have it. These attitudes are shown in the famous scenes of pigeon-shooting and lake fishing, and they are pointedly contrasted with the old values practiced by Natty and Chingachgook. The settlers need restraint; Judge Temple feels in himself the desire to overharvest the plentiful natural resources of Templeton and knows at firsthand the importance of restraining laws which will force the settlers to live by an approximation of the divine law by which Natty lives.

The central conflict in the seasonal ordering of the novel is between Natty, who lives by the old law, the natural law of the forest which reflects the divine law, and the settlers, who are comparatively lawless. This conflict is complicated as the new restraining civil laws come into effect and the lawless members of the community exploit and abuse those laws in order to harass Natty. Hiram Doolittle, a justice of the peace, and Richard Jones, the sheriff, become convinced that Natty is secretly mining silver on Judge Temple's land. In reality, Natty is concealing the aged and senile original white owner of this land, Major Effingham, helping to care for the old man until his grandson, Oliver Effingham, is able to move him to better circumstances. Doolittle succeeds at maneuvering the law and its institutions so that Judge Temple must fine and jail Natty for resisting an officer of the law. Thus, Natty becomes a victim of the very laws designed to enforce his own highest values, underlining the weakness of human nature and illustrating the cyclical pattern of anarchy, order, and repression and abuse of the law. When Doolittle's machinations are revealed and Natty is freed, he announces his intent to move west into the wilderness which is his proper home.

The conflict between the old order and the new is resolved only in part by Natty's apparent capitulation and retreat into the wilderness. Before Natty leaves, he performs a central function in the land transfer plot, a function which infuses the values of the old order into the new order. The land to which Judge Temple holds title was given to Major Effingham by a council

of the Delaware chiefs at the time of the French and Indian Wars. In recognition of his qualities as a faithful and brave warrior, Effingham was adopted
into the tribe as a son of Chingachgook. In this exchange, the best of native
American civilization recognized its own qualities in a superior form in
Effingham, a representative of the best of European Christian civilization.
This method of transfer is crucial because it amounts to a gentleman's agreement ratified by family ties; the transfer is a voluntary expression of values
and seems providentially ordained. The history of the land, as it passes from
the Major to his son, illustrates these same values. The Major confidently
gives his son control over his estates, knowing that his son will care for them
as a gentleman should. Generosity and honor rather than greed and violence
characterize these transfers.

For the transfer to be complete, the owners must be Americanized by
means of the American Revolution. This process is a purification which brings
to culmination in Oliver the traditions of American democracy and European
and Indian aristocracy. The Effinghams are a Tory family. Oliver's father and
Judge Temple are brothers in honor, a civilized reflection of Natty and Chingachgook. Temple is an example of Americanized aristocracy. His aristocratic
family had declined in the New World, but beginning with his father, they
reemerged as democratic "aristocrats," what Cooper referred to as gentlemen.
A gentleman is one whose superior talents are favored by education and
comparative leisure to fit him as a moral leader of the community. The gentleman differs from the Old World aristocrat in that he has no hereditary title
to political power. In the ideal republic, the gentleman is recognized for his
attainments by the common men, who may be expected to choose freely their
political leaders from among the gentry. The Effinghams have not undergone
this Americanizing process. The process is portrayed in the novel in Oliver
Effingham's resentful efforts to restore his grandfather to his accustomed way
of life.

Oliver labors under the mistaken idea that Temple has usurped his family's
land, but as the final revelations show, the Americanized gentleman has
remained faithful, holding the land in trust for the Effinghams to take once
they have become American. Oliver's deprivation, the military defeat of his
family, and his working in disguise for Judge Temple, are lessons in humility
which reveal to him the moral equality between himself and the Temples.
Without such an experience, he might well consider himself above the Judge's
daughter, Elizabeth, unable to marry her and unable to bring together the
two parts of the estate. The other main component of Oliver's transformation
comes under the tutelage of Natty and Chingachgook, who attempt to impress
upon Oliver, as well as upon Elizabeth, their obligations to the land and to
its previous owners. Through this two-pronged education, the aristocrat
becomes a gentleman and the breach caused by the American Revolution is
healed. This healing is manifested most clearly in the marriage of Oliver and

Elizabeth. The best of the Old World is recognized by the best of New World Indians and, by means of the Revolution, is purified of its antidemocratic prejudices; the aristocrat becomes a gentleman worthy to rule in America.

The transfer of title takes place within the context of inevitable seasonal change; its rhythm of tension and crisis reflects similar events within the seasons. The transition from the old order of Indian occupation to the new order of white democratic civilization is shown, despite local tensions and conflicts, to be providentially ordered when viewed from a sufficient distance. Within the seasons as well as in the human actions, the central theme of displacement underlines and elaborates the meaning of the overall movement.

The novel is filled with displaced persons. Remarkable Pettibone is displaced as mistress of the Temple mansion by Elizabeth. Natty and Chingachgook are displaced by white civilization. Oliver is displaced by the American Revolution, Le Quoi by the French Revolution. Finally, Judge Temple is displaced as the first power in the community. Within this thematic pattern, two general kinds of resolution occur. Oliver, Chingachgook, and Le Quoi are variously restored to their proper places, though Chingachgook must die in order to rejoin his tribe. Pettibone and Temple come to accept their displacement by their superiors. Natty is unique. His displacement seems destined for repetition until Providence finally civilizes the continent and no place is left that is really his home. For him, as for Chingachgook, only death seems to offer an end to displacement. Natty's legacy must live on, however, in those gentlemen who combine "nature and refinement," and there is some hope that in a mature American society, Natty as well as good Indians might find a home.

Critics tend to see Natty as an idealized epic hero who is too good for any society he encounters, but this is not quite true. In each of the books in which he appears, he acts as a conserver of essential values. This role is clearest when he teaches Elizabeth the ethics of fishing for one's food and when he saves her and Oliver from a fire on the mountain. His complaints about the "wasty ways" of civilization and about the laws which ought to be unnecessary are a part of this function. Though he fails to understand the weaknesses of civilized men and their need for the civil law, he still functions to further the best interests of civilization, not only by taming the wild, but also by performing a role like that of the Old Testament prophets. He constantly calls men's attention back to the first principles of civilized life. In this respect, Natty is much like Cooper.

The Pioneers is a hopeful novel, for in it Cooper reveals a confidence in a providential ordering of history which will lead to the fulfillment of his ideas of a rational republic. This novel resolves the central anarchic displacements of the native inhabitants and of the traditional European ruling class by asserting that the American republic is the fruition of these two traditions. Though far from perfect, the American experiment seems, in this novel, to be destined for a unique success.

The Last of the Mohicans is the best known of the Leatherstocking Tales, probably because it combines Cooper's most interesting characters and the relatively fast-paced adventure of *The Spy* and *The Pilot*. Set in the French and Indian Wars, this novel presents Natty and Chingachgook in their prime. Chingachgook's son, Uncas, is the last of the Mohican chiefs, the last of the line from which the Delaware nation is said to trace their origins. Although the novel moves straightforwardly through two adventures, it brings into these adventures a number of suggestive thematic elements.

The two main adventures are quests, with filial piety as their motive. Major Duncan Heyward attempts to escort Cora and Alice Munro to their father, commander of Fort William Henry on Horican Lake (Lake George). Led astray by Magua, an Indian who seeks revenge against Munro, the party, which comes to include a comic psalmodist, David Gamut, encounters and enlists the help of Natty and his Indian companions. This quest is fully successful. Magua joins the Hurons who are leagued with the besieging French forces at William Henry and captures the original party, which is then rescued by Natty and his friends to be delivered safely to the doomed fort. This adventure is followed by an interlude at the fort in which Heyward obtains Munro's permission to court Alice and learns, to his own secret pain, that Cora has black blood. Also in this interlude, Munro learns he will get no support from nearby British troops and realizes that he must surrender his position. Montcalm allows him to remove his men and equipment from the fort before it is destroyed, but the discontented Indians, provoked by Magua, break the truce and massacre the retreating and exposed people for booty and scalps. Magua precipitates the next quest by capturing Alice and Cora and taking them, along with David Gamut, north toward Canada. The second quest is the rescue mission of Natty, Chingachgook, Uncas, Heyward, and Munro. This attempt is only partly successful, for both Cora and Uncas are killed.

Cooper heightens the interest of these quests in part through a double love plot. During the first movement, Duncan and Alice come to love each other and Uncas is attracted to Cora. Though thematically important, the first couple is not very interesting. Except for the slight misunderstanding with Munro which reveals the secret of Cora's ancestry, the barriers between Heyward and Alice are physical and temporal. More complicated and puzzling is the relationship between Cora and Uncas. While Alice seems to spend most of the two quests calling on her father, weeping, and fainting, Cora shows a spirit and courage which make her an interesting character and which attract the admiration of Uncas. Magua is also interested in Cora, proposing in the first capture that if she will become his wife, he will cease his persecution of the rest of the family. Magua is primarily intent on revenge against Munro, but it seems clear that his interest in Cora as a woman grows until it may even supplant his revenge motive. Near the end of the novel, Natty offers himself in exchange for Cora, but even though Natty is a much more valuable prisoner, Magua prefers to keep Cora. When the hunted Magua's last remaining comrade kills Cora, Magua turns on him. Though there is no indication that Magua's is more than a physical passion, he seems strongly attracted to Cora, perhaps in part because of her courageous refusal to fear or to submit to him.

Critics have made much of the relationship between Cora, Uncas, and Magua, suggesting the Cooper gives Cora black blood to "sanitize" her potential relationship with Uncas and the heavenly marriage between them suggested in the final funeral service of the Indians. Cora becomes an early example of "the tragic mulatto" who has no place in the world where racial purity is highly valued. Natty insistently declares that even though he has adopted Indian ways, he is "a man without a cross"; his blood is pure white. On the other hand, the three-part pattern which seems to dominate Cooper's historical vision might imply a real fulfillment in the Indian funeral which is intended to bring Cora and Uncas together in the next life. This incident may be as close as Cooper came to a vision of a new America such as Lawrence hints at, in which even the races are drawn together into a new unity. The division between races is a symptom of a fallen and perverse world. Natty more than once asserts that there is one God over all and, perhaps, one afterlife for all.

The first meeting of Heyward's party with Natty's party in the forest has an allegorical quality that looks forward to the best of Nathaniel Hawthorne and begins the development of the theme of evil, which—in Cooper's vision— can enjoy only a temporary triumph. Lost in the forest, misled by the false guide, Magua, this party from civilization has entered a seemingly anarchic world in which they are babes "without the knowledge of men." This meeting introduces two major themes: the conception of the wilderness as a book one must know how to read if one is to survive, and the conception of Magua and his Hurons as devils who have tempted Heyward's party into this world in order to work their destruction. Though Magua is represented in Miltonic terms as Satan, he is not so much a rebel angel as a product of "the colonial wars of North America." Magua's home is the "neutral territory" which the rival forces must cross in order to fight each other; he desires revenge on Munro for an imprudent act, an act which symbolizes the whites' disturbance of Magua's way of life. As Magua asserts, Munro provided the alcohol that unbalanced him, then whipped him for succumbing to that alcohol. Magua has most of the qualities of the good men: courage, cunning, the ability to organize harmoniously talent and authority, and highly developed skills at reading the book of nature. He differs from Natty and his Indian companions, however, in that he allows himself to be governed by the evil passion of revenge rather than by unselfish rationality. Of his kind, the unselfishly rational men must be constantly suspicious. Montcalm's failure to control his Indian forces demonstrates that only the most concerted efforts can prevent great evil. The novel's end shows that ultimately only divine Providence can fully right the inevitable wrongs of this world.

Within this thematic context, a crucial event is David's response to Natty's promise to avenge his death if the Hurons dare to kill him. David will have no vengeance, only Christian forgiveness. Natty acknowledges the truth and beauty of the idea, but it is clear that his struggle is on another level. Those he fights are devils, the dark side of himself, of Chingachgook and Cora and Uncas—in fact, of all the main characters—for Magua is doubled with each of the main characters at some point in the novel. Magua comes to represent the evil in each character. In this forest world, the dark self takes shape in passionate savages who must be exterminated absolutely, like those who first capture Heyward's party. To show them pity is to endanger oneself; to neglect killing them is to open one to further jeopardy, such as the "descent into hell" to rescue the captured maidens, which is one element of the second quest. Only under the rule of civil law in civilization does human evil become a forgivable weakness rather than a metaphysical absolute.

Critics have noted the improbable plot of *The Prairie* while acknowledging its powerful and moving episodes. Ishmael Bush, an opponent of land ownership and of the civil law, has led onto the vast Western prairie his considerable family, including a wife, seven sons, and an unspecified number of daughters; his brother-in-law, Abiram White; a well-educated and distantly related orphan, Ellen Wade; Obed Battius, a comic naturalist and doctor; and Inez Middleton, whom Abiram has kidnaped for ransom. Bush's ostensible motive is to escape the various restraining regulations of civilization and, particularly, to set up his farm far from the irksome property law. It is never made clear why he has consented to join in the kidnaping or how anyone expects to collect a ransom. This expedition draws in its wake Paul Hover, a secret suitor of Ellen, and a party of soldiers led by Duncan Uncas Middleton, who seeks to recover his bride who was snatched between the ceremony and the consummation. On the prairie, they all meet the eighty-seven-year-old Natty, who has forsaken man-made clearings in order to avoid the sound of the axe and to die in a clearing made by God. The situation is complicated by the presence of feuding Indian bands: the bad Indians, the Hurons of the plains, are the Sioux, led by the treacherous Mahtoree; the good Indians are the Pawnee, led by the faithful Hard Heart. With these melodramatic materials, Cooper forges a moving tale which he makes significant in part by bringing into play issues of law and morality.

During the captivities and escapes which advance the novel's action, the white characters divide into two alliances which are then associated with the two Indian tribes. Both alliances are patriarchal, but their characters are significantly different. Bush is the patriarch of physical power. He lives by the "natural law" that "might makes right," establishing his dominance over his family through physical strength and his conviction of his own power and rectitude. This alliance is beset by internal danger and contradiction. The second alliance is a patriarchy of wisdom and virtue. Bound together by the faith of its members, it grows under the leadership of Natty to include Paul, Duncan, Ellen, Inez, and Dr. Battius. The conflict between these two groups is prefigured in the first confrontation between Natty and Ishmael. Ishmael is represented in the opening of the novel as being out of place on the prairie, for he is a farmer who has left the best farm land to take the route of those who, "deluded by their wishes," are "seeking for the Eldorado of the West." In one of the many great tableaux of this novel, Ishmael's group first sees Natty as a gigantic shadow cast toward them by the setting sun. He is a revelation who suggests to them the supernatural. Bush has come to the prairie in the pride of moral self-sufficiency, but Natty is an example of humble dependency on the wisdom of God. In part, through Natty's example, Ishmael finally leads his "wild brood" back to civilization at the novel's end.

Pride on the prairie, as in the wilderness of New York, leads to the subjection of reason to passion, to precipitate actions and death, whereas humility, though it may not save one from death, leads to the control of passion, to patience and probable survival. Natty teaches this lesson repeatedly to the group of which he becomes father and leader. Ishmael and the Sioux, "the Ishmaelites of the American deserts," learn the lesson through more bitter experience. The narrator implies that both Ishmael and Mahtoree, in attempting to be laws unto themselves, are playing God. In the central dialogue of the novel, Natty tells Dr. Battius in terms which echo *Essay on Man* that mankind's "gifts are not equal to his wishes . . . he would mount into the heavens with all his deformities about him if he only knew the road. . . . If his power is not equal to his will, it is because the wisdom of the Lord hath set bounds to his evil workings." Mahtoree, unrestrained by the traditional laws of his tribe, seeks through demagoguery to manipulate his people to effect his selfish desire for Inez. He and his band are destroyed in consequence. Bush's lesson comes when he discovers that Natty is not actually the murderer of Bush's eldest son, Asa.

The lesson Bush learns is always present to him. When his sons learn the well-kept secret that Ishmael is assisting Abiram in a kidnaping, they become indignant and rebellious. Cooper uses this conflict to demonstrate the precariousness of arbitrary power. Bush knows that he deserted his parents when he felt strong enough, and he is aware that only his strength keeps his sons with him in the present danger from Indians. This knowledge of instability becomes complete when he learns that Abiram has returned the blow he received from Asa by shooting the boy in the back. It is difficult to determine how fully Bush understands this revelation. He feels his dilemma, for he admits that while he suspected Natty, he had no doubt that the murderer deserved execution, but when he learned of his brother-in-law's guilt, he became unsure. The wound to his family can hardly be cured by killing another of its members. For the first time in his life, Bush feels the waste and solitude of the wilderness. He turns to his wife and to her Bible for authority. He feels the extent to which Ahiram has carried out Ishmael's own desire to punish his rebellious son, and thus he himself suffers as he carries out the execution of Abiram. This bitter lesson humbles him and sends him back to settled country and the restraints of civil law.

For Natty's informal family, there are gentler lessons. Paul and Duncan learn to be humble about their youthful strength, to realize their dependency on others, and to become better bridegrooms. Battius learns a little intellectual humility from Natty's practical knowledge of the wilderness. The center of Natty's teaching is that the legitimate use of power is for service rather than for self. This lesson arises out of the relationship between Natty and Hard Heart. Natty and the faithful Pawnee chief adopt each other when it appears the Sioux will kill Hard Heart. Natty later asserts that he became Hard Heart's father only to serve him, just as he becomes the figurative father of the more civilized fugitives in order to serve them. Once their relationship is established, it endures. Natty lives the last year of his life as a respected elder of the Pawnee and dies honored in their village. Having learned their lesson on the humble use of power in God's wilderness, Paul and Duncan carry their wisdom back to the high councils of the republic, where they become respected family men, property owners, and legislators. Like the Effinghams at Otsego Lake, the Hovers and the Middletons—the latter descending from the Heywards of *The Last of the Mohicans*—infuse the wisdom of the wilderness into the social order of America.

Cooper believed he had ended his Leatherstocking Tales when he completed *The Prairie*. Probably for this reason, he brought together his themes and characters and clarified the importance of Natty Bumppo to American civilization. Most critics have agreed that Cooper was drawn toward two ideals, the ability to exist in the wilderness and the ideal of a "natural aristocracy" of social and political order. It may be, however, that the first three of the Leatherstocking Tales are intended in part to create a history of America in which the wisdom of the wilderness is transferred to the social and political structure of the republic. Natty distrusts written tradition because "Mankind twist and turn the rules of the Lord to suit their own wickedness when their devilish cunning has had too much time to trifle with his commands." Natty's experience provides a fresh revelation which renews the best of the Christian tradition and which calls men back to basic Christian principles. That revelation consists essentially of a humble recognition of human limitations, justifying Cooper's vision of a republic where rulers are chosen for wisdom and faithfulness, where the tradition is not rigidly controlled by a hereditary elite but is constantly renewed by the unfettered ascendancy of the good and wise.

Throughout his career, Cooper worked within a general understanding of human history as a disordered phase of existence between two orders, and a particular vision of contemporary America as a disordered phase between the old aristocratic order and the new order to be dominated by the American gentleman. In the first three of the Leatherstocking Tales, Cooper reveals a desire to naturalize the aristocratic tradition through exposure to the wilderness and its prophet, the man who reads God's word in the landscape. The result of this process would be a mature natural order which, though far from divine perfection, would promise as much happiness as is possible for fallen mankind. In his later novels, Cooper gave increasing attention to the ways in which American society failed to understand and to actualize this purified tradition. He looked back often, especially in *The Deerslayer*, to the purity and goodness of those basic values. Although they are rarely read today, novels such as *Satanstoe* and *The Oak-Openings* among his later works are well worth reading, as is *The Bravo* from among his problem novels. In all of these works, Cooper continues to express his faith in the possibility of a high American civilization.

Terry Heller

Other major works

NONFICTION: *Notions of the Americans*, 1828; *A Letter to His Countrymen*, 1834; *Sketches of Switzerland*, 1836; *Gleanings in Europe: France*, 1837; *Gleanings in Europe: England*, 1837; *Gleanings in Europe: Italy*, 1838; *The American Democrat*, 1838; *Chronicles of Cooperstown*, 1838; *The History of the Navy of the United States of America*, 1839 (2 volumes); *Ned Meyers: Or, A Life Before the Mast*, 1843; *Lives of Distinguished American Naval Officers*, 1845; *New York*, 1851; *The Letters and Journals of James Fenimore Cooper*, 1960-1968 (J. F. Beard, editor, 6 volumes).

Bibliography
Clark, Robert, ed. *James Fenimore Cooper: New Critical Essays.* London: Vision, 1985. Each of the eight essays in this collection covers a different aspect of Cooper's fiction; most focus on a specific novel. A complete index helps the student find references to a particular work or theme.
Fields, W., ed. *James Fenimore Cooper: A Collection of Critical Essays*. Boston: G. K. Hall, 1979. The collection of new essays at the end of this book offers much of value to beginning students of Cooper, though there is no index to help them sift through the essays. The first section of the book is a selection of nineteenth century reviews of Cooper's novels.
Franklin, Wayne. *The New World of James Fenimore Cooper*. Chicago: Chicago University Press, 1982. For the more advanced student of Cooper. Develops a narrow thesis based on images of the wilderness in Cooper's

fiction and includes a chapter on each of Cooper's major novels, beginning with *The Pioneers* and ending with *The Last of the Mohicans*.

Long, Robert Emmett. *James Fenimore Cooper*. New York: Continuum, 1990. This general study of Cooper and his fiction touches on all the major works objectively. The five-page bibliography lists the most important studies of Cooper up to the 1990's.

Motley, Warren. *The American Abraham*. Cambridge, England: Cambridge University Press, 1987. Covers all Cooper's novels, but deals mostly with his patriarchal characters as an American archetype. Contains thorough bibliography and an index.

Ringe, Donald A. *James Fenimore Cooper*. 2d ed. New York: Twayne, 1988. The first edition of this work, in 1962, was a most succinct and helpful introduction to Cooper. Ringe's revision adds new information and updates the annotated bibliography to reflect another quarter-century of scholarship. Contains a complete chronology and index.

ROBERT COOVER

Born: Charles City, Iowa; February 4, 1932

Principal long fiction

The Origin of the Brunists, 1966; *The Universal Baseball Association, Inc. J. Henry Waugh, Prop.*, 1968; *The Public Burning*, 1977; *A Political Fable*, 1980; *Spanking the Maid*, 1981; *Gerald's Party*, 1985; *Whatever Happened to Gloomy Gus of the Chicago Bears?*, 1987; *Pinocchio in Venice*, 1991.

Other literary forms

In addition to his novels and novellas, Robert Coover has published numerous, usually experimental short fictions, most of which have been collected in *Pricksongs & Descants* (1969), *In Bed One Night* (1983), and *A Night at the Movies* (1987). His reviews and essays, while few in number, are exceptional in quality; his studies of Samuel Beckett ("The Last Quixote," in *New American Review*, 1970) and Gabriel García Márquez ("The Master's Voice," in *New American Review*, 1977), are, in addition to being important critical works in their own right, useful for the light they shed on Coover's interests and intentions in his own fiction. His plays, *The Kid* (1972), *Love Scene* (1972), *Rip Awake* (1972), and *A Theological Position* (1972), have been successfully staged in Paris and Los Angeles, and the New York production of *The Kid* at the American Place Theater in November, 1972, won for its director, Jack Gelber, an Obie award. Coover, who finds some relief from the fiction-writer's necessary isolation in the communal aspect of theater and motion-picture production, has also written, directed, and produced one film, *On a Confrontation in Iowa City* (1969), and published the script of another, *The Hair o' the Chine* (1980, but written some twenty years earlier). His poetry and one translation have appeared in various "little magazines."

Achievements

Although his work has not yet received widespread popular acclaim, Coover's preeminent place among innovative contemporary writers has already been firmly established by academic critics. His various honors include the William Faulkner Award for best first novel (1966), a Rockefeller Foundation grant (1969), two Guggenheim fellowships (1971, 1974), a citation in fiction from Brandeis University (1971), an Academy of Arts and Letters award (1975), and a National Book Award nomination for *The Public Burning* (1977). Even before its publication by The Viking Press, *The Public Burning* became a *succès de scandale* when Alfred A. Knopf, which had originally contracted for the novel, refused to publish it. The ensuing literary gossip undoubtedly fueled sales (including copies of the Book Club Edition), though not to the extent expected, and had the unfortunate result of bringing to both the book and its author the kind of notoriety neither deserved. The short-lived paperback editions of *The Public Burning* and *The Origin of the Brunists* (the latter novel had long been out of print) seemed to confirm that, except for *The Universal Baseball Association, Inc. J. Henry Waugh, Prop.*, which huo uttracted a diversified readership, Coover's works appeal to a fairly specialized audience.

Biography

Robert Lowell Coover was born in Charles City, Iowa, on February 4, 1932. His family later moved to Indiana and then to Herrin, Illinois, where his father, Grant Marion Coover, managed the town newspaper. (Both the newspaper and a local mining disaster figure prominently in Coover's first novel.) Small-town life as the son of a newspaperman gave Coover both an interest in journalism and a desire to travel. After beginning his college education at nearby Southern Illinois University (1949-1951), he transferred to Indiana University, where he received a B.A. in 1953, at which time he enlisted in the United States Naval Reserve, attaining the rank of lieutenant. While serving in Europe, he met Marie del Pilar San-Mallafre, whom he married on June 13, 1959. Coover's serious interest in fiction dates from the period immediately prior to his marriage, and his novel-writing followed the favorable response to his first published story, "Blackdamp" (1961), which he reworked and expanded into *The Origin of the Brunists*. Unable to make a living as a fiction-writer, Coover left Spain, his wife's native country, and began teaching in the United States; he has held positions at Bard College (1966-1967), the University of Iowa (1967-1969), Columbia University (1972), Princeton (1972-1973), Virginia Military Institute (1976), and Brown University (since 1981), and has served as writer-in-residence at Wisconsin State University—Superior (1968) and Washington University (1969).

Coover's attitude toward the university is similar to his attitude toward his native country. Contending that residence abroad stirs the memory and frees the imagination, Coover has, since 1953, spent more than half of his time and done most of his writing in Guatemala, Spain, and England. At a time when much of American literature no longer seems distinctly American, Coover has written plays and fiction about some of his country's most characteristic myths, traits, events, and institutions, including baseball, millenarianism, the West, Dr. Seuss, the Rosenberg spy case, and Rip Van Winkle. Currently, he is living in Providence, Rhode Island, where he teaches film and writing course at Brown University and continues to explore the relations between narrative possibilities and American popular culture, including film, pornography, and detective fiction.

Analysis

In Robert Coover's work, man is presented not as the center of the universe, the purpose of creation, but, instead, as the center of the fictions he himself creates to explain his existence. Only when he learns the crucial difference between these opposing viewpoints will he understand his possibilities and his limitations; only then will he be free to use his imagination to live his life fully and in all its perplexing variety.

Coover strongly distrusts man's reasoning faculty and, more particularly, the Enlightenment concept of human progress. As he explains in the Prologue to *Pricksongs & Descants*, Coover finds himself in the same position that Miguel de Cervantes was four hundred years before: at the end of one literary tradition and the beginning of another, where the culture's traditional way of perceiving the world is breaking down. Reading Ovid, Coover came to understand that man's basic and continual struggle is to resist these and other changes, to struggle "against giving in to the inevitability of process." Accordingly, his stories depict a constantly shifting or metamorphosizing world, one in which the sheer abundance of material implies the abundance of life and where the straight linear plot of conventional realistic fiction no longer suffices. In these works, the active imagination battles the deadening influence of various systems of thought—religious, political, literary—that are, as Larry McCaffery has pointed out, ideological rather than ontological in nature. Understanding this difference brings man to the edge of the abyss, from which he then recoils, seeking safety and comfort in various rituals and explanatory sytems that are necessary and, to some degree, related to the artistic process itself. These rituals and systems, however, are dangerous insofar as man allows himself to believe in them as other than self-generated imaginative constructs.

Coover urges his readers both to live in a more direct relationship to unmediated experience and to create fictions that will relieve them of their burden of anxiety in the indeterminate world. This balance of self-conscious fiction-making and unself-conscious participation in life is, however, not always achieved by Coover's characters. Even the best of them, the pattern-breakers, are often guilty of the same rigidity of the imagination that typifies their antagonists, the pattern-keepers. Refusing to accept their own mortality or that of their systems and beliefs, they venture forth on a spurious quest after immortality and platonic absolutes. Their terror of the void is real enough, but because their responses to it are ludicrous and absurd, the terror is rendered comically, fears turning into pratfalls, as in the misadventures of the Chaplinesque Charlie in the House of Rue. If, as Coover believes, existence does not have an ontological status, then life necessarily becomes not the serious business his characters make it but a kind of play, to which Johan Huizinga, author of *Homo Ludens: A Study of the Play Element in Culture* (1949), is the appropriate guide.

Coover is a fiction-writer who distrusts fiction—not because it is "exhausted," as John Barth has claimed, but because he feels that man's various fictions—not only his stories and novels, but also his histories and religions—

are always in danger of being confused with reality. He parodies myths, history, literary formulas, and elements of popular culture in an effort to expose their artifice. He imposes order on his fictions, both as structure and as subject, to undermine it effectively, to prove its arbitrariness, and thus lay bare the indeterminacy of the world. In place of the inadequate, narrowly conceived systems that some of his characters devise or even the more expansive but eventually imprisoning fantasies of others, Coover writes what one critic has called "cubist fictions," inviting the reader's participation in a work that is less a product than a process, a revelation of the instability and uncertainty of modern existence.

The parallels between Coover's fiction and process-oriented abstract expressionist art, modern physics, and post-existentialist philosophy mark Coover as a distinctly contemporary writer. His works are often discussed as leading examples of "metafiction," a formally experimental, highly reflexive literary mode which, as Robert Scholes has explained, "assimilates all the perspectives of criticism into the fiction itself." While many of Coover's shorter works are clearly metafictional in nature, in the novels and novellas formal inventiveness gives way to an interest in traditional narrative, in telling a good story. What results is a tension between contemporary and traditional narrative modes that is analogous to Coover's notion of the artist-audience relationship (dramatized in his story "The Hat Act"). In Coover's view, the fiction-maker is at once an anarchist and a priest: "He's the one who tears apart the old story, speaks the unspeakable, makes the ground shake, then shuffles the pieces back together into a new story. . . ." Coover's power to disturb is clearly evident in reviews of his work. More important, however, is the fact that these relationships between Coover and his readers, artist and audience, innovation and tradition, bear a striking similarity to the plight of his characters.

Coover's first novel, *The Origin of the Brunists*, is not "a vicious and dirty piece of writing," as one reviewer claimed; rather, it is a work in which Coover pays his dues (as he has said) to the naturalistic novel and exhaustively details the various ways in which man imaginatively responds to the randomness and variety of his world. Briefly stated, the story concerns a mining disaster that kills ninety-seven men, the formation of a millenarian cult around the sole survivor, Giovanni Bruno, and the reactions of the townspeople, especially Justin "Tiger" Miller, editor of the local newspaper, to the Brunists. An odd assortment of immigrant Italians, Protestant fundamentalists, a composer of folk songs, a numerologist, and a theosophist, the Brunists are drawn together by their desire to live meaningful lives in a comprehensible, cause-and-effect world, one in which they misinterpret random events as providential signs. Many of those who do not join the cult find a sense of purpose and a release from the frustations (often sexual) of living in a small, dying town by forming a Common Sense Committee. By accepting their roles as generally passive participants in these groups, the Brunists and their opponents gain the social approval, the feeling of power and significance, and the sense of communal purpose that makes their unimaginative lives bearable.

Miller suffers from the lack of purpose and sense of frustration that afflict the others—perhaps more so because he is able to articulate these feelings to a degree that they are not. This same consciousness, however, also frees Miller from delusions concerning the truth of the fictions they accept without question. Unlike the others, who read his headline "Miracle in West Condon" literally, Miller, the ironist, distinguishes between experience, on the one hand, and history and journalism, on the other, which he knows are not unmediated, factual accounts but imaginative constructions. The Brunists commit themselves to their version of reality and as a result become trapped within it. Miller, who is vaguely troubled by his own lack of commitment, joins the cult only to meet Bruno's attractive sister, relieve his boredom, and work up material for his paper. He does not serve the Brunists in the way his namesake, the apologist Justin, did the early Christians, for Miller only pretends to be a believer. In fact, as the movement's chronicler, he creates the cult and its members the way a novelist creates story and characters. Miller's problem, one which recurs throughout Coover's work, begins when his creation slips out of his control and takes on a life of its own, forcing its creator to assume an unwanted role: part antichrist, part blood sacrifice.

Life, of course, does not conform to the Brunist view. Yet even though the world does not end on the date predicted and despite the fact that their vigil on the Mount of Redemption turns into a Roman circus, the Brunists survive and prosper in their delusion. Growing into a worldwide religion with their own ecclesiastical hierarchy, the Brunists find a mass audience for their apocalyptic gospel. Miller also survives, resurrected by his author and comforted by his nurse, Happy Bottom, and it is their lusty, playful, and imaginative relationship, their finding the "living space between the two," that Coover holds forth as the alternative to Brunism and the denial of life it represents.

Coover is not the only contemporary American author to have written a novel about baseball and myth, but unlike Philip Roth's *The Great American Novel* (1973), which is played chiefly for laughs, or Bernard Malamud's *The Natural* (1952), where the mythic parallels seem forced, *The Universal Baseball Association, Inc. J. Henry Waugh, Prop.* successfully incorporates its various elements into a unified but complex and richly ambiguous work of narrative art. More than its baseball lore, mythic resonance, theological probings, stylistic virtuosity, or wordplay, it is the novel's blend of realism and fantasy and the elaborate development of its simple main idea or conceit that mark its achievement.

The novel focuses on a fifty-six-year-old bachelor named J. Henry Waugh and the table-top baseball game he invents: not only dice and charts, but also eight teams, players with full biographies, and fifty-five years of league records and history. Henry's fantasizing is not so much childish as necessary, given his environment, the urban equivalent of Miller's West Condon. Whereas the real world oppresses Henry with "a vague and somber sense of fatality and closed circuits," his fantasy liberates and fulfills him in several ways. For the meaningless routine of accounting, Henry substitutes the meaningful rituals of baseball and in this way finds the continuity, pastoral wholeness, and heroic purpose that his everyday existence lacks. In his Association, Henry directs and chronicles the course of history; outside it he is merely a loner, an anonymous clerk.

The advantages of his Association are not without their risks, however, for at the same time that Henry uses his imagination to enliven his moribund world he also reduces it to the narrow confines of his league: the USA miniaturized in the UBA, with its own "closed circuits." What is needed, Henry understands, is a balance of fact and fantasy, but in his attempt to right the imbalance that characterizes his life as an accountant, Henry goes to the opposite extreme, withdrawing into his fantasized realm. When a chance throw of the dice "kills" his rookie hero, Damon Rutherford ("His own man, yet at home in the world, part of it, involved, every inch of him a participant"), Henry despairs, choosing to exert that "unjustifiable control" which destroys the necessary balance of chance (dice) and order (imagination) and transforms his useful fiction into a version of the Brunists' providential universe. No longer a free, voluntary activity (according to Huizinga, a defining characteristic of true play), *The Universal Baseball Association* becomes repetitive work. Although the novel concludes with an unambiguous affirmation of the play spirit, the ending is itself ironic, for Henry, the godlike creator of his fiction (Jahweh), is no longer in control; having disappeared into the intricate mechanism of his Association, he is now controlled by it.

Henry's fate, which is very nearly Miller's in *The Origin of the Brunists*, represents for Coover the danger all writers face. As he has explained, *The Universal Baseball Association*, "as I wrote it, not necessarily as it ought to be read, is an act of exemplary writing, a book about the art of writing." In the light of Coover's belief that all men are fiction-makers insofar as they create systems to explain their world, the novel serves the related purpose of pointing out to the reader how difficult—and how necessary— is the task of distinguishing the real from the imaginary if one is to avoid Henry's fate. The need to make this distinction is the explicit subject of *The Universal Baseball Association*; the difficulty of making it is implicit in Coover's method. In the novel's opening pages, for example, Coover forces the reader to share Henry's predicament in the parallel act of reading about it. At first, the reader assumes Henry is actually at the ballpark where rookie pitcher Damon Rutherford is a few outs away from a no-hitter, but when Henry takes advantage of the seventh inning stretch to grab a sandwich at Diskin's delicatessen, one floor below, the reader corrects his mistake, perhaps unconsciously, now assuming that the game is being watched on television. Even when it becomes clear that the game is being played in Henry's mind and that Henry is himself having trouble separating fact from fiction, the reader does not stop his reading to consider what this means because, thanks to Coover's pacing, he, like Henry, is completely caught up in being "*in* there, *with* them." Once the game is over, he does have the opportunity to consider Henry's state of mind, but by the end of the first of the novel's eight chapters (seven for the days of creation plus one for the apocalypse), the reader again becomes lost in Coover's exuberant fantasy, as Henry, now in the guise of his imaginary hero Damon Rutherford, and local B-girl Hettie Irden (earth mother) play a ribald game of sexual baseball. Throughout the novel, the reader not only reads about Henry's dilemma but he is also made to experience it.

Tiger Miller understands that it is better to undertake numerous short "projects" than to commit himself to any one, as J. Henry Waugh does. Similarly, Coover has explained that the writing of short plays or stories involves very little commitment on the author's part—at most a few weeks, after which the work is either complete or discarded—whereas a novel requires not only a greater expenditure of time and energy but a certain risk as well. The starting point for each of Coover's works is not a character or plot but a metaphor, the "hidden complexities" of which he develops by means of some appropriate structural device, as in the play *The Kid* or the short stories "The Babysitter" and "The Elevator." At times, the demands of the metaphor exceed the limits of structural devices appropriate to these short forms, and here Coover turns to the novel; thus, the two early stories, "Black-damp" and "The Second Son" were transformed and expanded into *The Origin of the Brunists* and *The Universal Baseball Association*, respectively. The composition of Coover's third novel, *The Public Burning*, followed a similar but longer and more involved course, going from play to novella to novel over a difficult ten-year period during which Coover often questioned whether the expanding work would ever be completed.

One reason the novel took so long to write is that its main character, Richard Nixon, began taking real-life pratfalls in the Watergate scandal, out-stripping the ones that Coover had imagined for him in *The Public Burning*. A second reason lies in the nature of the work Coover chose to write: a densely textured compendium of American politics and popular culture in which literally thousands of details, quotations, names, and allusive echoes had to be painstakingly stitched together so as to suggest a communal work written by an entire nation. Against this incredible variety (or repetitive overabundance, as many reviewers complained) is the novel's tight and self-conscious structure: four parts of seven chapters each (magical numbers), framed by a prologue and epilogue and divided by three intermezzos. Using two alternating narrators—Vice-President Nixon and the sometimes reverent, sometimes befuddled, even frantic voice of America—Coover retells the familiar story of Ethel and Julius Rosenberg, specifically the three days leading up to their execution, which Coover sardonically moves from Sing Sing Prison to Times Square. Although it is clear that Coover is distressed by the injustice done the Rosenbergs, his aim is not to vindicate them; rather, he uses their case to expose American history as American fantasy.

Originally entitled "an historical romance," *The Public Burning* interweaves ostensible "facts," such as newspaper and magazine articles, courtroom transcripts, presidential speeches, personal letters, and obvious fantasy, including the superhero Uncle Sam and a ludicrous deathhouse love scene involving Nixon and Ethel Rosenberg. By creating "a mosaic of history," Coover provides the reader with a self-consciously fictive version of the Rosenberg case designed to compete with the supposedly historical view (as reiterated, for example, in Louis Nizer's *The Implosion Conspiracy*, 1973, which Coover reviewed in the February 11, 1973, issue of *The New York Times Book Review*). Coover's point is that, more often than not, man does not see experience directly (and therefore cannot presume to know its truth value) because he places that experience—or has it placed for him—in a context, an aesthetic frame, that determines its meaning. *The New York Times*, for example, is not shown printing "all the news that's fit to print"; rather, it selects and arranges the news on its pages ("tablets") in ways that, intentionally or not, determine the reader's ("pilgrim's") perception of what he assumes to be objective reality.

In sifting through the plethora of materials related to the Rosenberg case, Nixon comes very close to accepting Coover's view of history as essentially literary romance, or myth. He realizes that the Rosenberg conspiracy trial may actually be a government conspiracy against the accused (ritual scapegoats), depending chiefly on fabricated evidence, or stage props, and dress rehearsals for the prosecution; indeed, American life itself may be a kind of nationwide theatrical performance in which individuals play the roles assigned to them in the national scripts: Manifest Destiny, the Cold War, Westerns, and the Horatio Alger rags-to-riches plot. Nixon, however, is too much a believer in the American myths to break entirely free of them. Moreover, suffering from the same loneliness that afflicts Miller and Waugh, but being much less imaginative than they, Nixon desperately craves approval, and that requires his playing his part as it is written: "no ad-libbing," as the stage directions in *The Kid* make clear. To have a role in the Great American Plot, to be a part of the recorded "History" that he carefully distinguishes from merely personal "history," are the limited goals Nixon sets for himself because he is either unwilling or unable to imagine any other projects as being equally viable and fulfilling. As a result, he plays the role Coover has appropriately assigned him: chief clown in the national farce.

The Public Burning is not a piece of easy political satire of the sort Philip

Roth dashed off in his Nixon book, *Our Gang* (1971); in fact, Coover's Nixon is a surprisingly sympathetic character. Nor is it "a cowardly lie" which defames a nation and exonerates criminals, as one reviewer claimed. Coover's third novel, like all of his major works, is a warning to the reader concerning the uses and the dangers of the imagination: man must accept his role as fiction-maker and his responsibility for his fictions, or he will pay the penalty for confusing his facts with his fables.

Since 1978, Coover has continued to explore literary and "mythic" forms and to stretch generic classifications, revising or recycling a number of short fictions as "novels"—"A Working Day" (1979) as *Spanking the Maid* (1981), "The Cat in the Hat for President" (1968) as *A Political Fable* (1980), and "Whatever Happened to Gloomy Gus of the Chicago Bears?" (1968; novel, 1987)—and in an intertextual triple-feature of film parodies entitled *A Night at the Movies*, including previews, weekly serial episode, shorts, intermission, cartoon, travelogue, and musical interlude. All these texts manage to subvert the disclaimer which appears at the beginning of *A Night at the Movies*—"Ladies and Gentlemen May safely visit this Theatre as no Offensive Films are ever Shown Here"—but none so flagrantly as *Gerald's Party* (1985). Harking back to Coover's two "Lucky Pierre" stories about an aging pornographer, *Gerald's Party* constitutes a full-scale narrative onslaught, a playfully sadistic attack on its clownishly masochistic reader, and a vast recycling project which reverses the centrifugal reach of *The Public Burning*, moving centripetally in on itself to form Coover's fullest and most claustrophobic exploration of a single narrative metaphor.

Considered reductively, *Gerald's Party* parodies the English parlor mystery, but the parody here serves as little more than a vehicle for Coover's Rabelaisian exploitation in which John Barth's "literature of exhaustion" meets Roland Barthes' "plural text." The result is at once exhilarating and exhausting, freely combining murder mystery, pornography, film, theater, video, sex, puns, jokes, rituals, slapstick, clichés, fairy tales, party chatter, memory, desire, and aesthetic and philosophical speculation, all in one thickly embedded, endlessly interrupted yet unstoppable, ribald whole. The narrative is at once abundant (like the food and drink), full of holes (like the one in the victim Ros's breast), clogged (like the Gerald's upstairs toilet), and stuck (as Gerald becomes in one sex scene). Plots proliferate but do not progress in any conventional way. As Inspector Pardew tries to solve the murder mystery, Gerald pursues Alison; Sally Ann pursues Gerald; Jim, a doctor, attends to the dying; Steve, a plumber, fixes everything but the stopped-up toilet; Gerald's wife continues to prepare food, vacuum, and make wondrously inappropriate remarks ("I wish people wouldn't use guns in the house," she says after one guest has been fatally shot); and Gerald's mother-in-law, trying to put her grandson Mark to bed, looks on disapprovingly. These are but a few of the novel's myriad plots.

Gerald's efforts to understand what is happening, along with his inability to order the chaos, parallel the reader's. The novel in fact anticipates and thus short-circuits the reader's own efforts to understand Coover's bewildering but brilliant text, which seems to question its own purpose and seriousness and whose structure follows that of an all-night party, including the inevitable winding down to its anticlimactic end, or death. Not surprisingly, Pardew's solution resolves little and interests the reader not at all. Moreover, the most serious and philosophical comments in the novel—the ones upon which the conventional reader would like to seize for their power to explain and control the rest of the text—seem to be nothing more than additional false clues. Clearly, here as in all Coover's novels, stories, and plays, the reader can survive and in fact enjoy this narrative assault on his or her abilities and sensibilities only by resisting the Inspector's obsession with patterns and "holistic criminalistics." Yet even if the reader takes a pratfall or two, Coover's parodic range and supercharged narrative energy make the ride worth the risk.

Robert A. Morace

Other major works

SHORT FICTION: *Pricksongs & Descants*, 1969; *The Water Pourer*, 1972 (deleted from *The Origin of the Brunists*); *The Convention*, 1981; *In Bed One Night and Other Brief Encounters*, 1983; *A Night at the Movies: Or, You Must Remember This*, 1987.

PLAYS: *The Kid*, 1972; *Love Scene*, 1972; *Rip Awake*, 1972; *A Theological Position*, 1972.

Bibliography

Cope, Jackson I. *Robert Coover's Fictions*. Baltimore: The Johns Hopkins University Press, 1986. Cope's readings of selected texts are as provocative as they are unfocused; Cope considers the various ways in which Coover extends the literary forms within and against which he writes. The densely written chapter on *Gerald's Party* and the Bakhtinian reading of *The Public Burning* are especially noteworthy.

Couturier, Maurice, ed. *Delta* 28 (June, 1989). Special issue on Coover. Includes an introduction, a chronology, a bibliography, a previously unpublished Coover story and brief essay on why he writes, and critical essays on a wide variety of topics and fictions, including *Gerald's Party*.

Critique, 23, no. 1 (1982). Special issue devoted to essays on *The Public Burning*: Tom LeClair's (reprinted in expanded form in *The Art of Excess*; see below); Raymond Mazurek's on history, the novel, and metafiction; Louis Gallo's on a key scene in which a viewer exits from a 3-D motion picture; and John Ramage's on myth and monomyth.

Gordon, Lois. *Robert Coover: The Universal Fictionmaking Process*. Carbon-
    dale: Southern Illinois University Press, 1982. Focuses on Coover's preoc-
    cupation with the process by which man transforms the flux of random
    experience into order, fiction, and myth. Gordon's study is strictly intro-
    ductory but comprehensive and certainly far superior to Richard Ander-
    sen's *Robert Coover* in the Twayne's United States Authors series.
LeClair, Tom. *The Art of Excess: Mastery in Contemporary American Fic-
    tion*. Urbana: University of Illinois Press, 1989. LeClair discusses *The
    Public Burning* in terms of systems theory and the author's mastery of
    world, of reader, and of narrative technique. Like the rest of his book, the
    Coover chapter is intelligent and provocative despite, at times, the arbitrari-
    ness and obfuscations of the book's thesis.
McCaffery, Larry. *The Metafictional Muse: The Works of Robert Coover,
    Donald Barthelme, and William H. Gass*. Pittsburgh: University of Pitts-
    burgh Press, 1982. The three writers chosen represent different aspects of
    the metafictional approach. In his discussion of *Pricksongs & Descants* and
    the first three novels, McCaffery emphasizes the mythic impulse in Coo-
    ver's fiction as well as making an important observation concerning the
    characters' mistaking ideological fictions, or myths, for ontological truths.

JAMES GOULD COZZENS

Born: Chicago, Illinois; August 19, 1903
Died: Stuart, Florida; August 9, 1978

Principal long fiction

Confusion, 1924; *Michael Scarlett*, 1925; *Cock Pit*, 1928; *The Son of Perdition*, 1929; *S.S. San Pedro*, 1931; *The Last Adam*, 1933; *Castaway*, 1934; *Men and Brethren*, 1936; *Ask Me Tomorrow*, 1940; *The Just and the Unjust*, 1942; *Guard of Honor*, 1948; *By Love Possessed*, 1957; *Morning, Noon, and Night*, 1968.

Other literary forms

In addition to his thirteen novels, James Gould Cozzens published two collections of short stories, *Child's Play* (1958) and *Children and Others* (1964), which contain most of the twenty-seven stories he wrote between 1920 and 1950 for mass circulation magazines such as the *Saturday Evening Post*, *Colliers*, and *Redbook*. Cozzens also served as an associate editor for *Winged Foot*, a small in-house magazine published by the New York Athletic Club from 1928 to 1929, and for *Fortune* from 1937 to 1938. Matthew Bruccoli has edited a collection of some of these miscellaneous pieces, published under the title *Just Representations* (1978).

Achievements

Cozzens might best be characterized as a writer's writer. His work has traditionally been praised more highly by fellow writers and editors than it has by critics or book buyers. From the beginning of his writing career, when *The Atlantic* printed an essay he wrote as a sixteen year-old high school student, professionals have been drawn to his taut, disciplined style, his carefully structured plots, and his complex, precise renderings of character and background detail. His first novel, written during his freshman year at Harvard University, received a favorable review from *The New York Times*. His fifth, *S.S. San Pedro*, won the Scribner's Prize for fiction when he was but twenty-six. Most of his next eight novels were Book-of-the-Month Club selections. Cozzens won the O. Henry Award for a short story in 1936, a Pulitzer Prize for *Guard of Honor* in 1948, and in 1957, the Howells Medal, which the American Academy of Arts and Letters gives only once every five years for outstanding achievement in fiction, for *By Love Possessed*. In his nominating speech for the medal, Malcolm Cowley called the novel a solid achievement, written with a craftsmanship and intelligence which would be envied by all of Cozzens' fellow novelists. Orville Prescott claimed that at least three of Cozzens' novels were among the finest ever written in America, while C. P. Snow thought him one of the country's best realistic novelists. When John

Fischer reviewed *By Love Possessed* in *Harper's* in 1957, he suggested that Cozzens was one of the very few important serious novelists in the country. He claimed that the body of Cozzens' work clearly needed reevaluation, and he recommended it for a Nobel Prize. The editor who collected many of his shorter pieces, Matthew Bruccoli, compared him favorably to another Nobel Prize winner, claiming that Cozzen's work was often so distinguished that it could make even William Faulkner's prose look amateurish by comparison.

Despite such praise, Cozzens' novels did not fare well with the book-buying public or with the country's major reviewers during his lifetime. He achieved bestsellerdom only once, when *By Love Possessed* sold 170,000 copies during the first six weeks of publication.

Cozzens led a quiet, reclusive life, intentionally shying away from the channels of publicity through which many twentieth century authors have promoted their works. He wrote slowly, spending more than twenty-five years on his last three novels alone while doing little to keep his name before his audience or the publishing trade. More decisively, the novels themselves celebrated such a complex view of everyday human life that critics and readers alike regularly abandoned them unread, half-read, or misread. In print, Cozzens was frequently condemned not for what he wrote, but for what he did not write. Objections were regularly leveled against his choice of characters or his lack of social concern. The heroes of his fictions were most often professional men who lived unobtrusively in the small towns of the Atlantic seaboard. Their stories seldom showed the drama, outrage, alienation, terror, or rebellion which distinguished the characters of other mid-twentieth century writers. The tensions which preoccupied his contemporaries seemed not to touch Cozzens very deeply; their major solutions—social reform, rugged individuality, anarchy, or despair—did not accord with his complicated world view. For avoiding the fashionable in plot, character, and theme, he was often branded conservative, apathetic, bigoted, or reactionary—a spokesman for a traditional point of view far out of step with the realities of urban, industrial, and international America. Yet his intricate plots, complex ideas, and detailed psychological studies of modern men were, by the time of his death, beginning to be seen by critics and readers alike as the work not of a conservative mind, but of an independent thinker who simply took a broader and deeper view than most of his contemporaries.

Biography

James Gould Cozzens' life was as quiet, as competently professional, and as outwardly uneventful as the lives of the prosperous executives, lawyers, ministers, and generals who inhabit his fiction. He was born in Chicago, Illinois, on August 19, 1903, to a comfortable though not wealthy businessman, Henry William Cozzens, and his wife, Bertha. The family moved east, and Cozzens grew up on Staten Island. He attended private schools in New

York and, for six years, a preparatory school in Connecticut. By the time he was sixteen, he was already showing a precocious ability for writing. While still at Kent School, he managed to get his essay "A Democratic School" published by *The Atlantic*. A year later, he matriculated to Harvard University and spent much of his freshman year writing his first novel, *Confusion*. It was published in 1924 by B. J. Brimmer, and the success of it, he later admitted, went to his head. He immediately began a second, taking a leave of absence from school to complete it. *Michael Scarlett* was published in 1925 and received such favorable press from publications such as *The New York Times* that Cozzens gave himself over completely to writing. Instead of returning to college, he spent the next year in Cuba, planning his next fictions and earning pocket money by tutoring the children of American engineers. During the next eleven years, he published seven lengthy novels, the first three of which— *Cock Pit*, *The Son of Perdition*, and *S.S. San Pedro*—drew heavily on his experiences in the Caribbean. During 1926, he continued his wandering, spending more than a year in Europe; the trip eventually formed the basis for *Ask Me Tomorrow* (1940). He met Bernice Baumgarten, and on December 31, 1927, he married her. The Cozzens' settled into a quiet Connecticut suburb where Bernice could commute regularly to Manhattan for her career as a literary agent and where Cozzens could have the seclusion to continue writing full time.

The Cozzens' spent much of their next forty years single-mindedly dedicated to their professional endeavors, their careers intertwined: Bernice was Cozzens' first reader and his literary agent. In the little contact Cozzens allowed himself with the outside world, the troubled sense of duty and the gritty sense of honor which characterized many of his fictional heroes could be detected. When the Depression and a decline in his own royalties strained the family finances in the late 1930's, Cozzens took on an editorial job at *Fortune*. When patriotic idealism swept the country after the Japanese attack on Pearl Harbor in 1941, Cozzens—at age thirty-nine—volunteered to serve in the United States Army Air Corps and by 1945 had earned himself the rank of major. He avoided public appearances, shunned interviews, and allowed himself to be caught up in few causes. For most of his professional career, a career which spanned more than fifty years, Cozzens wrote. He died of pneumonia while vacationing in Florida on August 9, 1978.

Analysis

In an often quoted letter written to his English publishers, James Gould Cozzens defined the essence of his work, "the point of it all," as an attempt to give structure and understanding to "the immensity and the immense complexity" of human experience. This was more than a platitude for Cozzens; it was an obsession. "I wanted to show," he continued, "the peculiar effects of the interaction of innumerable individuals functioning in ways at once determined by and determining the functioning of innumerable others." Cozzens was sure that the key to understanding modern man lay not in exploring the individual psyche nor analyzing social institutions. Rather, he believed the key lay in exploring their interaction: the way tough-minded individuals gave shape to but were also shaped by the lives and destinies of many others. He saw society not as an organization, but as an organism "with life and purposes of its own" which threatened to leave little for a modern man to do in the complicated world he had created. He dissected the lives of ordinary men, probing their beliefs and decisions and weighing the outcomes of their failures and their successes. Beginning with *S.S. San Pedro* in 1931, and ending with his last novel, *Morning, Noon, and Night* in 1968, Cozzens singled out progressively smaller pieces of these ordinary lives and studied them more and more intensely. He was like a physicist, bent on unlocking the secrets of the social universe by examining smaller and smaller particles of matter with ever greater precision—and, like the modern physicist, Cozzens eventually resigned himself to the notion that chance and uncertainty played a disproportionately large share in the outcomes of the lives he studied. The networks of interaction, he warned, were infinitely more complex than a man could imagine. Yet novel by novel, he also groped toward an affirmation of the small but dignified role which a man could still play in the intricate world he had devised, if only he would live "rightly." This single-minded effort to define precisely how a man should live gave his novels many of their strengths and most of their weaknesses.

Studying the outlaw, the outcast, or the superhero did not suit these purposes. Neither did studying the pawn, the downtrodden, or the disadvantaged. Cozzens would not allow himself the luxury of writing about singularly interesting characters or immediately sympathetic ones. He focused instead on those everyday beings who were influential enough to be society's leaders and flawed enough to be its victims. In *S.S. San Pedro*, he fixed his attention on Anthony Bradell, the ship's senior second officer. In *The Last Adam*, he investigated a rural country doctor. In *Men and Brethren*, he studied a series of decisions made by one minister. In *The Just and the Unjust*, Cozzens finally combined the best qualities of these early characters. His hero, Abner Coats, is a reasonable and intelligent lawyer who can understand human weakness, who can distrust the excesses of his own emotionalism, who can use his honest realism to resist the commonplace responses of his fellow men, and yet finds his commitment to living dutifully and honorably sorely strained. For Coats, living well comes to mean trying to prevail over the randomness, the meanness, and the stupidity which surround him. As Cozzens' studies of how to live well grew more intricate, it took him longer to complete each of his novels. Cozzens' next novel, *Guard of Honor*, required six years of gestation; his last two novels, *By Love Possessed* and *Morning, Noon, and Night*, took him another twenty years to write.

As Cozzens examined his protagonists more slowly, he also narrowed his focus, plotting his novels more densely and condensing their actions to briefer segments of time. The action of *The Last Adam* takes place in exactly four weeks; the action in *Men and Brethren* spans about two days. In *Guard of Honor* and *By Love Possessed*, time is compressed even further, and by *Morning, Noon, and Night*, the action is reduced to a ten-hour stretch studied in more than four hundred pages of close analysis. At the same time, Cozzens progressively reduced the scope of his novels. His earliest fictions tended to be sprawling. *Michael Scarlett* was set in Elizabethan England, while *Cock Pit*, *The Son of Perdition*, and *S.S. San Pedro* wandered over much of the Caribbean. With *The Last Adam*, however, Cozzens began to understand what could be accomplished by limiting the events he studied to a tightly structured few and by exploring in depth all their intricate consequences. By the time he published *Morning, Noon, and Night*, his control of setting was so secure that the entire novel could be plotted from a single room, the downstairs study of Henry Dodd Worthington's management consultant firm.

Novel by novel, Cozzens continued to reduce the range of characters, incidents, and locales. Each novel examined more closely the tangled implications of human choice, developing a complex vision of man which at once admitted his smallness, helplessness, and isolation but which also celebrated the triumphs which right living still made attainable. Unlike many of his contemporaries, the more Cozzens came to understand and shape his material, the more quietly optimistic he grew. In *Michael Scarlett*, a dashing and intelligent Cambridge student, interested in poetry, dueling, brawling, and sex, and a friend of Christopher Marlowe, Thomas Nashe, Ben Jonson, John Donne, and William Shakespeare, uses his brilliance only to fashion for himself an early and violent death. Francis Ellery, the slightly autobiographical hero of *Ask Me Tomorrow*, comes to realize that his intelligence has limits, that his fate is bound up with a Europe whose complicated history and incomprehensible languages he might never understand, and that his only hope lies in continuing to survive. Gradually, Cozzens transforms the pessimism of these early efforts to affirmations of a quieter steadier path. The heroes of his last four novels come to share a deeper appreciation for the complications in their lives and their lack of clear-cut choices, but they learn also to confront their own fears openly and to strive for competence in spite of them. These quiet professionals seemed to have a greater impact on their world than the flashy heroes of the earlier novels. General Ira Beal's overcoming of his own weaknesses in *Guard of Honor* could have a small or perhaps an immeasurably large influence on the outcome of World War II. Arthur Winner's and Henry Worthington's honest confrontations with love, corruption, and human frailty in the last two novels benefit their families, their societies, and even themselves. Cozzens had set out to study the webs of men's interactions; he concluded that their world was far more difficult than most humans would allow themselves to believe, and far more ennobling.

Cozzens' early novels—*Confusion, Michael Scarlett, Cock Pit, The Son of Perdition, S.S. San Pedro, The Last Adam*, and *Castaway*—mark his development from a talented apprentice to a steady professional. It took him fourteen years to turn out these seven works and thirty-four years to write his next six. The mature Cozzens was not particularly proud of the early attempts, and he eventually convinced his publisher to remove the first four from his official list of works. Yet among these seven novels are some of his most accessible works; taken as a group, they show his steady growth toward the styles, themes, and characters which would come to dominate his mature fiction.

Most of the early novels feature a spokesman, usually one close to Cozzens' own age, who comments on the sometimes violent, sometimes melodramatic, but always hectic action. In *Confusion*, this role is played by Cerise D'Atree, a brilliant, young European woman on tour in America. In *Cock Pit*, Cozzens hides behind the same gender-distancing technique, creating in Ruth Micks a tough-minded intellectual who stands out from what one character in the book calls the muddled thinkers who create the novel's tensions. By *Cock Pit*, Cozzens was also showing interest in the flawed, influential, and willful professional. Ruth's father, Lancy Micks, is a field engineer for a sugar corporation; his company and his personality have the potential to shape the lives of hundreds of Cuban peasants.

Cozzens finally combined his honest and intelligent spokesman with his willful professional in *The Son of Perdition*, an ambitious, complicated novel which studies the cross-cultural effects of American imperialism. Joel Stellow, director of the United Sugar Company's Cuban holdings, exhibits the detached, unconventional, and brilliant mind that characterizes all of Cozzens' mature heroes. Though he is defeated by the anarchical forces of the island and by the footloose decadence of a wandering, ugly-American type, Stellow is beginning to develop the appreciation for the complex patterns governing men's lives which enables Cozzens' later heroes to achieve a measure of success.

S.S. San Pedro was the first novel Cozzens would officially admit to writing. Loosely based on the 1928 sinking of the *S.S. Vestris*, the novel focuses on another competent professional, Anthony Bradell, the ship's senior second officer. Like Stellow, Bradell finds himself all but powerless to check the intricate forces which lead to the destruction of the ship and many of its passengers. For the first of many times, Cozzens matches an ordinary, hardworking, and dedicated professional against a confluence of circumstances: the aging and largely incompetent captain, the purposeful and malicious ocean, and the enigmatic Doctor Percival, an old gentleman in black whose albatrosslike presence seems to make the other passengers nervous. The face of Dr. Percival haunts Bradell's dreams, and somehow, Cozzens suggests,

Percival is as responsible for the sinking as is any other single agent. By leaving this enigmatic figure unexplained, Cozzens emphasizes the role of chance and of inexplicable factors in human affairs: even his most intelligent heroes can be confounded by complex, natural patterns which are simply too complex to be understood.

The confined structure of *S.S. San Pedro*, with its limited crew, its closed environment, its concentrated span of time, and its focus on a single human event appealed to the craftsman and the philosopher in Cozzens. He learned what could be achieved by limiting the architecture of a novel to a compact segment of space and time; it was a lesson he would never forget. Moreover, *S.S. San Pedro* marked his turning inward, his abandonment of the pyrotechnics of fast-paced plots and his growing interest in deciphering the interactions of personality, irrationality, meanness, luck, weakness, and fate which influence every human act and which challenge even the most competent of men.

If *S.S. San Pedro* ends with Bradell still puzzled by the haunting presence of Dr. Percival, it also outlines the curriculum for Cozzens' further studies. In *The Last Adam*, he focuses on an enigmatic, small-town doctor. Moving from the sprawling geography of his earlier fiction, placing his competent professional in the controlled, laboratorylike environment of a Connecticut village, carefully scrutinizing the interior landscapes of his central characters' psyches, Cozzens' *The Last Adam* lays out the themes, techniques, and interests which would occupy him for the remainder of his career. The study of Dr. George Bull is focused on one critical month in one small, cliquish town. The doctor tries to understand the deaths of two women, the outbreak of a typhoid epidemic for which he is partially responsible, the increasingly strident charges against his own professional competence, and the miraculous recovery of a paralyzed patient whose bout with typhoid leaves him better than he has ever been. Cozzens' doctor finds no clear answers to the "whys" of this complicated chain of events. Why some should live, why some should hate, why some negative act should lead to some positive result, puzzles Bull as much as it had Bradell in *S.S. San Pedro*.

If Cozzens was no closer to answers, he was at least learning how to frame questions more precisely. His next novel, *Castaway*, explores the possibility of finding answers by studying in detail an individual psyche cut off from any social network. It is Cozzens' only exploration into the territory which fascinated many of his contemporaries. He examines the isolated, alienated soul of the intelligent but frightened Mr. Lecky. For reasons Cozzens felt were not important enough to explain, the character finds himself in a deserted department store, mysteriously cut off from his fellow men, from the social connections which puzzle Cozzens' earlier characters, and from the luck, chance, or providence which guides their lives. Cozzens' Mr. Lecky simply goes mad in his isolation, transforming himself into a homocidal maniac. The individual self, Cozzens seems to conclude, does not have the characteristics which others have so often attributed to it, no Emersonian store of answers which well up and reveal man's true direction. The fear which the unconnected self can generate leads instead to self-destruction.

Having ranged from the social criticism of *Cock Pit* to the expressionism of *Castaway*, Cozzens finally settled on a voice and a theme which was uniquely his own. In *Men and Brethren*, Cozzens turned back permanently to the investigations he had begun in *The Last Adam*. Focused on Earnest Cudlip, an Episcopalian minister, the novel is an intense, almost clinical study of the psychology of yet another competent professional. Cudlip has his flaws, but he has found solutions to the problems which stumped Bradell and Bull. Cudlip's sense of responsibility to others helps him maintain order in a complex world he can never fully understand. Like that of many of his predecessors, Cudlip's intelligence penetrates the shallow, emotional responses which most people allow to pass for truth, but more than any of his predecessors, he abandons an absolute faith in intellect and shows himself willing to let destiny, nature, or God guide the events which he acknowledges to be beyond his control. Foreshadowing the techniques Cozzens uses in his last four novels, *Men and Brethren* is plotted compactly: all the events dovetail into a series of decisions which Cudlip is forced to make during a hectic two-day period. He saves a woman from committing suicide by compromising his religious beliefs and helping her secure an abortion. He helps a minister who has been dismissed from his parish for homosexuality, but the minister turns ungrateful, strikes him, and brands him a hypocrite. He helps an alcoholic parishioner out of one problem, then watches her drown herself because of another. Cozzens concludes the novel ambiguously. Cudlip is resolutely dedicated to the duty of continuing to serve his flock and his God, but he realizes that his actions will seldom change the complicated, unfathomable courses of his parishioners' lives. All he can do, Cudlip concludes, is his best.

Unable to live with that resigned conclusion, Cozzens tried to break new ground. In *Ask Me Tomorrow*, he decided to explore a different kind of professional, choosing, for the first and last time, a novelist as his protagonist. Critics regard Frances Ellery as Cozzens' most autobiographical character. Like Cozzens himself, Ellery has known early success. The author of several well-received novels, Ellery turns out to be the least sympathetic of Cozzens' professionals. Losing himself on a grand tour of Europe, unsure of his writing, unsure of his purpose, unsure of his own attractiveness, Ellery stumbles through a series of romantic encounters trying desperately to understand what they mean to him and he to them. Cozzens invests Ellery with a keener intelligence than any of his previous case studies, but he gives him, too, less strength of will. The results prove to be disastrous for the youthful writer. Ellery fails in his romantic entanglements, in the tutoring duties through which he aimed to support himself, and in his ability to find peace or meaning in the accidents which befall him. As his novelist moves through his tour without deciphering his own life's complexities, Cozzens concludes that honesty and rationality are not sufficient for a man to live rightly: he needs the aid of some other faculty.

For *Men and Brethren*, Cozzens spent the better part of a year researching the theology and everyday workings of Episcopalianism. For *The Last Adam*, he carefully researched rural medicine. For *The Just and the Unjust*, he enmeshed himself in the study of law and the workings of a small county courthouse. In the case of the latter, this research helped Cozzens impart the vivid, precise, realistic detail which characterizes all his fiction about professionals while also providing a clue as to what a professional needs to reach the fulfillment which Frances Ellery fails to achieve. Abner Coats, a district attorney trying two men for murder, discovers the strength of will and sense of purpose which Ellery lacks. The novel advances an idea which is out of fashion: strength of character can overcome the limitations of intelligence.

The thesis of *Men and Brethren* was a startling and ultimately unpopular solution to the questions Cozzens had been raising in his previous fictions, implying that much of the ambiguity, much of the uncertainty, and much of the doubt experienced by his earlier professionals had actually been self-imposed. By giving too much credence to their own innocent ideals or innate fears, men such as Bradell, Bull, and Ellery had shut themselves off from a human network which seldom worked by the principles they had imagined. Abner Coats offers an alternative. In the brief three-day period chronicled by the novel, he is forced to learn that his ideas bear little relationship to the world. As he prepares a case against two men who have kidnaped and murdered a drug dealer, he has to acknowledge that the law can provide no absolute judgments about right and wrong, that judges and juries behave in unpredictable or downright ignorant ways, and that even the legal system, like all human creations, is best served by compromise rather than by absolute principle. Ideals and values, Coats concludes, are simplifications, abstract, almost featureless models of the complicated forces which lie behind human motivations. Outside the courtroom, abstract principles are even less reliable guides to understanding or empathy. Often, they prevent a man such as Coats from a meaningful participation in the lives around him. *The Just and the Unjust* confused many of Cozzens' readers. When Coats learns that the county's political boss is corrupt, readers accustomed to romantic fiction expect him to refuse to compromise his principles. Instead, Coats accepts the flaws of the world, allies himself with the party boss, and tries to use his skills to achieve what good he can. This moral ambiguity provoked criticism, and in his next novel, Cozzens defensively tired to explain his conclusions more fully.

Critics have usually called *Guard of Honor* one of Cozzens' two best novels. It is a densely plotted examination of a United States Army Air Corps general who faces the same sort of crisis which challenges Abner Coats. During a particularly critical Thursday, Friday, and Saturday during World War II, General Ira Beal has to confront both the destructiveness of his own fears and the inadequacies of his own intelligence—lessons which many of the characters in Cozzens' longest and most complicated novel have to learn. Set at Ocanara Army Air Corps Base in Florida in 1943, the novel presents Beal and his subordinates in a pattern of interconnected events, at once profoundly complicated, apparently random, and yet frighteningly powerful in their consequences. Beal freezes at the controls of a plane and comes close to causing a mid-air collision. The base's black pilots begin to protest the segregationist practices of the Officers Club. A colonel commits suicide; another assaults and wounds a black pilot who is scheduled to receive the Distinguished Flying Cross. A paratroop exercise, meant to help celebrate Beal's birthday, ends with several jumpers accidentally landing in a swamp and drowning. Beal has to deal with several episodes of impotence with his wife, while a captain and a lieutenant share an adulterous moment. These chance events create a six-hundred-page web for Beal to understand and overcome. He cannot fully explain why these events are happening, how they are related, or what their consequences for his future might be. Their energy and capriciousness paralyze him with fear, yet Cozzens allows Beal to redeem himself. He finds the strength of will to face each crisis; he has the luck to have an intelligent second-in-command officer to help cover for him, the humility to accept his limitations, and, most important, the resolve to continue doing his best.

In *By Love Possessed*, Cozzens amplifies the austere, rather stoic message of *Guard of Honor*. Returning to the familiar territory of a small county courthouse, Cozzens presents a collection of competent attorneys, prosecutors, judges, and victims who are confronted with a series of interactions far more complicated than anything faced by Beal. Each struggles to understand the tangled workings of four subplots from his own particular point of view, and amid such ambiguities, each tries to find the right way to act. As Cozzens moves more deeply into their psyches and away from the plot, he sustains tension not by adding dramatic incidents, but by contrasting the leading characters' different philosophical assumptions. Not much happens in this novel: for three days, Cozzens' characters chiefly talk to one another. Yet their discourses are so lucidly argued, their particular biases so honestly explored, and their interminglings of love, hate, and hurt so convincingly retold that the novel builds toward an intellectual climax as compelling as any of Cozzens' more dramatic ones. The novel juxtaposes the cool rationality of Julius Penrose, the fervid mysticism of Mrs. Pratt, the raw sexuality of Marjorie Penrose, the stifling love of Helen Detweiler, the opportunism of Jerry Brophy, the cynicism of Fred Dealy, the cowardice of Ralph Detweiler, and the despair of Noah Tuttle: all of them connected to the law firm of Winner, Tuttle, Winner, and Penrose; all of them crippled by their own unique certitudes. In the younger Winner, Cozzens develops fully the notion of remaining "of good heart" which informs *Guard of Honor*. Like Beal, Arthur Winner has learned painfully that each of the lives around him has weaknesses which affect the rest. Like Beal, Winner has to face the knowledge that his own weaknesses have added to the complications. Not intellect, not love, not good intentions, not intuition, he concludes, are enough to guide any of the characters to right choices. Early in the novel, the slow cancerous death of Winner's father teaches Winner that even the best of minds remains firmly rooted to a mortal body. Each of the four subplots explores the equally cancerous effects of depending too much on rationality or emotionalism. At the novel's end, Winner discovers a third and more reliable faculty: like Beal, Winner learns to trust his own strength of will and strength of character.

Still, Cozzens remained unsatisfied with the clarity of this recommendation. He was trying to understand and affirm an old abstraction and its relation to a modern setting. His last novel, *Morning, Noon, and Night*, tried to explain yet again the central thought which had informed *Guard of Honor* and *By Love Possessed*, a thought which was at once a cliché and an exciting discovery for Cozzens. Henry Dodd Worthington, founder of the nation's most successful management consulting firm and scion to landed New England gentry who for generations had amused themselves by becoming college professors, is twice a husband and once a father, and he is Cozzens' most complicated professional. Set entirely in Worthington's study, with its action concentrated in a ten-hour period of wide-ranging reminiscences, the novel centers itself on a precise definition of the strength of character advocated in Cozzens' previous novels.

By training, inheritance, temperament, and experience, Worthington is probably better equipped than any of Cozzens' previous creations to understand why complex human systems behave the way they do. As a specialist in organizational development, he has already learned that even the best human systems operate under the handicaps of inadequate ideals, reflexive emotional responses, and blind luck. Having enhanced his own fortune by capitalizing on these weaknesses in others, Worthington is ready to turn his intelligence on himself. In his late sixties, the eccentric consultant has arrived at the age where self-deception can no longer be tolerated. For ten demanding hours, he thinks through the consequences of his life's choices and comes resignedly to conclude that luck has largely determined his grandfather's career, his father's, his daughter's, his wives', and his own. Fortune and misfortune, he decides, have been the workings of chance: not skill, not intelligence, not idealism, and certainly not careful planning. His own failings as husband, father, businessman, and tawdry high school thief are enough to convince him that he is no better and no worse than other humans with whom he has shared the planet. Remembering a fool such as his grandfather, a sound businessman such as his uncle, or a failure such as his daughter convinces Worthington that neither victory nor defeat serve as clear guides to men's hearts. A man finds peace, he concludes, not in victory but in the nobility of doing whatever he does well.

Troubled, at the novel's end, that his intense examination has led to such trivial conclusions, Worthington cheers himself with the notion that life's great truths are usually trivial. Such is the consolation offered by Cozzens' mature novels.

Philip Woodard

Other major works

SHORT FICTION: *Child's Play*, 1958; *Children and Others*, 1964; *A Flower in Her Hair*, 1975.

NONFICTION: *Just Representations*, 1978 (Matthew Bruccoli, editor).

Bibliography

Bracher, Frederick. *The Novels of James Gould Cozzens*. New York: Harcourt, Brace, 1959. Of the eight novels by Cozzens published between 1931 and 1959, Bracher argues that at least four of them are of "major importance by any set of standards." Defends Cozzens from attacks by critics for his lack of personal commitment, showing him to be a novelist of intellect whose strength is storytelling. A thorough commentary on Cozzens' literary career.

Bruccoli, Matthew J. *James Gould Cozzens: A Life Apart*. New York: Harcourt Brace Jovanovich, 1983. This book-length story of Cozzens is essentially a biography with useful information on his upbringing and his development as a novelist. Includes a chapter each on *Guard of Honor* and *By Love Possessed* and an appendix containing excerpts from his notebooks. A must for any serious scholar of Cozzens.

Hicks, Granville. *James Gould Cozzens*. Minneapolis: University of Minnesota, 1966. An accessible introduction to Cozzens with some criticism of his novels from *Confusion* to *Guard of Honor*, winner of the Pulitzer prize, and *By Love Possessed*. Argues that the pretentiousness in Cozzens' early work was transformed in later novels to "competent, straightforward prose."

Mooney, John Harry, Jr. *James Gould Cozzens: Novelist of Intellect*. Pittsburgh: University of Pittsburgh Press, 1963. A straightforward, useful study. Each chapter focuses on a different novel, from *S.S. San Pedro* to *Castaway*, and the final chapter covers the critical material available on Cozzens.

STEPHEN CRANE

Born: Newark, New Jersey; November 1, 1871
Died: Badenweiler, Germany; June 5, 1900

Principal long fiction

Maggie: A Girl of the Streets, 1893; *The Red Badge of Courage: An Episode of the American Civil War*, 1895; *George's Mother*, 1896; *The Third Violet*, 1897; *Active Service*, 1899; *The Monster and Other Stories*, 1899; *The O'Ruddy: A Romance*, 1903 (with Robert Barr).

Other literary forms

Stephen Crane was an accomplished poet, short-story writer, and journalist as well as a novelist. His first collection of poems, *The Black Riders and Other Lines*, appeared in 1895; in 1896, a collection of seven poems and a sketch was published as *A Souvenir and a Medley*; and *War Is Kind*, another collection of poetry was published in 1899. Crane's uncollected poems form part of the tenth volume of *The University Press of Virginia Edition of the Works of Stephen Crane* (1970). *The Blood of the Martyr*, a closet drama believed to have been written in 1898, was not published until 1940. One other play, *The Ghost* (1899), wrtten for a Christmas party at Crane's home in England by Crane and others, has not survived in toto. Crane's shorts stories and sketches, of which there are many, began appearing in 1892 and have been discovered from time to time up to the present. His journalistic pieces occasionally have literary value.

Achievements

As one of the Impressionist writers—Joseph Conrad called him "The Impressionist"—Crane was among the first to express in writing a new way of looking at the world. A pivotal movement in the history of ideas, Impressionism grew out of scientific discoveries that showed how human physiology, particularly that of the eye, determines the way everything in the universe and everything outside the individual body and mind is perceived. People do not see the world as it is; the mind and the eye collaborate to interpret a chaotic universe as fundamentally unified, coherent, and explainable. The delusion is compounded when human beings agglomerate, for then they tend to create grander fabrications such as religion and history. Although Crane is also seen as one of the first American naturalistic writers, a symbolist, and imagist, and even a nihilist, the achievements designated by these labels all derive from his impressionistic world view.

Crane's major achievement, both as a fiction-writer and as a poet, was that he unflinchingly fought his way through established assumptions about the nature of life, eventually overcoming them. His perceptions were the logical end to the ideas of a long line of American Puritans and transcendentalists who believed in the individual pursuit of truth. The great and perhaps fitting irony of that logic is that Crane repudiated the truths in which his predecessors believed.

Rejecting much that was conventional about fiction in his day—elaborate plots, numerous and usually middle- or upper-class characters, romantic settings, moralizing narrators—Crane also denied values of much greater significance: nationalism, patriotism, the greatness of individual and collective man, and the existence of supernatural powers that care, protect, and guide.

In his best fiction, as in his life, Crane squarely faced the horror of a meaningless universe by exposing the blindness and egotism of concepts that deny that meaninglessness. He was, unfortunately, unable to build a new and positive vision on the rubble of the old; he died at age twenty-eight, his accomplishments genuinely astounding.

Biography

Born on November 1, 1871, in the Methodist parsonage in Newark, New Jersey, Stephen Crane was the fourteenth and last child of Mary Peck Crane and Reverend Jonathan Crane, whose family dated back more than two centuries on the American continent. On the Peck side, almost every male was a minister, one became a bishop. By the time his father died in 1880, Crane had lived in several places in New York and New Jersey and had been thoroughly indoctrinated in the faith he was soon to reject. Also around this time, he wrote his first poem, "I'd Rather Have." His first short story, "Uncle Jake and the Bell Handle," was written in 1885, and the same year he enrolled in Pennington Seminary, where he stayed until 1887. Between 1888 and 1891, he attended Claverack College, Hudson River Institute, Lafayette College, and Syracuse University. He was never graduated from any of these, preferring baseball to study. In 1892, the New York *Tribune* published many of his New York City sketches and more than a dozen Sullivan County tales. Having apparently forgotten Miss Helen Trent, his first love, he fell in love with Mrs. Lily Brandon Munroe. That same year, the mechanics union took exception to his article on their annual fete, which resulted in Crane's brother, Townley being fired from the *Tribune*.

In 1893, Crane published at his own expense an early version of *Maggie: A Girl of the Streets*. William Dean Howells introduced him to Emily Dickinson's poetry, and in the next year he met Hamlin Garland. Also in 1894, the Philadelphia *Press* published an abridged version of *The Red Badge of Courage*.

During the first half of 1895, Crane traveled in the West, where he met Willa Cather, and in Mexico for the Bachellor Syndicate; *The Black Riders and Other Lines* was published in May; *The Red Badge of Courage* appeared in October. By December, he was famous, having just turned twenty-four.

In 1896, he published *George's Mother*, *The Little Regiment and Other Stories*, and fell in love with Cora Stewart (Howarth), whom he never married but with whom he lived for the rest of his life.

In January, 1897, on the way to report the insurgency in Cuba, Crane was shipwrecked off the Florida coast. Four months later, he was in Greece, reporting on the Greco-Turkish War. Moving back to England, he became friends with Conrad, Henry James, Harold Frederic, H. G. Wells, and others. During that year, he wrote most of his great short stories: "The Open Boat," "The Bride Comes to Yellow Sky," and "The Blue Hotel."

Never very healthy, Crane began to weaken in 1898 as a result of malaria contracted in Cuba while he was reporting on the Spanish-American War. By 1899, Crane was back in England and living well above his means. Although he published *War Is Kind*, *Active Service*, and *The Monster and Other Stories*, he continued to fall more deeply in debt. By 1900, he was hopelessly debt-ridden and fatally ill. Exhausted from overwork, intestinal tuberculosis, malaria, and the experiences of an intense life, Crane died at the early age of twenty-eight, leaving works that fill ten sizable volumes.

Analysis

Stephen Crane's first novel, *Maggie: A Girl of the Streets*, was written before Crane had any intimate knowledge of the Bowery slums where the novel is set. It is the first American novel to portray realistically the chaos of the slums without either providing the protagonist with a "way out" or moralizing on the subject of social injustice. It obeys Aristotle's dictum that art imitates life and the more modern notion that art is simply a mirror held up to life. *Maggie: A Girl of the Streets* is the story of a young Irish-American girl who grows up in the slums of New York. The novel seems to belong to the tradition of the *Bildungsroman*, but its greatness lies in the irony that in this harsh environment, no one's quest is fulfilled, no one learns anything: the novel swings from chaos on the one side to complete illusion on the other.

By the time Maggie reaches physical maturity, her father and young brother have died, leaving only her mother, Mary—a maurauding drunken woman, and another brother, Jimmie, a young truck driver who scratches out a place for himself in the tenements. Living with an alcoholic and a bully, Maggie is faced with a series of choices that tragically lead her to self-destruction. First, she must choose between working long hours for little pay in the sweat shops or becoming a prostitute. She chooses the former, but the chaotic reality of home and work are so harsh that she succumbs to her own illusions about Pete, the bullying neighborhood bartender, and allows herself to be seduced by him. When this happens, Mary drives Maggie out of their home. For a short time, Maggie enjoys her life, but Pete soon abandons her to chase another woman. Driven from home and now a "fallen woman," Maggie must choose between prostitution and suicide. Deciding on the life of a prostitute,

Maggie survives for a time, but ultimately is unable to make a living. She commits suicide by jumping into the East River.

The form of the novel is that of a classical tragedy overlaid by nihilism that prevents the final optimism of tragedy from surfacing. The tragic "mistake," what the Greeks called hamartia, derives from a naturalistic credo: Maggie was unlucky enough to have been born a pretty girl in an environment she was unable to escape. Although she tries to make the best of her limited choices, she is inexorably driven to make choices that lead her to ruin and death. The novel's other characters are similarly trapped by their environment. Mary drinks herself into insensibility, drives her daughter into the street, and then, when Maggie kills herself, exclaims "I fergive her!" The irony of this line, the novel's last, is nihilistic. Classical tragedy ends on an optimistic note. Purged of sin by the sacrifice of the protagonist, mankind is given a reprieve by the gods, and life looks a little better for everyone. In *Maggie: A Girl of the Streets* there is no optimism. Mary has nothing upon which to base any forgiveness. It is Maggie who should forgive Mary. Jimmie is so egocentric that he cannot see that he owed his sister some help. At one point he wonders about the girls he has "ruined," but he quickly renounces any responsibility for them. Pete is a blind fool who is destroyed by his own illusions and the chaos of his environment.

For the first time in American fiction, a novel had appeared in which there clearly was no better world, no "nice" existence, no heaven on earth. There was only the world of the stinking tenements, only the chaos of sweat and alcohol and seduction, only hell. Also for the first time, everything was accomplished impressionistically. Maggie's sordid career as a prostitute would have required an earlier writer several chapters to describe. In *Maggie: A Girl of the Streets*, the description requires only a paragraph or two.

George's Mother, originally entitled *A Woman Without Weapons* and Crane's only other Bowery novel, is a companion piece to *Maggie: A Girl of the Streets*. Mrs. Keasy and her son George live in the same tenement as Mary Johnson, Maggie's mother. The story is more sentimental than that of the Maggie novel, and therefore less effective. George gradually succumbs to the destructive elements of the Bowery—drink and a subsequent inability to work—in spite of the valiant efforts of his mother to forestall and warn him. As Maggie has her "dream gardens" in the air above sordid reality, so young George has dreams of great feats while he actually lives in the midst of drunkenness and squalor. As drink provides a way out of reality for George, so the Church provides his mother with her escape. Both in *Maggie* and in *George's Mother*, illusions simultaneously provide the only way out of reality and a way to hasten the worsening of reality.

In his most famous novel, *The Red Badge of Courage*, Crane takes his themes of illusion and reality and his impressionistic method from the Bowery to a battlefield of the Civil War, usually considered to be the battle of Chancellorsville. A young farm boy named Henry Fleming hears tales of great battles, dreams of "Homeric" glory, and joins the Union Army. Published in 1895, the story of Henry Fleming's various trials took the literary world by storm, first in England and then in the United States. Crane became an immediate sensation, perhaps one of America's first media darlings, *The Red Badge of Courage* became a classic in its own time because it combined literary merit with a subject that captured the popular imagination. Never again did Crane reach the height of popularity which he achieved with *The Red Badge of Courage*.

Structurally, the novel is divided into two parts. In the first half, Henry's illusions disappear when confronted by the reality of battle. During the first skirmish, he sees vague figures before him, but they are driven away. In the next skirmish, he becomes so frightened that he runs away, becoming one of the first heroes in literature actually to desert his fellow soldiers in the field. Although Achilles had done something similar in the *Iliad* (c. 800 B.C), in the intervening millenia, few heroes had imitated him.

Separated from his regiment, Henry wanders through the forest behind the lines. There he experiences the kinds of illusions that predominate in all of Crane's writing. First, he convinces himself that nature is benevolent, that she does not blame him for running. Next, he finds himself in a part of the woods which he interprets as a kind of religious place—the insects are praying, and the forest has the appearance of a chapel. Comforted by this, Henry becomes satisfied with himself until he discovers a dead soldier in the very heart of the "chapel." In a beautiful passage—beautiful in the sense of conveying great emotion through minute detail—Henry sees an ant carrying a bundle across the face of the dead man. Shifting to a belief in nature as malevolent or indifferent, Henry moves back toward the front. He soon encounters a line of wounded soldiers, among whom is his friend Jim Conklin and another man called simply "the tattered man." Conklin, badly wounded, is dying. Trying to expiate his crime of desertion, Henry attempts to help Conklin, but is rebuffed. After Conklin dies, the tattered man probes deeply into Henry's conscience by repeatedly asking the youth "where ya hit?" The tattered man himself appears to be wounded, but Henry cannot abide his questions. He deserts the tattered man as well.

When Henry tries to stop another Union soldier to ask the novel's ubiquitous question "Why?," he is clubbed on the head for causing trouble. Ironically, this wound becomes his "red badge of courage." Guided back to his regiment by a "Cheery Soldier," who performs the same function as the ancient gods and goddesses who helped wandering heroes, Henry embarks on the novel's second half. Between receiving the lump on his head and returning to his regiment, Henry's internal wanderings are over. Not until the last chapter does Henry ask questions of the universe. Most of the repudiations are complete: heroes do not always act like heroes; no one understands the purpose of life or death; nature may be malevolent, probably indifferent, but is certainly not the benevolent, pantheistic realm of the transcendentalists; and God, at least the traditional Christian God, is simply nowhere to be found.

In the second half of the novel, Henry becomes a "war devil," the very Homeric hero he originally wanted to be. Wilson, his young friend, who was formally called "the loud soldier," has become a group leader, quiet, helpful, utterly devoted to the regiment. He becomes, in short, what Henry would have become had he not run from the battle. The idea of "Brotherhood," so prevalent in Crane's works, is embodied by Wilson. Henry is another kind of hero, an individual owing allegiance to no group; he leads a successful charge against the enemy with the spirit of a primitive warrior.

When the battle is over, however, all that Henry has accomplished is negated. Many critics have found the last chapter confused and muddled, for Henry's feelings range from remorse for the "sin" for which he is not responsible to pride in his valor as a great and glorious hero. Finally, he feels that "the world was a world for him," and he looks forward to "a soft and eternal peace." The beautiful lyricism of the novel's last paragraphs is, like that of many of Crane's conclusions, completely ironic. No one lives "eternally peacefully"; the world is not a world for Henry. As John Berryman says, Crane's "sole illusion was the heroic one, and not even that escaped his irony."

Thus, the novel's conclusion is not at all inconsistent. During the course of his experiences, Henry learns at firsthand of the indifference of the universe, the chaos of the world, the illusory nature of religion and patriotism and heroism, but he learns these lessons in the heat of the moment, when recognition is virtually forced on him. When the memory has an opportunity to apply itself to past experience, that experience is changed into what man wants it to be, not what it was. Henry, then, becomes representative of mankind. The individual memory becomes a metaphor for collective memory, history. Everything is a lie. Not even heroism can last.

Crane was only twenty-two when he began working on *The Third Violet*, and before it was published he had already written *Maggie: A Girl of the Streets*, *The Red Badge of Courage*, and *George's Mother*. Of the four, *The Third Violet* is by far the least successful. In Crane's attempt to portray middleclass manners, two things become clear: his best portraits, as well as his most admirable characters, are the simple farmer and the heiress; the others fall within the middle class and are more or less insipid; second, Crane should have left writing about the middle class to his friend and benefactor, William Dean Howells.

The protagonist of *The Third Violet*, Billie Hawker, is a young New York artist who returns to his family's farm for a summer vacation. While there, he falls in love with Grace Fanhall, a young heiress vacationing at a nearby resort hotel called the Hemlock Inn. The remainder of the novel recounts

Hawker's anxieties as he botches repeated attempts to declare his love and win the fair maiden at the hotel, during summer picnics, in New York studios, and in mansions. Aside from portraits of Hawker's father and the heiress, the most rewarding portraits are of a little boy and his dog. A memorable scene occurs when Grace Fanhall and Billie's father ride together in a farm wagon, their disparate social standings apparently freeing them from rigid middle-class stiffness. Equally worthwhile is the scene in the New York bohemian studio where Hawker's friends "Great Grief," "Wrinkles," and Pennoyer, manage to divert the landlord and concoct a meal in a manner reminiscent of the opening scenes of the opera *La Bohème* (1896). There is even a beautiful young model named "Splutter" O'Conner, whose easy and gay love for Hawker provides a contrast to his own doleful courtship of Fanhall.

The reality behind the mask of convention in *The Third Violet* is never sufficiently revealed. Reality in *The Third Violet* seems to be that love would predominate if only Hawker could free himself of his inferiority complex at having been born poor. While others might make great fiction from such a feeling, Crane could not.

The only great piece of fiction Crane produced from his experience of reporting the Greco-Turkish War of April and May, 1897, was "Death and the Child." By contrast, his Greek novel, *Active Service*, is lamentably bad. Following a creakingly conventional plot, *Active Service* relates the story of a boy and a girl in love: the girl's parents object; the boy pursues the girl and overcomes her parents' objections by rescuing the family from danger, and by manfully escaping the snares of another woman.

Crane's protagonist, Rufus Coleman, Sunday editor of the New York *Eclipse*, is in love with Marjory Wainright, the demure and lovely daughter of a classics professor at Washurst University. Disapproving of the match on the rather solid evidence that Coleman is "a gambler and a drunkard," Professor Wainright decides to include his daughter in a student tour of Greece, a tour the professor himself is to lead. While touring ruins near Arta in Epirus, the group is trapped between the Greek and Turkish lines. Meanwhile, back in the offices of the *Eclipse*, the not so mild-mannered reporter, Coleman, is discovering that he cannot exist without Marjory. Arranging to become the *Eclipse*'s correspondent in Greece, he heads for Europe. Temporarily distracted while traveling to Greece by a beautiful British actress and dancer, Nora Black, Coleman finally arrives in Athens and discovers that the Wainright party is in danger. He jauntily sets out to rescue them and equally as jauntily succeeds. So heroic and noble is Coleman, that the professor is quite won over. The novel finishes like hundreds of turn-of-the-century love-adventures with the hero and heroine sitting with the Aegean in the background while they declare their love for each other in the most adolescent manner.

Indeed, Crane intended to write a parody of love-adventures. The hero is too offhandedly heroic; the rival is too mean and nasty. The "other woman" wears too much perfume; the parents are too inept. The novel is banal and trite, however, because the characters lack interest, and the parody cannot sustain the reader's interest in the absence of a substantial form worthy of parody. The novel is probably bad for extraliterary reasons: Crane's poor health and finances. Crane began the book late in 1897 when he was still fairly healthy and when his finances were not yet completely chaotic. The effects of the malaria and the tuberculosis, however, were becoming increasingly debilitating and began to take their toll long before *The Third Violet* was finished in May, 1899. By then, too, his finances were depleted. Crane had the intellectual and cultural resources to write a first-rate book on this subject, but not the health and good fortune. One must agree with Crane: "May heaven help it for being so bad."

The Monster and Other Stories was Crane's last great work. A short book even when compared to his notably short novels, *The Monster and Other Stories* is often regarded as a novella rather than as a novel. Like *The Red Badge of Courage*, it is divided into twenty-four episodes, is divided in half structurally, and concerns a man caught in a straitjacket of fate. Like Maggie, Dr. Trescott, the hero, is led down a road which gradually leaves behind all side trails until his only choice is essentially made for him by his circumstances. Trescott is more intelligent and educated than Maggie, and he is certainly more conscious of his choices, but the most crucial difference lies in the intensity of the tragedy. While *Maggie: A Girl of the Streets* is about the individual facing chaos without the mediating power of a civilized group, *The Monster and Other Stories* concerns the conflict between individual ethics and the values of the group. For Crane, small towns in America exist to mediate between the individual and chaos. Ordered society blocks out reality, providing security.

Henry Johnson, the Trescott's black hostler, is badly burned while rescuing Jimmy, the doctor's young son, from the Trescott's burning house. This heroic act creates Trescott's tragic dilemma: personal ethics dictate that he care for the now horrific looking and simple-minded Henry; public security requires that Henry be "put away" or allowed to die, for civilization does not like to see reminders of what mankind would be like without the thin veneer of order. While Trescott faces his responsibility toward Henry, he fails to reckon with the task of forcing the community to face it as well. When he does, he consciously sets himself on a collision course with that society. Unlike Henry Fleming, Trescott cannot win even a temporary victory. The community defeats him utterly.

Trescott at first tries to avoid conflict by paying Alex Williams, a local black man who lives on the outskirts of town, to care for Henry. When Henry escapes into town and, although harmless, frightens little children, the community demands that Trescott do something. Standing by his obligation to Henry, Trescott is quickly ostracized by the community. At the novel's end, Trescott recognizes that he has lost. He cannot retain his moral and ethical stance toward Henry Johnson and remain within the community. He cannot concede defeat to the community without doing irrevocable damage to his own honor. The dilemma is a classical tragic one that must be faced by each individual. Ralph Ellison has called *The Monster and Other Stories* a metaphor for America's treatment of the black minority, but the greatness of the work lies in the fact that it is a larger metaphor for the human community's treatment of the individual.

The O'Ruddy is a parodic picaresque romance about English and Irish manners. Its humor belies the fact that Crane was writing on his deathbed, in great anguish and pain. Crane's only first-person novel, *The O'Ruddy* exposes the "dullness of the great mass of people, the frivolity of the gentry, the arrogance and wickedness of the court," and celebrates the notion that "real talent was usually engaged in some form of rascality." Similar to *Active Service* in that it recounts the story of an adventure-loving hero who overcomes the objections of a stuffy father and vehement mother for the hand of a somewhat demure, but beautiful young lady, *The O'Ruddy* is similarly unable to sustain greatness. Although sketchy as to the date of the events, *The O'Ruddy* seems to be set in late eighteenth century England, where young Tom O'Ruddy, a poor but noble Irishman, has come to return to the Earl of Wesport some papers given to Tom by his father. The reader learns more than half way through the novel that the papers give title to certain lands in Sussex. Smitten by Lady Mary, the Earl's daughter, Tom eventually trades the papers for her hand in marriage. Before the novel's conclusion, in which Tom and Mary are married, there are many duels, robberies, journeys through secret passages, and portraits of literary meetings and turnings at Kensington Gardens, all of which are parodied. Crane disliked the manners of many of the English, saying at one point that western New York farmers had better manners.

The parody is occasionally amusing, but since parody must mock form as well as content to be great, the novel fails. Understandably, given Crane's illness, and the reluctance of Robert Barr to finish the novel after Crane's death, there are numerous discrepancies, among which is a confusion as to whether Tom O'Ruddy can read and write. All in all, Crane's intensity is lacking in this slight novel, his freshness, his impressionistic insights, his accustomed power—gone. The last words he wrote in the novel before dying are lamentably apropos of the book itself: "This is no nice thing."

Chester L. Wolford

Other major works

SHORT FICTION: *The Little Regiment and Other Episodes of the American Civil War*, 1896; *The Open Boat and Other Tales of Adventure*, 1898; *Whilomville Stories*, 1900; *Wounds in the Rain: War Stories*, 1900; *Last Words*, 1902.

PLAYS: *The Ghost*, 1899 (with Henry James); *The Blood of the Martyr*, 1940.

POETRY: *The Black Riders and Other Lines*, 1895; *A Souvenir and a Medley*, 1896; *War Is Kind*, 1899; *The University Press of Virginia Edition of the Works of Stephen Crane*, 1970 (Vol. X).

NONFICTION: *The Great Battles of the World*, 1901.

Bibliography

Beer, Thomas. *Stephen Crane: A Study in American Letters*. New York: Alfred A. Knopf, 1923. Beer was Crane's first biographer, and his account contains many errors. Still, he had access to people who actually knew Crane, and so this book remains Crane's premier biography.

Cady, Edwin Harrison. *Stephen Crane*. Rev. ed. Boston: Twayne, 1980. An excellent reference tool for all students of Crane. Includes a short biography and an analysis of Crane's most famous work, *The Red Badge of Courage*, as well as his writing up to and following it. Provides an annotated bibliography for further study.

Halliburton, David. *The Color of the Sky: A Study of Stephen Crane*. New York: Cambridge University Press, 1989. A major study of Crane from point of view of a structuralist critic. Halliburton often dissects the stories at the expense of their spirit. Yet this book is valuable for the mid-level to advanced student of Crane.

Knapp, Bettina L. *Stephen Crane*. New York: Frederick Ungar, 1987. Includes a short biography and synopses of the major works. Knapp tends to interpret Crane's work allegorically, which works well for *The Red Badge of Courage* but not so well for other stories. Suitable for all students.

Linson, Corwin K. *My Stephen Crane*. Edited by Edwin H. Cady. Syracuse, N.Y.: Syracuse University Press, 1958. Linson was a painter and one of Crane's good friends, who tried to publish these memoirs many times during his life but failed. Eventually, his manuscript came to the attention of Syracuse University Press, which published it. Unfortunately, it is written from the point of view of a man who is looking back on his life, and his memories are not always accurate.

A. J. CRONIN

Born: Cardross, Scotland; July 19, 1896
Died: Montreux, Switzerland; January 6, 1981

Principal long fiction
Hatter's Castle, 1931; *Three Loves*, 1932; *The Grand Canary*, 1933; *The Stars Look Down*, 1935; *The Citadel*, 1937; *The Keys of the Kingdom*, 1941; *The Green Years*, 1944; *Shannon's Way*, 1948; *The Spanish Gardener*, 1950; *Beyond This Place*, 1953; *A Thing of Beauty*, 1956 (also known as *Crusader's Tomb*); *The Northern Light*, 1958; *The Judas Tree*, 1961; *A Song of Sixpence*, 1964; *A Pocketful of Rye*, 1969; *Desmonde*, 1975 (also known as *The Minstrel Boy*); *Lady with Carnations*, 1976; *Gracie Lindsay*, 1978; *Doctor Finlay of Tannochbrae*, 1978.

Other literary forms
In addition to the many novels he has published, A. J. Cronin has also written one play, *Jupiter Laughs*, which was produced in Glasgow and New York in 1940 and published in 1941. His autobiography—*Adventures in Two Worlds* (1952)—remains the best account of his formative years as well as an engaging vehicle for many of his opinions. In 1926, he also wrote two studies entitled *Report on First-Aid Conditions in British Coal Mines* and *Report on Dust Inhalation in Haematite Mines*. The outcome of his journeys to investigate the conditions said to prevail there became the fictional account of the mining communities found in *The Stars Look Down* and *The Citadel*.

Achievements
In the spring of 1930, a tall, sandy-haired, genial physician sold his London practice and home, moved with his family to an isolated farmhouse near Inverary, Scotland, and at the age of thirty-four wrote a novel for the first time in his life. *Hatter's Castle*, published the following year by Victor Gollancz, became an immediate success. It was the first novel to be chosen by the English Book Society for the book-of-the-month. It was later translated into many languages, dramatized, and made into a Paramount motion picture starring James Mason and Deborah Kerr. Before long, critics hailed Cronin as a new and important author, whose writing was comparable in content and style to that of Charles Dickens, Thomas Hardy, and Honoré de Balzac.

Cronin and his wife moved to a small apartment in London and then on to a modest cottage in Sussex, where he went to work on another novel, *Three Loves*. His popularity continued to increase following *Grand Canary* and *The Stars Look Down*; the ex-physician became something of a literary lion, in demand at dinners, bazaars, and book fairs. His writing launched him upon a literary career with such impetus that, once and for all, he "hung up

[his] stethoscope and put away that little black bag—[his] medical days were over."

The physician-novelist is of course by no means an unfamiliar literary figure. Arthur Conan Doyle, W. Somerset Maugham, C. S. Forester, Oliver Goldsmith, and the poet laureate of England, Robert Bridges, among others, had rich medical backgrounds into which they reached for ideas for their books. None of these examples, however, can quite parallel the dual career of Cronin. Medicine with him was not a stopgap or stepping-stone. He was an outstanding professional and financial success; moreover, he was ambitious, desperately tenacious, and single-minded in his pursuit of that success. It was hard won and well deserved. His second success, in an entirely different field, was equally substantial. Twenty novels (several of which were adapted to the cinema), a play, an autobiography, and one of the longest-running British television series represent a career that spans one-half of the twentieth century—1930 to 1978—and a life that was itself as engrossing and multifaceted as Cronin's fiction.

Perhaps just as remarkable as the extraordinary commercial success of the novels is the fact that most of them are much more than highly readable potboilers. Like Emily Brontë, Dickens, and Hardy—three writers with whom he is often compared—Cronin was a natural-born storyteller who transcended the category of "academic" fiction-writer. His novels are realistic, purporting to present the actual experiences of actual people. They present life not in the vacuum of timelessness, but in the timely flux of ordinary experience. They rely on a specific sense of place—interiors and exteriors—and reflect a rapid mastery of the different settings and environments to which Cronin's travels had taken him. Even in his most extreme formal experimentation—as in *The Stars Look Down*—Cronin's fiction retains accessibility and readability.

Although Cronin's popularity has somewhat waned, he was for many years one of the best-known and most controversial of British writers; through a number of books remarkable for their honesty and realism, he helped entertain and educate a generation of readers. As a writer, he was always promoting tolerance, integrity, and social justice. His favorite theme was that man should learn to be creative rather than acquisitive, altruistic rather than selfish.

Biography

Before Archibald Joseph Cronin's books can be appreciatively read, the reader must have a reasonable acquaintance with his life. This is not necessarily true in the case of many writers, whose private lives are less clearly reflected in their work than are those of writers such as Dickens and Maugham, to whom Cronin bears a resemblance in this matter. Throughout his career as a novelist, Cronin drew heavily on his memories of what he had actually observed. Henry James's argument that the writer of fiction should be "one upon whom nothing is lost" received an emphatic embodiment in the life of Cronin, whose experiences as a child, a medical student, and a physician are woven inextricably into the fabric of his novel.

As is the case with so many of his fictional characters, life for young Cronin was by no means idyllic. He was born in Cardross (Dumbarton), Scotland, on July 19, 1896, the only child of a middle-class family whose fortunes were soon to decline rapidly. His mother, Jessie Montgomerie, was a Scottish Protestant woman who had defied her family—and a host of ancestors—by marrying an Irishman and turning Catholic. His father, Patrick Cronin, was a mercantile agent who until his death was able to offer his family a fairly comfortable existence. After the death of his father, however, Cronin was forced to retreat with his penniless mother to the bitter and poverty-stricken home of her parents.

To most neighbors and relatives in the small, strictly moral and sternly Protestant town of Cardross, Jessie Montgomerie's marriage and conversion were considered a disgrace, and upon young Cronin they inflicted the inevitable ridicule and persecution. On the one hand, there was sectarian antagonism, not far short of that which has erupted in recent years in Northern Ireland as violence. On the other hand, was the stern Protestant morality. Cronin was permanently marked by an environment that was noisy, quarrelsome, profoundly unhappy, and emotionally dramatic—a source of endless tension and grief for the growing boy and of endless material for the future novelist.

Cronin's delight in reading and learning perhaps compensated for his frustrations. Among the authors he read were Robert Louis Stevenson (an only child like himself and a firm favorite right to the end of his life), Sir Walter Scott, Guy de Maupassant, Dickens, Maugham, and Samuel Butler—whose *The Way of All Flesh* (1903) Cronin cited as his favorite book. At Cardross Village School and later at the Dumbarton Academy—where literature was his best subject—the boy became something of a prodigy, repeatedly winning prizes and discovering in himself that love for learning which would be a source of stability all his life. Both as a student and, later in life, as a physician-writer, he spent enormous stretches of time at his desk, wrestling with his work. This compulsiveness, combined with his intelligence and his eagerness, won Cronin the approbation of his uncle—a poor, kindly Catholic priest who helped secure for him his education and who later became the model for Father Chisholm in *The Keys of the Kingdom*—and of his great-grandfather, who later became the model for Alexander Gow in *The Green Years*.

Yet Cronin's talent also meant he would suffer the emotions of premature loneliness that so often afflict an unusually bright boy. He was highly regarded by his teachers; however, other students—and their parents—sometimes resented his abilities. One father, whose young hopeful was beaten by Cronin in an important examination, became so enraged that years later *Hatter's*

Castle took shape around his domineering personality. The theme—"the tragic record of a man's egotism and bitter pride"—suggests the dark and often melodramatic atmosphere of Cronin's early novels. In them, some characters are drawn with humorous realism, but for the most part humor is dimmed by gloomy memories of his own neglected childhood, and sensational scenes are shrouded in an atmosphere genuinely eerie and sinister. Inevitably, Cronin clung to the notion that between the life of the mind and the life of the senses, between a disciplined commitment to scholarship and a need to share in the common pleasures of mankind, there is an irremediable conflict.

The religious bigotry, the family's unceasing poverty, the interest in learning—this trio of forces worked at shaping the young Cronin. A shy, sensitive, lonely boy, aware of his peculiarities yet hungry for the town's acceptance, he developed, like Robert Shannon of *The Green Years*, an overt mistrust for organized religion. Until his father's death, Cronin had been devout, and the question of his becoming a clergyman may have been considered; but if Cronin had entertained any such ambitions, his increasing indifference, which emerges very clearly in his novels, must have caused him to abandon such plans. Instead, he decided he would become a doctor—the only other thing for an ambitious poor boy living in Scotland to do—and in 1914 he entered Glasgow University Medical School.

Cronin had begun his medical studies when World War I took him into the Royal Navy Volunteer Reserve as a surgeon sublieutenant. Back at the university, he was struck forcefully by the contrast between his sincere idealism and the cynicism, selfishness, and muddled incompetency of many of the students and doctors he met. This conflict later found expression in his fiction, in which his idealized heroes' enthusiasm is contrasted sharply with the satirical descriptions of other doctors, civic officials, and small-town bigots. In *The Stars Look Down*, *The Citadel*, *The Green Years*, and *Shannon's Way*, for example, every aspect of the medical profession is criticized: medical schools, small-town practice, public health, fashionable clinics, and even research centers.

Having been graduated M.B., Ch.B. with honors in 1919, Cronin was appointed physician to the outpatients in Bellahouston war pensions hospital, and later medical superintendent at Lightburn Hospital, Glasgow. Two years later, he married Agnes Mary Gibson—also a medical school graduate—and entered into general practice in a mining area of South Wales from 1921 until 1924. In the latter year, he became a medical inspector of mines for Great Britain. In 1925, he took his M.D. degree with honors; a year later he prepared a report on first-aid conditions in British coal mines and another report on dust inhalation in haematite mines. After his service with the Ministry of Mines was completed, Cronin moved to London and built a practice in London's West End. Throughout these experiences and contacts with people of every kind, he continually thought of stories he could create. His patients and colleagues provided him with a dramatic cast of characters, a ready-made network of complex relationships, and a complete set of thunderous emotions. In all of this, he was not only an active participant but also, as the trusted doctor, an advantaged spectator.

"It has been said that the medical profession proves the best training ground for a novelist," Cronin wrote, "since there it is possible to see people with their masks off." Certainly, in his own writings, Cronin drew heavily upon his experiences as a doctor. The Glasgow medical school environment; the touch-and-go associations with mental patients at a suburban asylum; the medical practice in a Welsh mining village with its calls in the night and impromptu surgery on the kitchen tables and in mine shafts; the drama, pathos, and cynical worldliness that passed under his eyes as a medical practitioner in London—all these episodes were used as material for his novels.

The richest source of material for his novels, however—especially the later ones, beginning with *The Keys of the Kingdom*—was his newfound faith. At the height of financial prosperity and great reputation, in good health and with his work flowing smoothly and abundantly, Cronin felt a deep malaise, a feeling of emptiness and "interior desolation." For years he had ignored matters of the spirit; then, almost coinciding with the end of one career and the start of a new, even more successful one, he found himself confronted with a fundamental fact of existence. He had been born a Catholic, observing the outward practice of his faith, but had gradually drifted into a position where religion was something entirely outside his inner experience. In the years after World War II, he took his wife on pilgrimages to Vienna, Italy, and France, in particular Normandy. Each trip to war-battered Europe provided experiences which further crystallized Cronin's maturing faith. The source of his renewed strength can be summed up in a few words: "No matter how we try to escape, to lose ourselves from our divine source, there is no substitute for God." This is a simple statement of sincere faith by a man whose adventures in various environments were marked by a steady development in spirit and in art.

Analysis

Everything that A. J. Cronin wrote was stamped by his personality, his sincerity, his direct concern with ethical issues, his seemingly instinctive knowledge of ordinary people, and his tremendous gift for storytelling. An examination of five of his most popular novels—*Hatter's Castle, The Stars Look Down, The Citadel, The Keys of the Kingdom*, and *The Green Years*—reveals a consistent commitment to the value of the individual—the personal—and a remarkable development in narrative technique.

Hatter's Castle was in many ways a happy accident, securing for its author laudatory reviews and substantial earnings and establishing him as a writer of great promise. In its hero, readers found an outstanding personality: a hatter in Levenford, in strongly characterized surroundings, who lived through a destiny of suffering and tragedy. Readers were also treated to a return to the English novel in the grand tradition. Its themes—the rejected family, the struggle against poverty, the desire for wealth, the illusion of limitless opportunity, the conflict between personal desire and conventional restraint—were recurring ones throughout Cronin's fiction.

Cronin's fourth novel, *The Stars Look Down*, surpasses its predecessors by many standards. It develops in greater depth his major preoccupations—a concern with the chaos of life, its bitterness and desolation—but keeps under restraint the tendency toward melodrama without weakening the force of his instinct for drama. Characters reflect the special types to which Cronin is attracted, but the theme of the futility of the British working class against the greed and selfishness of the moneyed overlords receives fuller treatment here.

Set partly in the same atmosphere as *The Stars Look Down*—the dusky, dirty towns of the English coal-mining region—Cronin's fifth novel, *The Citadel*, is the savage and fiercely idealistic story of a young physician's struggle to achieve success in life. To many readers—doctors particularly—the novel's main interest lay in Cronin's indictment of both the unethical practices of the medical profession and the system under which the miners lived and worked. To other readers, the interest lay in the unmistakable similarity between the hero's personal philosophy and Cronin's own opinions. There is the same integrity of character, the same effort to focus public attention on social forces which are responsible for many of the ills of his patients, and the same deep concern as an individual for lessening human disaster. In the hero, these readers welcomed the titillating sense of being "inside" the medical profession. Reading Cronin, they enjoyed the especially comforting thought that they were being educated as well as entertained.

Perhaps his most popular novel, *The Keys of the Kingdom* emphasizes with incisiveness the problems encountered when a religious man rebels against the man-made rules, limitations, and barriers that are continually thrust between human beings and their God. Its merit lies precisely in its analysis of the conflicts between kindliness, sincere faith, and human understanding on the one side, and smugness, intolerance, bigotry, and assumed piety on the other side. Francis Chisholm is the medium through which Cronin presents his conception of what has been called the most difficult subject in the world: religion.

Finally, although *The Green Years* deals with traditional Cronin concerns, it marks another artistic departure in that the author uses as his "frame" the device of the novel of development or *Bildungsroman*. The protagonist encounters many guides and influences, and he must distinguish the true from the false. His own temperament, warped by self-distrust, spiritual uncertainty, and impatience, often makes him bring unnecessary suffering upon himself.

Like most heroes of this genre, however, he finally arrives at a philosophy that is tenable in the world he sees: a belief in the power of the human spirit to rise above conditions of the bleakest hopelessness.

To develop the plot of *Hatter's Castle*, Cronin used the familiar Victorian conventions available to all aspiring writers of the time: a straightforward linear chronology unfolded through the agency of the omniscient third-person narrator, with an emphasis on melodrama and horror. Added to these conventions is one of the most familiar themes of Greek tragedy: the retribution that attends overweening pride. James Brodie is a man whose inordinate self-love and unusually strong physique have made him the most feared person in town as well as the tyrant of a trembling household. He has deluded himself into believing that his hat shop is a thriving business, that his house is a romantic castle, and that he himself is related to the aristocracy. The novel proceeds almost consecutively from its beginning, with the hero at the "peak" of his power, to his decline into futility, frustration, and finally, alienation.

Woven through the book are patterns of developing images and symbols which serve important structural functions: they relate and unify the individual lives presented in the book; they support and embody its themes; and they are the means by which the texture of an event or feeling is conveyed. One cluster of these images grows out of the title, which refers, of course, literally to the house, and also to James Brodie himself and his career. The "castle," at once a physical structure and symbol of the Brodie family, is pictured early in the novel in terms which both symbolize the owner's pride and prophesy the dreadful environment and outcome of the story. It is a place of gloom and solitude, "more fitted for a prison than a home," "veiled, forbidding, sinister; its purpose likewise 'hidden and obscure.' " The pompous dignity of the gables greets the visitor with "cold severity." The parapet embraces the body of the house like a "manacle." Its windows are "secret, close-set eyes [which] grudgingly admitted light." Its doorway is "a thin repellent mouth." Not only does this description provide a haunting counterpoint to the action of *Hatter's Castle*, but also it establishes the essential character of Brodie well before he appears, before he is even named.

The members of the Brodie family share with the house a condition of imminent collapse. Typical of so many novelists, Cronin's device—here and elsewhere—is to put his minor characters in dire straits at the outset of the action so that they can be tested against the hardships life has to offer. This strategy he accomplishes by introducing the family members as they wait for Brodie, moving from grandmother to elder daughter, from younger daughter to mother, and each picture is presented as a miniature scene in a continuous drama of frustration. All along, the reader notes a strange absence of the usual signs of domesticity in a large country household.

The driving force of the book, however, is the portrayal of the successive disasters that Brodie brings upon himself and his family. Margaret, his feeble, downtrodden wife, is reduced to abjection and dies horribly of cancer. Mary, his elder daughter, is a lovely, gentle girl not quite able to cope with her father. She becomes pregnant, is thrown out of the house into a raging storm, and eventually marries the young doctor whom Brodie hates. Nessie, the younger daughter, is driven to insanity and suicide by Brodie's morbid determination that she shall win a scholarship and go to college. Matthew, Brodie's weakling son, robs his mother, lies to both of his parents, and runs off with his father's mistress. By the end of the novel, therefore, any manifestations of Brodie's supposed supremacy have vanished. Not only has he lost his family, but he has lost his business and has become a drunkard. He is left shattered, with no companion but his tragic, greedy old mother, and with no hope but death.

Although *Hatter's Castle* is in many ways a conventional novel, there are ideas, themes, and techniques in it which reappear in Cronin's later, more mature work. The characters are typical of Cronin: paradoxical mixtures of good and bad, weak and strong. Possessiveness, to the point of the pathological, is used as a catalyst to introduce a conflict and action, and, as in his later novels, it is always expressly condemned. The unrequited love theme which appears so often in Cronin's writing is present in the form of Mary's plight. Also, the central idea of rebellion against social pressures anticipates the kinds of revolt that motivate so many Cronin characters—including artists, seekers, and criminals.

Perhaps a legitimate criticism of the plot is that the sheer number of misfortunes suffered by Brodie and his family seems excessive and implausible. Possibly, but it seems to be a part of Cronin's philosophy that troubles never come singly, and, certainly, all of Brodie's misfortunes can be convincingly traced to his character and actions. "Character is Fate," quotes Thomas Hardy in *The Mayor of Casterbridge* (1886); and nemesis works unerringly through Brodie's own glaring defects. Imaginative belief in Brodie compels belief in what happens to him. As one critic observed, "the plot may creak, but Brodie lives."

Cronin's fourth novel *The Stars Look Down*, is by far his most intricate, both structurally and thematically. With action ranging over much of England, the novel takes in the period from 1903 to 1933. The story's center is the Neptune coal mine in Ryneside County. The plot moves back and forth between two families, the Fenwicks and Barrases, adding constantly to their widening circle of acquaintances. Working primarily (although not exclusively) within the minds of his characters, Cronin maintains a tightly unified texture as he changes focus from one character to another. The six main characters are rather schematically drawn: one character is paired off with another, usually to show contrasting versions of a general type. The six major characters fall into three pairs: David Fenwick and Joe Gowlan; Laura Millington and Jenny Sunley; Arthur Barras and his father, Richard. David,

Laura, and Arthur are the generally praiseworthy characters in the novel, the
ones who gain the greatest share of the reader's sympathy. The "evil" ones,
or those who obstruct the good characters, are Joe, Jenny, and Richard. The
good are characterized by genuineness, sincerity, and a general lack of pretense, the bad, on the other hand, continually disguise their motives and
present a false appearance.

If the six main characters have obvious symbolic import, so has the title
of the novel. Subject to their own laws and compulsions, heeding little outside
them, the stars look down upon a scene of chaos and social revolution—and
go on looking, unperturbed. " 'Did you ever look at the stars?' " asks the fat
man in Robert Louis Stevenson's *The Merry Men* (1887). " 'When a great
battle has been lost or a dear friend is dead, when we are hipped or in high
spirits, there they are, unweariedly shining overhead.' 'I see,' answered Will.
'We are in a mousetrap.' " This is the idea Cronin suggests in the title and
acts out through his characters, intending to convey something of the aloofness
of eternity compared to the chaos of the earth below.

Cronin conveys the atmosphere of a typical mining community by piling
up factual detail upon factual detail in an attempt to re-create the very look,
texture, and smell of the life of the miner. Frequently, he uses the slangy,
ungrammatical language of these people even in descriptive or explanatory
passages when the omniscient narrator is speaking. A work on a subject as
technical as coal mining is bound to have a somewhat specialized vocabulary,
and a reader without firsthand knowledge of life in the pits must search for
the meanings of such words as "collier," "hewer," "getter," "breaker," "pick-
man," and "pikeman." To come to grips with the actualities of life in the
mine, Cronin describes scenes such as the gaunt, unfriendly landscape, perpetually shrouded in grit; the silent and laconic manner of the miners; the
pervasive atmosphere of grim suffering and endurance. The town's very
name—"Sleesdale," suggesting "sleazy"—is emblematic. This, then, is the
backdrop to the human drama Cronin reconstructs—a drama about defeat
and disappointment, about how people are victims of the greed and selfishness
of others in power.

If there is any single clue as to Cronin's intention in *The Citadel*, it is in the
title. This simultaneously tragic and romantic novel was first called *Manson,
M.D.*, after its hero, but it was felt that the title finally chosen was a better
expression of the underlying meaning of the novel. Andrew Manson is a man
who in spite of great odds tries and ultimately succeeds in freeing himself
from materialistic influences. The word "citadel" stands for medical compe-
tency and medical integrity—the ideals to which Manson aspires. That this
symbol is central to the plot of the novel is made clear when Chris Manson
tells her husband: " 'Don't you remember how you used to speak of life, that
it was an attack on the unknown, an assault uphill . . . as though you had to
take some castle that you knew was there, but could not see, on the top?' "

At the end of the story, as Manson leaves Chris's grave, he sees in the sky before him a bank of clouds "bearing the shape of battlements." The reader is left to assume that Manson will once more assault the battlements, and that the conquest of them will be the greatest of all his achievements.

A large part of the novel's impressiveness stems from the way it functions throughout on a realistic level. Having grown out of Cronin's years as a physician and his experiences in Wales and London from 1921 to 1930, *The Citadel* may be read autobiographically—but with great caution. The reader may be sure that the greedy Mrs. Edward Page, the bitter Philip Denny, the incompetent but fashionable Doctors Ivory, Freedman, and Hampton, and a score of others had their living counterparts in Cronin's own experience. From a full spectrum of professional men and women, Cronin tells of the jealousies of the assistants and the scheming rivalries of their supervisors, of questionable medical practices, unsanitary conditions, hostile patients, rejected treatments, ephemeral successes and horrifying failures, and always the drudgery of endless plodding hackwork.

Significantly, these supporting characters remain stereotypes, since Cronin's main point is that, except for Denny, they ease through life, think and talk mostly of fees, and scheme to get ahead. The lazy among them learn little and continue to prescribe routine drugs and treatments. The ambitious think up tricks to entice rich patients, prompting them to believe they are sick whether or not they are. These antagonists—the nonprogressive, materialistic doctors—are mostly figures of straw, their outlines only vaguely discernible through the young doctor's self-concern. Relative to Manson's vigor and vitality, these characters appear flat and insipid.

Another striking achievement of the book is the solid underlayer of fact. Almost all of Cronin's books, including the poor ones, have this foundation, giving them a satisfying density and bulk. In *The Citadel*, the details of Manson's experiences—without the use of abstruse technical terms and too many scientific explanations—are tremendously appealing to the reader. His restoration to life of Joe Morgan's stillborn baby; his coal-pit amputation of a miner's arm in the perilous tunnel; his restoration to consciousness of hysterical Toppy Le Roy; and the shocking butchery of the operation by Dr. Ivory—all of these scenes rouse the emotions as a means of persuading the mind. With its sober factuality, it is not difficult to understand why this novel has been enormously popular in both America and Great Britain.

While *The Citadel* has much to say about a society which seems unwilling to allow Manson to do his best work, while it dilates upon the evil practices of other physicians, it is also an unusual love story, with Andrew and Chris Manson at the center. Chris is effectively presented as a frank, well-educated, levelheaded young woman whose instinctive enjoyment of life is the counterpart of Andrew's integrity and determination. She knows the secret of turning hardships into fun, of forgetting irritation in laughter. Hard work and poverty do not scare her. The passionate integrity her husband brings to his science she brings to human relations—above all to her husband. From him, she refuses to accept any compromise of principle, even though this course leads them for a time to obscurity and poverty. She is strongly opposed to materialism and its shabby, cheapening results. She fights as best she can against every influence which she thinks will hurt her husband either as a scientist or as a man.

If one demands purity of conception and unflagging precision of execution in a novel, then *The Citadel* is clearly disappointing. Cronin, however, surmounts these flaws as an artist to represent seriously, and at times movingly, some of the significant problems of his day. To one concerned with literary movements, part of the interest of the book lies in its representation of the many facets of its cultural and social milieu. It contains elements of romantic optimism, of realistic appraisal, of naturalistic pessimism. In attempting to trace in *The Citadel* the progression of his own attitudes toward life, Cronin makes a comment about human experience that frequently strikes home with compelling force.

In *The Keys of the Kingdom*, it is not the profession of medicine, but that of the priesthood which is held up to examination. The verdict, however, is much the same as that found in *The Citadel*. The priest who serves God according to the teachings of Christ, viewing himself as the selfless shepherd and servant of man, accepting poverty, humility, and perhaps even martyrdom, is likely to be misunderstood, undervalued, and cruelly censored by his brethren. The more worldly priest, on the other hand, will win the power and the glory that the Church has to bestow. Cronin's priest, like Cronin's doctor, is an individualist with the courage to accept the guidance of his conscience rather than his self-interest. In the Church, as in the medical profession, such courage may put one at a disadvantage, often bringing disappointment and disillusionment. *The Keys of the Kingdom*, therefore, is an entrancing story, but also an expression of personal faith.

The title for this novel comes from the words of Christ to Peter—"'And I will give to thee the keys of the kingdom of heaven'"—and the central theme comes from Geoffrey Chaucer's famous description of the poor parson of the town, which ends, "'But Christes' lore and his apostles twelve/ He taught, but first he followed it himself.'" Thus, the keys, according to Cronin and his mouthpiece, Francis Chisholm, are one's knowledge and use of the fundamentals of tolerance, humility, charity, and kindness. Where creeds divide, deeds of love and sympathy unite.

Like the great Victorians from whose rich tradition they spring, Cronin's characters, according to his modest moral aims, are unmistakably "good" or "bad." The reader knows as soon as he meets them that Aunt Polly, Nora Bannon, Mr. Chia, Dr. Willie Tullock, and Bishop McNabb are "good." He also can be reasonably sure that these people will endure their share of misfortune. The reader can find in these characters a schooling in generous humanity. Also easily recognizable are the unsympathetic characters: Bishop Mealey, Father Kezer, Mrs. Glennie, and Monsignor Sleeth. The reader always knows where he stands with Cronin.

This contrast between the "good" and the "bad" is apparent especially through the comparison of Francis Chisholm and his lifelong associate, Anselm Mealey, who lacks the feeling and innate spirituality of his friend, but who uses a certain veneer and his commanding appearance to get himself elevated to the bishopric. As a picture of the worldly priest, Mealey is eloquent in his sermons, popular with the women of the parish, and especially assiduous in those good works which gain him the approbation of his superiors. He attracts large donations, makes many converts, and fights the outward battles of the Church. He is even willing to capitalize on a "miracle" that proves to be no miracle at all.

Francis Chisholm, on the other hand, is the dissenter, the man who is different and therefore doomed to disappointment and failure in the eyes of the world. Through him, however, Cronin celebrates a central conviction: the significance—in possibility and promise, in striving if not in attainment—of tolerance and compassion and of encouragement for those striving to be true to their aspirations. Francis wins the priesthood the hard way: being plain, outspoken, and unprepossessing in appearance, he never gets far in the Church. While Mealey attends to the social affairs of the Church, Francis works with the poor and lonely. While Mealey complies with all of the Church's teachings, Francis speaks his mind. Christ-like yet human, Francis believes in tolerance rather than dogma, and he holds humility above pride and ambition.

It is doubtful that a book has ever been more timely. Appearing as it did when most of the world was at war, and with most writers preoccupied with that topic, a book with religion as its background was most refreshing. When religion is presented logically and unpretentiously, as in *The Keys of the Kingdom*, without mawkishness or condescension, it is sufficiently novel to make the reading public take notice. In this atmosphere and with these attributes, Cronin's most popular novel achieved its immense success.

Until *The Green Years*, most of Cronin's attention had been focused on the absurdities and complications of the adult world. In *The Green Years*, however, Cronin set himself the added difficulty of working within the limited consciousness of a small child while at the same time avoiding the sentimentalities of so many books about childhood written for adults. To accomplish all of this Cronin takes his hero quite seriously, and often describes his experiences with the same gravity as Robert, the protagonist, would view them. What is more, the novel consists of a grown man's remembered experience, for the story is told in retrospect of a man who looks back to a particular period of intense meaning and insight. "Our purpose," the author says, "is to reveal [the young Robert] truthfully, to expose him in all his dreams, strivings and follies." This double focus—the boy who first experiences, and the man who has not forgotten—provides for the dramatic rendering of a story told by a narrator who, with his wider, adult vision, can employ the sophisticated use of irony and symbolic imagery necessary to reveal the story's meaning.

The Green Years is a story of initiation, of a boy's quest for knowledge. The plot covers a period of ten years (1902 to 1912) and falls into three sections of nearly equal length as the hero progresses from innocence to perception to purpose. In the early chapters, Robert's innocence is expressed as a mixture of bewilderment and ignorance. The opening establishes with Proustian overtures the desolation which haunts him upon his arrival at his new home, Levenford, with his new "mama," Grandma Leckie: "I was inclined to trust Mama, who, until today, I had never seen before and whose worn, troubled face with faded blue eyes bore no resemblance to my mother's face." Robert's sensitivity to his new surroundings is apparent in his acute perception of details. At the dinner table, Papa says "a long, strange grace which I had never heard before." Robert has difficulty managing "the strange bare-handled knife and fork," does not like the cabbage, and finds the beef "terribly salty and stringy." He wonders why he is "such a curiosity" to all these people. The feeling of "being watched" is an experience that is repeated and a notion that reverberates throughout the novel. Suggested here is his continual need to perform for others and to be evaluated by others. Robert is the typical uncomprehending child caught in an uncomfortable situation. Lonely, imaginative, and isolated, he lacks the understanding necessary for evaluation and perspective.

Robert's gradual development into a perceptive young man functions, in large part, as a kind of organizing principle in the novel, uniting the common interest of a variety of disparate characters. These figures include Papa and Mama Leckie, Uncle Murdock, Adam Leckie—all of whom are caught by marked shifts in their lives: illness, the death of those close to them, the breakup of careers, and the discovery of new opportunities. To compensate for this unhappy environment, Robert turns in part to nature and literature. His appreciation of nature, for example, may be attributed to his friend, Gavin Blair, in whom he discovers the companionship he craves. Like the companions of so many of Cronin's protagonists, Gavin is intelligent, gifted, and handsome. Particularly appealing to Robert is Gavin's "inner fibre, that spiritual substance for which no words suitable can be found."

While Cronin makes it clear that there is great comfort in all this, he also shows that this friendship initiates a problem that haunts Robert for much of the novel: a weakness for idealism. For Cronin, the great struggle of youth coming to maturity is the search for reality. This process involves disillusionment and pain. Robert endures a great deal of anguish each time one of his illusions is destroyed, but these disillusionments are necessary if he is to achieve intellectual and emotional independence. Once he must fight with his best friend, Gavin, to stop the taunts of his fellow classmates. At night, he is terrified by his grandmother's tales of Satan. He witnesses Gavin's death and on the same day fails the important Marshall examinations. All of this contributes to his temporary loss of faith in himself and his God.

Helping to shape Robert's purpose and philosophy is Alexander Gow, the one character with whom Robert feels secure. Robert quite naturally takes to Gow, with his apocryphal tales of the Zulu War, his eye for the ladies, his orotund views of human frailty, and his love for drink. Gow possesses "those faint ennobling virtues—never to be mean, always kind and inspiring affection." He defends Robert's right to Catholicism and to an education. Robert sees him as the reader sees him: erratic, not always dependable, yet—as one reviewer wrote—"still with an unquenchable zest for experience, an insatiable hunger for vital and beautiful things, an instinctive understanding of the human heart, especially a heart in trouble or in extreme youth."

In retrospect, *Hatter's Castle*, *The Stars Look Down*, *The Citadel*, *The Keys of the Kingdom*, and *The Green Years* fall into a pattern, illustrating Cronin's recurring themes. Each of the five novels features a protagonist who has glimpses of values beyond the reach of his environment and who must struggle to achieve them. All five novels focus with dramatic force on the essential evil of injustice: the personal suffering that is the real reason for hating such injustice. Cronin's humanitarian sympathies, his reaction against political, social, and religious injustice in his time, led him to a philosophical position somewhat akin to Thomas Carlyle's. He believed that it is man's responsibility to work, to prove his worth in whatever social stratum he happens to find himself.

Dale Salwak

Other major works

PLAY: *Jupiter Laughs*, 1940.

NONFICTION: *Report on First-Aid Conditions in British Coal Mines*, 1926; *Report on Dust Inhalation in Haematite Mines*, 1926; *Adventures in Two Worlds*, 1952.

Bibliography

Bartlett, Arthur. "A. J. Cronin: The Writing Doctor." *Coronet* 35 (March, 1954): 165-169. This readable, entertaining piece provides biographical details concerning Cronin's transition from life as a doctor to life as a writer.

Cronin, Vincent. "Recollection of a Writer." *Tablet* 235 (February 21, 1981): 175-176. One of Cronin's surviving sons writes a moving appreciation of his father with biographical details and a discussion of *Hatter's Castle* through *The Spanish Gardener*. His novels were both "indictments of social injustice" and expressions of "a deep religious faith." From the latter stemmed "the warm humanity which gave his novels a worldwide appeal." Quotes from two messages of sympathy sent to the family.

Davies, Daniel Horton. *A Mirror of the Ministry in Modern Novels*. New York: Oxford University Press, 1959. This perceptive piece compares and contrasts the portrayal of a Protestant missionary in W. Somerset Maugham's "Rain" and Cronin's *The Grand Canary* and *The Keys of the Kingdom*.

Frederick, John T. "A. J. Cronin." *College English* 3 (November, 1941): 121-129. One of the earliest important considerations of Cronin's reputation in the light of his flaws as a writer. Discusses *Hatter's Castle, The Grand Canary, The Citadel, The Stars Look Down*, and *The Keys of the Kingdom*. Judges Cronin's novels to suffer from a lack of humor, an absence of stylistic grace, an obvious construction, and some feeble characters. On the positive side, finds a "deliberate choice of fictional material of the highest value and importance, unquestionable earnestness of purpose and—most important of all—positive evidence of capacity for self-criticism and for growth."

Fytton, Francis. "Dr. Cronin: An Essay in Victoriana." *Catholic World* 183 (August, 1956): 356-362. This important discussion covers the man behind the novels and his religious thinking since his return to the Faith. Divides the works into two groups: those before *The Keys of the Kingdom* (which grow in quality) and those after (which descend in quality). "And the descent exactly corresponds with the author's growth in religious conviction."

Salwak, Dale. *A. J. Cronin*. Boston: Twayne, 1985. The only published book-length study of Cronin, offering a full introduction to his life and works. After a discussion of his life as a doctor and his transition to that of a writer, examines each of Cronin's novels and concludes with an assessment of his career since his death. Supplemented by a chronology, notes, a comprehensive bibliography (listing primary as well as secondary sources with brief annotations), and an index.

_____. *A. J. Cronin: A Reference Guide*. Boston: G. K. Hall, 1982. This annotated bibliography is an indispensable research tool for those interested in tracing the judgments passed on Cronin, the writer and the man, by his English and American readers from 1931 until his death in 1981. The annotations are descriptive, not evaluative, and are fully indexed, and the introduction traces the development of Cronin's literary reputation.

ROBERTSON DAVIES

Born: Thamesville, Ontario, Canada; August 28, 1913

Principal long fiction

Tempest-Tost, 1951; *Leaven of Malice*, 1954; *A Mixture of Frailties*, 1958; *Fifth Business*, 1970; *The Manticore*, 1972; *World of Wonders*, 1975; *The Rebel Angels*, 1981; *What's Bred in the Bone*, 1985; *The Lyre of Orpheus*, 1988.

Other literary forms

Dramatist, journalist, and essayist, Robertson Davies has written plays such as *Fortune, My Foe* (1948), *A Jig for the Gypsy* (1954), *Hunting Stuart* (1955), and dramatizations of some of his novels; histories (notably *Shakespeare's Boy Actors*, 1939); numerous newspaper commentaries and columns (often for the *Peterborough Examiner* and the *Toronto Star*); and essays of all kinds, including many for volume 6 (covering the years 1750-1880) of *The Revels History of Drama in English*.

Achievements

Davies is considered the foremost Canadian man of letters, achieving virtually every literary distinction his country offers, including the Governor-General's Award for Fiction and fellowship in the Royal Society of Literature. He is the first Canadian honorary member of the American Academy and Institute of Arts and Letters. Professor emeritus of the faculty of the University of Toronto, he held the Edgar Stone Lecturership in Dramatic Literature (as its first recipient); he was also the first master of Massey College.

Biography

Born on August 28, 1913, in the town of Thamesville, Ontario, into a family of enterprising and individualistic Canadian entrepreneurs and newspaper publishers, the third child of Rupert and Florence MacKay Davies was to inherit the verbal skills and high-energy work ethic of his parents, along with their Welsh temperament. Receiving a cultural education that included frequent visits to the opera and theater, balanced with a presbyterian love of music, Robertson learned to love words very early, from the family habit of reading aloud. He learned to read at the age of six and promptly began consuming the classics as well as popular newspaper and magazine fare.

When his family moved to Renfrew, young Davies was forced to attend a country grade school, where ruffians and jealous peers made his quiet, bookish life miserable. These times were to be recalled in some of his best fiction. Travel with his father, in Europe as well as throughout Canada, convinced him of the importance of a British education; after undergraduate work at Upper Canada College, he spent 1932 to 1938 at Queen's College and the University of Oxford, reading literature, drama, and history. A predilection for acting led him to the Old Vic (1938-1939), until the war sent him back to Canada, to begin a journalistic career, following his father's financial interests. By 1942 he was editor of the *Peterborough Examiner*, a man of great interests and broad education trapped by circumstance in a fairly provincial town in Canada, forced to deal daily with the pedestrian affairs of journalism. Far from fading into the woods, however, he found his creative voice and energy in the contradiction, and began a fruitful writing career.

At the center of Davies' strange reconciliation of apparent opposites was his ability to live moderately, sanely, while expressing his outrageous imagination in writing. He took on the journalistic persona of Samuel Marchbanks, an outspoken man of letters, at once the antithesis and the complement of Davies the man. So successful was his ability to generate a reality for Marchbanks that for eleven years the Marchbanks columns of the *Peterborough Examiner* were syndicated in Canadian papers.

Responding to his love of theater, Davies wrote several plays as well during this period, notably *Eros at Breakfast* (1948) and *Fortune, My Foe*. He was also instrumental in founding the Shakespeare Festival in Stratford. While his plays were only modestly successful outside Canada, in his homeland he is highly respected for his original stagework and his adaptations of classics such as Ben Jonson's *Bartholomew Fair* (1614).

Davies experienced a major career change in 1960, when he joined the faculty of Trinity College, University of Toronto, first as a visiting professor and, in 1961, as first master of Massey College, a new branch of the University of Toronto. While his new duties meant giving up his editorship (his father died in 1967 and the business was sold), the change of career allowed him time to begin a long and full fiction-writing career, while continuing his stage and essay work. He had become disenchanted with theater as a full-bodied medium when his stage adaptation of *Leaven of Malice* failed to enjoy a long run on Broadway in 1960. Now he began to pursue the novel form as more independent of outside interference and the uncertain financial fortunes of the stage. A trio of novels, sometimes called the Salterton novels, demonstrated the transition in Davies' own life, by concentrating on the backstage events, mostly humorous, of amateur and professional acting companies trying to put on classic and modern plays. However successful these novels were, it remained for Davies to find in his next trilogy the permanent setting and cast of characters to inform his novels.

Davies' most interesting and, according to many critics, long-lasting writing began with his 1970 publication of the novel *Fifth Business*, the first of the so-called Deptford Trilogy, to be followed by *The Manticore* in 1972 and *World of Wonders* in 1975. These novels combined Davies' previous experiences in rural Canada and cosmopolitan Europe, his familiarity with academic circles, and his love of the world of theater to bring to life a series of characters that would appear over and over in his subsequent fiction.

During the next ten years of Davies' academic life, a second trilogy appeared, examining in depth a Canadian family so similar to his own that some critics consider it an autobiographical series. *The Rebel Angels* (1981) and *What's Bred in the Bone* (1985) were followed by *The Lyre of Orpheus* in 1988; these works continued in fresh perspective the only nominally altered lives and adventures of the central characters in the previous trilogy. Readers of Davies' work enjoy his habit of moving his characters from peripheral to central positions in a retrospective reintroduction of their favorite narratives, sometimes serving support roles and sometimes taking center stage in exciting, humorous, and erudite stories that can be read separately, in any order, or enjoyed in their entirety.

Full-bearded and Jovian in appearance, Davies continues to pursue a literary life set against his academic retirement, sought after by interviewers and cultural clubs of all kinds, not only the most successful Canadian writer of fiction but indeed an international man of letters.

Analysis

At the core of Robertson Davies' novels is a sense of humor that reduces pompous institutional values to a refreshing individuality. Interplays of the formal with the specific—officious academia versus lovable satyr-professor, self-important charitable foundation versus reclusive forger-artist, elaborately constructed "magic" paraphernalia versus truly gifted magician, Viennese Jungian psychology versus painfully intimate self-exploration—are the pairings that make the novels come alive. The theatrical metaphors from his early work come forward whenever Davies' novels are to be described: behind the scenes, his cast of characters perform their roles even more effectively than on the stage of their professional lives, but Davies, often in his fictive personas of Dunstan Ramsay and, in the later trilogy, Simon Darcourt, is there to unmask them and make them laugh at themselves.

Davies perceives a basic duality in human nature and exploits the tensions between the two sides to produce novelistic excitement and philosophical insight. Another way to clarify the duality of Davies' view is to make use of the central "grid" in *The Manticore*: reason versus feeling. Giving both human impulses their proper due, Davies finds the fissure in their marriage and wedges his humor into the gap, penetrating the surface of their union to reveal the weakness of one and the domination of the other. The "gypsy" in each individual (a subject at the center of *Rebel Angels*) must be answered to, or else an imbalance will turn life sour. For David Staunton in *The Manticore*, reason has overpowered his ability to feel; for Parlabane in *Rebel Angels*, feelings and emotions have made his intellectual life a hollow pretense. Davies finds and repairs the imbalances, giving to each novel a closure of reconciliation between feeling and reason. Thus, despite the intertwining of characters and incidents, providing a "perspectivist," kaleidoscopic view of both, each novel stands apart, complete, while at the same time the richness of the situations promises more.

Coupled with Davies' vast erudition and education (he is called a "polymath" by more than one critic) is a fine sense of how the English language works; these qualities combined provide both the broad stroke and the marvelous attention to detail that make his novels successful. One unusual feature of all of his work is the very high level of education enjoyed by virtually all the characters, an intellectual *mise-en-scène* that allows the reader and Davies to share all kinds of sophisticated observations. The title *Rebel Angels* subtly suggests its subject, François Rabelais; *What's Bred in the Bone* echoes the "paleopsychology" of a character in *Rebel Angels*; and the character Magnus prepares the reader for the fact that another character, Pargetter, will be called a "Magus" in a subsequent novel. The puns and plays on words are polylingual and are never spelled out (the character names "Parlabane," "Cruikshank," and "Magnus Eisengrim" are examples ready to hand); Davies does not patronize his readers. Ramsay lost his leg in World War II; he may be David Staunton's biological father, having been in love with Leola Cruikshank Staunton (her maiden name means "crooked leg"). These few examples point to a general trend: metaphor before bald statement, reflected heat before direct blast, euphemism before naked statement. When Dr. von Haller refers to a man's age as "a psalmist's span," she makes no apologies. To appreciate fully what Davies is getting at in his work, a fairly comprehensive cultural literacy is required of the reader.

Yet the earthiness of real life is never lost among the intellectual conceits: a plot line of one whole novel deals with the quality of dung to improve the tonal qualities of stringed instruments. When the time is right for describing sexual aberrations or cadaverish details, Davies is ready. It is true that Ramsay's vast knowledge of arts and letters (Davies himself is famous among his colleagues for extemporaneous but highly informative lectures on obscure subjects of every kind) gives glimpses, if not insights, into such a broad range of cultures and historical periods that Davies' full canon can almost serve as a checklist of gaps in the reader's erudition. Still, as Ramsay himself points out while speaking of his own book in *World of Wonders*, Davies' novels are "readable by the educated, but not rebuffing to somebody who simply wanted a lively, spicy tale."

Dunstan Ramsay is clearly the authorial persona in the Deptford novels, as actor and audience; whether taking part in the plot directly, as in *Fifth Business*, or as observer and narrator in *World of Wonders*, or as a coincidental facilitator in *The Manticore*, Ramsay emerges as having the closest to Davies' own fine sense of the observably ridiculous, along with a forgiving spirit that makes Davies' work uplifting and lighthearted, despite its relent-less examination and criticism of everything spurious and mediocre in the human spirit. Simon Darcourt, a priest and academician in the later novels, is yet another Davies persona, recognizable by his penetration into (and forgive-ness of) the foibles of the rest of the characters.

Fifth Business, the first novel of what has become known as the Deptford Trilogy, has been cited by many critics as the real beginning of Davies' major work, a "miracle of art." The novel marks Davies' first real "thickening" of plots and details, and a list of the subjects dealt with reads like a tally sheet of Western civilization's accomplishments to date: saints' lives, psychology, mythology, folk art, place-names and family lineages, magic arts, medieval brazen heads and other tricks of the trade, and the complex workings of nineteenth century theater. It is the autobiography of Dunstan Ramsay him-self, at age seventy, looking backward at the impulses that formed his life and character, beginning with an accident in a winter snowball fight, in which a passerby, Mary Dempster, was injured, causing the premature birth of her son. The "friend/enemy" relationship between Ramsay and Boy Staunton (intended target and careless launcher, respectively) is the singular metaphor for Davies' pursuit of the dichotomy in every person: a drive for worldly success foiled by a need for spiritual or aesthetic grace. For Ramsay, the reverse is true: his life is so affected by the snowball-throwing incident that he never succumbs to merely material reward, but spends his life in self-examination. In this novel, all the major characters for the next two are introduced in some form or another: David Staunton (Boy's son) is the central figure in *The Manticore*; the stunted child of Mary Dempster, now Magnus Eisengrim, centers the third novel, *World of Wonders*.

The Manticore, an examination of Jungian psychology, serves as *dramatis personae* for all Davies' novels: the archetypes appear again and again in various disguises, from the shadow figure to the father figure to the hero, from the anima to all of its component parts. David Staunton's analyst, Dr. von Haller, a woman truly balanced between reason and feelings, helps him find the missing part of his life and represents the Davies character that appears in every novel: the grown woman, wise, often not beautiful but very attractive nevertheless, who leads the central figure past his conventional assumptions about all women into a deeper, more substantive appreciation of the Eternally Feminine. As Staunton describes the death of his "swordsman" father, Boy Staunton (the name's significance becomes clearer as the analysis progresses), he learns to recognize all sorts of shadows in his past that have led to his celibacy, his indifference to feelings, and his essential loneliness. Ramsay was one of David's tutors, and their reunion at the novel's end, also in the presence of Magnus Eisengrim and Liesl Naegeli, an "ogress," is another example of the sense of reconciliation and closure that each novel offers, despite the interrelationship of the trilogies themselves. The reader is treated to a full-length portrait of the major characters and then finds them, like old friends, reappearing in other places, other novels, so that the reader is in fact dwelling in the same regions as the heroes of the books. It is a reassuring and comforting realization that, once a book is finished, the characters will be back to reacquaint themselves with the reader in future volumes.

World of Wonders follows Magnus' career up to the point at which Ramsay is asked to write a fictional autobiography of Magnus, as part of a large commercial enterprise that includes a film on the life of Harry Houdini, with Magnus in the title role. The central metaphor is once again a duality, the division of illusion and reality, for Magnus' real genius lies not in the tricks of the trade but in a spiritual gift, given to him at his unusual birth. Now the story of Ramsay and Boy Staunton and Mary Dempster is told from yet another perspective, that of the putative victim, enriched beyond measure by the accident of the stone-filled snowball. The stone inside the snowball, like the knives of Spanish literature, is almost alive, with a mind and a direction all its own; Boy Staunton's body will be found in the river with the stone in his mouth; at the end of *The Manticore*, Ramsay had tossed the stone down a mountain, remarking almost in passing, "I hope it didn't hit anybody." In this way Davies looks at the cause-effect duality apparently at work on the plane of reality, reflecting a larger karmic cause-effect relationship on the spiritual plane. Magnus' life and success, unforeseen at his birth, tell the listeners (they gather each night to continue the story) that human beings can neither foresee nor alter the future by conscious acts, but they affect the future nevertheless by their own facticity. That is the "world of wonders" the book's title introduces.

A special and very important motif for Davies is the mentor-protégé relationship, dealt with in every novel in some form or another. *The Rebel Angels*, beginning a new trilogy, is an example. The protagonists are three professors who have been asked to oversee the distribution of a vast collection of art and manuscripts, left to a charitable foundation by Francis Cornish (the subject of the next novel in the trilogy, *What's Bred in the Bone*). Their contentions and agreements form the framework for a deeper discussion of the nature of human achievement. Simon Darcourt is one of the executors, the kindest and broadest in his interests; he shares the narration with his gifted student Maria Magdalena Theotoky, a young student about to venture on the same academic, "reasoned" path as her tutors. Her Gypsy mother insists, however, on a larger image of her life, and in the reexamination of her values, she discovers the Rabelaisian side of her, in the person of Parlabane, a dissolute, perverted, and most warmhearted individual, a murderer and a suicide, who gives her a great gift in his dying wish.

At least three plots join and part as the book progresses, even the two narrative voices alternating as the story unfolds. Parlabane is a modern manifestation of the seventeenth century Rabelais, Maria's dissertation topic and the author of three valuable letters stolen by one of the three executors. A thoroughly unlikable character named McVarish serves as a foil to the larger, more humanitarian lives of the other professors and the idealized free-enterprise benefactor, Arthur Cornish. Cornish eventually marries Maria, but not before her idol, Clement Hollier, almost absentmindedly has his way with her on the office couch (a false start in the mentor-protégé relationship). In the process of telling four or five stories at once, Davies manages to give the reader a tour of dozens of cultural worlds, including the care and feeding of rare violins, the cataloging of art collections, the literary secrets of seventeenth century letter-writers, the habits of obscure monastic cults, and the fine points of academic infighting.

The second novel in the trilogy, *What's Bred in the Bone*, moves backward one generation, to Canada and Europe just before World War II. Francis Cornish, a member of the Cornish clan, recognizably similar to but different from the Staunton clan, is the scion of a rich Canadian entrepreneur. Brought up both Catholic and Protestant (like Davies), Francis combines a quiet talent for drawing with an uncanny ability to imitate the brush strokes of the masters. A series of circumstances finds him forging paintings in a German castle, painting his own personal life story into large canvases (a metaphor for Davies' own work), and spying for the British government by counting the clacks of the passing Nazi trains on their way to concentration camps. This mild form of spying is inherited from his military father, in the mold of Boy Staunton, a great diplomatic success but something of a failure as a nurturing parent and an aesthetic model.

Most valuable to scholars seeking biographical references are Davies' descriptions of Francis' childhood in rural Canada, especially his gradual, painful understanding about class differences and the sexual indiscretions of adults (a theme examined more fully in *The Manticore*). Simon Darcourt, academic-priest, has been commissioned to write a biography of Francis Cornish, but has turned up some questionable material about his European experiences: he may have forged some drawings, now in the possession of a prestigious public museum. Davies uses the device of splitting the narration (as he does in *Rebel Angels*) between two supernatural beings, one Zadkiel, the "angel of biography," and the other the Daimon Maimas, a dark but energetic manifestation of the artistic conscience. Their otherworldly debate as Cornish's story unfolds allows Davies to investigate once again the necessity of balancing human dualities for sanity and satisfaction.

The Lyre of Orpheus finds a musical theme for Davies, a lost and incomplete E. T. A. Hoffmann musical treatment of the Arthurian legend. The music student Hulda, indirectly under Simon Darcourt's tutelage, decides to complete the opera, and Darcourt is asked to supply a text—his choice of Sir Walter Scott's poetic rendition of the legend makes for an excellent example of how Davies winds the arts around themselves into a whole act of achievement. Here the mentor-protégé relation is developed fully, not only between the narrator and Hulda but also between the student and a visiting composer/conductor, Gunilla, one of Davies' strong, ugly (but attractive), mature women. The "ominous" Professor Pfeiffer, called in as external examiner to Hulda's examination, provides Davies with an opportunity to lampoon all that is disagreeable about certain academics of his acquaintance.

Whatever the manufacture of Davies' novels, they are witty, informed, insightful portraits of intellectuals no longer in touch with their feelings, an imbalance made right by novel's end. The stories are told and retold, in pairs that act as shadows of each other, alternately figure and ground, told in a perspectivist style that gradually gives full dimension to every event and every character. Whether Davies will ever ring the changes on the world he has entered is problematic; the reader will never tire of hearing the same incidents over and over, told from yet another point of view, in another voice, and with another metaphorical lesson in tow. Davies seems to be enjoying himself immensely in this genre. The end is nowhere in sight.

Thomas J. Taylor

Other major works

PLAYS: *Overlaid*, 1947; *Fortune, My Foe*, 1948 (teleplay); *Eros at Breakfast*, 1948; *Hope Deferred*, 1948; *The Voice of the People*, 1948; *At the Gates of the Righteous*, 1948; *At My Heart's Core*, 1950; *King Phoenix*, 1950; *A Masque of Aesop*, 1952; *A Jig for the Gypsy*, 1954; *Hunting Stuart*, 1955; *Love and Libel: Or, The Ogre of the Provincial World*, 1960; *A Masque of Mr. Punch*, 1962; *Hunting Stuart and Other Plays*, 1972 (includes *King Phoenix* and *General Confession*); *Question Time*, 1975.

NONFICTION: *Shakespeare's Boy Actors*, 1939; *Shakespeare for Younger Players: A Junior Course*, 1942; *The Diary of Samuel Marchbanks*, 1947; *The Table Talk of Samuel Marchbanks*, 1949; *Renown at Stratford: A Record of the Shakespeare Festival in Canada, 1953*, 1953 (with Tyrone Guthrie); *Twice Have the Trumpets Sounded: LA Record of the Stratford Shakespearean Festival in Canada, 1954*, 1954 (with Guthrie); *Thrice the Brinded Cat Hath Mew'd: A Record of the Stratford Shakespearean Festival in Canada, 1955*, 1955 (with Guthrie); *A Voice from the Attic*, 1960; *The Personal Art: Reading to Good Purpose*, 1961; *Marchbanks' Almanack*, 1967; *Stephen Leacock: Feast of Stephen*, 1970; *One Half of Robertson Davies*, 1977; *The Enthusiasms of Robertson Davies*, 1979.

Bibliography

Davis, J. Madison, ed. *Conversations with Robertson Davies*. Jackson: University Press of Mississippi, 1989. This collection of various media interviews is the best way to compare and contrast Davies the man with the central characters in his novels. Far from the Tory throwback some critics have assumed because of his academic background, Davies emerges in these interviews as an iconoclastic and daring investigator of the possible.

Heintzman, Ralph H., ed. *Journal of Canadian Studies* 12 (February, 1977). A special issue of Davies criticism; much of the scholarly work on Davies appears only in Canadian publications. This special edition includes a valuable Davies log of writing and important events, with six other essays examining the Deptford Trilogy.

Lawrence, Robert G., and Samuel L. Macey, eds. *Studies in Robertson Davies' Deptford Trilogy*. Victoria, Canada: English Literary Studies, University of Victoria, 1980. Davies introduces this collection with a personal retrospective of the creative impulses that resulted in the Deptford Trilogy. The studies range from traditional historical criticism to folklore backgrounds to Jungian analysis to examinations of law. An opening article surveying the Salterton novels brings the reader up to the Deptford novels.

Monk, Patricia. *The Smaller Infinity: The Jungian Self in the Novels of Robertson Davies*. Toronto: University of Toronto Press, 1982. The most thorough book-length study of Jungian influences in all Davies' writing, but especially concentrating on *The Manticore*. Monk finds the archetypal constructions of the characters a more overpowering leitmotif than Davies' own autobiographical renditions, and she systematizes the Deptford Trilogy's characters around the traditional figures of Jungian psychology. This study was begun in her essay "Davies and the Drachenloch," in Lawrence and Macey, above.

Peterman, Michael. *Robertson Davies*. Boston: Twayne, 1986. The first four chapters deal with Davies' journalistic and dramatic careers; the last chapters discuss the Salterton novels, the Deptford Trilogy, and *The Rebel Angels*. Peterman explains well the importance of Davies' Canadian birth and childhood. Valuable bibliography (to 1985) and index.

H. L. DAVIS

Born: Roane's Mill, Oregon; October 18, 1896
Died: San Antonio, Texas; October 31, 1960

Principal long fiction
Honey in the Horn, 1935; *Harp of a Thousand Strings*, 1947; *Beulah Land*, 1949; *Winds of Morning*, 1952; *The Distant Music*, 1957.

Other literary forms
H. L. Davis first gained public and critical notice as a poet. His earliest poems were published in *Poetry* magazine and were much admired by such writers as Carl Sandburg and James Stevens. Most of Davis' work in fiction before 1947 was in the short-story form. At first, he collaborated with Stevens, but in the late 1920's he began publishing on his own, establishing a reputation as a writer of Westerns. Both his poetry and short fiction focus on western American themes. Davis's poetry is sensitive to the experiences of the people who lived on the Western frontier; among his short stories are a number that retain considerable literary merit. These are notable for the universality of their themes and sensitivity to human character.

Achievements
Davis won the Pulitzer Prize in 1936 for his first novel, *Honey in the Horn*. His subsequent novels enhanced his reputation, yet he has received little serious scholarly attention. Western genre fiction has long been regarded as inferior: Westerns are often formulaic, poorly written, and insubstantial. Davis' complex novels have been unappropriately associated by many critics with the typical products of the genre; at his best, Davis imbues the Western with a universality achieved by few of its practitioners.

Biography
Harold Lenoir Davis was born in Roane's Mill, Oregon, on October 18, 1896. The town was a small one and has not survived. Many of the details of Davis' early years are confused by events that he fabricated in later accounts of his life. For example, he turned a few weeks of herding sheep when a youngster into a tale of a job as a cowpuncher; and he turned a short tenure as a military clerk into an adventure with the cavalry in pursuit of Pancho Villa. One can read psychological import into Davis' romanticizing of his youth—perhaps he did so to compensate for his feelings of inadequacy among the elite writers of his day—but he might simply have been following the frontier tradition of duping outsiders with outlandish anecdotes and contradictory details of his life. Davis' work is full of tall tales; his telling such tales about his life should not be surprising.

His parents were James Alexander and Ruth Bridges Davis. Although James Davis had only one leg (the other having been lost in an accident in a sawmill when he was six years old), he was a vigorous man. He was a schoolteacher who taught in one-room schools and took on other jobs when he could in order to support a family that began with Harold and included three other boys. The Davis family moved from town to town in Oregon while James Davis moved from job to job, finally settling in The Dalles, where in 1908, James was made principal of the high school.

James Davis had a taste for literature and wrote poetry. Even though H. L. Davis does not seem to have liked his father, James Davis inculcated in him an interest in literature. Writing was initially a secondary interest for Davis. After working and saving money for college, he went, in 1917, to Stanford University with the hope of training to be an engineer. The school was too expensive, however, and he returned to The Dalles.

In 1918, Davis, nearly twenty-four years old, was drafted into the army and sent to Fort McDowell in California. He served as a clerk from September to December, 1918, at which time he was discharged. During 1918, he submitted poems to *Poetry*; they were published in 1919 and won for Davis a moderate recognition among other poets. He worked at various jobs until he began earning money by collaborating on stories with James Stevens.

In 1926, Davis and Stevens alienated much of the Northwest's small literary establishment by writing *Status Rerum: A Manifesto upon the Present Condition of Northwestern Literature Containing Several Near Libelous Utterances upon Persons in the Public Eye*. The pamphlet assaulted the members of the literary community of Washington and Oregon for low standards and nepotism, and earned for Davis the long-lasting enmity of many Northwestern writers and scholars. He had happier collaborations with Stevens on short stories. Davis needed money, and Stevens was a well-known writer who commanded a higher rate of pay than Davis could expect. (Paul T. Bryant, in his *H. L. Davis*, 1978, suggests that two stories were written entirely by Davis and published under Stevens' name.) Encouraged by H. L. Mencken and others, faced with difficulty earning money, and newly married in 1928 to Marion Lay, Davis committed himself to writing professionally and began publishing stories under his own name.

Davis and his wife moved to Washington, then to Arizona, back to Washington, and then to Mexico, where they lived on a grant from the Guggenheim Foundation which enabled Davis to concentrate on a major work. The result was his first novel, *Honey in the Horn*, which appeared in 1935 and won both the Harper Novel Prize and the Pulitzer Prize. In his forties, Davis received recognition as a writer with a promising future, and his next novel was highly anticipated. This second novel, however, was delayed for eleven years by a quarrel with Harper and Brothers, publishers of *Honey in the Horn*, and the breakup of Davis' marriage.

Always a private man, Davis refused Harper and Brothers' offer of an all-expenses-paid trip to New York to receive the Pulitzer Prize. This initiated a strain on his relationship with the publishing house that developed into a dispute over royalty payments and the right to publish his next book. The dispute, combined with Marion's suit for divorce in 1942 and Davis' recurring ill-health, made the period from 1936 to 1947 unproductive for Davis, save for some short stories published before 1941—although he may have had the manuscript for *Beulah Land* ready in the late 1930's. Davis earned money during this period by writing screenplays.

With the publication of *Harp of a Thousand Strings* by William Morrow in 1947, Davis' career and life took a turn for the better. The publication of *Beulah Land* in 1949 secured his place in American letters. His subsequent novels generally enhanced his reputation and gave him financial security. In 1953, he married Elizabeth Tonkin Martin del Campo, and their relationship was a happy one.

While the 1950's brought Davis hard-earned success and happiness, they also saw the worsening of his health. Doctors amputated his left leg in 1956 because of arteriosclerosis. Almost incessant pain did not prevent him from writing essays, finishing his last novel, *The Distant Music*, and pursuing his interest in literature. In October, 1960, he suffered two heart attacks while visiting San Antonio, Texas; he died on October 31.

Analysis

The novels of H. L. Davis are unified by common themes and a common structure: in each novel save his last, movement from one place to another provides the various backgrounds for the conflicts and growth of his characters. The themes of flight and pursuit dominate each of Davis' novels, even *The Distant Music*, which structurally is an inverted reflection of its predecessors. In it, Davis focuses on what happens to people who are tied to one place and contrasts them to those who are free.

Honey in the Horn relates the adventures of Clay Calvert, Wade Shively, Uncle Preston Shively, Luce, and Luce's father, a horse trader. Typical of Davis' novels, it is populated by many minor characters in addition to the main characters on whom the action focuses. The book is the creation of a mature author who had been writing for most of his adult life, and thus its themes are those that concerned Davis most, and its style is consistent and representative of the author's work. Davis was more interested in characters than in plots, more interested in universal human realities than in local customs. In *Honey in the Horn*, the principal characters act out their drama in a plot that twists and turns almost as if at random; the plot relies heavily on coincidences and is held together primarily by Clay Calvert's travels. The novel faithfully depicts the Oregonian settings and the social customs of the time, but broad Christian symbolism sometimes dominates the novel's imagery. Through symbolism, Davis tries to point out the universal significance of his characters.

Honey in the Horn is set in Oregon in the early part of the twentieth century. The principal events are the murder of a gambler, the development of a relationship between Luce and Clay, Clay's accidental killing of a man, the hanging of Wade Shively, and the discovery that Luce had killed the gambler. These often violent events are set against a background of rural areas and wilderness and mark the growth to maturity of Clay and Luce. They are surrounded by violence and the threat of violence; even the meeting with an old tyrannical owner of a lumber mill about the use of land for camping overnight is fraught with overtones of menace and threats of physical harm. Clay, who initially flees violence, is trapped in it; Luce, too, cannot evade the violence in her nature. As the couple learn to accept each other, they also learn to accept the dark aspects of their own natures; not wholly good nor wholly evil, they are fully human. Focusing on the relationship of Clay and Luce, the novel emphasizes spiritual trial and growth and presents a sad, slightly world-weary view of humanity typical of Davis' novels.

The appearance of symbolism in *Honey in the Horn* is sporadic; it almost totally commands some events and disappears afterward. The most striking example of Christian symbolism is the killing of Wade Shively. Although he is an evil man, he plays the role of Christ in his death: he is captured at night, hanged under false pretenses, and buried in a manner suggesting the burial of Christ. The irony of such symbolism serves Davis' purposes well: human beings are mixtures of good and evil, Satanic at one moment and Christlike the next.

The use of characters to represent ideas is even more pronounced in the presentation of Melancthon Crawford, Commodore Robinette, Apeyahola (Indian Jory), Jean-Lambert Tallien, and Thérèse de Fontenay of *Harp of a Thousand Strings*. These characters are used to illustrate the theme of the title: Each life is part of a vast instrument, the tones of which reverberate from the past, through the present, and into the future. The broad theme of the interrelationships of human lives dominates the novel to the extent that some of Davis' literary strengths are blunted. The satirical humor which enlivens many of his works is almost nonexistent in *Harp of a Thousand Strings*; his characters sometimes move awkwardly as they fulfill their assigned roles and thus lose some of the natural humanity found in Davis' characters in other novels.

Harp of a Thousand Strings is an ambitious work that portrays the broad sweep of history from the French Revolution to Tripoli in 1805, to the American prairie in the mid-nineteenth century. In flashbacks, the story details how Tallien and Fontenay lived through the French Revolution; came to Tripoli and saved Crawford, Robinette, and Apeyahola; and how the three saved men eventually built a town on the American prairie and named it after

Fontenay.

The novel begins with Crawford being declared mentally incompetent and then being shipped from the town he helped to found back to his grasping relatives in Pennsylvania. Dismayed by the mistreatment of Crawford, Robinette and Apeyahola discuss their collective fates and recall the events that led them to the prairie. They had met during the attack by American forces on Tripoli—after they had escaped from the Barbary forces, which had held them prisoner. They are met by Tallien, the French consul, and Fontenay. Tallien tells his life story to the three men and notes how it illustrates that the pursuit of love, revenge, and ambition leads to failure: He wins as his wife a woman who does not love him; he finds that avenging personal injustices is silly because of the changes in those he hated; and he finds that power, once gained, controls him rather than his controlling it. In their lives, Apeyahola, Crawford, and Robinette represent the desires for love, revenge, and ambition, and their lives illustrate the futility of their efforts to reach their goals. Apeyahola wants to return to his wife; he ends up murdering her because of her infidelity. Crawford at first suffers failures in his quest to become rich and return to his hometown as an important man; he ultimately returns as a wealthy man in name only because his greedy relatives have made him their ward. Robinette's ambitious military career ends in ignominy: the killing of unarmed Mexican soldiers in Texas.

Harp of a Thousand Strings shows Davis' interest in the large issues that confront human beings and humanity as a whole. It also shows that those issues are important on a personal level as well as on the dauntingly huge scale of human history. In later novels, the impact of great issues on personal life is more subtly handled. In *Beulah Land*, the scale of events remains large; the novel sweeps from Tennessee through the forced migration of the Cherokee nation to Oklahoma, through the Civil War, and to Oregon. The novel has a sadly compassionate tone, and is pervaded by a gentle sense of humor that enlightens rather than mocks. The central theme of the novel is the failure of love. The characters of *Beulah Land* seek homes—places where they can live in peace. In the Bible, Beulah Land is the prosperous and peaceful home promised to the children of Israel. In Davis' book, it is both a place and a state of mind. Indians and white people both want lands of their own, and they dispute over who owns what land. The rivalry for land leads to betrayal, hatred, and death from the beginning. Sedayah Gallet saves her people, the citizens of Crow Town, from the Cherokee Trail of Tears by helping the army find hiding Indians. She is motivated by love of land and people; the citizens of Crow Town reject her because of her help to the army, even though the army then spares them from the forced march to the Indian Territory. She eventually flees to Ewen Warne and dies after bearing him a daughter.

Love is pursued throughout the novel as if it were a spiritual Beulah Land.

Love of children, love of parents, love of wife, love of people, and love of land are sought with determination, in spite of repeated disasters. Ewen Warne, an independent man who works for the Cherokees, wants to take his daughter Elison with him when he moves. She has been living with the Cargills, who want to keep her. In an argument, Warne kills a Cargill and flees, thus losing his daughter. His other daughter, Ruhama, whose mother was an Indian, and a white boy reared by the Cherokees, Askwani, flee with him. The efforts of Ruhama and Askwani to find peace and fulfilling love serve as focus for much of the novel. Their efforts are sometimes misguided and blind and pull them apart. Their dedication to their search for Beulah Land is at once admirable and pathetic; unlike Clay Calvert and Luce in *Honey in the Horn*, they do not grow into a common understanding. Ruhama seems to have gained some resigned understanding of life and an acceptance of its disppointments, but Askwani is still puzzled, even if a bit wiser. As if to emphasize the divergence of Ruhama and Askwani, Davis has their daughters choose two very different lives: one on a reservation and the other with an Englishman.

Beulah Land shares with *Harp of a Thousand Strings* the generally happy notion that people live beyond themselves in the effects they have on others; humanity shares each person's dreams and sorrows. The characters in *Beulah Land* live on through those they meet and their children, but the notion that love leads to vulnerability, then wounds, and then failure, creates a background of universal futility. No worthwhile alternative goals to love are presented.

In contrast to *Beulah Land*, *Winds of Morning* portrays a cynical young man's discovery of innocence and the good in life. The novel blends folktales, humor, a love story, a murder mystery, and travel into a story about injustice and redemption. The cynical young man is Amos Clarke, a deputy sheriff. The other principal character is Pap Hendricks, an old man who seems younger in spirit than Clarke. The relationship between Clarke and Hendricks is the focus of the book. Clarke arrests Sylvester Busick for killing an Indian. Busick's trial is rigged so that he is acquitted of manslaughter, and Clarke is made to appear a liar. The sheriff sends Clarke to help Hendricks move some horses to high country. To further complicate Clarke's life, the young man is interested in Calanthe, Busick's daughter, who might have helped set Clarke up for his fall. The journey to the high country is marked by the help Hendricks and Clarke provide for those they meet and by clues to the mysterious murder of Farrand, a rancher. They discover that their companion, Estéban d'Andreas, is the supposed murderer. Later, they determine that d'Andreas was tricked by Farrand's wife, who is also Hendrick's daughter. Busick reappears as her foreman; he is blackmailing her because he knows Mrs. Farrand had lied about the murder. Hendricks, who has long—and for good reason—kept his distance from his daughter, speaks with her and reveals the strength of a father's love. His help saves his daughter from Busick and d'Andreas from execution.

One of the novel's important themes is that of reconciliation. Although his daughter had falsely accused him of raping her, Hendricks helps her. Whatever her faults, she remains his daughter and his responsibility. The theme of responsibility is also important. Hendricks finds peace within himself when he acknowledges his responsibility for the death of his wife. Reconciliation between friends and relatives is possible thorugh acknowledgment of love and responsibility; reconciliation with one's own past and spirit is also possible. The ultimate reconciliation comes when Hendricks acknowledges Busick as his son. The peace of spirit he attains comes through his acceptance of the consequences of his acts. Clarke learns from observing Hendricks that he can reconcile with Calanthe.

Winds of Morning is set in Oregon in 1927. The scenes are primarily rural and serve to create a pastoral tone for the background of the novel. While traveling through the semiwilderness, Clarke learns that violence and treachery should indeed be watched for, but that they are not all that is to be found in humanity. Oregon provides wide-open spaces for the opening of his spirit.

In *The Distant Music*, Davis uses Oregon for opposite purposes. In *Winds of Morning*, the land seems liberating, but in *The Distant Music*, it imprisons and rules the main characters. The plot focuses on successive generations of the Mulock family. The first Ranse Mulock settles his homestead along the Columbia River; his wife is a white woman purchased out of bondage from Indians and has a miscarriage of a pregnancy sired by an Indian. An angry, resentful man, the first Ranse Mulock bears a grudge against the Indian and another against the snooping, self-righteous citizens of the local town, Clark's Landing. He drives himself to build his land into something of value. He dies of exposure after gunning down the Indian responsible for his wife's first pregnancy. Mulock seems at peace with himself for the first time after murdering the Indian. The succeeding Mulocks are bound to the land by their struggle to preserve it. Claib, the elder son of the first Ranse Mulock, dies when he leaves the land; without it, his life seems to lack meaning. His younger brother, the second Ranse Mulock, takes over the land, even though he wants to leave it. He spends his life subdividing the land and managing it. Betrayed by his supposed friends and business partners and abandoned by an ungrateful wife, he is left with only his land. He never escapes from it.

The hold of the land extends to the next generation, even though the third Ranse Mulock temporarily escapes to work for the railroad. His old father makes his own ineffectual attempt to escape, is beaten by thieves, and is found by young Ranse and Nina, daughter of the elder Ranse's housekeeper, who is in turn the daughter of one of the people who had betrayed the elder Ranse. Young Ranse returns to the land to help his father and, like his father, is trapped.

Travelers, wanderers, and the broad horizon contrast with the lives of bondage of the Mulocks throughout *The Distant Music*. Davis portrays what happened to the settlers of Oregon, their change from free spirits to parochial ones. The book is sketchy; it lacks the depth and detail that a story covering three generations of people should command. The darkness of *The Distant Music* resembles that of *Beulah Land*, but without the hubris that the pursuit of a great—if empty—goal provides the characters of the earlier book. The movement from one generation to the next is worthy of Davis' other novels; *The Distant Music* is broad in its vision of time and of individual people caught in social change.

Davis was a writer of great ambition. He drew on his experiences to create novels that speak of universal human problems. They are consistent in their portrayal of the universality of human experience, whether in France, Tripoli, the Midwest, or Oregon; in their presentation of individual men and women as part of the large family and history of humanity; and in their sympathetic understanding for people, whatever their weaknesses.

Kirk H. Beetz

Other major works

SHORT FICTION: *Team Bells Woke Me*, 1953.

POETRY: *Proud Riders*, 1942; *The Selected Poems of H. L. Davis*, 1978.

NONFICTION: *Status Rerum: A Manifesto upon the Present Condition of Northwestern Literature Containing Several Near Libelous Utterances upon Persons in the Public Eye*, 1926; *Kettle of Fire*, 1959.

Bibliography

Armstrong, George M. "H. L. Davis's *Beulah Land:* A Revisionist's Novel of Westering," In *The Westering Experience in American Literature: Bicentennial Essays*, edited by Merrill Lewis and L. L. Lee. Bellingham: Western Washington University, 1977. Maintains that *Beulah Land* is Davis' only novel to make a direct presentation of settling the West as a foolish effort to achieve impossible goals, as compared with *Harp of a Thousand Strings*. Davis used history to challenge the conventions of fiction, as his treatment of the Civil War and Indians in *Beulah Land* illustrates. The Cherokee Removal is displayed for its brutal reality as a force in the history of settling the American West.

——————. "An Unworn and Edged Tool: H. L. Davis's Last Word on the West, 'The Kettle of Fire.'" In *Northwest Perspectives: Essays on the Culture of the Pacific Northwest*, edited by Edwin Bingham and Glen A. Love. Seattle: University of Washington Press, 1979. A study of Davis' last published work, "Kettle of Fire," the title story for a collection of short prose in 1959. The simple plot is analyzed as a satire of the Promethean myth, which expands the meaning of the story. Davis' story argues that western fiction should aim for the complications and ambiguities of true human experience, not for simplification and surface action of the kind which has dominated the genre.

Bryant, Paul T. "H. L. Davis." In *A Literary History of the American West*. Fort Worth: Texas Christian University Press, 1987. Although brief, this article appears in a significant book of scholarship for American literary history, examining Davis' place within it. He is presented as a paradox: a fine stylist who chose to work in a genre of clichés, and a narrator of Western tales who insisted that there was nothing special about the Western experience. One result of his attitude about style and substance is that his writing is uneven, in both the short and long fiction. Throughout, however, he wrote of life as a human comedy in which people can be foolish and cowardly, but also loving and unselfish. Contains a selected bibliography of primary and secondary sources.

—————. *H. L. Davis*. Boston: Twayne, 1978. After a biographical sketch, first examines Davis' poetry from 1918 to 1928, and then looks at his short prose from 1927 through 1941, including stories developed from narrative poetry. Chapter 4 focuses on *Honey in the Horn*, a difficult novel to write which failed to realize fully its central character. The next four chapters analyze Davis' next four novels, from *Harp of a Thousand Strings* to *The Distant Music*, analyzing their main themes and describing the critical reception of each. The last chapter assesses the achievement of Davis through analysis of his style, structural techniques, use of folklore and natural landscape, basic themes, and symbolism. Contains a chronology, notes and references, a selected, annotated bibliography, and an index.

Kohler, Dayton. "H. L. Davis: Writer in the West." *College English* 14 (December, 1952: 133-140. Sketches events in Davis' early life in Oregon to explain his fictional world. Argues that he carefully examines the sociology of the West as a drifting society on a static frontier. Analyzes *Honey in the Horn, Harp of a Thousand Strings, Beulah Land*, and *Winds of Morning* (which is narrower in scope than its predecessors). Davis' style sets him apart from more popular writers in the genre, and he writes with a strong sense of the interrelationship among rhythm, tone, imagery, scene, and character.

DANIEL DEFOE

Born: London, England; 1660
Died: London, England; April 26, 1731

Principal long fiction

The Life and Strange Surprizing Adventures of Robinson Crusoe, of York, Mariner, Written by Himself, 1719; *The Farther Adventures of Robinson Crusoe: Being the Second and Last Part of His Life*, 1719; *The History of the Life and Adventures of Mr. Duncan Campbell, a Gentleman Who, Tho' Deaf and Dumb, Writes Down Any Stranger's Name at First Sight, with Their Future Contingencies of Fortune*, 1720; *The Life, Adventures and Pyracies of the Famous Captain Singleton*, 1720; *Memoirs of a Cavalier: Or, A Military Journal of the Wars in Germany, and the Wars in England, from the Year 1632 to the Year 1648*, 1720; *The Fortunes and Misfortunes of the Famous Moll Flanders, Written from Her Own Memorandums*, 1722; *The History and Remarkable Life of the Truly Honourable Col Jacque, Commonly Call'd Col Jack*, 1722; *A Journal of the Plague Year: Being Observations or Memorials of the Most Remarkable Occurrences, as Well Publick as Private, Which Happened in London, During the Last Great Visitation in 1665*, 1722 (also known as *The History of the Great Plague in London*); *The Fortunate Mistress: Or, A History of the Life and Vast Variety of Fortunes of Mademoiselle de Beleau, Afterwards Call'd the Countess de Wintselsheim, in Germany, Being the Person Known by the Name of the Lady Roxana, in the Time of King Charles II*, 1724 (also known as *Roxana*); *The Memoirs of an English Officer Who Serv'd in the Dutch War in 1672, to the Peace of Utrecht in 1713, by Capt George Carleton*, 1728 (also known as *A True and Genuine History of the Last Two Wars* and *The Memoirs of Cap George Carleton*).

Other literary forms

Although Daniel Defoe is mainly remembered as the author of *The Life and Strange Surprizing Adventures of Robinson Crusoe, of York, Mariner, Written by Himself*, more commonly known as *Robinson Crusoe*, he did not begin to write fiction until he was fifty-nine. The earlier part of his writing career was spent primarily in producing essays and political pamphlets and working for strongly partisan newspapers. He also wrote travel books, poetry (usually on political or topical issues), and biographies of rogues and criminals.

Achievements

Defoe's principal contribution to English literature is in the novel, and he has been called the first English novelist. The extent of his contribution, however, has been debated. A contemporary of Defoe, Charles Gildon, wrote an attack on *Robinson Crusoe*, criticizing, in part, inconsistencies in the narrative. Such problems are not infrequent in Defoe's long and episodic plots. Nevertheless, the reader of almost any of Defoe's works finds himself in a real and solid world, and Defoe's constant enumeration of *things*—the layettes for Moll's illegitimate children, the objects she steals, even her escape routes through London—has earned for Defoe a reputation as a realist and for his style the label "circumstantial realism." To see Defoe as a photographic realist, however, is also to see his limitations, and some of his critics argue that the formlessness of his novels shows his lack of the very shaping power that belongs to great art. Further, even his circumstantial realism is not of the visual sort: once Moll has named an object, for example, she rarely goes on to describe it in such detail that the reader may visualize it.

More recently, Defoe's novels have undergone a reassessment, and critics are starting to see him as more than a mere assembler of objects. Although these critics diverge widely in their interpretation of his techniques, they do agree that Defoe consciously developed the themes and used his narratives to shape these themes, all of which center around the conflict between spiritual and earthly values. Instead of viewing Defoe as a plodding literalist, some critics see a keen irony in his work: Moll's actions and her commentary on those actions, they argue, do not always agree. Thus, the reader is allowed to cultivate a certain ironic detachment about Moll. While few readers would judge Defoe to be a deeply psychological novelist, this double perspective does contribute to a rudimentary analysis of character. Others see a religious vision in his works, one that underwrites an almost allegorical interpretation of his novels: the ending of *Robinson Crusoe*, the killing of the wolves, is seen as Crusoe slaying his earthly passions. While such a reading may seem forced, one should perhaps remember that John Bunyan was a near contemporary of Defoe—he even preached at Morton's Academy at Stoke Newington while Defoe was a student there—and that readers in his time were accustomed to reading allegorically.

Part of the fascination—and achievement—of Defoe may well lie in the tension between realism and allegory which informs his work. Using natural dialogue and a kind of realistic detail, he can yet go beyond these to create events and characters which are, finally, mythic.

Biography

Daniel Defoe was born in the parish of St. Giles, London, the son of James Foe, a Dissenter and a tallow-chandler. (Only after the age of forty did Defoe change his last name, perhaps to seem more aristocratic.) The date of his birth is conjectural: in 1683, he listed his age on his marriage license as twenty-four, but since his sister, Elizabeth, was born in 1659, it is probable that Defoe was born the next year. Not much is known of his early childhood, but his education was certainly important in molding his interests. Being a Dissenter,

Defoe was not allowed to attend Oxford or Cambridge; instead, he went to a dissenting academy presided over by the Reverend Charles Morton. While offering a study of the classics, the academy also stressed modern languages, geography, and mathematics, practical subjects neglected at the universities. This interest in the practical seems to have stayed with Defoe all his life: when his library was sold after his death, the advertisements listed "several hundred Curious, Scarce Tracts on . . . Husbandry, Trade, Voyages, Natural History, Mines, Minerals, etc." Defoe's appreciation of the objects and processes by which one is enabled to live in the world is obvious: after making a table and chair, Crusoe reflects that "by stating and squaring everything by reason and by making the most rational judgment of things, every man may be in time master of every mechanic art."

Although his father intended him for the ministry, Defoe became a merchant after leaving school and probably traveled on the Continent as part of his business. In 1684, he married the daughter of another dissenting merchant and she brought him a considerable dowry. Defoe's fortunes seemed to be rising, but in 1685, he was briefly involved in the Duke of Monmouth's rebellion, a Protestant uprising. Athough he escaped the king's soldiers, this event illustrates his willingness to espouse dangerous political causes: three former schoolmates who joined the rebellion were caught and hanged. While his affairs seemed to prosper during this time, there were disquieting lawsuits—eight between 1688 and 1694, one by his mother-in-law, whom he seems to have swindled—that cast doubt on both his economic stability and moral character. In fact, by 1692 he was bankrupt, a victim of losses at sea and his own speculations. Defoe's character is always difficult to label; while the lawsuits show his unsavory side, he did make arrangements after his ruin to repay his creditors, which he seems to have done with surprising thoroughness.

Defoe then began building a brick factory on some land that he owned in Tilbury. This enterprise went well and, with William and Mary on the throne, Defoe could praise the government with a clear conscience. He admired William's religious toleration, foreign policy, and encouragement of English trade. He wrote several pamphlets supporting William's policy of containing Louis XIV's political aspirations, a policy not always popular in England. When William's followers from Holland were harassed by the English, Defoe wrote *The True-Born Englishman: A Satyr* (1701), a long poem arguing that the English are themselves a mixed race who cannot afford to deride other nationalities.

With the accession of Queen Anne of England in 1702, the Dissenters— and Defoe—suffered serious political grievances. Fiercely loyal to the Church of England, Anne looked with disfavor on other religious groups, and bills were introduced to limit the freedom of Dissenters. While both houses of parliament debated the Occasional Conformity Bill in 1702—a bill that would have effectually prevented Dissenters from holding political office—Defoe published "The Shortest Way with the Dissenters," an ironic pamphlet urging the government to annihilate this group entirely. At first it was taken at face value and applauded by the High Church party but, when its irony was perceived, a warrant was issued for Defoe's arrest and he went into hiding.

Fearful of imprisonment and the pillory, Defoe sent letters to Daniel Finch, Second Earl of Nottingham, the Secretary of State, trying to negotiate a pardon: he would raise a troop of horses for the government at his own expense; he would volunteer to fight—and possibly die—in the Netherlands. Nottingham was inflexible, however, and when Defoe was found, he was imprisoned in Newgate, the scene of Moll's incarceration. Two months later, he was fined two hundred marks, forced to stand in the pillory three times, imprisoned at the Queen's discretion, and forced to provide sureties for his good behavior for the next seven years. This experience helps, perhaps, to explain Defoe's later political views, which seemed to his contemporaries based on expediency rather than conviction: in a letter to a friend he said that, after Newgate, he would never feel himself maligned if called a coward. When Defoe describes Moll's stay in prison, he knows whereof he speaks.

How long Defoe might have remained in Newgate at the Queen's discretion cannot, of course, be known; certainly the government showed no sign of releasing him during the summer nor in the fall. He appealed to Robert Harley, a man destined to take Nottingham's place when the latter had been dismissed by the Queen. After leisurely negotiations—perhaps to render Defoe more grateful when his pardon finally did come—Harley obtained Defoe's release in November, 1703, the Queen even going so far as to send money to Mrs. Defoe and another sum to Defoe to settle his debt.

Harley continued to be influential in Defoe's life; indeed, popular opinion seems to have been that Defoe prostituted himself, abandoning all political ideals for Harley. Still, it is hard to imagine how a forty three-year-old ruined businessman, with a wife and seven children to support, could begin life over if not with the help of a powerful ally. Defoe's letters to Harley also suggest that Harley sometimes kept him short of funds on purpose, perhaps to make him more compliant. In any case, Defoe's career was definitely the writing of political pamphlets—usually in favor of Harley's policies—and he also edited and wrote most of *A Weekly Review*, which ran from 1704 to 1713. Perhaps Defoe's most significant work for Harley was the establishment of a spy system in England to determine what the national sentiment was for the government. This project—which was Defoe's own idea—began in 1704 when Harley sent him on a preliminary reconnaissance trip through the country. This was the first of several such trips, including one to Edinburgh, Scotland, in 1706, to determine local opinion about the proposed union of the English and Scottish parliaments. On all of these trips, Defoe had to assume fictitious identities, and he seems to have relished this subterfuge; it is perhaps signif-icant that Defoe's characters usually are forced to assume many varied disguises in the course of their eventual lives. Even Defoe's tracts and pamphlets bear witness to his fascination with assuming various roles: one critic has estimated that Defoe created eighty-seven personae in these works.

After Harley's political decline and Queen Anne's death, Defoe continued to work for the government characteristically in a role requiring deception. Pretending to be a Tory out of favor with the government, he obtained a job on *Mist's Weekly Journal*, one of the most influential Tory papers. In this way, he was able to temper the writing so that its attacks on the government became less virulent. Defoe's shadowy activities are difficult to follow, but it seems that he was also performing the same service to the government on other papers: *Dyer's News-Letter*, *Dormer's News-Letter*, *Mist's Weekly Journal*, and *Mercurius Politicus*. Defoe's easy transition from Harley's Tory government to the succeeding Whig regime angered many people, who claimed that he had no principles. Defoe's reply, difficult to counter, was always that he was working for moderation, no matter on which side.

Only toward the end of his life did Defoe begin to write prose fiction: *Robinson Crusoe* (1719) and its sequels: *The Life, Adventures and Pyracies of the Famous Captain Singleton* (1720), *The Fortunes and Misfortunes of the Famous Moll Flanders, Written from Her Own Memorandums* (1722), *A Journal of the Plague Year* (1722), *The History and Remarkable Life of the Truly Honourable Col Jacque, Commonly Call'd Col Jack* (1722), and *The Fortunate Mistress* or *Roxana* (1724). Even after completing this enormous output, he continued to produce biographies of criminals and imaginary biographies of soldiers and sailors.

To all appearances, Defoe seemed to embark on a comfortable old age; Henry Baker, his son-in-law, reported that he had retired from London to a handsome house in Stoke Newington, where he lived a leisurely life, growing a garden, pursuing his studies, and writing. In 1730, however, Defoe vanished from his home and, in a rather cryptic letter to Baker, wrote about his "Load of insupportable Sorrows," a "wicked, perjur'd, and contemptible Enemy," and the "inhuman dealing of my own son" who reduced his "dying Mother to beg . . . Bread at his Door." The enemy seems to have been Mary Brooke, the wife of one of Defoe's former creditors. Although Defoe appears to have paid Brooke—at least Brooke's executor accepted Defoe's story—Brooke died before destroying his record of the debt and his wife was determined to collect it. Once again, Defoe was being hounded by a creditor. His reference to his unnatural son is a bit more puzzling but may show that he had transferred most of his money and property to his son to keep it out of Mary Brooke's hands; if so, his son seems to have abused the trust placed in him. Defoe died in April, 1731, while hiding in a lodging house in Ropemaker's Alley.

Although Defoe's colorful life almost calls too much attention to itself—some critics have tried to deduce his exact birthdate by events in his characters' lives—it is hard not to see a link between the elements of disguise and trickery in so many of his novels and his own eventful life, spent, in large part, in fabricating identities for himself in his government work. Like his character Moll Flanders, Defoe had personal experience with Newgate, and his biographies of criminals and rogues show a fascination with the inventive powers that allow one to thrive in a treacherous world. In this respect, Defoe and his characters seem to have a great deal in common: they are all survivors in an often hostile environment. This sense of alienation may also have a link with Defoe's religion, a creed that was sometimes tolerated but rarely encouraged by the Crown.

Analysis

Although *A Journal of the Plague Year* is not Daniel Defoe's first work of fiction, it does offer an interesting perspective from which to examine the novels. Purporting to be a journal, one man's view of a period in a city's history, it shows especially well the nexus between realistic reporting and imaginative invention that is the hallmark of Defoe's novels. Defoe himself lived through one seige of the plague, and although he was only five years old when the disease swept through London, he presumably would have retained some recollections of this catastrophic event, even if only through conversations he would have heard in his family. He also refers frequently to the mortality list, drawing on actual documents of the time to give his narrative a sense of reality. In spite of the realistic foundations of the work, however, its imaginative—not to say fantastic—elements outweigh its realism. Defoe, in fact, often shows a surprising interest in the occult or grotesque for one who is supposedly forging the realistic novels in English. Dreams and premonitions often assail his characters—Crusoe's dream of the angel; Moll's telepathic contact with her Lancashire husband; Roxana's precognitive vision of the dead jeweler—and the utter incomprehensibility of the plague takes this work far beyond cause-and-effect realism.

Perhaps the main thing to consider in *A Journal of the Plague Year* is the narrator, who, like many of Defoe's characters, is divided spiritually: he must decide whether to flee London or stay and trust God's divine providence. Like Crusoe, H. L. in times of stress opens the Bible randomly and applies its words to to his immediate situation. A problem with theme—often Defoe's weakness—immediately arises, for while the passage that he finds in the Bible convinces him to stay, by the end of the novel he has decided that flight is the only sensible alternative. His stay in the city is not developed as a moral flaw, however, although given the religious concerns of the novel it seems as though it should be: some critics even see him guilty of overstraining God's providence. This view seems inconsistent with the overall sympathetic character of H. L., and one feels that Defoe is not, perhaps, completely in control of his theme.

Even more significant for theme is the origin of the plague. H. L., a sensible, levelheaded man, insists that the plague's cause is natural; he is just as insistent, however, that God has used natural means to bring about the plague. In fact, he makes frequent biblical references which, if not providing specific emblematic types for the plague, do give it a resonance beyond that of a mere disease. Thus, the narrator's insistence on seeing all the horrors of the plague for himself—even though he admits he would be safer at home—has led some critics to see his curiosity as a desire to understand God's workings directly. Again, one encounters an awkward thematic problem. Is H. L. really curious about God's wisdom, or is his seeming inability to stay home simply a narrative necessity? There would, after all, be no journal without an eyewitness. Like many thematic problems in Defoe's works, this only becomes one in retrospect; H. L.'s emphasis on the particulars he describes can be so interesting— even if gruesome—that it is not until the reader has finished the book that these problems surface.

Two episodes from this work show how effective Defoe can be with detail. The first involves H. L.'s journey to the post office. Walking through silent and deserted streets, he arrives at his destination, where he sees "In the middle of the yard . . . a small leather purse with two keys hanging at it, with money in it, but nobody would meddle with it." There are three men around the courtyard who tell H. L. that they are leaving it there in case the owner returns. As H. L. is about to leave, one of the men finally offers to take it "so that if the right owner came for it he should be sure to have it," and he proceeds to an elaborate process of disinfection. This episode, on the surface merely straightforward description, is fraught with drama and ambiguity.

While it is realistic that the streets be deserted as people take to the safety of their houses, the silence lends an eerie backdrop to this scene. Furthermore, the men's motivations are hardly straightforward. Are they leaving the purse there out of honesty or are they fearful of contamination? Are they simply playing a waiting game with one another to see who leaves first? Does one man finally take the purse to keep it for the owner or for himself? Finally, why does he have all the disinfecting materials—including red-hot tongs— immediately available? Was he about to take the purse before H. L. arrived? H. L.'s remarks about the money found in the purse—"as I remember . . . about thirteen shillings and some smooth groats and brass farthings"—complete this episode: the particularity of the amount is typical of Defoe's realism, and H. L.'s hesitant "as I remember" also persuades the reader that he is witnessing the mental processes of a scrupulously honest narrator. In fact, this whole passage is so effective that one tends to overlook an internal inconsistency: early in the paragraph H. L. says that the sum of money was not so large "that I had any inclination to meddle with it," yet he only discovers the sum at the end of this episode. Defoe is prone to narrative slips of this kind but, like this one, they are usually unimportant and inconspicuous.

Another vivid episode concerns H. L. going to check on his brother's house while he is away. Next to the house is a warehouse, and as H. L. approaches it, he finds that it has been broken into and is full of women trying on hats. Thievery is by no means uncommon during the plague, although the women's interest in fashion does seem bizarre. What is remarkable about this description, however, is its ambience. instead of grabbing the hats and fleeing, the women are behaving as if they are at a milliner's, trying on hats until they find those that are most becoming. This scene shows Defoe ostensibly writing realistically, but in fact, he is creating a picture that borders on the surreal.

A Journal of the Plague Year does not always achieve the degree of success that these two episodes display; much of the book is filled with descriptions of the cries and lamentation the narrator hears as he walks the streets. Even horror, if undifferentiated, can become monotonous, and Defoe does not always know how to be selective about details. One device that he employs to better effect here than in his other works is the keeping of lists. Defoe's characters often keep balance sheets of their profits and expenditures, and while this may indicate, as Ian Watt contends, Defoe's essentially materialistic bias, these lists often seem examples of the crudest form of realism. In *A Journal of the Plague Year*, however, the mortality lists scattered throughout are rather more successful and provide almost a thudding rhythm to what is being described: God's terrible visitation.

Robinson Crusoe, like *A Journal of the Plague Year* and much of Defoe's fiction, is based on a factual event: Alexander Selkirk, a Scottish sailor, lived for four years on the island of Juan Fernandez until he was rescued in 1709. Defoe supplemented accounts of Selkirk's adventures with travel books: Richard Hakluyt's *Voyages* (1589); William Dampier's *New Voyage Round the World* (1697); and Robert Knox's *An Historical Relation of Ceylon* (1681). Nevertheless, it is as fiction—not a pastiche of other people's books—that *Robinson Crusoe* engrosses the reader. Since the story centers around one character, it depends on that character for much of its success, and critics have tended to divide into two groups: those who see Crusoe as the new middle-class economic man with only perfunctory religious feelings, and those who see him as a deeply spiritual person whose narrative is essentially that of a conversion experience. The answer, perhaps, is that both views of Crusoe coexist in this novel, that Defoe was not sure in this early work exactly where his story was taking him. This ambiguity is not surprising since the same problem surfaces in *The Fortunes and Misfortunes of the Famous Moll Flanders* (more popularly known as *Moll Flanders*); it was not until *Roxana* that Defoe seems to have worked out his themes fully.

The opening frame to Crusoe's island adventure provides a logical starting point for examining his character. Writing in retrospect, Crusoe blames his shipwreck and subsequent sufferings on his "propension of nature" which made him reject his father's counsel of moderation and prompted him to go to sea. His father's speech seems to echo the idea of a great chain of being:

Crusoe's life belongs to the "middle state" and he should not endanger himself by reckless acts. If Crusoe's filial disobedience seems trivial to modern readers, it was not to Defoe: his *The Family Instructor, in Two Parts* (1715) and *A New Family Instructor* (1727) make clear how important the mutual obligations of parents and children are. Crusoe himself, recounting his exile from the perspective of old age, talks about his father in biblical terms: after Crusoe's first shipwreck he is "an emblem of our blessed Saviour's parable, [and] had even killed the fatted calf for me." When Crusoe reflects, then, on his sinful and vicious life, the reader has to accept Defoe's given: that Defoe's early giddy nature is a serious moral flaw.

Even with this assumption, however, the reader may have problems understanding Crusoe's character. Throughout the novel, for example, there are images of prison and capture. This makes sense, for the island is both a prison and, if the reader believes in Crusoe's conversion, a means of attaining spiritual freedom. Crusoe himself is imprisoned early in the novel by some Moors and only escapes after two years (which, like many long stretches of time in Defoe's novels, are only briefly summarized) with a boy named Xury, a captive who soon becomes Crusoe's helpmate and friend. Once Crusoe is free, however, he sells Xury willingly and only misses him when his plantation grows so large that he needs extra labor. Indeed, it is indicative of his relations with other people that, when Crusoe meets Friday, Friday abases himself to Crusoe and Crusoe gives his own name as "Master." Perhaps one should not expect enlightened social attitudes about slavery or race in an eighteenth century author. Even so, there seems pointed irony—presumably unintended by Defoe—in Crusoe gaining his freedom only to imprison others; Crusoe's attitude does not seem sufficient for the themes and imagery that Defoe himself has woven into this work.

Crusoe does not behave appreciably better with Europeans. When he rescues Friday and his father, he also rescues a Spaniard who, with a group of Spaniards and Portuguese, has been living peaceably with Friday's tribe. Crusoe begins to think about trying to return to civilization with the Europeans and sends the Spaniard back to Friday's tribe to consult with the others. Before he returns, however, a ship with a mutinous crew arrives on the island: Crusoe rescues the captain and regains control of most of the mutineers. They leave the worst mutineers on the island and sail off for civilization; Crusoe apparently gives no thought to the Spaniard, who will return to the island only to find a motley collection of renegades. Defoe may, of course, simply have forgotten momentarily about the Spaniard as his narrative progressed to new adventures, but if so, this is an unfortunate lapse because it confuses the reader about character and, therefore, about Crusoe's humanity.

Another problem—this time having to do with theme—occurs at the end of the novel. After being delivered to Spain, Crusoe and another group of travelers set out to cross the Pyrenees, where they are beset by fierce wolves.

They manage to escape, and Crusoe returns to England, marries, has three children, travels back to his island, and continues having adventures, which, he says, "I may perhaps give a farther account of hereafter." One might argue that the adventures after he leaves the island are anticlimactic, although some critics try to justify them on thematic grounds, the killing of the wolves thus being the extermination of Crusoe's earthly passions. The question remains whether the narrative can bear the weight of such a symbolic—indeed, allegorical—reading. The fact that the sequels to *Robinson Crusoe* are merely about external journeys—not internal spiritual states—shows, perhaps, that Defoe was not as conscious an allegorist as some critics imagine.

Given these thematic problems, it may seem odd that the novel has enjoyed the popularity it has over the centuries. In part, this may simply be due to the element of suspense involved in Crusoe's plight. On one level, the reader wonders how Crusoe is going to survive, although the minute rendering of the day-to-day activities involved in survival can become tedious. Of more interest are Crusoe's mental states: his fluctuating moods after he finds the footprint, for example, have a psychological reality about them. Further, the very traits that make Crusoe unappealing in certain situations lend the novel interest: Crusoe is a survivor, and, while one sometimes wishes he were more compassionate or humane, his will to endure is a universal one with which the reader can empathize.

Aside from the basic appeal of allowing the reader to experience vicariously Crusoe's struggles to survive, the novel also offers the reader a glimpse of Crusoe's soul; while some of Crusoe's pieties seem perfunctory, Defoe is capable of portraying his internal states in sophisticated ways. For example, early in his stay he discovers twelve ears of barley growing, which convinces him "that God had miraculously caused this grain to grow without any help of seed sown and that it was so directed purely for my sustenance on that wild miserable place." Two paragraphs later, however, "it occurred to my thoughts that I had shook a bag of chicken's meal out in that place, and then the wonder began to cease; and I must confess, my religious thankfulness to God's Providence began to abate too. . . ." The mature Crusoe who is narrating this story can see in retrospect that "I ought to have been as thankful for so strange and unforeseen Providence as if it had been miraculous; for it was really the work of Providence as to me" that God allowed the seed to take hold and grow. Here the reader finds Defoe using a sophisticated narrative situation as the older Crusoe recounts—and comments upon—the spiritual states of the young Crusoe. Indeed, one problem in the novel is determining when Crusoe's egocentric outlook simply reflects this early unregenerate state of which his mature self would presumably disapprove, and when it reflects a healthy individualism in which Defoe acquiesces. Perhaps Crusoe is most appealing when he is aware of his foibles—for example, when he prides himself on building a gigantic canoe, only to find that he cannot possibly transport it to water.

If *Robinson Crusoe* shows an uneasy balance between egocentricity and spiritual humility, materialism and religion, Defoe's next novel, *The Life, Adventures and Pyracies of the Famous Captain Singleton*, more commonly known as *Captain Singleton*, displays what Everett Zimmerman calls a "soggy amalgam of the picaresque and Puritan." This problem reappears in Defoe's next novel *The History and Remarkable Life of the Truly Honourable Col Jacque, Commonly Call'd Col Jack*, known to readers simply as *Colonel Jack*. Jack's motives are often suspect. When he becomes an overseer in Virginia, for example, he finds that he cannot whip his slaves because the action hurts his arms. Instead, he tells the slaves they will be severely punished by an absentee master and then pretends to have solicited their pardon. Grateful for this mercy, the slaves then work for Jack willingly and cheerfully. While Jack describes this whole episode in words denoting charity and mercy, the reader is uneasily aware that Jack is simply playing on the slaves' ignorance. It is method rather than mercy that triumphs here.

The confusion in *Captain Singleton* and *Colonel Jack* between expediency and morality can also be found in *Moll Flanders* and, to a lesser extent, in *Roxana*. What makes these latter novels enduring is the power of their central characters. Both Moll and Roxana bear many children, and although they manage to dispose of their offspring conveniently so that they are not hampered in any way, their physical fertility sets them apart from Defoe's more sterile male heroes. This fertility may, of course, be ironic—Dorothy Van Ghent calls Moll an Earth Mother but only insofar as she is a "progenitrix of the wasteland"—but it adds a dimension to the characters that both Jack and Singleton lack. One also feels that Defoe allows his female characters greater depth of feeling: each one takes husbands and lovers for whom they have no regard, but Moll's telepathic communication with her Lancashire husband and Roxana's precognitive vision of the jeweler's death imply that both of these women are involved deeply in these relationships—even though Roxana manages to use the jeweler's death as a way of rising in the world by becoming the Prince's mistress. Defoe's heroines may mourn their losses yet also use them to their advantage.

Another difference between the female and male protagonists is that neither Moll nor Roxana descend to murder, whereas Defoe's male picaros often do. Although Moll can occasionally rejoice when a criminal cohort capable of exposing her is hanged, she feels only horror when she contemplates murdering a child from whom she steals a necklace. Similarly, while Roxana may share an emotional complicity in Amy's murder of her importunate daughter, she explicitly tells Amy that she will tolerate no such crime. *Roxana* also seems to have more thematic unity than Defoe's other novels: instead of advocating an uneasy balance between spiritual and material values, *Roxana* shows a tragic awareness that these are finally irreconcilable opposites. Roxana, although recognizing her weaknesses, cannot stop herself from indulging in them, and her keen awareness of what she calls her "secret Hell within" aligns her more with John Milton's Satan than with Defoe's earlier protagonists.

If Defoe begins to solve the thematic problems of his earlier novels in *Moll Flanders* and *Roxana*, he does so through fairly dissimilar characters. Moll equivocates and justifies her actions much more than does Roxana: when she steals the child's necklace, she reflects that "as I did the poor child no harm, I only thought I had given the parents a just reproof for their negligence in leaving the poor lamb to come home by itself, and it would teach them to take more care another time." She also shows a tendency to solve moral dilemmas by the simple expedient of maintaining two opposing moral stances simultaneously. When she meets a man at Bartholomew Fair who is intoxicated, she sleeps with him and then robs him. She later reflects on his "honest, virtuous wife and innocent children" who are probably worrying about him, and she and the woman who disposes of her stolen goods both cry at the pitiable domestic scene Moll has painted. Within a few pages, however, she has found tha man again and taken him as her lover, a relationship that lasts for several years.

Moll seems to see no conflicts in her attitudes. Her speech also shows her ability to rationalize moral problems, and she often uses a type of equivocation that allows her to justify her own actions. When a thief is pursued through a crowd of people, he throws his bundle of stolen goods to Moll. She feels herself free to keep them "for these things I did not steal, but they were stolen to my hand."

Contrary to the character of Moll, Roxana recognizes her failings. After her first husband leaves her in poverty, her landlord offers to become her lover. Although he has a wife from whom he is separated, he argues that he will treat Roxana in every way as his legal wife. Throughout their life together, Roxana distinguishes between their guilt: the landlord, she says, has convinced himself that their relationship is moral; she, however, knows that it is not and is thus the greater sinner.

Indeed, Roxana is portrayed in much greater psychological depth than is Moll; one measure of this is the relationship between Roxana and her maid, Amy. While Defoe's characters often have close friends or confidants—Friday in *Robinson Crusoe*; the midwife in *Moll Flanders*; Dr. Heath in *A Journal of the Plague Year*—it is only in *Roxana* that the friend appears in the novel from the beginning to the end and provides an alter ego for the main character. When Roxana is deciding whether to take the landlord as her lover, for example, Amy volunteers several times to sleep with him if Roxana refuses. Once the landlord and Roxana are living together, Roxana decides to put Amy into bed with the landlord, which she does—literally tearing off Amy's clothes and watching their sexual performance. By the next day, the landlord's lust for Amy has turned to hatred and Amy is suitably penitent. The logical question is why Roxana does this destructive deed, and the answer seems to be that, since she herself feels intense guilt at sleeping with the landlord, she wants to degrade Amy and the landlord as well.

Amy, similarly manipulative, is less passive than Roxana. At the end of the novel, Susan, one of Roxana's daughters, appears, guesses her mother's identity, and begs Roxana to acknowledge her. Amy's suggestion is that she kill Susan, who alone can reveal Roxana's past, having been, unknowingly, a maid in her mother's household when Roxana had many lovers. Roxana recoils from this idea although she admits that Amy "effected all afterwards, without my knowledge, for which I gave her my hearty Curse, tho' I could do little more; for to have fall'n upon Amy, had been to have murther'd myself. . . ." Some critics argue that Roxana actually acquiesces in Susan's murder, even though she forbids Amy to do it; her statement that to fall upon Amy would be to destroy herself does lend credence to this view. Amy, perhaps, acts out the desires that Roxana will not admit, even to herself.

In fact, both *Moll Flanders* and *Roxana* seem to hint at an irrational perverseness in their characters that explains, in part, their crimes. At one point after beginning her life as a thief, Moll actually tries to earn her living with her needle and admits that she can do so, but temptation makes her return to crime. She appears to enjoy living outside the law, no matter how much she may talk of her fears of Newgate. Similarly, she once steals a horse simply because it is there; she has no way to dispose of it, but the irrational impulse in her that leads her to crime causes her to commit this theft anyway. Defoe is not given to high comedy, but the picture of Moll leading the horse through the streets, wondering how she is ever going to rid herself of it, is a memorably comic scene. The frequent irrationality of Moll's behavior seems reiterated in the actions of *Roxana*; without Moll's self-justifying rationalizations, however, Roxana becomes a tragic figure who knows that her behavior is wrong but who cannot stop it. About halfway through the novel, for example, she meets a Dutch merchant, who helps her out of some difficulties; she sleeps with him, but, when he proposes marriage, she refuses him on the grounds that marriage is a kind of slavery for women. Actually, she fears that he is trying to take over her fortune. When he answers this unspoken objection, promising not to touch her wealth, she is left in the uncomfortable position of having to admit that her initial reluctance was based solely on financial considerations, or else continuing her spirited defense of female freedom. Moll chooses the latter option, arguing until the merchant admits defeat. After she is left alone, Roxana regrets her decision and wishes the merchant back, arguing that no "Woman in her Senses" would ever behave as she did. In these two novels, Defoe seems to be exploring the nature of evil, and it is seen repeatedly as an irrational drive that can deprive its victims of free choice.

In fact, *Roxana* is noteworthy for the ambiguously dark atmosphere that pervades the novel, even apart from Roxana's actions. Although *Moll Flanders* touches on incest, madness, and murder, these seem to be the understandable results of understandable causes: if you do not know your mother, you may marry your brother; if your brother-husband discovers your identity, he may go mad with grief; if you steal from a child, you may contemplate murder to cover up your crime. In *Roxana*, however, many of the characters seem motivelessly malignant, obscurely evil. The midwife whom the Prince hires for Roxana seems so murderous that Roxana has him dismiss her; yet there has been no suggestion in the novel that the Prince intends Roxana harm. On the contrary, he seems delighted with her pregnancy and even spends some time with her during labor. The sexual promiscuity found in *Moll Flanders* turns to sexual perversion in *Roxana*: Roxana's final lover before she goes to live with the Quaker disgusts her "on some Accounts, which, if I cou'd suffer myself to publish them, wou'd fully justifie my Conduct; but that Part of the Story will not bear telling. . . ."

Even the Quaker is an ambiguous figure. Although strictly truthful—Roxana states several times that the woman will not tell a lie—she hardly seems above reproach: she shows a surprising adeptness at bringing together Roxana and her former lover; she knows how to disguise the smell of alcohol on one's breath; she says at one point that she is almost tempted to abandon her sober Quaker attire and wear Roxana's Turkish costume, although the costume by this time has come to be an emblem of Roxana's sinful life.

Perhaps Defoe's darkening vision can best be seen by comparing the conclusions of *Moll Flanders* and *Roxana*. After a life of crime—by which she becomes quite wealthy—Moll is finally caught and sent to Newgate. Sentenced to die, she is instead transported, but not before meeting Jemmy, her Lancashire husband, who has been a highwayman and who also ends up in Newgate. They leave for America together, and since they have enough money to pay the captain of the ship handsomely, they are treated like gentry on their voyage. Once in America, they prosper, only returning to England at the end of the novel, presumably repentant but certainly wealthy from their life of crime.

The uneasy balance of religion and roguery in *Moll Flanders*—Moll's pieties interspersed throughout the work sometimes sound as perfunctory as Crusoe's—shifts in *Roxana*, where Defoe's character finally realizes that one cannot reconcile sin and prosperity in the easygoing synthesis that Moll seems to achieve. The novel ends with Susan's death and Amy's desertion; the final paragraph tells the reader that Roxana and her husband prospered for a while but that a "Blast from Heaven" finally destroyed her tranquility and she ended her days miserably. The abruptness of this conclusion makes for an unsatisfactory ending, but at least it does show Defoe solving the thematic problems inherent in all his earlier novels: Roxana recognizes a higher power but is unable to obey it. Instead of having the best of two worlds—prosperity and religion—she is doomed by a just providence which punishes her unrepentance.

If, like Defoe's heroes and heroines, the reader is given to keeping balance sheets, he could summarize easily Defoe's weaknesses and strengths. On a basic level, Defoe is often slipshod in his handling of narrative: at one point Moll tells the reader how many lovers she has had in her life, but Moll's list of lovers falls far short of the number she mentions in her own narrative. More serious are the thematic problems that Defoe seems to solve only in his final novel. Finally, his realism is quite crude in some places: descriptions of objects assail the reader without having any sensuous reality to them. To Defoe's credit, he is able to establish a convincing conversational tone for most of his characters, and they often have an energy which far exceeds their function as counters through whom Defoe can manipulate his episodic plots. When reading Defoe, however, one does not tend to think in terms of balance sheets. In his best works, the problems in Defoe's writings are so far masked by the vitality of his fiction as to be unnoticeable. Like all artists, Defoe has the ability to make his readers suspend disbelief.

Carole Moses

Other major works

SHORT FICTION: *A True Relation of the Apparition of One Mrs. Veal*, 1706.
POETRY: *The True-Born Englishman: A Satyr*, 1701.
NONFICTION: *An Essay Upon Projects*, 1697; *The Shortest Way with the Dissenters*, 1702; *The Family Instructor, in Three Parts*, 1715; *A New Family Instructor*, 1727.
MISCELLANEOUS: *A General History of the Robberies and Murders of the Most Notorious Pyrates*, 1724-1728 (2 volumes); *A New Voyage Round the World by a Course Never Sailed*, 1724; *A Tour Thro' the Whole Island of Great Britain*, 1724-1727 (3 volumes); *The Complete English Tradesman*, 1725-1727 (2 volumes); *The Four Years Voyages of Capt George Roberts*, 1726; *Augusta Triumphans: Or, The Way to Make London the Most Flourishing City in the Universe*, 1728; *A Plan of the English Commerce*, 1728; *The Novels and Miscellaneous Works of Daniel Defoe*, 1840-1841 (Walter Scott, editor, 20 volumes); *Romances and Narratives by Daniel Defoe*, 1895 (George Aitken, editor, 16 volumes); *The Shakespeare Head Edition of the Novels and Selected Writings of Daniel Defoe*, 1927-1928 (14 volumes).

Bibliography
Backscheider, Paula R. *Daniel Defoe: Ambition and Innovation*. Lexington: University Press of Kentucky, 1986. Argues for Defoe's conscious artistry, seeing a consistency of outlook throughout his writing. Places him at the

beginning of the English novelistic tradition and maintains that the historical novel is among his inventions. A fine survey of Defoe's entire oeuvre, including many pieces generally ignored.

_____. *Daniel Defoe: His Life*. Baltimore: The Johns Hopkins University Press, 1989. Excellent, detailed biography of Defoe. Sets the man and his writings in his political, social, and economic milieu. Includes a full bibliography of Defoe's writing and an extensive bibliography (thirty pages) of works about him from the eighteenth century through the 1980's.

Blewett, David. *Defoe's Art of Fiction: "Robinson Crusoe," "Moll Flanders," "Colonel Jack," and "Roxana."* Toronto: University of Toronto Press, 1979. In Defoe's letters and nonfiction, Blewett finds a worldview that sees the individual as isolated in an indifferent or hostile universe. Shows how four of Defoe's novels artfully voice this outlook. An epilogue considers Defoe's contribution to the development of prose fiction.

Hunter, J. Paul. *The Reluctant Pilgrim: Defoe's Emblematic Method and Quest for Form in "Robinson Crusoe."* Baltimore: The Johns Hopkins University Press, 1966. Examines *Robinson Crusoe* to understand not only that work but also the nature of the early English novel. Looks at the way Defoe used Puritan ideas, especially as they were expressed in seventeenth and early eighteenth century tracts.

Novak, Maximillian E. *Defoe and the Nature of Man*. London: Oxford University Press, 1963. Traces the sources of Defoe's ideas about natural law and then discusses how Defoe demonstrates those views in *Robinson Crusoe, Moll Flanders, Colonel Jack*, and *Roxana*.

_____. *Realism, Myth, and History in Defoe's Fiction*. Lincoln: University of Nebraska Press, 1983. A collection of previously published essays by a leading Defoe scholar. Treats various aspects of Defoe's artistry: the psychological realism of *Roxana*, the use of history in *A Journal of the Plague Year* and *Memoirs of a Cavalier*, and myth-making in *Robinson Crusoe*.

Richetti, John J. *Daniel Defoe*. Boston: Twayne, 1987. A good general introduction to Defoe, with three of the seven chapters devoted to the novels. Includes a useful selective, annotated bibliography.

Shinagel, Michael. *Daniel Defoe and Middle-Class Gentility*. Cambridge, Mass.: Harvard University Press, 1968. A major theme in Defoe's fiction and life is the quest for financial security and social acceptance. Drawing on historical, biographical, and literary evidence, Shinagel explores this aspect of Defoe's writing.

Starr, George A. *Defoe and Spiritual Autobiography*. Princeton, N.J.: Princeton University Press, 1965. Explores the role that religion and religious conversion play in Defoe's fiction, treating *Robinson Crusoe, Moll Flanders*, and *Roxana* as outgrowths of spiritual autobiographies.

Sutherland, James. *Daniel Defoe: A Critical Study*. Cambridge, Mass.: Har vard University Press, 1971. An excellent overview of all of Defoe's work. Offers commonsensical readings of the works and provides helpful historical and biographical background as well as a useful bibliography for further study.

Watt, Ian. *The Rise of the Novel: Studies in Defoe, Richardson, and Fielding*. Berkeley: University of California Press, 1957. Discusses *Robinson Crusoe, Moll Flanders*, and Defoe's contribution to the realistic novel. Relates Defoe's fiction to the social and economic conditions of the age.

Zimmerman, Everett. *Defoe and the Novel*. Berkeley: University of California Press, 1975. Discusses Defoe's six novels in terms of the growing self-awareness of the principal character in each. Also seeks to use the fiction to analyze Defoe.

JOHN WILLIAM DE FOREST

Born: Humphreysville (now Seymour), Connecticut; March 31, 1826
Died: New Haven, Connecticut; July 17, 1906

Principal long fiction

Witching Times, 1856-1857 (published in its entirety in 1966); *Seacliff: Or, The Mystery of the Westervelts*, 1859; *Miss Ravenel's Conversion from Secession to Loyalty*, 1867; *Overland*, 1871; *Kate Beaumont*, 1872; *The Wetherel Affair*, 1873; *Honest John Vane*, 1875; *Playing the Mischief*, 1875; *Justine's Lovers*, 1878; *Irene the Missionary*, 1879; *The Bloody Chasm*, 1881; *A Lover's Revolt*, 1898.

Other literary forms

John William De Forest was interested in history; he began his career as a writer with *History of the Indians of Connecticut from the Earliest Known Period to 1850* (1851). He contributed a number of historical essays to leading magazines such as *The Atlantic Monthly, Harper's New Monthly Magazine*, and *Galaxy*. A few years before his death, he published a family history, *The De Forests of Avesnes (and of New Netherland)*, 1900. His first long work of fiction, *Witching Times*, and his last, *A Lover's Revolt*, are essentially historical novels. He wrote two travelogues (*Oriental Acquaintance: Or, Letters from Syria*, 1856, and *European Acquaintance: Being Sketches of People in Europe*, 1858) and important accounts of his experience in the Civil War (*A Volunteer's Adventures: A Union Captain's Record of the Civil War*, 1946) and in the Reconstruction (*A Union Officer in the Reconstruction*, 1948). He published rather undistinguished poetry (*The Downing Legends: Stories in Rhyme*, 1901, and *Poems: Medley and Palestina*, 1902); much short fiction of uneven quality which has not been published in book form; and a variety of uncollected essays, the title of the best known of which, "The Great American Novel," has become a famous phrase.

Achievements

Gordon S. Haight, who rescued De Forest from oblivion by republishing *Miss Ravenel's Conversion from Secession to Loyalty* in 1939, declared that De Forest was "the first American writer to deserve the name of realist." Bold as that declaration may sound, it follows William Dean Howells's earlier conviction that De Forest was a major novelist but that the reading public did not appreciate him because he did not conform to the literary fashion of his time. Indeed, De Forest's strong and often unvarnished realistic treatment of battle scenes, political corruption, and sexual morals frequently brought him critical acclaim but hardly ever any popularity. Modern criticism tends to be less enthusiastic about De Forest than Howells but does recognize him as an important precursor of literary realism in America. De Forest's personal experience as a Union officer and his evenhanded treatment of both sides of the conflict give a balance, authenticity, and honesty to *Miss Ravenel's Conversion from Secession to Loyalty* that make it perhaps the best novel ever written about the Civil War.

Biography

Descended from Huguenot immigrants of earliest colonial times, John William De Forest was born on March 31, 1826, in Humphreysville (now Seymour), Connecticut. His father was president of a local manufacturing company and in other ways, too, one of the small town's most important citizens; his mother was noted for her strong religious beliefs. Thus, De Forest's background was paradigmatically characteristic of the Protestant ethic, and throughout his entire life he attempted to prove himself worthy of its religion-derived ideology of hard work. An early illness made it impossible for him to attend college; in order to expand his private schooling into an education approximately equivalent to that which he would normally have received at Yale University, and in order to improve his health at the same time, he traveled for some years in the Near East (especially Lebanon, where his brother was a missionary) and Central and Southern Europe. However formative these years abroad were, they did not lastingly restore his health or significantly broaden his ideological perspective. Not healthy enough or temperamentally suited for a career in business but very conscious of having to do something, De Forest decided to become a writer.

After his return from Europe, De Forest met Harriet Silliman Shepard, the attractive daughter of Dr. Charles Upham Shepard, a famous scientist who taught part of the year in Charleston, South Carolina, and part in Amherst, Massachusetts. De Forest's courtship of and marriage to Harriet brought him into contact with the antebellum South, and his firsthand experience of slavery and Southern life made him a more knowledgeable and rational participant in the Civil War than most Union volunteers. He served as a captain in Louisiana and Virginia and, after his discharge, joined the Veteran Reserve Corps with assignments first in Washington and then with the Freedmen's Bureau in the western district of South Carolina. His experience in the war and in the Reconstruction led to his best writing.

De Forest returned to New Haven in 1869 and for a decade attempted to make a living as a writer. He began to realize that the Gilded Age following the Civil War was characterized not by great collective strides toward perfect nationhood but rather by selfish and frequently corrupt business schemes which merely lined the pockets of individual entrepreneurs. De Forest's ideology increasingly came into conflict with his need for royalties: on the one hand, he urged his countrymen in his best though rarely remunerative work—through analysis of regional heritage and through political satire—to fulfill

America's manifest destiny as the leader and hope of the world; on the other hand, in order to survive financially, he tried to cater to the reading public's taste with artistically weak novels, novelettes, and short stories, some of which are little better than formula fiction and pulp literature.

The unresponsiveness of the reading public, the death of his wife in 1878, intermittent financial difficulties, and advancing age made a disillusioned and sometimes bitter recluse of De Forest for much of the remainder of his life. He abandoned his notion of being an intellectual and artistic herald to his country and reluctantly contented himself with writing of essentially private import. A forgotten man and author, he died in New Haven, Connecticut, on July 17, 1906.

Analysis

John William De Forest's works accurately reflect the phases of his ideology, beginning with high optimism about progress, reaching mature though still visionary belief in America's destiny as a light to the world, passing on to disillusionment about and satirical criticism of the actual course America was taking after the Civil War, and ending in melancholy and private resignation over the country's failure to fulfill the American dream.

Although the panic of 1837 lastingly damaged the fortunes of the family business, De Forest's youth saw a period of phenomenal growth in every area of the economy and constant technological inventions and improvements. Intoxicated by the magnitude and rapidity of progress in America, De Forest believed devoutly in the country's future and its mission as the coming leader of the world. While he was alive to the cultural and architectural attractions of Europe and the Near East, he compensated for any feelings of cultural inferiority by noticing and describing in detail the many and varied signs of decadence and decay in the Old World and holding them up for comparison with American progress. His travelogues about Central and Southern Europe and the Eastern Mediterranean reaffirm the worth and superiority of American democracy, just as his *History of the Indians of Connecticut from the Earliest Known Period to 1850* concludes that it was morally right and historically inevitable for white American civilization to have superseded the anachronistic, barbarous mode of living of the native American Indians.

In the development of De Forest's ideology, the moral element is of particular importance for he had been exposed to a religious environment in his childhood. Somewhat later, he read John Bunyan's *Grace Abounding to the Chief of Sinners* (1666) and *The Pilgrim's Progress* (1678) as well as Nathaniel Hawthorne's New England romances (1850-1852). These works tempered his easy belief in progress by their insistence on the moral weakness of all human beings. De Forest began to understand that outward progress was hollow unless it was accompanied by inward progress: it was not only the gross national product that needed to grow but man's soul as well. In his first novels,

Witching Times and *Seacliff*, De Forest outlines the nature of this inward growth and establishes the cultivation of the virtues of the New Testament—faith, hope, and charity—as the moral equivalent of economic progress and as the most important requirement for America's impending role as world leader.

During his courtship of Harriet Shepard and during the first few years of their marriage, De Forest spent considerable time in Charleston, South Carolina. Firsthand observation of the blacks and a realization of the magnitude of the problem that emancipation would present, kept him from becoming an abolitionist; he felt instead that slavery might melt into serfage and finally disappear altogether over a span of six generations. Nor did he consider Southern white society contemptible because of its adherence to slavery: he saw that the system was indefensible, but he also recognized and respected the personal dignity and integrity of high-toned Southerners. De Forest never doubted, however, that slavery had to cease: it was morally wrong; it had been the subject of harsh criticism by the Europeans that De Forest had met during his early travels abroad; and it had become so topical an issue that it might become a real crisis at any time.

The outbreak of the Civil War destroyed De Forest's hopes for a gradual disappearance of slavery, and making a virtue of necessity, he came to see the war as something of a godsend, as an opportunity for America to mend the one great imperfection in the national fabric. The extraordinary sacrifices required by the war could indeed be made to appear sensible only if they served a great end, the unimpeded progress of the United States to human and societal perfection. Yet, De Forest's actual experience in the war and the Reconstruction, together with his interest in the theories of Charles Darwin and Herbert Spencer on biological and societal evolution, confirmed him in his opinion that racial equality in America would be achieved gradually rather than swiftly and that the fostering of individual worthiness and responsibility was the prerequisite for the ultimate realization of a perfect society. The United States, De Forest concluded, had a long way to go after all, and along the way she would need the guidance of the best and the brightest of her citizens.

Accordingly, De Forest developed in his novels from *Miss Ravenel's Conversion from Secession to Loyalty* to *The Wetherel Affair*, as well as in several essays, the concept of the worthy gentleman of democracy. It is particularly noteworthy that this concept is not purely Northern but rather a synthesis of Northern morals and Southern manners. *Miss Ravenel's Conversion from Secession to Loyalty* describes America's breakthrough of a new relationship between North and South, the end of all bitterness, and the renewed hope for a great national future. The essays "Two Girls" and "The 'High-Toned Gentleman'" (1868) suggest ways to draw upon the abilities of the American woman and the high character of the defeated Southerners in the continuing and indeed renewed effort to realize the American dream; "The Great American Novel" of the same year defines the function of the American writer as that of a spiritual goal-setter, leader, and educator of the vast mediocre masses of democracy and thus expresses the same sentiments Walt Whitman would put forward more poetically in *Democratic Vistas* (1871). In *Overland* and *Kate Beaumont*, De Forest turns West and South, back to the days before the war, in search of a heritage to energize the moral and economic progress of the country after Appomattox. He finds this heritage in exemplary men and women who are just as worthy as their Northern postwar counterparts, whom he discusses in *The Wetherel Affair*.

When it appeared, however, that most Americans were interested in more mundane matters than the moral and intellectual progress of civilization, De Forest attacked the rampant political corruption of the Grant Administration and the underlying money-grubbing philosophy of the postwar Gilded Age in two satirical novels, *Honest John Vane* and *Playing the Mischief*. Increasingly, he had to admit to himself that the lofty goal of the American millennium was in reality taking on the shape of the lowly goal of the American millionairium, that the Civil War had in fact opened the way not to moral glory but to materialistic go-getting instead, that the great dream was being perverted to what would become the Horatio Alger myth, and that the worthy gentleman of democracy was being pushed aside by the political boss.

The defeat of his mission also meant De Forest's defeat as a writer. His final works were nostalgic (*A Lover's Revolt*, for example, invokes the glorious spirit of the Founding Fathers through a highly idealized portrayal of General Washington during the early stages of the War of Independence), and they increasingly served only the purpose of De Forest's demonstrating to himself and to the few people who still cared to read him that he himself had at least always attempted and generally managed to follow his ideal of the worthy gentleman of democracy.

De Forest's technical development as a writer seems by and large to parallel the phases of his ideology from youth to old age. As the message of his early writings is overconfident and youthfully chauvinistic, so their technique is imitative and their tone sentimental, melodramatic, and brash. His work of the war years and the early 1870's gives a well-balanced assessment of the state of the nation; personal maturity and significant firsthand experience find their stylistic equivalent in reasoned, realistic, pointed expression which generally frees itself from its literary models and becomes authentic. De Forest's late works stylistically resemble his early ones, except that in keeping with the change from relatively unquestioned belief in the American dream to severe disappointment over its failure, their tone is mostly muted and resigned.

De Forest had begun his career as a writer with a scholarly but ideologically biased *History of the Indians of Connecticut from the Earliest Known Period*

to 1850; he had there ascribed the decline of the Indians to their own weaknesses and had cited the inevitability of progress to justify the takeover by
the white man. The accounts of his foreign travels, *Oriental Acquaintance* and
European Acquaintance, take a sometimes chauvinistically pro-American
stance. His first piece of long fiction, *Witching Times* (serialized but never
published in book form during De Forest's lifetime), returns to an epoch of
American colonial history but draws no racial or international comparisons.
Disturbed by his reading of Nathaniel Hawthorne's *The House of the Seven
Gables* (1851), De Forest investigated the Salem witchcraft trials of 1692-1693,
probing the various layers of sin and evil present in the leading historical
figures of that occurrence. Magistrates such as Stoughton and Hawthorne's
ancestor are shown to corrupt justice, but even greater blame is reserved for
those Puritan ministers who, purporting to do battle for Christ, forget Christian virtue. Elder Parris is a glutton ruled by jealousy and hate; Elder Noyse
is a scheming lecher; Cotton Mather is almost Antichrist because of his pride,
ruthlessness, and excessive ambition. De Forest charges the threesome with
a complete perversion of true ministry.

A group of four characters opposes these perverted Puritan leaders: the
physically and intellectually strong, fiercely independent Henry More; his
daughter Rachel; her husband Mark Stanton; and gentle Elder Higginson.
Henry More strongly resists the witchcraft delusion but has too much of a
temper, too much pride, and not enough understanding of and rapport with
the common people to succeed; on the contrary, he becomes the most prominent victim. Rachel and Mark are more balanced; where More is hopelessly
idealistic and unbending and goes to his death, they are practical without
sacrificing their integrity, and thus they survive. Higginson, however, is the
true minister, who lives and pronounces the book's message, namely that life
and therefore progress must be directed by the three cardinal virtues of the
New Testament: faith, hope, and charity.

De Forest became active in the Civil War as a Connecticut volunteer in
January, 1862, completing his active duty in December, 1864. During that
time, he saw much action in Louisiana and in Virginia. He described his war
experience in a number of articles, short stories, and poems, but most extensively in letters to his family which he later organized into a book manuscript
that was not published until forty years after his death (*A Volunteer's Adventures*). Much of this observation of war entered his novel *Miss Ravenel's
Conversion from Secession to Loyalty*, but it would be erroneous to assume,
as some critics have done, that De Forest wrote the novel in order to give
the reading public a true picture of what war was really like, and that he
added the characters and the love plot only to satisfy the most elementary
formal requirements of a novel of the time. Quite on the contrary, De Forest
insists auctorially that the book is concerned with a great change in the life
of his heroine and that the military aspects of the war are not the book's main

theme.

Edward Colburne is an upright but somewhat shy young man from "New Boston," where he makes the acquaintance of Dr. Ravenel, a scientist and abolitionist, and his daughter Lillie, who have had to leave secessionist New Orleans. Colburne falls in love with Lillie, who has much of the charm and attitude of a young Southern belle, but Lillie is attracted to the dashing, virile Colonel Carter, whom she marries after her return to New Orleans. Carter is a gentleman from Virginia by birth, a West Point graduate, and an officer in the Union army. He is a good soldier but unfortunately has little moral fiber: he swears, drinks, has an affair with a French Creole widow, and embezzles government funds. Not entirely a negative character, Carter has enough integrity to regret his fraud and his unfaithfulness, and De Forest gives him an honorable death on the battlefield.

The course of her marriage, the course of the war, the moral authority of her father, and the devotion of Colburne—which is as steady to her as it is to the Union—ultimately affect Lillie's conversion from secession to loyalty: just as her early adherence to the South changes to an understanding and acceptance of the Union cause, so her private allegiance shifts from the memory of the unworthy Carter to the living presence of the worthy Colburne. Lillie's marriage to Colburne in the end symbolizes the reunion of the repentant and matured South with the forgiving and faithful North. Lillie's and Carter's little boy, who resembles his maternal grandfather, is no hindrance to Colburne but a joy instead: the end of the war also means the end of the sins of the fathers, and no previous errors are held against those whose new life is before them.

De Forest integrates the ideological, military, and amatory elements of his narrative into a convincing whole; *Miss Ravenel's Conversion from Secession to Loyalty* is the summary of a painful but necessary and highly gratifying process of individual and national maturing, at the end of which stands a hard-won reaffirmation of the great purpose and promise of the United States of America as the true and tested leader in the progress of the human race.

De Forest's firsthand experience of the South before, during, and after the war made him understand more fully its strengths and shortcomings. Evaluating these, he gives in *Kate Beaumont* a balanced picture of those Southern elements it had been necessary to destroy and those it was necessary to preserve for the good of the nation.

De Forest's Protestant ethic is offended by the unwillingness of the antebellum planters to work and by their failure to make slavery a truly profitable enterprise. The Southern economic system encourages idleness on the part of the ruling class; idleness in turn leads to vice. The Beaumonts are a typical South Carolina planter family; they are basically good but headstrong and misguided people who have few goals in life. Although two of the young Beaumonts have a professional education, they rarely use it, instead whiling away the day with drink and cultivating the family feud with the McAlisters.

Noble Frank McAlister and sweet Kate Beaumont are De Forest's Romeo and Juliet, except that they finally overcome the barbarian senselessness of the *code duello* by their marriage. Through Kate and Frank but especially through Kate's grandfather Colonel Kershaw, De Forest makes the point that there is much that is admirable about the high-toned Southerner; both Frank and Kershaw are likened to the archetypal American gentleman, George Washington himself, and both are depicted as men of high moral and intellectual caliber. The South's real problem, De Forest suggests, is its frivolity, which in turn stems from a wrong attitude toward work; its great contribution to the nation's fabric is the highly civilized character of the best members of its aristocracy, a contribution much needed to keep the level of democracy high. Frank and Kershaw are more progressive than their relatives; Frank in particular is ready to put his scientific education to use for the economy of the South the moment it becomes acceptable for a gentleman to concern himself with something other than cotton.

Kate Beaumont is an important book primarily because of De Forest's careful analysis of the Old South. He excoriates the weaknesses of the South but also (and more constructively) identifies its strengths and insists upon making them fruitful for the entire nation. Despite the unhappiness of some contemporaneous Southern reviewers, it is hard to deny that De Forest was successful in his attempt to give a fair and balanced view of the Old South. The thematic and analytic merit is matched by the technical quality of the book. It provides an impressive range of realistically drawn characters and situations, including an authentic use of dialect; from William Dean Howells's favorite De Forest heroine Nellie Armitage and her drunken husband to Peyton Beaumont, the reader is given such a comprehensive and forthright picture of the Old South that he cannot help but forgive the sentimentality of the love story.

The indispensability of men such as Edward Colburne or Frank McAlister for the advance of American democracy became painfully evident in the political scandals of the Grant Administration. The Crédit Mobilier affair in particular made it obvious to De Forest that patient persuading of the American public to assert itself against corrupt leadership had to give way to sound scolding. In *Honest John Vane*, De Forest functions in the manner of an irate Puritan preacher who thunders a jeremiad at his stubborn congregation. Modeling his story on Bunyan's *The Life and Death of Mr. Badman* (1680), De Forest chronicles the rise of his title character from unassuming small-town citizen to fraudulent and hypocritical congressman.

Unfortunately, Vane is not an isolated case, nor does De Forest imply that the fault lies solely or even primarily with politics. The real villain is the gullible, plebeian American public that is too comfortable in its moral mediocrity to desire the leadership of the elite. The modern American woman also comes in for severe criticism: Vane's wife Olympia not only does not work, but also spends extravagantly and therefore drives her husband, whose moral bulwarks are weak to begin with, into debt and then into venality. Still, De Forest shows that he has not given up hope; he still believes in the basic soundness of the democratic enterprise and of the American people, whom he expects to clean house, reform, and then continue on their way toward the great national goal, the perfection of the American dream.

Frank Bergmann

Other major works

POETRY: *The Downing Legends: Stories in Rhyme*, 1901; *Poems: Medley and Palestina*, 1902.

NONFICTION: *History of the Indians of Connecticut from the Earliest Known Period to 1850*, 1851; *Oriental Acquaintance: Or, Letters from Syria*, 1856; *European Acquaintance: Being Sketches of People in Europe*, 1858; *The De Forests of Avesnes (and of New Netherland)*, 1900; *A Volunteer's Adventures: A Union Captain's Record of the Civil War*, 1946; *A Union Officer in the Reconstruction*, 1948.

Bibliography

Bergmann, Frank. *The Worthy Gentleman of Democracy: John William De Forest and the American Dream*. Heidelberg, West Germany: C. Winter, 1971. A revision of Bergmann's graduate thesis, this short (112-page) work reads more smoothly than most academic exercises and is useful even to the beginning student of De Forest's fiction.

Gargano, James W., ed. *Critical Essays on John William De Forest*. Boston: G. K. Hall, 1981. Though the twentieth century essays in this collection are mostly aimed at scholars, the rich selection of early reviews, written in De Forest's own time, is a boon to students at any level.

Haight, Gordon S. "Realism Defined: William Dean Howells." In *Literary History of the United States*, edited by Robert E. Spiller, et al. 2 vols. 4th rev. ed. New York: Macmillan, 1974. A compact discussion of De Forest's major works, this essay speaks of him as "the first American writer to deserve the name of realist."

Hijiya, James A. *John William De Forest and the Rise of American Gentility*. Hanover, N.H.: University Press of New England, 1988. There are some intersting references to De Forest's novels in this study, but most of the analysis is biographical and social.

Light, James F. *John William De Forest*. New York: Twayne, 1965. The only book-length study of De Forest not limited to a specific theme, this volume comments briefly on each of his novels. Provides a chronology and an annotated bibliography.

Wilson, Edmond. *Patriotic Gore*. New York: Oxford University Press, 1966. A study of the literature of the American Civil War, this massive work contains a long (107-page) chapter on De Forest and "The Chastening of American Prose Style," one of the most succinct introductions to De Forest in print.

WALTER DE LA MARE

Born: Charlton, England: April 25, 1873
Died: Twickenham, England; June 22, 1956

Principal long fiction

Henry Brocken, 1904; *The Return*, 1910; *The Three Mulla-Mulgars*, 1910 (reprinted as *The Three Royal Monkeys: Or, The Three Mulla-Mulgars*, 1935); *Memoirs of a Midget*, 1921; *At First Sight: A Novel*, 1928.

Other literary forms

Walter de la Mare was a prolific author of poetry, short stories, and non-fiction. Like his novels, de la Mare's poetry and short fiction range from works written explicitly for children (for which he is best remembered) to works intended for adults. Poetry collections such as *Songs of Childhood* (1902) and *A Child's Day: A Book of Rhymes* (1912) reveal his understanding of the pleasures and frustrations of childhood, an understanding that made *The Three Mulla-Mulgars* a favorite with children. De la Mare's poetry for adults embodies his belief that human beings live in two coexistent worlds: the world of everyday experience and the world of the spirit, which is akin to dreaming.

Dreams and the nature of the imagination are frequent themes in both his fiction and poetry. These and other interests are more explicitly revealed in his essays and in his work as an editor. Not much given to analysis, de la Mare was primarily an appreciative critic. Of the anthologies he edited, *Behold, This Dreamer!* (1939) is perhaps the most revealing of the influences that shaped his work.

Achievements

De la Mare published only five novels, one of which, *At First Sight*, is more a long short story than a true novel. His fiction is metaphorical and resembles his poetry in its concerns. Much of what he wanted to communicate in his writing is best suited to short works, and therefore his novels are haphazardly successful. In spite of the difficulties of the novels of de la Mare, his contemporary critics in general had a high regard for him as a novelist. Edward Wagenknecht, an important historian of the novel, ranked *Memoirs of a Midget* as one of the best twentieth century English novels. Indeed, in his essay on de la Mare in *Cyclopedia of World Authors* (1958), Wagenknecht emphasizes *Memoirs of a Midget* at the expense of de la Mare's other writings.

De la Mare's novels, however, were not as widely read in their time as his poetry and short fiction, and today they are seldom read at all. The lack of modern attention to de la Mare's novels is caused less by any absence of merit than by the predictable drop in reputation which many authors undergo in the literary generation after their deaths. Although his novels are unlikely to regain their popularity with a general readership, serious students of twentieth century English literature will almost certainly return to de la Mare's novels as his generation's writings are rehabilitated among scholars.

Biography

No full-length biography of Walter de la Mare has as yet been published. He was, by the few published accounts of those who knew him, a quiet and unpretentious man. One can reasonably infer from the absence of autobiographical material from an otherwise prolific writer that he was a private man. He seems to have lived his adventures through his writing, and his primary interests seem to have been of the intellect and spirit.

He was born in 1873 to James Edward de la Mare and Lucy Sophia Browning de la Mare, a Scot. While attending St. Paul's Cathedral Choir School, Walter de la Mare founded and edited *The Choiristers' Journal*, a school magazine. In 1890, he entered the employ of the Anglo-American Oil Company, for which he served as a bookkeeper until 1908. During these years, he wrote essays, stories, and poetry, which appeared in various magazines, including *Black and White* and *The Sketch*. In 1902, his first book—and one of his most lastingly popular—was published, *Songs of Childhood*, a collection of poetry. He used the pseudonym, "Walter Ramal," which he also used for the publication of the novel *Henry Brocken* in 1904, then dropped. He married Constance Elfrida Igpen in 1899, with whom he had two sons and two daughters. His wife died in 1943.

De la Mare's employment at the Anglo-American Oil Company ended in 1908, when he was granted a Civil List pension of a yearly one hundred pounds by the British government. Thus encouraged, he embarked on a life of letters during which he produced novels, poetry, short stories, essays, one play, and edited volumes of poetry and essays. These many works reveal something of de la Mare's intellect, if not of his character. They reveal a preoccupation with inspiration and dreams, an irritation with Freudians and psychologists in general (too simplistic in their analyses, he believed), a love of romance, and a love for the child in people. The works indicate a complex mind that preferred appreciation to analysis and observation to explanation.

Analysis

Walter de la Mare's novels are diverse in structure, although unified by his recurring themes. *Henry Brocken* is episodic, with its protagonist moving from one encounter to another. *The Return* has all the trappings of the Gothic, with mysterious strangers, supernatural events, and unexplained happenings. *The Three Mulla-Mulgars* is a children's story, with a direct narrative and a clear objective toward which the novel's actions are directed. *Memoirs of a Midget* is Victorian in structure and is filled with incidents and coincidences;

it emphasizes character over the other aspects of novel-writing. *At First Sight: A Novel* is really a long short story, what some might call a novella; its plot is simple, the problem its protagonist faces is straightforward, and it has only the barest attempt at a subplot.

Early in his literary career, de la Mare concluded that there were two ways of observing the world: inductive and deductive. Induction was a child's way of understanding his environment, through direct experience, whereas deduction was associated with adolescents and adults—the environment was kept at an emotional and intellectual distance. De la Mare believed that reality is best understood in relation to the self, and best interpreted through imagination; childlike—as opposed to *childish*—observation is subjective, and childlike imagination can make and remake reality according to the imaginer's desires. Henry Brocken, the eponymous protagonist of de la Mare's first novel, is such a childlike observer. Critics are often confused by his adult behavior; they fail to understand that Brocken is intended to be childlike rather than childish.

Dreams are a part of the human experience that can be made and remade according to the subjective dictates of the self; de la Mare believed that dreams revealed a truer reality than that found in the waking experience. Given de la Mare's beliefs, Brocken's use of dreams to meet with famous literary characters seems almost natural. Brocken is able to converse with characters from the works of such authors as Geoffrey Chaucer, Jonathan Swift, and Charlotte Brontë. The characters are often living lives that were barely implied in their original author's works. Jane Eyre, for instance, is with Rochester long after the conclusion of Brontë's *Jane Eyre* (1847). *Henry Brocken* is about imagination and what it can do to reality. Great literary characters can seem more real than many living people. De la Mare represents this aspect of the imaginative response to literature by showing characters maturing and changing in ways not necessarily envisioned by their creators. Chaucer's Criseyde, for example, is not only older but also wiser than in *Troilus and Criseyde* (c. 1385). What is imagined can have a life of its own, just as dreams can be more alive than waking experience.

The Three Mulla-Mulgars seems to be an interruption in the development of de la Mare's themes of imagination, dreams, and reality. In it, three monkeys—called "Mulgars"—search for the Valley of Tishnar and the kingdom of their uncle Assasimmon. During their travels, the three—Nod, Thimble, and Thumb—have adventures among the various monkey species of the world and encounter danger in the form of Immanala, the source of darkness and cruelty. Although a children's story, and although humorous and generally lighthearted, *The Three Mulla-Mulgars* contains the spiritual themes typical of de la Mare's best work. Nod, although physically the weakest of the three monkeys, is spiritually gifted; he can contact the supernatural world in his dreams and is able to use the Moonstone, a talisman. Immanala is essentially a spiritual force; it can strike anywhere and can take any form; it can make dreams—which in the ethos of de la Mare are always akin to death—into the "Third Sleep," death. The quest for the Valley of Tishnar is a search for meaning in the Mulla-Mulgar's lives; their use of dreams, a talisman, and their conflict with Immanala make the quest spiritual as well as adventurous.

The Return represents a major shift in de la Mare's approach to fiction, both long and short. Before *The Return*, he presented his iconoclastic views in the guise of children's stories and allegories—as if his ideas would be more palatable in inoffensive fantasies than in the form of the adult novel. In *The Return*, de la Mare took an important step toward his masterpiece, *Memoirs of a Midget*, by creating a novel featuring adult characters with adult problems.

The Return seems Gothic on its surface. Arthur Lawford, weak from a previous illness, tires while walking in a graveyard. He naps beside the grave of Nicholas Sabathier, a man who committed suicide in 1739. Lawford awakens refreshed and vigorous, but to his dismay he discovers that his face and physique have changed. Later, a mysterious stranger, Herbert Herbert, reveals that Lawford resembles a portrait of Sabathier, and Herbert's sister Grisel becomes a powerful attraction for Lawford—she seems to be an incarnation of the lover who may have driven Sabathier to kill himself. The plot, when examined by itself, seems trite and melodramatic, yet de la Mare makes the events frightening, in part because he imbues the novel with genuine metaphysical questions and in part because he believes in his story.

Belief is always a problem in fiction, particularly fantastic fiction. Part of what makes hackwork poor literature is insincerity in the author; the author does not believe that his work is valid, important, or worthy of belief. De la Mare clearly believes that the love story in *The Return* is important, that the novel's themes are valid, and that its events can be believed. His sincerity endows the novel's events with poetic power. Thus, the question of Lawford's identity becomes disturbing for the reader: de la Mare is saying that no one's identity is certain. Soon after Lawford's physical metamorphosis, his speech takes on a dual sound, as if he and Sabathier were speaking simultaneously. His conversations with Grisel are discussions between the corporeal Lawford and Grisel and between Sabathier and his past love.

In *The Return*, de la Mare's notions about the human spirit being part of two coexistent worlds are made graphic. Lawford becomes a citizen of everyday reality and of the greater reality of the spirit. He can see the world out of time, past and present; he battles both corporeal and supernatural foes; he is at once Sabathier and an ordinary, middle-aged Englishman. Although a part of two realities, he is accepted by neither. His friends and neighbors want him jailed or locked up in a madhouse; Grisel tells him that he cannot have her, although she shares his love, because he is not free of the burdens of his old world. The dilemma of Lawford, trapped as he is between the two worlds, is representative of the human condition: everyone is trapped between two realities because everyone, whether he chooses to recognize it or not, is spiritual as well as physical. So thick with double meanings and disturbing confusions is *The Return* that its almost too convenient resolution—on All Angels Eve, the night on which Sabathier had committed suicide, Lawford is freed of Sabathier's spiritual tug—is a relief. Lawford is free to pretend that what he sees is all that exists, and so is the novel's reader.

Greeted from its publication with praise for its characterization and graceful prose, *Memoirs of a Midget* is generally regarded by critics as de la Mare's masterpiece. The novel allows multiple readings; most critics readily recognize de la Mare's unusually successful development of a character's point of view, and they note the subtlety of his social commentary, but they often fail to recognize the novel's informing purpose. The story is simple on its surface. Miss M., also known as Midgetina, is a perfectly formed midget. The novel describes her childhood and emergence as an adult. Her point of view as a small adult is carefully created. The bulk of the novel is devoted to her twentieth year, during which she confronts her selfhood and comes to understand that there is a world of the spirit that is greater than the physical one in which she is a social amusement.

The novel has a Victorian flavor, and many of the characters have a Dickensian vitality. One of the most memorable characters is Mr. Anon, a misshapen hunchback who is only a little taller than Miss M. Mr. Anon transforms Miss M. from a social manipulator into a thoughtful person. He loves her—probably, he says, because she is one of the few people close to his size. His ugliness is repulsive, and Miss M. wants to keep him as a friend, but not as a lover. She joins a circus in order to become independent and quickly becomes a main attraction. In order to save Miss M. from possible recognition when Mrs. Monncrie, Miss M.'s former patroness, attends the circus, Mr. Anon takes her place in a pony-riding act. He is thrown from the pony and later dies in Miss M.'s arms. Some critics contend that at Mr. Anon's death Miss M. finally loves him. What is probable is that she believes that his inner self—his spirit—is beautiful and more real than his ugly physical form. Later, Miss M. disappears from a locked room. Her housekeeper, Mrs. Bowater, who commands the only entrance and exit to the room, hears a male voice from within, even though no one had entered through the door. Upon investigation, Mrs. Bowater finds a note which reads "I have been called away."

The character of Miss M. is well suited to de la Mare's purposes. She is small and treated like a child by other characters, and thus her perspective is like that of a child. Reared in seclusion by indulgent parents, she emerges into society with much of her childlike ability to experience the world inductively still intact. She is an adult with an adult's thinking capacity, enabling her to understand as well as know the world. She is an excellent vehicle for de la Mare's ideas about the nature of the human spirit. She observes the best and worst in people, and she sees that the unhappiest people are those who see the world as something to be manipulated, who take without giving. Mr. Anon gives all he has without expectation of receiving what he wants, Miss M.'s love. *Memoirs of a Midget* is more than a story of a social outcast's view of society, it is a depiction of spiritual conflict and revelation.

De la Mare was a seeker, a questioner, and an observer, the endings of his novels are suggestive but provide few answers. A skilled and demanding craftsman, he never failed to entertain his readers, but he employed his storyteller's gift in the service of the lifelong spiritual quest which animated all of his works.

Kirk H. Beetz

Other major works

SHORT FICTION: *Story and Rhyme: A Selection*, 1921; *The Riddle and Other Stories*, 1923; *Ding Dong Bell*, 1924; *Broomsticks and Other Tales*, 1925; *Miss Jemima*, 1925; *Readings*, 1925-1926 (2 volumes); *The Connoisseur and Other Tales*, 1926; *Told Again: Traditional Tales*, 1927; *Old Joe*, 1927; *On the Edge*, 1930; *Seven Short Stories*, 1931; *The Lord Fish*, 1933; *The Nap and Other Stories*, 1936; *The Wind Blows Over*, 1936; *Animal Stories*, 1939; *The Picnic*, 1941; *The Best Stories of Walter de la Mare*, 1942; *The Old Lion and Other Stories*, 1942; *The Magic Jacket and Other Stories*, 1943; *The Scarecrow and Other Stories*, 1945; *The Dutch Cheese and Other Stories*, 1946; *Collected Stories for Children*, 1947; *A Beginning and Other Stories*, 1955; *Ghost Stories*, 1956.

POETRY: *Songs of Childhood*, 1902; *Poems*, 1906; *The Listeners and Other Poems*, 1912; *A Child's Day: A Book of Rhymes*, 1912; *Peacock Pie: A Book of Rhymes*, 1913; *The Sunken Garden and Other Poems*, 1917; *Motley and Other Poems*, 1918; *Flora: A Book of Drawings*, 1919; *Poems 1901 to 1918*, 1920; *Story and Rhyme*, 1921; *The Veil and Other Poems*, 1921; *Down-Adown-Derry: A Book of Fairy Poems*, 1922; *Thus Her Tale*, 1923; *A Ballad of Christmas*, 1924; *Stuff and Nonsense and So On*, 1927; *Self to Self*, 1928; *The Snowdrop*, 1929; *News*, 1930; *Poems for Children*, 1930; *Lucy*, 1931; *Old Rhymes and New*, 1932; *The Fleeting and Other Poems*, 1933; *Poems 1919 to 1934*, 1935; *This Year, Next Year*, 1937; *Memory and Other Poems*, 1938; *Haunted*, 1939; *Bells and Grass*, 1941; *Collected Poems*, 1941; *Collected Rhymes and Verses*, 1944; *The Burning-Glass and Other Poems*, 1945; *The Traveller*, 1946; *Rhymes and Verses: Collected Poems for Young People*, 1947; *Inward Companion*, 1950; *Winged Chariot*, 1951; *O Lovely England and Other Poems*, 1953; *The Complete Poems*, 1969.

NONFICTION: *Rupert Brooke and the Intellectual Imagination*, 1919; *The Printing of Poetry*, 1931; *Lewis Carroll*, 1932; *Poetry in Prose*, 1936; *Pleasures and Speculations*, 1940; *Chardin, J.B.S. 1699-1779*, 1948; *Private View*, 1953.

ANTHOLOGIES: *Come Hither*, 1923; *The Shakespeare Songs*, 1929; *Christina*

Rossetti's Poems, 1930; *Desert Islands and Robinson Crusoe*, 1930; *Stories from the Bible*, 1930; *Early One Morning in the Spring*, 1935; *Animal Stories*, 1939; *Behold, This Dreamer!*, 1939; *Love*, 1943.

Bibliography

Atkins, John. *Walter de la Mare: An Exploration*. London: C. & J. Temple, 1947. A brief but useful analysis of de la Mare's works.

Duffin, Henry Charles. *Walter de la Mare: A Study of His Poetry.* London: Sidgwick & Jackson, 1949. The first full-length critical study of de la Mare's poetry. Unfortunately the repetition and effusive style detract from the main points of criticism.

Hopkins, Kenneth. *Walter de la Mare*. London: Longman, 1954. A brief but excellent overview of de la Mare. Includes a bibliography.

McCrosson, Doris Ross. *Walter de la Mare*. New York: Twayne, 1966. Focuses on his novels as being the clearest statement of de la Mare's vision, giving particular emphasis to his imagination and dreams. McCrosson hopes to correct the popular notion that de la Mare is primarily a children's author. A helpful study, in part because there is so little current criticism on de la Mare.

Reid, Robert. *Walter de la Mare: A Critical Study*. New York: Henry Holt, 1929. An important study of de la Mare that discusses both his prose and his poetry. Also focuses on the later tales, which Reid divides into various groups according to themes, including six tales of the supernatural.

SAMUEL R. DELANY

Born: New York, New York; April 1, 1942

Principal long fiction

The Jewels of Aptor, 1962, 1968; *Captives of the Flame*, 1963; *The Towers of Toron*, 1964, 1966; *City of a Thousand Suns*, 1965, 1966; *The Ballad of Beta-2*, 1965; *Empire Star*, 1966; *Babel-17*, 1966; *The Einstein Intersection*, 1967; *Nova*, 1968; *Out of the Dead City*, 1968; *The Fall of the Towers*, 1970; *The Tides of Lust*, 1973 (originally entitled *Equinox*); *Dhalgren*, 1975; *Triton*, 1976 (originally entitled *Trouble on Triton*); *Empire*, 1978; *Tales of Nevèrÿon*, 1979; *Neveryóna: Or, The Tale of Signs and Cities*, 1983; *Stars in My Pocket Like Grains of Sand*, 1984; *Flight from Nevèrÿon*, 1985; *The Bridge of Lost Desire*, 1987.

Other literary forms

Samuel R. Delany has worked in a number of other literary forms, including those of the short story, autobiography, and, most notably, literary criticism and theory. Delany's short stories have been collected in *Driftglass: Ten Tales of Speculative Fiction* (1971), and some have been reprinted along with new stories in *The Distant Stars* (1981). *Heavenly Breakfast: An Essay on the Winter of Love* (1979) is a memoir describing Delany's experiences as a member of a commune in New York. *The Straits of Messina* (1987) is a memoir based on his travels in the eastern Mediterranean. *The Motion of Light in Water: Sex and Science-Fiction Writing in the East Village, 1957-1965* (1988) is an autobiography covering Delany's youth and the early part of his writing career. Delany has also published a number of important essays on science fiction, some of which have been collected in *The Jewel-Hinged Jaw* (1977) and *Starboard Wine* (1984). In addition to other, uncollected essays, introductions, and speeches, Delany has written *The American Shore: Meditations on a Tale of Science Fiction by Thomas M. Disch* (1978), a structuralist/semiotic study of Disch's short story "Angouleme." Delany has worked in other forms as well: with his then-wife, Marilyn Hacker, he co-edited the speculative-fiction journal *Quark* from 1970 to 1971; he has also written for comic books, including a large-format "visual novel" *Empire* (1978); and has made two experimental films, "Tiresias" (1970) and "The Orchid" (1971).

Achievements

Delany is one of a handful of science-fiction writers to be recognized by the academic community as well as by authors and fans of the genre (he has won both the Hugo and Nebula Awards). Delany has studied and taught at the State University of New York-Buffalo and the University of Wisconsin-Milwaukee and is a contributing editor to the scholarly journal *Science-Fiction Studies*. Unlike mainstream (or "mundane," as Delany prefers) authors such as Walker Percy and John Barth who have dabbled in science fiction, or science-fiction writers such as Kurt Vonnegut who now reject that label, Delany is a vigorous defender and promoter of the superiority of science fiction to other writing. In his criticism as well as in his practice, he has continually stressed the importance of care, thought, and craft in writing. His own work, like that of those writers he most consistently praises (including especially Joanna Russ, Thomas Disch, and Roger Zelazny), is marked by its attention to language and its concern with issues beyond "hard science" and technology, particularly with the roles of language and myth in society and the potential of and constraints on human behavior within different social constructs.

Delany's own background informs these social concerns: he is one of a handful of black science-fiction writers, he is a committed feminist, and he has also come out as a gay writer and parent. His graphic depictions of sex and violence often exceed the usual limits of his genre (he has even published an explicitly pornographic novel). On the other hand, his criticism and his writing have over the years increasingly come together, as Delany has sought to popularize his theoretical interests by publishing them in formats accessible to science-fiction fans and by incorporating them into the very structures of his fiction. While Delany's theoretical stance sometimes alienates those very fans, he must be seen as one of the foremost contemporary writers and critics of science fiction or, indeed, of any type of fiction.

Biography

Samuel Ray Delany was born in Harlem in New York City on April 1, 1942, to an upper-middle-class black family. His father was a prominent Harlem funeral director and was active in the N.A.A.C.P. Delany attended grade school at the prestigious Dalton School, noted for its progressive curriculum and   eccentric teachers and staff. Tensions with his father and a learning disability that would later be diagnosed as dyslexia kept Delany's childhood and teen years from being particularly happy. In turn, though, he was attracted to theater, science, gymnastics (all of which figure in his novels), and especially writing.

Toward the end of his Dalton years, Delany began to write short stories. He also began reading science fiction, including the works of such writers as Theodore Sturgeon, Alfred Bester, and Robert Heinlein. After being graduated from Dalton in 1956, Delany attended the Bronx High School of Science, where he was encouraged in his writing by some of his teachers and by a fellow student and aspiring poet, Marilyn Hacker. After high school graduation in 1960, Delany received a fellowship to the Breadloaf Writers Conference in Vermont, where he met Robert Frost and other professional writers.

In 1960, Delany enrolled in City College of New York but dropped out in 1961. He continued to write, supporting himself as a folksinger in Greenwich Village clubs and cafés. On August 24, 1961, he and Marilyn Hacker were married. Although their marriage of more than thirteen years was open and loosely structured (the couple often lived apart), Hacker and Delany were highly influential on each other as he developed his fiction and she her poetry (Hacker's influence is especially strong in *Babel-17*). Delany submitted his first published book, *The Jewels of Aptor*, to Ace Books, where Hacker worked, at her suggestion. Hacker herself is the model for Rydra Wong, the heroine of *Babel-17*.

Delany's life in New York over the next several years, including his personal relationships and a near nervous breakdown in 1964, figures in a number of his works from *Empire Star* to *Dhalgren*. After *The Jewels of Aptor*, he completed a trilogy, *The Fall of the Towers*, and in 1964 reenrolled at City College of New York, where he edited the campus poetry magazine, *The Promethean*. He soon dropped out again and in 1965, after completing *The Ballad of Beta-2*, went with a friend to work on shrimp boats in the Gulf of Mexico.

At this point, Delany's writing was beginning to return enough to help support him, and, after completing *Babel-17* and *Empire Star*, he used the advance money to tour Europe and Turkey during 1965 and 1966, an experience which influenced both *The Einstein Intersection* and *Nova*. When he returned to the United States, Delany became more involved in the science-fiction community, which was beginning to take notice of his work. He attended conferences and workshops and met both established science-fiction writers and younger authors, including Joanna Russ and Thomas Disch, who would both become good friends. In 1967, The Science Fiction Writers of America awarded *Babel-17* the Nebula Award for best novel (shared with *Flowers for Algernon* by Daniel Keyes), and in 1968 the award again went to Delany, this time for both *The Einstein Intersection* and the short story "Aye, and Gomorrah. . . ."

During the winter of 1967, while Hacker was living in San Francisco, Delany moved in with a New York rock group called The Heavenly Breakfast, who lived communally. This experiment in living, recorded in *Heavenly Breakfast*, is reflected in *Dhalgren*. By 1968, Delany was becoming firmly established as an important science-fiction writer. He had won three Nebulas, had a new book—*Nova*—published in hardcover, had begun to receive critical acclaim from outside science-fiction circles, and had spoken at the Modern Language Association's annual meeting in New York. During the next few years, while working on *Dhalgren*, he devoted himself to a number of other projects, including reviewing and filmmaking. He received the Hugo Award in 1970 for his short story "Time Considered as a Helix of Semi-Precious Stones," and in the same year began coediting, with Marilyn Hacker, *Quark: A Quarterly of Speculative Fiction*. The journal—which published writers such as Russ, Disch, R. A. Lafferty, and others who experimented with both form and content in the genre—ceased publication in 1971 after four issues.

In 1972, Delany worked for D. C. Comics, writing the stories for two issues of *Wonder Woman* and the Introduction of an anthology of *Green Lantern/ Green Arrow* comics. In 1973, he joined Hacker in London, where he continued to work on *Dhalgren* and sat in at the University of London on classes in language and philosophy which profoundly influenced his later writing. Completing *Dhalgren*, Delany began work on his next novel, *Triton*, which was published in 1976.

On January 14, 1974, Hacker gave birth to a daughter, Iva Hacker-Delany, in London. Delany, with his family, returned to the United States late in 1974 to take the position of Visiting Butler Chair Professor of English, SUNY-Buffalo, a post offered him by Leslie Fiedler. At this time, Hacker and Delany agreed to a separation and Hacker returned to London (they were divorced in 1980). Delany completed *Triton* and in September, 1976, accepted a fellowship at the University of Wisconsin-Milwaukee's Center for Twentieth Century Studies. In 1977, he collected some of his critical essays in *The Jewel-Hinged Jaw* and in 1978 published *The American Shore*, a book-length study of a Disch short story.

During the 1980's, Delany spent much of his time in New York, writing, looking after Iva, and attending conferences and conventions. His major project in that decade was the creation of a "sword-and-sorcery" fantasy series, comprising *Tales of Nevèrÿon*, *Neveryóna*, *Flight from Nevèrÿon*, and *The Bridge of Lost Desire*. The impact of the AIDS crisis is seen in the latter two books, especially *Flight from Nevèrÿon*. In 1984, Delany collected more of his criticism in *Starboard Wine* and also received the Pilgrim Award for achievement in science-fiction criticism from the Science Fiction Research Association.

Delany's only science-fiction work in that decade was *Stars in My Pocket Like Grains of Sand*, the first part of a planned "dyptich." (In an afterword to the 1990 paperback edition of *Stars in My Pocket Like Grains of Sand*, Delany announced that the second part of the dyptich—*The Splendor and Misery of Bodies, of Cities*—would probably be completed by 1993.) In 1988, he published his autobiographical recollections about his earlier years in *The Motion of Light in Water*.

Analysis

T. S. Eliot has remarked that a poet's criticism of other writers often reveals as much or more about that poet's own work as about that of the writers being discussed. This observation certainly holds true for Samuel R. Delany, perhaps the most vocal and certainly among the most intellectual of science-fiction author-critics. All too often, science fiction has been regarded by mainstream critics as an adolescent subgenre, a form to be lumped with mysteries, Westerns, and Gothic romances, barely literate and hardly deserving of serious attention. Of course, the genre does have its apologists, whose defense takes many forms. Some treat science fiction thematically and historically, as the latest manifestation of a great tradition of heroic and mock-heroic fantasy and utopian literature, running in a line from the epic of Gilgamesh through Homer's *Odyssey* (c. 800 B.C.) and Ludovico Ariosto's *Orlando Furioso* (1516) and including the works of Thomas More, Jonathan Swift, François Rabelais, and Edward Bellamy. Others take a more pragmatic approach, centered on science fiction as a predictive form, able to explore the implications of new technologies and new social forms, as in the works of Jules Verne, H. G. Wells, George Orwell, and Aldous Huxley. Still others point to the literary merits of an elite handful of science-fiction writers from Wells to Ursula K. Le Guin.

What all these approaches have in common is an assumption that science fiction is a form which can and occasionally does live up to the standards of "true" literature. Delany, though, turns the premises of such critics upside down. Rather than seeking the meaning and value of science fiction by detecting the presence of "literary" elements and properties, Delany insists, the reader and critic must employ a set of "reading protocols" as a methodology for tapping the richness and complexity of science fiction. The protocols one applies to reading science fiction of necessity must be different from the protocols one applies to "mundane" literature, if only in how the reader must constitute whole worlds and universes as background for any narrative.

As an example, first noted by Harlan Ellison, Delany frequently cites a sentence from a Robert Heinlein novel: "The door dilated." Given only these three words, one can make a wealth of suppositions about a culture which needs doors that dilate rather than swing or slide open and shut and which has the technology to manufacture and operate them. The more profound implications of the "protocol of reading" which science fiction necessitates can be seen in another example often mentioned by Delany. In another Heinlein novel, *Starship Troopers* (1959), it is casually revealed two-thirds of the way through the book that the first-person narrator is Hispanic, not white. Placed so casually in the narrative and read in the context of American society in the 1950's—when Delany himself read it—such a revelation must be disruptive, all the more so for a reader such as Delany, who is black. The fact that a society can be imagined in which race is no longer a major factor in determining social position opens to question the social fabric of the society in which the book is read and thereby generates potentials for change. Indeed, it may come as a surprise that requires such a shift in understanding for some of Delany's readers to realize that virtually none of his major protagonists is white.

Such a protocol of reading has the power to affect the reader's reaction to the language itself; Delany's own writing virtually confronts the reader with the need to watch for cues and read carefully for complexity and variety. Mollya, a character in *Babel-17*, explains her desire to aid the heroine, Rydra Wong, by stating. "I was dead. She made me alive." In a mainstream novel, such a statement would be merely a clichéd metaphor. In *Babel-17*, though, Mollya means what she says quite literally: she had been "discorporate" before she was revitalized by Rydra, who needed a new crew member. With this new weight of literal meaning, the cliché is refreshed and itself given new life as a metaphor as well as existing as a factual statement. It is through such potential to refresh the language, Delany suggests, that science fiction is the form of prose which is closest to poetry, even, through its popularity, coming to usurp some of poetry's traditional social functions.

Delany's critical comments and theoretical observations have three effects. First, they are an incitement to the literary critic to accept science fiction as a serious genre. (His essay "Letter to a Critic" was prompted by his offense at Leslie Fiedler's expressed hope that science fiction would not lose its "sloppiness" or "vulgarity.") Second, he has insisted that science-fiction writers give greater care to their art, in the texture of their prose as well as in the precision with which they render their imagined worlds. (His attack on Ursula K. LeGuin's highly praised novel in "To Read *The Dispossessed*" takes the author to task precisely for the book's weaknesses on both counts.) Finally, these observations are above all a comment on the standards which Delany has set for himself.

To read through Delany's novels is to trace the growth and coming to maturity of a literary artist as well as to see the development and mutation of prevalent themes and images. Up through *Dhalgren*, his works usually center on a quest for identity undertaken or observed by a young man (*Babel-17*, with its female hero, is a notable exception). More often than not, the novel's center of consciousness is an artist, usually a writer or musician. These characters themselves are in varying stages of development and their quest usually culminates in their reaching a new level of awareness. In *The Ballad of Beta-2*, the young scholar-protagonist not only discovers behind an apparently trivial piece of space folklore a meaning which will alter humanity's future and knowledge of the universe but also discovers the dangers of glib preconceptions and the value of dedicated work. In *Empire Star*, the young Comet Jo advances from "simplex" to "multiplex" levels of thought in a tale which is also a neat twist on the paradoxes of time travel.

A major concern throughout Delany's career up through *Tales of Nevèrÿon* has been the function of language and myth. The power of language in shaping awareness is the major thematic concern of *Babel-17*. Its heroine, the poet and space captain Rydra Wong (fluent in many languages, including those of body movements) is sent to interpret and discover the source of an enemy alien language, Babel-17. In so doing, she discovers a way of thinking which is highly analytical and marvelously efficient and compact but which is also dangerous—having no concept of "I" or "you," the language can induce psychotic and sociopathic behavior in those who use it.

Myth is employed to varying degrees in Delany's novels, most heavily in *The Einstein Intersection*, *Nova*, and *Dhalgren*—so much so that the three almost form a trilogy of meditations on the subject. In *The Einstein Intersection*, aliens have populated a ruined earth deserted by human beings. Before these new inhabitants can create their own culture, though, they must first act through the myths—from those of Orpheus and Jesus to those of Billy the Kid and Jean Harlow—which they have inherited from humanity. In *Nova*, space captain Lorq von Ray self-consciously sets out on a Grail-like quest for Illyrion, an element found at the heart of exploding stars, in order to change the social and economic structure of the entire universe. In *Dhalgren*, media and rumor elevate characters to legendary status almost overnight. The book effectively examines the disjuncture between myth and experience without denying the reality or validity of either.

Myth reappears in a different form in the Nevèrÿon cycle. Although three of the books—*Tales of Nevérÿon*, *Flight from Nevèrÿon*, and *The Bridge of Lost Desire* (in addition to *Neveryóna*)—are collections of "tales," they have to be read as complete fictions whose individual parts create a greater whole. In fact, the tetralogy can be considered one complete text in itself; however, in keeping with Delany's insistence on the importance of the provisional, the random, and the contradictory as features to be accepted in life and in literature, the parts do not always cohere and may be read in different orders. Myth is the very subject of these writings, inspired in part by Robert Howard's Conan the Barbarian books but also playing with numerous utopian concepts. (The name Nevèrÿon itself—"never/there"—is a play on the word utopia—"no place.") The books themselves are further framed within the context of an ongoing mock-scholarly analysis, "Some Informal Remarks Toward the Modular Calculus" (which actually began as part of *Triton*), suggesting that Nevèrÿon is an extrapolation of an ancient text, possibly the beginning and source of all writing.

In his mature works, from *Babel-17* on, Delany has become increasingly "multiplex" as his characterizations take on new levels of depth and complexity. Delany has moved increasingly to the realization that neither the individual nor society is a stable, unitary entity and that meaning is not to be derived from either or both of these forces in themselves, but from the relationships and interactions between them. This realization is manifested in two images which recur throughout Delany's fiction and criticism. The first is the palimpsest—the inscribed sheet which has been imperfectly erased and reinscribed several times, creating a rich and difficult multilayered text whose meanings may be incomplete and can never be reduced to any one reading.

The Nevèrÿon cycle, as an extreme instance, is a densely layered text that comments on its own narrative, its generic counterparts and origins, and its own composition.

The second image is that of the web, which is multidirectional rather than linear and in which the individual points are no more important than the connections between them. To recognize the web is to understand its structure and learn how to use it or at least work within it, possibly even to break or reshape it. On the literal level, such understanding allows Rydra Wong to break free of a web which straps her down; on the figurative level, recognition of the web allows one to understand and function within a culture. Katin, the protonovelist of *Nova*, comes to realize that his society, far from being impoverished and lacking a necessary center of tradition (a common complaint of modern artists), is actually rich and overdetermined, multilayered, when one looks at the interrelationships of points within the culture rather than at any single point. The fatal mistake of Bron Helstrom, the protagonist of *Triton*, is his inability to recognize the web, his attempt to seek a sense of unitary being which is increasingly elusive instead of accepting the flux and flow which characterize Triton's society. In *Stars in My Pocket Like Grains of Sand*, the Web is the name of the information and communication network that spans the universe, affecting its operations in mysterious ways.

In these images of palimpsest and web, Delany echoes modern thought in many disciplines. Some psychiatrists assert that the individual ego is illusory, a construct to give the semblance of unity to the multiple and conflicting layers of desire and repression which constitute the subject. Anthropologists and sociologists define society by the interactions within its patterns and structures rather than as a unitary and seamless "culture" or even a collection of such cultures. Linguists stipulate that the meanings of individual utterances cannot be determined by isolating individual parts of speech, that in fact the concepts "noun" and "verb" have no individual meaning except in relation to whole statements and the context within which they occur. Finally, post-Einsteinian physics has demonstrated that matter itself is not composed of stable, unitary particles but that atoms and their components are actually "energy packets" whose characteristics and behavior depend upon the expectations of observers and the contexts in which they are observed. Delany is aware of all these intellectual currents, and is in fact a part of this "web" of thought himself; within this pattern of relationships he has set a standard for all writers, whether fantastic or mainstream. Two of the novels that explore the implications of these assumptions are *Dhalgren* and *Triton*.

Dhalgren begins with an archetypal scenario: a young man, wearing only one sandal and unable to remember his name, wanders into Bellona, a Midwestern city which has suffered some nameless catastrophe. In the course of the novel's 880 pages, he encounters the city's remaining residents; goes through mental, physical, and sexual adventures; becomes a local legend; and leaves. In its complexity and its ambitious scope, *Dhalgren* invites comparison with a handful of contemporary novels, including Vladimir Nabokov's *Ada or Ardor* (1969) and Thomas Pynchon's *Gravity's Rainbow* (1973), which make Joycean demands of the reader. Unlike many other science-fiction novels set in a post-holocaust society, *Dhalgren* is not concerned with the causes of the breakdown nor does it tell of an attempt to create a new society out of the ashes of the old. There is no need for such a reconstruction. Bellona's catastrophe was unique; the rest of the country and the world has been unaffected. Separated from outside electronic communication and simply abandoned by the larger society, Bellona has become a center of attraction for outcasts and drifters of all descriptions as well as remaining a home to its own disenfranchised, notably the city's black population. The city has become a place of absolute freedom, where all can do and be whatever they choose, yet it is not in a state of anarchy. There are rules and laws which govern the city, but they are not recorded or codified.

To the newcomer (and to a first reader of the book), these "rules" seem random and unpredictable. Clouds obscure the sky, so that time of day has little meaning, and the days themselves are named arbitrarily. Direction in this city seems constantly to shift, in part because people change the street signs at whim. Fires burn throughout the city, but listlessly and without pattern. When the clouds do part, they might reveal two moons in the night sky or a sun which covers half the sky. The protagonist (who comes to be known simply as The Kid) must define his identity in terms of these shifting relationships, coping with the ever-fluid patterns Bellona offers.

The price of failing to work within the web and to accommodate reality—even an unreal reality—is exemplified by the Richards family, white middle-class citizens who try to maintain a semblance of the life they had known and are going mad as a result. The Kid begins his stay in Bellona by working for the Richards, helping them to move upstairs in their apartment complex, away from a "nest" of "Scorpions," the mostly black street gangs who wander through the city. (The Scorpions themselves are almost as annoyed and bothered by the Richards.) The move is futile—the Richards are no happier or saner in their new apartment, and their son accidentally dies during the move; The Kid is not paid his promised wages (in any case, money is useless in Bellona). Still, the job has helped The Kid to adjust to Bellona's society, and he has begun to write poetry in a notebook he has found. As he nears the end of his job, he finds himself becoming, almost by accident, a Scorpion and eventually the leader of a "nest." His poetry is published, and he becomes, within the city, famous.

The characters and events of *Dhalgren* are rich and detailed enough in themselves to make the book notable. It is Delany's attention to form, though, that makes the book so complex and the act of reading it so disruptive. Not only are the city and its events seemingly random, but the plot and charac-

terization are likewise unpredictable. Questions remain unanswered, few elements are fully resolved, and the answers and resolutions which are given are
tentative and possibly misleading. Near the end of the novel, The Kid believes
that he has discovered his name, but this is never confirmed. He leaves Bellona
at the end of the book, but his fate is left obscure. The Kid is, moreover, an
unreliable center of consciousness. He was once in a mental institution, so
the reader must doubt his perceptions (he unaccountably loses stretches of
time; after his first sexual encounter early in the book, he sees the woman
he was with turn into a tree). He is also ambidextrous and possibly dyslexic,
so that the random ways in which Bellona seems to rearrange itself may be
the result of The Kid's own confusion. At the same time, though, Delany
gives the reader reason to believe The Kid's perception; others, for example,
also witness the impossible double moons and giant sun.

Dhalgren is not a book which will explain itself. A palimpsest, it offers new
explanations on each reading. The Kid's notebook contains observations by
an unknown author which tempt the reader to think that they are notes for
the novel *Dhalgren*; there are minor but significant differences, however,
between notes and text. The last phrase of the novel, ". . . I have come to,"
runs into the first, "to wound the autumnal city," recalling the circular construction of *Finnegans Wake* (1939). Unlike the riverrun of James Joyce's
dream book, though, *Dhalgren* does not offer the solace of such a unitary
construction. The two phrases do not, after all, cohere, but overlap on the
word "to." If anything, the construction of the book echoes the "optical chain"
made of mirrors, prisms, and lenses which The Kid and other characters wear.
Events and phrases within the book do not exactly repeat, but imprecisely
mirror one another. Certain events and phenomena, such as the giant sun,
are magnified as if by a lens; others are fragmented and dispersed, as a prism
fragments light into the visible spectrum.

Ultimately, Delany's Bellona is a paradigm of contemporary society. Within
this seeming wasteland, though, the author finds not solace and refuge in art
and love, as so many modern authors have, but the very source and taproot
of art and love. Delany's epigraph reads, "You have confused the true and
the real." Whatever the "reality" of the city, the book's events, or The Kid's
ultimate fate, "truth" has been discovered. The Kid no longer needs the city,
and his place is taken by a young woman entering Bellona in a scene that
mirrors The Kid's own entrance. Even the "reality" of this scene is not assured,
as The Kid's speech fragments into the unfinished sentences of the notebook.
"Truth," finally, is provisional, whatever is sufficient for one's needs, and
requires to be actively sought and separated from the "real."

Delany's next novel, *Triton*, has some similarities to *Dhalgren* but turns
the premises of the earlier novel inside out. Once again, a protagonist is
introduced into a society of near-total freedom. This time, however, the
setting is an established, deliberately and elaborately planned society on Nep-

tune's moon Triton in the year 2112, and the protagonist, Bron Helstrom, is a worker in "metalogics" for a company (termed a "hegemony") on that moon. Triton is at least as free a society as Bellona—indeed, more so, since people are not only free to behave and live in almost any social, sexual, or religious pattern but also may change their residences, their physical sex, and their psychological sexual orientation almost at will.

In the novel's course, Triton joins with the other Outer Satellites of the worlds beyond Jupiter in a war against Mars and Earth, but Delany subverts one's expectations in his treatment of this conflict. The war involves no soldiers, causes the deaths of millions, and is over quickly; it is also peripheral to the book's main focus, a psychological study of Bron Helstrom. Helstrom, a seemingly normal individual and a recent emigrant from Mars, is out of place on this moon which has a place for everybody. He meets a roaming actress and theatrical producer called The Spike and becomes romantically obsessed with her, but she ultimately rejects him. This rejection, caused by and coupled with Helstrom's narcissism and obsession with correct responses to codes, conventions, and patterns of behavior, drives him deeper into himself. Unable, as he thinks, to find a woman who will suit his ideal, he has a sex-change operation to become that ideal himself, one who will then be available for a man like himself. His (or now her) rules of conduct, though, require complete passivity. Helstrom must wait for the right man and can make no sign to him, so she must wait forever, all the more so because she has falsely idealized a code of "correct" male and female behavior. The end reveals a total solipsism: the one man who could meet Bron Helstrom's standards is himself, just as she is the one woman who could meet his.

Triton is, in its way, an illustration of Gödel's theorem: no logical system is sufficient to explain itself, and thus every system is incomplete and open to paradox. Triton's social system, designed to accommodate everyone (one of its rules even requires a place where no rules apply) still cannot accommodate someone such as Helstrom who, coming from Mars, does not share the presuppositions on which that system is founded. Helstrom's logic of male-female relationships, on the other hand, stems from his failure to operate on Triton's terms and is paradoxical and incomplete within itself too.

Triton, subtitled *An Ambiguous Heterotopia*, is in some ways a reply to Ursula K. LeGuin's *The Dispossessed* (1974, subtitled *An Ambiguous Utopia*). While Triton's society is in certain aspects utopian, offering a nearly ideal model of a future society, that model—like all utopias, including LeGuin's—is insufficient. Thus Delany alludes to the notion of the "heterotopia" advanced by the French philosopher Michel Foucault. In contrast to utopias, which provide consolation, heterotopias disturb and disrupt, refusing to allow things to hold together. Triton can not "hold together" metaphorically or literally. It cannot anticipate a Helstrom; it also may lose its artificial gravity by a random coherence of the subatomic particles in its energy field.

The contradictions of modern American society—tending toward libertarianism on the one hand and repression on the other—are extrapolated into the future interplanetary society of *Triton*. Triton itself is an idealized extension of aspects of Delany's experiences in New York's East Village, San Francisco, and elsewhere in the 1960's and early 1970's. Earth, however, remains mired in its dominant hierarchical, patriarchal culture. Helstrom, from Mars, is sufficiently distant from Earth's culture to be shocked at its brutality and bemused by its adherence to money. Helstrom, though, patterns his own models of sex role behavior on sexist and patriarchal assumptions about the supposedly innate natures of men and women, behavior which is rendered ridiculous by a society in which "male" and "female" are simply categories of choice. It should be noted that in its depictions of Helstrom's behavior, *Triton* is often richly comic.

Delany's probing goes even further. He reminds the reader that *he* is presenting models too. The novel includes two appendices, one a collection of notes and omitted segments from the novel and the other a segment of lectures by a Martian scholar, Ashima Slade, entitled "Some Informal Remarks Toward the Modular Calculus, Part Two." These additions are integral to the novel. They serve to remind the reader that the book is a made object, subject to work and revision, and they also comment on the method of the models provided in the "novel" itself. They also give hints of possible answers to some of the questions raised by the text while raising new ones in turn.

As noted above, the Nevèrÿon series continues Delany's radical examination of narrative formats, in this case the sword-and-sorcery fantasy narrative, through the various tales and plot lines within the four books of the series and through a continuation of the "Informal Remarks Toward the Modular Calculus." In the category of science fiction itself, *Stars in My Pocket Like Grains of Sand* continually tests readers' assumptions. The two major protagonists, Rat Korga and Marq Dyeth—the former an illiterate slave who has become filled with knowledge thanks to technological information devices and the latter a descendant of an ancient family and "industrial diplomat"— become lovers. The reader is uncertain, though, of their genders until well into the novel; both are male, but in this future universe people are usually classed as "women" and referred to as "she" regardless of actual sex, as in English (until recently) "man" has been assumed to refer to humanity in general and "he" could refer generically to men or women. One paradox the book presents is that travel and communication can cut across vast distances between planets and galaxies, thus making the universe a smaller place, while the social complexities and contradictions among differing groups on one planet can make a world a very large place. Marq Dyeth travels to and communicates with different interstellar planets with relative ease; it is much harder, though, for social and practical reasons to travel on his own home planet. Marq's family grouping (and the word "family" is a richly complex term) includes Evelmi, the planet's aboriginal insectoid beings, who are enslaved on the same planet's other hemisphere.

The love between Marq and Rat is complicated by the social and political structures within which they exist. Throughout the inhabited worlds there is a power struggle between two factions, the Family and the Sygn. The Family seeks dominance to impose what a contemporary person might call "traditional moral values"—a restrictive, authoritarian system of beliefs and behaviors. The Sygn is a looser, almost ideally anarchic force; if it gains power, it will avoid the use of power in any social sense. Complicating this contention of forces are the roles of the Web, the information link that connects the planets, and the Xlv, a nonhuman species that is capable of space travel and may have destroyed Rat's home planet. At the novel's end, little is resolved; Marq and Rat have been forcibly separated, the Xlv threaten Marq's planet, and the social issues have yet to reach a peak. It is not even certain that these and other issues will be resolved in the promised second part of the "dyptich," *The Splendor and Misery of Bodies, of Cities*. That book may not be a sequel or continuation of the first, but a complementary portrait, like a second painting in a dyptich. In any event, *Stars in My Pocket Like Grains of Sand* leaves room for many explorations of the rich and dazzling cultures that Delany presents or hints at in addition to the novel's complex narrative threads.

Delany has been referred to in jest by some as the "ultimate marginal writer"—a black, gay, poststructuralist writing in a marginal literary form—but those very margins serve to offer a critique of what is missing in the center and a vision of what could be found there instead. Increasingly, Delany's work has come to stand for openness, diversity, randomness, and the provisional; it opposes closedness and stagnation, hierarchies and fixities. Delany's fiction is a continuing challenge to assumptions about sex, race, and social roles as well as to assumptions about what fiction is and how it should be read. This "marginal" writer is also one of the great writers of our time.

Donald F. Larsson

Other major works
SHORT FICTION: *Driftglass: Ten Tales of Speculative Fiction*, 1971; *The Distant Stars*, 1981.

NONFICTION: *The Jewel-Hinged Jaw*, 1977; *The American Shore: Meditations on a Tale of Science Fiction by Thomas M. Disch*, 1978; *Heavenly Breakfast: An Essay on the Winter of Love*, 1979; *Starboard Wine: More Notes on the Language of Science Fiction*, 1984; *The Straits of Messina*, 1987; *The Motion of Light in Water: Sex and Science-Fiction Writing in the East Village, 1957-1965*, 1988.

MISCELLANEOUS: *Quark: A Quarterly of Speculative Fiction*, 1970-1971 (edited with Marilyn Hacker).

Bibliography

Barbour, Douglas. *Worlds Out of Words: The SF Novels of Samuel R. Delany*. London: Bran's Head Books, 1979. An examination of Delany's full-length fiction through *Triton*. Includes bibliographical references to Delany's works that are otherwise hard to find.

Gawron, Jean Mark. *Introduction to Dhalgren*, by Samuel R. Delany. Reprint. Boston: Gregg Press, 1977. Gawron's forty-three-page introduction to this edition is an excellent starting point for readers wishing to deal with the complexities of Delany's longest single work. The Gregg Press reprint series includes textually accurate hardbound editions of Delany's major works through *Triton*. The introductions by various critics and scholars are especially helpful.

McEvoy, Seth. *Samuel R. Delany*. New York: Frederick Unger, 1984. An accessible overview which concentrates on Delany's work through *Dhalgren*, though some later works are discussed briefly. Emphasizes the impact of Delany's dyslexia on his development as a writer and corrects some biographical inaccuracies in earlier critical studies. Includes sketchy notes; the bibliography merely consists of a listing of Delany's books in print as of 1983, though it does refer the reader to Peplow and Bravard's bibliography (see below).

Peplow, Michael W., and Robert S. Bravard. *Samuel R. Delany: A Primary Bibliography, 1962-1979*. Boston: G. K. Hall, 1980. This exhaustive bibliography is the best starting reference book about Delany's early life and career. The introduction includes a lengthy biographical sketch, and the primary and secondary bibliographies list virtually all writings by and about Delany up to 1979.

Slusser, George Edgar. *The Delany Intersection: Samuel R. Delany Considered as a Writer of Semi-Precious Words*. San Bernardino, Calif.: Borgo Press, 1977. This sixty-four-page pamphlet briefly discusses Delany's early work, particularly *Nova*, from a structuralist perspective. The comments on his later work, including *Dhalgren* and *Triton*, are very brief and negative.

Weedman, Jane. *Samuel R. Delany*. Mercer Island, Wash.: Starmont House, 1982. This work, adapted from Weedman's doctoral dissertation, discusses Delany's work through *Dhalgren*, with emphasis on the biographical and social elements in his fiction. Includes annotated bibliographies of Delany's fiction and secondary works about him.

DON DeLILLO

Born: New York, New York; November 20, 1936

Principal long fiction

Americana, 1971; *End Zone*, 1972; *Great Jones Street*, 1973; *Ratner's Star*, 1976; *Players*, 1977; *Running Dog*, 1978; *The Names*, 1982; *White Noise*, 1985; *Libra*, 1988; *Mao II*, 1991.

Other literary forms

Although Don DeLillo's major literary efforts have centered on the novel, he has contributed short stories to periodicals including *The New Yorker*, *Esquire*, *Sports Illustrated*, and *The Atlantic*, and has written several plays.

Achievements

The publication in 1971 of DeLillo's first novel, *Americana*, launched the career of one of America's most innovative and intriguing writers. DeLillo produces satirical novels, novels that drill into and hammer at the chaos of modern society, the lack of coherence and order in institutions, the breakdown of personal relationships, and particularly the failure of language in the world today. He writes a driving, mercurial, upbeat prose that at times smacks of an idiosyncratic pedantry yet abounds in lyricism and musicality. Some readers have labeled his prose "mandarin," after the fashion of Donald Barthelme and Thomas Pynchon. Pynchon definitely influenced him, but DeLillo pushes far beyond the limits of imitation or even derivation and asserts a truly independent voice. The promise of prodigious talent inherent in his first novel has flowered in the later works. In 1984, the American Academy and the National Institute of Arts and Letters presented to DeLillo their Award in Literature. DeLillo's novels, although often criticized as plotless disquisitions that never produce anything but comic-strip characters, nevertheless stimulate and excite readers with their musicality, their rhetorical rigor, and their philosophical depth.

Biography

Don DeLillo was born in New York City in November of 1936. He spent his childhood and adolescence in Pennsylvania and the South Bronx. After studying at Fordham University, he lived for a while in Canada and then returned to New York, where he has lived ever since.

Analysis

What little there is of traditional narrative structure in the Don DeLillo novel appears to serve principally as a vehicle for introspective meanderings, a thin framework for the knotting together of the author's preoccupations about life and the world. Thematically, each novel is a profound reworking of the familiar precepts that make up the core of his literary belief system. This basic set of ideas includes the function (misfunction) of language as it relates to being, the absurdity of death and the meaning of apocalypse, the complications and chaotic workings of societies (particularly governments and institutions), the ontological purity of women and children, the notion of sacred spaces, and the interrelatedness of time, history, and myth. DeLillo's great facility with a language perfectly tuned for irony and satire allows him to range the breadth and depth of these themes.

All these thematic strains are present in *Americana*. The problem of language and meaning finds a penetrating focus in the conversation between the protagonist, David Bell, a dissatisfied minor network executive who seizes upon a documentary assignment to make a cross-country odyssey of self discovery, and Carol Deming, a distracted yet aggressive young actress who reads a part for David's film: The encounter is set up to be sexual but proves to be nothing more than a bizarre verbal tryst, a duel of wacky hyperbole laced with sarcasm. Beneath the words fired rapidly back and forth between David and Carol, there are the levels of behavior and intensity normally associated with seduction. In this case, words appear to substitute for the great diversity of emotional responses associated with the sex act. The reader, however, knows that verbal intercourse is no substitute for sexual intercourse and commiserates with David on his lack of fulfillment; words are false images that can be made to disguise the multilayered nature of reality. In the end, however, the word is destroyed by the meaning it tries to mask.

This verbal affair takes place in the middle of America, in a town called Fort Curtis, the designated location for the filming of David's documentary. He has been commissioned to film the Navajo Indians but decides that the town will be the backdrop for a film about the central moment of his own childhood, the moment he learned that his mother, for him the bastion of health and security, would soon face disintegration and death. Each stop on his "sacred journey" out West holds a numinous attraction for him: the starting point, the chaotic craziness of the network office with its mad memo writer; the garage of Bobby Brand (a friend who uses his van for the trip); Fort Curtis; and ultimately Rooster, Texas, where David's pilgrimage of self-exploration ends in a boozy orgy in the dust. In Fort Curtis, David hires local people to read absurd lines and then has traveling companion Sullivan, an enigmatic sculptor, play the part of his mother on the day he learned, in the pantry of his parents' home, the tragic truth that women were not what he expected and wanted them to be: They cannot be held as an anodyne against the fear of death. In David's hands, the camera has the power to create from the union of a special place and a particular moment an image that is again an illusion of reality. When he later tries to make a created image real (that is, make Sullivan a real mother figure by having her tell him a precoital bed-time story), he is again instructed in the misalignment between images and the world. DeLillo, by constantly emphasizing the impossibility of the world's true representation in time and place via the word (history), mythologizes his characters and frees them from the bounds of historicity.

One of these mythic characters, Myna Corbett, appears in *End Zone*, the one DeLillo novel that most of the author's critics agree is a brilliant piece. Myna, a student at Logos College in West Texas, is typical of DeLillo's female characters: She is big, carrying 165 pounds, which she refuses to shed because of her desire not to have the "responsibility" of being beautiful; she fills her mind with trivial matter (she reads science-fiction novels); and she has large breasts in which Gary Harkness, the protagonist, hopes to find sol-ace from the world.

Gary is a talented but eccentric footballer at Logos College who, because of his strange behavior, has been cut from the team rosters of larger institu-tions such as Penn State and Syracuse. He does not change his ways at Lo-gos, walking off the field during the last game, high on marijuana and very hungry. He has a fascination with war and audits the Reserve Officers' Train-ing Corps classes that have to do with mass killing strategy. When Colonel Staley asks him to become a cadet, Gary refuses, saying that he wants only to fantasize about nuclear war. He enjoys playing nuclear destruction games with the colonel, but he will not prepare himself to become an Air Force offi-cer: He will not drop real bombs.

When not engaged in his graphic war daydreams, Gary is either playing football, an abstraction of war, or having picnics with Myna. If war is or-ganized, palpable death, then Myna must be its opposite, an image of life and a defense against the fear of death. The tension between women (as the word or image of antideath) and harsh reality finds expression in the scene in which Gary undresses Myna in the library stacks. He says to himself that it is important to have her completely nude in the midst of the books containing millions of words. He must see her as the word (the image of harmless, uncomplicated femaleness) made flesh. He wants to see Myna, as the em-bodiment of the illusion of safety that words give, appear to belie the truth behind the image, the truth that women are not immune from the dread of death and therefore cannot offer the security that he seeks. He does not want to confront the mystery and lure of feminine beauty: He is upset when Myna loses weight. When she returns from vacation slender, it is he who does not want the responsibility of Myna's beauty. Women's love can lead to death and words can have deadly connotations.

DeLillo further explores his themes dealing with language, death, women, and time in *Great Jones Street*, the story of a rock star, Bucky, who grows tired of the business, leaves his band in Houston, and returns to a hovel of an apartment in New York City. There his seclusion is destroyed when Skippy, a hippie girl, leaves with him a box full of a special kind of dope that is untested but is thought to be extremely powerful, and therefore of great interest to the drug people. The rest of the novel focuses on the many people who want to get the drugs. One of the agents sent for the drugs is Opel, who eventually dies in Bucky's bed. She is only an image of a living woman as she lies in the bed; the anti-image, death, is the reality of her being there. When she dies, Bucky can contemplate only her dead self; once people leave one extreme of being, they must become the other.

Bucky tries to make his apartment a refuge from the relentless roll of time and the world. He talks into a dead phone, stifling any possibility that words can reach their destination and complete the communication process. He refuses to wind the clock, hoping to arrest time, that hard reality that lies beneath the illusory image of stasis. Opel, although safe in bed in Bucky's timeless, wordless (telephoneless) world of the apartment, dies nevertheless.

The song that has made Bucky famous, "Pee-Pee-Maw-Maw," provides grist for another favorite DeLillo theme, that children, because of their few years, have no thoughts or fears of dying and therefore are immune from death. Bucky sings in the simple, life-giving syllables of children. The Mountain Tapes, traded for the drugs by a boy named Hanes, bring the same release as do the drugs in the box: They reduce language to nonmeaning. Later, when Bucky is injected against his will with the drug, he loses the power of speech; he is silent. Childish babble and wordlessness are equated with a loss of the fear of death and consequently, a loss of humanity. Only humans fear death, says Bucky.

A child is the central character in *Ratner's Star*, a dense and overly long novel about the shortcomings of modern science. Billy, a fourteen-year-old mathematical genius who has just won the first ever Nobel Prize for Mathematics, is called to a futuristic think tank to help decipher a signal presumed to be a communication from Ratner's Star. The boy eventually finds the answer: The pulses of the message are really from the Earth as it existed long ago. The meaning of the mathematical "words," the exact time of day as Billy looks at the clock on the wall (and coincidentally the exact time as an unscheduled eclipse of the sun), is that the secret of all knowledge is what one has at a particular place at the present time. All the supposed power of the modern scientific community can be reduced to the utter simplicity of the time of day in a child's room on our own planet in our own time. When a spontaneous heavenly movement takes place, it is announced first to the child's mind.

The adult scientists with whom Billy is obliged to interact by their utter egregiousness offer DeLillo myriad openings for the insertion of his biting satirical barbs. Endor, for example, the world's greatest mathematician, has given up solving the mystery of the pulses and has gone to live in a mud hole, living off worms and roots which he digs from the ground. Fitzroy-Tapps, the rat-talk scholar, hails from Crutchly-on-Podge, pronounced Croaking-on-Pidgett. Hoy Hing Toy, the obstetrician who once ate a newborn placenta; Grbk, who has to be officially reprimanded for showing his nipples to young children; and Armand Verbene, S.J., a practitioner of red-ant metaphysics, are representative of the resident staff. Of these bizarre characters, one in particular provides DeLillo with an excellent opportunity to hold forth on the meaning of language. Young Billy, a Nobel laureate by virtue of his having conceived the mathematical notion of the zorg (an entity reduced as far as it can be—that is, to nothing), confronts the astronomical mind of Lazarus Ratner. It is necessary to say that Billy confronts the "mind" of Ratner, because that is practically all that is left of the man. He is kept from collapsing in on himself by constant silicone injections, and his bodily functions are kept going mechanically inside a protective bubble. Billy sits astride the biotank, talks to Ratner (who will speak to nobody but the child), and translates what the great scientist says for those who stand near.

DeLillo uses this conversation between the old man and the boy to explore provocative notions about language, knowledge, and God. Ratner tells the boy about the Cabala: The hidden and unknowable name of God is a literal contraction of the superdivinity. The contraction of divine anti- or other-being, *en sof*, makes possible the existence of the world. Being (God) is somewhere on a spectrum between light and darkness, something and nothing, between an integer and a zorg, in Billy's mathematical code. Divinity (pure being) is revealed in the expansion of matter. As the universe expands, human beings, as part of that expansion, come into existence. Existence, then, is like the birth and death of stars, says Ratner: It is manifested with the expansion and perishes with the contraction of its mass. Thus, as elements, or *sephiroth* of the primal being, humans are like tiny sparks of Ratner's Star. Human names, the words that equate with human existence, are merely artificial and abstract images of a constant expansion and contraction. Real being consists of the flux and levels of being behind the image.

Billy puts this theory into simple, incomplete terminology which, complains Ratner, is not fully expressive of the reality of that which is being communicated. Here again is the old problem: Words, as images of reality, cannot possible convey the entire dimension of the meaning of the world. Those who listen to Billy as he interprets Ratner are able to glean only a small portion of the content of Ratner's words.

Of the later novels, *The Names* and *White Noise* offer the most moving and powerful treatment of DeLillo's recurring themes. *The Names* features the decay of the typical American marriage. James and Kathryn are married, have a son named Tap, and live happily for a time on an island in the Eastern United States. They live peacefully until the bright image of marital bliss splinters, broken into a multileveled subset of hard problems, the first of which is separation. Kathryn, yielding to the fascination for digging in the ground in search of lost messages, commits herself to a life of archaeological digging. She joins an excavation site on an island in Greece; James, wanting to be near his fractured family, gets a job in Greece as a so-called risk analyst. Even though this bit of darkness has tarnished the core of the little family, they live on a reasonably even keel until archaeologist Owen Brademas begins an investigation of a cult of hammer killers. These cultists occasionally pound to death a chosen victim who happens to wander into a town, the initials of whose name match the initials of the victim's name: For example, they kill Michaelis Kalliambestos as he enters Mikro Kamini. Brademas, whose profession it is to find and translate ancient script written in stone, really is more interested in the cabalistic power of the alphabet as it is combined and recombined to reveal the hidden names of God. He finds the Names, as the members of the hammer cult refer to themselves, becomes one of them in spirit, witnesses a ritual hammer murder (death comes to him who finds, even if by accident, correspondence in letters and reality), and then retires to read stones and live unmolested in his final sacred place, a hotel room in Bombay. Owen Brademas seems to be merely a mythic extension of an innocent, babbling language spoken by Kathryn and her sister as children, and used by Kathryn and her son: The language inserts the syllable "ob" among the syllables of real words to create a special code. The initials of wordmonger Owen Brademas' name happen to be O.B. OB seeks the meaning of alphabetic combinations even when they lead to death: He is the one who figures out the workings of the Names. In many ways, he is the shadow image of her husband, a writer, who lives by the combinations of words and who follows Brademas in search of the cult. James finds his place of revelation in a Roman ruin just as Brademas finds his in a hotel room. Brademas is also an alter ego of Kathryn, who seeks hidden wisdom by a kind of mindless digging at the site, yet he takes archaeological inquiry to the ultimate degree and ends in a room with nothing but ordered space, a perfect stasis, a state much like death.

In the same way, James's job is nothing but a cover for a CIA operation. His image of a harmless and rather pleasant way of life in Greece is destroyed: He experiences a dark underside of intrigue and deception. It seems that the surface of daily life can never remain innocuously in place; there is always a seepage of antilife. His wife and profession appear to be entities resting on shifting sands; only his son, the child, who writes away at a nonfiction novel, can be counted on for authenticity.

White Noise is a thematic duplicate of *The Names*. The characters are cartoons. Babette is the physically large wife to whom Jack Gladney, her husband, looks for a peaceful domestic life totally removed from danger. Babette, also called Baba, appears to be very capable of fulfilling her husband's needs: She is the perfect image of easygoing housewifery. She volunteers for community service, she shops constantly in the supermarket, and she lovingly cares for the children. The children are precocious and serious-minded. Heinrich, the oldest boy, seems to know much more than his father, a college professor, about the real world. The girls, especially Denise, are concerned about Babette's health, hiding her drugs and looking for hidden habits that might bring her danger or death. Husband and wife, lost in triviality, make inconsequential or erroneous statements, while the children speak with precision and maturity. There is a reversal in the parent-child roles; these children, therefore, are not as innocent as the typical DeLillo child figure. Only Wilder, the baby, embodies the ideal of the deathless child hero: At the end of the novel, he rides his tricycle into the street, across a four-lane street teeming with speeding vehicles, into the grass of the opposite shoulder, miraculously escaping death.

Babette crumbles as the symbolic shield against fear; she is exposed as a woman so terrified of death that she trades sex for a special kind of drug that causes one to forget about the fact that one must die. She takes these pills on the sly and is finally found out by her snooping family. Jack has been happy with Babette because she is open and guileless, unlike his previous wives, who were mysterious, complicated secret agents who worked for the CIA. His illusion is destroyed when he finds out about her pills. Her complicity in this kind of intrigue reinforces his recently discovered vulnerability to death (a physical examination has revealed that his exposure to the toxic chemical spill may leave him only a short time to live). Even Baba, the large, comfortable, unbeautiful, unmysterious, faithful wife, who has consoled Jack as he has lain with his face between her large breasts, proves to be full of duplicity and treachery.

This complication leads Jack to reflect on what Murray Siskind, a fellow faculty member, has told him regarding death; death, says Siskind, can only be purged by killing. Jack has already intuited this precept on his own: His success as a professor of "Hitler studies" (which he established as a full-fledged academic discipline) depends in part on his awareness of the peculiar fascination of the Nazis. Ultimately, Jack shoots Willie Mink, a seedy drug dealer who dispenses death-forgetting pills to women in exchange for sex. He enjoys the bleeding of his wife's seducer for a while but then has pity on the mindless Mink, a victim of his own pills, and drags him by the foot to a hospital. The nuns who attend the wounded man destroy the last great image of security that Jack has left: Jack learns that those whom he had always thought of as sainted women, women firm in their faith that death's dominion has been crushed by the resurrection of Christ, have no more faith in salvation than he, his wife, or anybody else. The white noise of death silences any voice that would offer human beings a verbal sanctuary from its assault.

DeLillo followed *White Noise* with *Libra,* a novel about the assassination of President John F. Kennedy; atypically for DeLillo, the novel enjoyed a run on the national best-seller lists while winning critical acclaim. *Libra* is, in a sense, two novels in one. It is, first, a fictional re-creation of the assassination and the events leading up to it. In the book's opening pages, and at intervals throughout, the reader shares the consciousness of Lee Harvey Oswald. From Oswald's point of view and many others as well, DeLillo constructs his scenario of this still-enigmatic and much-disputed moment in American history. While DeLillo's version departs from the conclusions of the Warren Report (he posits a second gunman and a fortuitous confluence of conspirators, including rogue CIA agents and Cuban exiles who want Fidel Castro overthrown), much of the speculation is grounded in the public record.

At the same time, *Libra* is a novel about the making of fiction and, more broadly, about the way in which people make sense of their lives. The novelist's alter ego is Nicholas Branch, a retired senior analyst for the CIA, hired by the agency in the 1980's to write the "secret history" of the assassination. This device allows DeLillo to sketch for the reader the process he went through in order to re-create happenings of the 1960's: sifting through the incredible profusion of evidence (he describes the twenty-six-volume Warren Report as "the Joycean Book of America, . . . the novel in which nothing is left out"), discovering strange patterns of coincidence. Novelists and conspiracy theorists, DeLillo suggests, are in the same business.

Not unlike many other writers, Don DeLillo writes the same novel over and over, each time with a bit more force in the dissection and probing of the human spirit. For this reason, the later novels seem more sinister and joyless than the earlier ones. Yet he writes with such brilliance that one never tires of his reiteration of theme. Reading DeLillo continues to be a delightful experience.

Watson Holloway

Other major works

PLAYS: *The Engineer of Moonlight*, 1979; *The Day Room*, 1986; *A Visit from Dr. Bazelon*, 1986.

Bibliography

Bosworth, David. "The Fiction of Don DeLillo." *Boston Review* 8, no. 2 (1983): 29-30. A scholarly review comparing *The Names* to DeLillo's previous work. Bosworth sees DeLillo as a "keen chronicler of our fragmentary existence" and refers to him as an author with driving purpose and ambition.

Bryant, Paula. "Discussing the Untellable: Don DeLillo's *The Names.*" *Critique: Studies in Modern Fiction* 29 (Fall, 1987): 16-29. Discusses DeLillo's avocation of language in his novel *The Names.* Bryant cites DeLillo as a writer who uses "idiosyncratic expression within the existing language system." Well worth reading; Bryant writes with knowledge and confidence.

Johnson, Stuart. "Extraphilosophical Instigation in Don DeLillo's *Running Dog.*" *Contemporary Literature* 26 (1985): 74-90. In this study, Johnson relates DeLillo's *Running Dog* to Wittgenstein's theories of language and context, where meaning is essentially immediate rather than analytic. Gives another angle to the wealth of information available on DeLillo's use of language.

LeClair, Tom. *In the Loop: Don DeLillo and the Systems Novel.* Urbana: University of Illinois Press, 1987. Currently the only study devoted solely to DeLillo's work and therefore a valuable resource. LeClair argues for placing DeLillo in the genre of what he calls the "systems novel." Compares postmodernists with systems theory novelists, whom he applauds as being concerned with regeneration rather than deconstruction. LeClair's lively study contains a bibliographical checklist, including a useful list of titles on systems theory.

Nadeau, Robert L. "Don DeLillo." In *Readings from the New Book on Nature: Physics and Metaphysics in the Modern Novel.* Amherst: University of Massachusetts Press, 1981. Nadeau's study closely examines DeLillo's novels up to *Running Dog* in the context of the new physics. Discusses how DeLillo's work, in turning away from closed systems to a more "primal awareness," approaches the immediate function of the word.

Oriard, Michael. "Don DeLillo's Search for Walden Pond." *Critique: Studies in Modern Fiction* 20, no. 1 (1978): 5-24. According to Oriard, DeLillo is recording the "modern American's futile search for the mystery of existence," a vision of life that upholds chaos rather than order. Discusses DeLillo's fifth novel, *Players*, and its acceptance of ambiguity rather than embracing the simplistic harmony of *Walden*.

ANITA DESAI

Born: Mussoorie, India; June 24, 1937

Principal long fiction

Cry, The Peacock, 1963; *Voices in the City*, 1965; *Bye-Bye, Blackbird*, 1971; *Where Shall We Go This Summer?*, 1975; *Fire on the Mountain*, 1977; *Clear Light of Day*, 1980; *In Custody*, 1984; *Baumgartner's Bombay*, 1988.

Other literary forms

Anita Desai is a well-known short-story writer as well as a novelist. Her first story was published in 1957, when she was twenty years old. Since then, she has contributed stories to magazines and periodicals such as *Envoy* (London), *Quest* (Bombay), *The Illustrated Weekly of India* (Bombay), and *Miscellany* (Calcutta). A collection of short stories, *Games at Twilight and Other Stories*, appeared in 1978. Desai has written three books for children, *The Peacock Garden* (1974), *Cat on a Houseboat* (1976), and *The Village by the Sea: An Indian Family Story* (1982). Finally, she has written a few articles, sketches, and reviews for some of the periodicals mentioned above.

Achievements

Desai is one of the more prominent contemporary Indian English novelists. With her first novel, *Cry, The Peacock* (1963), she added a new psychological dimension to Indian English fiction. Desai is probably the first Indian English novelist to be primarily concerned with the inner life of her characters—their fleeting moods, wisps of memory, subtle cerebrations. In her novels, Desai succeeds in capturing these evanescent moments of consciousness, preserving them from oblivion and investing them with the permanence of art. The result is that Desai not only creates something of value for herself out of the endless flux of her own psyche, but also provides for her reader an opportunity to share this rich inner life through her characters.

Desai's stylistic accomplishment is noteworthy as well. Unlike many other Indian English novelists, she does not find it necessary to experiment with language. In her novels, no clash between English, her medium of expression, and the Indian subject matter is apparent. Indeed, her use of the language is natural and unself-conscious. Her writing is both supple and precise. Though each sentence is carefully crafted, the overall manner is easy, not precious or labored. Stylistically, Desai is thus in the mainstream of twentieth century English novelists.

With her novels, books for children, and collection of short stories, Desai is a writer of considerable achievement, perhaps the best contemporary Indian English woman novelist. Critical interest in her work has steadily grown since her first novel was published. Desai received the Royal Society of Literature Winifred Holtby Prize in 1978 and the Sahitya Akademi of India Award in 1979; she has been a member of the Sahitya Akademi English Board since 1972 and a fellow of the Royal Society of Literature since 1978.

Biography

Though born in Mussoorie, Anita Desai grew up in Delhi. Her father, D. N. Mazumdar, was Bengali, a businessman, and her mother, Toni, was German. Desai's mother met her father when the latter was a student in Germany. They were married and then moved to India in the late 1920's. As a child, Desai spoke German at home and Hindi to her friends and neighbors. She then learned English once she started school. She grew up during the war years of the late 1930's and the 1940's, sensing the anxiety in her mother about the situation in Germany. Fearing the devastation and change wrought by World War II, Desai's mother never returned to Germany, probably inspiring some of the facets of the character Hugo Baumgartner in *Baumgartner's Bombay*.

Desai was educated at Queen Mary's School, Delhi, and then at Miranda House at the University of Delhi. At Miranda House she studied English literature, receiving her B.A. in 1957. Her studies helped to fuel her passion for writing, a compulsion which began at the age of seven. After working for a year in Max Muller Bhavan, Calcutta, she married Ashwin Desai, a business executive, in 1958. Since then, she has lived in Calcutta, Bombay, Chandigarh, Delhi, and Pune. She has four children, Rahul, Tani, Arjun, and Kiran.

Desai's work is respected worldwide. In Great Britain, she was Visiting Fellow at Girton College, Cambridge, in the late 1980's, during which time she wrote *Baumgartner's Bombay*, and both *Clear Light of Day* and *In Custody* have been short-listed for the prestigious Booker Prize. She has taught writing at both Smith and Mount Holyoke colleges in the United States.

Analysis

Anita Desai's novels reveal certain recurring patterns in plot, setting, and characterization. The plots of her novels fuse two opposing propensities—one toward the Gothic mystery, and the other toward the philosophical novel. The Gothic orientation, which Desai probably derived from Emily Brontë's *Wuthering Heights* (1847), is evident in varying degrees in all her novels. *Fire on the Mountain*, the novel that comes closest to being purely a psychological thriller, ends with a half-insane, reptilelike child setting fire to the forest surrounding her house; in *Cry, The Peacock*, Maya, the neurotic heroine, kills her husband, thereby fulfilling the prophecy of an albino sorcerer; in *Voices in the City*, Monisha, an unsettled, manic-depressive housewife, pours kerosene over herself and burns herself to death. On the other hand, most of

Desai's novels also contain a deep-rooted, philosophical concern about the meaning of life. From Maya to Bim, most of Desai's protagonists, dissatisfied with their routine existence, search for a more meaningful life. Such a spiritual orientation is reminiscent of similar concerns in novels such as E. M. Forster's *Howard's End* (1910) or Virginia Woolf's *Between the Acts* (1941).

Desai's novels also evolve a typical setting or "world" of their own. Most are set in the city, which comes to represent the undesirable, unimaginative reality; most also have a romantic counterpoint to the city in a hill-station or an island, which seems to represent the remote, romantic, ideal, but which is revealed to be an unreal or unsatisfying delusion. At the heart of the novels there is usually a big, old house with several verandas, green shutters, a garden, servants, and pets. The garden is extremely important in Desai's world because her characters show an unusual sensitivity to it. Trees, creepers, tendrils, flowers, fruits, seasons, pets—the concerns of the so-called "woman's world"—are more vividly perceived in Desasi's novels than anywhere else in Indian English fiction. Also in Desai's world is a brooding, Faulknerian obsession with the past: the present is usually seen by the characters as a decadent remnant, a husk of a glamorous past. Finally, the characters are all upperclass, belonging to once affluent, now decaying families. The city, the hillstation, the big house with a garden, a decadent family, an obsession with the past—these make up the typical world of a Desai novel.

Desai's protagonists can be divided into essentially two types: one type possesses a neurotic, hypersensitive, artistic sensibility; the other is cynical, tough, and acerbic. Maya, Monisha, Sarah, Sita, and Tara belong to the first category, while Nirode, Amla, Dev, Nanda, and Bim belong to the second. In addition to these are two types of supporting characters: the old, ugly, sterile crone, who has been a failure; and the mysterious, insulated character, intriguing but ultimately inscrutable. The best example of the former is Ila Das of *Fire on the Mountain*, of the latter, Dharma of *Voices in the City*. The rest of the characters are the common crowd against whom the protagonist defines himself: they have given up trying to make their lives meaningful and have accepted the full mediocrity of a futile existence.

Against such a backdrop, Desai's protagonists struggle to come to terms with their lives. They are usually in a state of conflict, either with themselves or with their environment. The results of this basic conflict are murder, insanity, suicide, compromise, death, or, in the rare instance of Desai's best novel, *Clear Light of Day*, balance, reconciliation, rich acceptance of reality, and a resolution of the conflict.

Cry, The Peacock, Desai's first novel, is divided into three sections: a short introduction and conclusion in objective, third-person narrative, and a long subjective middle section narrated by the neurotic heroine, Maya. In Maya's narrative, Desai employs stream of consciousness to fill in details of Maya's past and to chronicle the progressive deterioration of both Maya's relationship with her husband, Gautama, and her own mental poise and sanity. In the climax, Maya, a slave to the fate she has feared, kills Gautama in accordance with the prophecy of an astrologer. The novel ends with her total mental collapse.

Maya is the sensitive, poetic, intuitive, and unstable type of personality that appears consistently in Desai's fiction. She is extremely sensitive to the beauty around her—the flowers and fruits in the garden, the trees and plants, the sky and the seasons, her pets and other animals—in brief, the whole gamut of nature. Gautama, her husband, is her opposite: he is insensitive to transient beauty; a pure rationalist, he is only concerned with absolutes. The characters' names themselves epitomize their irreconcilability: Maya means "illusion," and Gautama is the name of the Buddha, who was able to rend the veil of maya. Thus, while Maya revels in the world of the senses, Gautama rejects it entirely. According to the astrologer's prophecy, one of them must die. Maya decides to kill Gautama because, in her view, he has rejected all that makes life worth living; hence, to her, he is already "dead." Unable to resolve her conflict with Gautama, Maya pushes him from a terrace, thereby terminating her struggle.

Desai's second novel, *Voices in the City*, is more ambitious than her first but also noticeably flawed. The narrative centers on the effect of Calcutta on Nirode and his two sisters, Monisha and Amla. Like the previous novel, it is divided into three sections: "Nirode," "Monisha," and "Amla." Nirode is the first of Desai's tough, cynical protagonists, a type that finds fruition in Bim, the heroine of *Clear Light of Day*, fifteen years later. Nirode, realizing that his uncreative job at a respectable newspaper will never allow him to live meaningfully, quits. He refuses support from his rich, widowed mother, who lives in the hills; instead, he sinks from failure to failure, cynically awaiting the bottom. Thus, his magazine fails after a brief run; his subsequent attempts to be a writer fail too, when his brutally honest play is rejected by a theater group. Nirode envisions himself as fighting Calcutta, the city of Kali, the city that destroys all that is worthwhile in her denizens. Surrounded by quitters, he refuses to compromise, to succumb to an existence he despises.

Monisha, his elder sister, is the sensitive, neurotic type, like Maya in *Cry, The Peacock*. Married into a traditional Bengali family, she has, to all appearances, accepted the compromise of a routine existence. In fact, however, Monisha leads a secretive inner life, which is inviolate despite the ugliness of her surroundings. For example, her inability to bear a child symbolizes her refusal to allow another life into what is, to her, a meaningless and loathsome world. Her section is in the form of a diary, a sort of compressed version of Maya's long narrative in *Cry, The Peacock*.

Amla, the youngest sibling, is a muted version of Nirode. Beneath the surface, all three characters struggle against Calcutta, fighting to preserve their inner integrity. Of the three, Amla seems the most likely to succeed because she has neither the excessive cynicism of Nirode nor the neurosis of Monisha.

An interesting minor character is Dharma ("righteousness"), the unflappable painter who has left Calcutta, but who, upon discovering an ideal model in Amla, returns, following a drastic revolution in his painting. Though he is shown to be the only character who has survived against Calcutta, his inscrutability renders him incomprehensible to Nirode and Amla, as well as to the reader.

The novel has a sensational climax and a somewhat contrived ending. Monisha triumphs by burning herself to death in her bathroom. Her death brings her mother down to Calcutta from the hills. Nirode has a vision of his mother as Kali, the preserver and the destroyer; apparently, his conflict is thus resolved. Nirode, therefore, becomes the initiate, and Amla's more promising efforts at wisdom are sidestepped. In fact, Amla is the only character out of the three whose spiritual growth is utterly convincing; after her encounter with Dharma, she becomes more reconciled to Calcutta. Disregarding the triviality of her job in an advertising agency, she manages to do something which truly satisfies her—making sketches for Professor Bose's translations from the *Panchatantra*. Amla's progress, however, is not allowed fruition, but is neglected in favor of the more artificial vision of Nirode. Part of the problem is in Desai's definition of the central conflict in the novel; by pitting three individuals against an entire city, the novelist, in effect, disallows the possibility of a single creative, balanced, and happy person in the whole city. Such an opposition is precarious because the reader questions the stance of the protagonists, instead of accepting the destructiveness of their environment. Thus, when Nirode's very ordinary mother, who has retreated to the hills, is suddenly revealed to be the Goddess Kali, Nirode's vision and the novel's resolution seem to be mere impositions of the novelist.

In Desai's third novel, *Bye-Bye, Blackbird*, the action shifts to England. The novel, again, has a tripartite structure: arrival, "Discovery and Recognition," and "Departure." The three main characters are Dev, who has recently arrived in London when the novel begins, his friend Adit, with whom he is staying, and Adit's British wife, Sarah. All three characters are in conflict with their environment. Sarah is an unstable wife (in the tradition of Maya and Monisha) who finds herself playing two roles, that of an Indian at home and that of a Britisher outside; all the while, she questions who she really is. Dev and Adit are, in a sense, doubles like Nirode and Amla. Dev is the more cynical and aggressive of the two, while Adit, though essentially the same, is muted at the beginning. The novel follows a pattern like that of Henry James's *The Ambassadors* (1903): Adit, who thought he had felt at home in England, returns to India, while Dev, the militant cynic who has reviled Adit for staying, takes Adit's place (he accepts a job in Adit's firm and moves to his apartment) after his departure.

Bye-Bye, Blackbird is a satisfying novel partly because Desai builds an inevitability into the narrative; characters are subordinated to pattern and rhythm. Dev's and Adit's decisions, hence, do not have to be fully explained. Their conflicts are not resolved so much as exchanged; the pleasure at the end is as much formal as it is emotional.

In Desai's fourth novel, *Where Shall We Go This Summer?*, all of her pervasive themes return: the neurotic heroine, the dissatisfaction with the here and now, the obsessive search for the meaning of existence. Sita, the wife of an industrialist, is disgusted with her indifferent husband, her meaningless life in their Bombay flat, and her selfish, uncaring children. Her memory of an idyllic childhood with her father on a nearby island, Manori, keeps haunting her as a reminder of what life can be. After becoming pregnant with a fifth child, she decides not to continue the charade; she visits the island again, to regain the secret magic of life that she had experienced as a child. To her dismay, she realizes that her father, instead of being the great leader that she has thought him to be, was really a charlatan. She has glamorized the past, and she now realizes that her memory has deceived her. Completely disillusioned, she waits for her drab husband to take her back to Bombay.

Toward the close of the novel, Sita's conflict appears to have found its solution when she recalls a verse from D. H. Lawrence which has eluded her for a long time. With the recollection, she feels she knows all the answers and can explain everything to her husband. This euphoria, however, is short-lived, ending with her realization that she cannot connect psychologically with her husband. Thus, the novel ends with a compromise after a false resolution; Sita is back where she began. Commenting that if she had been younger, she might have ended the novel with Sita's suicide, Desai has explained that her less melodramatic conclusion is more in keeping with the realities of middle age. Hence, although Sita continues living, her conflict is not resolved; instead, she accepts defeat and compromise.

In her fifth novel, *Fire on the Mountain*, Desai reverts to the psychological thriller that is exemplified by her first novel. The narrative builds to a superb pitch of suspense and tension, only to end in sensational melodrama: the murder and rape of an old, ugly woman, and a forest fire started by a demented child.

Embittered by the indifference and infidelity of her husband, worn-out from the rearing of several children and grandchildren, and now abandoned by her relatives, Nanda Kaul lives alone in her mountaintop cottage "Carignano," in Kasauli, surrounded by a pine forest. She tries to conceal her bitterness and loneliness behind a facade of cold, cynical aloofness, pretending that she does not need anyone, that she is living in Kasauli out of choice, that she is in happy retirement after a rich and fulfilling life. When Raka, her great-granddaughter, comes to live with her, Nanda's craving for contact is revived. She tries to win the child by various devices, telling her wild stories, going for walks with her, and bribing her with food. Raka, who is as inscrutable and self-sufficient as a reptile, rebuffs the old woman. Into this situation steps Ila Das, Nanda's childhood friend, a complete failure, a pathetic harridan who has descended into desperate poverty after the ruin of her once rich, decadent family. It is only when Ila is raped and murdered that Nanda is willing to acknowledge the lie at the core of her life; just then, Raka, the strange, half-crazy child, informs her that she has set the forest on fire.

Fire on the Mountain is superbly narrated, but does not aim at being much more than a thriller. Nanda's quest for a meaningful life is subordinated to the demands of the plot. The novel is interesting, however, for at least two reasons. First, the hill-station, usually the romantic contrast to the anticreative life of the city, here becomes a horrifying place for ghosts, mad dogs, demented women, impoverished hags, lonely great-grandmothers living in illusions, and demented children; the fantasy has turned into a nightmare. To the Kasauli of *Fire on the Mountain*, even the Calcutta of *Voices in the City* seems preferable. Second, Ila and Raka are two of Desai's most disturbing characters: both are consistently sketched in animal and reptile imagery, and both are, in a sense, unhinged. Both represent the extremes of the fondness for the bizarre that lurks in all of Desai's fiction.

Clear Light of Day is one of her most accomplished novels. In it, the typical elements of her art merge to create a unique artistic triumph. The plot, for example, is a fine blend of the Gothic and the philosophical, each strengthening the other. The mysterious well in the back, the drowned cow, Mira Masi's alcoholic disintegration, Tara's fear that her mother was murdered by her father, Baba's idiocy—all these contribute to the final resolution of the novel. One by one, these events are put into their place by the two heroines, Bim and Tara; the mystery, horror, or shame enveloping these events is slowly peeled away, and the past emerges in a new light of clarity and understanding by the end of the novel.

The setting, too, has the typical Desai elements—the ugly city, the large house with verandas, the garden, the servants' quarters, upper-class characters, and decadent families. These elements, however, are augmented by acute social observation and particularity of place and time. Not only the inner life of the characters but also their milieu is fully developed. Perhaps no other English novel so successfully immortalizes mid-twentieth century Delhi and its locales—Civil Lines, the old Delhi convent school, the Jamuna, Connaught Circus, Hindu College, Darya Ganj, Chandni Chowk, the Ridge, and the Lodi Gardens, *Clear Light of Day* is thus also valuable as a sociohistorical document, a feat rare in Desai's canon.

Desai's main concern, of course, remains with the characters and their conflicts. Bim is the tough, cynical heroine, the one who refuses to compromise. Tara is her softer, more sensitive, counterpart. Raja, the deserter, their brother, is Bim's double. Mira Masi and the sisters next door are the hags.

Bakul, Tara's husband, is a shallower, stupider version of Gautama. Bim, Tara, and Raja share the same determination to live meaningfully, without compromise. At the beginning of the novel, when Tara returns to the old house, both sisters are equally distant from resolving their conflicts: while Tara is too weak, Bim is too harsh, too bitter. Both are uncertain about their past, about their relationships to each other and Raja, about the meaningfulness of their lives. Together, they slowly relive their entire past, which leads to the marvelous reconciliation in the last few pages of the novel. Bim, to her astonishment, realizes that Tara—despite her marriage to Bakul and several mundane years as the wife of a diplomat—whom she has always despised, is just like her, and that Tara, too, has managed to preserve her integrity. Tara and Bim reach a new understanding for the first time; through Tara, Bim at last relinquishes her grudge against Raja, reconciling herself to him again. After Tara's departure, Bim and Baba listen to Mulk and his Guru; Mulk is not after all merely a slothful drunkard as Bim has thought—he *can* sing, he is an artiste. Bim realizes that she does not have to degenerate into another Mira Masi; she fathoms the truth of T. S. Eliot's line from *Four Quartets* (1943): "Time the destroyer is also time the preserver."

Bim's conflict ceases, dissolves; she transcends her duality and her contradictions. She can face reality without bitterness or neurosis. Her fancy ceases to cheat her; her imagination no longer makes her despise the reality around her; instead, she realizes that ordinary life has its moments of fulfillment too. *Clear Light of Day* thus ends in balance, harmony, reconciliation, resolution, not in murder, suicide, death, insanity, or compromise, as did all of Desai's previous novels, and as did her *Baumgartner's Bombay*.

In *Baumgartner's Bombay*, the main character is neither Indian nor English—he is a German Jew. The story follows Hugo Baumgartner from childhood in pre-World War II Germany to his death in Bombay, India. The novel, however, starts with the ending (though the reader cannot realize it until the actual end of the book) and then jumps to the middle of the story. Baumgartner's past is relayed in a series of flashbacks from his time in India.

Baumgartner is forced to leave Germany when the Nazis' rise to power can no longer be ignored. Indeed, by the time Baumgartner leaves, his father has already committed suicide after being sent to a concentration camp, though he was later released. Interestingly, Desai has said about *Baumgartner's Bombay* that she "wasn't writing about the Nazis. I was writing about random evil." Baumgartner himself never expresses much feeling about the injustices done to him; about his six years in a British internment camp for German nationals, Baumgartner protests that "they were not such bad days."

Baumgartner's escape from Germany takes him to Venice, where he is to catch a boat for India. Venice remains in Baumgartner's mind as a kind of paradise, despite the troubles he has there and the fact that he is in the city for less than a week. These fabled and probably half-imagined qualities of Venice contrast sharply with the squalor and degradation of Bombay and of Baumgartner's life there. In fact, he spends most of his time going from restaurant to restaurant trying to find scraps for the multitude of cats with which he shares his dingy little flat.

Ironically, Baumgartner does die at the hands of a German, though not a Nazi, rather, a German junkie whom Baumgartner has offered a place to stay kills him for his silver trophies. *Baumgartner's Bombay* marks a return for Desai to the twin themes of hopelessness and despair. Baumgartner, his aging friend Lotte, Julius Roth—all are stranded in India; none can return to Germany because the old Germany is gone forever, and they do not fit into the new Germany. Indeed, it is the new Germany that becomes the death of Baumgartner in the shape of the brutal junkie. Desai's picture of foreigners, or *firanghi*, as the Indians label these outcasts, is that they can never fit into Indian society no matter how hard they try. It is Desai's great talent, however, to be able to make these characters compelling despite their obvious fate, which is to be forgotten. They leave no mark or memory when they die, though Desai ensures that they do remain with the reader long past the end of the novel.

Makarand Paranjape

Other major works
SHORT FICTION: *Games at Twilight and Other Stories*, 1978.
CHILDREN'S LITERATURE: *The Peacock Garden*, 1974; *Cat on a Houseboat*, 1976; *The Village by the Sea: An Indian Family Story*, 1982.

Bibliography
Bande, Usha. *The Novels of Anita Desai: A Study in Character and Conflict*. New Delhi: Prestige Books, 1988. Bande briefly surveys the critical material written on Desai before going on to detailed discussions of each of her novels up to *In Custody*. Desai's works are explored mainly in the context of her characters' various personality disorders. Each chapter has an extensive list of references, some of which are briefly annotated. Also includes both primary and secondary bibliographies and an index.

Jain, Jasbir. *Stairs to the Attic: The Novels of Anita Desai*. Jaipur, India: Printwell, 1987. Desai's novels are approached through detailed comparisons between the plots, characters, and settings of each of her works up to *In Custody*. An extensive list of references at the end of the book is given for each chapter. Also includes both a primary and a secondary bibliography, as well as an index.

Jena, Seema. *Voice and Vision of Anita Desai*. New Delhi: Ashish Publishing House, 1989. First written as Jena's dissertation, this text concentrates on the place of Desai among female Indian novelists, but also includes plot and character discussion. Notes and references are provided at the end of each chapter, as well as a list of books by and about Desai, reviews of her work, interviews with her, and an index.

PETER DE VRIES

Born: Chicago, Illinois; February 27, 1910

Principal long fiction

But Who Wakes the Bugler?, 1940; *The Handsome Heart*, 1943; *Angels Can't Do Better*, 1944; *The Tunnel of Love*, 1954; *Comfort Me with Apples*, 1956; *The Mackerel Plaza*, 1958; *The Tents of Wickedness*, 1959; *Through the Fields of Clover*, 1961; *The Blood of the Lamb*, 1962; *Reuben, Reuben*, 1964; *Let Me Count the Ways*, 1965; *The Vale of Laughter*, 1967; *The Cat's Pajamas and Witch's Milk*, 1968; *Mrs. Wallop*, 1970; *Into Your Tent I'll Creep*, 1971; *Forever Panting*, 1973; *The Glory of the Hummingbird*, 1974; *I Hear America Swinging*, 1976; *Madder Music*, 1977; *Consenting Adults: Or, The Dutchess Will Be Furious*, 1980; *Sauce for the Goose*, 1981; *Slouching Towards Kalamazoo*, 1983; *The Prick of Noon*, 1985; *Peckham's Marbles*, 1986.

Other literary forms

Peter De Vries is also a short-story writer of some repute; a number of his stories are collected in *No, But I Saw the Movie* (1952) and *Without a Stitch in Time: A Selection of the Best Humorous Short Pieces* (1972). He has also collaborated with Joseph Fields in writing a stage version of one of his novels, *The Tunnel of Love: A Play* (1957). Finally, he has published a handful of essays and interviews.

Achievements

In the 1950's, Kingsley Amis called De Vries the "funniest serious writer to be found either side of the Atlantic." De Vries is certainly a clever punster and wit, a master of situation comedy, and a devastating observer of the foibles of suburbia. His droll humor often involves the amorous adventures of the middle-aged suburban male, torn between the sophisticated mores of Connecticut suburbia and his simpler childhood roots, usually in the Dutch Reformed Church or some other equally strict background. De Vries writes knowingly about the same suburban milieu as that of John Updike and John Cheever, but with less overt seriousness and more sheer fun. In fact, he resists the label of "serious writer" (or, for that matter, "religious writer"), although he has dealt extensively with serious topics, including religion, in most of his works. The predominant tone of his writing, with the exception of *The Blood of the Lamb*, is comic and even lighthearted.

De Vries has been a prolific novelist, with more than two dozen novels published, along with several collections of short stories reprinted from *The New Yorker*. With so many novels to his credit, there is bound to be some repetitiveness, and De Vries often uses the same basic plot situation—the comic mischances of the lecherous suburban male who is thwarted by his moral scruples, his underlying decency, the vestiges of his past, or simply by unlucky circumstances. There is a sameness about so many of his protagonists—particularly in their recollections of their strict religious backgrounds and their ambiguous attempts to "liberate" themselves from middle-class conventionality—that De Vries has been accused by some critics of being too autobiographical. What saves his novels from redundancy is the variety of his humor: the puns, witticisms, drollery, repartee, lampoons, parodies, caricatures, and spoofs. De Vries has the comic instincts of a cartoonist or a comedian, the ability to coin phrases or epigrams so funny that they are almost distracting. His fictional scenes seem to be built around the humorous or witty line, sometimes to the detriment of his plot, narrative, or characterization. Yet since De Vries has repeatedly insisted that his primary purpose as a humorist is to entertain, the loose structure of his work may be judged a necessary evil.

The targets of De Vries's humor are the pretenses and absurdities of modern, affluent suburbia. In an interview he once commented, "I'm a regionalist, like Thomas Hardy. And I love those yokels who get off the same bar car at the same time every night and have never swum in anything but a pool in their own backyards. It's really a new provincialism." His "Avalon" and "Decency" are the fictional counterparts of the wealthy, exclusive suburbs such as Greenwich, Darien, Stamford, and Westport along Connecticut's "Gold Coast." His characters—or sometimes caricatures—show all of the vanities, postures, and affectations of wealth, education, and good breeding that might be expected of sophisticated Connecticut suburbanites, yet De Vries is never harsh or satirical, commenting that the purpose of humor, unlike satire, is not to kill one's prey but to bring it back alive to be released. De Vries's humor is thus more charitable than satire; he invites mankind "to laugh at itself."

De Vries is a master of the humorous scene and the comic caricature. Many of his characters are immediately recognizable as "types"—the ultraliberal clergyman, the suave newspaper columnist, the lecherous poet, the hick farmer, the small-town atheist, the unsuccessful artist, and the television game show host—and they behave in predictable ways. The humor occurs as De Vries builds his scenes toward a hilarious climax—such as the cup of bourbon switched with the teacups at the church ladies' reception in *The Mackerel Plaza* or the social worker's visit to a disorganized family in *The Tunnel of Love*. Often the comedy takes the form of a continuation of James Thurber's "battle of the sexes," with De Vries's male characters seeking a worldly sophistication and urbanity in which to live out their fantasies, only to be thwarted by the forces of female respectability. Virtually all of De Vries's novels have a male protagonist, and he writes from a decidedly male perspective on the themes of sex and marriage, explaining once in an interview that bawdy literature is written predominantly by men. His characters *think* they want the freedom and irresponsibility of a carefree bachelor life, with its worldliness and sophistication, but seem bewildered or disappointed if they get what they seek. The theme of many of his comic novels (and hence the source of their humor) is the shallowness and superficiality of the sophisticated suburban life.

Perhaps the key to De Vries's best work is in the tragicomic tone of his humor—that urge to laugh so as not to cry that marks the grotesque "as a blend of the tragic and comic." Too often in De Vries's novels, however, the comic is present without the tragic, the burlesque and farcical without the serious note which redeems his work from being merely superficial entertainment. De Vries's inferior works always seem to verge upon situation comedy, with their frequently contrived or manufactured scenes, and it is not surprising that he collaborated on a successful Broadway production based upon his novel *The Tunnel of Love*. *The Blood of the Lamb* is incomparably De Vries's best novel, with its poignant mixture of humor and pathos; coming at midcareer, it is the touchstone against which the remainder of his novels must be measured. The earlier works in comparison seem to strain after a false sophistication, and the more recent novels appear increasingly superficial, employing forced gags and contrived situations and depending too heavily on topical humor and burlesque of current trends and fashions.

Biography

Peter De Vries was born in Chicago, Illinois, on February 27, 1910. His parents, Joost and Henrietta De Vries, immigrated from Holland and settled in a closely knit Dutch Calvinist community on Chicago's South Side. De Vries's father was an iceman and furniture mover who started with "a one-horse outfit that he gradually built to a sizeable warehouse business." During De Vries's boyhood, the family lived in a three-room apartment behind his father's business office.

The De Vries family were members of the strict Dutch Reformed Church, and their domestic life was probably much like that described in the autobiographical *The Blood of the Lamb*: a large, contentious family with parents and in-laws forever arguing about some obscure point of theology or church doctrine. Apparently, such disagreements were commonplace in the Dutch Reformed Church, for in the novel *The Mackerel Plaza*, when someone boasts to the protagonist's father that *his* denomination has not had a schism in the past one hundred years, he replies, "Rotten wood you can't split." De Vries's parents were also strict about forbidding any form of worldliness: motion pictures and card-playing were forbidden, and instead Bible-reading and theological discussions were encouraged. During his adolescence, De Vries rebelled against these strictures, but he later expressed fond memories of the Dutch-language services and hymns of his childhood.

Young De Vries attended the Chicago Christian High School of the Dutch Reformed Church and then entered Calvin College in Grand Rapids, Michigan, a private liberal arts college founded by the same denomination. There he won a Michigan state extemporaneous speaking contest and was graduated with an English major in 1931. That summer he also studied briefly at Northwestern University. His family had hoped that he would enter the ministry after graduation, but instead he decided to become a writer and embarked upon a series of odd jobs in Chicago to support himself. He edited a community newspaper, tended vending machines, peddled candy apples, served as a radio actor, and spoke before women's clubs.

From 1938 to 1944, he served capably as an editor of *Poetry* magazine. There he met his future wife, Katinka Loeser, who was a poetry contributor and later became a short-story writer of some note. They were married on October 16, 1943. During this time, De Vries had published three early novels, *Who Wakes the Bugler?*, *Handsome Heart*, and *Angels Can't Do Better*, which earned him some critical notice but met with only limited financial success. In 1943, De Vries invited James Thurber to speak at a Chicago benefit for *Poetry* magazine and Thurber subsequently persuaded De Vries to go East and write for *The New Yorker*. De Vries joined the staff of *The New Yorker* in 1944 and has served as a contributor and cartoon editor ever since. At *The New Yorker*, he worked with editor Harold Ross and such famous humorists as E. B. White and James Thurber, on a staff that had once included Robert Benchley and S. J. Perelman. He continues to work part-time with *The New Yorker* and commutes to his office several times a week.

De Vries settled with his wife in suburban Westport, Connecticut, where they live comfortably in a ten-room house on one acre of land. They have three children—Jan, Peter Jon, and Derek. A fourth child, Emily, died of leukemia before adolescence, a deep personal loss registered in De Vries's most serious novel, *The Blood of the Lamb*, where a similar event occurs. Unlike the zany characters in many of his novels, De Vries is a man of conventional tastes, happily married and devoted to his family.

During his long career, De Vries has published more than two dozen novels, along with his collections of short stories. He is still actively writing, though not at the pace at which he worked during the 1960's, when he wrote virtually a novel a year. He has won wide critical acclaim for his humorous novels, including a grant from the American Academy of Arts and Letters and the National Institute of Arts and Letters, of which he is a member.

Analysis

"If I spent my time portraying life as it actually is," Peter De Vries once remarked, "I think I would go insane with boredom inside of two weeks." Eschewing the realistic novel, De Vries has instead concentrated on entertaining his readers with witty and humorous works, filled with hilarious but highly improbable incidents. He has been satisfied to write a good comic novel without aiming for any higher artistic qualities. This self-acknowledged limitation has been the source of much of the unevenness in De Vries's work, with the overemphasis on humor weakening the structure of his novels—often to the neglect of narrative continuity, consistent point of view, clear transitions, and strong characterizations. In fact, many of his novels are so seriously flawed as scarcely to be considered novels at all; rather, they are loosely constructed narratives that simply provide a framework for his comic genius. Beyond the purpose of sheer entertainment, De Vries has been ambiguous about the intent of his humor, minimizing the social commentary and underlying seriousness of his work so that it is difficult to categorize him as a comic novelist of manners or a satirist. Like his mentor, James Thurber, De Vries has chosen to limit the scope of his humor and to evoke laughter through grotesque or absurd depictions of modern suburban life, but as his later novels suggest, he risks reducing his work to formulaic entertainment, or worse, self-parody. Stylistically, De Vries is not as original as Thurber, but is perhaps at his best as a parodist of other writers, or as a writer of brilliant puns and epigrams rather than as the creator of a unified and coherent comic vision. His weakness as a comic novelist comes from his failure to unify his material and to offer an implicit corrective vision to the world he ridicules.

De Vries's first three novels are of slight artistic value. His first novel of note, and still perhaps his most popular, is *The Tunnel of Love*. Here one enters the affluent world of Connecticut suburbia as seen through the eyes of the first-person narrator, a New York magazine cartoon editor much like De Vries himself. The focus of the novel, however, is on the comic imbroglios of his next-door neighbors, Augie and Isolde Poole, a young, well-to-do, "artistic" couple who try to adopt a child to save their marriage. The novel alternates between Manhattan and Avalon, Connecticut, through a round of weekend cocktail parties and dinners that provide a backdrop for De Vries's wit and cleverness. De Vries peoples the book with a humorous collage of "artsy" types—would-be actresses and directors, abstract painters, mediocre illustrators, poets *manqués*, affected snobs, precious aesthetes, and other rarefied types. In short, one finds all of the empty worldliness of "Vanity Fair," which De Vries is quick to mimic and satirize, yet one also feels the narrator's attraction to these values, which lends the novel a curiously mixed tone of admiration and ridicule. De Vries is a shrewd observer of suburban language and behavior, with a good ear for nuances of conversation, and he creates a wonderful satire of the pretentious cocktail chitchat about creativity and neuroses that the characters employ to boost their sagging egos and disguise from themselves the truth of their mediocrity.

The protagonist, Augie Poole, is a good gag writer though a poor cartoonist who cannot sell his work, so he turns to profligacy to salve his ego. A self-confessed "rotter," he is never quite as wicked as he pretends to be. Superficially a glib and literate ladies' man, he is basically shallow and conceited, though not beyond eventual redemption through the responsibilities of parenthood. The Pooles ironically adopt the illegitimate child of Augie and his artist mistress, but not before a comic series of mishaps during the adoption process. Augie is forced to compromise his "artistic integrity" and sells his gags without the cartoons to prove himself a responsible prospective parent with a steady income. Much of the humor is generated in the domestic life of the narrator, however, in a genial "battle of the sexes" with his wife and family. In conversations with his wife, the narrator of course defends Augie, while she defends Isolde, with predictable results.

In *The Tunnel of Love*, husbands and wives are torn between the routines of respectable suburban life and the allure of a self-indulgent and liberated "artistic" life, with its glamour and sophistication. De Vries contrasts the romantic myth of personal creativity and self-indulgence with the more staid world of middle-class marriage and commuter life. His characters enjoy all of the luxuries of suburban affluence, yet they seem to yearn for a vague "something more"—a vicarious excitement missing from their lives and beckoning from the bohemian life or from the narrator's vicarious dreamworld of "Moot Point," a Hollywood fantasy-world of cinema clichés. The comedy is generated by the clash of illusion and reality as Augie and the narrator slowly learn to accept the world as it is; "Moot Point" is eventually replaced by "Drowsy Dell," the summer cabin on a New Hampshire lake that both families enjoy.

After De Vries's commercial success with *The Tunnel of Love*, he adapted the novel for stage and screen, and the play ran for a year on Broadway. His fiction writing continued in the same comic vein with his next three novels, *Comfort Me with Apples*, *The Mackerel Plaza*, and *The Tents of Wickedness*. Once more he took aim at the hollow values and assumptions of modern suburbia, particularly the jargon of psychology and adjustment, though not necessarily to replace them with more traditional values, but simply to show their comic inadequacy. The protagonist of *The Mackerel Plaza* is a pompous, ultraliberal minister, the Reverend Andrew Mackerel, as rigid and narrow in his "advanced thinking" as the fundamentalists he opposes. His People's Liberal Church, a nondenominational congregation, is the "first split-level church in America," with a church clinic and psychiatric facilities designed to meet all of the needs of modern man. Mackerel preaches short, iconoclastic sermons intended to demolish whatever remains of his parishioners' traditional Christian beliefs, though he is the one who ultimately loses his faith in unbelief. A young widower, he is thwarted in his desire to marry an aspiring actress by the forces of New England respectability in his congregation and by an elderly parishioner's desire to erect a memorial to his late wife.

None of the characters is really convincing in this book, and De Vries seems to play off orthodox beliefs against liberal Christianity merely for laughs, without either appearing credible. Mackerel loses his actress, Molly Calico, to a Rumanian director and ends up marrying his own sister-in-law, Hester, a caricature of New England primness and domesticity. Like Flannery O'Connor, De Vries uses the humor of the grotesque to show the inadequacy of secular humanism and to point to religious concerns, though not with as much intensity, conviction, or originality as the Georgia writer.

In *Comfort Me with Apples* and *The Tents of Wickedness*, De Vries introduces Chick Swallow, a suave newspaper columnist who dispenses inept advice to his readers and generally muddles their lives with his well-intentioned but wrongheaded amateur therapy. Chick and his brother-in-law, Nickie Sherman, are self-styled Oscar Wilde types, adept at café repartee and clever rejoinders but unable to manage their lives or marriages. The pair continually confuse literature and life, and Swallow, who narrates *The Tents of Wickedness*, insists upon viewing his personal crises through the eyes of famous writers, which allows De Vries to display his clever parodies of the styles of Thurber, J. P. Marquand, William Faulkner, Marcel Proust, Ernest Hemingway, Graham Greene, Henry James, Theodore Dreiser, Franz Kafka, James Joyce, and others. The plot consists of a series of thinly contrived situations involving Swallow's blundering attempts to mend his brother-in-law's split personality and to advise Sweetie Appleyard, an innocent young poetess whom he urges to take up the bohemian life, with disastrous results. Nickie vacillates between private detective and a Raffles-like jewel thief, while Sweetie is transformed from a Pre-Raphaelite poetaster to a liberated Greenwich Village type who persuades Swallow to father the child she wants in order to fulfill herself as an "emancipated woman." The action alternates between Greenwich Village and Decency, Connecticut, with De Vries predictably contrasting middle-class and beatnik life-styles. Without De Vries's clever stylistic parodies and his brilliant verbal wit, this would be unlikely material even for a comic novel. *The Tents of Wickedness* strains credulity with its clumsy social satire and wooden characterizations. Unfortunately, De Vries never allows his characters lives of their own; instead, they serve merely as mouthpieces for his humor. These same flaws are evident in *Through the Fields of Clover*, which takes as its occasion a New England family's fortieth wedding anniversary for De Vries's satire of modern notions of family and marriage.

De Vries's next novel, *The Blood of the Lamb*, marked a sharp departure from the slapstick comedy of his earlier novels. In what is undoubtedly his finest book, he blends comedy and pathos in the story of Don Wanderhope, an obviously autobiographical character who breaks away from Chicago and his strict Dutch Calvinist background and goes East to work in a New York advertising agency. The focus of the novel is on the relationship between the protagonist and his daughter Carol, a graceful and precocious child who is stricken with leukemia. Her illness, suffering, and eventual death test Wanderhope's faith, and, through the example of his daughter's courage, lead him back to grace. *The Blood of the Lamb* contains a depth and seriousness otherwise missing in De Vries's work, since it is based on the author's loss of his own daughter Emily to the same disease. Here De Vries finds a theme that permits him to move beyond cleverness for its own sake and create characters of substance and credibility.

"What people believe is a measure of what they suffer," remarks Don Wanderhope, who is himself tried by a series of misfortunes, including the death of his older brother Louie, his father's insanity, his wife's suicide, and finally his daughter's death. Since De Vries's characters are for the most part unable to accept the consolations of traditional belief, and since they are uneasy with modern, relativistic assumptions, their suffering often seems grotesque, and it is from this quality that De Vries extracts much of his humor. This "gallows humor" is what ultimately saves Wanderhope from despair, as when, in a scene of bitter poignancy after he learns of his daughter's death, he pitches her birthday cake at a statue of the suffering Christ. The theme of the novel seems to be that, contrary to received opinion, suffering does not teach one anything; hence, laughter is the best antidote to despair.

There are some very funny episodes in *The Blood of the Lamb*, such as when Wanderhope and his future wife, Greta, are caught in bed together by Greta's parents in a model home that her parents are showing to a client. The emotional center of the book, however, is Carol, especially after her mother's suicide. Carol is the most compelling and believable character in any of De Vries's books. She is, of course, the "Lamb," and her blood is shed gratuitously to a disease for which there is no cure. "The blood of the Lamb" does not redeem anything (except perhaps the protagonist, though that point remains deliberately ambiguous) and hence her suffering and that of the other children in the leukemia hospital remains meaningless. It recalls Herod's slaughter of the innocents. One's only defense against such realities is to laugh at the tragic absurdity of life; this tragicomic note is best illustrated by the birthday party in the hospital for the young leukemia patients. Once Carol's illness has been diagnosed, Wanderhope must race against time to cherish every moment with his daughter while sparing her the truth of her condition. As he observes, in such a case "the greatest experience open to man is the recovery of the commonplace." In another moment of bitter emotional truth, a parent remarks to Wanderhope that grief does not unite but separates people. De Vries's personal credo may be reflected in the philosophical statement written by Wanderhope for his alma mater, which is read back to him in a tape recording by his daughter Carol: that man has only "Reason, Courage, and Grace" to see him through.

Though De Vries never achieved the same artistic success with any of the novels that followed *The Blood of the Lamb*, he managed in several books to temper the humor with serious themes. In *Reuben, Reuben*, his longest novel, De Vries returned to suburban situation comedy and his burlesque of artsy sophistication. Written in three parts, the novel shifts from Frank Spofford, a shrewd chicken farmer, to Gowen McGland, a crude and dissolute Welsh poet, to Alvin Mopworth, a hapless English journalist, all of whose lives become entangled in a humorous chain of events.

In *Let Me Count the Ways*, agnostic piano mover Stan Waltz is pitted against his fundamentalist wife Elsie. *The Vale of Laughter* finds comedian Joe Sandwich trading witticisms with his humorless rival, Wally Hines, a dull professor of humor; and the novellas *The Cat's Pajamas* and *Witch's Milk* deal with characters dissatisfied with their professions or marriages. *Mrs. Wallop*, another situation comedy, finds a middle-aged woman taking on the forces of modernism.

Following the publication of these novels, De Vries proceeded to lampoon modern art and the sexual revolution in a short-story collection, *Without a Stitch in Time*, and a series of unimpressive novels: *Into Your Tent I'll Creep*, *Forever Panting*, *I Hear American Swinging*, *Madder Music*, and *Consenting Adults*.

One of De Vries's few novels that does not deal with sexual comedy is *The Glory of the Hummingbird*, an account of a likable young couple of Dutch Reformed background who, unable to have a child of their own, decide to adopt a teenage juvenile delinquent in hopes of reforming him. The protagonist, Jim Tickler, gravitates from advertising to television, where he eventually comes to host a rigged game show called the "Little Red Poolroom," where in a variation of the "Fortunate Fall," as one critic points out, he wins his foster son's affection after the show is exposed and Jim and his wife Amy are shown to be fallible.

De Vries's novels of the 1980s have continued to play out clever variations of the battle of the sexes in a world of changing social mores. In *Sauce for the Goose*, Daisy Dobbin, a young feminist writer from Terre Haute, Indiana, escapes to New York to take a position at the *Metropole* magazine in order to expose the sexual harassment of women and ends by falling in love with the publisher, Dirk Dolfin, a wealthy Dutch businessman. An unconvincing feminist, Daisy betrays her "cause" in a conflict between head and heart, implying that her feminism is an inadequate substitute "religion." In *Slouching Towards Kalamazoo*, Maggie Doubloon, another liberated heroine, attempts to capitalize on her unwed motherhood by marketing T-shirts emblazoned with a scarlet "A+" after she is impregnated by one of her students. Despite its many puns and literary allusions, the novel teeters between comedy and vulgarity.

The Prick of Noon and *Peckham's Marbles* both involve picaresque rascals who attempt to rise in social class or redeem their failed literary careers by using others. In *The Prick of Noon*, Eddie Teeters, a successful pornographic film director from Backbone, Arkansas, attempts to crash into the genteel country-club society of Merrymount, Connecticut, through his affair with socially prominent Cynthia Pickles. Teeters yearns for a world that he cannot enter. Since marriage with Cynthia is out of the question, Teeters eventually settles for an attractive waitress, Toby Snapper, who shares his modest background. In *Peckham's Marbles,* Earl Peckham, a failed novelist, pursues Nelly DelBelly, the wealthy, overweight owner of the Dappled Shade rest home, and Poppy McCloud, the young author of best-selling romances, in a humorous quest for love and money.

Despite the large number of books he has written, De Vries is essentially a one-book novelist, with *The Blood of the Lamb* rising above the level of his other works, which remain primarily entertainment. Distracted by his own cleverness, De Vries has not employed his humor in the service of any coherent social vision. Unlike Miguel de Cervantes, William Shakespeare, Mark Twain, or any of the other great comic writers, De Vries does not humanize his reader so much as divert him temporarily from the human condition. Because his characters are for the most part weakly drawn, one does not empathize with them, merely enjoying a laugh at their expense and turning away from the book without having gained in any measure. This lack of depth, along with the sameness of so much of his work, marks the failure of De Vries to move beyond wit to an underlying seriousness of purpose in his art.

Andrew J. Angyal

Other major works

SHORT FICTION: *No, But I Saw the Movie*, 1952; *Without a Stitch in Time: A Selection of the Best Humorous Short Pieces*, 1972.

PLAY: *The Tunnel of Love: A Play*, 1957 (with Joseph Fields).

Bibliography

Bowden, Edwin T. *Peter De Vries.* Boston: Twayne, 1983. A concise critical biography that provides a useful overview of De Vries's life and works. After an introductory biographical chapter, Bowden discusses each of De Vries's major novels. The text is supplemented by a chronology, notes, and a selected bibliography of primary and secondary works.

David, Douglas M. "An Interview with Peter De Vries." *College English* 28 (April, 1967): 524-530. A lively interview in which the author raises some interesting questions about De Vries's style of humor. De Vries discusses his use of suburban settings, his character types, and his humorous attitude toward sexuality.

Hasley, Louis. "The Hamlet of Peter De Vries: To Wit or Not to Wit." *South Atlantic Quarterly* 70 (1971): 467-476. Hasley examines De Vries's excessive use of wit and wordplay, which some readers may find distracting, and suggests that De Vries's novels may function primarily as a forum for his jokes and gags.

Higgins, William R. "Peter De Vries." In *American Novelists Since World War II.* Vol. 6 in *Dictionary of Literary Biography.* (Detroit: Gale, 1980) A standard author entry that provides a useful profile of De Vries's life and works. It includes a list of primary and secondary sources.

Jellema, Roderick. *Peter De Vries: A Critical Essay.* Grand Rapids, Mich.: William B. Eerdmans, 1966. This monograph in the Contemporary Writers in Christian Perspective series includes a critical study of De Vries's first eight novels. This study points to the religious issues that are often overlooked in discussions of De Vries as a humorist.

Sale, Richard B. "An Interview in New York with Peter De Vries." *Studies in the Novel* 1 (1969): 364-369. This interview touches on De Vries's writing habits and includes questions about the type of humor in his novels and his view of the world. De Vries discusses the question of whether he is a black humorist.

Yagoda, Ben. "Being Seriously Funny." *The New York Times Magazine,* June 12, 1983, 42-44. A feature article that presents a portrait of De Vries and an overview of his literary career. Yagoda's article offers a good introduction to the writer and his work.

PHILIP K. DICK

Born: Chicago, Illinois; December 16, 1928
Died: Santa Ana, California; March 2, 1982

Principal long fiction

Solar Lottery, 1955; *The World Jones Made*, 1956; *The Man Who Japed*, 1956; *Eye in the Sky*, 1957; *Time Out of Joint*, 1959; *Dr. Futurity*, 1960; *Vulcan's Hammer*, 1960; *The Man in the High Castle*, 1962; *The Game-Players of Titan*, 1963; *Martian Time-Slip*, 1964; *The Three Stigmata of Palmer Eldritch*, 1964; *The Simulacra*, 1964; *The Penultimate Truth*, 1964; *Clans of the Alphane Moon*, 1964; *Dr. Bloodmoney: Or, How We Got Along After the Bomb*, 1965; *The Crack in Space (Cantata 140)*, 1966; *Now Wait for Last Year*, 1966; *The Unteleported Man*, 1966; *Counter-Clock World*, 1967; *The Zap Gun*, 1967; *The Ganymede Takeover*, 1967 (with Ray Nelson); *Do Androids Dream of Electric Sheep?*, 1968; *Ubik*, 1969; *Galactic Pot-Healer*, 1969; *The Philip K. Dick Omnibus*, 1970; *A Maze of Death*, 1970; *Our Friends from Frolix 8*, 1979; *We Can Build You*, 1972; *Flow My Tears, the Policeman Said*, 1974; *Confessions of a Crap Artist*, 1975; *Deus Irae*, 1976 (with Roger Zelazny); *A Scanner Darkly*, 1977; *The Divine Invasion*, 1981; *Valis*, 1981; *The Transmigration of Timothy Archer*, 1982; *Lies, Inc.*, 1984; *The Man Whose Teeth Were All Exactly Alike*, 1984; *Radio Free Albemuth*, 1985; *In Milton Lumky Territory*, 1985; *Puttering About in a Small Land*, 1985; *Humpty Dumpty in Oakland*, 1986; *Mary and the Giant*, 1987; *The Broken Bubble*, 1988.

Other literary forms

Before he began writing long fiction, in 1955, Philip K. Dick went through an extraordinarily prolific period as a short-story writer. His first story, "Beyond Lies the Wub," appeared in 1952. In both 1953 and 1954 Dick published twenty-eight short stories a year. His total output in this genre is more than one hundred stories, most of which he wrote early in his career. Many have been reprinted in his collections *A Handful of Darkness* (1955), *The Variable Man and Other Stories* (1957), *The Preserving Machine and Other Stories* (1969), *I Hope I Shall Arrive Soon* (1985), and elsewhere. A five-volume collection, *The Collected Stories of Philip K. Dick*, was published in 1987. He has also collaborated on novels, including *The Ganymede Takeover* (with Ray Nelson) and *Deus Irae* (with Roger Zelazny).

Achievements

In all histories of science fiction, Dick is hailed as one of the greatest and most distinctive exponents of the genre. Literary awards, however, came his way surprisingly rarely. He received the Hugo Award (which is decided by vote of science-fiction fans attending the World Science Fiction Convention) for the best novel of the year 1962, for *The Man in the High Castle*. He received the John W. Campbell Award (decided by a panel of writers and critics, and also administered by the World Science Fiction Convention) for *Flow My Tears, the Policeman Said*, in 1975. More recognition might have been expected, and would surely have been forthcoming, if it were not for two things. One is that Dick was, for a while, an amazingly prolific author (five novels were published, for example, in 1964), yet one who wrote very few evidently weak or minor novels. His high level of productivity and consistency have accordingly made it difficult for single novels to be chosen as superior to others. Probably few critics would agree even on which are the best ten of his nearly forty novels. A further point is that Dick, while a writer of amazing power and fertility, is also prone to convolution and to the pursuit of personal obsessions.

Biography

Philip Kindred Dick was born in Chicago in 1928, but he lived most of his life in California. He studied for one year at the University of California at Berkeley, but he did not take a degree. Dick held several jobs for short periods, then began writing science fiction with great speed and immediate success, first short stories and then novels. His output slowed markedly at the beginning of the 1970's, as a result of personal problems, involvement with drugs, strong discontent with American society in the Vietnam era, and a sequence of failed relationships. When he resumed writing, his books were significantly more personal and more propagandist. He died on March 2, 1982, following a stroke.

Analysis

Philip K. Dick's novels are, without exception, distinctive in style and theme. Their style may be characterized relatively easily: Dick writes clearly and plainly, and is a master of realistic dialogue. He is, however, also a master of the art of "cutting." Frequently a chapter or a scene will end with a short summary statement, often of doubt, bewilderment, or unease, only to be followed in the next chapter by a longish sentence introducing a new character going about his daily concerns in a manner which seems—but only seems—to have no connection with the foregoing. For all of his plainness, Dick furthermore makes considerable use of words of his own coinage—for example, "flapple," "quibble" (a kind of vehicle), "thungly," "gubbish," or "kipple." The latter has even achieved a certain currency outside its novel, *Do Androids Dream of Electric Sheep?*, to mean the morass of useless objects, such as gum wrappers or junk mail, which seems to reproduce by itself in any modern dwelling. The overall effect of Dick's style is to give an impression of plainness and superficial normality, but to suggest strongly that beneath this surface things are going on which are ominous, disastrous, inexplicable.

This preoccupation is clearly mirrored in Dick's characteristic themes, many of which are shared with the body of science fiction at large. He often writes of androids, simulacra, mechanical men. He bases several plots on consciousness-raising drugs. His later works in particular tend toward the dystopian, presenting visions of a future America as a vast gulag or a slave-labor state. The notions of alternate worlds and of post-Holocaust societies are often exploited. Where Dick differs from other users of these themes is in the strange insecurity which he generates while handling them. Androids are common in science fiction, and so are plots in which androids cannot be told from people. Only Dick produces plots in which the test to distinguish human from android is so deeply infected with the bureaucratic mentality that even people are likely to fail, and be eliminated. Only Dick has a hero giving himself his own test, having come (for good reason) to doubt his own humanity. Similarly, Dick is capable of writing a story which appears to be set in an alternate world, but then begins to suggest that the real world never existed and is merely a drug-induced hallucination—only to switch back again, deny its own hypothesis, and leave the reader quite unsure even of the bases of judgment. Dick is fascinated by forgeries, and by coincidences. In scene after scene, he presents a hero doubting even his own identity, and doing so with total rationality on the basis of all the evidence in the world around him. Most readers soon realize that the common concern that binds Dick's repeated themes and plot elements is the very nature of reality itself, and that Dick doubts common notions of reality more sincerely and more corrosively than almost any writer in any genre. Dick could be described as the poet of paranoia. Yet his cool and sensible style enables him to present horrifying alienations in a way with which even the sanest reader can sympathize.

Dick's overriding concerns are quite apparent in even his earliest novels. *Solar Lottery*, his first novel, presents a future society which is dedicated entirely to chance, as a result of "extrapolation" first of the then-new phenomenon of television quiz shows, and second (as one might have expected) of the "Uncertainty Principle" as a basic rule of the universe. In this world, all authority devolves on "the Quizmaster," but the Quizmaster may be deposed at any moment from his position by a "twitch of the bottle," an event determined by the intrinsically unpredictable forces of submolecular physics. The bottle twitches. Reese Verrick the Quizmaster is deposed. His place goes to an unknown fanatic called Cartwright, whose only interest is the search for a (mythical?) tenth planet. Caught up in all these events is a hero who has had the colossal bad luck to swear irrevocable fealty to Verrick just before he fell from power. Already the sense of an unpredictable world where anything can go wrong is very marked. Even more revealing is *Eye in the Sky*, in which eight characters caught up in a scientific accident find themselves exploring what they slowly realize are the worlds of one another's minds: first that of a total believer in an obscure fundamentalist sect, then that of an inhibited housewife, a borderline paranoid, a fanatical Communist, and so on. The worlds themselves are presented with great verve. In the first, for example, a man going for a job asks not about pay but about credits for salvation, and if he presses is told that in his position the God of this world, "(Tetragrammaton)," will probably grant his prayers to the extent of four hundred (dollars?) a week. The job may be constructing a grace reservoir, or improving the wire to Heaven. There is in fact an "eye in the sky," belonging to the unnameable (Tetragrammaton). Underlying the structure of the whole novel, though, is the notion that each person's individual universe is not only private but unreachable; most people are mad. In view of Dick's later development it is also interesting that the novel is strongly anti-McCarthyite, even though one of the characters (ironically a security chief) is indeed a Communist agent.

The novel which best sums up Dick's earliest phase as a novelist, however, is *Time Out of Joint*. This appears for quite some time not to be science fiction at all. It reads instead as a pleasantly pastoral, perhaps rather dull, account of life in a small American town of the 1950's. The only odd feature is that the hero, Ragle Gumm, makes his living by continually winning a newspaper contest "Where Will the Little Green Man be Next?" Slowly, however, this idyllic setting begins to drift by quarter-tones to nightmare. Gumm does not recognize a picture of Marilyn Monroe (something unthinkable if he were really of that time and place). An old phone book found in some ruins has his name in it, with eight phone numbers for all hours of the day and night. A boy's crystal radio picks up voices saying in effect "That's *him* down there, Ragle Gumm." It transpires that the small town with its idealized families is a total deception, all created to shield Ragle Gumm and maintain him in his stress-free delusion while he performs his real job—using extra-sensory powers to predict the fall of enemy rockets on Earth, under the fiction of the newspaper contest.

Gumm is mad at the start. When he thinks he is going mad, he is learning the truth. There is no way to prove that reality is not a perfectly rehearsed plot. This latter is a classic Dick conclusion. In *The Man in the High Castle*—Dick's most famous but not most characteristic work—the reader is plunged into an alternate reality where the Allies lost World War II, California is occupied by the Japanese, and the inhabitants rather like it. The hero here, Robert Childan, is a seller of "ethnic" American curios, such as Mickey Mouse watches, or Civil War handguns, for which the conquerors have an insatiable appetite. His problem is that some of the guns are fakes. The faker's problem is that he is a Jew, and could be deported to German-controlled areas. Still, the predictable theme of resistance, triumph, escape to the real universe where the right side won, hardly materializes. Instead, the reader is presented with a complex argument in favor of Japanese sensitivity, and with strong underlying hints that even the "alternate worlds" of this "alternate world" would not be the same as our world. The novel suggests powerfully that history is chance, merely one possibility among a potential infinity of realities.

By this time Dick was at the height of his power as a writer, and almost any of the sixteen novels published between 1964 and 1969, including *The Simulacra*, *Dr. Bloodmoney*, *Counter-Clock World*, or *Galactic Pot-Healer*, would find admirers. Some especially significant themes emerge, however, from five novels in this group: *The Penultimate Truth*, *Martian Time-Slip*, *The Three Stigmata of Palmer Eldritch*, *Do Androids Dream of Electric Sheep?*, and *Ubik*. The first of these returns to the theme of total, deliberate illusion. In the future imagined in this novel, most of the inhabitants of Earth live underground, in ant-tanks, under the conviction that World War III is still going on and that if they emerge from hiding they will die from the Bag Plague, the Stink of Shrink, Raw-Claw-Paw, or one of a multitude of man-made viruses. In reality, though, the war stopped long ago, and the Earth is a park, divided up into the demesnes of the ruling classes. Like Ragle Gumm, one character digs his way out to discover the truth and to try to lead these latter-day Morlocks up to the light. The particular point which Dick wishes to rub in here, though, is that even outside science fiction people are genuinely at the mercy of their television screens. They cannot tell whether they are watching truth or a construct. They usually have no way of telling true history from the false varieties which Dick makes up. The end of the novel declares that what is essential—and not only in the novel—is a ferocious skepticism. People are too gullible, too easily deceived.

There is no such overt political thesis in *Martian Time-Slip*, of the same year, but in this Dick creates one of his most likable sets of characters, in Jack Bohlen, the Martian repairman, and Arnie Kott, senior member of the Waterworkers' Union—naturally a privileged body on arid Mars, though no one had previously been mundane enough to say so. Dick also brings into the novel what seems to be a personal image of "the Tomb World," a world in which everything is rotten and decaying, with buildings sliding to ruin, and bodies to corruption. This world is perceived only by an autistic child, but that child's perceptions seem stronger than the grandiose claims of governments and land speculators. Still another route into horror is via drugs.

The Three Stigmata of Palmer Eldritch moves rapidly from a protagonist who has the seemingly harmless job of guessing fashion for dolls and dollhouses to the notion of exploitation—for these "Perky Pat Layouts," as they are called, can be experienced only by people who take the drug Can-D to let them into the doll-world—to menace and terror. Can-D is about to be superseded by Chew-Z, a drug allegedly harmless, nonaddictive, government sponsored. This drug, however, puts its users (as in *Eye in the Sky*) in the world of Palmer Eldritch, a demon-figure with steel teeth, artificial hand, and mechanical eyes. Nor can they return from it. Chew-Z takes one into a variant, one might say, of "Tomb World."

Ubik prolongs this theme. Its hero, Joe Chip, finds the "Tomb World" happening around him, as it were. Cigarettes he touches fall into dust; cream turns sour; mold grows on his coffee; even his coins turn out of date. Then he himself starts to age. The only thing that can cure him is a spray of "Ubik," a material which halts the race to corruption and obsolescence. In a memorable scene near the end, Joe Chip reaches a drugstore just before it closes, to demand Ubik, only to find that the store is closing, the stock is out, spray cans too have aged, becoming cardboard packets. What force is doing all this? Are the characters in fact already dead, now existing only in a bizarre afterlife? For whose benefit is the spectacle being played out? Once again, Dick creates a happy ending, but more strongly than usual, one believes that this ending is demanded by the conventions of the field rather than by the logic of the plot.

For depth of paranoia, though, the prize should go to *Do Androids Dream of Electric Sheep?* This novel is best known as the original of the 1982 film *Blade Runner*, both book and film centering on a bounty hunter whose job is to kill androids. What the film could not do is show the depth of devotion which the characters in the book—who live in a world so radioactive that almost all unprotected creatures have died—give to their pets. Deckard the bounty hunter has a counterfeit electric sheep because he is too poor to afford a real one, but like everyone in the book he consistently consults the manual of animal prices. If he kills three more androids, could he buy a goat? If he spares one, will they give him an owl (thought to be extinct)? Would it be an artificial owl? The pitiless slaughter of androids is balanced against the extraordinary cosseting of every nonartificial creature, down to spiders. Yet what is the basis of the division? In a heartrending scene, after Deckard has wiped out his androids, another android comes and kills his goat. Before then, though, Deckard himself has been accused of being an android, been taken to the Hall of Justice, and been quite unable to prove his own identity—because, as soon becomes clear, all the authorities are themselves androids. The notions of undetectable forgery, total illusion, and unanimous conspiracy combine to make the central scenes of this novel as disorienting as any in Dick's work. In the background, a silent struggle goes on in "Tomb World."

Somewhere near this point, Dick's development was cut off. He wrote most movingly on the subject in the "Author's Note" to *A Scanner Darkly*. This novel, he says, is "about some people who were punished entirely too much for what they did." They were real people, the author's friends. They took drugs, like children playing; it was not a disease, it was an error of judgment, called a "life-style." He then lists seven of his friends who have died, three more with permanent brain damage, two with permanent psychosis, one with permanent pancreatic damage . . . the list goes on. How deeply Dick himself was involved in late 1960's California "drug culture," one cannot say. He himself insists this was exaggerated. Yet for whatever cause, Dick wrote less; and his mood became angrier, less playful.

Even so, the great surprise of *Flow My Tears, the Policeman Said* is its ending. In this world—a dystopia based on Nixon-era America—students are persecuted, the "nats" and the "pols" run identification checks in the streets, a quota is taken off daily to slave camps, civil liberties have vanished. Through the world wanders Jason Taverner, in the first chapter a rich and fantastically successful entertainer, who finds himself suddenly (in dream? psychosis? alternate reality?) in a place where everything is familiar, but no one knows him. His hunter is Police General Felix Buckman, as it were the arch-bogey of the liberal conscience, the policy-maker for the police-state. Yet at the end, with his sister dead and Taverner arrested, Buckman, weeping, finds himself at an all-night garage. He climbs out of his "quibble" and goes over to hug a lonely black—one of the very few black people in this world to have got through the sterilization programs. The moral is totally unexpected, as a reaction to incidents such as the Kent State University shootings. It is that even policemen can love. Even men systematically evil can abandon the system. The ending of this novel comes over as an extraordinarily generous gesture from an embittered man. As with the very strongly anti-drug stance of *A Scanner Darkly*, this scene shows that Dick, for all of his liberalism, is not prepared to accept the complete "anti-Establishment" package.

Nevertheless, from this point his works grow weirder, and more connected. Some of his later novels, such as the posthumously issued *Radio Free Albemuth*, were either not submitted or not accepted for publication. This group also includes the best of Dick's non-science-fiction novels, *Humpty Dumpty in Oakland*, a book most easily described as a sequel to John Steinbeck's *The Grapes of Wrath* (1939), recounting what happened after the "Okies" got to California: They settled down, lost their way, ran used-car lots, became "humpty dumpties," passive spectators of the American Dream. The central idea of the last set of Dick's science-fiction novels, however, is a form of Gnosticism, the ancient Christian heresy which insists that the world contains two forces, of good and evil, in eternal conflict, with only a remote or absent God trying occasionally to get through. Dick writes variations on this theme in *Valis, The Divine Invasion, The Transmigration of Timothy Archer*, and *Radio Free Albemuth*, mentioned above.

Valis, at least, makes a direct assault on the reader by including the character "Horselover Fat," a transparent translation of Philip K. Dick. He hears voices, very like the characters from Berkeley in *Radio Free Albemuth*, who believe they are being contacted by a sort of divine transmission satellite. What the voices say are variations on the view that the world is ruled by a Black Iron Empire, by secret fraternities in Rome or the United States; that the President of the United States, Ferris F. Fremont, has "the number of the beast" in his name; that true believers are exiles from another world. Is this mere madness? Horselover Fat remarks himself that the simplest explanation is that the drugs he took in the 1970's have addled his mind in the 1980's. Still, he has to believe his voices. One might say that Dick's corrosive skepticism has finally developed a blind spot; or alternatively, that the novelist has become a sadder and a wiser man. Whatever the decision, Dick's last novels could be characterized not as science fiction, but as theological fiction.

Dick's work as a whole shows clear evidence of his deep social concerns, reacting against Senator McCarthy and President Nixon, first praising and then condemning drugs, testing one notion after another concerning the limits of government. Yet it also remained solidly consistent in its private and personal quest for a definition of reality which will stand any trial. It could be said that Dick's work is obsessive, introspective, even paranoid. It has also to be said that it very rarely loses gentleness, kindness, even a rather wistful humor. Dick has certainly contributed more first-class novels to science fiction than anyone else in the field, and has convinced many also of the genre's ability to cope with serious reflections on the nature of humanity, and of perception.

T. A. Shippey

Other major works
SHORT FICTION: *A Handful of Darkness*, 1955; *The Variable Man and Other Stories*, 1957; *The Preserving Machine and Other Stories*, 1969; *The Book of Philip K. Dick*, 1973; *The Best of Philip K. Dick*, 1977; *I Hope I Shall Arrive Soon*, 1985; *The Collected Stories of Philip K. Dick*, 1987.
MISCELLANEOUS: *The Dark-Haired Girl*, 1988.

Bibliography
Greenberg, Martin Henry, and Joseph D. Olander, eds. *Philip K. Dick*. New York: Taplinger, 1983. Contains excellent essays by Aldiss, Disch, Hayles, Warren, Warrick, and Dick himself, supplemented by notes on the essays, a biographical note, a comprehensive bibliography of primary sources, a selected bibliography of criticism, notes on the contributors, and an index.
Mackey, Douglas A. *Philip K. Dick*. Boston: Twayne, 1988. A book-length study of Dick. After a sketch of Dick's life, Mackey provides a comprehensive survey of his fiction from the 1950's through the 1980's. Supplemented by a chronology, notes, an extensive bibliography of primary sources, an annotated list of selected secondary sources, and an index.

The Philip K. Dick Newsletter. Glen Ellen, Calif.: Philip K. Dick Society, 1983-   . An essential, well-edited newsletter featuring extracts from Dick's unpublished writings, news of forthcoming publications by and about Dick, photographs, interviews, and letters.

Robinson, Kim Stanley. *The Novels of Philip K. Dick.* Ann Arbor, Mich.: UMI Research Press, 1984. A survey of Dick's narrative structures and fictional techniques by a highly respected science-fiction writer.

Warrick, Patricia S. *Mind in Motion: The Fiction of Philip K. Dick.* Carbondale: Southern Illinois University Press, 1987. Contains excellent studies of eight of Dick's major novels.

CHARLES DICKENS

Born: Portsmouth, England; February 7, 1812
Died: Rochester, England; June 9, 1870

Principal long fiction

Pickwick Papers, 1836-1837 (originally published as *The Posthumous Papers of the Pickwick Club*); *Oliver Twist*, 1837-1839 (originally published as *The Adventures of Oliver Twist*); *Nicholas Nickleby*, 1838-1839 (originally published as *The Life and Adventures of Nicholas Nickleby*); *The Old Curiosity Shop*, 1840-1841; *Barnaby Rudge: A Tale of the Riots of '80*, 1841; *Martin Chuzzlewit*, 1843-1844 (originally published as *The Life and Adventures of Martin Chuzzlewit*); *Dombey and Son*, 1846-1848 (originally published as *Dealings with the Firm of Dombey and Son, Wholesale, Retail, and for Exportation*); *David Copperfield*, 1849-1850 (originally published as *The Personal History of David Copperfield*); *Bleak House*, 1852-1853; *Hard Times*, 1854 (originally published as *Hard Times for These Times*); *Little Dorrit*, 1855-1857; *A Tale of Two Cities*, 1859; *Great Expectations*, 1860-1861; *Our Mutual Friend*, 1864-1865; *The Mystery of Edwin Drood*, 1870.

Other literary forms

All of Charles Dickens' novels were published in bound form after serialization, the Oxford edition being the most complete modern collection. A prolific writer, Dickens also published a number of other works. He founded and edited the periodicals *Master Humphrey's Clock* (1840-1841), *Household Words* (1850-1859), and *All the Year Round* (1859-1870), in which many of his essays, collaborative works, and Christmas stories were originally published. Some of the essays have been collected: *Sketches by Boz* (1836), for example, comprises Dickens' periodical contributions from 1833 to 1836, and *The Uncommercial Traveller* (1860) reprints essays from *All the Year Round*. In addition to the Christmas stories, Dickens published five Christmas books, all collected in 1852. He recorded his travel experiences as well: *American Notes* (1842) depicts his first American tour, and *Pictures from Italy* (1846) is a collection of essays first printed in the *Daily News*. Finally, the texts of his public readings have appeared, along with reprints of his dramatic productions. Many of Dickens' works have been anthologized and adapted for stage and screen and the definitive Pilgrim Edition of his letters is in preparation.

Achievements

Known for his biting satire of social conditions as well as for his comic world view, Dickens began, with *Pickwick Papers*, to establish an enduring novelistic reputation. In fourteen completed novels and countless essays, sketches, and stories, he emerged as the champion of generosity and warmth of spirit, those human traits most likely to atrophy in an industrialized society. In his own day, he appealed to all levels of society but especially to the growing middle class, whose newfound literacy made them educable to eradicate the social evils they themselves had fostered. Dickens was extremely popular in America, despite his ongoing attack on the lack of an international copyright agreement, an attack directed in part against the Americans who had a financial stake in pirated editions of his works.

Above all, Dickens appealed to his readers' emotions, and through them, to an awakened social sense. To be sure, Dickens' sentimentality oends as many modern readers as it pleased Victorian ones. Indeed, the twentieth century reader may study his novels primarily for the enjoyment of his craft, but to do so is to ignore Dickens' purpose: to argue on the side of intuition against materialism, as Angus Wilson puts it, or on the side of the individual against the system, as Philip Hosbaum has commented. In his facility for comic language, for example, Dickens created the unforgettable Sairey Gamp, Flora Finching, and Alfred Jingle, whose manic lingo creates worlds with a preposterous logic of their own, but such lingo is sometimes a shield for a warm heart and sometimes an indicator of fragmentation and despair. The reader also finds that Dickens' attacks on certain social institutions, such as the Poor Law in *Oliver Twist* or the Court of Chancery in *Bleak House*, are actually attacks on universal human evils—the greed, hypocrisy, and lust for power that lead to dehumanization, that make, for example, a "species of frozen gentleman" out of Mr. Dombey instead of a warm, affectionate human being.

Biography

Born on February 7, 1812, in Landport, district of Portsmouth, on Portsea Island, England, Charles Dickens was the son of John Dickens, a Naval Pay Office employee, and Elizabeth Barrow, the daughter of the Naval Conductor of Moneys. John Dickens' largely unsuccessful struggle to gain middle-class respectability was hampered not only by his parents' career in domestic service, but also by the disgrace of his father-in-law, who left the country to avoid the consequences of a petty embezzlement. John Dickens' seaport life left a lasting impression on his son to be recorded partly in Rogue Riderhood's river activities in *Our Mutual Friend*, and partly in metaphor, as in *Dombey and Son*, where the running of the river into the ocean is the passage of life into immortality. John Dickens' improvidence and inevitable bankruptcy is reflected in the impecunious but absurdly hopeful Mr. Micawber and, more abstractly, in Dickens' ambiguous attitude toward wealth, which he viewed as a highly desirable tool but worthless as a gauge of human value, as in *Our Mutual Friend*, in which money is equated with an excremental dust heap. An inordinate number of his deserving characters acquire wealth fortuitously: Oliver Twist, the parish boy, finds his near relatives; Nicholas Nickleby becomes clerk to the generous Cheerybles; Esther Summerson comes under the protection of the well-to-do Jarndyce. Other childhood associations were incorporated as well. His nurse, Mary Weller, by her own dogmatic adherence, inculcated in him a distaste for Chapel Christianity; his childhood taste for theatricals blossomed into a lifelong fascination. (In fact, in 1832, only illness prevented him from auditioning at Covent Garden.) Perhaps no other circumstance, however, had so profound an effect on Dickens as his father's imprisonment in the Marshalsea for bankruptcy, well-chronicled in *David Copperfield*. John Forster, Dickens' friend and biographer, records the author's bitterness at being put to work at Warren's Blacking Factory. Even worse than the degradation of the job for the young Dickens was the feeling that he had been abandoned. While his period of employment in the factory could be measured in months, the psychological scars lasted for the rest of Dickens' life, as witnessed by his novelistic preoccupation with orphans and adopted families: Oliver Twist, Amy Dorrit, Pip, Little Nell—all abandoned in some sense and forced into precosity, some, in effect, reversing roles with their parents or guardians to become their protectors.

At the age of fifteen, Dickens was apprenticed as a law clerk in Doctor's Commons, certainly the source of his profound dislike for the pettifoggery exhibited in the Jarndyce case in *Bleak House*. He then became a reporter in Parliament, and, at the age of seventeen, fell in love with Maria Beadnell, the daughter of a banking family who discouraged the attentions of the impoverished young man. This experience, as well as his unsuccessful marriage to Catherine Hogarth, daughter of the editor of the *Morning Chronicle*, contributed much to his alternate idealization of women (such as Dora in *David Copperfield*) and mockery of their foibles.

At the time of his marriage, Dickens had been writing a serial for Robert Seymour's sporting drawings—a work that became *Pickwick Papers* upon Seymour's suicide. Dickens' success came quickly: he became editor of *Bentley's Miscellany* (1836), and in February, 1837, *Oliver Twist* began to appear, one month after the birth of the first of his ten children. Before *Oliver Twist* had finished its serial run, Dickens had begun *Nicholas Nickleby*, in which he drew on his dramatic interests to create the Crummles provincial acting company. Then, in 1840, Dickens arranged to edit *Master Humphrey's Clock*, which became a vehicle for both *The Old Curiosity Shop* and *Barnaby Rudge* (the story of the 1780 Gordon Riots). Some of his immense creative energy came from the early happiness of his marriage, but some also came from an effort to forget the death of his beloved sister-in-law Mary, who died in his arms when she was seventeen.

This period of activity ended in 1842 with a six-month visit to the United States. In letters, in *American Notes*, and in *Martin Chuzzlewit*, Dickens reveals his double vision of America. Welcomed in Boston by such literati as

Henry Wadsworth Longfellow, Dickens moved from the cultivated blue-stocking milieu into a furious newspaper war that was battling over the lack of an International Copyright. Dickens came to believe that while democracy did exist in such model factory towns as Lowell, Massachusetts, America's much-vaunted freedom was an excuse for vulgarity on the one hand and hypocrisy on the other. He was appalled at the conditions of slavery in St. Louis and dismayed by the flat stretches of the Great Plains and by the ever-present concern for partisan politics, money, and power. All of these he satirized bitterly in the American section of *Martin Chuzzlewit*.

At home again, he installed his sister-in-law Georgina in her lifelong role of housekeeper to counter what he judged to be Catherine's growing indolence, surely symptomatic of their growing disillusionment with each other. Two years later, he began publication of *Dombey and Son*, his first planned novel. His next, the autobiographical *David Copperfield*, contains advice by the novel's heroine, Agnes, that he applied to his own life: "Your growing power and success enlarge your power of doing good." In March, 1850, Dickens founded *Household Words*, a periodical that featured short stories, serialized novels, poetry, and essays. Dickens and his writers published exposés of hospitals, sanitary conditions, political affairs, education, law, and religion, all expressed in a characteristically fanciful style. In these years, Dickens was engaged in amateur theatricals, partly to raise money to endow an impoverished actors' home. Between 1852 and 1857, he wrote three novels: *Bleak House*, his experiment in first-person narration; *Hard Times*, an attack on utilitarianism; and *Little Dorrit*, a semiautobiographical work. Becoming more and more estranged from his wife, he engaged in a strenuous and highly popular series of readings from his works, again bringing his dramatic talent into play. In June, 1858, he published a much-criticized apologia for his marital separation; then, chafing at the restrictions imposed on *Household Words* by the publishers, Edward Chapman and William Hall, Dickens severed the connection and began *All the Year Round*, a new periodical of the same type.

His liaison with the actress Ellen Ternan continued in this period, during which he wrote *A Tale of Two Cities*, *Great Expectations*, and *Our Mutual Friend*, his last completed novel. He undertook another exhausting series of public readings, his reenactment of Nancy's murder in *Oliver Twist* proving the most demanding. In 1867, he left for a successful tour of the United States. He continued public readings until the end of his life.

Dickens died at Gad's Hill in Rochester on June 9, 1870, and is buried in Westminster Abbey. His last unfinished novel, *The Mystery of Edwin Drood*, appeared posthumously.

Analysis

The "Dickens World," as Humphrey House calls it, is one of sharp moral contrast, a world in which the self-seeking—imprisoned in their egotism—

rub shoulders with the altruistic, freed from the demands of self by concern for others; a world in which the individual achieves selfhood by creating a "home" whose virtues of honesty and compassion are proof against the dehumanizing "System"; a world in which all things are animate and where, indeed, metaphors for moral perversity take lives of their own, like the miasma of evil that hangs above the houses in *Dombey and Son*.

Many of Charles Dickens' most memorable characters are those whose language or personality traits are superbly comic: Sairey Gamp, the bibulous nurse in *Martin Chuzzlewit*, with her constant reference to the fictitious Mrs. 'Arris; Flora Finching, the parodic reincarnation of a stout, garrulous Maria Beadnell in *Little Dorrit*; and Turveydrop, the antediluvian Beau Brummel in *Bleak House*. To provide characters with distinguishing traits is, of course, a dramatic device (to see red hair and a handkerchief is to be reminded of Fagin, and knitting, of Mme. DeFarge); more important, however, such traits carry a moral resonance. While Dickens' villains grow more complex as his writing matures, most share an overriding egotism that causes them to treat people as things. Perhaps that is why things become animate; in a world in which human traits are undervalued, objects achieve a life and controlling power of their own. The miser Harmon disposes of Bella Wilfer in *Our Mutual Friend* as if she were a property to be willed away; the convict Jaggers creates a "gentleman" out of Pip in *Great Expectations*; both Carker and Dombey see Edith as a valuable objet d'art in *Dombey and Son*.

Dickens' later heroes and heroines are characterized by their movement toward self-actualization. In the early novels, Rose Maylie, Mr. Brownlow, Tom Pinch, Nicholas Nickleby, and even Pickwick represent compassionate but stereotyped models. Later, however, Dombey is thawed by his daughter Florence's love; Eugene Wrayburn, the blasé lawyer, is humanized by Lizzie Hexam; and Bella Wilfer gives up self-seeking for John Rokesmith. Some, however, must go through the reverse process of acquiring self-assertiveness. Florence Dombey is such a one; only by fleeing her father's household and establishing a family of her own can she achieve perspective. Amy Dorrit is another; she must grow up and then willfully become as a child again for the benefit of Arthur Clennam, who needs to be convinced of his worth. Esther Summerson is yet a third; persuaded of her worthlessness because of her illegitimacy, she must learn a sense of self-worth before she can marry Allan Woodstone.

Many of the heroes and heroines are tested by touchstone figures, such as Smike, Jo, Mr. Toots, Maggie, and Sloppy—unfortunates whose lack of mental capability or personal disfavor provide a test for altruism. Many of Dickens' child characters serve a similar purpose, from Oliver Twist and his famous request for more gruel to the itinerant Little Nell.

All of the characters are subject to the effects of the "System," in whatever shape it takes: Dotheboys Hall and the Gradgrind's school, the Circumlocution Office, the middle-class complacency of Podsnappery, the unsanitary conditions of Tom All Alone's, the financial shenanigans of Montague Tigg's Anglo-Bengalee Disinterested Loan and Life Insurance Company. Far worse are the hypocrisy of Pecksniff, the concupiscence of Gride, the utilitarianism of Gradgrind, and the lovelessness of Estella, but all are personal evocations of the evils of the system. Even as early as *Oliver Twist*, Dickens seemed to recognize that no one individual could rectify the evil; as Stephen Marcus comments, "*Pickwick Papers* is Dickens' one novel in which wickedness, though it exists, is not a threat. The unfortunate and the deprived . . . have only to catch a glimpse of Pickwick in order to be renewed, for this is the world of the 'good heart', that thaumaturgic resource of spirit." When Nicholas breaks up Dotheboys Hall by whipping Squeers, all that one can do is succor the runaways; when the law is befogged by obscurities as in the Jarndyce case, all one can do is provide a warm, loving household. This, in fact, seems to be Dickens' solution; for despite his call for reforms, he was, at heart, a conservative, more likely to help Angela Burdett-Coutts set up a home for "fallen women" and to campaign against public executions than to lead riots in the streets. Dickens, then, might say with Voltaire's Candide, "Let us cultivate our garden."

Nicholas Nickleby, an ebullient novel loosely patterned after such picaresque models as Henry Fielding's *Tom Jones* (1749), is ostensibly an attack on the abusive Yorkshire schools that served as repositories for unwanted children. It is, as well, a depiction of Dickens' theatrical concerns, a condemnation of greed, a mystery story, and a conventional romance. To be sure, as Bernard Bergonzi points out, it has been criticized for its lack of a tightly woven plot as well as for its lack of a "significant moral pattern"; nevertheless it stands as the first of Dickens' full-scale, complex novels.

Dickens went to some trouble to establish the realistic fabric of the novel. Dotheboys Hall is modeled on William Shaw's notorious Bowes Academy, and the generous Cheeryble brothers, who give employment to the titular hero, mirrors the merchants William and Daniel Grant. More important than the realistic antecedents, however, is what they represent: the schoolmaster Squeers and the Cheerybles are at opposite moral poles. Indeed, Nicholas' encounter with Dotheboys, his self-defense against Squeers, and his decision to "adopt" the enfeebled and mistreated Smike are preparation to confront his uncle Ralph, whose ungenerous nature is pardigmatic of moral usury. Even Nicholas' accidental joining with the Crummleses and their Infant Phenomenon is a way for him to act out his confrontation with pasteboard sword, for certainly, despite Crummles' benevolence, the closed world of the theater betrays as much selfishness as the world Nicholas eventually joins.

As Angus Wilson suggests, the foe that Nicholas confronts is more complex than generally recognized. Ralph, driven by the desire for money, is also driven by a desire for power. His belittlement of his clerk, Newman Noggs, is comically reflected in Miss Knag's spitefulness and in Mr. Lillyvick's patronizing attitude toward his relatives, and more seriously in Arthur Gride, the miser who charily serves an old wine—"liquid gold"—on his wedding day, and in Walter Bray, who affiances his daughter Madeline to Gride for a retirement stipend. Ralph is powerless, however, against generosity. Cast off by his uncle, Nicholas, like a hero in a French comedy of manners, rescues his sister Kate from the unwelcome advances of Sir Mulberry Hawk, one of Ralph's procurers; he is befriended by Noggs, with whose help he eventually rescues Madeline; and he is given a livelihood by the Cheerybles. In setting up a home for his mother, sister, and Smike, Nicholas establishes a center of domestic harmony independent of his uncle's world yet connected to that of the Cheerybles who inculcate similar homely virtues in their business. Indeed, as Nicholas gathers friends around him, Ralph is slowly denuded of his power. Both plot strands meet in the Gride/Bray association, where Ralph faces a double loss, material and psychological: not only does Gride's loss of valuable deeds spell the beginning of Ralph's financial downfall, but Ralph's scheme to marry Madeline to Bray is also foiled by his nephew, against whom he feels growing resentment.

Nicholas' circle of friends thus comes to dominate Ralph's circle of power. Ralph's bankruptcy is, moreover, symbolic of spiritual bankruptcy, for his ultimate ignominy is discovering that Smike, whom he had persecuted in an attempt to wound Nicholas, is his own son. That the enfeebled boy turned to Nicholas for help is, for Ralph, a final, inescapable bitterness. As Ralph's wheel of fortune reaches its nadir, he hangs himself, cursing the hope of the New Year which brings to Nicholas a marriage and a new family.

Partly the product of Dickens' 1842 trip to America, *Martin Chuzzlewit* takes as its theme the effects of selfishness. Some critics, such as Barbara Hardy, find this theme to be fragmented, insofar as the characters are so isolated that their moral conversions produce no resonance; or according to critic John Lucas, locate the flaws not only in narrative sprawl and faulty timing but also in Dickens' indecision as to "whether he is writing a realistic study or a moral and prescriptive fable." The fabular element is indeed strong. Young Martin is a developing hero whose American experiences and the selflessness of his companion Mark Tapley bring him to recognize his flaws, while his father, Old Martin, serves in his wealth and eccentricity as a touchstone for cupidity. In studying the cumulative effects of selfishness, Dickens portrays a number of family groups and also presents an effective psychological study of a murderer.

Pecksniff, ostensibly an architect and Young Martin's teacher, is the root of hypocrisy in the novel. He imposes on the gullible Tom Pinch; he raises his daughters, Charity and Mercy, to be spiteful and thoughtless; he tries to seduce Martin's fiancée, and then accuses Tom of the action; he attempts to influence Old Martin to disinherit his grandson. Like Molière's Tartuffe,

Pecksniff only appears to be virtuous. His assistant, Tom Pinch, is the reader's surrogate; honest, consistent, and generous, Pinch is exiled from Pecksniff's house and goes to London, where he is aided by John Westlock, a former pupil who has come into his inheritance. Tom's household, where he installs his sister Ruth (rescued from being a governess to a highly inconsiderate family), is in direct contrast to Pecksniff's in its innocent, loving companionship. Other family groups appear as contrasts as well, not the least being that of Anthony Chuzzlewit, brother to Old Martin. Anthony's miserly ways have inculcated in his son Jonas so grasping a nature that Jonas attempts to poison his father. Another kind of family group may be seen at Todgers' Commercial Boarding House, where the Pecksniffs stay and where Mercy, eventually married to the brutal Jonas, finds understanding from Mrs. Todgers. The association between young Martin and Mark Tapley may be contrasted with that between Pecksniff and Pinch, for Mark moves from the character of servant to that of friend. While Mark's Pollyanna attitude—that one must be "jolly" under all circumstances—has annoyed many critics, he is a descendant of the comedy of humors and serves as an important antidote to Martin's selfishness. In setting Martin's conversion (a purgative illness) in the swamps of America, Dickens suggests that hypocrisy, greed, and false pride are not simply manifestations of the British social milieu but flourish even in the "City of Eden," which that worshiper of freedom, Major Hannibal Chollop, praises so highly.

Jonas, on the other hand, undergoes no such conversion, although Mercy fills a role similar to that of Mark. As an investor in a pyramid scheme, the Anglo-Bengalee Company, he is blackmailed into procuring Pecksniff as an investor by Montague Tigg, who is privy to Jonas' poisoning scheme. Fearing exposure, Jonas murders Tigg. Dickens' portrayal of the murderer's frame of mind is exceptional, accompanied as it is by a study of Nadgett, the self-effacing paid informer who shadows Jonas like conscience itself. Even more telling is the disclosure that the deed was unnecessary, for Anthony, who had discovered his son's scheme and foiled it, is said to have died of a broken heart.

The regrouping that occurs at the end when Old Martin confesses his own kind of selfishness, that of suspicion of others, is a reestablishment of an extended family and a casting out of Pecksniff as a kind of scapegoat. Martin and Mary, Ruth Pinch and John Westlock are affianced; only Tom Pinch, hopelessly in love with Mary, remains unwed, to be a source of financial support for Pecksniff and Charity, who cadge small amounts from him. In the final analysis, Dickens has performed an "anatomy of selfishness" that is especially powerful because some of his characters have exhibited moral development. To be sure, Old Martin's pretended subservience to Pecksniff and final revelations may be seen as contrivances making possible a *deus ex machina* ending; yet, for all their artificiality, the conversions seem as true in spirit as do Jonas' terrified and cowardly maunderings.

Dombey and Son is considered to be the first novel of Dickens' maturity. Indeed, as John Butt and Kathleen Tillotson point out, it is the first for which he worked out a complete plot outline; therefore, the subplots are controlled and a fully orchestrated set of symbols emerges. Importantly, John Lucas notes that *Dombey and Son* presents the social panorama of the new, industrialized England, allowing "patterns of behavior and language to suggest connections more deeply insistent than blood-ties."

In this story of a middle-class merchant prince who must learn to place heart above head, Dickens produces one of his most moving and powerful studies of childhood, not only in Florence, the neglected daughter, but also in Paul, whom Dombey regards as a small version of himself. Paul is portrayed as an "old fashioned" boy, one who astonishes his father by asking what money is. Unlike Oliver Twist, who seeks to find a way into society, Paul runs counter to its expectations, resisting his father's attempt to make him into a grown-up before he has been a child. Alive to the world of the imagination, Paul is left untouched by Blimber's educational establishment, described as a hothouse where young minds are forced to produce before their time. Mr. Toots, one of Dickens' divine fools, is intellectually blasted by the process, but retains a sweetness of soul that adds poignancy to his comic diction.

When Paul dies in Florence's arms, Dickens illustrates his pervasive water imagery in a masterly way. Paul, rocked gently out to sea in a flood of divine love, has come "to terms with the watery element," as noted by Julian Moynihan; only by close association with the sea is anyone in Dombey saved from an atrophying of the affections. Paul's death is but one step in the education of Dombey, whom it initially hardens rather than softens: Dombey blames all of those Paul loved—Polly Toodle, his wet nurse; Walter Gay, one of Dombey's clerks in love with Florence; and Florence herself—for alienating Paul's affections. Another important step comes from Dombey's second marriage, which is to Edith Granger, a young widow put on the marriage market by her Regency mother, the artificial Mrs. Skewton. Bought for her accomplishments and ability to bear sons, Edith sets her will against Dombey's, determined to scorn his material success. She elopes with John Carker, the manager to whom Dombey had entrusted not only his domestic troubles but also his business affairs. Outraged, Dombey strikes Florence when she tries to comfort him. Florence runs away, taking refuge with a friend of Walter's uncle. Edith, eventually runs away from Carker, for her motive was not adultery but vengeance. Carker, while trying to escape from the pursuing Dombey, is hit by a train. As Marcus notes, the railroad is Dickens' "great symbol of social transformation" as well as Carker's nemesis.

That Florence takes refuge with Captain Cuttle, a friend of Walter's uncle, shows the way in which the ocean theme is invoked even in a comic way, for

Captain Cuttle is a peg-legged, Bible-quoting sea dog, yet he proves to be a tenderhearted surrogate father to Florence. Her affiancement to Walter, who, at Dombey's instigation, has been sent to the West Indies and shipwrecked, is another blow to Dombey, for it allies him not only with a class he shuns but also with an individual he believes had stolen his son's affections.

The last step in the education of Dombey is the failure of his business, largely through Carker's machinations. Left alone in his empty mansion to be pitied by Miss Tox, an old-maid figure whose ridiculousness, like Captain Cuttle's, is belied by her warmth of heart, Dombey meditates on the remembered figure of his daughter. His contemplation of suicide is interrupted, however, when Florence unexpectedly returns. For Dickens, Florence serves as the model of Christian, womanly behavior, of unselfish self-abnegation that, founded upon love, redeems her father. She returns because, as a mother, she can imagine what desertion by a child would be like.

The story of Dombey was a powerful parable for the middle classes, for whom, Dickens believed, overconcentration on such firms as Dombey and Son led to dehumanization, to a buying and selling not of goods but of people. That Paul's old-fashioned, loving nature could evoke responses in such un- likely quarters as in the pinched and spare Miss Tox or in the schoolmarmish Cornelia Blimber, or that Florence could melt both the disdainful Edith and her hardhearted father, is testimony to Dickens' optimism. In keeping with the theme, all of the characters, no matter how comic, are invariably treated as more than comic elements. Mr. Toots and his fascination with the boxer, the Game Chicken; Miss Tox's futile hope to become Mrs. Dombey; even the straitlaced Mrs. Pipchin; and the seaman's caricature, Captain Cuttle himself are integrated with the plot and ranged on the side of heart.

While *David Copperfield* is considered to be Dickens' autobiographical novel *par excellence*, *Little Dorrit* explores some of the same themes through the metaphor of the imprisonment that had so deep an effect on the Dickens' family fortunes. Critical opinion ranges from Angus Wilson's comment that the "overcomplicated plot" weakens the imprisonment/release theme, to Lionel Trilling's assessment that the novel is "one of the most profound . . . and most significant works of the nineteenth century." In *Little Dorrit*, imprisonment has many facets. The initial and end scenes are set in the Marshalsea, where William Dorrit, imprisoned like Dickens' father for debt, has set up a social circle whose obsequiousness and class consciousness is simply a reflection of the society outside the prison. The resemblance suggests, in fact, that the large, self-seeking society without is itself a prison, for even when William Dorrit is freed by a legacy (as was John Dickens), he carries the taint of the Marshalsea with him, attempting to conform to social conventions so rigid that they dehumanize him, and hiring the "prunes and prisms" Mrs. General to tutor his daughters. That Dorrit, in ill health, should break down at Mrs. Merdle's state dinner to babble about the prison is indicative that he has never, indeed, left it but has merely called it by different names.

Some prisons are built to contain those like Blandois, an evocation of the evil principle; others are less obvious, like the workhouse, for example, where old Nandy lives, or Bleeding Heart Yard, whose tenants are imposed upon by the patriarchal landlord Casby, or the Circumlocution Office, an accurate representation of the futile motions of a government bound by red tape. People, as well, create their own prisons: Miss Wade, for example, writes "The History of a Self-Tormentor"; Flora Finching is an "embodiment of romantic love that persists against all reason and propriety," as Wilson calls her; even Cavalletto is sequesterd by his inability to speak English fluently. Amy, or Little Dorrit, is held in bondage not only by her selfless love for her father but also by her neurotic refusal to be anything but a child. Her sister Fanny willfully contracts a marriage with the dandified Edmund Sparkler, a marriage that guarantees her social respectability at the price of a fool for a husband. Fanny's prison becomes even smaller when her father-in-law, Mr. Merdle, commits suicide before his financial chicanery is discovered; without the emollient of money, Fanny spends her days in social battle with her mother-in-law, leaving her children in Little Dorrit's care.

For Arthur Clennam, to return home to his mother's house is to return to imprisonment, where the walls are walls of the spirit, built of her unforgiving nature and her Calvinism that judges by the letter, not by the spirit of the ethical law. Clennam, however, carries his prison with him in the form of diffidence, for it is a lack of self-confidence that prevents him from proposing to Pet Meagles and almost prevents him from believing in the redeeming love of Little Dorrit herself (whom Lionel Trilling sees finally as "the Paraclete in female form"). In the end, he deliberately takes responsibility for his friend Doyce's financial trouble and is imprisoned in William Dorrit's old room. It is fitting that Amy should tend him there, for just as she held the key of affection to lead her father from the prison of self, so she holds the key of love that frees Clennam. In this respect, she radically differs from Clennam's mother, who, knowing that Arthur Clennam is her husband's illegitimate child, takes her vengeance accordingly.

Clearly, in *Little Dorrit*, the individual is both the jailer and the jailed, the cause of suffering and the sufferer; perhaps nowhere else does Dickens so emphasize the intertwined fates of all humans. At this stage in his life, when he was actively involving himself in a number of projects and coming to understand that his marriage was failing, Dickens' view of the human condition had little of the sunny hope exhibited, for example, in *Pickwick Papers*, or little of the simplistic interpretation of motivation found in *Nicholas Nickleby*. Indeed, the last lines of the novel sound a quiet note; Little Dorrit and Clennam go down into the midst of those who fret and chafe as if entering a prison; their only hope is "a modest life of usefulness and happiness." Their ability to quell the "usual uproar" seems severely limited.

For J. Hillis Miller, "*Our Mutual Friend* presents a fully elaborated definition of what it means to be interlaced with the world." In this last completed novel, Dickens has indeed relinquished the idea that evil or, in fact, the redemption of society resides in any one individual or institution. The Poor Law in *Oliver Twist*, the effects of education in *Nicholas Nickleby*, the law itself in *Bleak House* represent abuses that are manifestations of a larger illness permeating society. This view, which Dickens begins to develop in *Little Dorrit* is clear in *Our Mutual Friend*. From the violent, repressed sexuality of the schoolmaster Bradley Headstone to the cool indifference of Eugene Wrayburn, who would despoil Lizzie Hexam to satisfy a whim, all society is affected with a kind of moral (and financial) selfishness that was a matter of parody in *Martin Chuzzlewit*. Even the heroine, Bella Wilfer, becomes, as she calls herself, a "mercenary little wretch," consciously weighing her desire for a wealthy marriage against love for John Rokesmith. The exuberance of subplotting evident in Dickens' early novels is again evident here, although in this case he provides a more disciplined framework, giving the reader not only a central symbol—money (represented as an excremental dust-heap) inherited by the Boffins from the miser John Harmon—but also a central character, the enigmatic John Rokesmith, Harmon's son and therefore rightful heir to the fortune.

The central plot that devolves from a single generous act—the Boffins' returning to Rokesmith his inheritance—is illustrative of the title, whose significance Arnold Kettle explores in terms of the mutuality of relationships, insofar as the activities of Rokesmith/Harmon interweave all social levels, from Wegg and Venus to the Podsnaps. The novel, moreover, contains elements of the masquerade in *Martin Chuzzlewit* as well as the motif of educating the affections in *Dombey and Son*. Boffin pretends to be a miser and Rokesmith an impoverished clerk to convince Bella that grasping for wealth deadens the heart. Her happy marriage is contrasted with that of her mother, whose perpetual toothache, tender temperament, and mortuarylike deportment minister to her pride but not to the comfort of her family. Indeed, other marriages in the book are hardly preferable: the nouveau-riche Veneerings, who make good friends of strangers in order to entertain them at a sumptuous board, are one example; another is the Lammles, who, sadly deceived in their original estimate of each other's wealth, set out to defraud the world. Likewise, the Podsnaps, an embodiment of the solid, tasteless, and pretentious middle class, are concerned not, for example, with the emotional state of the much-repressed Georgiana but rather with their place on the social scale, and they are therefore willing to entrust her to the Lammles, whose intention it is to procure her in marriage for the moneylender "Fascination Fledgeby."

The novel is about the use and misuse of childhood as well. It offers a panoply of unnatural parents: Jesse Hexam, who forces Lizzie to dredge corpses from the Thames; the bibulous "Mr. Dolls," whose crippled daughter

Fanny ("Jenny Wren") is a dolls' dressmaker. There are adoptive parents as well—some, like the Lammles, shamming affection to benefit themselves; others, like Lizzie, mothering her selfish brother Charley; or Riah, giving Lizzie fatherly protection; or Betty Higden, showing kindness to her diminutive boarders. The prime example is, of course, the Boffins, who nurture a series of children, young and old, beginning with John Harmon, for whom their kindness created a home in his father's cold house; then Bella, who they felt had been harmed by the dictates of Harmon's will, being, as she was, ceded in marriage to a stranger, then Johnny, the orphan who dies; and finally, Sloppy, an idiot foundling. Their adoption of Sloppy, an unprepossessing individual, is the key to the series, for Sloppy is another of Dickens' touchstone figures.

The subplot which runs parallel to the education of Bella is that of Lizzie Hexam's wooing by Eugene Wrayburn. While Bella originally refuses Rokesmith because of his supposed poverty, Lizzie evades Wrayburn because of his wealth, fearing that she will become his mistress rather than his wife. Again, while Bella can accept Rokesmith's proposal without knowing his true identity, Lizzie flees Wrayburn to a factory town (perhaps an evocation of Lowell, Massachusetts, where Dickens visited on his American tour). Even Bella's moment of bravery, in which she relinquishes all hope of inheriting the Boffins' money in favor of defending Rokesmith, whose dignity she thinks Boffin is maligning, has a parallel, albeit on a more earthy level; Lizzie rescues Wrayburn from the murderous attack of Headstone, thereby putting to use the skills she had learned when working with her father. Wrayburn's proposal of marriage to her is his recognition that financial and class standing are irrelevant in matters of the heart.

It is, in fact, their marriage that is central to the "trial" scene at the end of the novel, in which the Veneerings convene their friends to pass judgment on Wrayburn's action. Mr. Twemlow, a minor character with romantic notions and little apparent strength of character, nevertheless rises to the occasion, as he had in agreeing to help warn the Podsnaps that their daughter was in danger of a mercenary scheme. He asserts, with finality and against the general disparagement, that if Wrayburn followed his "feeling of gratitude, of respect, of admiration and affection," then he is "the greater gentleman for the action." Twemlow's voice is clearly not the voice of society; rather, it is the voice of the heart, and it is to him that Dickens gives the closing word.

Patricia Marks

Other major works

SHORT FICTION: *Sketches by Boz*, 1836; *A Christmas Carol*, 1843; *The Chimes*, 1844; *The Cricket on the Hearth*, 1845; *The Battle of Life*, 1846; *The Haunted Man*, 1848; *Reprinted Pieces*, 1858; *The Uncommercial Traveller*, 1860; *George*

Silverman's Explanation, 1868; *Christmas Stories*, 1871.

PLAYS: *The Strange Gentleman*, 1836; *The Village Coquettes*, 1836; *Mr. Nightingale's Diary*, 1851 (with Mark Lemon); *No Thoroughfare*, 1867 (with Wilkie Collins).

NONFICTION: *American Notes*, 1842; *Pictures from Italy*, 1846.

CHILDREN'S LITERATURE: *A Child's History of England*, 1852-1854; *The Life of Our Lord*, 1934.

MISCELLANEOUS: *Master Humphrey's Clock*, 1840-1841 (periodical, edited); *Household Words*, 1850-1859 (periodical, edited); *All the Year Round*, 1859-1870 (periodical, edited).

Bibliography

Flint, Kate. *Dickens*. Brighton, England: Harvester Press, 1986. One of the Harvester New Readings, attempting to generate fresh insights into Dickens by looking at paradoxes within his novels and beween his novels and his culture. Includes a select bibliography and an index.

Johnson, Edgar. *Charles Dickens: His Tragedy and Triumph*. 2 vols. Boston: Little, Brown, 1952. Still the best biographical account of Dickens, evaluating each of his novels, placing them firmly within his career, and relating them to his life and times. A full bibliography and an index are provided.

Marcus, Steven. *From Pickwick to Dombey*. London: Chatto & Windus, 1965. Traces Dickens' development as a novelist over the first half of his career, relating fiction, life, and culture. Contains a bibliography and an index.

Miller, J. Hillis. *Charles Dickens: The World of His Novels*. Cambridge, Mass.: Harvard University Press, 1959. Traces the development of Dickens' imagination through nine of his major novels. Includes a select bibliography and an index.

Page, Norman. *A Dickens Companion*. Basingstoke, England: Macmillan, 1984. This mini-encyclopedia gives a full account of all Dickens' writings (including critical responses), the main characters of each novel, a chronology, a topography, a select bibliography, and a filmography.

JAMES DICKEY

Born: Atlanta, Georgia; February 2, 1923

Principal long fiction
Deliverance, 1970; *Alnilam*, 1987.

Other literary forms
James Dickey's early fame as a writer was based on several volumes of poetry. He has also published books of criticism and of children's poetry.

Achievements
At the age of thirty-eight, in the midst of a successful career as an advertising executive, Dickey became a full-time poet. Five years later, in 1966, he won the National Book Award for a collection of poems entitled *Buckdancer's Choice* (1965), and he was appointed Poetry Consultant to the Library of Congress. In 1967, his collection *Poems, 1957-1967* won critical praise. Dickey's first novel, *Deliverance*, was published in 1970 and was a best-seller. His second novel, *Alnilam*, appeared in 1987 after a seventeen-year conception.

Biography
Born and reared in Atlanta, Georgia, James Dickey attended public schools and experienced a typical twentieth century boyhood and adolescence. He excelled in sports and became a notable football player at Clemson University. During World War II and the Korean War, Dickey flew more than one hundred night combat missions. Returning to the United States after World War II, he enrolled at Vanderbilt University. There the subjects of his compositions for a writing course, based on his war experiences, made Dickey stand out from other students, who were writing about their summer vacations. At Vanderbilt, Dickey absorbed the literary tradition established by the Fugitive Poets, such as John Crowe Ransom, Allen Tate, and Robert Penn Warren, and discovered himself to be a poet. He was graduated with honors and went on to finish a master's degree before taking a job teaching English in college. He left teaching for immediate success in advertising, first in New York and later in Atlanta. A grant allowed him to retire from advertising in his mid-thirties and pursue writing full-time. He became convinced of the absolute necessity and worth of writing, of writing as a calling demanding total commitment and absorption. His poems were the narration of intense experiences both imaginary and real, whether the dreamlike falling of an airline stewardess into a Midwestern cornfield or the shark-fishing experience of young boys. As he wrote his poems as extended narratives, it was natural for Dickey also to write novels. Like his poems, his novels deal with human

intensities on a visceral level where the limits of human vulnerability and endurance are explored.

Analysis

James Dickey's novels *Deliverance* and *Alnilam* were published seventeen years apart, and the chronological separation parallels the levels of difference in their content and style. *Deliverance*, written by Dickey when he was in his forties, is more conventional in form and more accessible to a popular readership. The reader is quickly plunged into the equivalent of an adventure story, as four middle-aged men take a canoe trip in North Georgia and a malevolent pair of mountain men force them into a primal life-or-death encounter. *Alnilam*, a formidably physical book of 682 pages, defies the reader in many ways, including the intermittent use of experimental double-column pages where the simultaneous narration of the blind character's perception and the seeing narrator is developed. The blind man, Frank Cahill, is physically incapable of the more conventionally heroic feats performed by the narrator of *Deliverance*. This limitation of the main character seems a deliberate aim of Dickey, as he is writing a book about the delusions human beings sustain in their assumed youth and strength. Yet Dickey is also concerned with physical reality, and the task of characterizing the blind Cahill gives Dickey's imagination a broad field of sensations to explore.

Though different in many ways, the novels share a concern with men struggling to survive. *Deliverance* considers the angst of middle-aged suburban males and the efforts they make to escape their civilized imprisonment while dreading the alternative of survival in the wild. *Alnilam* takes the he-man Cahill—a carpenter and lover of boards and nails—and, by making him become blind, places him in a wilderness of greater darkness than the North Georgia forests of *Deliverance*; the normal world becomes as mysterious and untrustworthy as wild nature. Both novels consider the questions quoted from David Hume in an epigraph to *Alnilam*: "Where am I, or what? From what causes do I derive my existence, and to what condition do I return? Whose favour shall I court, and whose anger must I dread? What beings surround me?"

Deliverance conjures the world of modern America in the commercial South of the 1960's. The four male characters have jobs which are typical of this world: bottle distribution, mutual fund sales, advertising, and apartment rental. The main character, Ed Gentry, becomes increasingly aware that running an advertising agency is death-in-life. He admires the survivalist Lewis, who has honed his body to a muscular perfection through constant exercise and is devoted to a hypothetical future fantasy in which his physical superiority will keep him alive. Dickey is both critical and supportive of Lewis' point of view. He suggests there is in men a need to be tested, to be physically pitted against stress, as a daily fact of life. The modern world has eliminated this part of what it means to be human, and the restlessness of men such as Ed and Lewis to polish their survival skills and instincts indicates a real human need. The modern world has replaced the world where such skills were practiced, however, and men look ridiculous if they believe and behave as sincerely as Lewis. Thus, Lewis must manufacture his own wilderness, must find it before it is buried by developers.

Lewis discovers his dangerous place in North Georgia: a river to explore by canoe. Ed and Lewis are joined by Bobby and Drew, who are less avid but ready for a change of scene. Though the river has treacherous places and does damage to the novice canoers, it is human ugliness which is revealed to be the main danger. Two hillbillies appear to Bobby and Ed on the second day. They are repulsive, lacking teeth and manners, and they sodomize Bobby and prepare to do worse to Ed before Lewis kills one of the mountain men with an arrow through his chest. The four suburbanites are faced with a decision: do what civilization dictates and face the local authorities, or bury "the evidence" and hope to escape. Lewis argues that survival dictates the latter, and Bobby and Ed agree. After burying the attacker and continuing down the river, Drew is shot and killed by the other hillbilly, the two canoes capsize, and the three survivors are battered by water and stones before landing in a gorge. With Lewis' broken leg and Bobby's general cowardice, Ed is left to scale the gorge walls and kill the sniper with his bow and arrow. The three make it to a town, ultimately escape the local law, and live to savor the next year's damming of the river, creating a recreational lake which hides all evidence of their experience.

Ed has been tested—a good thing, as implied by the title of the novel, but horrible. Ed has taken the blood and life of another man who had wanted his own. Had he not, he and his friends would have perished. He has also been delivered into an understanding of something disturbing about being human, about what humans carry inside them. This knowledge is good because it is truth, and nothing more. Dickey is aware that men in World War II learned to kill thousands from bombers without seeing their faces or hearing their screams. *Deliverance* presents its main character with an enemy who must be killed face-to-face, as men killed one another before modern warfare. There is a kind of joy for Ed in this combat, but he must return to Atlanta for a lifetime of remembering while he pursues the art of advertising. Dickey intimates that, after such a deliverance experience, the spiritual corrosions of civilization—designing ads for women's underwear—will not so completely dampen Ed Gentry's spirit, as they had before.

Deliverance is an unabashedly self-reflective book. At the time that he wrote it, Dickey's passions for archery and the guitar, which Drew plays in the novel, were well documented in magazine articles. Ed Gentry, the narrator, works in the field of advertising, where Dickey spent many successful years. With *Alnilam*, however, Dickey projects a persona whose similarities to himself are more metaphorical than literal. Frank Cahill is an Atlanta carpenter with a high school education who loves to build things, look at blueprints, construct an amusement park labyrinth with his bare hands, and run a swimming pool for the public. Then, in middle age, he becomes blind from diabetes. Suddenly, a man who had loved to be in the visible world, making new things appear with hammer, wood, and nails, is now closed off permanently from being that man. Cahill does not complain and listens to the doctor, who suggests that blindness, rather than killing him, can make Cahill alive in a new way. Another epigraph from David Hume suggests how this might occur: "May I not clearly and distinctly conceive that a body, falling from the clouds, and which, in all other respects, resembles snow, has yet the taste of salt or feeling of fire?"

The reader senses the test Dickey is giving himself as a writer. All characterization demands empathy, but it is more difficult to imagine what one is not than what one is. Also, Dickey is passionate about the world, and a blind narrator forces him to view it through a new dimension. Blindness, while closing off the visible, sharpens touch, smell, hearing, and, most satisfying to Cahill, memory. Cahill's memory, whether of roller skating all day on Atlanta streets, watching a boy fly a rubber band airplane in a park, or coming upon a waterfall during a picnic hike, becomes an etched message which repeatedly appears and a measure for all the unseeableness of his present world. Cahill in his blindness is a metaphor for the private consciousness to which everyone is confined, and the replays of memory allow Dickey to emphasize this point. Cahill, divorced, having never seen his son, and regretting neither the divorce nor the sonlessness, has unashamedly accepted his privacy and distance. Blinded, however, he makes a pilgrimage into the land of other selves.

With Cahill drawn in such a manner that he cannot be easily identified with the author, Dickey places him in a world very familiar to the younger Dickey: a training base for World War II pilots. Cahill's son, Joel, a pilot trainee, has died in a crash during a forest fire in the North Carolina hills. Cahill comes to the base in his new blindness accompanied by his version of a Seeing Eye dog. Zack is not a graduate from a training school for guide dogs but part shepherd and part wolf; Cahill and a friend trained him before Cahill went blind. Zack possesses a blend of viciousness and loyalty that Cahill adores.

Mystery surrounds the death of Joel, and initially Cahill suspects foul play. Joel has been an inspiration to his fellow trainees, and a secret society has developed, with Joel as the leader. Cahill's conversations with Joel's friends reveals the society's name, Alnilam (the middle star of the constellation Orion's belt), and intention: the mystical union with other young pilots across the nation leading to a destruction of all war and the means to wage war.

By novel's end, this scheme will be revealed for what it is—high-minded but naïve youthful rebellion against authority. Yet Joel was an extraordinary young man. He innately grasped the subtleties of flying and developed a hypnotic training called "Death's Baby Machine," which struggling young pilots received sitting in an ordinary chair. In his mind, Cahill is able to create a psychological and physical portrait of Joel from questioning those who knew him on the base, and he realizes that giftedness mixed with unwillingness to obey rules constituted Joel's essence. Cahill, who never saw Joel alive or made any effort to that end, can now clutch the few personal remnants of his son in his coat pockets: the broken pilot's goggles, a burned zipper from his boot found near the crash, a piece of wire from the airplane. Cahill steadily contemplates the tangible remains while absorbing the memory fragments from the other pilots. His boy is alive in his head. Cahill, in this blitz of story and memorabilia, is learning to love, but the word does little to indicate the combination of physical impressions and the straining for meaning which come to make up Joel in Cahill's consciousness.

Dickey's creation of a blind character allows him to exploit his bias toward the physical. The world has never been so mediated as felt. Even when the seeing, right-hand column is being read, the experience is emphatically visceral. A bus drives away at the novel's end: "The gears gathered, smashed and crowded, found each other; the bus straightened onto the highway, . . . The highway came to exist in the bodies of the passengers, as the driver brought it into himself, and with it made the engine hoarse and large."

Dickey shows that Cahill, while now blind, has never been so fully *in* the world, and a dead son has never been more alive for him. Joel's Alnilam brothers show a film of their group's arrival at the base. Cahill, privy to their secrets because of their perception of his own arrival as part of Joel's master plan, is present at the showing and asks for a description of Joel when the projector sends out his image. Hearing of a curl of hair across the forehead, Cahill strains out of his chair in an effort to see his son. Later, taking a bath and speaking aloud of the wondrous good things there are in the world, such as a hot bath to soak in and a bottle of gin to swallow, Cahill hears Joel speak. Zack hears him as well and tears up the room. A ghost is as real and sensible as hot water. The world is full of marvels, and human beings are rich creatures both to be and to know.

This message might be a summation of what Dickey writes fiction about. He will not leave disenchanted suburbanites amid unmitigated ennui. *Deliverance* claims that a man has things to prove to himself. *Alnilam* claims that a man is composed of more than he knows and lives in a world of presences and forces which he tends to ignore or disbelieve. In Cahill, Dickey creates a primal character, a sort of caveman, through whom Dickey as a writer can imagine all sensations anew, from the feeling of snowflakes to the taste of water. Dickey wants to go back to man before he was dulled by civilization, and in *Deliverance* and *Alnilam* he imagines characters who experience their basic vitality as living creatures.

Bruce Wiebe

Other major works

POETRY: *Into the Stone and Other Poems*, 1960; *Drowning with Others*, 1962; *Helmets*, 1964; *Two Poems of the Air*, 1964; *Buckdancer's Choice*, 1965; *Poems, 1957-1967*, 1967; *The Achievement of James Dickey: A Comprehensive Selection of His Poems, with a Critical Introduction*, 1968; *The Eye-Beaters, Blood, Victory, Madness, Buckhead and Mercy*, 1970; *The Zodiac*, 1976; *The Strength of Fields*, 1977, revised 1979; *Veteran Birth: The Gadfly Poems, 1947-1949*, 1978; *Head-Deep in Strange Sounds: Free-Flight Improvisations from the UnEnglish*, 1979; *Fading Falling, May Day Sermon, and Other Poems*, 1981; *The Early Motion*, 1981; *Puella*, 1982; *The Central Motion: Poems, 1968-1979*, 1983.

PLAYS: *Deliverance*, 1972 (screenplay), 1981 (published); *The Call of the Wild*, 1976 (teleplay, based on the novel by Jack London).

NONFICTION: *The Suspect in Poetry*, 1964; *A Private Brinksmanship*, 1965 (address); *Spinning the Crystal Ball: Some Guesses at the Future of American Poetry*, 1967; *Metaphor as Pure Adventure*, 1968 (lecture); *Babel to Byzantium: Poets and Poetry Now*, 1968; *Self-Interviews*, 1970; *Sorties*, 1971 (essays); *Exchanges . . . Being in the Form of a Dialogue with Joseph Trumbull Stickney*, 1971; *Jericho: The South Beheld*, 1974; *God's Images: The Bible— A New Vision*, 1977; *The Enemy from Eden*, 1978; *In Pursuit of the Grey Soul*, 1979; *The Water-Bug's Mitten's: Ezra Pound, What We Can Use*, 1979 (lecture); *The Starry Place Between the Antlers: Why I Live in South Carolina*, 1981; *The Eagle's Mile*, 1981; *False Youth: Four Seasons*, 1982; *The Poet Turns on Himself*, 1982; *For a Time and Place*, 1983; *Night Hurdling: Poems, Essays, Conversations, Commencements, and Afterwords*, 1983; *Sorties*, 1984.

CHILDREN'S LITERATURE: *Tucky the Hunter*, 1979.

TRANSLATION: *Stolen Apples*, by Yevgeny Yevtushenko, 1971.

Bibliography

Batchelor, John Calvin. "James Dickey's Odyssey of Death and Deception." *Book World—The Washington Post Magazine*, May 24, 1987, 1-2. A worthwhile review that draws connections between *Deliverance* and *Alnilam*.

Dickey, James. *Self-Interviews*. Edited by Barbara Reiss and James Reiss. Garden City, N.Y.: Doubleday, 1970. The most interesting commentary on Dickey is that of the writer himself. A collection of transcribed tapes of Dickey talking about his life and poetry. Includes an informative piece of autobiography on Dickey's life before he became a full-time writer and straightforward analyses of poems that Dickey wrote in the 1950's and 1960's.

_____. *Sorties*. Garden City, N.Y.: Doubleday, 1971. Divided into two sections. The first is a daily journal Dickey wrote in the late 1960's, which contains an interesting mix of ruminations on everything from archery to the nature of love, as well as lengthy character and plot sketching from what was to be published as *Alnilam* sixteen years later. These entries provide a firsthand glimpse into the extensive planning and rearranging that occur in the creation of a novel. The second section contains essays on other poets, including Theodore Roethke.

_____. *The Voiced Connections of James Dickey.* Edited by Ronald Baughman. Columbia: University of South Carolina Press, 1989. Baughman has selected portions of interviews with Dickey from 1965 to 1987. The range of selections includes Dickey talking about his poetry, his writing process, his fascination with sextants and celestial navigation, the work of other poets, and lengthy discussion of *Deliverance* and *Alnilam*. The image of a fascinating writer emerges, one who speaks plainly about the most sublime things.

Kirschten, Robert. *James Dickey and the Gentle Ecstasy of Earth: A Reading of the Poems.* Baton Rouge: Louisiana State University Press, 1988. Treats Dickey's poetry rather his novels, but a source rich in insight on the poems and Dickey's preoccupations as a writer in general.

JOAN DIDION

Born: Sacramento, California; December 5, 1934

Principal long fiction
Run River, 1963; *Play It As It Lays*, 1970; *A Book of Common Prayer*, 1977; *Democracy*, 1984.

Other literary forms
Joan Didion is respected as a novelist, but she has been even more highly acclaimed as an essayist. Her career as a writer was launched by a piece of nonfiction; in 1956, during her senior year at the University of California at Berkeley, her article on the San Francisco architect William Wilson Wurster won *Vogue*'s Prix de Paris contest for young writers, and she was awarded a job with that magazine. Although she resigned her position at *Vogue* in 1963 to devote more time to her fiction, she continued as a film critic for the magazine and began publishing regularly in the *Saturday Evening Post*. She has also written articles for periodicals such as *The American Scholar*, *The New York Times Magazine*, *National Review*, *Esquire*, *New West*, and *The New York Review of Books*. Didion has also collaborated with her husband, John Gregory Dunne, on several screenplays.

Didion achieved national recognition with her first collection of essays, *Slouching Towards Bethlehem* (1968); her second collection, *The White Album* (1979), was a best-seller. Her books *Salvador* (1983) and *Miami* (1987) are more overtly political and have aroused considerable controversy.

Achievements
Didion's achievements are somewhat paradoxical. Despite her claims that she speaks only for herself, she has become a spokesperson for the anxiety-ridden generation of the late 1960's and early 1970's; as surely as F. Scott Fitzgerald became the chronicler of the jazz age, she has become the chronicler of a generation living, in her terms, "close to the edge." Didion has developed a reputation for cool, detached observation and for her syncopated but elegant style. James Dickey has called her "the finest woman prose stylist writing in English today," and even some who dismiss her as intellectually shallow respect her craftsmanship.

Didion has her detractors, as all writers have. Some, pointing to her detachment, have criticized her for not taking stronger moral and political stands. Others maintain that her pessimism is too overriding and that her criticism of society is too shrill. Whether one shares Didion's pessimistic outlook, however, her integrity and her style deserve respect. She published her first novel in 1963; given her unflinching eye and sense of style, it might well be that her best books are yet to come.

Biography

Joan Didion was born to Frank Reese and Eduene Jarret Didion on December 5, 1934, in Sacramento, California. Both the date and the place are significant. Though Didion had just turned seven when Pearl Harbor was attacked, she is not, strictly speaking, a child of the postwar generation. This fact might explain some of her detachment from the 1960's and some of the nostalgia she evidently feels even when she is pointing out the shortcomings of the more traditional and more orderly values of pre-World War II America.

Didion's place of birth is even more important. Didion is a child of the West—not the West of Los Angeles, but of the more pastoral Sacramento Valley. The land on which Didion lived had been in her family for five generations, and as a child, she was expected to absorb the myth that America was a new Eden. In *Slouching Towards Bethlehem*, Didion reports that her Episcopal Sunday school teacher used to ask the children, "In what ways does the Holy Land resemble the Sacramento Valley?" Didion explores—and largely explodes—the myth of the Sacramento Valley as Eden in her first novel, *Run River*. Eden, however, is not lost—or rejected—without some sense of regret, and Didion's novel reflects a nostalgia for the lost paradise and the passing of innocence.

Didion's intellectual break from a more traditional world may have begun in high school, when she discovered literature, and it must have been accelerated by her studies at the University of California at Berkeley, where she majored in literature, read Ernest Hemingway, Joseph Conrad, Henry James, and Albert Camus, moved out of her sorority house, and did not, as she points out with some regret, make Phi Beta Kappa. She did, however, win first prize in *Vogue*'s Prix de Paris contest. Given as an award the choice of a trip to Paris or a job on the magazine, Didion chose the more practical option and moved to New York.

At *Vogue*, Didion learned to write for the general public, and she began writing for several other magazines as well. She also seriously began writing fiction, and *Run River* was published in 1963. Her time in New York, then, was important for her development as a writer, and, judging from her essay "Good-bye to All That," she enjoyed her first few years there. Unfortunately, as the essay continues, she began to believe that "it is distinctly possible to stay too long at the fair." Disenchantment turned to depression. In January, 1964, in lieu of seeing a psychiatrist, she married John Gregory Dunne, also a writer, and the couple moved to Los Angeles.

In Los Angeles, Didion's writing continued to go well—she published *Slouching Towards Bethlehem* in 1968, and she and Dunne wrote the screenplay for *The Panic in Needle Park* (1971)—but for some time, she continued to suffer from the depression and sense of disorientation she describes in *The White Album*. Her marital problems were publicized in her own essays and in Dunne's. In the 1970's, however, both her marriage and her emotional state improved, and her literary success continued to grow: *Play It As It Lays, The White Album*, and *A Book of Common Prayer* were all best-sellers. Financial success also came, not so much from the books as from Didion and Dunne's collaboration on screenplays. Besides *The Panic in Needle Park* and the film adaptation of Dunne's novel *True Confessions*, the couple worked on the script for *A Star Is Born* (1976). According to Dunne, that motion picture "made us a fortune."

At present, Didion and Dunne are comfortably entrenched in the affluent Brentwood section of Los Angeles. They have one adopted daughter, Quintana Roo, who apparently has been a source of great happiness for Didion. One might well be happy for Didion, unless one is John Lahr, who has viciously attacked Didion and Dunne for their hypocrisy in criticizing the lifestyle of California while enjoying all its material benefits. Didion's response to Lahr's attack is simple: "It's here, in the face of what many people believe to be a moral vacuum, that we are actually forging a little community. Friends. Family. You have a sense that you're actually doing it where it counts." Didion's life seems to be proving that even living close to the edge gets easier, if one survives it long enough.

Analysis

Almost all of Joan Didion's works are concerned with similar themes, and there is an interesting complementary relationship between her essays and her novels. Her essays generally seem intended to force the reader to strip away his illusions about contemporary life and accept realities, even if they are bleak. The novels are generally explorations of characters crippled by illusions. To some extent, in each novel, the heroine is disabused of her illusions. The fragile hope that each novel holds out, however, is not offered in terms of this disillusionment, but in terms of new illusions and almost meaningless gestures. Each novel ends with the heroine learning to care for others—for a husband, for children, for friends—and yet this caring is generally based on illusion and seems doomed to failure. Didion's final implication, then, seems to be that people need to strip away all illusions, except those which help them to care for others. Such illusions—even though they are doomed to lead to failure—are sacred. These sacred illusions might be fictional, as stories are fictional, but, as Didion has said, "We tell ourselves stories in order to live . . . or at least we do for a while."

Although Didion's first novel, *Run River*, is not autobiographical, it does explore the myth she absorbed in her childhood, the myth of America as the new Eden, the new Promised Land. This myth was brought to the New World by the earliest settlers of Virginia and Massachusetts, but it took special form with the westward expansion. Lily Knight, the heroine of *Run River*, expresses her faith directly: "She believed that it was America's mission to make manifest to the world the wishes of an Episcopal God, [and] that her father would one day be Governor of California." The novel can be quickly summarized. It begins—and finally ends—on the night that Everett McClellan, Lily's husband, kills Ryder Channing, Lily's lover, and then himself. The novel backtracks to trace the lives of the main characters, and returns full circle to the murder and suicide. Along the way, it suggests that Lily, Everett, and Everett's sister Martha have been shattered because of a misplaced faith in traditional, romantic notions about their lives and about their home, the Sacramento Valley.

Lily, after she admits to herself that she probably will not be offered the lead in *Gone with the Wind*, accepts a traditional, passive woman's role. After passively "accepting" Everett twenty-seven times, she agrees to marry him: "It seemed as inescapable as the ripening of the pears, as fated as the exile from Eden." Unfortunately, she finds the role of river matron less than satisfactory, and she continues to accept men—first Joe Templeton and later Ryder Channing—for little more reason than that they desire her. Through it all, Lily fails to come to terms with who she is and what she really wants.

The traditional dream of ranch and family no longer works for Everett, either. Ironically, he seems happy only when he runs away from the ranch, his wife, and his sister, to join the army during World War II. When his father dies, however, he feels bound by duty to return to the ranch, to try to make it work, and to take care of his wife and sister. It does not work; his wife is unfaithful, his sister is destroyed by the "lack of honor" in the world, and his son obviously intends to abandon the homestead.

Martha, Everett's sister, is perhaps the most utterly destroyed character in the novel. She cannot act out her incestuous feelings for her brother, and the man she does accept for a lover, Ryder Channing, is no gentleman. After he is married to another woman and their affair is over, he almost brutally "seduces" her again. Martha is forced to admit that she is not a "lady"—their affair had not been a great romantic passion, but what Ann Landers might describe as "chemistry." Stripped of her illusions, she cannot live. Her brother cannot protect her—a fact that will make him, a romantic gallant, feel even more guilty—and she kills herself.

All of the romantic illusions of the traditional world come crashing down when Everett kills Ryder Channing and then himself. It could be argued that it is not the traditional world that has failed these characters; it is rather that they have failed it. After all, a good river matron should not have an affair while her husband is serving his country; Everett should have been stronger; and Martha should have had more self-respect than to take up with a man such as Ryder. Such an argument, however, would simply ignore too much of the characters' background. Lily's father, Walter Knight, was not so shining as Lily had thought. He does not become governor of California. He is a near alcoholic, and he carries on an adulterous relationship with Rita Blanchard, another "good spinster" who proves no better and no worse than

Martha. Walter is no more a rancher than Everett; his Mexican foreman Gomez is the one who keeps the place going. Finally, he can no more protect his Rita than Everett can protect Martha; both he and Rita drown when he accidentally drives into the Sacramento River.

The novel, then, shows the myth of the Sacramento Valley as a second Eden to be a second-generation failure. The book might seem to imply that it is World War II that renders this idyllic world "gone with the wind," but it is doubtful that Didion believes that things were really better in the old days. Her vision of the settling of the West seems centered on the Donner-Reed party; her great-great-great grandmother had been part of that party originally, but she left it before they were stranded by winter snows and forced to eat their own dead to survive. In her essay "On Morality," Didion equates morality with not leaving the dead to the coyotes, and she writes of the Donner-Reed party: "We were taught instead that they had somewhere abdicated their responsibilities, somehow breached their primal loyalties or they would not have found themselves helpless in the mountain winter . . . would not have failed." At the end of *Run River*, all three major characters have failed to live up to their primal loyalties of wife to husband, husband to wife, brother to sister, sister to sister-in-law. They have been "immoral," not because of their sexual misconduct, but because they have failed to take care of one another.

There is, perhaps, some hope for Lily at the end. She has survived, not by virtue but by luck, and she may have learned. Looking at Everett's body, she finally—perhaps for the first time—tries to talk to him. She recalls the good times and realizes the importance of their love: "She hoped that . . . he would rise thinking of her, *we were each other, we were each other, not that it mattered much in the long run but what else mattered as much.*" "Not that it mattered much" is vintage Didion, but the "what else mattered as much" seems heartfelt. The hope that lovers will rise thinking of each other "through all eternity" has the ring of romantic illusion, but at this point, such a hope constitutes the only possible relationship left for Lily and Everett. At the end of the novel, she is left thinking about what she will say to her children. To sustain them, she will probably be compelled to sustain an illusion about the man she has come to love too late: "She did not know what she could tell anyone except that he had been a good man. She was not certain that he had been but it was what she would have wished for him, if they gave her one wish."

The ease with which *Run River* can be explained as an explosion of traditional American myths probably suggests why the novel is generally considered Didion's most modest achievement. So many people have exploded traditional American myths since 1963 that it does not seem necessary to reread *Run River* to see it done again. In *Play It As It Lays*, however, Didion does something few writers have done as well as she; she turns the tables and explodes the myths and illusions of the contemporary sensibility.

Perhaps no setting could be more appropriate for an illusion-hunter than Los Angeles. In *Play It As It Lays*, Didion places her heroine Maria (pronounced "Mar-eye-ah," like the west wind in the musical) squarely in the fast lane of life in Southern California. The novel opens with Maria in a psychiatric ward. She has been placed there, presumably, for her failure to attempt to stop a friend from committing suicide in her presence. As the novel unfolds (like *Run River*) backwards into the past, however, the reader comes to realize that if Maria has become unhinged, it is probably a result of the cumulative effect of her abortion, her divorce, and the miscellaneous acts of casual sex, drugs, and other perversities one might expect in a novel about Hollywood.

Didion does not condemn the fast lane from a traditional moral perspective; that would have been too easy, and probably not very convincing or interesting. Besides, Didion's target is not simply the sexual mores of contemporary culture. Rather, she explores the popular "philosophy" or world view that so many have accepted since the collapse of the traditional morality—a "philosophy" which might be called sloppy existentialism, extreme relativism, or simply nihilism. Maria states the key tenet of this philosophy on the second page of the novel: "NOTHING APPLIES."

Maria herself was not reared with the traditional American values. Instead of the Puritan work ethic ("God helps those who help themselves"), she was taught the gambler's code: "My father advised me that life itself was a crap game." That view was infused with a faith in good luck: "I was raised to believe that what came in on the next roll would always be better than what went on the last." For a long time, Maria was content to wait for the rolls, to go with the flow, and to "play it as it lays."

Unfortunately, Maria's luck runs out. The bad roll is an unwanted pregnancy. She thinks, but is not sure, that Carter, her husband, is not the father. He demands that she have an abortion and threatens to take away Kate, their brain-damaged daughter, if she refuses. Maria acquiesces, and her mental deterioration begins.

If Maria could completely accept the mores of her set, she would have no problem; for them, neither abortion nor divorce is anything to lose one's composure over. Maria, however, does cling to one traditional dream; she wants a family. She fantasizes about living a simple life with Kate and some man—in almost identical fantasies, the man is either Ivan or Les, two of her steadier lovers. Abortion—the termination of another possible child—is almost more than Maria can contemplate, yet she undergoes it.

Maria's reaction to the abortion is not philosophical, moral, or religious: it is emotional, physical, and psychological. She cries; she hemorrhages; she reaches a point where she cannot easily use plumbing because she imagines pipes clogged with chopped-up pieces of flesh.

Didion does not attempt to make an abstract moral issue out of abortion. Maria's reaction is almost primitive, in the sense of being immediate and unreflecting. In a real sense, however, to return to Didion's essay "On Morality," abortion is a denial of the most basic social responsibility, that of mother to child (it is hard here not to recall Didion's own traumatic miscarriage and her devotion to her adopted daughter). In *Play It As It Lays*, even more emphatically than in *Run River*, characters fail to fulfill their primal social responsibilities. Carter, Les (even Les' wife), Maria's friends, Helene and BZ, and a number of others all say that they are "seriously worried" about Maria as she slips more and more into self-destructive behavior; they say that they care, but none of them can reach her, none of them can take care of her. Some of their protestations are hard to take seriously; Carter humiliates Maria on a number of occasions, and Helene and BZ use her—while she is drunk and only half-conscious—for obscure and unpleasant sexual purposes.

Most of these characters profess not to be concerned with the sexual conduct of their spouses. When Helene, BZ's wife, drifts into an affair with Carter, BZ asks Maria if she cares. For a time, Maria tries to insist that she does care, but as the novel draws to a conclusion, BZ forces her more and more to a nihilistic position: "'Tell me what matters,' BZ said. 'Nothing,' Maria said." The "nothing" here is Ernest Hemingway's "nada," and at the end of the novel, BZ, like Hemingway, kills himself. BZ, however, does not use a gun. He goes out with a bottle of vodka and a grain-and-a-half of Seconal. When Helene and Carter force their way into the room, BZ is dead and Maria is asleep next to him, holding his hand.

On the last page of the novel, Maria, from the psychiatric ward, affirms BZ's nihilism, if not his suicide: "I know what 'nothing' means, and keep on playing. Why, BZ would say. Why not, I say." That, however, is not all there is to it. Maria has already made it clear that she is playing for Kate. She wants to take Kate away from the hospital; she wants them to have a home by the sea where they can live a simple life. Given Kate's condition—to say nothing of Maria's—this future does not sound very likely. Despite her acceptance of nihilism, Maria holds on to one last romantic notion. Perhaps she realizes how illusory her hope is, but, like Lily's hope that Everett will rise thinking of her, the illusion and the hope are necessary. They keep her in the game and away from the Seconal.

Run River and *Play It As It Lays*, then, demonstrate the failures both of traditional American myths and of more current nihilistic life-styles. Lily Knight McClellan and Maria Wyeth both survive, but both are sustained by hopes that seem largely based on illusion. In Didion's third novel, *A Book of Common Prayer*, the reader is told on the first page that the protagonist, Charlotte Douglas, does not survive. The narrator, however, comments that "she died, hopeful." Whether Charlotte's hope is also illusory is a central question of the novel.

It is the question that the narrator, Grace Strasser-Mendana, nee Tabor, is trying to answer throughout the novel. Grace, originally from the United

States, "married into one of the three or four solvent families in Boca Grande," the small central American republic in which Charlotte Douglas is finally killed (or murdered; as Grace says, neither word seems to work). The death of Grace's husband has left her "in putative control of fifty-nine-point-eight percent of the arable land and about the same percentage of the decision-making process in La República." From this position of power, Grace observes the political scheming of her family. She also watches Charlotte walk bare-footed into the scene and become caught up in it. Grace leaves the country before Charlotte dies, and the novel is her attempt to understand Charlotte. As she says, "Call it my witness to Charlotte Douglas."

At the very beginning of her witness, Grace comments that Charlotte "dreamed her life," and much of what Grace says makes Charlotte seem a woman even more given to illusion than was Lily Knight McClellan or Maria Wyeth. Grace insists that Charlotte was the "usual child of comfortable family in the temperate zone." She had been supplied with all the material benefits and easy optimism of an affluent American. As a child, she was given a carved Austrian angel which listened to her bedside prayers: "In these prayers the child Charlotte routinely asked that 'it' turn out all right, 'it' being unspecified and all-inclusive, and she had been an adult for some years before the possibility occurred to her that 'it' might not."

Like Maria, Charlotte loses some of the optimism; her luck runs out. The more traditional life-style fails her. Her first husband, Warren Bogart (per-haps the name is meant to be half-way between Warren Beatty and Humphrey Bogart) had been "raised to believe not in 'hard work' or 'self reliance' but in the infinite power of the personal appeal." He is also sadistic, sexually perverse, and alcoholic. Charlotte is not perfect, either; one Easter, while their child Marin is still a baby, she gets drunk and sleeps with a man she does not even like (she later conveniently forgets the episode). Warren hits her, and she finally walks away from the marriage.

Her second marriage is not unlike Maria's life in the fast lane, except that the game is no longer motion pictures but radical politics. Her husband is not a director but a radical chic lawyer who flies from one center of revolution to another. Leonard does seem genuinely to care for Charlotte, but there are complications. Marin, Charlotte's child by Warren, turns revolutionary; she and her friends hijack a jetliner, burn it in the desert, and join the underground.

Charlotte's main illusion, like Maria's, is centered around her daughter. She later tells Grace that she and Marin were "inseparable" (a term she also uses to describe her relationship with Warren), and she spins out fantastic accounts of their visit to the Tivoli Gardens. As might be expected, the revolutionary Marin claims to have little use for her bourgeois mother.

After a disastrous reunion with Warren and after the birth and almost immediate death of her child by Leonard, Charlotte drifts to Boca Grande, where she meets Grace. At first, Charlotte gives Grace every reason to think that she is dreaming her life; for quite a while, she goes to the airport every day, on the offhand chance that Marin will pass through Central America; she drifts aimlessly into sexual relations with Victor, Grace's brother-in-law, and then with Gerardo, Grace's son; she seems not to notice the growing signs of revolution; she refuses the attempts of Gerardo, Leonard, and Grace to persuade her to leave; finally, the revolution begins, and she is arrested and killed. Her body is dumped on the lawn of the American embassy.

All this does seem to add up to a life of dreams and illusions, yet throughout the novel, Charlotte proves herself to be capable of very practical behavior. She kills a chicken with her bare hands; she skins an iguana for stew; she performs an emergency tracheotomy with a penknife; and she inoculates people against an epidemic of cholera for thirty-four hours without a break. Although Charlotte often seems not to notice what is going on around her, she corrects people who claim to know what is happening: she reminds a reporter that Marin's comrade killed himself in Arizona, not Mexico, and she later corrects Gerardo on a technical point: "'Carmen wasn't using a M-3.' Charlotte said. She leaned forward slightly and her face was entirely grave. 'Antonio was. Carmen was using an M-16.'"

If Charlotte is not as out of touch as she seems, why then does she stay in Boca Grande and risk her life? In her last conversation with Leonard, she says very simply, "I walked away from places all my life and I'm not going to walk away from here." In another context, one could imagine John Wayne speaking those lines. In this context, however, there is no sense of the heroic. For a moment, Leonard seems to misunderstand this, and he warns her, "You don't get any real points for staying here, Charlotte." Charlotte understands perfectly: "'I can't seem to tell what you do get the real points for,' Charlotte said. 'So I guess I'll stick around for a while.'" Didion does not glorify Charlotte's decision to stay; it is not a self-defining existential act. She simply returns to her work at a birth control clinic (an ironic job for a woman whose passport lists her occupation as "*madré*"). Her work is not particularly meaningful, since Charlotte routinely advises women to use the diaphragm while the clinic stocks only IUD's. In any event, no clients come on Charlotte's last day of work, the last day of her life. In deciding to stay, Charlotte maintains something of her integrity, what Didion would call "character," but Didion allows the reader no illusions about the act; it is the integrity of a cardplayer playing out a losing hand.

Charlotte's integrity can only be appreciated in comparison to the values of the other characters, particularly Grace. Even though Grace has been trying to understand Charlotte throughout the novel, she is as much a victim of delusion as Charlotte is. For some time, Grace has realized the difficulty in understanding things, in trying to get the story straight. She had abandoned her first discipline before the beginning of the novel: "I am an anthropologist who lost faith in her own method, who stopped believing that observable activity defined anthros." She turned to biochemistry, but that, too, failed: "Give me the molecular structure of the protein which defined Charlotte Douglas." When Leonard reveals to her that her husband Edgar had been involved with the guerrillas himself, Grace is finally forced to realize that her life, as much as Charlotte's, has been one of delusion.

Grace's statement, "We all remember what we need to remember," is one of the lessons of the novel; all people prefer to believe their own versions of the stories in which they are trapped; all people accept delusions. Grace finally realizes that, "I am more like Charlotte Douglas than I thought I was." Perhaps Charlotte's death was something of a meaningless gesture, but beside her coffin, Grace can only make a small meaningless gesture of love; she places a T-shirt painted like an American flag on the casket. By way of comment, she borrows a phrase from Charlotte and Leonard: "There were no real points in that either."

Neither Grace nor Charlotte—perhaps none of Didion's characters in any of her novels—scores any real points in the end. They try to take care of one another, but they fail. Grace and Leonard try to take care of Charlotte, but they fail. Charlotte would like to take care of Marin, but she cannot. Warren wants Charlotte to take care of him, but it does not work. As cynical as Warren is, he may have the final judgment in the novel: "It doesn't matter whether you take care of somebody or somebody takes care of you. . . . It's all the same in the end. It's all the same." Warren dies alone; Charlotte dies alone. Grace will die—as she says—very soon, and she will be alone. It is all the same in the end. At least Charlotte does to some degree shape her own life toward the end. The night she was arrested, she was, Grace imagines, "walking very deliberately."

The protagonist of Didion's fourth novel, *Democracy*, is Inez Christian Victor, the daughter of a prominent Honolulu family and the wife of a liberal California senator who narrowly lost the Democratic nomination for president in 1972. The love of her life, however, is a shadowy soldier of fortune named Jack Lovett. She follows him to Southeast Asia on the eve of the fall of Vietnam (to retrieve her daughter—a heroin addict who has drifted to Saigon because she hears that employment opportunities are good there) and sees him drown in a hotel pool in Jakarta. She brings the body back to Hawaii to be buried under a jacaranda tree at Schofield Barracks and returns to Kuala Lampur to work with refugees.

In *Democracy*, one finds evidence of two of Didion's most prominent characteristics as a writer—her acute sense of place and her fascination with the American West. While these twin aspects of her muse have always been evident in her writings about California, she has occasionally cast her glance farther westward to Hawaii. In *Slouching Towards Bethlehem*, she wrote: "I sat as a child on California beaches and imagined that I saw Hawaii, a certain shimmer in the sunset, a barely perceptible irregularity glimpsed intermittently through squinted eyes." In a column for *New West* magazine, written more than a decade later, she revealed that she keeps a clock in her bedroom in Los Angeles, set at Honolulu time.

When Didion, however, tried to write a novel about feudal Hawaii (originally entitled *Pacific Distances*), she produced a book that is only marginally about that subject. In *Democracy*, Hawaii is less important as a society in transition than as a way station between the Mainland and America's ultimate western frontier, Southeast Asia. (In *Slouching Towards Bethlehem*, she speaks of sailors who got drunk in Honolulu because "they were no longer in Des Moines and not yet in Da Nang.") As Walt Whitman proclaimed more than a century earlier in his poem "Passage to India" (1871), the roundness of the Earth leads not to some apocalyptic West but back east whence we came. America's Manifest Destiny, however, has not even produced a mystical passage to India, but rather helicopters lifting off the roof of the American embassy in Saigon during the final days of the only war the United States has ever lost.

In this imagistic, elliptical novel, much is left to conjecture. More than in any of her previous works, Didion has helped fuel this conjecture by an almost compulsive literary allusiveness. Certainly the most significant allusion is to Henry Adams, who in 1880 published a novel entitled *Democracy*. Although Mary McCarthy made nothing of the novels' having the same name, Thomas R. Edwards saw both Didion and Adams as displaced aristocrats who with "irony and subtlety confront a chaotic new reality that shatters the orderings of simpler, older ways."

From a purely technical standpoint, the most controversial and problematic aspect of *Democracy* is its point of view. Departing from the more conventional narrative techniques of her earlier novels, Didion inserts herself into *Democracy* and claims to have been acquainted personally with her characters. Although this device may appear to make Didion's tale a postmodernist novel about novel writing, it also places her in the decidedly premodernist company of George Eliot and William Makepeace Thackeray, who both inserted themselves into their fiction.

By revealing her problems in writing this book and by treating her characters as if they were as real as the figures in her journalism, Didion may be trying to collapse the distinction between fiction and nonfiction narrative. If the new journalism brings the techniques of fiction to the writing of fact, this novel brings the illusion of fact to the writing of fiction. Such a device is for *Democracy* what the title *A Book of Common Prayer* was for Didion's earlier novel—a reason for telling the story. Yet one suspects that, like Grace Strasser-Mendana, "Joan Didion" has not been the witness she wanted to be.

James Reynolds Kinzey

Other major works

SCREENPLAYS: *The Panic in Needle Park*, 1971 (with John Gregory Dunne); *Play It As It Lays*, 1972 (with John Gregory Dunne); *A Star Is Born*, 1976 (with John Gregory Dunne and Frank Pierson); *True Confessions*, 1981 (with John Gregory Dunne).

NONFICTION: *Slouching Towards Bethlehem*, 1968; *The White Album*, 1979; *Salvador*, 1983; *Miami*, 1987.

SHORT FICTION: *Telling Stories*, 1978.

Bibliography

Friedman, Ellen G., ed. *Joan Didion: Essays and Conversations*. Princeton, N.J.: Ontario Review Press, 1984. This collection contains Didion's essay "Why I Write," three conversations with the author, and fourteen essays by various hands. Although several of the contributions are first-rate, the book is marred by anachronisms and careless editing.

Henderson, Katherine Usher. *Joan Didion*. New York: Ungar, 1981. A brief but helpful introductory study of Didion's life and work up through *The White Album*, this book is written for a general audience of nonspecialists.

Kasindorf, Martin. "New Directions for the First Family of Angst." *Saturday Review* 9 (April, 1982): 14-18. Based on an interview with Didion and Dunne, this feature article was written to coincide with the publication of Dunne's second novel, *Dutch Shea, Jr.*

Kazin, Alfred. "Joan Didion: Portrait of a Professional." *Harper's* 243 (December, 1971): 112-114. This influential biographical and critical article appeared shortly after the publication of *Play It As It Lays*. Part of this piece was later published in Kazin's *Bright Book of Life: American Novelists and Storytellers from Hemingway to Mailer* (1973).

Lahr, John. "Entrepreneurs of Anxiety." *Horizon* 24 (January, 1981): 36-39. This vitriolic attack on Didion and Dunne as "brilliant mirrors of the California bourgeoisie" reveals less about its ostensible subject than about Lahr's own distaste for the jacuzzi culture of Los Angeles.

Olendorf, Donna. "Joan Didion: A Checklist, 1955-1980." *Bulletin of Bibliography* 32 (January-March, 1981): 32-44. Although more than a decade out of date, this bibliography is still the most thorough and accurate of both primary and secondary material on Didion.

Winchell, Mark Royden. *Joan Didion*. Rev. ed. Boston: Twayne, 1989. A revised and updated version of the first book ever written on Didion, this study follows its subject's career up through *Miami* (1987). Although his work is accessible to the general reader, Winchell writes for a more scholarly audience than Henderson.

E. L. DOCTOROW

Born: New York, New York; January 6, 1931

Principal long fiction

Welcome to Hard Times, 1960; *Big as Life*, 1966; *The Book of Daniel*, 1971; *Ragtime*, 1975; *Loon Lake*, 1980; *World's Fair*, 1985; *Billy Bathgate*, 1989.

Other literary forms

E. L. Doctorow has ventured outside the novel genre very seldom: in a play, *Drinks Before Dinner* (1978), and a collection of short stories, *Lives of the Poets* (1984).

Achievements

Ragtime, a popular and critical success, catapulted E. L. Doctorow into prominence as one of the finest and most exciting novelists of his generation. With *Welcome to Hard Times* and *The Book of Daniel*, he had already established a solid reputation, but the rave reviews of *Ragtime* and the subsequent film adaptation of the novel secured his place in the contemporary culture. *World's Fair* won the American Book Award in 1986, and *Billy Bathgate*— nearly as successful as *Ragtime*—suggests that Doctorow continues to explore the astute blending of fact and fiction and of history and literature that has distinguished his most important novels.

Biography

Born in the Bronx in 1931, Edgar Laurence Doctorow has returned again and again to urban themes, particularly to the life of New York City at the turn of the century and in the 1920's and 1930's when he was growing up. He was graduated from Kenyon College with a major in philosophy, and after serving in the army he worked for publishers in New York City, editing important writers such as Norman Mailer. His philosophical training is evident in his novels, in which he tries to infuse serious ideas into popular genres such as the Western (*Welcome to Hard Times*) and science fiction (*Big as Life*).

Identifying with the downtrodden, with immigrants, criminals, and political protesters, he has fashioned fiction with a leftist orientation, and on occasion he has joined his voice to public protests against government censorship and other forms of tyranny. With residences in New York City and New Rochelle, New York, he has divided his time between the city and the suburbs. He has taught at Sarah Lawrence College and New York University.

Analysis

E. L. Doctorow is a political novelist and is concerned with those stories, myths, public figures, and literary and historical forms that have shaped public consciousness. Even when his subject was not overtly political—as in his first novel, *Welcome to Hard Times*—he chose the genre of the Western to comment upon the American sense of crime and justice. Knowing that the Western has often been the vehicle for the celebration of American individualism and morality, Doctorow purposely writes a fablelike novel in which he questions American faith in fairness and democracy. At the same time, he writes from within the genre by maintaining the customary strong opposition between good and evil, between the "bad guys" and the "good guys," and by fashioning a simple but compelling plot line.

The struggle in *Welcome to Hard Times* is between the Man from Bodie, who in a fit of rage destroys a town in a single day, and Blue, the tragic old man who almost singlehandedly tries to rebuild it. The plot and characters echo classic Western films such as *High Noon* (1952) with their solitary heroes who oppose villains' tyrannizing of a community. Doctorow's vision, however, is much bleaker than that of the traditional Western and cannot be encompassed by the usual shootout or confrontation between the sheriff and the outlaw. In fact, Doctorow's novel implies, the West was chaotic and demonic, and order was not usually restored in the fashion of a Hollywood Western. The reality of American history has been much grimmer than its literature or its popular entertainment has ever acknowledged. Indeed, Doctorow's fiction shows again and again an America whose myths do not square with its history.

It is a paradoxical aspect of Doctorow's success that his parodies of popular genres are themselves usually best-sellers. Perhaps the reason is that alongside his ironic use of popular genres runs a deep affection for the literary forms he burlesques. The title of the novel, for example, is a kind of genial welcome, an invitation to have some fun with the pieties and clichés of the Western. Doctorow is deadly serious about the "hard times" and grave flaws in American culture, but he usually finds a way to present his criticism in a comic vein.

Doctorow's fiction is often set in the past, during an identifiable historical period—the 1920's, the Depression, the 1950's and 1960's. When he has turned to contemporary life, as in his second novel, *Big as Life*, his effort to use the genre of science fiction is less successful. The novel is a kind of spoof about monsters who destroy New York City. Doctorow has acknowledged it as a failed work. Indeed, its theme—the malaise of modern life—is difficult to dramatize.

Much more characteristic of Doctorow's deft handling of important political themes and historical periods is *The Book of Daniel*, a major political novel about the Cold War period of the 1950's. Centering on a couple (who bear a striking resemblance to Ethel and Julius Rosenberg) who were executed for espionage (they were accused of stealing the "secret" of the atomic bomb for the Soviet Union), the story is narrated by one of their children, Daniel. He sets out to investigate what happened to his parents while trying to come to terms with his own 1960's brand of radicalism. Concerned less with whether the couple were actually guilty of spying than with uncovering his own identity, Daniel tracks down and interviews those who had been closest to his parents.

Through this personal story, Doctorow conducts an analysis of the failure of American radicalism, of one generation to speak to another. By and large, 1960's radicals did not know much about the history of the Left, and the traditional Left has done little to pass on its past, so that young men like Daniel feel isolated, bereft, and angry about their lack of connection to a heritage of social protest.

Daniel mourns the loss of his family. Unable to cope with his parents' sacrifice of themselves to a political movement, he allows his own marriage to deteriorate as he is racked by memories of what it was like for his parents to be constantly harassed for their political beliefs. The human costs of political activism are what embitter Daniel, but those costs are also what make him fiercely determined to gain some truth out of what happened to his parents and to confront those relatives who seem to have collaborated in his parents' execution.

From the point of view of 1960's radicalism, Daniel has a certain contempt for his parents and their attorney, who tried scrupulously to accommodate themselves to the American judicial system rather than challenging that system outright by calling the trial political and acting in court—as protesters did in the 1960's—as defiant political prisoners. Politics serves as the metaphor for the divisions in family life. In other words, there is a merging between the private and public realms, between individuals and political movements, just as the narrative swings between Daniel's first-person (intimate) and third-person (impersonal) points of view. In his great trilogy, *U.S.A.* (1937), John Dos Passos separated elements of history and fiction by creating discrete sections called "Camera Eye" and "Newsreel." It is Doctorow's achievement to have fused the personal and the public, the fictional and the historical, into one narrative voice, suggesting the indivisibility of history and the individual's perceptions of it. There is no "history" out there, he implies; there is only the "history" within the minds of the people who live it and re-create it.

Near the end of *The Book of Daniel* there is a brilliant set-piece description of Disneyland, which comes to stand for the forces in American life that threaten any complex sense of history. On the Disneyland lot, which resembles a film set, are arranged figures and artifacts of American history, the symbols and the tokens of the national heritage, wrenched from their social and historical context, abstracted into a series of entertainments for customers who do not have to analyze what is presented to them. This spectacle of history substitutes for the real thing, demeaning the past and replacing it with a comfortable, pacific, and convenient product that need only be enjoyed and consumed.

In *Ragtime*, Doctorow goes even further in suggesting that much of American history has been turned into a myth. In this novel historical figures have the same status as fictional creations. The novelist's Sigmund Freud, who appears in *Ragtime* going through the Tunnel of Love with Carl Jung, one of his disciples (later a rival), and the historical Freud are equally products of the imagination, of the language that is used to invent both history and fiction. So convincing is Doctorow in inserting famous people such as J. P. Morgan, Henry Ford, and Emma Goldman into his narrative that he has caused many people to wonder which incidents in the novel are "true." Doctorow has implied in interviews that in a sense it is all "true," since the imagination has such power to reconfigure history. *Ragtime* is surely one of the most subversive novels ever written by an American, for it suggests that history can be viewed as a consummate fiction.

Like *The Book of Daniel*, *Ragtime* is anchored in the story of a family—this time of a boy who grows up at the turn of the century during the time of polar exploration, the development of great inventions such as motion pictures, and political upheavals led by radicals such as Emma Goldman. From his naïve viewpoint, the small boy observes the explosive changes and the stresses of a society that does not know how to handle its own dissenting elements—such as Coalhouse Walker, a proud black man who is insulted by a group of white firemen and who resorts to violence and hostage-taking, demanding that society recognize his rights.

If the actions of Coalhouse Walker seem more appropriate to the 1960's than to turn-of-the-century America, it is Doctorow's way of exaggerating those elements of the future that inhere in the past. The rage that Walker feels is both a personal and a historical rage. The insult is to him and to his race. If a black man in the age of J. P. Morgan would not in fact take over the financier's library full of art treasures, the truth is (Doctorow implies) that the conditions for such a terrorist act have been a long time coming in the United States. Such an act could almost have happened then. That the seemingly stable world before World War I was actually on the verge of cataclysm is suggested at the end of the novel's first chapter, when the boy exclaims, "Warn the duke"—referring to the assassination of the Archduke Ferdinand, the event that precipitated World War I.

Ragtime is similar to *Welcome to Hard Times* in that it has a fairy-tale quality. The prose is quite simple, descriptive, and declarative, so that Doctorow could almost begin with the phrase "once upon a time." It is clear, however, that his point is to link the past and the present, to show that the craving for mass entertainment at the turn of the century naturally had its outlet in the invention of motion pictures, just as the urge of Robert Peary and other explorers to roam the world had its counterpart in the mass production of the automobile. Repeatedly, Doctorow links the innovations in domestic life with great public adventures and events, fusing public and private affairs in an almost magical, uncanny manner.

The very title of the novel, *Ragtime*, refers not merely to the syncopated, accented music of the time but also to the quality of the period, with its fragmented, volatile changes that transformed the character of the country. This was the beat, the rhythm of the period, Doctorow implies. Time was being given a different tempo by the inventions, innovations, and struggles of the immigrants, the underclass, and the blacks, even as Americans of an earlier generation took refuge in patriotism and public displays that excluded these new groups.

The class distinctions that play an important role in *Ragtime* become the focal element of *Loon Lake*, which, like *The Book of Daniel*, contains a double narrative perspective. *Loon Lake* shifts between the experience of a poet on a rich man's isolated estate and a poor man's picaresque adventures across 1930's America. Somehow the power of the materialist, the millionaire capitalist, is meant to be balanced by the imagination of the poet, but the novel fails to measure up to *Ragtime*'s astonishing feat of fusing the different realms of fiction and history. The poetic interludes in *Loon Lake* are reminiscent of the stream-of-consciousness "Camera Eye" sections of the U.S.A. trilogy, but they seem excessively obscure, introverted, and disruptive of the novel's narrative pace.

Nevertheless, *Loon Lake* has a haunting, ineffable quality, evoking a metaphorical but almost tangible sense of history that is akin to the novel's image of the lake: a dazzling surface of ever-shifting and widening perspectives and hinted-at depths. History as mirror—refracting, distorting, highlighting, and obscuring human actions—is a palpable presence. A great social novelist, Doctorow manages to describe every level and grouping of society in the soup kitchens, monasteries, mansions, and assembly lines in the United States between the two world wars.

In comparison to his earlier novels, *World's Fair* seems remarkably straightforward. It resembles a work of conventional nonfiction, and like a memoir it is largely bound by a chronological structure. Much of the action is seen through the consciousness of a young boy, Edgar, growing up in the Bronx during the 1939-1940 World's Fair. Given the character's name and background, it is difficult not to conclude that Doctorow has himself and his family in mind. He had already used his New Rochelle house as a model for the house in *Ragtime* and the mind of a young boy as the intuitive medium through which many of the domestic, private events of that novel would be filtered. Doctorow's interest in the way the fictional and factual impinge upon each other would naturally lead to this exercise in quasi-autobiography, in which the materials from his own background underpin the plot. The World's

Fair becomes a metaphor for the boy's growing up and for the country's maturation.

Unlike many American novelists, Doctorow does not merely criticize American materialism, seeing in the emphasis on things a soul-deadening culture that is antithetical to the artist's imagination. On the contrary, he enjoys playing with and observing the materiality of America, decrying, to be sure, the way in which the culture turns its important figures and events into toys and commercials for capitalism, but also capturing—and honoring—the American delight in inventiveness and machinery. In *World's Fair*, he triumphantly combines the personal and familial aspects of life with the way a society celebrates itself. In doing so, he recovers the synthesis of history and literature that made *Ragtime* such a resounding success.

The artist and the material world are not opposites of each other in Doctorow's fiction, even though art is often turned into a commodity. In *Ragtime*, for example, the Jewish immigrant Tateh transforms his gift for making moving picture books into a position of prominence in the motion-picture industry. He is a film director, a capitalist, and an artist. In *Lives of the Poets*, a collection of short stories, Doctorow takes this theme of the artist in society, which is only one of the many themes in his novels, and makes it a paramount question: how is the writer able to sustain the process of literary creation in a commercial culture?

In most of Doctorow's work there is a tension between a naïve, childlike point of view, which is often fresh with perception, and an older, ironic, detached perspective. Sometimes this split gets expressed in terms of first- and third-person narration, as in *The Book of Daniel*. In *Ragtime*, the narrator seems to be simultaneously the little boy and his older self, both observing for the first time and remembering the past. Like *World's Fair*, *Billy Bathgate* seems more conventional than earlier novels, for it is told from the standpoint of its main character, a mature man reviewing his past. Yet the novel unfolds with such immediacy that it appears to be taking place as the narrator tells it.

The first long sentence of *Billy Bathgate* launches right into the excitement of a scene in which Dutch Schultz is disposing of a disloyal associate, Bo Weinberg. The setting is described by fifteen-year-old Billy Bathgate, the novel's narrator, who is impressed with the smooth running of the Dutchman's criminal enterprise. A car drives up to a dark dock, and without using any light or making a sound, Schultz's crew gets on the boat with Bo and his girl, Drew Preston. Schultz's control over the situation is awesome and inspiring for the young boy, who has been given the honor of running errands and performing other chores for the famous gang. He becomes their mascot and good-luck charm.

Doctorow handles exquisitely the feeling of an adult remembering his adolescent self and the sheer excitement of being privy to the most secret counsels of criminals. Billy describes, in fascinating detail, the process by which Bo's feet are encased in concrete. Facing the torture of drowning, Bo taunts Schultz, hoping to provoke his famous temper so that Schultz will shoot him quickly rather than make him suffer the agony of a slow death. Schultz keeps calm, however, while Bo retails instances of Schultz's violent and ungiving nature. Schultz takes his revenge by appropriating Bo's mistress, Preston.

Billy fears but is also fascinated by Schultz's violence, for Schultz cuts a great figure in the world, with minions to serve him and women to fawn over him. Billy's Irish mother has occasional periods of dementia (pushing around a baby carriage full of broken eggshells and other garbage), and his Jewish father long ago abandoned his family. Schultz provides a glamorous alternative to this grim life, and the gang a surrogate family for the neglected boy. Billy is on his own in the East Bronx, with no prospects of a better life, until the Dutchman sees him juggling on the street and takes a shine to him, eventually calling Billy his "pro-to-jay." Billy is, in Schultz's words, "a capable boy." Praise from the gangster and inclusion in the gang's activities make Billy feel important. His eager willingness to learn from the gang, to accept any assignment without complaint, earns for him special marks of favor.

Schultz has a way of utterly changing the face of things, and for a long time working for him has a fairy-tale quality to it. Billy is enchanted by the sheer magic of the way Schultz gets things done. No sooner is Bo Weinberg overboard with his cement overshoes than Schultz is making love to Drew Preston—a socialite who is fascinated, for a while, by his presence and energy. She even accompanies him to Onondaga in Upstate New York, where Schultz takes over a town, plying the locals with gifts and setting up a cozy atmosphere in preparation for what he rightly expects will be a favorable jury verdict in the case the government has brought against him for tax evasion.

Schultz has the power to create his own world, staying for days at a time in his hotel room with Preston. Not bound by conventional moral values, he is an exhilarating person to be around. There is something very engaging and down-to-earth in his crude, raw energy, which is perhaps why Preston finds herself attracted to a man so unlike her husband and his rich cronies. Preston's involvement with Schultz is reminiscent of Evelyn Nesbit's fascination with Tateh, the Jewish immigrant, and his beautiful little daughter in *Ragtime*, for they represent a life of the streets, a flavor of what is going on in the lower orders, that is at once alien and appealing to those living a highly stylized and often-repressed life in the upper classes. In *Billy Bathgate*, the gang is a kind of tribe with Schultz as chief, and their reason for existence is tied up with preserving and extending his power, which has a sexual component that Preston finds irresistible.

Schultz's great strength is also his great weakness. By making all of his business revolve around himself, he fails to see how crime is becoming organized and corporate. His way of doing business is almost feudal—depending almost entirely on violence and on the loyalty of subordinates—and he has no grasp of how to put together an organization that can compete with the combinations of power being amassed by the government and by his rival, Lucky Luciano. Schultz wants to personalize everything, so that it all evolves out of his own ego. Yet that ego is unstable. On an impulse, he kills an uncooperative colleague in an Onondaga hotel, and this is only one of many instances when he goes berserk and pounds his opponents into the floor.

Members of Schultz's gang—particularly his accountant, Abbadabba Berman—sense that the old ways of doing things are nearly finished. Bo's defection is only the beginning of events that put Schultz on the defensive and that culminate in his gangland murder near the end of the novel. Berman tries to convince Schultz to do business in the new way, to recognize that he is part of a larger crime network, but Schultz can think only in terms of his own ambitions and calls off plans to amalgamate with Lucky Luciano and other gangsters. In compensation, perhaps, for Schultz's inability to adapt to new times, Berman turns to Billy, making him an apprentice and lavishing attention on the boy. Berman plies Billy with advice, gives him assignments that build his confidence and extend his knowledge of the business.

Through Berman and Preston, Billy gains perspective on Schultz. Preston, Billy finds, has her own sort of power and sense of ease. When she tires of Schultz, she simply leaves him, conveying to Billy the impression that Schultz's charisma has its limits. Billy never dares to think of actually leaving the gang, but he keeps his own counsel and is prepared to take care of himself when Schultz is murdered. At the death scene, in which Schultz, Berman, Lulu, and Irving have been shot, Billy learns from Berman the combination of the safe where Schultz has stashed much of his loot. Evasive about his subsequent career, Billy intimates at the end of the novel that he has indeed gained the Dutchman's fortune, but he does not explain what he will do with it.

Billy's reticence is a perfect foil to the Dutchman's very public career: even Schultz's last delirious words are taken down by a stenographer and published in the papers. Schultz never learns to be circumspect and even plans to assassinate Thomas E. Dewey, the district attorney who has made it his mission to put Schultz in prison. By the end of his career, not only has Schultz alienated his gangland associates, but he has also made it impossible for corrupt Tammany politicians to accept his bribes. He is a relic of an earlier age of unbridled individualism. Billy, on the other hand, hides Schultz's fortune, goes back to school, is graduated from an Ivy League college, and becomes first an army officer in World War II and then a business entrepreneur—an inconceivable career in Dutch Schultz's world.

Billy Bathgate is a combination of Huck Finn, Tom Sawyer, and Horatio Alger. He is a hero who is prudent, yet an adventurer who risks making love to Drew Preston, even though he knows that it means certain death if the

Dutchman finds out. He keeps a cool head even when the Dutchman is punishing him for not having provided a piece of vital information sooner. Billy is a romantic, melting at the sight of Preston and hardly believing that they have been sexual partners. He is also a rationalist, realizing that his best chance of survival is to play the role of the loyal Bronx kid.

In this fast-paced adventure novel, which takes quick tours of the Bronx, Upstate New York, Saratoga, and the docks of Manhattan, Doctorow supplies the color and the feel of the 1930's. As Billy prospers and gets to know these different worlds, he finds it impossible to return as he was to his old neighborhood. There he is immediately perceived as a different person. He dresses differently, carries himself differently, and has a consciousness of a world that extends far beyond the Bathgate Avenue from which he has derived his assumed name. Billy becomes, in other words, a self-invented figure, transcending his origins not only in the actions he narrates but also in his very language, which is at once colloquial and formal, a blend of popular and sophisticated vocabulary that precisely captures the boy and the man who has become the narrator of this novel. In this quintessential American story, Doctorow has managed yet another stunning version of the hero's quest for identity and success.

In nearly all Doctorow's novels there is a certain nostalgia for the past. In some ways that past does seem simpler and less threatening. Dutch Schultz is evil, yet his brand of evil has its limitations; it cannot spread in the insidious way organized crime has done in taking over American institutions. *Ragtime* glows with yearning for a seemingly uncomplicated past in a style that often eschews subordinate clauses and complex grammar, as if to mirror in a straightforward style the innocence of an earlier era in which, for example, patriotism could be easily celebrated and not called into question. If people had a mind to, they could easily ignore the waves of immigrants and the growing urban population of blacks, the narrator notes in the novel's first chapter.

Such nostalgia is not surprising, since memories of the past are often selective, and Doctorow is acutely perceptive of the way the public makes its selections—aided by the film industry and Disneylands of the culture. Gangsters, film stars, cowboys—all have a certain glamour in Doctorow's fiction, because they have that glamour in the popular genres he mimics. As models for a rational, democratic society, these stock types fail, and Doctorow is fully aware of that reality. Yet he cannot abandon them, for these amusements reflect the core of the American psyche, the overwhelming urge to mythologize history, to make it amenable to human desires and hopes.

Carl Rollyson

Other major works

SHORT FICTION: *Lives of the Poets*, 1984.
PLAY: *Drinks Before Dinner*, 1978.

Bibliography

Kakutani, Michiko. "Do Facts and Fiction Mix?" *The New York Times Book Review*, January 27, 1980, 2-3, 28-29. A comprehensive and objective discussion of the development of the "nonfiction novel," treating Doctorow in the context of his contemporaries' experiments with the form. Besides reporting on the phenomenon of blending history and fiction, Kakutani suggests certain principles that should be applied in assessing the value of both fiction and journalism.

Levine, Paul. *E. L. Doctorow*. London: Methuen, 1985. The first full-length study of the novelist's career. Levine provides sound and often-insightful readings of individual novels as well as substantial discussions of the recurring themes in the fiction: politics, the nature of fiction and history, and Doctorow's critique of the "American dream." A useful bibliography and a discussion of film adaptations of Doctorow's work make this a comprehensive study.

Strout, Cushing. "Historizing Fiction and Fictionalizing History: The Case of E. L. Doctorow." *Prospects*, 1980, 423-437. A detailed analysis of the strengths and limitations of Doctorow's handling of fiction and history. Should be read in conjunction with Barbara Foley's article "From *U.S.A.* to *Ragtime*: Notes on the Forms of Historical Consciousness in Modern Fiction," which is included in Trenner's volume (see below).

Trenner, Richard. *E. L. Doctorow: Essays and Conversations*. Princeton, N.J.: Ontario Review Press, 1983. This collection yields valuable biographical and critical insights into the novelist's work. Includes several of his important essays as well as articles by others about his fiction. The pieces are well chosen to reflect the range of critical opinion on Doctorow, the variety of his themes and techniques, and the historical background required to read his novels.

Weber, Richard. "E. L. Doctorow: Myth Maker." *The New York Times Magazine*, October 20, 1985, 25-26, 42-43, 74-77. Primarily useful as an overview of the novelist's life and career, with special emphasis on *World's Fair* and on the growth of his reputation. This profile emphasizes Doctorow's growing importance in contemporary fiction.

J. P. DONLEAVY

Born: Brooklyn, New York; April 23, 1926

Principal long fiction

The Ginger Man, 1955, 1965; *A Singular Man*, 1963; *The Saddest Summer of Samuel S.*, 1966; *The Beastly Beatitudes of Balthazar B.*, 1968; *The Onion Eaters*, 1971; *A Fairy Tale of New York*, 1973; *The Destinies of Darcy Dancer, Gentleman*, 1977; *Schultz*, 1979; *Leila: Further in the Destinies of Darcy Dancer, Gentleman*, 1983; *De Alfonce Tennis, the Superlative Game of Eccentric Champions: Its History, Accoutrements, Conduct, Rules, and Regimen*, 1984; *Are You Listening, Rabbi Löw?*, 1987.

Other literary forms

All of J. P. Donleavy's principal works are novels, but some of the protagonists and central situations of these novels have been explored in other literary forms. *A Fairy Tale of New York* is derived from the play *Fairy Tales of New York* (1961) and the short story, "A Fairy Tale of New York" (1961), later collected in Donleavy's only collection of short stories, *Meet My Maker the Mad Molecule* (1964). Donleavy has adapted three published novels for the stage: *The Ginger Man* (1961), *A Singular Man* (1965), and *The Saddest Summer of Samuel S.* (1972). He has also written one book of satirical nonfiction, *The Unexpurgated Code: A Complete Manual of Survival and Manners* (1975). Among Donleavy's limited production of occasional pieces there are two important autobiographical essays: "What They Did in Dublin with *The Ginger Man*," an introduction to that play, and "An Expatriate Looks at America," which appeared in *The Atlantic Monthly* in 1976. He explored his Irish heritage in *J. P. Donleavy's Ireland: In All of Her Sins and Some of Her Graces* (1986).

Achievements

The prevailing literary image of Donleavy is that of the one-book author: he gained celebrity status of a notorious sort with his first novel, *The Ginger Man*, but his subsequent novels failed to generate equal interest. Reactions to *The Ginger Man*, a book which only appeared in an unexpurgated edition ten years after first publication, ranged from outraged condemnations of it as obscene in language and immoral in content to later appreciations of it as a comic masterpiece. The later novels have been received with moderate praise for their style and humor and with slight dismay for their lack of structure or apparent intent. Donleavy himself has remained confidently aloof from all critical condemnation, exaltation, and condescension. He continues to pursue his private interests in fiction, to discourage academic interest in his work, and to express, when pressed, bemusement at literary frays of any sort. To some extent, his aloofness has been left undisturbed because he is difficult to place in standard literary traditions: his residency in Ireland and fondness for Irish settings seem to place his work outside of American literature, but his birth and use of American protagonists seem to place it outside of Anglo-Irish literature as well.

Biography

James Patrick Donleavy was born of Irish parents in Brooklyn, New York, on April 23, 1926. After being educated at private schools, he served in the United States Navy during World War II. He saw no action in the service, but he did encounter the work of James Joyce through an English instructor at the Naval Preparatory School in Maryland. This combination of family background and reading interests led to his enrollment in Dublin's Trinity College in 1945, on funds provided by the American G.I. Bill. There he was registered to read natural sciences, but he readily admits that most of his energies were devoted to pub crawls with fellow American students such as Gainor Crist, the model for Sebastian Dangerfield in *The Ginger Man*, and A. K. O'Donoghue, the model for O'Keefe in the same novel.

Donleavy returned to the United States in 1952, as did Crist and O'Donoghue, and he wrote most of *The Ginger Man* during the following year in New York City, Boston, and Bridgewater, Connecticut. On his return to Dublin in 1954, he became friends with playwright and man-about-town Brendan Behan. Through Behan's efforts, *The Ginger Man*, already rejected as unpublishable because of obscene language by Charles Schribner's Sons in New York, was accepted for publication in 1954 by the Olympia Press of Paris, a house whose main list of pornography enabled it to gamble on unusual literary properties such as Behan's works and Samuel Beckett's novel *Watt* (1953). Donleavy's book was greeted rudely by the British press and by its courts, where it was prosecuted for censorship violations, but the ensuing publicity led to the publication of an English edition in 1956 that brought Donleavy financial stability and an enviable literary reputation for a first novelist. After that time, he continued to make his home in Ireland, on Lough Owel in Westmeath, in rather baronial circumstances that resembled the affluence of his later characters rather than the student poverty of *The Ginger Man*.

After his marriage to Valerie Heron ended in divorce, Donleavy married Mary Wilson Price. Each of his marriages produced one son and one daughter.

Analysis

In his *Journal of Irish Literature* interview published in 1979, J. P. Donleavy said: "I suppose one has been influenced by people like Joyce. But also possibly—and this is not too apparent in my work—by Henry Miller who was then literally a private god." Appreciation of Donleavy's work is indeed improved by cognizance of these two acknowledged predecessors, and it is entirely appropriate that the former is Irish and the latter American and that all three expatriates have been subject to censorship litigation.

The influence of James Joyce is most apparent in Donleavy's style, and it should be noted that the Ireland of Donleavy's work scarcely overlaps with that of Joyce's work. Joyce made self-conscious and even self-indulgent style a necessity for the serious modern novelist, and Donleavy creates his own evocation of Dublin and other Irish environs in an intricate prose style characterized by minimal punctuation, strings of sentence fragments, frequent shifts of tense, and lapses from standard third-person narration into first-person stream of consciousness. The single most obvious indication of Donleavy's stylistic ambitions is his habit of ending his chapters with brief poems.

The influence of Miller is most apparent in the fact that Donleavy's novels, for all their supposedly "graphic" language and sexual encounters, create a world that is a patent fantasy. As in Miller's case, the primary aspect of the fantasy is a distinctly male fabrication based on unending sexual potency and invariably satisfying liaisons with uniformly passionate and voluptuous women. To this, Donleavy adds fantasies about immense wealth, requited infantile eroticism, Dionysian thirst, and spectacular barroom brawls. Because of this comic freedom from actual contingencies, his work satirizes absurd caricatures of recognizable social evils.

The central concern of all of Donleavy's novels is the fortune of a single male protagonist isolated from family and country and pursuing a life-style that is improvised and erratic. The great exemplar of this essential situation is *The Ginger Man*, a novel that weighs the joys of decadent drunkenness and ecstatic sex against spiritual fears of loneliness and death. Since that first novel, which left the future of its protagonist ambiguous, Donleavy has gone through a period of bleak despair over the viability of a free life-style and has emerged from it into a period of wholehearted endorsement of its pleasures. In the process, his view of the world has changed from a belief in its essential malevolence to an assertion of its essential benevolence. He has, then, confronted the problem of the value of independence from social conformity from two wholly different perspectives.

The Ginger Man, Donleavy's famous first novel, opens with a pair of subordinate clauses; the first celebrates the spring sun, and the second laments Dublin's workaday horse carts and wretched child beggars. It is between these two emotional poles that the Ginger Man, Sebastian Dangerfield, vacillates throughout the novel. He will be exalted by visions of freedom and possibility, but he will also be crushed by fears and depressions. In *The Ginger Man*, freedom is revolt against the forces of social conformity and rigidity, a casting over of the bulwark virtues of thrift, reverence, and self-discipline. The fear, however, is of the ultimate victory of those same forces and values. The novel refuses to resolve neatly these oppositions. Dangerfield, subject to reckless extremes throughout, finally remains both the Ginger Man, an alias suggestive of spirit and mettle, and Sebastian, the namesake of a betrayed and martyred saint.

One of the novel's achievements is its candid admission of the most deplorable aspects of a quest for freedom such as Dangerfield's. It is appropriate and commonplace in contemporary fiction that an alienated protagonist should court his wife for her dowry and run into debt with landlords, shopkeepers, and other pillars of middle-class society. Donleavy, however, proceeds beyond this comfortable degree of roguery to a proposal of a more complete anarchy that is the novel's most compelling and disturbing quality. Dangerfield also beats his wife, abuses his child, senselessly vandalizes the property of strangers, and is otherwise selfishly destructive because of a self-proclaimed natural aristocracy, a phrase crucial to Donleavy's later novels. In this respect, he sins far more than he is sinned against, and one measure of the novel's complexity is the fact that its most sympathetic character is a matronly Miss Frost, who is devoted to Sebastian but is abandoned by him when her finances have been consumed. *The Ginger Man* is superior to many contemporary novels contemptuous of society because of this admission of the sheer egotism and selfishness underlying such contempt.

Dangerfield's redeeming features, which make him an anti-hero rather than a villain, are his invigorating bohemian bravura and his true appreciation of life's quiet beauties. The novel is appropriately set in Dublin, mirroring a fine appetite for great talk and plentiful drink. On one level, the novel is about the meeting of the vital New World with the stagnant Old World, for Dangerfield and his Irish-American cronies flamboyantly out-talk and out-drink the Irish, who are portrayed as a mean and frugal people who can only be bettered by insult. Dangerfield's appreciation of more subtle sensual delights, however, is as essential to his character as those more raucous tastes. His love of the smell of freshly ground coffee wafting from Bewley's in Grafton Street is as important to this novel as its more notorious adventures with whiskey and women. In these aesthetic moments, including the appreciation of the rising sun in the opening of the novel, Sebastian provisionally justifies his sense of aristocracy and demonstrates a kind of moral purity not shared by the novel's other characters.

In conjunction with the picaresque comedy and titillation of Dangerfield's more preposterous adventures, there remains the essentially naïve and ultimately unfulfilled desire for a simpler, solitary bliss. *The Ginger Man* is Donleavy's salient novel because it manages this balance between frivolity and remorse, between freedom and surrender, an opposition resolved in different ways in all of his subsequent novels.

In his second novel, *A Singular Man*, Donleavy left the bohemian life-style that gave Sebastian Dangerfield vitality for the opulent but gloomy existence of George Smith, whose freedoms have been lost to the encroachments of great wealth. The premise of the novel has obvious autobiographical relevance to the success of *The Ginger Man*; George Smith is accused by his estranged wife of sneaking into society, and he is in fact bewildered by his inexplicable attainment of sudden wealth and fame. The novel frustrates autobiographical interpretation, however, because it represents the emergence in Donleavy's work of the caricatured environment common in his later novels. The nature of Smith's industrial empire is mysterious, but he travels through surroundings with names such as Dynamo House, Electricity Street, and Cinder Village, and makes his home in Merry Mansions.

Smith's only obvious claim to singularity is his solitary appreciation of the hollowness of material wealth, and the novel records his increasing disillusionment and despair. The only satisfying one of his several love affairs is with the sassy Sally Thompson, doomed by the sorrowful machinations of the plot to death in an automobile accident. Smith's only respite from the responsibilities of his financial empire is the construction of a fabulous mausoleum under the pseudonym "Doctor Fear." *A Singular Man* is controlled completely by the obsession with death that was always counterpointed in *The Ginger Man* with a potential for sudden joy, and its style reflects this severe introversion in its reliance on more extended passages of stream-of-consciousness narration than is common in Donleavy's novels.

While *A Singular Man* explored the despair of wealth, *The Saddest Summer of Samuel S.* broadened the gloom of Donleavy's post-*Ginger Man* novels by exploring the despair of a vagrant life-style. An expatriate American living in Vienna, Samuel S. is an overage Ginger Man whose misery is caused by the stubborn isolation from society that was at least a mixed virtue in Donleavy's first novel. In this novel, the only humor is provided by Samuel's bleak confessions to his shocked psychoanalyst Herr S., who functions as a socially acclimated if complacent foil to the alienated but determined Samuel S. The comedy is, however, completely overwhelmed by Samuel's inability to accept the apparent happiness of a relationship with an invigorating American student named Abigail. It is as if Donleavy set out to correct simplistic praise for *The Ginger Man* as an unambiguous paean to rootlessness by stressing in Samuel S. the costs of bohemian disregard for domestic and social comforts. The novel presents no acceptable alternative to Samuel's self-destructive insistence on alienation for its own sake, none of the moments of happy appreciation of life that redeemed Sebastian Dangerfield.

Balthazar B. is Donleavy's most withdrawn and morbid protagonist, and the novel named for him represents the author's most consistent use of religious resignation as a metaphor for a passive secular disengagement from a malevolent world. The presence of his prep school and college classmate Beefy adds a raucous dimension reminiscent of *The Ginger Man*, however, and *The Beastly Beatitudes of Balthazar B.* resuscitates the power of outrageous farce in Donleavy's work. Balthazar, another Donleavy protagonist who is fatherless and without a surname, progresses only from childhood fantasies about African pythons to more adult but equally futile ones about sex in aristocratic surroundings. Throughout the novel, he provides naïve perspective that enables Donleavy to satirize social pretensions and rampant materialism. The beatitudes that govern most of the novel are Beefy's, which bless the beastly virtues of complete decadence and joyful carnality but prove inadequate in the face of repressive social conformity. The ultimate beatitudes of the novel, however, are Balthazar's, which emerge late in the work and resemble those delivered in the sermon on the mount. Having accompanied Beefy on his salacious adventures and seen his companion undone, Balthazar—who, like Donleavy's other early protagonists, identifies with martyrs—is left only with a saintly hope for later rewards such as those in the beatitudes recorded in Matthew's gospel.

Like Balthazar B., Clementine of *The Onion Eaters* is a protagonist plagued by lonely remorse and surrounded by a dynamism in others that he is unable to emulate. He is a young American heir to a medieval British estate, a situation whose effect is that of placing an introspective and morose modern sensibility in the raucous world of the eighteenth century novel. As in most of Donleavy's novels, the central theme is the vicissitudes of a natural aristocracy, here represented by the fortunes of Clementine of the Three Glands in a chaotic world of eccentric hangers-on and orgiastic British nobility. The emotional tension of the novel is based on a deep desire for the freedom of complete decadence in conflict with a more romantic yearning for quieter satisfactions. That conflict enables Donleavy, as in parts of *The Ginger Man*, to create a titillating fantasy while concurrently insisting on a sort of innocence, for Clementine survives his picaresque adventures with his essential purity intact. The significant contemporary revision of an older morality, however, lies in the fact that in Donleavy's fiction such virtue goes unrewarded.

In Donleavy's later work, fantasy is allowed to prevail over remorse, and this new direction emerges first in *A Fairy Tale of New York*, in which a protagonist named Christian is tempted by the evils of the modern metropolis much as the traveler Christian is tempted in John Bunyan's *The Pilgrim's Progress* (1678). This novel has a special interest within Donleavy's work for its description of a return from Ireland to New York City, which is characterized in the novel by gross consumerism. In *A Fairy Tale of New York*, Christian is more a protector of real virtues than a seeker of them, and the novel ends with a comment on life's minor and earthy beauties rather than the plea for mercy that is common in Donleavy's earlier works. A brief vignette of the same title published a decade earlier provided the opening of *A Fairy Tale of New York*, and the intervening years saw a change in Donleavy's literary interests that enabled him to pursue a fulfilling fantasy beyond the limits of vignette. The result, however it may finally be judged, is a sacrifice of the emotional tension of his finest earlier work in favor of the pleasure of unconstrained fabrication, a surrender of psychological depth for a freer play of literary imagination.

Returning to the spirit of the eighteenth century novel which animated *The Onion Eaters*, *The Destinies of Darcy Dancer, Gentleman* evokes a world of baronial splendor, earthy servants, seductive governesses, and naïve tutors without apparent concern for the forces of modern technology and consequential social ills common to the contemporary novel. It is a stylish and literate entertainment without moral pretensions, a vein of fiction entirely appropriate to the alliance with freedom of imagination arduously explored in the course of Donleavy's work.

There are allusions to a darker world beyond the novel's immediate environs, such as housekeeper Miss von B.'s wartime experiences in Europe, but these serve only to stress the value of the free life-style pursued by Darcy Dancer without guilt and without controls beyond a decent sense of chivalry. One indication of the shift from morbidity to frivolity apparent in Donleavy's work is the fact that the setting here is Andromeda Park, named for a goddess whose miseries were relieved rather than for a saint who was martyred. Yet *Leila*, sequel to *The Destinies of Darcy Dancer, Gentleman*, retains the tone of upperclass superficiality while reintroducing a darker view: in this novel, Dancer becomes enamored of a woman but is left helpless when his love is married to another.

Schultz is similar to *The Ginger Man* but expresses no remorse or recrimination. Its operative assumption and central motif is a concept of the world as a pointless Jewish joke, and this permits the London theatrical impresario Sigmund Schultz to exploit materialism without moral doubts and Donleavy to create a world in which even the sinfully rich prove ultimately benevolent. Class consciousness and privilege are a matter for comedy rather than bitterness in this novel, and the foul-mouthed American social climber Schultz is accepted with amusement rather than repelled with horror by English royalty.

The perspective of the novel is so completely comic that venereal diseases are presented as mere inconveniences, the political world is represented by the monarch of an African nation named Buggybooiamcheesetoo, and the romantic liaisons are unabashed and masturbatory fantasies. The most important distinction between *The Ginger Man* and *Schultz* is that in Donleavy's first novel the world was seen as malevolent and in his latest it is seen as benign. In accordance with this movement, the author has shifted from a celebration of gallant but doomed improvised life-styles to a forthright assertion of their superiority to accepted and inherited modes of behavior.

The style and structure of Donleavy's work continued to evolve: *De Alfonce Tennis, the Superlative Game of Eccentric Champions*, for example, is such a mishmash of story, satire, and whimsy that the reader is hard-pressed to categorize it. Donleavy's later fiction deliberately deprives itself of the emotional conflicts central to his earlier, saintlier protagonists. It represents as well an insolent abrogation of the traditional concerns of "serious" fiction. By contrast, *The Ginger Man* was superior to the bulk of postwar novels about bohemian expatriates in Europe because of its sense of the limitations of that life-style as well as its potential.

John P. Harrington

Other major works

SHORT FICTION: *Meet My Maker the Mad Molecule*, 1964.

PLAYS: *The Ginger Man*, 1959 (also known as *What They Did in Dublin, with The Ginger Man: A Play*); *Fairy Tales of New York*, 1961; *A Singular Man*, 1965; *The Saddest Summer of Samuel S.*, 1972; *The Plays of J. P. Donleavy: With a Preface by the Author*, 1972.

NONFICTION: *The Unexpurgated Code: A Complete Manual of Survival and Manners*, 1975; *J. P. Donleavy's Ireland: In All Her Sins and Some of Her Graces*, 1986; *A Singular Country*, 1990.

Bibliography

Donleavy, J. P. "The Art of Fiction LIII: J. P. Donleavy." Interview by Molly McKaughan. *Paris Review* 16 (Fall, 1975): 122-166. In this lengthiest of interviews with Donleavy, he discusses the complex publishing history of *The Ginger Man*, the painful process of writing, the differences between his characters and himself, his preference for reading newspapers and magazines rather than novels, his life on his Irish farm, and his attitudes toward critics, New York, and death.

_____. "An Interview with J. P. Donleavy." Interview by Kurt Jacobson. *Journal of Irish Literature* 8 (January, 1979): 39-48. Donleavy explains how he evolved from student of natural science to painter to writer and discusses the origins of some of the characters and events in *The Ginger Man* and that novel's controversial reception.

LeClair, Thomas. "A Case of Death: The Fiction of J. P. Donleavy." *Contemporary Literature* 12 (Summer, 1971): 329-344. Shows how Donleavy's protagonists are both classical rogues in the tradition of Henry Fielding's Tom Jones and modern victims resembling Franz Kafka's Joseph K. Perhaps the best analysis of Donleavy's obsession with death, identified as the controlling element in his fiction.

Masinton, Charles G. *J. P. Donleavy: The Style of His Sadness and Humor.* Bowling Green, Ohio: Bowling Green University Popular Press, 1975. This pamphlet-length study of Donleavy's fiction through *A Fairy Tale of New York* places him in the American black humor tradition. Explains that while

Donleavy's characters become increasingly morose and withdrawn, his fiction is most notable for its humor and irony. This most complete interpretation of Donleavy includes a brief bibliography.

Norstedt, Johann A. "Irishmen and Irish-Americans in the Fiction of J. P. Donleavy." In *Irish-American Fiction: Essays in Criticism*, edited by Daniel J. Casey and Robert E. Rhodes. New York: AMS Press, 1979. Donleavy's attitudes toward his native and adopted countries in *The Ginger Man*, *The Beastly Beatitudes of Balthazar B.*, and other works are examined with the conclusion that he has grown more hostile toward America while gradually accepting a romanticized view of Ireland. This eleven-page essay is the best consideration of Donleavy's use of Ireland. A bibliography is included.

JOHN DOS PASSOS

Born: Chicago, Illinois; January 14, 1896
Died: Baltimore, Maryland; September 28, 1970

Principal long fiction
One Man's Initiation—1917, 1920; *Three Soldiers*, 1921; *Streets of Night*, 1923; *Manhattan Transfer*, 1925; *U.S.A.*, 1937 (includes *The 42nd Parallel*, 1930, *1919*, 1932, *The Big Money*, 1936); *Adventures of a Young Man*, 1939; *Number One*, 1943; *The Grand Design*, 1949; *Chosen Country*, 1951; *Most Likely to Succeed*, 1954; *The Great Days*, 1958; *Midcentury*, 1961; *World in a Glass*, 1966; *Century's Ebb: The Thirteenth Chronicle*, 1975 (posthumous).

Other literary forms
John Dos Passos published only one collection of poetry, *A Pushcart at the Curb* (1922), which re-creates a journey through crowded streets and countrysides of Spain and the Near East. He also published a collection of plays, *Three Plays* (1934), written and produced during the author's experimentation with the expressionistic techniques of the New Playwright's Theatre group.

In addition to Dos Passos' many long fictions, which he called contemporary chronicles, he also published many volumes of historical narratives, essays, and reportage. Among his books of travel and reportage, which spanned his entire career, were *Rosinante to the Road Again* (1922), *Orient Express* (1927), *In All Countries* (1934), *Journeys Between Wars* (1938), *State of the Nation* (1944), *Tour of Duty* (1946), *The Prospect Before Us* (1950), *District of Columbia* (1952), *Brazil on the Move* (1963), *The Portugal Story* (1969), and *Easter Island: Island of Enigmas* (1971).

Most of Dos Passos' historical narratives were written in his later years and reflect the shift in his political stance; they include *The Ground We Stand On: Some Examples from the History of a Political Creed* (1941), *The Head and Heart of Thomas Jefferson* (1954), *The Men Who Made the Nation* (1957), *Mr. Wilson's War* (1962), *Thomas Jefferson: The Making of a President* (1964), and *The Shackles of Power: Three Jeffersonian Decades* (1966).

Achievements
Dos Passos' importance can neither be highlighted with one literary accomplishment nor summarized with a list of singular achievements. Rather, he offered a constant but integrated response to the nation and to the new. Throughout his writing career of fifty years, Dos Passos was committed to exploring individual freedom and utilized every literary means to that end. Combining his interest in history with his experience as a journalist and as an artist, Dos Passos produced a remarkable number of novels, poems, plays, essays, and various nonfictional pieces. They are important for their intrinsic

merit as well as for their great documentary value. In addition to his extensive list of publications, Dos Passos was a loyal and impassioned correspondent; his letters to significant literary figures and friends also serve as chronicles of the age.

Finally, and unknown to many of his readers, Dos Passos was a talented painter. His sketchbooks, watercolors, and drawings—which date from his youth to his last days—are evidence of Dos Passos' fascination with the visual innovations and artistic movements of his lifetime. His painting had a significant influence on his methods as a writer.

Although Dos Passos experienced a decline in popularity when the critics believed he had abruptly shifted his political views to the right, there is now a revived interest in his best works, which are acknowledged as among the most inventive pieces of the twentieth century.

Biography

From the start of his life, John Roderigo Dos Passos was the victim of circumstances which would set him on an isolated course. In 1896, he was illegitimately born in a Chicago hospital. His father, John R. Dos Passos, Sr., was a famous defense lawyer and stock-market expert. He was also a writer of brokerage texts. His mother, Lucy Addison Sprigg, was of a fine Southern stock. Apparently, his birth was never recorded: this would have meant a scandal for Dos Passos, senior, whose Catholic wife, Mary Dyckman Hays Dos Passos, was an invalid.

For the most part, Dos Passos' childhood was spent with his mother in Brussels, London, or on the Continent, where reunions with his father were possible. From time to time, he was able to visit his father along the New Jersey shore or in New York, but only in a formal gathering where the affections of the boy for his "guardian" were repressed. Dos Passos' own account of his father's rare presence and peculiar hold are captured poignantly in *The Best Times* (1966).

Dos Passos' father, however, managed to shape the boy's intellect and attitudes, not through fatherly attentions, but with books and clear opinions about politics and through his son's elitist schooling. Dos Passos attended Peterborough Lodge, outside London, and the Choate School after returning to the United States. In 1910, Mary Dos Passos died; the boy's mother and father were married, and Dos Passos was given his actual surname. This new life and early schooling culminated in a grand tour of Europe and the Near and Middle East, complete with a mentor—Virgil Jones, a Dominican candidate. At this point, Dos Passos' great interest in art, architecture, and history was kindled. Ironically, he returned home to find that his mother, like Mary, had become an invalid.

The following autumn, Dos Passos entered Harvard, and the great avenues were opened for the nurturing of his writing, his political and social tendencies, and his artistic abilities. He ardently read both the classics and the moderns, as well as *Insurgent Mexico* (1914) by John Reed, an activist and a Harvard contemporary. Outside Harvard's walls, Dos Passos and his friends absorbed such artistic events as the Boston Opera, Sergei Diaghilev's ballet, the sensational Armory Show of modernist paintings, and the approach of world war.

Dos Passos' final year in school was somewhat sad, for his mother died, deepening his sense of isolation. It was also a springboard for his literary career, since it afforded the opportunity to collect and edit material and negotiate funds from his father for *Eight Harvard Poets*. He wrote for various Harvard publications, especially *The Harvard Monthly*, for which he was secretary and editor.

In 1916, Dos Passos studied architecture in Spain—an experience which would color his perspective on the Civil War there and alienate him from his friend, Ernest Hemingway. It was at this time, too, that Dos Passos' father died of pneumonia; his subsequent feeling of abandonment can be traced through correspondence with friends in *The Fourteenth Chronicle* (1973).

During "Mr. Wilson's War," as he dubbed it, Dos Passos, like many writer friends, joined the selective Norton-Harjes Ambulance Unit, serving France and Italy. Following the war, he was considered to be a member of the so-called Lost Generation, but always remained somewhat apart. Dos Passos immersed himself in and contributed to the artistic excitement in Paris. Designing and painting sets for the ballet and writing consistently for the first time, Dos Passos also observed the Peace Conference and the postwar unrest.

Travels took Dos Passos to the Basque country, to New York, and to the Near East on the Transiberian Railroad. There, the danger of the desert, the stench of the cities, and the exotic activity greatly affected Dos Passos' creative notions. Back in New York by 1924, Dos Passos rode on the wave of socialism, jazz, and the fragmentation of the postwar period—precisely the right mixture for his highly stylized work, *Manhattan Transfer*. Simultaneously, he directed the New Playwright's Theatre group, which produced his dazzling, expressionistic productions on labor issues: *The Moon Is a Gong* (1926); *Airways, Inc.* (1928); and *Fortune Heights* (1933).

In 1928, Dos Passos met and married Katy Smith, a writer and friend of the Hemingways. Her temperament, wit, and goodness seemed to be the perfect match for Dos Passos' solitary nature and restless spirit. The couple enjoyed years of extensive travel and literary success before Katy was killed in a tragic automobile accident, in which her husband was driving. As for his political development during these years, Dos Passos supported the labor cause and the more universal cause for justice and individual freedom. When the Spanish Civil War broke out, however, and the making of a film rallied writers to Spain, Dos Passos' reaction to the execution of his friend, the poet José Robles, caused a serious rift with Hemingway.

The 1940's and 1950's marked a transition away from the political left: for

Dos Passos, it was a natural shift to maintain his defense of freedom; for others, it remained a puzzling and outrageous movement to the right. During this period, Dos Passos was a war correspondent in the Pacific; after the war, he married a widow, Elizabeth Holdridge, and fathered a daughter, Lucy. He spent his remaining years traveling widely—particularly to South American countries such as Chile, Argentina, Brazil, and also around the United States. A serious heart condition plagued him with discomfort.

On September 28, 1970, John Dos Passos died of a heart attack in an apartment near Baltimore. He is buried near Spence's Point, his family's home in the Northern Neck of Virginia.

Analysis

Readers of John Dos Passos' unusual novels have attempted to define the writer as a chronicler, a historian, or a critic of twentieth century America. To these titles, Dos Passos added another dimension by calling himself "an architect of history." Indeed, his works move in skillfully drawn directions— horizontally across continents, vertically through socioeconomic strata, temporally to the deepest places of memory. Considering further Dos Passos' training in architecture and painting, it is not solely by conventional literary means that students can come to grips with his novels; the reader must also be a good viewer. In fact, in the best of his long fiction—*Three Soldiers*, *Manhattan Transfer*, and the *U.S.A.* triology—the image and the word are often synonymous.

Three Soldiers emerged from Dos Passos' post-World War I travels through Italy, Portugal, and Spain. Published in 1921, it was not the writer's first novel, but it refined an artistic process he had begun during his ambulance service, a process which yielded his first novel, *One Man's Initiation*, in 1920. Both this novel and *Three Soldiers* were drawn from sketchbooks of notes, highly descriptive entries, diagrams and sketches of landscapes, characters, and confrontations. While they are both antiwar books, *Three Soldiers* is clearly a better experiment in realism. Recalling Stephen Crane's *The Red Badge of Courage* (1895), the novel presents war through the eyes of the common soldier in France. Widening the range, Dos Passos poignantly captures the disillusionment and dehumanization of war for all soldiers.

True to his architectural design, Dos Passos allows for three geographical and individual perspectives—that of Dan Fuselli, a Californian; that of Chrisfield, a restless Indiana farmer boy; and that of Andrews, a Virginian and a composer. Through a thick buildup of violent encounters, he vividly portrays the army's destruction of the individual. Each responds to the regimentation and absurd conformity in different ways. Dan accepts the fantasy that conforming will result in promotion and the ultimate possession of his girl. Chrisfield plans to avenge himself on the hated sergeant. Andrews, the artist, struggles to find his creative place. In a series of violent confrontations, each soldier fails miserably to achieve his personal goals. Dan is promoted to corporal, but only after total exploitation by his superiors; Mabe, his girl, has married another man. Chrisfield vows to murder the sergeant. Having practiced on a solitary German in an abandoned house, he throws his last two grenades at the wounded sergeant in the woods. Dos Passos focuses on the artist, Andrews, who has managed to study legitimately in Paris and meet a sympathizer, Geneviève. Finally, he decides to go A.W.O.L. and is discovered and beaten by the military police. As Andrews is dramatically removed from his hiding place, a gust of wind scatters his unfinished composition entitled "John Brown," an homage to the liberator of slaves.

Although simplistic when compared to the later works, *Three Soldiers* is an exercise in an important visual process. First, he planned his novel from collected verbal and visual sketches. Second, his strong sense of painterly composition allowed for three diverse perspectives in Chrisfield, Fuselli, and Andrews. The reader will discover this geographical interest later in the *U.S.A.* trilogy, as well. Finally, he positioned images of violent confrontations against serene French landscapes. The violent action is shockingly portrayed while the images of the countryside are almost nostagically impressionistic. The effect is similar to the anxiety created in cubist paintings, where familiar objects and spaces are reshaped and limited. In the juxtaposition of images, the reader will sense Dos Passos' extreme personal disdain for war and his appreciation of a lost world.

The writing which followed *Three Soldiers* was not so much a futher refinement as it was a sudden explosion of artistic innovation, yet the germination of *Manhattan Transfer* was like that which produced Dos Passos' first two novels: a rich collage of images, impressions, notes, and sketches. Just as *Three Soldiers* is critical of war, so *Manhattan Transfer* focuses on the dehumanizing effects of the city, particularly on immigrants or outsiders. To convey his theme, Dos Passos transformed the conventional components of character, setting, and plot in much the same way that cubist painters distorted familiar objects and transformed the viewer's perception of them. New York, for example, is not really a setting or a backdrop, to use a visual term, but a major and monstrous character. Similarly, while there are approximately twelve identifiable characters out of the masses, they are important only as facets of the portrait of the real antagonist, the city. Finally, while there is a complicated network of overlapping and chaotic activities among and between the characters, there is no single plot. Instead, the novel is like a roller coaster or rapid transit ride; the reader experiences flashes of sense, sound, color, and conflict. It is, then, a collective novel—a compilation of the notes and pictures created while Dos Passos himself was in motion as a traveler.

The novel is divided into three sections, demarcated not by logical, literary closures but by highly visual introductory commentaries. Each section also contains several divisions, the headings of which allude to the metals and myths of great cities: "Ferryslip," "Tracks," "Rollercoaster," "Steamroller," "Revolving Doors," "Skyscrapers," and "The Burthen of Nineveh." What occurs within each division is not an unfolding of ideas or action, but an envelopment of the reader into a frenzy of lives colliding in the city's mainstream.

To create this collage, Dos Passos welds fragments of dialogue, action, newspaper clippings, signs, city sights, and time. In "Ferryslip," a child is born to an uncertain father, Ed Thatcher, and a hysterical mother, Susie. The child suddenly becomes Ellie, Ellen, or Elaine, depending upon the fortunes and fame of the gentlemen she lures. In "Tracks," the reader meets Jimmy Herf, an immigrant newspaper reporter who is the only figure eventually to escape the city's grasp. There is George Baldwin, a manipulative attorney who turns politician; Congo and Emile, two Frenchmen who represent the extremes of survival in a new land—one marries and conforms while the other returns to sea. Joe O'Keefe, a labor organizer, is juxtaposed with a successful Broadway producer, Harry Goldweiser. Almost all the characters collide with one another or else their adventures are butted against one another's in the same section of the novel. Herf provides the final view as he waits for a ferry to take him from Manhattan. Broken by every component of life in New York, he decides to hitchhike out of the city on a furniture truck, glistening and yellow. He provides the reader with an uncertain perspective; when asked how far he is going, Herf replies aimlessly that he wants to go far away.

Recalling the collective portrayal of the army in *Three Soldiers*, *Manhattan Transfer* captures the entirety and enormity of the city. The realism of *Three Soldiers*, however, was brilliantly and vividly transformed into a masterful expressionistic style. Instead of a conventional linear narrative about the dehumanization of the modern city, Dos Passos chose to re-create the eclectic experience of Manhattan. He verbally reproduced the rhythms, forms, plasticity, and chaotic activity of the city without the traditional literary processes of describing, developing, or narrating. The novel initially shocks the reader, forces a complicated sensual experience, and convinces the reader of the city's power by its sheer visual frenzy. The innovative techniques of *Manhattan Transfer* won for Dos Passos the praise of eminent contemporaries; Sinclair Lewis compared the novel to the modernist masterpieces of Gertrude Stein, Marcel Proust, and James Joyce. Certainly, Dos Passos had concocted a work in which the mass of the image and the word were of equal weight.

If *Manhattan Transfer* represented a heightened style and structure in comparison to *Three Soldiers*, then the *U.S.A.* trilogy was the apex of Dos Passos' expressionistic novels; generally acknowledged as his masterpiece, it is on this work that his reputation will rest. The trilogy is a panoramic fictional history of America in the first three decades of the twentieth century. The title of the first novel in the trilogy, *The 42nd Parallel*, suggests the sweep of the work, across the United States from Plymouth, Massachusetts, through the industrial centers of Detroit and Chicago, over to the gold coast of northern California. Along the way, history is not remembered or narrated, but reproduced by a series of modernist devices.

Dos Passos composed his trilogy with fragments of American life—newsreels, headlines, songs, letters, placards, colloquialisms, and biographical pieces of fictional and nonfictional figures. These fragments click away like an early film or newsreel itself, which captures the reader's attention for the narrative that follows. Dos Passos embellished this superstructure, more elaborate in scope than the divisions of *Manhattan Transfer*, with illustrations and with the ingenious and provocative device of the "Camera Eye." Interspersed and intruding into the narrative, the Camera Eye is composed of images in such a way as to reproduce memory, probably the writer's memory. The voice seems both deterministic and vulnerable to all that happens around it. Its focus set, the epic catalog of characters, real and imagined, is called to action.

The characters in the trilogy are representative figures intended to form a composite of the American soul. In *The 42nd Parallel*, there is Mac McCreary, a printer who eventually joins the revolutionary movement in Mexico, following disillusionment with marriage. J. Ward Moorehouse, a charismatic and powerful figure, is then introduced; the reader follows him throughout the trilogy as he is transformed from a public relations man and government servant in France to a wealthy advertising executive. Among the female characters is Eleanor Stoddard, an artsy interior decorator at Marshall Field's in Chicago; she eventually makes the acquaintance of Moorehouse. There is also Charley Anderson, an opportunist whose mechanical inventiveness leads him to become an airplane manufacturer. The reader observes his steady decline through the trilogy. These are but a few of the many contrasting characters sketched throughout the trilogy.

The historical portraits are of eloquent and eccentric figures of the period: Eugene V. Debs, the labor organizer jailed by President Woodrow Wilson; William Jennings Bryan, the silver-tongued Midwestern orator and frequent presidential candidate; the socialist mathematician Charles Proteus Steinmetz, who, as the property of General Electric, developed the law of hysteresis that produced electrical transformers for the world. The novel is a portrait collection of real and imagined people. Some are creative, cunning, impassioned; most are naïve. To link them, Dos Passos develops a kind of self-portrait through the Camera Eye series. The reader traces the Eye's consciousness from young and constant traveler in Europe and feisty adolescent to observer of labor rallies. The very last Camera Eye in *The 42nd Parallel* parallels the final sequence of Charley Anderson's crossing to war-torn France. The Eye pans out on the *Espagne*, dangerously crossing the Atlantic, its passengers caught in ironic responses to the great fear of destruction. The Eye moves quickly to death in the trenches, to the prosperity of vinegrowers, to a town in France unpleasantly interrupted by agents searching bags in well-known hotels. Through one Eye, then, and through the other biographies, the reader views rather than reviews the transition of Americans from naïveté to anticipation of some inevitable doom.

If *The 42nd Parallel* finishes in fearful anticipation, then *1919* fills the void with the thunder of World War I and the frightened inner voices of the characters. Far more tragic and total a portrayal of war than *Three Soldiers*, this second volume in the trilogy unmasks the entire absurdity, debauchery, and waste of "Mr. Wilson's War" at home and abroad. *1919* opens with a grimly ironic headline concerning the "great" battle of Verdun. The horror implicit in this headline is counterpointed by domestic suffering, by scenes of an America in which the wealthy few prosper at the expense of the masses.

Against this panorama of war and an industrializing nation, Dos Passos paints his imaginary portraits. There is Dick Savage, a literary Harvard graduate who resembles the author in several ways. He serves in the ambulance corps, caring for the mutilated and deranged. His horror is juxtaposed with a farcical censuring and punishment by the army for his mild criticism of war in a letter to a friend. In a similar incident, Dos Passos himself had been expelled from the Red Cross. Dick eventually finds his way into J. Ward Moorehouse's association after the war. There is also Ben Compton, the son of a Jewish immigrant, who travels north, south, east, and west as a political agitator at home. He is jailed, persecuted, and finally broken by the forces of law and order. Eleanor Stoddard begins her climb to the top through a series of affairs ultimately leading to J. Ward Moorehouse in Paris. Together, they exploit all around them to buy into the power of "Big Business" back home.

The historical figures expand Dos Passos' portrayal of this contradictory world at war. There is Jack Reed, the Harvard man who spoke and wrote revolution. Theodore Roosevelt is portrayed by a series of vivid anecdotes. He was, for Dos Passos, the last major figure of everything American, what Teddy characterized as "bully." The great J. P. Morgan is last. His family's empire built upon warmongering, Morgan's portrait prepares the reader for the monsters to come in *The Big Money*.

Just as in *The 42nd Parallel*, the Camera Eye moves the reader's view from the dying and dead in ambulance vans, to harlots, to soldiers running for cover in city streets, and finally to civilians collecting scrap iron at the war's end. Moreover, Dos Passos adds to the collage scraps of headlines of suicides and murders at home; uprisings of the workers; bits of melancholy American and French war songs. These grim scraps are collected for the future recycling of postwar industrial and political figures in *The Big Money*. The reader experiences the change in American consciousness from innocent anticipation to horror.

The end of *1919* is quite poignant both in technique and in meaning. Dos Passos blends the essence of the "newsreels," the Camera Eye, and the biographies to create a moving elegiac portrait of the Unknown Soldier. From the almost flippant choosing among pieces of bodies in France, to the imagined home and youth of the anonymous man, to the placing of Wilson's bouquet of poppies at the Tomb, Dos Passos movingly portrays the common dehumanizing experience of all soldiers and the unique and sacred individuality of every human being.

Following the brilliant design of the first two volumes of the trilogy, *The Big Money* picks up the pace of *1919* and brings the author's rather cynical perspective into perfect focus. Against the scenes of war's end and the anticipation of the great Depression, Dos Passos draws his ultimate conclusion—that the simple individual, as an American ideal, was not strong enough to confront the new powers of the modern world. It is not so much the individual against the world that is of importance here, however, as it is the composite view of America as one character after all, a collection of all the victims and aggressors of the early twentieth century. America is both protagonist and antagonist in *The Big Money*; both Dos Passos' subject and his means of painting it are unsettling.

Exploiting the technical innovations of the previous volumes, Dos Passos paints a pessimistic picture of Americans coming to terms with the twentieth century. Charley Anderson, corrupted by money, booze, and sexual affairs, drives south and dies in a car crash in Florida. Eveline Johnson, reaching her lowest point of boredom with Moorehouse and company, takes her life with sleeping pills. Margo Dowling, the ultimate plastic Hollywood starlet, is created and controlled by her powerful producer-husband, Sam Mongolies. In contrast, Mary French remains honest, constant, and determined in her work for the Communist party, particularly in her protest against the executions of Nicola Sacco and Bartolomeo Vanzetti. Among the real biographies, there is Isadora Duncan, who danced for the sake of art, accidentally drowned her children, and died in a joyride when her neck scarf caught in the wheel of an automobile. There is Frank Lloyd Wright, whose functional designs for the rich were not beauty enough to disguise his ugly family squabbles, bankruptcy, and scandalous affairs. Even the Wright Brothers, whose flying machine becomes a new war machine, present no triumph for the common man—at least, not at first—but they are admiringly portrayed.

The Camera Eye seems surer, more direct than before, more focused as it captures the Depression era. The man behind the camera was older, more experienced. The Eye in *The Big Money* is not reminiscent, as in *The 42nd Parallel*, or horrified, as in *1919*, but strong and clear about the plight of the social worker, the immigrant, and the laborer; about the triumph of the rich, the powerful, and the political. In fact, one of the last Camera Eyes of the trilogy forces the reader to view finally two nations in one, two languages, two experiences—that of the poor and that of the wealthy. Somehow, nevertheless, through Dos Passos' concentration on the common American, the nation seems on the brink of renewal.

The use of the now familiar experimental tools of Newsreels and cultural fragments is also sharper in *The Big Money*, especially in Dos Passos' juxtapositions of realities and absurdities, a technique begun in *1919*. One Newsreel, for example, proclaims in archaic speech and images that the steel corporation is a marvelous colossus, while bomb scares, suicides, and Georgia's new controversial dance, Shake That Thing, are stated matter of factly. Another announces America's air supremacy and a boom year ahead while it simultaneously lists a massacre of six hundred in Canton, the production of gas for warfare, the use of machine guns and steamrollers on strikers. The musical fragments come from the blues and from poetic choruses written for the unemployed. What seems hidden in the portrayal of America as shaken, explosive, and cruelly challenged is a wishful portrait of America as diversified, creative, and positively evolving.

Although Dos Passos continued to explore the themes of his great trilogy in seven subsequent novels, none of them was as provocative, as innovative in visual techniques, or as critically acclaimed as his masterpiece, *U.S.A.*

Mary Ellen Stumpf

Other major works
PLAYS: *The Garbage Man*, 1926; *Three Plays*, 1934.
POETRY: *A Pushcart at the Curb*, 1922.
NONFICTION: *Rosinante to the Road Again*, 1922; *Orient Express*, 1927; *In All Countries*, 1934; *Journeys Between Wars*, 1938; *The Ground We Stand On: Some Examples from the History of a Political Creed*, 1941; *State of the Nation*, 1944; *Tour of Duty*, 1946; *The General*, 1949; *The Prospect Before Us*, 1950; *District of Columbia*, 1952; *The Head and Heart of Thomas Jefferson*, 1954; *The Theme Is Freedom*, 1956; *The Men Who Made the Nation*, 1957; *Prospects of a Golden Age*, 1959; *Mr. Wilson's War*, 1962; *Brazil on the Move*, 1963; *Occasions and Protests*, 1964; *Lincoln and the Gettysburg Address*, 1964; *Thomas Jefferson: The Making of a President*, 1964; *The Shackles of Power: Three Jeffersonian Decades*, 1966; *The Best Times: An Informal Memoir*, 1966; *The Portugal Story*, 1969; *Easter Island: Island of Enigmas*, 1971; *The Fourteenth Chronicle*, 1973.

Bibliography
Becker, George J. *John Dos Passos*. New York: Frederick Ungar, 1974. A critical biography, this short book links Dos Passos' major works, his artistic observations, and his treatment of American social institutions.
Carr, Virginia Spencer. *Dos Passos: A Life*. Garden City, N.Y.: Doubleday, 1984. Presents a detailed biography with critical insights into the personal and political influences on Dos Passos' fiction.

Colley, Iain. *Dos Passos and the Fiction of Despair.* Totowa, N.J.: Rowan & Littlefield, 1978. This short but important book traces Dos Passos' maturation as an artist through his major works.

Hook, Andrew. *Dos Passos: A Collection of Critical Essays.* Englewood Cliffs, N.J.: Prentice-Hall, 1974. This excellent collection of essays explores topics such as Dos Passos' politics and his artistry.

Maine, Barry. "*U.S.A.*: Dos Passos and the Rhetoric of History." *South Atlantic Review* 50, no. 1 (1985): 75-86. This important article treats the role of narrative in conveying history in the first of Dos Passos' trilogy, with attention to the relationship between narrative and film.

Wagner, Linda W. *Dos Passos: Artist as American.* Austin: University of Texas Press, 1979. A comprehensive (624-page) study of Dos Passos' development as artist/observer, treating his quest for an American hero through his major works.

ARTHUR CONAN DOYLE

Born: Edinburgh, Scotland; May 22, 1859
Died: Crowborough, England; July 7, 1930

Principal long fiction

A Study in Scarlet, 1887; *The Mystery of Cloomber*, 1888; *The Firm of Girdlestone*, 1889; *Micah Clarke*, 1889; *The Sign of the Four*, 1890; *Beyond the City*, 1891; *The Doings of Raffles Haw*, 1891; *The White Company*, 1891; *The Great Shadow*, 1892; *The Refugees*, 1893; *The Parasite*, 1894; *The Stark Munro Letters*, 1895; *The Surgeon of Gaster Fell*, 1895; *Rodney Stone*, 1896; *The Tragedy of the Koroska*, 1897 (also as *A Desert Drama*); *Uncle Bernac*, 1897; *A Duet, with an Occasional Chorus*, 1899, revised 1910; *The Hound of the Baskervilles*, 1902; *Sir Nigel*, 1906; *The Lost World*, 1912; *The Poison Belt*, 1913; *The Valley of Fear*, 1915; *The Land of Mist*, 1926.

Other literary forms

In his lifetime, Arthur Conan Doyle was far better known for his short stories than for his novels. Until he became interested in science fiction, after 1900 (a medium he found better suited to shorter fiction), Doyle concentrated his creative energies on his novels, those works he felt posterity would judge him by, and took a purely monetary interest in the short-story format. Ironically, contemporary readers and critics continue to value the Sherlock Holmes short stories and largely ignore Doyle's historical novels.

One of the most prolific in an era of prolific authors, Doyle also dabbled in the theater. The most commercially successful of his dramas was the stage version of *Sherlock Holmes*, starring William Gillette. Doyle frequently financed his own plays, such as the violent and realistic *The Fires of Fate* (from his novel *The Tragedy of the Koroska*), a dramatization of a river-pirate raid on a party of English tourists in Egypt, an adventure based—like so many of Doyle's works—on his own experiences.

Doyle's nonfiction was largely polemic. The course of the British involvement in the Boer War was chronicled and defended in his *The Great Boer War*, written in 1900, and *The War in South Africa: Its Causes and Conduct* (1902). His efforts at defending government policy, as well as his own medical service during the war, were largely responsible for his knighthood. He also wrote extensively about other causes: the reform of the divorce laws, the denial of the vote for women, the abolition of ostrich feather hats. He reserved his greatest energy, however, for his popularizing and propagandizing of spiritualism, a doctrine with which he had toyed from his youth and to which he became devoted after the death of his oldest son in World War I. Indeed, the last fifteen years of his life were spent in furthering the spiritualist cause through writings and lectures.

Achievements

"Come, Watson. The game's afoot." Few words by any author evoke a clearer picture in the public's mind. Individuals who have never read a Sherlock Holmes story can immediately conjure up a vision of two distinctive figures leaving the fog-shrouded entrance to 221-B Baker Street: Sherlock Holmes, tall and skeletal, pale from his sedentary existence and haggard from his addiction to cocaine, wearing his famous deerstalker cap; Dr. Watson, short and stolid, though limping from an old bullet wound, one hand nervously hovering over the pocket that holds his trusted revolver. Indeed, few, if any, imaginary addresses have received the bulk of mail which continues to be sent to Holmes's Baker Street apartment; few fictional characters have been the subject of even a single "biography," let alone the great number of books which purport to document the life of Sherlock Holmes; and certainly few authors have cursed the success of one of their creations as much as Doyle did that of Sherlock Holmes.

When the struggling young Portsmouth physician first wrote down the name of "Sherringford Hope," soon changed to "Sherlock Holmes" in honor of the American writer Oliver Wendell Holmes, he did not dream of fame or literary immortality but merely of some means of augmenting his income, for he had a wife as well as a younger brother and an impoverished mother to support. In fact, as soon as *A Study in Scarlet* had been sent off to a prospective publisher in early 1887, Doyle was hard at work on *Micah Clarke*, the novel he felt would represent "a door . . . opened for me into the Temple of the Muses." Two years later, Doyle wrote the second Holmes novel, *The Sign of the Four*, as a jeu d'esprit after a convivial dinner with Oscar Wilde, an unlikely admirer of *Micah Clarke*, and James Stoddart, the editor of *Lippincott's Monthly Magazine*, who challenged both Doyle and Wilde to supply him with suitable mystery manuscripts. Doyle's real interest at this time was in the completion of his "masterpiece," the historical novel *The White Company*, and its acceptance for serialization in the *Cornhill Magazine*, beginning in January, 1891, seemed to him a far better harbinger of literary fame.

The unexpected success of Sherlock Holmes stories as they appeared in *Strand Magazine* in the early 1890's quickly established Doyle's reputation, in the opinion of Greenough Smith, the literary editor of that magazine, as the greatest short-story writer since Edgar Allan Poe, but he continued to churn out a seemingly endless series of historical and semi-autobiographical novels, most of which are read today only by scholars. The commercial success of these novels (*The Firm of Girdlestone*, *The Refugees*, *Beyond the City*, *The Great Shadow*, *The Stark Munro Letters*, *The Parasite*, *Uncle Bernac*, *Rodney Stone*, and *Sir Nigel*, among others), of his numerous collections of short stories, of his occasional ventures into drama, and of his essays and pamphlets on social and political issues (such as reform of the divorce laws and the conduct of the Boer War), all depended in large part on Doyle's popularity as the creator of Sherlock Holmes. Yet throughout his life, he never saw the stories and novels featuring Holmes and Watson as much more than pot-boilers. Even the famous "resurrection" of Holmes in 1903 was an attempt to capitalize financially on the success of the London opening of the play *Sherlock Holmes*, starring William Gillette. Doyle saw his real life's work, up until he became a propagandist for spiritualism at the end of his life, as writing fiction which would amuse and distract "the sick and the dull and the weary" through the evocation of the heroic past.

Biography

The idealization of the past served other purposes for Arthur Conan Doyle, who had been born into genteel poverty in Edinburgh on May 22, 1859, and named for King Arthur: it gave him a model to live by and to instill in his sons, and it diverted him from the disappointments of life which frequently threatened to overwhelm him. From his earliest childhood, his mother, Mary Doyle, the daughter of a lodging-house keeper who believed herself the descendant of the Plantagenets, indoctrinated her oldest son in tales of his aristocratic ancestry and the virtues of medieval chivalry. Doyle's father Charles, although employed throughout his son's childhood as a municipal architect in Edinburgh, was the youngest son of a highly gifted and artistic family. Charles Doyle's father John Doyle was the talented caricaturist "H. B."; his maternal uncle Michael Edward Conan was an artist as well as the art and drama critic and Paris correspondent for *Art Journal*; his brother Richard was a graphic artist for *Punch* and later an illustrator for John Ruskin, Charles Dickens, and William Makepeace Thackeray; another brother Henry was a painter before becoming director of the National Gallery of Ireland; a third brother James was a famous mid-Victorian portrait painter. Charles Doyle himself, who had suffered since early childhood from epilepsy and emotional disturbances, supplemented his salary with sketches of famous criminal trials and illustrations of fairy tales and historical romances. By the time his older son reached adulthood, Charles Doyle had descended through alcoholism into incurable insanity, retreating from a world he found uncongenial to his artistic temperament.

Mary Doyle necessarily became the central figure in her children's lives and continued to be so after they grew up. When Doyle first considered killing off Sherlock Holmes in November, 1891, his mother convinced him not to do so, thus reprieving the famous detective for a year. She also supplied her son with ideas for the Holmes stories. Throughout his childhood, Doyle's mother managed the practical necessities of life for an improvident husband and eight children on £180 per year and also instilled a vision of the ideal gentleman into her oldest son. In contrast to his father's instability and impracticality, Doyle grew into the epitome of the Victorian male: respectable, decent, cautious, thrifty, stolid. Only his writing—with its predilection for the codes of chivalry and honor and its preoccupation with a romantic past and his later obsession with spiritualism—betrayed the influences of Doyle's belief in his descent from kings and his father's retreat into a world of fantasy.

Doyle's family was Catholic, and he was educated first at a Catholic preparatory school and then at Stonyhurst, the foremost Jesuit educational institution in England. He hated both, finding Stonyhurst rigid, backward, superstitious, narrow, and, above all, dull. Unpopular with the masters because of his frequent protests against physical punishment, Doyle survived his school days because of his ability at games, his preeminence among his schoolmates, and his aptitude at diverting himself through reading and writing about a more glorious and exciting past. In his five years at Stonyhurst, he had no formal holidays but managed one visit to his uncle Richard Doyle in London, where the highlight of his stay was a visit to the Chamber of Horrors at Mme. Tussaud's on Baker Street. During this period, he began to read the short stories of Poe, which later influenced him through their fascination with the macabre as well as through the characterization of Poe's intellectual detective, M. Auguste Dupin, who was one of the models for Sherlock Holmes. When Doyle entered Stonyhurst, the Jesuits had offered free tuition if he would train for the priesthood; fortunately, his mother refused the offer for him in spite of the advantages such an arrangement would have held. Ironically, the reactionary atmosphere at Stonyhurst contributed to his loss of faith, a faith he would not regain until his adoption of spiritualism forty years later.

Leaving school, Doyle found himself with three choices: the priesthood, law, or medicine. His loss of faith ruled out the first alternative, his lack of influential connections the second, so he entered Edinburgh University to study medicine in 1877. Although he was once again not a particularly brilliant student, he was deeply influenced by two of his professors, Dr. Joseph Bell, who became a prototype for Sherlock Holmes, and Dr. Andrew Maclagan, an instructor of forensic medicine, who served as a model for Professor Challenger in Doyle's later science-fiction novels. The School of Medicine at Edinburgh formed both the setting and the subject of his early and happily forgotten novel, *The Firm of Girdlestone*.

His university days were punctuated with two spells as a ship's surgeon. The first voyage was aboard the *Hope*, an Arctic fishing boat. The seven-month-long trip was one of the highlights of Doyle's life. Seemingly indifferent to the bloody spectacle of the slaughter of whales and seals, he remembered only the sense of adventure and camaraderie among the crew. After graduation, he took a similar job aboard the passenger ship *Mayumba* on a voyage to the Gold Coast. This trip was in stark contrast to the first. Passengers and crew were struck down with tropical fevers that the young doctor was unable to treat. This experience so depressed Doyle that he gave up his plans for a career as a ship's surgeon and took up a position as an assistant to a doctor who turned out to be incompetent. When Mary Doyle objected to this association, her son left his employer and went to Portsmouth, where he opened his first practice.

Since the first years of his practice were not prosperous, Doyle returned to writing to occupy his time and to supplement his earnings. He also began to toy with an interest in the supernatural that is reflected in his later fiction and in his obsession with spiritualism. He attended his first séance in 1879 and worked on a number of bizarre stories which were included in his anthology *Dreamland and Ghostland* (1886). His poverty was such (he earned only about fifty pounds a year from his writing, and not much more from his practice) that his nine-year-old brother Innes, who was living with him at the time, had to usher patients into his surgery. His mother sent sheets and other household necessities from Edinburgh.

One of Doyle's greatest strokes of good fortune was the death of a patient. When a young boy collapsed of meningitis, then an incurable illness, outside his office, Doyle took the patient in and nursed him until his death. The boy's mother was so grateful for the doctor's solicitude, if not his medical skill, that she introduced Doyle to her daughter Louise (Touie) Hawkins. The young couple was married on August 6, 1885, and Touie Doyle became the perfect Victorian wife. Not only was she gentle, undemanding, submissive, and industrious, but also she possessed a small yearly income which nicely supplemented her husband's earnings. The Doyles eventually had two children, Mary Louise and Alleyne Kingsley, before Touie developed consumption, the disease which doomed her to an early death and Doyle to years of celibacy.

Doyle's *Beyond the City* and *A Duet* chronicle their married life. *Beyond the City* is set in Upper Norwood, the London suburb to which they moved in 1891, and details the days of their early married life: quiet afternoons spent bicycling together, equally quiet evenings with Touie sewing and her husband reading or writing. *A Duet*, written after Touie's fatal illness had been diagnosed, is silly and sentimental but ends with the deaths of the main characters in a train crash. Although Doyle remained devoted to assuring his wife's happiness until her death in 1906, he had fallen in love again in the mid-1890's. How much the fictionalized death of Touie in *A Duet* may have represented wish fulfillment remains conjecture.

The 1890's were years of contradiction for Doyle. His rise to literary prominence was paralleled by great personal distress. Although he had enjoyed moderate success as an author beginning with the publication of *A Study in Scarlet* in 1887, he still doubted that he could support his family by his pen. Early in 1891, he and Touie went to Austria, where he attempted to study ophthalmology; unsuccessful in this, he returned to England and moved his wife and daughter to London, where he set up a practice that drew even fewer patients than the one in Portsmouth. He had arrived back in England at a fortuitous moment for his career as a writer, however, as *Strand Magazine* had decided to bolster its circulation by abandoning the traditional serial novel for a series of short stories featuring a continuing character. Hearing of this, Doyle decided to revive his Sherlock Holmes character. In less than two weeks, he wrote two more Holmes stories, "A Scandal in Bohemia" and "The Red-Headed League," which were immediately accepted by Greenough Smith, the literary editor of *Strand Magazine*. With Sidney Paget as illustrator, the two stories were instant and enormous successes. Doyle found himself an overnight celebrity.

This, however, was not the type of literary fame for which Doyle had hoped. Although he continued to turn out Holmes stories for *Strand Magazine*, he worked more diligently on two new novels, *The Refugees*, another historical tale, and *Beyond the City*. By November, 1891, just five months after Holmes first appeared in *Strand Magazine*, his creator had decided to end the detective's life. Only the influence of Mary Doyle and the temptation of the one thousand pounds *Strand Magazine* was offering for a new series to run throughout 1892 made Doyle reconsider.

The second Holmes series confirmed Greenough Smith's opinion that Doyle was among the masters of the short-story form. Doyle himself found the format tedious; he always thought up the solution to the mystery first and then concocted the story in such a fashion as to obscure the true outcome from the reader as long as possible. His real affinity was for the historical novel, which he felt comfortable in writing and which he felt represented the true and highest purposes of art. In 1893, *The Great Shadow*, another example of his fondness for this genre, was published. It was extremely popular only because its author was the creator of Sherlock Holmes.

The continued ill-health of Doyle's wife (her tuberculosis was finally diagnosed in 1893) required frequent journeys to the Continent. Churning out a story a month to meet his commitment to *Strand Magazine*, concerned about Touie's health, constantly on the move, unhappy with the format in which he was forced to write, Doyle became more and more dissatisfied with his literary detective. If he did not exactly grow to hate Sherlock Holmes, he found the process of inventing new adventures for him more and more distasteful. He informed *Strand Magazine* that Holmes's final case, recorded in "The Final Problem," would appear in their December, 1893 issue. No entreaties or offers of higher payments would change his mind. After the account of Holmes's death was published, more than twenty thousand *Strand Magazine* readers canceled their subscriptions.

With Sherlock Holmes seemingly permanently out of his life, Doyle devoted himself to a renewed interest in the psychical research of his youth and to public affairs. Since his wife's illness precluded sexual intercourse, Doyle's writings of this period reverted to his earlier preoccupation, reflected in the *Dreamland and Ghostland* stories, with a connection between sex and death.

The 1894 novel, *The Parasite*, deals with the relationship between Professor Gilroy, a Holmesian figure who has retreated to the world of the intellect, and Helen Penclosa, a beautiful clairvoyant. At first a skeptic, Gilroy becomes increasingly obsessed with the beautiful young woman until, unable to withstand the passion that has made him lock himself in his own room, he rushes to her flat and makes love to her. Overcome immediately by guilt, he flees from her room, only to discover later that she has mesmerized him and forced him to rob a bank. As his obsession grows, Gilroy is dismissed from his post at the university and becomes increasingly erratic in his behavior. The more unstable Gilroy becomes, the weaker Penclosa grows, her power obviously transferring itself into his mind. In a moment of madness, Gilroy attempts to murder his fiancée, then decides to free himself by killing Penclosa. When he arrives at her flat, he finds her already dead and himself returned to sanity.

The public Doyle, however, continued to be the respectable man of affairs. Another historical novel, *Rodney Stone*, the story of a Regency dandy who becomes a "man" in the end, appeared in 1896. *Round the Red Lamp*, a collection of ghost stories Doyle wrote for his children, was published in 1894. He continued his travels in search of renewed health for Touie, journeying back and forth to Switzerland and spending the winter of 1896-1897 in Egypt.

In private, Doyle was increasingly troubled by the complications of his love for Jean Leckie, to whom he was originally attracted because of her descent from the Scottish hero Rob Roy. Although he confessed his love for Jean to his mother and other family members, he resisted all their advice that he divorce Touie. Vowing never to consummate his relationship with Jean until Touie's death, he instructed his family never even to hint of the affair to his wife. His "code of honor" as a gentleman mandated that he cherish and protect Touie at the cost of his own happiness. Jean, with whom he had never and would never quarrel, agreed. They continued to see each other, but Touie was kept ignorant of her husband's love for another woman. Doyle and Jean even waited the requisite year of mourning after Touie's death before they were finally married in 1907.

Although he had returned to an English setting for *Rodney Stone*, Doyle was fascinated by the events of the French Revolution and the Napoleonic Wars. In 1896 and 1897, after a spell in Egypt as a war correspondent during the Sudanese War, he published *The Exploits of Brigadier Gerard*, the first of a series of stories about the picaresque hero to appear in novel form. He also wrote *Uncle Bernac*, another Napoleonic novel, and *The Tragedy of the Koroska*, a melodrama about his adventures with paddleboat bandits in Egypt. Later dramatized as *The Fires of Fate* (1909), the scene depicting the flagellation of tourists by their Egyptian captors was so realistic that several members of the audience had to be restrained from going to the assistance of the actors.

In the late 1890's and the first years of the new century, Doyle increasingly turned to the horror story. One particular story, "Playing with Fire," published in 1900, combined his interest in psychic phenomena with his love for animals and suggested that animals, too, survive the grave. "The King of Foxes" (1903) dealt with Jean Leckie's favorite sport, foxhunting, in a bizarre and macabre form. To make money and to forestall another dramatist from seizing on the idea, he adapted the character of Sherlock Holmes for the American stage, emphasizing that the play which would make William Gillette famous was not a new adventure but related events that had occurred before Holmes's "death."

The outbreak of the Boer War in October, 1899, gave Doyle the outlet he needed for his interest in public affairs. He first attempted to enlist and then accepted the position of senior surgeon with John Longman's private field hospital. He saw his service at Bloemfontein in 1900 as that of a medieval knight seeking to help those less fortunate than he. His heroic efforts with inadequate equipment, his propaganda pamphlet *The War in South Africa: Its Cause and Conduct*, and later his history of the war, *The Great Boer War*, combined to win him his knighthood in 1902.

While in South Africa, Doyle had read of the story of the Cabell family, which was haunted by a ghostly hound. He saw in this the germ of a new Holmes novel, and *The Hound of the Baskervilles* was duly published in 1902. He was still not committed to reviving Holmes from beneath the Reidenbach Falls and insisted once again that *The Hound of the Baskervilles* was an earlier adventure only now coming to light. Although he continued to write horror stories, he was unable to resist the financial lure of more Holmes tales, and, consequently, in October, 1903, the first adventure of the "resurrected" Sherlock Holmes appeared.

During the last two decades of Doyle's life, his fame and finances were assured by the popularity of Sherlock Holmes. His private life, after his marriage to Jean Leckie and the birth of their three children, was that of an Edwardian paterfamilias. With the exception of *Sir Nigel*, he finally abandoned the historical novel in favor of science fiction. Politically reactionary, Doyle nevertheless was respected for his warnings about the outbreak of World War I. His greatest preoccupation, however, was with the cause of spiritualism; his final "conversion" to absolute belief in the phenomena which had fascinated him for years resulted from the deaths of his brother Innes and oldest son Kingsley during World War I. To the end of his life, he was convinced that he was in frequent touch with the spirits of his loved ones and thus devoted all the proceeds from his novels and lectures to the "cause." In the early 1920's, he once again announced Holmes's departure, this time to honorable retirement as a beekeeper on the Sussex Downs. Doyle brought him back only once, in a 1924 story written expressly for Queen Mary's Dollhouse. His literary reputation suffered because of his involvement in spiritualism, and his excellent science-fiction novels, many of which rival those of Jules Verne, were ridiculed by the critics more for their author's peculiarities than for their own lack of merit. Doyle died on July 7, 1930; his wife Jean claimed to receive a spirit message from him less than twenty-four hours later. His epitaph, however, looked back to earlier decades, to the little boy named after King Arthur who had resolved to live his life according to knightly ideals: "STEEL TRUE/BLADE STRAIGHT."

Analysis

Arthur Conan Doyle's epitaph can also serve as an introduction to the themes of his novels, both those that feature actual medieval settings and those that center on Sherlock Holmes. Doyle's central character is always the knight on a quest, living and battling according to chivalric ideals. Micah Clarke, Alleyne Edricson, Sir Nigel Loring all engage in real battles; Sherlock Holmes combats villains on behalf of distressed young women and naïve and frightened young men; Professor Challenger takes on the unknown: a prehistoric world, the realm of the spirit, the threatened extinction of life on Earth.

Doyle's first historical novel, *Micah Clarke*, is set in seventeenth century England against the background of Monmouth's Rebellion. As he always did in his historical fiction, in which he intended to portray the actual conditions of life at the time the novels were set, he paid meticulous attention to actual detail. In the Sherlock Holmes stories, Doyle seems not to have cared whether Dr. Watson's old war wound was in his shoulder or his knee, whether the good doctor's Christian name was John or James, whether there were one or two Mrs. Watsons, but his period novels show none of this casualness. For *Micah Clarke*, the author had carefully explored the area around Portsmouth, where most of the action takes place. He also did careful research into the dress, customs, and speech of the era. Indeed, it was its "mode of speech" that caused both Blackwoods and Bentley, Ltd. to reject the novel; this same period diction makes the novel extremely slow going for the modern reader.

Like most of Doyle's characters, those in *Micah Clarke* are modeled on real individuals. Micah Clarke, the gallant young man fighting zealously for a lost cause, is largely based on young Doyle himself, protesting hopelessly at Stonyhurst against outmoded courses of study, unfair punishments, and censorship of his letters home. Ruth Timewell, the cloyingly sweet young heroine, depicts the quiet, meek Touie Doyle, who at the time the novel was written represented her husband's ideal of womanhood. In spite of the critical acclaim *Micah Clarke* received when it was originally published, few people would consider it the stirring tale of adventure that its author did, although parts of it, especially the description of the climactic Battle of Sedgmoor and the portrait of the evil Judge Jeffreys, retain some interest for the modern reader.

The White Company, Doyle's second venture into the historical genre, and its companion piece, *Sir Nigel*, have worn slightly better. Like its predecessor, *The White Company* is distinguished by its scrupulous re-creation of the entire spectrum of life in fourteenth century England. Once again, Doyle's preoccupation with noble causes is reflected in the interests of his characters, members of a small but dedicated mercenary company who set off for the Continent to fight for England during the Hundred Years War.

The hero of *The White Company*, after whom Doyle later named his oldest son, is Alleyne Edricson, a landless young squire who leaves the monastery where he has been reared with his two companions, the lapsed monk Hortle John and the former serf Samkin Aylward, to join the White Company under the command of Sir Nigel Loring. Alleyne, his friends, his leader, and later his prince represent a microcosm of English society in the Middle Ages, depicting an idealized vision of the English character and contrasting with that of the country's main enemies: the French, the Spanish, and the Germans. Departing from his usual historical accuracy, Doyle presents the Germans as the worst foes of the English, reflecting his own late-Victorian perspective. Alleyne and his friend are mercenaries who live by their wits, but their fighting, looting, and pillaging are always conducted according to the rules of the chivalric game. At the end of the novel, Alleyne wins his knighthood, his inheritance, and his lady fair in the person of Sir Nigel's daughter Maude. The virtues Sir Nigel embodies and Alleyne learns are those that Doyle taught his own sons: sympathetic treatment of social inferiors, courtesy and respect for women, and honesty in financial dealings.

The novel is particularly interesting for its two main themes: the rise of the English middle class and of English patriotism. *The White Company* depicts a world where individuals are not judged by their birth but by their accomplishments, in much the same manner as Doyle rose from poverty to affluence through his own efforts. The book, however, also reflects its author's belief that the English character was the best in the world; Doyle clearly insists that language, history, customs, and beliefs of England are far superior to those of any other nation.

At first glance, the four Sherlock Holmes novels (*A Study in Scarlet, The Sign of the Four, The Hound of the Baskervilles, The Valley of Fear*) might seem to have little in common with Doyle's historical fiction. A closer look, however, shows that whatever the surface differences, the author's underlying concerns and prejudices are the same. Indeed, Sherlock Holmes can be seen as a knight-errant who ventures forth from Baker Street on a series of quests. In the earlier novels and stories, he battles dragons of crime on behalf of individuals. Mary Morstan in *The Sign of the Four* is the epitome of a damsel in distress. In Holmes's later adventures, both the suppliants and the dragons are different. There is an increasing tendency for those seeking Holmes's assistance to be representatives of the government itself or, as in "The Illustrious Client," a person no less exalted than King Edward VII himself, and for the villains to be international criminals or even foreign governments.

Holmes's relationship with Dr. Watson reflects that of a knight and his squire. The detective and his intellect operate according to the rules of detection which Holmes has himself established at the beginning of *The Sign of the Four*, rules analogous to the chivalric code, and squire Watson accompanies Holmes as much to learn how to conduct himself according to these rules as to assist in the solution of the crime. Dull, plodding, faithful Watson may never win his spurs, but at least he wins the hand of Mary Morstan.

The Holmes novels also exhibit Doyle's characteristic xenophobia. With the possible exception of Moriarty, who, after all, is an international rather than an English criminal, the villains Holmes contends with frequently are foreigners or else the crimes he deals with have their origins in foreign or distant events. *A Study in Scarlet* is a story of the revenge exacted for a crime committed in the mountains of Utah twenty years earlier. The novel's "victims" are in fact villains who have mistreated an old man and a young girl, those most deserving of protection, and so deserve their own deaths, while its "villain" is a just avenger who is saved from the gallows by a "higher judge" and dies with a smile upon his face as if looking back on a deed well done. The crime in *The Sign of the Four* similarly has its origins years before in India, and its victims also turn out to have brought their doom upon themselves. Rodger Baskerville, the father of Stapleton the naturalist who perpetrated the hoax in *The Hound of the Baskervilles*, had fled to South America before his son was born. As in the fictional press report at the end of *A Study in Scarlet*, Doyle appears eager to distance the true Englishman from responsibility for crime.

Although Doyle himself favored his historical fiction while the public preferred the Sherlock Holmes adventures, the author's finest works have largely been ignored. *The Lost World*, *The Poison Belt*, and *The Land of Mist* are novels which belong to a series of science-fiction works featuring the eccentric Professor George Edward Challenger. By the time *The Lost World* was published in 1912, Doyle was already becoming a figure of fun among the intelligensia because of his ardent defense of psychic phenomena and his reactionary political views. The critics' disdain for this series unfortunately affected its popularity, and there has been a consequent tendency to overlook them as examples of Doyle's literary skill at its finest.

The Lost World resulted from Doyle's interest in prehistoric footprints near his home in the New Forest. After he made casts of the prints, he consulted with zoologist Edwin Ray Lankester and came away with the idea for the novel. *The Lost World* is narrated by Edward Dunn Malone, a journalist who comes to act as a Watson-like chronicler of the exploits of Professor Challenger, an eccentric scientist with a great physical resemblance to Arthur Conan Doyle. After knocking Malone down the stairs at their first meeting, Challenger recruits him for a proposed expedition to South America in search of a prehistoric monster believed to exist on a plateau in the Amazon River basin.

Doyle's penchant for realistic description deserts him in *The Lost World*. His details are fifty years out of date; he instead presents a fantastically imaginative vision of the unexplored jungle wilderness. The beauty of the jungle vanishes as the explorers reach the historic plateau. With almost surrealistic horror, Doyle depicts the filthy, fetid nesting ground of the pterodactyls and the dank and dirty caves of the ape-men who inhabit the plateau. A marvelous comic ending has Challenger revealing the results of the expedition to a skeptical London audience of pedants by releasing a captured pterodactyl over their heads.

The characterization in *The Lost World* is among Doyle's finest achievements. The members of the expedition are well-balanced: the eccentric and pugnacious Challenger, the naïve and incredulous Malone, the cynical and touchy Summerlee, and the great white hunter Lord John Roxton. The one woman in the novel, Malone's fiancée Gladys, bears no resemblance to the Ruth Timewells and Lady Maudes of Doyle's earlier work. She is spunky and independent, refusing to marry Malone until he has done something worth admiring, and in his absence marrying someone else because she decides money is a more practical basis for marriage than fame.

The series retains its high quality in *The Poison Belt*, but the subsequent related works are less consequential. In *The Land of Mist*, Challenger becomes a spiritualist convert when the spirits of two men whom he believes he has killed return to tell him of his innocence. "When the World Screamed," one of the stories in *The Maracot Deep and Other Stories* (1929), reverts to the morbid sexuality of *The Parasite*. When Challenger attempts to drill a hole to the center of the Earth, the world turns out to be a living female organism. When Challenger's shaft penetrates the cortex of her brain, she screams, setting off earthquakes and tidal waves.

Few of Doyle's writings from the last decade of his life are read by other than specialists, dealing as they do with the propagation of spiritualism. The canon of his fiction can thus be said to have ended with science-fiction novels. These novels too all deal with Doyle's characteristic themes and concerns. Challenger and Maracot uncover hidden truths about the nature of the past, the present, the future, and life after death much in the same way as Sherlock Holmes discovered the truth about human nature in the course of his investigation of crime. The historical fiction had sought to explore the truth about a specialized human nature, that of the archetypal Englishman, in the same manner. Even the obsession with spiritualism which cost him his credibility among intellectual circles was but another example of Doyle's lifelong search for the truth about human existence.

In whatever guise he portrayed that search, Doyle never deviated from the devotion to the ideals that had been instilled in him in childhood and which

were recorded on his gravestone: "STEEL TRUE/BLADE STRAIGHT."
Similarly, all his literary protagonists embodied these same ideals: a devotion
to truth and a belief in the rightness of their cause. Few other authors have
managed to create such a coherent body of work as did Arthur Conan Doyle,
and fewer have matched the content of their work so closely to the conduct
of their lives.

Mary Anne Hutchinson

Other major works

SHORT FICTION: *Mysteries and Adventures*, 1889 (also as *The Gully of Blue-
mansdyke and Other Stories*); *The Captain of Polestar and Other Tales*, 1890;
The Adventures of Sherlock Holmes, 1892; *My Friend the Murderer and Other
Mysteries and Adventures*, 1893; *The Great Keinplatz Experiment and Other
Stories*, 1894; *The Memoirs of Sherlock Holmes*, 1894; *Round the Red Lamp:
Being Fact and Fancies of Medical Life*, 1894; *The Exploits of Brigadier
General*, 1896; *The Man from Archangel and Other Stories*, 1898; *The Green
Flag and Other Stories of War and Sport*, 1900; *The Adventures of Gerard*,
1903; *The Return of Sherlock Holmes*, 1905; *Round the Fire Stories*, 1908;
The Last Galley: Impressions and Tales, 1911; *One Crowded Hour*, 1911; *His
Last Bow*, 1917; *Danger! and Other Stories*, 1918; *Tales of the Ring and
Camp*, 1922 (also as *The Croxley Master and Other Tales of the Ring and
Camp*); *Tales of Terror and Mystery*, 1922 (also as *The Black Doctor and
Other Tales of Terror and Mystery*); *Tales of Twilight and the Unseen*, 1922
(also as *The Great Keinplatz Experiment and Other Tales of Twilight and the
Unseen*); *Three of Them*, 1923; *The Dealings of Captain Sharkey and Other
Tales of Pirates*, 1925; *Last of the Legions and Other Tales of Long Ago*,
1925; *The Case-Book of Sherlock Holmes*, 1927; *The Maracot Deep and
Other Stories*, 1929; *The Final Adventures of Sherlock Holmes*, 1981; *Un-
collected Stories: The Unknown Conan Doyle*, 1982.

PLAYS: *Foreign Policy*, 1893; *Jane Annie: Or, The Good Conduct Prize*,
1893 (with J. M. Barrie); *Waterloo*, 1894 (also as *A Story of Waterloo*);
Halves, 1899; *Sherlock Holmes*, 1899 (with William Gillette); *A Duet*, 1903;
Brigadier Gerard, 1906; *The Fires of Fate*, 1909; *The House of Temperley*,
1909; *The Pot of Caviare*, 1910; *The Speckled Band*, 1910; *The Crown
Diamond*, 1921; *Exile: A Drama of Christmas Eve*, 1925; *It's Time Something
Happened*, 1925.

POETRY: *Songs of Action*, 1898; *Songs of the Road*, 1911; *The Guards Came
Through and Other Poems*, 1919; *The Poems: Collected Edition*, 1922.

NONFICTION: *The Great Boer War*, 1900; *The War in South Africa: Its
Causes and Conduct*, 1902; *The Case of Mr. George Edalji*, 1907; *Through
the Magic Door*, 1907; *The Crime of the Congo*, 1909; *The Case of Oscar
Slater*, 1912; *Great Britain and the Next War*, 1914; *In Quest of Truth, Being*

a Correspondence Between Sir Arthur Conan Doyle and Captain H. Stansbury, 1914; *To Arms!*, 1914; *The German War: Some Sidelights and Reflections*, 1915; *Western Wanderings*, 1915; *The Origin and Outbreak of the War*, 1916; *A Petition to the Prime Minister on Behalf of Roger Casement*, 1916(?); *A Visit to Three Fronts*, 1916; *The British Campaign in France and Flanders*, 1916-1919 (6 volumes); *The New Revelation*, 1918; *The Vital Message*, 1919; *Our Reply to the Cleric*, 1920; *Spiritualism and Rationalism*, 1920; *A Debate on Spiritualism*, 1920 (with Joseph McCabe); *The Evidence for Fairies*, 1921; *Fairies Photographed*, 1921; *The Wanderings of a Spiritualist*, 1921; *The Coming of the Fairies*, 1922; *The Case for Spirit Photography*, 1922 (with others); *Our American Adventure*, 1923; *My Memories and Adventures*, 1924; *Our Second American Adventure*, 1924; *The Early Christian Church and Modern Spiritualism*, 1925; *Psychic Experiences*, 1925; *The History of Spiritualism*, 1926, (2 volumes); *Pheneas Speaks: Direct Spirit Communications*, 1927; *What Does Spiritualism Actually Teach and Stand For?*, 1928; *A Word of Warning*, 1928; *An Open Letter to Those of My Generation*, 1929; *Our African Winter*, 1929; *The Roman Catholic Church: A Rejoinder*, 1929; *The Edge of the Unknown*, 1930; *Arthur Conan Doyle on Sherlock Holmes*, 1981; *Essays on Photography*, 1982; *Letters to the Press*, 1984.

TRANSLATION: *The Mystery of Joan of Arc*, 1924 (by Léon Denis).

EDITED TEXTS: *D. D. Home: His Life and Mission*, 1921 (by Mrs. Douglas Home); *The Spiritualist's Reader*, 1924.

ANTHOLOGY: *Dreamland and Ghostland*, 1886.

Bibliography

Baring-Gould, W. S. *Sherlock Holmes of Baker Street: A Life of the World's First Consulting Detective*. New York: Bramhall House, 1962. A "biography" of Doyle's most popular creation, Sherlock Holmes. Based upon the Sherlock Holmes stories and numerous secondary sources. A chronological outline of Holmes's life as created by Baring-Gould is also included.

Carr, John Dickson. *The Life of Sir Arthur Conan Doyle*. New York: Harper & Brothers, 1949. Well researched and written by a distinguished mystery writer, this is a highly readable biography. Carr had access to Doyle's personal papers and enjoyed the cooperation of Doyle's children. A good place to begin further study.

Edwards, Owen Dudley. *The Quest for Sherlock Holmes: A Biographical Study of Arthur Conan Doyle*. New York: Barnes & Noble Books, 1983. Concentrates on the first twenty-three years of Doyle's life in an attempt to unravel the influence of various forces in his early life on his writing, such as his early love of history and Celtic lore, the impoverished and Catholic Edinburgh of his youth, and his alcoholic father.

Green, Richard Lancelyn. *A Bibliography of A. Conan Doyle*. New York: Oxford University Press, 1983. Provides a massive (712-page) bibliography of all that Doyle wrote, including obscure short pieces. Illustrated and containing a seventy-five-page index, this book includes a list of more than one hundred books of biographical, bibliographical, and critical interest for the study of Doyle.

Higham, Sir Charles. *The Adventures of Conan Doyle: The Life of the Creator of Sherlock Holmes*. New York: W. W. Norton, 1976. A popular biography which attempts to establish a link between Doyle's detective fiction and events in his own life, such as his use of actual criminal cases, the mental collapse of his father, and his interest in spiritualism. Indexed and illustrated. Includes a bibliography.

Jaffe, Jacqueline A. *Arthur Conan Doyle*. Boston: Twayne, 1987. Jaffe provides a brief (148-page) scholarly biography of Doyle.

Symons, Julian. *Conan Doyle: Portrait of an Artist*. New York: Mysterious Press, 1979. This biography is particularly useful, as it tries to present Doyle as much more than the creator of Sherlock Holmes. Only 135 pages, it contains 122 illustrations, a chronology of Doyle's life, and a bibliography of his writings.